Comparative Economic Systems

Comparative Economic Systems

Third Edition

Paul R. Gregory
University of Houston

Robert C. Stuart
Rutgers University

HOUGHTON MIFFLIN COMPANY   BOSTON
Dallas   Geneva, Illinois   Palo Alto   Princeton, New Jersey

DEDICATION

To Peter and Elizabeth Gregory
and Floyd and Gladys McCaig

Cover illustration by Dorothea Rockburne,
MOZART AND MOZART UPSIDEDOWN AND BACKWARD
Copyright © 1985 by Dorothea Rockburne

Printed in the U.S.A.

Library of Congress Catalog Card Number: 88-81332

ISBN: 0-395-43332-0

BCDEFGHIJ-KR-89

Contents

Preface

The first edition of this work was written in the mid 1970s, a period of stagflation, energy shocks, and general unease concerning the long-run future of market capitalism. Although the planned socialist economies were experiencing their own troubles, the problems of capitalism appeared to be most pressing. The second edition was written in the early 1980s, during the unexpectedly rapid reduction of the rate of inflation and the acceleration of economic growth in the West. The remarkable economic performance of Japan had become a topic of everyday conversation. These situations both seemed to highlight the declining economic fortunes of parts of the East. Although talk of meaningful economic reform continued in the East, only the Chinese reform appeared to be yielding real benefits.

This edition was written in 1988. The mid to late 1980s has been an era of conservative economic policy in the West. In virtually all the major industrialized capitalist countries, conservative governments have come to power to pursue policies of privatization and reducing the scope of government. Japan continues to be the envy of the West with its strong currency, rapid growth, low unemployment, and positive trade balances. The "four tigers" of Asia (Taiwan, Singapore, South Korea, and Hong Kong) have gained strong footholds in world manufacturing markets and threaten to one day replace Japan. The major economic story of the late 1980s has been the East's decision to attempt serious reform of planned socialism. It is much too early to know whether these attempts, spearheaded by the Soviet General Secretary Gorbachev, will lead to lasting change of the planned socialist economic systems. We must wait for subsequent editions to answer this question.

The renewed emphasis on economic reform has caused us to introduce an entire chapter on economic reform in East and West. This chapter describes the ongoing reform attempts in the East and focuses on changes in the West as well. Otherwise, this edition follows the same chapter outline as the previous edition. An expanded instructor's manual, which includes a computerized test bank, is available for instructors.

We are grateful to comments from readers of earlier editions of this work. We especially wish to thank: Frank Holzman of Tufts University, Fred Zapp, Irwin Collier of the University of Houston, Gertrude Schroeder-Greenslade of the University of Virginia, Marvin Jackson of Arizona State University, Roger Morefield of the University of St. Thomas, Jan Svejnar of the University of Pittsburgh and Ira Gang of Rutgers University.

P.R.G.
R.C.S.

Comparative Economic Systems

PART I

ECONOMIC SYSTEMS: DEFINITION, COMPARISON, THEORY

Chapter 1
Economic Systems: Definition, Classification

Comparative economic systems is a subject that is more difficult to characterize than other fields of economics. It has been described as "a field in search of a definition."[1]

Comparative economics studies economic problems across comparable economic settings. Comparative economists might compare the growth rates of industrialized countries or labor force participation rates in developing countries. In either case, the forces influencing the variables are studied in a transnational setting. Comparative economic *systems* studies economic outcomes in different economic settings. In comparing economic problems across economic settings, the comparative economist must isolate and measure the impact of the economic system itself on the observed outcomes. The economic system is treated as an important input to the economic process along with the conventional inputs — land, labor, and capital. The economic system is assumed to matter in observable and understandable ways.

How might the economic system affect economic outcomes? Economic outcomes are influenced by social, economic, geographical, political, and random forces. The comparative economist must develop methods to understand and control (hold constant) all relevant variables in order to understand the role of the economic system.[2] For example, we know that level of economic development is an important factor in explaining many observable economic outcomes.[3] We expect an economy with a low per capita income to have a relatively large share of its labor force in agriculture; we would expect just the reverse for an economy with a high per capita income. Level of development is a characteristic that can be measured, albeit imperfectly, and its impact on economic outcomes can be investigated. But what about less-measurable factors such as ideology; institutional arrangements; and social, cultural, and historical forces? Although they transcend the traditional economic inputs that normally enter into such an analysis, they are likely to be important in accounting for economic outcomes.[4]

Here, then, is the puzzle that the analyst of comparative economic systems must solve: how to deal in a systematic manner with the totality of economic and noneconomic factors, including the economic system, that affect economic outcomes.

ECONOMIC SYSTEMS: DEFINITION

Countries have organizational arrangements termed economic systems, which are used to allocate resources to achieve economic objectives. To the extent that we believe outcomes may differ as economic systems differ, we must isolate the economic system from its country setting and from other variables that may influence outcomes. Further, we must be able to measure the system's impact, so that observed differences in outcomes can be related to differences in systems. Before we can do either, however, we must have a working definition of an economic system.

Traditional and Modern Approaches to Definition

People seem to know what an economic system is, but there is little agreement about how to describe one in objective terms. The traditional approach has devoted little attention to problems of definition and measurement, dealing instead with a number of stylized economic systems — fascism, socialism, capitalism, feudalism. The isms are either not defined at all, or they are defined in terms of one or two key characteristics — for example, socialism is defined in terms of the social ownership of the means of production.

The modern approach defines economic systems in terms of a broad series of characteristics — property ownership, processing and utilization of information, decision-making processes, behavior rules, and so on. Today, the notion that an economic system is either "capitalist" or "socialist" is rejected. Instead, what type of economic system a country has is determined by a number of characteristics. Economic systems can blend characteristics so that there is a large variety of possible economic systems, depending upon how the characteristics are mixed.

There are two drawbacks to the modern approach. The first is that developing unanimous definitions or descriptions of the characteristics of economic systems is extremely difficult. The second drawback is that people have been brought up on the isms, and definitions. After all, the contemporary world is divided into economic and political blocs known loosely as capitalist, socialist, and communist systems. What ultimately interests people is how and how well capitalist and socialist economic systems solve the problem of resource allocation. Any approach that relies exclusively on technical characteristics to define economic systems and avoids the communism-capitalism issue will surely disappoint the student. Moreover, a technical approach tends to neglect the issue of change in economic systems. As J. M. Montias writes:

Capitalism, communism, socialism, and kindred terms, whatever system traits they may in actuality represent, have a life of their own. They live as symbols or clusters of symbols in the minds of participants in all modern systems..., and they may have a profound influence on the way actual systems change or on the reasons why they fail to change.[5]

A Compromise Solution

As Frederic Pryor has noted, "the concept of an 'economic system' is almost impossible to define exactly."[6] However, definition is essential for measurement and comparison. We compromise by dealing with three stylized economic systems — capitalism, market socialism, and centrally planned socialism. Each system is defined within the multidimensional framework of the modern approach. We limit our definitions to modern economic systems. We shall not deal with slave, feudal, and traditional societies or with variants such as utopian socialism. The emphasis is on what we consider to be the prime focus of a course on modern comparative economic systems — namely, capitalism and socialism.

Definition of the Economic System

We adopt with some modification the definition of an economic system proposed by Assar Lindbeck.[7] This definition emphasizes the multidimensional nature of an economic system; and it represents a reasonable consensus of current thinking.

> **Definition:** An *economic system* is a set of mechanisms and institutions for decision making and the implementation of decisions concerning production, income, and consumption within a given geographic area.

Broadly speaking, then, the economic system consists of mechanisms, organizational arrangements, and rules for making and executing decisions about the allocation of scarce resources. An economic system can vary in any of its dimensions, particularly in its structure, its operation, and its adaptability to change through time. As Pryor has written, it "includes all those institutions, organizations, laws and rules, traditions, beliefs, attitudes, values, taboos, and the resulting behavior patterns which directly or indirectly affect economic behavior and outcomes."[8]

Economic systems are **multidimensional**, a feature that can be conveniently formalized in the following manner:

$$ES = f(A_1, A_2, \ldots, A_n)\tag{1.1}$$

As equation 1.1 indicates, an economic system (ES) is defined by its attributes (A_i) or characteristics, where there are n such attributes. This means that an economic system cannot be defined fully in terms of a single characteristic such as property ownership; rather, the full set of characteristics must be known before ES is specified. We shall focus upon four general (and often overlapping) attributes $(n = 4)$ that are critical in differentiating economic systems:

1. Organization of decision-making arrangements
2. Mechanisms for the provision of information and coordination: market and plan
3. Property rights: control and income
4. Mechanisms for setting goals and for inducing people to act (incentives)

The four characteristics have been chosen because we *expect* economic systems to differ with respect to them. These characteristics have been chosen, also, because they are believed to affect economic outcomes. We do not list features that are relatively uniform across systems — for example, the organization of production in factory units.

FOUR CHARACTERISTICS OF ECONOMIC SYSTEMS

We shall now examine each of the four characteristics and explain why economic outcomes differ with resepct to them. Initially, the characteristics appear to have little in common with ordinary characterizations of economic systems as capitalist or socialist. However, later in this chapter we shall bring together the traditional and modern approaches to formulate working definitions of capitalism and socialism.

The Organization of Decision-Making Arrangements

Nobel laureate Herbert Simon writes that "organization refers to the complex pattern of communications and other relations in a group of human beings."[9] According to Montias, "an organization consists of a set of participants (members) regularly interacting in the process of carrying on one or more activities...."[10] The organization must be allowed to have some turnover in its membership and be able to change the activities it pursues. It is generally accepted that there are advantages to organized as opposed to unorganized behavior. In an organization, goals exist, information is created, and assumptions and attitudes are formed, all of which play a part in the making of decisions.

Organizations typically have a hierarchy in which some individuals issue commands or orders to other members of the organization, who must comply with the orders. One reason for this common arrangement is suggested by Armen Alchian and Harold Demsetz.[11] Technology requires members of the organization (say, the firm) to work together in "team production." Because output is produced as a team effort, it is difficult to assess each individual's contribution. There may be a tendency to slacken effort in such a work environment unless someone (a boss) monitors work effort and determines the rewards of individual members.

An economic system is one of the most complex organizations studied by social scientists. Economic systems, by definition, facilitate decisions concerning the allocation of resources. One way to describe an economic system is the level at which resource-allocation decisions are made. Economic systems are decentralized if decisions are made primarily at low levels in the organization; they are centralized if decisions are made primarily at upper levels.[12]

The agents who operate in an economic system are grouped into subunits or smaller organizations. A private enterprise may be a branch of a company that is owned by a conglomerate corporation. A government enterprise may be subordinated to a branch department which is subordinated to a ministry. The actual allocation of resources takes place in the enterprise, yet the decisions that determine resource allocation may be made either at the enterprise level or above. The resource-allocation decision could be made either at the lowest level (at the enterprise), at an intermediate level (the company or the branch department), or at a high level (the conglomerate corporation or the ministry).

Two factors determine at what level resource-allocation decisions will be made. They are the manner in which authority is distributed within the hierarchy and the manner in which the hierarchy utilizes information.

In a perfectly centralized economy, the authority to make decisions would rest in a single central command, which would issue orders to lower units in the organization. The perfectly decentralized case would be a structure where all decision-making authority rests with the lowest subunits (households and individual firms), independent of superior authorities. Economic systems can be characterized as centralized or decentralized on the basis of where the authority to make decisions lies. In the real world authority is typically spread through various levels in the hierarchy, and its locus changes over time.

The level of decision making also depends on the handling of information. According to Leonid Hurwicz, perfect centralization of information means that a single decision maker possesses all information about all participants, their actions, and their environment.[13] Decentralization implies that such a decision maker possesses less than complete information. In simplest terms, an "informationally decentralized" system is one that generates, processes, and utilizes information at the lowest level in the organization without exchanging information with higher levels in the organization. In a decentralized system, for example, information on prices is exchanged only among the lowest units. Conversely, an "informationally centralized" system involves the generation, processing, and utilization of information by superior agencies and the subsequent transmission of only limited pieces of information to lower subunits.

Identifying levels of decision making in terms of a formal organizational chart can be misleading. Figure 1.1 shows why. In column A, there are three levels in the hierarchy. In column B, there are two — resulting, say, from eliminating the intermediate level or from combining the lower and intermediate levels. At first glance, the change from A to B appears to be a move toward the centralization of decision making. The removal of the intermediate organization seems to concentrate

Figure 1.1 Levels of Decision Making in an Economic System

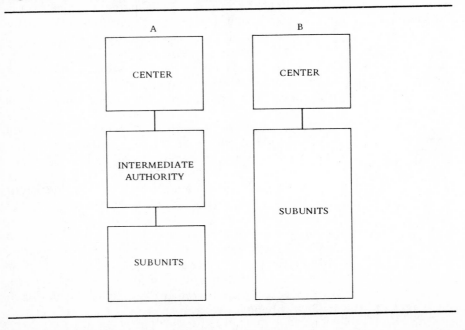

decision-making authority at the center. But the elimination of the intermediate organization might cause authority to devolve to the sub-units. Clearly, formal organizational changes do not necessarily affect the distribution of authority and the utilization of information. Organization charts may not describe the de facto organization of an economic system.

Mechanisms for the Provision of Information and Coordination: Market and Plan

The **market** and the **plan** provide information and coordinate decisions in economic systems. It is common to identify centralization with plan and decentralization with market, but there is no simple relationship between the level of decision making and the use of market or plan as a coordinating mechanism. In market economies, it is possible to combine considerable concentration of decision-making authority and information in a few large corporations with substantial state involvement, and yet have no system of planning as such.[14] On the other hand, economies that are characterized as planned can vary substantially. As examples, one might cite centralized planning in the Soviet Union, the "indicative" planning system of France, and the combination of plan and market found in Yugoslavia. To identify an economy as planned does not necessarily reveal the prevalent coordinating mechanism or, for that matter, the degree of centralization in decision making. Both will depend on the type of planning mechanism.

The many uses of the term **planning** contribute considerably to the confusion over market and planning as coordinating mechanisms. A **planned economy** is one where subunits are coordinated by specific instructions or directives formulated by a superior agency (a planning board) and disseminated through a document called a plan. The participants are induced to carry out the directives by appropriate incentives, which are designed by the planning authorities. The specifics differ from one case to another. The basic point, however, is that in a planned economy, economic activity is guided by instructions or directives devised by higher units and subsequently transmitted to lower units. Rewards depend on the achievement of plan directives. A planned economy (defined in this sense) and a market economy are mutually exclusive: In the former, resources are allocated by the instructions of planners, thereby usurping the role of the market as an allocator of resources.

Indicative planning is a second form of national economic planning. The market serves as the principal instrument for resource allocation, but a plan is prepared to guide decision making. An indicative plan is one in which planners seek to project aggregate or sectoral trends and provide additional information beyond that normally supplied by the market. An indicative plan is *not* broken down into directives or instructions for individual production units; enterprises are free to make use of the information contained in the indicative plan as they see fit, though indirect means are used to influence economic activity.

In the case of a market economy, the market — or, broadly speaking, the impact of the interaction of supply and demand on prices — provides signals that trigger subunits in the system to make resource utilization decisions. The market thereby coordinates the activities of different decision-making units. For example, households earn income by providing land, labor, and capital, and with this income they generate demand schedules to which firms respond in pursuit of profit. The subunits, here firms and households, work through and respond to the market. Other mechanisms for information or coordination are not necessary, and decision-making authority is vested at the lowest level of the economic system.

In planned and market economies, the ultimate decision makers are different. In a market economy, the consumer can "vote" in the marketplace and exercise **consumer sovereignty**. If consumer sovereignty prevails, then the basic decision of what to produce will be dominated by consumers in the marketplace. On the other hand, in a planned economy decisions are made by the planners, and hence **planners' preferences** prevail. Where planners' preferences prevail, the basic decision of what to produce is made by planners.

In a planned economy, planners must base their instructions to production units on some social preference function (that is, some known ordering of society's desires). At least to some degree, for political reasons or to promote incentives, planners may well have to take into account consumers' preferences. Thus it is difficult to envision a pure planners' preference system, where the wishes of the consumer are totally disregarded.

Neither would one expect pure consumer sovereignty to prevail in a market economy. In market economies, governments exercise considerable influence over the mix of goods and services produced. Furthermore, factors such as public goods, externalities, and the market power of large concentrated firms are said to abridge the consumer's ability to dictate resource allocation.

Property Rights: Control and Income

J. M. Montias has written that "the word **ownership** refers to an amalgam of rights that individuals may have over objects or claims on objects or services" and that "these rights may affect an object's disposition or its utilization."[15] Ownership rights may be divided into three broad types. First is the **disposition** of the object in question —

the transfer of ownership rights to others as in the selling of a privately owned automobile. Second, ownership may include the right to **utilization,** whereby the owner can use the object in question in any manner deemed appropriate. Third, ownership may imply **the right to use the products and/or services** generated by the object in question.

Ownership rights may be temporary or permanent, and the three types just mentioned may well rest with different individuals at any point in time. Thus the individual who rents an automobile has the right (within regulated limits) to the *utilization* of that automobile, but not to its *disposition.* The owners of a private firm have a claim over the profits of the firm, even though the operation may be significantly circumscribed by government rules and regulations. De jure ownership rights may differ significantly from de facto rights. For example, although members of Soviet collective farms "own" the assets of the farm in the form of kolkhoz-cooperative property, departing members cannot sell their share of these broad assets.

Broadly speaking, there are three forms of property ownership — private, public, and collective (cooperative). Under private ownership, each of the three ownership rights would belong to individuals, whereas under public ownership, these rights would belong to the state.

How do differences in ownership rights and in the distribution of these rights affect economic outcomes? Consider an economic system in which capital is owned by individuals (all three ownership rights belong to individuals). As the owners seek to maximize their lifetime incomes, capital will be disbursed so as to yield the highest rate of return commensurate with the risk involved. If capital is owned by the state, capital allocation rules may be different. Greater attention may be paid to long-term social rates of return. Moreover, time preferences may differ substantially according to whether individuals or the state owns the capital. The distribution of income will differ according to state or private ownership: Property income will accrue to private owners in the one case, to the state in the other. Finally, as the allocation of capital will ultimately determine the direction of economic activity, the ownership of capital will determine whether allocation is done by private individuals or by the state.

It is clear why property rights are used to characterize economic systems. Traditionally, the classification of economic systems has been in terms of isms — capitalism, socialism, feudalism — where the nature of the property rights distinguishes each system. In the Marxian schema (discussed in Chapter 4), changes in the economic system are signaled by changes in the ownership of the means of production. Indeed, property ownership patterns are typically more measurable than the other criteria, although the impact of the ideology of property rights on economic outcomes is less certain than one might expect.[16]

Incentives

An economic system can also be characterized in terms of the incentives that motivate people. As Frederic Pryor has written: "Goals and incentives are...vital links in understanding the transformation of property rights and informational inputs into effective actions."[17]

An incentive mechanism should induce participants at lower levels to fulfill the directives of participants at higher levels. As Montias notes, an effective mechanism must fulfill three conditions.[18] First, the person who is to receive the reward must be able to influence the outcomes for which the reward will be given. Second, the upper-level participant must be able to check on the lower-level participant to see whether tasks have been executed properly. Third, the potential rewards must matter to the lower-level participant.

In a hierarchy in which superiors issue binding directives to their subordinates, incentives would not be necessary if the superior had perfect information. Armed with perfect information, the superior would automatically know whether the subordinate is carrying out designated tasks properly. In complex organizations, however, superiors typically lack such perfect information. The subordinate knows much more about local circumstances than the superior, and the superior cannot issue perfectly detailed instructions to the subordinate. Because of the imperfect information of the superior, the subordinate gains local decision-making authority in a number of realms. The superior needs to devise an incentive system that will induce the subordinate to act in the interests of the superior when the subordinate makes such local decisions. If the superior's incentive system is flawed, the subordinate will not act in the interest of the superior.

The superior can devise and use either material or moral incentives to motivate the subordinate. Material incentives have typically been dominant in modern economic systems; yet some systems have attempted to emphasize moral rewards. **Material incentives** promote desirable behavior by giving the recipient a greater claim over material goods. **Moral incentives** reward desirable behavior by appealing to the recipient's responsibility to society (or the company) and accordingly raising the recipient's social stature within the community. Moral incentives do not give recipients greater command over material goods. In simpler terms, the difference between material and moral incentives is the difference between a cash bonus and a medal for an outstanding job.

Different justifications for material rewards have been advanced. According to the neoclassical theory of distribution, those who provide inputs to the system (private owners in a market system) are rewarded according to their productivity. Material incentives are a reward for higher productivity. The Marxian explanation of income differentials in a capitalist society is discussed in Chapter 4. A case for material incentives can be made even when capital is not privately owned. Marx argues that material rewards will be necessary for socialist societies to progress. When ownership of the means of production becomes public and socialism is attained, differential material rewards should persist, but moral incentives (to build socialism for future generations) will become more important. Eventually, when a stage of material abundance is reached, distribution can be based on the notion "from each according to his ability, to each according to his needs." Thus, in the Marxian framework under conditions of social ownership, one would expect material rewards to be gradually replaced by moral incentives.

Comparing Economic Systems: A Mode of Classification

We have examined the features that characterize different economic systems. Figure 1.2 summarizes the alternative options available for each feature. We have selected four criteria for distinguishing among economic systems. Although additional criteria could have been

Figure 1.2 Features of Economic Systems

Feature:	Options:
Organization of Decision Making	Centralization Decentralization } MIXED
Provision of Information and Coordination	Market Plan } MIXED
Property Rights	Private Cooperative Public } MIXED
Incentive System	Moral Material } MIXED

introduced, these four are especially important and useful. We use a three-fold classification of economic systems in three stylized variants: *capitalism*, *market socialism*, and *planned socialism*. As Figure 1.3 shows, each system is characterized multidimensionally in terms of the four characteristics.

- **Capitalism** is an economic system characterized by the private ownership of the factors of production. Decision making is decentralized and rests with the owners of the factors of production. Their decision making is coordinated by the market mechanism, which provides the necessary information. Material incentives are used to motivate participants.
- **Market socialism** is an economic system characterized by the public ownership of the factors of production. Decision making is decentralized and is coordinated by the market mechanism. Both material and moral incentives are used to motivate participants.
- **Planned socialism** is an economic system characterized by public ownership of the factors of production. Decision making is centralized and is coordinated by a central plan, which issues binding directives to the system's participants. Both material and moral incentives are used to motivate participants.

Figure 1.3 The Classification of Economic Systems

	CAPITALISM	MARKET SOCIALISM	PLANNED SOCIALISM
Decision-making Structure	Primarily Decentralized	Primarily Decentralized	Primarily Centralized
Mechanisms for Information and Coordination	Primarily Market	Primarily Market	Primarily Plan
Property Rights	Primarily Private Ownership	State and/or Collective Ownership	Primarily State Ownership
Incentives	Primarily Material	Material and Moral	Material and Moral

Providing definitions raises as many questions as it answers. These definitions merely state the most important characteristics of economic systems; they do not tell us how and how well each system solves the economic problem of resource allocation. Under capitalism, how do the owners of the factors of production actually allocate their resources, according to what rules, and so on? Under market socialism, how can public ownership of the factors of production be made compatible with market coordination? In fact, is public ownership ever compatible with market coordination? Can market coordination be simulated? Under planned socialism, how is sufficient information gathered and processed to allocate resources effectively from the center? How can one be sure that the center's directives will be followed by the system's participants? These are all questions we deal with in chapters on the theory of capitalism and socialism.

SUMMARY: ECONOMIC SYSTEMS

1. The subject of comparative economic systems studies the effect of the economic system on economic outcomes.
2. An economic system makes and implements decisions concerning production, income, and consumption.
3. Economic systems are multidimensional. The four main characteristics of an economic system are: how decision-making arrangements are organized, whether coordination is determined by market or plan, how property rights are maintained, and what the incentive system is.
4. Economic systems can be classified as three pure systems: capitalism, planned socialism, and market socialism.

NOTES

1. Alexander Eckstein, "Introduction," in Alexander Eckstein, ed., *Comparison of Economic Systems: Theoretical and Methodological Approaches* (Berkeley: University of California Press, 1971), p. 1. On defining the field of comparative economic systems, the reader is also referrred to Morris Bornstein, "An Integration," ibid., pp. 339–355; and John Michael Montias, *The Structure of Economic Systems* (New Haven: Yale University Press, 1976).
2. The objectives of an economic system (nation) may be formulated in different ways — for example, by a single person (dictator) or on the basis of some democratic process. On the question of social choice, the classic work is Kenneth Arrow, *Social Choice and Individual Values*, 2nd ed. (New York: Wiley, 1963). See also G. M. Heal, *The Theory of Economic Planning* (New York: North Holland, 1973), ch. 2.
3. For a study that attempts to analyze differences in outcomes in terms of differing levels of economic development, see Hollis Chenery and Moises Syrquin, *Patterns of Development, 1950-1970* (New York: Oxford University Press, 1975).

4. Neoclassical economic theory focuses on land, labor, and capital as the traditional inputs to the production process. Although nontraditional inputs such as organization and management are thought to be important, economists have largely been unsuccessful in measuring their impact. For a discussion of these issues in the context of economic development, see Charles P. Kindleberger and Bruce Herrick, *Economic Development*, 3rd ed. (New York: McGraw-Hill, 1977).

5. Montias, *The Structure of Economic Systems*, p. 8.

6. Frederic Pryor, *Property and Industrial Organization in Communist and Capitalist Nations* (Bloomington: Indiana University Press, 1973), p. 337.

7. See Assar Lindbeck, *The Political Economy of the New Left: An Outsider's View*, 2nd ed. (New York: Harper & Row, 1977), p. 214.

8. Pryor, *Property and Industrial Organization*, p. 337, adapted from T. C. Koopmans and J. M. Montias, "On the Description and Comparison of Economic Systems," in Eckstein, *Comparison of Economic Systems*, pp. 27–78.

9. Herbert A. Simon, *Administrative Behavior*, 2nd ed. (New York: Free Press, 1966), p. xvi.

10. Montias, *The Structure of Economic Systems*, p. 8. For a discussion of the relation between organization and comparative economics, see Benjamin Ward, "Organization and Comparative Economics: Some Approaches," in Eckstein, *Comparison of Economic Systems*, pp. 103–133.

11. A. A. Alchian and H. Demsetz, "Production, Information, Costs and Economic Organizations," *American Economic Review*, 62 (December 1972), 777–795. For a survey of organizations, see Marcus Alexis and Charles Z. Wilson, *Organizational Decision Making* (Englewood Cliffs, N.J.: Prentice-Hall, 1967), ch. 1. For a discussion of organizational principles, see Simon, *Administrative Behavior*.

12. This section relies heavily on the pioneering work of Leonid Hurwicz, Thomas Marschak, and others. See, for example, Leonid Hurwicz, "Centralization and Decentralization in Economic Processes," in Eckstein, *Comparison of Economic Systems*, pp. 79–102; Leonid Hurwicz, "Conditions for Economic Efficiency of Centralized and Decentralized Structures," in Gregory Grossman, ed., *Value and Plan* (Berkeley: University of California Press, 1960), pp. 162–183; and Thomas Marschak, "Centralization and Decentralization in Economic Organizations," *Econometrica*, 27, no. 3 (1959), pp. 399–430.

13. Hurwicz, "Centralization and Decentralization in Economic Processes," p. 96. For a discussion of various meanings of the concepts of centralization and decentralization, see Pryor, *Property and Industrial Organization*, ch. 8.

14. A classic case would be John Kenneth Galbraith's view of the contemporary American economy. See John Kenneth Galbraith, *Economics and the Public Purpose* (Boston: Houghton Mifflin, 1973).

15. Montias, *The Structure of Economic Systems*, p. 116. For a useful survey of recent literature on the subject of property rights, see Eirik Furubotn and Svetozar Pejovich, "Property Rights and Economic Theory: A Survey of Recent Literature," *Journal of Economic Literature*, 10 (December 1972), pp. 1137–1162; for a discussion of these issues in a comparative context, see Pryor, *Property and Industrial Organization*.

16. For a discussion of ideology as a system determinant, see Alexander Gerschenkron, "Ideology as a System Determinant," and the discussion thereafter in Eckstein, *Comparison of Economic Systems*, pp. 269–299.

17. Pryor, *Property and Industrial Organization*, p. 338.

18. Montias, *The Structure of Economic Systems*, ch. 13.

RECOMMENDED READINGS

Alexander Eckstein, ed., *Comparison of Economic Systems: Theoretical and Methodological Approaches* (Berkeley: University of California Press, 1971).

Gregory Grossman, *Economic Systems* (Englewood Cliffs, N.J.: Prentice-Hall, 1967), chs. 2–3.

Vaclav Holesovsky, *Economic Systems: Analysis and Comparison* (New York: McGraw-Hill, 1977), ch. 2.

John Michael Montias, *The Structure of Economic Systems* (New Haven: Yale University Press, 1976).

Egon Neuberger, "Classifying Economic Systems," in Morris Bornstein, ed., *Comparative Economic Systems: Models and Cases*, 4th ed. (Homewood, Ill.: Irwin, 1978).

Egon Neuberger and William J. Duffy, *Comparative Economic Systems: A Decision-Making Approach* (Boston: Allyn and Bacon, 1976).

Frederic Pryor, *Property and Industrial Organization in Communist and Capitalist Nations* (Bloomington: Indiana University Press, 1973).

———, *A Guidebook to the Comparative Study of Economic Systems* (Englewood Cliffs, N.J.: Prentice-Hall, 1985).

P. J. D. Wiles, *Economic Institutions Compared* (New York: Halsted Press, 1977).

Andrew Zimbalist and Howard Sherman, *Comparing Economic Systems: A Political-Economic Approach* (New York: Academic Press, 1984).

Chapter 2
The Economic System and the Evaluation of Economic Outcomes

In Chapter 1 we considered the nature of an economic system and presented several possible definitions. Four major characteristics were presented that might be used to identify an economic system — the decision-making structure (levels of decision making), mechanisms for information and coordination (market versus plan), property rights (private versus public), and incentives (material versus moral). Finally, a broad mode of systems classification was presented including capitalism, market socialism, and centrally planned socialism.

This chapter considers how observed economic outcomes — or, put another way, real-world economic performance, might be systematically related to differences in the nature of the economic system. This, after all is what the comparison of economic systems is all about.

In this chapter we consider three issues: first, some questions of method; second, what we mean by economic outcomes or economic performance; and, finally, how we might control for nonsystem forces (for example, the resource base and policy differences) when relating outcomes to system differences.

METHODS OF COMPARISON: MODELS VERSUS REALITY

For most students of comparative economic systems, the niceties of differing theoretical models are unrecognized and uninteresting. The question of whether the United States conforms to market capitalism and the Soviet Union conforms to centrally planned socialism is far outweighed by a simple interest in knowing whether, on some particular ground (the rate of growth of consumption, for example), one country outperforms the other. However, if we wish to associate an observed performance difference with different system characteristics, one must have a complete understanding of observed differences in outcomes. For example, suppose we analyze unemployment rates in socialist and capitalist economic systems, concluding that such rates are lower in socialist systems. Are we then justified in concluding that the socialist economic system is the main force driving this observed outcome?

Clearly, in the absence of a study isolating the many forces which influence employment patterns, such a conclusion would be premature.

The field of comparative economic systems tends to be structured on two levels: **models** and **reality**.[1] It is frequently argued that models, though highly abstract, are useful for comparing the theoretical differences in systems, for providing a common terminology, and finally for providing a "norm" against which actual performance can be judged. At the same time, it is the reality of real-world systems that is of interest, not the theoretical models. While theories or models may provide useful predictions about outcomes, which may then be compared with actual results, most observers are more interested in finding out how well a particular system performs in the real world.[2] While our major interest is to compare one real-world system with another, we realize that no single set of criteria will satisfy all observers. It is for this reason that we will ultimately characterize our comparisons in terms of a variety of widely used criteria such as growth, consumer well-being, and inflation.

THE FORCES INFLUENCING ECONOMIC OUTCOMES

Real-world economies do not fit the neat theoretical molds of the pure models. Instead, the real world is populated by **mixed economies**, which combine elements of market and plan, public and private ownership, material and moral incentives, and so on. Furthermore, economic outcomes are also the result of forces beyond the economic system per se — for example, the level of economic development and resource endowment.

The measurement of how closely a particular economy conforms to the imposed theoretical ideal is a complex and, in most cases, insoluble problem. Moreover, in empirical applications it is very difficult, if not impossible, to provide a quantitative measure of the economic system. Thus to study the impact of the economic system on outcomes in empirical applications, we most often must deal with generalized groupings of capitalist, planned socialist, and market socialist countries.

Another fundamental aspect of the measurement issue must be raised. Let us assume that we are somehow able to measure the system component in an adequate manner, and let us refer to this measure as ES. Our interest is how ES affects economic outcomes, which we denote as O. Yet economic outcomes depend on factors other than the economic system — natural resource endowments, the level of economic development, the size of the economy, labor and capital inputs, random events, and so on — termed **environmental factors**[3] and denoted as ENV. Finally, economic outcomes depend on the **policies** that the policy makers in economic systems choose to follow, which we denote as POL. In notational form, we have

$$O = f(ES, ENV, POL) \tag{2.1}$$

where

O   denotes economic outcomes
ES   denotes the economic system
ENV denotes environmental factors
POL denotes policies pursued by the economic system

This equation and Figure 2.1 highlight the methodological problems of determining the impact of ES on O (the *ceteris paribus* problem). Insofar as outcomes depend on factors in addition to the economic system, one cannot isolate the impact of ES without first understanding and controlling for (holding constant) ENV and POL. Let us illustrate this problem with some examples.

It has been rather well established that labor productivity (the "outcome") in the Soviet Union is low relative to that of the United States and industrialized Western Europe.[4] Is this low productivity a consequence of the system of planned socialism, environmental and policy factors, or some combination thereof? This question cannot be easily answered, primarily because the level of economic development of the Soviet Union (as measured, say, by per capita income) is still behind that of the United States and Western Europe, and productivity is positively associated with the level of development. Can the Soviet

Figure 2.1 Forces Influencing Economic Outcomes

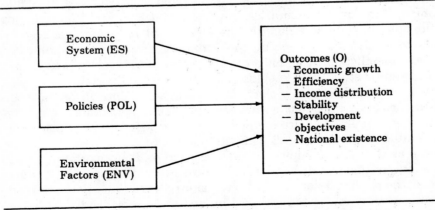

productivity gap be accounted for entirely by environmental factors, or is the economic system itself partially or fully to blame? These issues are central to the problem of evaluating the performance of economic systems. Our methods for dealing with the *ceteris paribus* problem are discussed in Chapter 12.

What do we mean by policy factors, and what is their relationship to the economic system? This distinction is difficult to elaborate and define with precision. Let us consider two examples, which illustrate the complexity of the relationship. The tendency of the planned socialist economies to pursue rapid economic growth as a top priority is well known. This choice will have an impact on economic outcomes, for the planned socialist economies will adopt a pattern of resource allocation designed to achieve the growth objective. Yet is the priority of growth a policy or is it inherent in the system of planned socialism? A second example is the tendency (see Chapter 11) of the planned socialist economies to underutilize foreign trade potential (trade aversion). Trade aversion will affect economic outcomes through its impact on industrial structure, relative prices, and economic efficiency in general. Again, one must ask: Is trade aversion a policy or is it inherent in the planned socialist model?

The answer is that a factor may be appropriately classified as policy if it could be significantly changed without changing the underlying economic system. It must be classified as a direct attribute of the economic system (the A variables) if it cannot conceivably be altered without an alteration of the economic system. Such an approach provides us with some conception of how policy and system influences might differ.

These methodological problems are difficult because policies tend to be closely intertwined with the economic system. They are nonetheless important to the evaluation of economic systems. In most instances trade aversion leads to a lower standard of living than would have prevailed had there been free international specialization. As the standard of living is often used as a performance indicator, should this weakness be attributed to the economic system or to policies pursued by the economic system?

To understand the impact of the economic system on economic outcomes one must understand the impacts of all other significant environmental and policy factors. In other fields of economics, the economic system may be taken as "given," and one can better isolate the effect of changes in particular variables on economic outcomes. The comparative economist must determine the impact both of economic systems and of other factors on economic outcomes. Appendix 2A, at the end of this chapter, discusses the statistical methods for analyzing the effect of the economic outcomes.

THE EVALUATION OF OUTCOMES:
THE SUCCESS CRITERIA PROBLEM

When the outcomes of differing economic systems are compared, one must know, first, what forces have influenced the observed outcome, and second, which economic system performs "best" in achieving its goals. How are we to evaluate the differing outcomes to decide which is "best"? Two crucial problems must be faced.

First, to evaluate the outcomes of differing economic systems, we must select a set of performance criteria. Because people will typically not agree on the appropriate criteria, the selection will be subjective.

Second, even if agreement could be reached on a list of criteria for evaluating outcomes, how will the criteria be added together, if (as is quite likely) economic systems yield different results on each of them? In such instances, one must somehow add the disparate results together by selecting **weights** for aggregation. This produces a **single index** of achievement, which can then be compared across systems. Clearly the weights selected will determine the value of the index of achievement, but they are themselves subjective and will depend on the values held by the particular observer.[5]

It is logical to think that the economic system should have as its objective the achievement of a maximum value of the economic outcome (O), subject to the constraints imposed by the economic system (ES), policies (POL), and environmental factors (ENV), where the last includes technology and resource constraints. In notational form, the objective is to

$$\text{Maximize:} \quad O \qquad\qquad (2.2)$$
$$\text{Subject to (ES, ENV, POL)}$$

From this, it would seem that the evaluation of the performance of economic systems would be (theoretically at least) a rather simple matter. After adjusting for differences in environment and policy, one would only have to determine which system achieved the highest economic outcome. If there were agreement on the measurement of outcome, it would work this way. Instead, the economic outcome (O) is a function of a series of performance indicators:

$$O = \sum_{j=i}^{k} a_j o_j \qquad\qquad (2.3)$$

where

o_j = desirable (or undesirable if negative) economic outcomes
a_j = the relative importance of the various outcomes

Consider the following example, in which economic systems designated A and B both generate two outcomes designated 5 and 9. If system A assigns weights of .2 and .8 to the outcomes 5 and 9 respectively, the weighted sum of the outcomes in this system will be 8.2. At the same time, if system B assigns weights of .7 and .3 to the outcomes 5 and 9 respectively, then the weighted sum of the outcomes in system B will be 6.2. Although the outcomes are identical in system A and system B, the use of a weighted sum clearly indicates that system A is superior to system B. Thus the selection of weights is crucial.

Just as individuals assign different weights (a_j) to different economic goals, so one would expect economic systems to assign different weights to those goals.[6] And one would not expect the evaluation of these goals to remain constant in a given economic system over time. One need only note the changing priority of economic goals in the United States or the fact that capitalist societies attach different weights to a rather similar list of economic goals or objectives.

Equation 2.3 summarizes the crux of the problem. As different societies will assign different subjective weights (a_j) to the list of economic outcomes (o_j), the measurement of economic performance will depend not only on o_j, which we assume for the moment can be measured objectively, but also on a_j, which must remain subjective. For example, one economic system may assign priority to economic growth and allocate resources accordingly. In so doing, it attaches relatively low weights to the other goals. Another economic system may attach a dominant weight to price stability and allocate its resources accordingly. It is likely, in this scenario, that the first system will perform better in terms of the growth objective, and the second system will outperform the first in terms of price stability. Which system has outperformed the other? The answer depends on one's personal judgment of which goal is more important.

THE DETERMINATION OF SYSTEM PRIORITIES

How are national priorities determined in practice? The involvement of substantial subjective elements does not mean that priorities are not in fact established, although they do change over time partly as a function of change in the economic system itself.[7]

The determination of national priorities differs from system to system. In societies where political power is largely centralized, the prevailing political authority will exercise decisive control over the formation of national goals. In the Soviet Union, for example, the Communist party plays a dominant role in goal formation.[8] This does not mean that other forces have no influence, but their roles are relatively limited. (In socialist societies, where political power is substantially concentrated, the process of modernization itself leads to some pluralization of the society and to the formation of influential interest groups.)[9]

In democratic capitalist societies, establishing priorities is more complicated. The complexity is reflected in part by various arrangements through which individuals can express preferences by voting. The vote may indicate a preference among political candidates with differing positions on major national issues, or it may be a vote cast in the marketplace indicating what goods and services are desired. However, pressure groups such as trade unions, manufacturers' associations, and professional associations can and do exercise substantial influence. Even though majority voting prevails, special interest legislation that favors minority interest may be passed.[10] Also, as many have argued, even in a pluralistic democratic society, as power becomes concentrated — whether in the hands of individuals in the form of wealth or in the hands of lobby groups, corporations, or whomever — there is a tendency for the goal formation process to change.[11] In a democratic society, the change may take place rather slowly. In a society where power is relatively centralized, change may be more sudden, though not necessarily revolutionary.

Before we consider the goals that an economic system might pursue, another matter must be raised. The reader might well ask: If various goals are laudable, why not pursue all of them? The problem is that there exist tradeoffs among goals, and specific goals can often be achieved only by sacrificing other, less important, goals. The necessity to trade off goals is a consequence of the fundamental scarcity of resources, a fact that exists in any economic system and prevents an economy from producing unlimited quantities of goods and services. Instead, choices must be made among alternate goals.

The nature of the tradeoffs is not always measurable. Can unemployment in the United States be lowered without increasing inflation? Is sustained economic growth compatible with a cleaner environment? Can the Soviet Union sustain rapid growth of both GNP and military power? The existence of tradeoffs is important in at least two dimensions. First, the performance of economic systems cannot be assesssed without some insights into the nature of the tradeoff among alternatives. Second, when one goal must in some degree be sacrificed to achieve another, we should not criticize a system for not achieving a goal that it is not, in fact, pursuing.

PERFORMANCE CRITERIA

We have selected a set of performance criteria that can be generally applied to assess economic outcomes. We know, however, that such a list will omit some criteria (military power, for example) that are important to some observers. We shall use the following criteria to evaluate economic outcomes:

1. Economic growth
2. Efficiency
3. Income distribution
4. Stability (cyclical stability, inflation, unemployment)
5. Development objectives
6. Continuation of national existence

In utilizing these six performance criteria, we shall proceed with a three-stage order of development. First, we shall examine each criterion and attempt to assess interrelationships and tradeoffs among them. Second, as we build our stylized models of capitalism and socialism, we shall generate hypotheses about how we expect each system to perform with regard to each criterion. Third, as we later look at real-world economic systems in action, we shall compare their performance in terms of these criteria.

Economic Growth

Probably the most widely used indicator of economic performance is economic growth. **Economic growth** refers to increases in the volume of output that an economy generates over time or to increases in output per capita.[12] We are interested in economic output and its growth because, for a particular economic system at a point in time, the material well-being or welfare of its population can be approximated by the volume of goods and services per capita at its disposal.[13] Changes in the volume of output per capita over time will normally bring about changes in the welfare of the population in the same direction. Using this interpretation, levels of well-being of different systems can be compared at a point in time, or over time, to evaluate the rate at which progress is being made.

The sorts of comparisons and interpretations that we are suggesting are complex in the real world. Because economic growth is such a widely used performance indicator, it is useful to spell out some complications:

First, in assessing economic growth, there are severe measurement problems, especially when different economic systems are compared. These sorts of problems have been discussed at length in specialized literature on economic growth.[14]

Second, it is difficult to untangle the causes of differences in economic growth. Growth differences may be the consequence of the economic system, but they may also be due to environmental and policy factors. The process of economic growth is so complex that it defies easy description; therefore, we can never be sure of the system's impact on growth. For example, our analysis in Chapter 12 indicates that economic growth is related to level of development.[15] If one compares the growth of two economic systems over time, when each system begins with a different **base**, one may expect, *ceteris paribus*, differences in growth performance.

Third, the uncertain linkage between the growth of output and increases in welfare of the population should be emphasized. Economic growth is enhanced by capital formation, but to expand the capital stock, saving (refraining from current consumption) is required. It may well be that the savings of the present generation will bear fruit in the form of welfare increases only for later generations. The decision to postpone present consumption in favor of future consumption must be confronted in any economic system, whether the choice is made primarily by consumer or by planner. The outcome of this decision will have an impact on growth performance and current welfare. It is even possible for the output of an economy to grow while welfare (as measured by available consumer goods) is declining.

It has been argued that capitalist systems consistently underrate the merits of future vis-à-vis present consumption and hence save too little to make adequate provision for the future.[16] Thus we could anticipate higher savings ratios in socialist systems and, accordingly, a more rapid rate of growth of the capital stock and, *ceteris paribus*, a higher rate of growth of output.

Efficiency

A second measure of system performance is economic efficiency. The concept of **efficiency** refers to the effectiveness with which a system utilizes its available resources (including knowledge) at a particular point in time (**static efficiency**) or through time (**dynamic efficiency**).[17] Static and dynamic efficiency are interrelated in a complex manner, but both are multidimensional in the sense that they depend on a wide variety of factors. Economists have a technical definition of efficiency called Pareto optimality. The conditions of Pareto optimality are given in the next chapter (pp. 47–48).

The concept of efficiency can be conveniently illustrated by the production possibilities schedule, as shown in Figure 2.2. The initial possibilities schedule (*AB*) illustrates all feasible combinations of producer and consumer goods capable of being produced by a particular economic system at a particular point in time using all available resources at maximum efficiency. The production possibilities schedule shows that, given its existing resources, the system has a menu of production choices open to it. Economic systems must choose where to locate on the schedule. In capitalist societies, the consumer-voter dominates this choice. In planned socialist societies, planners make the decision.

It is worth emphasizing that the labels we have attached to the axes in Figure 2.2 are arbitrary. We could have chosen other goals and examined a number of possible tradeoffs among goals. However, the *shape* of the production possibilities frontier is not accidental. The fact that it is a curve convex from the origin illustrates a basic fact of economic life: As one attempts to produce increasing amounts of, say, consumer goods, ever larger amounts of producer goods will have to be given up to obtain indentical increases in consumer goods. In more technical terms, there is a diminishing marginal rate of technical substitution between the production of consumer goods and the production of producer goods.

The production possibilities schedule is a useful device for illustrating the concept of efficiency. We have already indicated that AB represents the capacity of a particular economic system at a particular point in time. Static efficiency requires an economic system to be operating on

Figure 2.2 The Production Possibilities Schedule

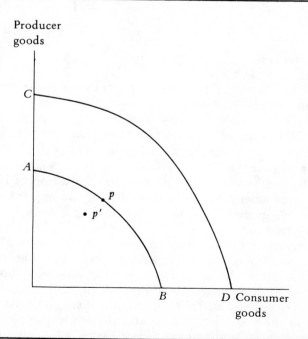

its production possibilities frontier, for example, at point p. Output combinations beyond AB are impossible at that time; combinations inside AB are feasible but inefficient. An economic system that has the capacity AB but is producing at p' is statically inefficient, because it could move to point p and produce *more of both* goods with no increase in available resources.

Dynamic efficiency refers to the ability of an economic system to enhance its capacity to produce goods and services over time without an increase in capital and labor inputs. Dynamic efficiency is indicated by the movement of the frontier outward from AB to CD (without an underlying increase in resources available), the distance of this movement indicating the rate of change of efficiency.

Like other indicators of system performance, static and dynamic efficiency are subject to complex measurement problems. The basic approach to measuring static efficiency is to make productivity calculations, as measured by the ratio of the output of an economic system to the inputs available. Dynamic efficiency is measured by changes in this ratio over time.

Economic growth and dynamic efficiency are not the same. The output of a system may grow through increases in efficiency (that is, better ways of doing things with the same resources) or by expanding the amount of, say, labor but using that labor at a constant rate of effectiveness. The former is often termed **intensive growth**, the latter **extensive growth**.

Income Distribution

How well an economic system distributes income among the participants in the system is the third criterion for assessing economic performance. Technically, income distribution is measured by the well-known Lorenz curve or Gini coefficient, as shown in Figure 2.3. The availability of techniques to measure income distributions does not, however, answer the question of what constitutes good distribution. There may be substantial agreement on the definition of bad income distributions (for example, where 1 percent of the population receives 95 percent of all income); judgments concerning intermediate cases are more difficult to make.

What constitutes an equitable distribution of income?[18] Equity involves fairness, though what is considered fair will differ from case to case and will likely evolve over time as a social judgment. For example, one criterion of fairness might involve reward according to contribution to the production process. In a capitalist society, personal income is determined by the volume of human and physical capital one owns and by their prices as determined by factor markets. Income differences reflect differences in effort (provision of labor services), differences in frugality (provision of capital), inheritance of physical and human capital, luck, and so on. The market distribution of income may be modified by action through the tax system and the provision of social services. The extent to which government redistributive action is justified on equity grounds is a matter of continuing controversy in capitalist societies. Under socialism, the factors of production are, with the exception of labor, publicly owned. Thus even if Marxian ideology did not dictate that labor be the only productive input, the distribution of incomes would differ under socialism and capitalism. Capital and land are both socially owned in a socialist society. Even if they were

Figure 2.3 Measuring Income Inequality: The Lorenz Curve

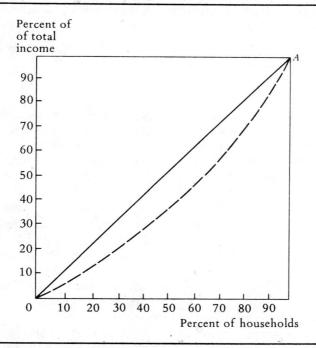

Explanation: Percent of households is measured on the horizontal axis, percent of income on the vertical axis. Perfect equality would be, for example, where 10 percent of households received 10 percent of all income. This would be illustrated by a 45-degree line between the origin (0) and point *A*. Inequality can be illustrated by the dashed line. The further the dashed line bows away from the 45-degree line, the more unequal the distribution of income. In the diagram, for example, the bottom 20 percent of households receive 10 percent of income. A comprehensive measure, known as the *Gini coefficient*, is typically used to measure income inequality. The Gini coefficient is the area between the 45-degree line and the dashed line divided by the entire area under the 45-degree line.

allocated to the production process on the basis of prices and thereafter received a reward, that reward would belong to the state, not to individuals.

What is the relationship between the efficiency of an economic system and its distribution of income? In particular, to what degree is it possible to lessen income inequality in a capitalist (or even socialist) system without retarding effort, capital inputs, and risk taking? The theme is familiar: Do steeply progressive taxes (capitalism) or state-dictated wage equality (socialism) limit personal incentives and motivations? This matter is of more than theoretical interest. First, we have already noted that system goals may conflict and that choices must be made. Can social goals — for example, the elimination of poverty — be pursued without impairing efficiency? Second, the analysis of differing economic systems may provide us with important evidence on the equity-efficiency tradeoff, evidence that is difficult to accumulate from one particular system.

Stability

The fourth criterion by which to assess the performance of economic systems is economic stability. By **stability** we mean the absence of significant fluctuations in growth rates, the maintenance of acceptable rates of unemployment, and the avoidance of excessive inflation whether or not the inflation and unemployment are cyclical. Economic stability is a desirable objective for two reasons. The first is that various segments of the population are damaged by instability. Individuals on fixed incomes are hurt by unanticipated inflation; the poorly trained are hurt by unemployment. Second, cyclical instability can lead to losses of potential output, making the economic system operate inside its production possibilities schedule.

Capitalist economies have historically been subject to fluctuations in the level of economic activity, in other words, to business cycles.[19] In planned socialist economies, aggregate economic activity (including investment) is more subject to the control of planners. Although cyclical activity could arise in a planned socialist society — for example, through planning errors or transmission through the foreign sector — the economic growth of a socialist society is less likely to suffer cyclical fluctuations than that of a capitalist society (this hypothesis will be elaborated in Chapter 5).

The matter of stability in economic growth is of practical importance. Potential lost at any point in time is lost forever. A system that, because of cyclical instability, does not reach its potential at various points in time, cannot be expected to achieve its potential rate of growth through time. This waste is evident in concrete terms, for example, unemployment. Thus the matter of cyclical instability, the length and the severity of cycles, and the forms in which they find expression must be important indicators of the relative success of economic systems.

Inflation, a second manifestation of instability, may appear in open form as a general rise in the price level, or it may occur in repressed form as lengthening lines for goods and services, regional and sectoral shortages, and the like. In capitalist economies, inflation typically occurs in the first form; in the planned socialist economies (where planners set prices), it typically occurs in the repressed form. In any event, excessive inflation is viewed as an undesirable phenomenon insofar as it can distort economic calculation (where relative prices are used as sources of information), cause increased use of barter, and alter the anticipated income distribution.

Unemployment is undesirable. It implies, along with the personal hardships of those unemployed, less than full utilization of a system's resources. It is difficult, however, to measure causal factors and to compare unemployment rates across economic systems because the planned socialist economies do not maintain records on unemployment (which is said to have been "liquidated"). Moreover, the standard definition of unemployment (those seeking employment but unable to find jobs) leaves room for differences in interpretation. Economists recognize that there are different types of unemployment, ranging from unemployment associated with the normal changing of jobs to chronic hard-core unemployment.

These sorts of definitions relate to individuals and jobs. They do not relate to the more subtle but possibly more important concept of **underemployment**, or the employment of individuals on a full-time basis at work in which they utilize their skills at less than their full potential. Underemployment (which may be most common in the planned socialist economies) is less visible than unemployment, but it can have a similarly adverse effect on capacity utilization. It typically takes the form of overstaffing, a situation in which ten people are employed for a job that could be accomplished just as well by five people.

At first glance, stability appears to be one performance criterion that is unambiguously good because desirable goals need not be sacrificed to attain it. Closer inspection, however, reveals possible tradeoffs. Consider an economy that guarantees employment (underemployment?) to all. What effect will this have on incentives and job performance? Moreover, in such a system the temptation would exist to keep inefficient firms in operation for the sake of stable employment, and this would have a negative impact on efficiency.

Development Objectives

The performance criteria we have been discussing are familiar to most and uncontroversial to many. Few would argue that economic growth, efficiency, stability, and a "good" distribution of income are unimportant, despite disagreement on the weights that should be assigned to each. But what about development objectives? What are they, and why should they be included as a separate performance criterion?

Most of the world's people live in poverty, and their primary concern is economic development. Although the industrialized nations have tended to assign a rather small weight to the problems of the less-developed countries (LDCs), those countries would be most interested in comparing economic systems in a development context. What can be learned from the development paths of capitalist and socialist economic systems that might help LDCs? Does one economic system offer a means to rapid economic development not present in other economic systems?

It could be argued that it is redundant to evaluate economic systems according to their success in achieving development objectives — economic systems that achieve the first four objectives (particularly rapid growth) with also achieve development goals. It could also be maintained that the industrialized capitalist systems developed early without conscious developmental objectives. The planned socialist economies, on the other hand, have maintained a consistent set of priorities that emphasize rapid economic development ("building socialism") above other goals. It is in this light that one can understand Soviet emphasis on the growth objective. Thus, to some extent, we are up against the success criterion problem, for the planned socialist economies have placed greater emphasis on development goals than have their capitalist counterparts.

The planned socialist economies would likely argue that there is a distinction between growth objectives and development objectives, for they view economic development as the growth of particular branches and particular structural changes. This view is shared by Western economists, who also view development as a combination of economic growth and structural change. The question is: Can one economic system perform "better" in producing the structural changes required for economic development?

Although there is controversy over what caused economic development, statistically the pattern that emerges from nations that have been or are developing shows a remarkable degree of consistency.[20] The sectoral patterns of development are familiar: The product and labor force shares of industry increase while those of agriculture decline; the urban sector grows proportionally while the rural sector declines proportionally; and so on. When these structural features are examined across systems at a point in time and over time, they reveal a good deal about the development paths followed by a particular economic system. Western authorities have identified a "socialist path" of development in which at given levels of economic development investment shares are high relative to what one might observe in capitalist systems and there is a tendency to favor industry over agriculture in investment shares, to promote heavy industry over light industry, to keep agriculture relatively labor-intensive and industry relatively capital-intensive, and to minimize the size (and costs) of the urban sector.[21]

In a planned economy, it has been argued, concentration of power in the hands of the planner facilitates rapid adjustments in the structural features of the economy. In the capitalist economy, on the other hand, those sorts of structural change take place relatively slowly in response to changing market forces. We shall compare systems, therefore, not only in terms of their structural features at given levels of development, but also in terms of the speed with which these features change. In particular, we shall examine the possibility that eventually there will be structural convergence so that quite apart from structural differences at a particular point in time (controlling for level of development) structural features will become increasingly similar at increasingly high levels of economic development.

Continuation of National Existence

An obvious goal of all economic systems is to continue their national existence. In fact, this goal would override the other five goals in all but unusual circumstances. Continuation of national existence requires the political, military, and social power necessary to turn back forces that threaten national existence. From an economic point of view, continuation of national existence requires being able to devote sufficient human and capital resources to national defense (in a hostile world) to prevent the overthrow of the system by external forces. Sufficient internal cohesion and strength are also necessary to prevent the collapse of the system from within. Thus, if economic growth were to become negative for a long period of time or if the income distribution became intolerable to a sufficient number of people, continuation of national existence could be threatened.

There can be tradeoffs between the goal of continuation of national existence and the other five goals. If the external world is so hostile that the major portion of resources must be devoted to national defense, the goal of economic growth would have to be sacrificed. If for some reason a highly unequal distribution of income and wealth were desired, this goal might have to be sacrificed to guarantee continuation of national existence.

SUMMARY: THE ECONOMIC SYSTEM AND ECONOMIC OUTCOMES

1. The field of comparative economic systems has generally been in flux. Models of economic systems are not well defined, making comparisons difficult, even on an abstract theoretical level. As one turns to real-world economic systems, the many forces which influence observed outcomes make comparisons difficult. It is especially difficult to relate differences in observed outcomes to differences in the economic system as opposed to other factors, such as the resource base.
2. The economic system is an organizational arrangement that influences resource allocation. The task of comparative economics is to relate differences in economic systems to observed differences in outcomes.
3. Both the economic system and other factors affect observed outcomes. The other factors are policies and environmental factors. The latter factor is a catchall for a variety of influences, for example, resource endowment.
4. There are two major problems in comparing the performance of economic systems: first, how to select the criteria that will be used to make the performance comparison; second, once the criteria have been selected, how to add them together (select appropriate weights) to come to an unequivocal conclusion about the relative performance of economic systems. The criteria, and the importance attached to them, are subjective, so there are bound to be differences of opinion when system performance is assessed.
5. Six criteria — economic growth, efficiency, income distribution, stability, development objectives, and continuation of national existence can be used to measure economic performance. Each performance indicator was described, and we discussed how each indicator could be used to evaluate the performance of economic systems. We emphasized that not all goals could be achieved simultaneously, necessitating tradeoffs among objectives. The existence of these tradeoffs makes the evaluation of economic performance difficult because different economic systems have emphasized different objectives.

NOTES

1. For a survey of these issues, see, for example, Morris Bornstein, ed., *Comparative Economic Systems: Models and Cases*, 3rd ed. (Homewood, Ill.: Irwin, 1974), ch. 1.

2. The use of deductive models is criticized in a recent work by Trevor Buck. Buck argues that the *predictions* derived from utopian models (in particular those of perfect capitalism, central planning, and self-management) are identical. Further, he argues that "empirical evidence cannot test utopian models." For elaboration, see Trevor Buck, *Comparative Industrial Systems* (New York: St. Martin's, 1982), ch. 1.

3. Here we are following the approach suggested in Tjalling C. Koopmans and John Michael Montias, "On the Description and Comparison of Economic Systems," in Alexander Eckstein, ed., *Comparison of Economic Systems: Theoretical and Methodological Approaches* (Berkeley: University of California Press, 1971), ch. 2.

4. The reader is referred to Abram Bergson's studies of comparative Soviet-United States factor productivity: Abram Bergson, *The Economics of Soviet Planning* (New Haven: Yale University Press, 1964), ch. 14; Abram Bergson, *Planning and Productivity Under Soviet Socialism* (New York: Columbia University Press, 1968); and Abram Bergson, "Comparative Productivity," *American Economic Review*, 77 (June 1987), pp. 342-357.

5. For a recent attempt to develop a framework in which to analyze outcomes, see Koopmans and Montias, "On the Description and Comparison of Economic Systems," pp. 27-78; for an earlier survey of the problem, see Bela Balassa, "Success Criteria for Economic Systems," in Morris Bornstein, ed., *Comparative Economic Systems: Models and Cases*, rev. ed. (Homewood, Ill.: Irwin, 1969), pp. 2-18.

6. There is a considerable body of literature on system goals. See, for example, John Michael Montias, *The Structure of Economic Systems* (New Haven: Yale University Press, 1976), ch. 3; Kenneth Arrow, *Social Choice and Individual Values*, 2nd ed. (New York: Wiley, 1963); G. M. Heal, *The Theory of Economic Planning* (New York: North Holland, 1973), ch. 2.

7. One of the difficult aspects of goal formation in economic systems is the fact that goals and system structure are not independent of each other. For a discussion of this point see Montias, *The Structure of Economic Systems.*

8. For a detailed treatment, see Leonard Shapiro, *The Communist Party of the Soviet Union* (New York: Random House, 1971); for a brief treatment of the Communist party in relation to the formation of economic policy, see Paul R. Gregory and Robert C. Stuart, *Soviet Economic Structure and Performance*, 3rd ed. (New York: Harper & Row, 1986), ch. 7.

9. The standard work on this question is H. Gordon Skilling and Franklyn Griffiths, eds., *Interest Groups in Soviet Politics* (Princeton, N.J.: Princeton University Press, 1971); for the case argued with regard to industrial managers, see Jeremy R. Azrael, *Managerial Power and Soviet Politics* (Cambridge, Mass.: Harvard University Press, 1966).

10. The literature of modern public choice has reached some disturbing conclusions about the rationality of majority-rule voting procedures in single- and multi-issue settings. On this, see James Buchanan and Gordon Tullock, *The Calculus of Consent* (Ann Arbor: University of Michigan Press, 1962).

11. This is a fairly standard critique of capitalism — namely, that the impact of the consumer is quite limited and, in fact, is replaced over time by the views of powerful lobby groups, large corporations, and so on. This view has been expressed by a number of authors, among them John Kenneth Galbraith, *The New Industrial State* (Boston: Houghton Mifflin, 1967); Assar Lindbeck, *The Political Economy of the New Left: An Outsider's View*, 2nd ed. (New York: Harper & Row, 1977); Samuel Bowles, David M. Gordon, and Thomas E. Weisskopf, *Beyond the Waste Land: A Democratic Alternative to Economic Decline* (New York: Anchor Press/Doubleday, 1983).

12. For a discussion of economic growth, see, for example, Charles P. Kindleberger and Bruce Herrick, *Economic Development*, 3rd ed. (New York: McGraw-Hill, 1977), ch. 3; and Phillip A. Neher, *Economic Growth and Development: A Mathematical Introduction* (New York: Wiley, 1971).

13. On the technical aspects of measurement, see Abram Bergson, *The Real National Income of Soviet Russia Since 1928* (Cambridge, Mass.: Harvard University Press, 1961), ch. 3; on the general question of how to measure the well-being of a nation, see Kindleberger and Herrick, *Economic Development*, ch. 1.

14. The question of cross-country comparisons has been discussed in great detail, especially for the tricky though interesting case of comparisons between the Soviet Union and the United States. For a discussion of some of the major issues, see Robert W. Campbell, N. Mark Earle, Jr., Herbert S. Levine, and Francis W. Dresch, "Methodological Problems Comparing the U.S. and U.S.S.R. Economies," in U.S., Congress, Joint Economic Committee, *Soviet Economic Prospects for the Seventies* (Washington, D.C.: Government Printing Office, 1973), pp. 122-146.

15. For an analysis of growth patterns, see Hollis Chenery and Moises Syrquin, *Patterns of Development, 1950-1970* (London: Oxford University Press, 1975).

16. This is a standard socialist critique of capitalism. See, for example, A. C. Pigou, *Socialism Versus Capitalism* (London: Macmillan, 1960), ch. 8; for a summary statement of this view, see Heinz Kohler, *Welfare and Planning: An Analysis of Capitalism Versus Socialism* (New York: Wiley, 1966), ch. 5; for an in-depth treatment, see Maurice Dobb, *Welfare Economics and the Economics of Socialism* (Cambridge: Cambridge University Press, 1969).

17. For a discussion of these concepts in the comparative context, see Bergson, *Planning and Productivity Under Soviet Socialism*.

18. For an introductory discussion of income inequality, see Roy Ruffin and Paul Gregory, *Economics* (Glenview, Ill.: Scott, Foresman, 1983), ch. 22; see also Paul Taubman, *Income Distribution and Redistribution* (Reading, Mass.: Addison-Wesley, 1978).

19. There is a large body of literature pertaining to stability. For an introduction, see Rudigor Dornbusch and Stanley Fischer, *Macroeconomics*, 4th ed. (New York: McGraw-Hill, 1987).

20. See Chenery and Syrquin, *Patterns of Development*.

21. Much of the analysis of socialist development has been from the examples of the Soviet Union and the East European countries. For a summary of this position, see Gregory and Stuart, *Soviet Economic Structure and Performance*, ch. 12.

RECOMMENDED READINGS

Kenneth Arrow, *Social Change and Individual Values*, 2nd ed. (New York: Wiley, 1963).

Bela Balassa, "Success Criteria for Economic Systems," in Morris Bornstein, ed., *Comparative Economic Systems: Models and Cases*, rev. ed. (Homewood, Ill.: Irwin, 1964).

Trevor Buck, *Comparative Industrial Systems* (New York: St. Martin's, 1982).

Etienne Kirschen and Lucian Morissens, "The Objectives and Instruments of Economic Policy," in Morris Bornstein, ed., *Comparative Economic Systems: Models and Cases*, 4th ed. (Homewood, Ill.: Irwin, 1978).

Assar Lindbeck, *The Political Economy of the New Left: An Outsider's View*, 2nd ed. (New York: Harper & Row, 1977).

John Michael Montias, *The Structure of Economic Systems* (New Haven: Yale University Press, 1976).

APPENDIX 2A: MEASUREMENT OF THE SYSTEM IMPACT

At this juncture, the idea of actually measuring the impact of the economic system might seem to be highly artificial. Nevertheless, to try to do so would seem justified, insofar as economists are always interested in understanding the nature of the forces that influence observed outcomes. The issue is of great importance. Consider, for example, a typical characterization of the Soviet economic system: It is a system which, over the years, has stressed the development of industry at the expense of the consumer, and heavy industry at the expense of light industry. This description of the Soviet economy (albeit in a very simplistic form) is derived not from casual observation, but rather from careful consideration of Soviet development. Specifically, the share of consumption in total Soviet output can be examined, while controlling in some fashion for the level of Soviet development, since we know such factors as share of economic output vary through time. This approach certainly does not prove that the economic system caused the outcome. However, it does provide a mechanism for attempting to discover systematic differences in observed outcomes between capitalist and socialist economic systems.

A number of outcomes in the Soviet (socialist) case are commonly said to result from the influence of particular Soviet resource allocation arrangements, for example, the importance of foreign trade and the role of consumer goods. However, let us consider for the moment the matter of urbanization. We have chosen urbanization in part for expository convenience, though, in fact, urbanization patterns in various economic systems are a matter of considerable real-world interest.

Comparative Urbanization Patterns: System Influences

Analysis of historical data provides a model of the relationship between economic development, as measured by per capita gross national product (GNP) and the proportion of a country's population living in urban areas (URB). This relationship is depicted diagrammatically in Figure 2.A1.

Suppose we wish to consider whether there are systematic differences in urbanization patterns in socialist and capitalist systems, and to infer that, if there are, the system differences may have been influential. The reader might well ask: how urbanized is the Soviet Union (for example), and how does its level of urbanization compare, say, to that of the United States? An examination of relevant data for the mid-1980s would reveal that, according to existing definitions, about 65 percent of the Soviet population lives in urban centers, while for the United States the equivalent number is about 75 percent. Aside from the critical issue of differences in definition, can we conclude that the Soviet Union is less urbanized than the United States? Such a conclusion may be warranted, yet from Figure 2.A1 we know that some difference should be expected, since the Soviet Union is at a lower level of economic development than the United States. Clearly there are two possible explanations for the patterns we observe. Each is developed in Figure 2.A2 (see p. 40).

Panel A of Figure 2.A2 provides us with one possible explanation of the observed urbanization pattern: Urbanization patterns are similar in socialist and capitalist economic systems; differences are accounted for by the simple fact that urbanization *levels* are related to levels of economic development. Thus, since the Soviet Union is at a lower level of economic development than the United States, the Soviet level of urbanization is also lower.

Panel B suggests a different interpretation: Socialist and capitalist urbanization patterns are systematically different. Even when we con-

Figure 2.A1 Urbanization and Economic Development

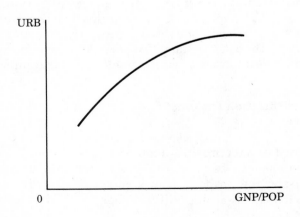

trol for the level of economic development, socialist systems are less urbanized, suggesting that there are characteristic features of socialism, possibly aspects of the economic system or policies, which systematically influence urbanization. To resolve this issue, we need to examine empirical evidence relating to the forces within each system influencing the observed outcomes. Let us consider this question in greater detail.

In Chapter 1, we elaborated an approach to the study of differing economic systems. This approach is based on the desirability of isolating the impact of the economic system and assessing that impact (both direction and magnitude) on observed outcomes. In notational form, the following approach was suggested:

$$O = f(\text{ES, ENV, POL}) \qquad\qquad (2A.1)$$

Thus we argued that outcomes (O) are a function of the nature of the economic system (ES), the nature of the environment in which the economic system functions (ENV), and, finally, the nature of the policies (POL). But can we, in practice, empirically estimate the above relationship for real-world economic systems? Within certain limitations we can in fact estimate the above relationship and thus give empirical content to the comparison of economic systems. In this particular case, the outcome (O) is the level of urbanization, measured by the percentage of population living in urban areas; the environmental or controlling factor (ENV) is the level of economic development measured by per capita gross national product; the economic system (ES) is considered explicitly, in our case capitalist or socialist. Thus we argue that proxies can be developed for the variables in equation 2A.1 and an explicit functional relationship can be posited as follows:

$$\text{URB}_i = a + b(\text{GNP/POP})_i + u_i \qquad\qquad (2A.2)$$

This relationship is assumed to have the usual characteristics (a positive relationship between per capita income and urbanization), though it is not a theory of urbanization. It is simply a relationship through which to examine statistical regularities or irregularities across a number of systems (countries). In practice, there are several ways to estimate equation 2A.2 to give explicit consideration to the economic system. Fundamentally, our task is to observe a particular relationship (in this case urbanization) in samples drawn from two populations, capitalist and socialist, and to consider, on the basis of the available statistical evidence, whether the results that we obtain can be assumed to have come from two different populations.

Figure 2.A2 Urbanization in Different Economic Systems

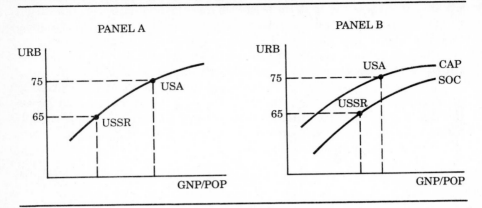

THE FORECASTING APPROACH

Equation 2A.2 can be estimated from data drawn from a sample of capitalist or market systems. Having derived estimates for the parameters of the equation (the constant a and the coefficient b), we then have a simple model from which predictions can be derived. Specifically, using sample data on per capita gross national product from capitalist systems, we would use the predictive equation to forecast values for URB_i in socialist systems. The forecast values tell us the expected level of urbanization of each socialist country assuming that they follow the "normal" capitalist relationship between income and urbanization. We can then compare the actual socialist values of URB_i with those predicted by our equation. Assuming that our predictive equation captures the "normal" capitalist relationship, differences between predicted and actual values of URB_i would tell us whether socialist countries are, relative to capitalist countries, underurbanized, overurbanized, or about the same.

This approach has the distinct advantage of indicating how particular socialist countries behave relative to "normal" patterns. As it stands, however, we have no test of the statistical significance of our results. Finally, should we observe that the deviations are not uniformly positive or negative, some additional criterion of evaluation would be necessary.

THE DUMMY VARIABLE APPROACH

An appealing method for handling many discrete differences (in this case whether a system is capitalist or socialist) is the use of the dummy variables.[1] In this approach, equation 2A.2 would be respecified as follows:

$$URB_i = a + b(GNP/POP)_i + cDUM + u_i \qquad (2A.3)$$

The dummy variable would be assigned the value 1 for socialist systems, and 0 for capitalist systems and then estimated using an aggregated sample (socialist and capitalist) of countries. The statistical importance of the economic system in influencing urbanization levels as defined here would be assessed by determining the significance and magnitude of the coefficient attached to the dummy variable.

A useful variant of the dummy variable approach would be the use of the dummy variable to isolate differences in *both* the intercept and the slope, thus providing a better explanation of why the socialist and capitalist patterns differ. In our present example, the dummy variable would be defined as before, namely 1 for socialist systems and 0 for capitalist systems. A second dummy variable would be defined as follows:

$$DUMG = (DUM)\,(GNP/POP)$$

In this variant, the equation to be tested would be as follows:

$$URB_i = a + b(GNP/POP)_i + cDUM + dDUMG + u_i \qquad (2A.4)$$

As before, this equation would be estimated using data from capitalist and socialist systems, and the results would be assessed by examining the magnitude and significance of the coefficients. While equation 2A.4 provides the observer with more information than equation 2A.3, the potential for multicollinearity (for example between DUM and DUMG) may introduce undesirable bias.

THE CHOW TEST

A third method for examining system differences in a relationship such as equation 2A.2 is the Chow test.[2] In this approach, equation 2A.2 would be estimated separately using capitalist and socialist sample data. Two sets of parameter estimates, a and b, would exist, one for the socialist, the other for the capitalist sample. The Chow test would be used to determine if the coefficients (for example, the coefficient b in equation 2A.2) are in fact statistically different in the sense that they can be said to come from different populations. If the Chow test shows the parameters to be statistically different, the conclusion is that the economic system acts to render the relationship between per capita income and urbanization different.[3] The empirical evidence seems to support the outcome postulated in Panel B of Figure 2.5.[4] However, while considerable emphasis is placed upon this sort of analysis in our characterization of different outcomes across economic systems, it should be emphasized that the analysis presents a number of problems. The modeling of the relationship between systems and outcomes remains simplistic. Moreover, econometric issues such as appropriate specification, along with the usual problems of data availability in the international context, complicate our attempts to analyze these relationships.

NOTES

1. For a discussion of dummy variables, see, for example, Gregory C. Chow, *Econometrics* (New York: McGraw-Hill, 1983), ch. 2.
2. For a discussion of the Chow test, see Edward J. Kane, *An Introduction to Statistics and Econometrics* (New York: Harper & Row, 1968), p. 341.
3. For a useful comparison of various approaches, see Edward A. Hewett, "Alternative Econometric Approaches for Studying the Link Between Economic Systems and Economic Outcomes," *Journal of Comparative Economics*, 4, no. 3 (September 1980), pp. 274-294. Also see John Michael Montias, *The Structure of Economic Systems* (New Haven: Yale University Press, 1976), ch. 5.
4. See Gur Ofer, "Economizing on Urbanization in Socialist Countries: Historical Necessity or Socialist Strategy," in Alan A. Brown and Egon Neuberger, eds., *Internal Migration: A Comparative Perspective* (New York: Academic, 1977), ch. 16. For a broader discussion, see Henry W. Morton and Robert C. Stuart, *The Contemporary Soviet City* (Armonk, N.Y.: M. E. Sharpe, 1984).

Chapter 3
The Theory of Capitalism

There is no single theoretical model of capitalism, and no two capitalist economies are alike. Controversy exists over the role of the state, the role of market imperfections (externalities, monopoly, public goods), and the inherent cyclical instability of capitalism.

This chapter is about the theory of capitalism. Subsequent chapters discuss capitalism in practice. This chapter asks: How well should capitalist market economies *in theory* resolve the problem of allocating scarce resources among competing ends? This issue is important for two reasons. The first is that the theories of capitalism and socialism yield hypotheses concerning expected performance differences among systems, and those hypotheses can be tested against the experiences of capitalist and socialist nations. The second is that one may be most interested in the theoretical models themselves and in what they suggest about the performance of economic systems under **ideal conditions** (say, of perfect competition or central planning with perfect information and control). Because actual economies will diverge from the ideal, it could be argued that their performance cannot be used as a test of the system's "true" performance and that the performance issue must be resolved at the theoretical level.[1]

At the end of this chapter, we shall return to the performance criteria discussed in Chapters 1 and 2 and consider the hypotheses concerning the performance criteria used to evaluate economic systems that can be derived from the theory of capitalism.

HOW MARKETS WORK

The theory of capitalism has focused on how a market economy works. It examines the role of prices in harmonizing the wishes of consumers and producers.

Equilibrium and the "Invisible Hand"

The pioneering analysis of market capitalism is Adam Smith's *The Wealth of Nations*, published in 1776.[2] Speaking against the mercantilist position that free trade could lead to a country's ruin, Adam Smith argued that a highly efficient and harmonious economic system would emerge if competitive markets were left to function freely without government intervention and if government acted to protect property rights.

Smith's underlying notion was that, if individuals were given free rein to pursue their own selfish interests, an "invisible hand" (that is, the competitive market) would cause them to behave in a socially responsible manner. Products desired by consumers would be produced in the appropriate assortments and quantities, and the most efficient means of production would be used. No government or social action would be required to bring about this desirable state of affairs, for each individual acting in pursuit of his or her own gain could be counted on to do the right thing. In fact, government action would be likely to interfere with this natural process, thus government should be limited to providing essential public services — national defense, a legal system to protect private property, and others — which private enterprise could not produce on its own. An equilibrium of consumers and producers would be created spontaneously in the competitive marketplace, for if the actions of consumers and producers were not in harmony, the market price would adjust to bring the two groups into equilibrium.

Smith's notion of a natural tendency toward an efficient economic equilibrium formed the foundation for the liberal economic thought of the nineteenth century. In the words of one authority, Smith's most important triumph was that "he put into the center of economics the systematic analysis of the behavior of individuals pursuing their self-interest under conditions of competition," and this remains "the foundation of the theory of resource allocation."[3] Most of the later theorizing aimed at a further elaboration and then partial criticism of Smith's vision of market capitalism. This theorizing became known as neoclassical economics.

Partial Equilibrium

Adam Smith's description of markets was informal and incomplete, and it was left to his successors to provide more formal analyses of the workings of markets and the price system. The partial equilibrium approach pioneered by Alfred Marshall and developed more fully by J. R. Hicks and Paul Samuelson suggests a more formal way to describe the "invisible hand."[4]

It is assumed that two motivating forces drive market capitalism: the desire of producers to maximize profits and the desire of consumers to maximize their own welfare (utility) subject to the constraint of limited income. Under competitive conditions, producers will be prepared to supply larger quantities at higher prices, combining inputs to minimize costs. Consumers, seeking to maximize their welfare, will be prepared to purchase less at higher prices. The producer and consumer meet in the marketplace, where their conflicting objectives are brought into equilibrium. If the quantity demanded exceeds the quantity supplied at the prevailing price, the price will automatically rise, thereby squeezing out some demand and evoking a larger supply response until all those willing to buy and sell at the prevailing price can do so. At this point, an equilibrium price is established, the market clears, and there is no tendency to depart from the equilibrium unless it is disrupted by some exogenous change (see Figure 3.1).

This description underscores how market resource allocation works under competitive conditions. All other things being equal, an increase in consumer demand for a particular product will disrupt the established equilibrium, and the price will start to rise. As the price rises, producers will find it in their interest to supply a larger quantity of the product. If at the new price larger profits can be obtained, additional producers will enter the market. On the demand side, the rise in the price will cause substitution (substitution of now less expensive

Figure 3.1 Market Equilibrium in a Competitive Economy

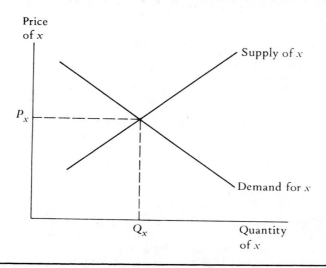

Explanation: In a competitive market economy the price at which x sells will be P_x. If the price were *below* this level, the quantity demanded would exceed the quantity supplied. The *shortage* of x would cause the price of x to rise. If the price were *above* P_x, the quantity supplied would exceed the quantity demanded. The surplus of x would then cause the price of x to fall. Only at P_x is the quantity supplied equal to the quantity demanded (Q_x).

commodities) and income effects (the effect of lower real income), thereby reducing the quantity demanded (see Figure 3.2). In sum, the increase in demand causes resources to be shifted automatically to the product in greater demand, and the wants of the consuming public are met without intervention from outside forces. In this manner, consumers are said to be sovereign as the economy responds to changes in their demand.

General Equilibrium

Partial equilibrium analysis of competitive markets suggests that markets for individual products can function smoothly in isolation from the remainder of the economy. However, economies consist of thousands or even millions of distinct but interrelated markets in a constant

Figure 3.2 Consumer Sovereignty in a Competitive Economy

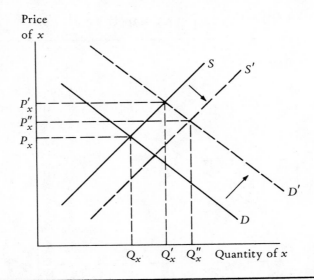

Explanation: We begin with the market for x in equilibrium at price P_x and quantity Q_x. There is an increase in consumer demand from D to D'. As a consequence, the price of x rises to P'_x and the equilibrium quantity *rises* to Q'_x. If economic profits are being made at this new price, new firms will enter the market and the supply curve will eventually shift to S'. Now a new long-run equilibrium is established at price P''_x and quantity Q''_x. An increase in consumer demand *automatically* leads to an increase in the quantity produced. The long-run effect on market prices will depend on the entry of new firms at the higher price.

state of change. It remains to be established whether a harmonious general equilibrium of all markets can be expected or whether disequilibrium forces will disrupt the neat harmony of the partial equilibrium model. A French economist, Leon Walras, was one of the first theorists to address this question. He arrived at the sanguine conclusion that in theory, at least, competitive capitalism would be able to generate a set of general equilibrium prices that could clear all markets simultaneously.[5] Walras's theory demonstrates that despite the enormous complexity of market interactions, a general equilibrium can be obtained. This **general equilibrium** means that the divergent interests of consumers and producers can be harmonized not only for single markets, but for all markets simultaneously.

Subsequent research in general equilibrium economics has built on and elaborated the Walrasian system with similar but less general results, none denying the possibility of a general equilibrium under conditions of competitive capitalism.[6]

Optimality of Competitive Capitalism (Pareto)

Demonstrating that a general equilibrium can exist does not prove that it will be desirable or optimal. The Italian economist Vilfredo Pareto formulated a set of conditions, now called **Pareto optimality**.[7] A "Pareto-optimal" allocation of resources exists when "production and distribution cannot be reorganized to increase the utility of one or more individuals without decreasing the utility of others."[8]

The direct approach of defining optimality as the maximization of the total satisfaction of all members of society would require a subjective evaluation of the importance of one individual's satisfaction vis-à-vis another's (interpersonal utility comparisons). Should resources be allocated from the rich to the poor because the increase in the satisfaction of the poor would be greater than the decrease in satisfaction of the rich? We have no objective method for answering such questions. What we have is Pareto's indirect definition. Under a Pareto optimal allocation of resources, a **maximum output** is being produced from available resources.

Pareto optimality forms the core of modern welfare economic theory, which seeks to evaluate the desirability of various economic states. The issue of special interest here — whether market capitalism can be expected to yield optimal resource allocations — is also central to the study of welfare economics. The answer is that under certain conditions — perfect competition in production and consumption, equality of private and social costs (or benefits), and taxation systems that do not alter competitive decisions — capitalist resource allocation will indeed be Pareto optimal.[9]

In simplest terms, this can be demonstrated by noting that, under perfect competition, the price P (reflecting the marginal utility of consumption) of each commodity will be equated with its marginal cost of production, MC, and this is the necessary general condition for welfare maximization. This follows because MC will reflect society's opportunity cost of producing the last unit of production and P will reflect its marginal benefit. If costs and benefits are not equal at the margin, welfare can be increased by a redistribution of resources.

The competitive form of capitalism is Pareto optimal. Some important limitations must be mentioned, however. Pareto optimality does not serve as a clear guide to determining the single "best" allocation of resources. In fact an almost infinite number of resource allocations may be compatible with Pareto optimality, some of them calling for highly unequal distributions of income. Moreover, the "optimal" distribution of income is not even considered. In some manner, then, society must select, from all possible allocations of resources, that allocation (and underlying income distribution) that it judges to be "best."[10]

Capitalism under conditions of monopoly and other forms of imperfect competition violates Pareto optimality. Figure 3.3 compares competitive and monopolist price and output determination. A capitalist economy that includes imperfectly competitive industries where price is greater than marginal cost will be suboptimal. How suboptimal would seem to depend on the strength of monopolistic forces in the economy, but it is difficult to provide a rigorous proof of this intuitive logic. "Second best" solutions cannot be proven without exception to represent an unambiguous improvement over more monopolistic arrangements. For example, it cannot be demonstrated that in *all* cases an economy that is, say, 90 percent perfectly competitive is "better" than one that is 80 percent. Nevertheless, under certain likely conditions, it can be demonstrated that a change to more competition does make an economy more "optimal."

A perfectly competitive economy violates Pareto optimality in the case of market failures caused by the presence of public goods and externalities of production and consumption. (These issues will be discussed later.)

The Efficiency of Capitalism: Hayek and Mises

The noted Austrian economists, Friedrich Hayek and Ludwig von Mises have written about the *relative* superiority of market economies over planned socialist economies.[11] Their arguments rest on the efficient manner in which market economies mobilize and utilize information, in contrast to the inefficient use of information in planned socialist and market socialist economies. Hayek writes that the principal

Figure 3.3 The Competitive and Monopolistic Capitalist Models
(Partial Equilibrium Analysis)

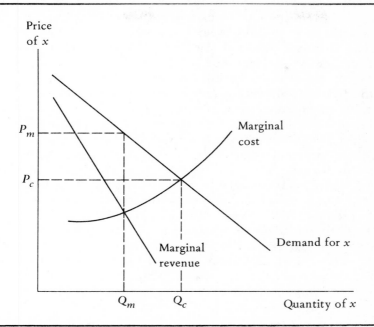

Explanation: This diagram presents the theoretical models of price and output
determination under conditions of perfect competition and monopoly.

Let us suppose that industry X could be organized either as a monopoly (with a
single producer) or as a competitive industry (with a large number of producers).
The marginal costs of production are the same whether the industry is a monopoly
or is perfectly competitive. The industry demand schedule and the industry marginal cost schedule are given in the diagram. The latter is the marginal cost schedule of
the monopolist (in the case of the monopolistic industry) or is the sum of the
individual marginal cost schedules of the competitive producers (in the case of the
competitive industry).

Because the demand schedule is negatively sloped, the monopolist's marginal
revenue will be less than the product price. To maximize profits, the monopolist
will produce that output (Q_m) at which marginal cost and marginal revenue are
equated and will sell this output at the price dictated by the market (P_m). Competitive producers will produce output levels at which the product price and
marginal costs are equal; therefore, the supply schedule of the competitive industry
will be the industry marginal cost schedule. The competitively organized industry
will produce Q_c, and the product will sell for P_c.

As this analysis demonstrates, the monopoly will produce less than the competitive industry and will charge a higher price. The monopolist will charge a price
greater than the marginal costs of production; whereas the competitive industry will
equate price and marginal cost. Because price and marginal revenue are not equal,
an economy comprised of monopolies will not be Pareto optimal.

economic problem is not how to allocate given resources (the problem posed by Pareto), but "how to secure the best use of resources known to any member of society, for ends whose relative importance only these individuals know. Or, to put it briefly, it is a problem of the utilization of knowledge not given to anyone in its totality." Economic agents (consumers and producers) specialize in information about prices, products, and location that is relevant to them in their daily lives. Economic agents need not know all prices, products, and locations to behave efficiently in the marketplace. According to Hayek and Mises, the fact that market economies efficiently generate information in the form of market prices, which enable producers and consumers to plan their actions in a rational manner, is the principal advantage of capitalism and will ensure its relative superiority over planned socialism. This is their argument for the theoretical and practical superiority of market capitalism.

The picture of capitalism that we have developed is one of a harmonious resource allocation system, strongly inclined toward equilibrium in production (especially under competitive conditions), and proceeding at a high degree of efficiency. This harmony occurs without the benefit of government intervention and control. Critics of the harmonious model of capitalism point to the need for state intervention to deal with monopoly power, externalities, public goods, and income distribution problems. They also stress the inherent cyclical instability of capitalism and the problems of making rational public choices.

REASONS FOR STATE INTERVENTION

The appropriate level of state intervention into the affairs of private enterprise is one of the most disputed issues in the theory of capitalism. The neoclassical position, descended directly from Adam Smith, is that, in the absence of monopoly and other forms of imperfect competition, and in the absence of external effects, the economic role of the state should be strictly limited. In particular, the state should supply only those public goods — such as national defense, public roads, a legal system, and foreign policy — that private enterprise on its own would not be able to provide in optimal proportions. The theory of public goods, first articulated formally by Nobel laureate Paul Samuelson, explains why laissez faire capitalism will underproduce such goods.[12] The question we wish to consider here is in what instances state intervention is called for to correct deficiencies in the activity of private enterprise.

Monopoly and Imperfect Competition

The nonoptimality of monopoly has been emphasized by economists since, and even before, the publication of *The Wealth of Nations*. Formally analyzed by Alfred Marshall around the turn of the century, the theory of monopoly is a standard feature of introductory economics courses.[13] The crux of the monopoly problem is the monopolist's inclination to restrict output below the level that would be reached in a competitive situation. Because competitive outputs and prices are Pareto optimal, the existence of monopoly necessarily means a suboptimal allocation of resources. Monopolists will underproduce and overcharge relative to competitive producers. Monopoly will cause a deadweight loss, in that the gains of the monopolist will be less than the losses to consumers. Figure 3.3 demonstrated that monopolies produce less and charge higher prices than competitive markets.

Monopoly behavior is not explained by the extraordinary greed of the monopolist, who is simply attempting to maximize profits. By definition, the monopolist is the sole producer in a particular market. Therefore, the demand for output will follow the law of demand, and to sell a large volume of output, the monopolist must lower the price. If less is produced, the price will rise. This situation contrasts with the perfectly competitive producer, who, as a price taker, can sell all he or she desires at the price established by the market. Monopolists fail to expand their output to the point where the marginal cost (which measures the marginal cost of output in terms of society's resources) equals price (which measures the marginal benefit of output to society). Rather, monopolists who wish to maximize profits must restrict their output.

Economists such as Edward Chamberlin and Joan Robinson have evaluated market arrangements between perfect competition and monopoly.[14] The two intermediate market forms are oligopoly and monopolistic competition.[15] It is beyond the scope of this work to describe them in detail. All we shall say is that both oligopoly and monopolistic competition (like monopoly) violate the criteria of Pareto optimality, although they probably deviate less from optimality than does pure monopoly. Because of the greater degree of competition facing monopolistic competitive firms, the degree of monopoly power at their disposal (as measured by the gap between P and MC) is likely to be small. Some may argue that they represent a reasonable approximation of perfect competition. In the case of oligopoly, it is difficult to draw general conclusions because the outcome depends on the manner in which a small number of large, interdependent firms behave. In some instances (collusive oligopoly, for example), the degree of monopoly power may be the same as that of pure monopoly; in other cases (price-warring oligopolists), the degree of monopoly power may be small.

Social Control of Monopoly Power:
Taxes and Regulation

Economic theory suggests four approaches to the control of monopoly, three of which require collective intervention. The first is to use the state's authority to tax and subsidize to correct the underutilization of resources by monopolistic producers. The basic idea, proposed by A. C. Pigou and Arnold Harberger, is to combine subsidization with consumer and producer taxation to induce the monopolist to expand output to the competitive level, while at the same time producing a social tax dividend for society. A graphical description of this approach is provided in the accompanying note.[16]

The obvious difficulty with this scheme is that tax authorities must make quite sophisticated calculations for its implementation. The use of subsidies and taxes to obtain an optimal allocation of resources from a monopolist does not seem too practical, although the theory of how to do so is clear.

The second form of state intervention is direct regulation of monopoly. Theoretically, state regulatory authorities could dictate that the regulated natural monopoly produce the efficient quantity of output at which P equals MC and force the monopolist to charge a regulated price equal to marginal costs. In this manner, the regulators could dictate directly an efficient allocation of resources. There are two practical difficulties with this approach, however. How are regulators to determine market demand and monopoly marginal costs? The monopoly might be tempted to inflate its costs by lax management or other means to obtain a higher regulated price. The second difficulty is that marginal cost pricing would likely force the monopolist to operate at a loss (if marginal costs were still declining at the output where P equals MC). The existence of regulated losses would require a system of subsidization, which would tend to disrupt the optimal allocation of resources.

The third approach is that recommended by Milton Friedman — namely, to leave natural monopolies alone because regulation would be poorly managed and would encourage monopolists to be inefficient.[17] The unregulated monopoly, prompted by the desire to maximize profits and to keep potential competitors out of the market, would, according to this theory, supply a larger quantity at a lower price than that charged by a regulated monopoly. Moreover, even monopolists must face some form of competition in the long run and cannot get by indefinitely with an inefficient use of resources.

The final collective approach applies to cases where competitive production is also possible. The state through enforcement of antitrust and anticartel legislation and through the removal of legal obstacles to competition can serve to transform the industry from monopolistic to competitive.

External Effects and Collective Action

The notion of **external effects** was pioneered by the English economist A. C. Pigou.[18] It refers to situations where the actions of one producer (or consumer) directly affect the costs (utility) of a second producer (or consumer). By **direct effects**, we mean effects that take place outside of the price system. These external effects may be harmful, in which case they are called an **external diseconomy**; or they may be salutary, in which case they are known as an **external economy**. An example of an external diseconomy of production would be the dumping of wastes into a river by one producer, requiring a producer downstream to increase costs by installing water purification equipment.

When external effects are present, the allocation of resources will not be optimal, even if the economy is perfectly competitive. Producers of the external effect will not be required to take the external impact of their actions into account when making decisions. Rather they will seek to maximize their private profit on the basis of the private costs of production, not on the basis of social costs. The producer of an external harmful effect will therefore produce an output level in excess of the optimum, for a private producer tends to underestimate the true social costs of production (Figure 3.4). There can also be instances of a producer's creating external economies for others. In this case, the private costs exceed social costs, and the producer will underproduce relative to the optimal output level.

Corrective Action in the Case of Externalities

Economic theory suggests remedies to correct for misallocations caused by external effects. One is the internalization of such effects, for example, by combining the enterprises both producing and being affected by external effects. Consider the example of the waste-dumping factory. If it merged with the downstream factory, the water purification costs would become private costs for the combined enterprise, and waste dumping would be limited as a natural consequence of profit maximization.

In the absence of opportunities for internalization, remedies involving state action have been suggested, the most prominent being taxation and subsidies to equate private and social costs. For example, if an excise tax equal to the value of the external diseconomy were levied on the producer of the external effect, his or her private costs would equal the full social costs of production. Thus, to maximize private profits, the producer would be forced to limit output to the level at which price and marginal *social* costs are equal — the condition required for an efficient allocation of resources. Producers creating external economies would be paid a subsidy equal to the value of the positive external effect and would be encouraged to expand output to the socially optimal level.

When appropriate taxes and subsidies cannot be levied, one alternative is state regulation. Government regulators would determine the optimal allocation of resources and administratively decree that producers supply the optimal output mix. The major drawback of this approach is that enforcement and policing costs may be quite high, for it is not clear how one would obtain compliance with regulations. Moreover, there is the enormous problem of calculating private and social marginal costs — the data required for effective regulation.

A third approach to the externality problem is voluntary agreements among the parties involved. This notion was first suggested by Ronald Coase.[19] He contends that under certain conditions the creator and recipient of the external effect will be able to come to a mutually

Figure 3.4 The Inefficiency of External Costs

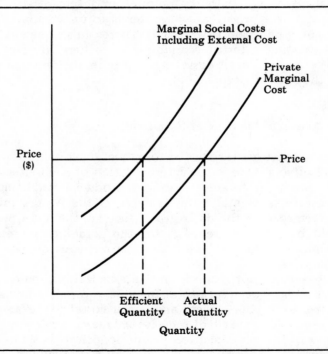

satisfactory agreement, which will restore an optimal allocation of resources. Whenever harmful effects from externalities exist, the parties involved will have opportunities for gains from trade. In the absence of legal obstacles, the amount of shared gains from an agreement must exceed the costs of transacting the agreement, if an agreement is to be reached. Coase's novel conclusion, therefore, is that, if the transaction costs of reaching an agreement are small, the market will on its own correct the misallocation of resources caused by external effects. And if mutually acceptable bargains are not reached in the presence of small transaction costs, the divergence between private and social costs is probably inconsequential. As E. J. Mishan, another pioneer in the theory of externalities, comments: "Rationalizing the *status quo* in this way brings the economist perilously close to defending it."[20]

The most important drawback to the notion of voluntary agreements is exactly the problem of transaction costs and other impediments to agreement, especially when the number of parties involved is large. When only several parties are concerned, then voluntary agreements do seem feasible, but when a large number of parties must participate in the agreement, some of whom have relatively small stakes in the matter, the probability of a mutually acceptable agreement is small. In those cases, external effects will lead to a misallocation of resources, which can be corrected only by social action.

PROBLEMS OF PUBLIC CHOICE

Theorists of capitalism agree that in some instances government must supply certain goods and services. There is widespread agreement that public goods — national defense, police protection and a legal system, dams, flood-control projects, and the like — will not be supplied in efficient quantities by the private economy. The private economy will undersupply public goods for two principal reasons: Nonpayers (called free riders) cannot be prevented from enjoying the benefits of the public good; and one person's use of the good does not usually prevent others from enjoying it. Both of these features make it difficult for the private sector to produce public goods.

How efficiently will government supply such public goods? How rational is public choice? Public choice theorists, such as James Buchanan and Gordon Tullock and Kenneth Arrow, have concluded that certain factors prevent public choices in a democratic (majority-rule) society from being made in an efficient manner.[21]

Efficiency in the case of a public good requires, at a minimum, that the marginal benefits enjoyed by users of the good equal or exceed the marginal costs of supplying the good. Will this necessarily be the case in a society in which public choice decisions are made by majority rule voting? Public choice theory outlines a number of potential problems: First, majority voting fails to take into consideration the intensity of preferences among voters. A number of voters may have intense feeling about a specific public expenditure decision, while others may be virtually indifferent. Yet each person's vote counts equally and changes in preferences typically will not change the voting outcome (the median voter rule). Second, there may be a tendency toward vote trading when voters must decide on a number of public choice issues. A group that wishes one public expenditure program may offer its support for the public expenditure program of a second group if that group will form a majority coalition. Through such logrolling techniques, public expenditure programs may be enacted where marginal costs exceed marginal benefits. Moreover, politicians are in the business of getting reelected and are likely to serve special interest groups who are instrumental in financing election campaigns. The voter, on the other hand, does not have a great incentive to be well informed about public choice issues. The individual voter is aware that his or her vote is unlikely to change any outcome, and the costs of gathering information on the large number of technically detailed government programs are high. It is therefore in the rational voter's economic interest to remain "rationally ignorant."

Economist Kenneth Arrow points out yet another problem of majority-rule decision making, called the Arrow paradox. When different voters rank public choice programs differently, there is no guarantee that such decisions will be consistent. That is, voters may choose program A over program B, program B over program C; yet when confronted with the choice of A and C, they may choose C.

INCOME DISTRIBUTION

It is clear how income is initially distributed in a capitalist economy. Members of society who own resources that command a high price in the marketplace will have higher incomes than those who own resources that command low prices in the marketplace. The major source of income is labor income, and one's labor income depends on natural ability, human capital, and amount of time worked.

The more interesting question is the optimal distribution of income. How equally or unequally should income be distributed? This question raises another: To what extent should the capitalist state redistribute income?

The marginal productivity theory of income distribution follows from the fact that the private owners of labor, land, and capital will be paid the marginal revenue product of their factor. If the factor market is perfectly competitive, the owner receives the actual value of the marginal product of the factor. Thus, argue some economists, the resulting distribution of income is "just" because owners of the factors of production (especially in the perfectly competitive case) receive a reward that is equal to the factor's marginal contribution to society's output.

Critics of this view of natural justice point out that the marginal productivity of any factor depends on the presence of cooperating factors. For example, an American coal miner may work with millions of dollars of capital equipment, while the Indian coal miner who works just as hard works with only a pick and shovel. The marginal productivity of the American coal miner will therefore be many times that of the Indian coal miner. Moreover, the marginal productivity of labor is affected by human capital investment, and not everyone has equal access to education.

The major argument against income redistribution by the state is that a system that rewards according to marginal productivity encourages the owners of the factors of production to raise the productivity of their factors. If the state were to alter this distribution scheme markedly, there would be less incentive to raise the marginal productivity of one's own factors. There would be less investment in human capital, less risk taking, and accordingly society's output would be less.

There are a number of arguments in favor of a redistributive role for the state. First, there is the argument that people are not indifferent to the welfare of others. They are basically altruistic, and their own welfare is diminished by the existence of poverty around them. Given the altruistic motives of people, one would expect there to be considerable income redistribution through private charitable contributions; yet there are strong incentives against charitable contributions. Any individual knows that his or her own contribution can have only a negligible effect on poverty. Only if a large number of people in the upper income brackets give will there be a noticeable impact. If I give and everyone else does not give, then the poor are no better off. If I fail to give, and everyone else gives, then the poor will be better off. The insignificance of any one donor creates a substantial free-rider problem, which means that it is unlikely for voluntary contributions to have a significant impact on the distribution of income.

However, if the state embarks on an income redistribution program through the tax system, the free-rider problem is eliminated. Each person knows that the other must do his or her share. Only the state is in a position to alter the distribution of income.

The philosopher John Rawls has advanced another argument in favor of a more equal distribution of income under capitalism.[22] Basically, Rawls argues that an unequal distribution of income persists because those who benefit from income inequality are unwilling to accept changes that favor the poor. People are unwilling to agree to redistribution because those who will be rich know fairly early in life their chances of being rich. For this reason, a social consensus can never be formed to the effect that the rich agree to redistribute income to the poor.

Rawls asks: How would people behave if they did not know in advance their lifetime endowment of resources? How would they react if they operated behind a "veil of ignorance"? Rawls maintains that under this condition people would naturally act to minimize the risks of being poor and would therefore reach a social consensus in favor of a fairly equal distribution of income. If people, operating behind a veil of ignorance, would naturally favor an equal distribution of income, then society should have an equal distribution of income. Insofar as voluntary charitable giving will not effect this result, the state is justified in redistributing income from the rich to the poor.

MACROECONOMIC INSTABILITY

A major challenge to the neoclassical vision of self-regulating capitalism was mounted by John Maynard Keynes in *The General Theory of Employment, Interest, and Money*, published in 1936 against the backdrop of the world depression.[23] The depression seemed to deny neoclassical notions of an automatic tendency toward equilibrium over time. Keynes's assertion that positive government action was required to stabilize capitalist economics represents his major contribution to capitalist thought.

Keynes

Keynes focused on the mainstay of classical equilibrium theory — namely, Say's law.[24] **Say's law** maintained that there could be no lasting deficiency of aggregate demand because the act of producing a given value of output creates an equivalent amount of income. If that income were not spent directly on consumer goods, it would be saved. The savings would end up being spent as well, for interest rates would adjust to equate *ex ante* savings and *ex ante* investment. Accordingly, depressions could not be caused by deficiencies in aggregate demand. If one were only patient, eventually prices and wages would adjust to bring about an equilibrium at full employment. If unemployment did exist, it was because workers were unwilling to accept the lower real wages required for labor market equilibrium. As long as prices and wages are flexible, there will be an automatic adjustment mechanism to restore full employment.

Keynes argued that there was no assurance that equilibrium would occur at full employment or that the automatic adjustment mechanism would work with reasonable speed. Thus — and this was the foundation of the Keynesian revolution — it was the responsibilty of government to ensure the full employment of the nation's resources.

Keynes disputed the conclusions of the neoclassical school in the following manner. First, he argued that wages and prices were not nearly as flexible (especially downward) as the neoclassical economists believed. He pointed to the fact that money wages were not falling in England in the 1920s and 1930s despite considerable unemployment. Second, he argued that aggregate saving is not significantly affected by the interest rate, rather it is principally dependent on the level of income. According to Keynes, the investment-savings relationship would be especially troublesome because of the cyclical instability of investment expenditures; only by chance would enough investment be forthcoming to guarantee full employment.

Keynes saw no reason why macroequilibrium should occur at a rate of output sufficient to ensure full employment. Therefore, it is the responsibility of government, by appropriately raising or lowering its spending and taxes (fiscal policy) or by controlling investment spending (through monetary policy), to ensure that equilibrium occurs near full employment. Because investment spending is quite unstable, government must be prepared to counteract investment fluctuations with compensatory actions.

After the Second World War, Keynes's advocacy of discretionary monetary and fiscal policy came to be widely accepted by economists and public officials, who felt justified in abandoning the traditional hands-off policies favored by the neoclassical school. Federal budgets could be openly in deficit in order to stimulate the economy. In the United States, for example, tax cuts and tax increases were imposed for the express purpose of manipulating aggregate demand. The practice of demand management has become standard procedure in Western Europe, Japan, and Canada. Monetary policy has also become an instrument of macroeconomic regulation. In the height of optimism in the mid-1960s there was talk of being able to "fine-tune" the economy, and the business cycle was declared dead. The general acceptance of these notions is called the **Keynesian revolution**.

Self-Correcting Capitalism: Monetarism and Rational Expectations

Keynes and his contemporary followers questioned the cyclical stability of capitalism. Without government intervention to moderate business cycles, there will be a significant loss of output and employment.

Activist monetary and fiscal policy is required to keep the economy on an even keel.

The monetarists, under the intellectual leadership of Milton Friedman, and rational expectations economists, led by Robert Lucas, argue against the use of activist macroeconomic policy to combat capitalism's cyclical instability.[25] They argue that capitalism is considerably more stable than Keynes had thought. In fact, the Great Depression was an aberration caused in large part by economic policy blunders. The capitalist economy has a built-in self-correcting mechanism that will restore it to full employment, or to the natural rate of unemployment. If the economy is operating at an unemployment rate above the natural rate, a slowing down of the inflation rate (or even deflation in extreme cases) will restore the economy to full employment. Lower prices raise aggregate supply, and aggregate employment rises until the natural rate is reached.

The monetarists argue against the use of activist policy. Because fiscal policy is decided primarily by politics rather than economics, monetary policy has been the most flexible tool of activist policy. Monetarists maintain that activist monetary policy is as likely to do harm as good. There are lengthy and indeterminate lags between the recognition of a macroeconomic problem, the taking of necessary monetary action, and then the effect of that action on the economy. An anti-inflationary policy adopted during a period of rising prices may begin to affect the economy at the very time an expansionary monetary policy is required. Rather than running the risk of policy mistakes, the monetarists favor a fixed monetary growth rule, which would bind monetary authorities to expand the money supply by a fixed rate each year (roughly equal to the real growth of the economy) regardless of the state of the economy.

Rational expectations economists also argue against activist policy. They maintain that activist policy will have the desired effect on the economy only if the policy catches people off guard. If taxes are lowered for the purpose of stimulating employment — and people know from experience that lower taxes raise inflation — people will take actions to defeat the policy. If monetary authorities expand the money supply to raise employment and workers and employees know that more monetary growth means more inflation, the higher wages and prices will not raise employment or real output.

The basic message of the monetarists and rational expectations economists is that capitalism is much more stable than Keynes had thought and that activist policies are likely to harm the economy. It is better to rely on the self-correcting forces of the capitalist economy to restore it to equilibrium than to count on government policy makers to do so.

THE PERFORMANCE OF CAPITALIST
ECONOMIC SYSTEMS: HYPOTHESES

Chapter 2 discussed five criteria by which to judge the performance of economic systems: economic growth, efficiency, income distribution, stability, and development objectives. What hypotheses, if any, can be derived from the theory of capitalism in each of these areas? First, let us say that it is difficult to formulate hypotheses at this point because our principal concern is the efficiency of capitalism vis-à-vis other economic systems; these hypotheses would be best stated in relative terms. Nevertheless, we shall proceed with caution and begin with what we believe to be the more apparent hypotheses.

Efficiency

Capitalism should provide a high level of efficiency, especially in the static case. The more competitive the economy, the more efficient the economy. The producer's desire to maximize profits and the consumer's desire to maximize utility will lead to a maximum output from available resources under conditions of perfect competition. Imperfect competition and external effects will reduce this efficiency, but evidence suggests that in the first instance, at least, these effects are not very large. Another point promoting static efficiency is capitalism's apparent ability to process and utilize information more effectively than an economic system in which the market is lacking. Probably the most important point is that profit maximization, under all market arrangements, strongly encourages the efficient (least-cost) combination of resources to produce output.

Stability

Stability is the ability of an economic system to grow without undue fluctuations in the rate of growth and without excessive inflation and unemployment. Of course, it is a relative matter to judge what "undue" and "excessive" mean in such a context. Nevertheless, the current consensus seems to be that capitalist economies are not stable, at least in terms of short-run automatic equilibrating forces. This is the major thrust of Keynesian economics. Monetarists and rational expectations theorists, on the other hand, believe that capitalist economies are (or could be) inherently more stable if left to their own devices; so there is considerable disagreement on this point. However, theoretical arguments and the historical record convince us that capitalism is unstable in the sense that it suffers from periodic bouts of inflation, unemployment, and growth fluctuations, which the general public regards as excessive.

Income Distribution

The theory of capitalism cannot make definitive judgments about equity and how resources should be divided among the members of capitalist societies. This is an area where only value judgments can provide answers. We lack a consensus about "fairness," and without an agreed-upon definition it is difficult to arrive at hypotheses. Instead, we can only consider empirical measures of income distribution and make statements like the following: Income is distributed more equally in society X than in society Y. It is difficult to proceed further and say income is distributed "better" ("more fairly") in X or in Y.

The theory of capitalism, however, does suggest the likelihood of significant inequalities in the distribution of income. The factors of production are owned predominantly by private individuals, and the relative value of these factors is determined by the market. Insofar as human and physical capital and natural ability are not likely to be evenly distributed throughout the population, especially when such things can be passed from one generation to another, private ownership of the factors of production raises the likelihood of an uneven distribution of income and wealth among the members of capitalist societies. Exactly how unevenly income and wealth are distributed will depend on the distribution of human and physical capital, which will depend on the education system, inheritance laws, and chance. It will also depend on the redistributive role of the state within a capitalist society.

Economic Growth

One of the advantages of planned socialist economies is their ability to direct resources to specific goals, such as economic growth and military power (see Chapter 5). Thus to a greater extent than capitalist economies, they can marshal resources for economic growth, if they so desire, by controlling the investment rate and the growth rate of the labor force. Although capitalist governments can and do affect the investment rate, the amount saved and invested is largely a matter of individual choice, and it is likely that individual choice will result in lower saving rates than a planned socialist economy, emphasizing the growth objective, would choose. Thus if the growth of factor inputs is left to individuals, one would hypothesize a slower rate of growth of factor inputs and hence of economic growth *ceteris paribus* under capitalism.

A counterbalancing factor must be considered: namely, the hypothesized efficiency of capitalist economies. Static efficiency means that a maximum output is produced from available resources and (with a given saving rate) a greater volume of savings is available relative to less efficient production methods. Moreover, there is the unresolved matter of the dynamic efficiency of capitalist economic systems. To this point, capitalist theory has relatively little to say about dynamic efficiency. It is conceivable that the greater static and dynamic efficiency of capitalism can compensate for the lesser control over the growth of productive resources.

Development Objectives

What can we hypothesize about the nature of development objectives under capitalism? Growth is obviously an important component of the development process. Examination of developed capitalist economic systems suggests, moreover, a pattern of structural change and factor proportions controlled primarily by market forces with only limited intervention by central authorities. The result is a fairly even pattern of sectoral adjustment. The question of sectoral adjustment is tied to the debate between the advocates of balanced and unbalanced growth and there is considerable controversy about the appropriate role for capital in the development process. Nevertheless, the industrial sectors of capitalist countries do not receive the attention or the capital intensity that they receive under socialism. Capital accumulation in capitalist countries is typically slower, paying greater attention to the consumer sector. This is all expected, since the market mechanism plays a domi-

Table 3.1 Hypotheses on the Performance of Capitalist Economic Systems

Criteria	Performance
Efficiency	Good
Stability	Potentially poor; debate over government role
Income distribution	Unequal in the absence of state action
Economic growth	No clear a priori hypothesis: greater efficiency versus potentially lower capital formation
Development objectives	No clear hypothesis

nant role in the development process. Finally, to the extent that central authorities play only a limited role in directing economic activity, there is less emphasis on economic development as a central policy objective. These hypotheses are summarized in Table 3.1.

SUMMARY: THE THEORY OF CAPITALISM

1. The theory of capitalism discusses how well capitalism solves the problem of resource allocation, and what economic role the state should play in the capitalist system. The mainstream approach maintains that, if one is prepared to accept the underlying distribution of income, resource allocation will be optimal if the economy is perfectly competitive. Optimality is defined as an allocation of resources that cannot be changed to make at least one person "better off" without making at least one other person "worse off" (Pareto optimality). If the economy is reasonably competitive, capitalism will be self-regulating and will yield "good" allocation of resources, ignoring any problems of "unfair" distributions of income. The policy prescription is that the role of government should be strictly limited and government should maintain a hands-off policy toward business.

2. Critics of this model of self-regulating capitalism have focused on several perceived weaknesses. Keynes attempted to demonstrate that the economy could establish a stable macroequilibrium at less than (or greater than) full employment. It was, therefore, the government's responsibility to bring about an appropriate macroequilibrium. Critics have also emphasized that with imperfect competition, resource allocation could not be optimal and the government would therefore have to step in to correct the abuses of monopoly power through regulation and taxation. Moreover, other economists have demonstrated that resources will be misallocated whenever externalities are present; government must therefore ensure that social as well as private costs and benefits are considered in private economic decisions.

3. The notion of self-regulating capitalism has its contemporary defenders as well as its critics. The monetarists, under the leadership of Friedman, have mounted an important counterattack on the Keynesian revolution. Some have even argued that capitalism will automatically take care of its monopoly and externality problems without government intervention.

4. Capitalism should perform well in the efficiency area but will tend to be unstable. The distribution of income will be more unequal than under social ownership (although the state can redis-

tribute income). No firm hypothesis could be put forward concerning economic growth.

In Chapter 4 we turn to the most important challenge to capitalist theory — the Marxian critique. Marx, Engels, Lenin, and the New Left all reject outright the notion of a stable, self-regulating form of capitalism, capable of moving toward an optimal allocation of resources over time.

NOTES

1. Examples of how the latter approach has been applied are found in Abram Bergson, *The Economics of Soviet Planning* (New Haven: Yale University Press, 1964); Jaroslav Vanek, *The Participatory Economy* (Ithaca, N.Y.: Cornell University Press, 1971), chs. 2-3; and Benjamin Ward, *The Socialist Economy* (New York: Random House, 1967), chs. 8-9. We also refer the reader to our discussion of the socialist controversy in Chapter 5.
2. Adam Smith, *The Wealth of Nations*, ed. Edwin Cannan (New York: Modern Library, 1937).
3. George Stigler, "The Successes and Failures of Professor Smith," *Journal of Political Economy*, 84 (December 1976), pp. 1199-1214.
4. Of course, it is difficult to single out a few individuals and claim that they are the major contributors to partial equilibrium analysis, but these three would likely appear on most lists: Alfred Marshall, *Principles of Economics*, 8th ed. (New York: Macmillan, 1948); J. R. Hicks, *Value and Capital*, 2nd ed. (Oxford: Oxford University Press, 1946); and Paul Samuelson, *Foundations of Economic Analysis* (Cambridge, Mass.: Harvard University Press, 1948).
5. Leon Walras, *Elements of Pure Economics*, Jaffe translation (London: Allen and Unwin, 1954). Walras demonstrated this proposition by noting that in a general equilibrium framework the demand and supply schedules in each market (let us assume m such markets) will be functions of their own price and the prices of all other commodities in the economy. This follows from the fact that when all markets are allowed to interact simultaneously, changes in commodity prices can affect demands and supplies in other markets because of the existence of substitute and complementary relationships. As formulated by Walras, the general equilibrium system will consist of m equations and m unknowns — a seemingly desirable state of affairs, mathematically speaking, for it suggests the existence of an equilibrium set of prices (under certain conditions it was later demonstrated), which will cause all markets to clear simultaneously.

    At this point, Walras introduced and then resolved an important indeterminacy in the model, and this resolution is his major contribution to general equilibrium analysis. Because the value of purchases in the economy must *identically* equal the value of sales (Walras's identity), the general equilibrium system actually consists of only $m - 1$ independent equations, a concession that at first appears to leave the solution for the set of equilibrium prices indeterminate. Walras's resolution of this problem was to demonstrate that, in actuality, the number of unknown prices is also $m - 1$, for only *relative* prices affect supply and demand. Accordingly, one commodity must be singled out as a numeraire, and the system can then be solved for a consistent set of *relative* equilbrium prices.
6. Subsequent research on general equilibrium has addressed the issues of existence and stability. The *existence* literature addresses the point that the mere

equality of equations and unknowns does not ensure the existence of a set of equilibrium prices, for existence will depend on functional forms of utility and production functions, and realistic values (zero or positive prices and quantities) are required for an acceptable general equilibrium solution. The research of Kenneth Arrow and Gerard Debreu reveals that a general equilibrium does exist under certain conditions associated with perfect competition and orderly utility and production functions. The second literature addresses the issue of the *stability* of the general equilibrium — that is, whether there is an automatic tendency for the economy to return to a general equilibrium after this equilibrium has been disrupted.

7. For a detailed treatment of Pareto's economics and philosophy, see Vincent Tarascio, *Pareto's Methodological Approach to Economics: A Study in the History of Some Scientific Aspects of Economic Thought* (Chapel Hill: University of North Carolina Press, 1968).

8. James Henderson and Richard Quandt, *Microeconomic Theory: A Mathematical Approach*, 2nd ed. (New York: McGraw-Hill, 1971), ch. 7.

9. For a simple presentation of the conditions of Pareto optimality, see F. M. Bator, "The Simple Analytics of Welfare Maximization," *American Economic Review*, 47 (March 1957), pp. 22-59. For more sophisticated treatments, see Henderson and Quandt, *Microeconomic Theory*, ch. 7.

10. Henderson and Quandt, *Microeconomic Theory*, pp. 280-286. The discussion of second best is also based on Henderson and Quandt, pp. 286-288. The standard reference on the second best hypothesis is R. G. Lipsey and Kelvin Lancaster, "The General Theory of the Second Best," *Review of Economic Studies*, 24 (1956-1957), pp. 11-32.

11. Friedrich Hayek, "The Price System as a Mechanism for Using Knowledge," *American Economic Review*, 35 (September 1945), pp. 519-530; and Ludwig von Mises, *Socialism: An Economic and Sociological Analysis* (New Haven: Yale University Press, 1951).

12. Paul Samuelson, "The Pure Theory of Public Expenditure," *Review of Economics and Statistics*, 36 (November 1954), pp. 26-30.

13. For a brief but lucid discussion of monopoly theory, see George Stigler, *The Theory of Price*, rev. ed. (New York: Macmillan, 1952), pp. 204-222. For a discussion at the introductory level, see Samuelson, *Economics*, ch. 25.

14. Joan Robinson, *The Economics of Imperfect Competition* (London: Macmillan, 1933); Edward Chamberlin, *The Theory of Monopolistic Competition*, 6th ed. (Cambridge, Mass.: Harvard University Press, 1948).

15. *Oligopoly* is defined as a market comprised of a few sellers, interdependent in their output and pricing decisions, producing either a homogeneous or differentiated product. *Monopolistic competition* is defined as a market consisting of a large number of producers, producing a slightly differentiated product, with limited barriers to entry.

16. Figure 3.5 (shown on p. 67) is adapted from Henderson and Quandt, *Microeconomic Theory*, pp. 277-279. It assumes (for purposes of simplification) constant marginal costs (MC) equal to average total costs (ATC).

   In order to induce the monopolist to increase output to Q_c, he or she must be paid a unit subsidy equal to EC, the total subsidy being the area of the rectangle $FECP_c$. The monopolist's increase in costs from going from Q_m to Q_c is $Q_m BQ_c C$ while the increase in revenues is the area under the MR curve, or $Q_m BEQ_c$. Therefore, the monopolist's profits decline by the difference between the increase in revenues and costs, or the area BCE, which should equal the original profits $P_m ABP_c$, because we have constructed the example so that the monopolist is now making zero profits at Q_c. The monopolist will be just as well off at Q_c as at Q_m if the state charges a lump-sum tax equal to $P_c BEF$, for that will leave the original profits intact, the BCE triangle.

Consumers have been made better off as a consequence of the expansion of output from Q_m to Q_c and decline in price from P_m to P_c. Assuming zero income elasticities (to avoid shifts in the demand schedule as prices change), the increase in consumer surplus is measured by the area under the demand schedule between Q_m and Q_c, or the area $Q_m ACQ_c$. However, consumers pay only the area under the MR curve, or $Q_m BEQ_c$ to the producer, leaving them with a surplus of $ABEC$. The state can therefore tax this surplus away without reducing consumers' satisfaction below its original level at A, and the state is required only to make a net payment to the producer equal to BCE to keep the producer at the original level of profit. Therefore, the state has generated a surplus equal to the triangle ABC as a consequence of moving the producer from Q_m to Q_c, the Pareto optimal output and price level.

17. Milton Friedman, "Monopoly and Social Responsibility of Business and Labor," in Edwin Mansfield, ed., *Monopoly Power and Economic Performance*, 3rd ed. (New York: Norton, 1974), pp. 57-68 George J. Stigler, "The Government of the Economy," in Paul Samuelson, ed., *Readings in Economics*, 7th ed. (New York: McGraw-Hill, 1973), pp. 73-77.

18. The discussion of externalities is based on the following sources: Henderson and Quandt, *Microeconomic Theory*, pp. 267-275; E. J. Mishan, "The Postwar Literature on Externalities: An Interpretive Essay," *Journal of Economic Literature*, 9 (March 1971), pp. 1-28; George Daly, "The Coase Theorem: Assumptions, Applications, and Ambiguities," *Economic Inquiry*, 12 (June 1974), pp. 203-213; and Eirik Furobotin and Svetozar Pejovich, "Property Rights and Economic Theory: A Survey of Recent Literature," *Journal of Economic Literature*, 12 (December 1972), pp. 1137-1162.

19. R. H. Coase, "The Problem of Social Costs," *Journal of Law and Economics*, 3 (October 1960), pp. 1-44.

20. Mishan, "The Postwar Literature on Externalities," p. 17.

Figure 3.5 The Social Control of Monopoly

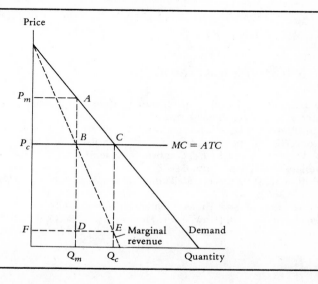

21. James Buchanan and Gordon Tullock, *The Calculus of Consent* (Ann Arbor: University of Michigan Press, 1974); Kenneth Arrow, *Social Choice and Individual Values* (New Haven: Yale University Press, 1976).

22. John Rawls, *Theory of Justice* (Oxford: Clarendon, 1976).

23. John Maynard Keynes, *The General Theory of Employment, Interest, and Money* (New York: Harcourt Brace Jovanovich, 1936). The most important early work to interpret Keynes's general theory for nonspecialists was Alvin Hansen, *A Guide to Keynes* (New York: McGraw-Hill, 1953).

24. There is considerable controversy over what Keynes actually meant to say in *General Theory*, and some authorities argue that the more popular interpretations of Keynes are incorrect. For discussion of this controversy, see Don Patinkin, *Money, Interest, and Prices*, 2nd ed. (New York: Harper & Row, 1965); Axel Leijonhufvud, *On Keynesian Economics and the Economics of Keynes* (New York: Oxford University Press, 1968); Herschel Grossman, "Was Keynes a 'Keynesian'? A Review Article," *Journal of Economic Literature*, 10 (March 1972), pp. 26–30; and Alan Coddington, "Keynesian Economics: The Search for First Principles," *Journal of Economic Literature*, 14 (December 1976), pp. 1258–1338. For a historical perspective on the Keynesian revolution, see Alan Sweezy et al., "The Keynesian Revolution and Its Pioneers," *American Economic Review, Papers and Proceedings*, 62 (May 1972), pp. 116–141.

25. The discussion of the monetarist school is based on the following sources: Milton Friedman, ed., *Studies in the Quantity Theory of Money* (Chicago: University of Chicago Press, 1956); Milton Friedman and A. J. Schwartz, *A Monetary History of the United States* (Princeton, N.J.: Princeton University Press 1963); Milton Friedman, *Dollars and Deficits* (Englewood Cliffs, N.J.: Prentice-Hall, 1968); Franco Modigliani, "The Monetarist Controversy, or, Should We Forsake Stabilization Policies?" *American Economic Review*, 67 (March 1977), 13; Edmund Phelps, *Microeconomic Foundations of Employment and Inflation Theory* (London: Macmillan, 1974); Milton Friedman, "Inflation and Unemployment," *Journal of Political Economy*, 85 (June 1977), pp. 451–472.

RECOMMENDED READINGS

THE NEOCLASSICAL MODEL

F. M. Bator, "The Simple Analytics of Welfare Maximization," *American Economic Review*, 47 (March 1957), pp. 22–59.

Abram Bergson, "A Reformulation of Certain Aspects of Welfare Economics," *Quarterly Journal of Economics*, 52 (February 1938), pp. 310–334; reprinted in R. V. Clemence, ed., *Readings in Economic Analysis* (Reading, Mass.: Addison Wesley, 1950), vol. I, pp. 61–85.

J. de V. Graaff, *Theoretical Welfare Economics* (London: Cambridge University Press, 1957).

James Henderson and Richard Quandt, *Microeconomic Theory: A Mathematical Approach*, 2nd ed. (New York: McGraw-Hill, 1971), chs. 5–7.

J. R. Hicks, *Value and Capital*, 2nd ed. (Oxford: Oxford University Press, 1946).

Paul Samuelson, *Foundations of Economic Analysis* (Cambridge, Mass.: Harvard University Press, 1948).

Tibor Scitovsky, *Welfare and Competition*, rev. ed. (Homewood, Ill.: Irwin, 1971), chs. 20-21.

Adam Smith, *The Wealth of Nations*, ed. Edwin Cannan (New York: Modern Library, 1937).

MACROECONOMIC THEORY

Martin Bailey, *National Income and the Price Level*, 2nd ed. (New York: McGraw-Hill, 1971).

Alan Coddington, "Keynesian Economics: The Search for First Principles," *Journal of Economic Literature*, 14 (December 1976), pp. 1258-1338.

Paul Davidson, *Money and the Real World* (London: Macmillan, 1972).

Rudiger Dornbusch and Stanley Fischer, *Macroeconomics*, 4th ed. (New York: McGraw-Hill, 1987).

A. S. Eicher and J. A. Kregel, "An Essay on Post-Keynesian Theory: A New Paradigm in Economics," *Journal of Economic Literature*, 13 (December 1975), pp. 1293-1314.

Milton Friedman, *Dollars and Deficits* (Englewood Cliffs, N.J.: Prentice-Hall, 1968).

——, ed., *Studies in the Quantity Theory of Money* (Chicago: University of Chicago Press, 1956).

Robert J. Gordon, *Macroeconomics*, 4th ed. (Boston: Little, Brown, 1986).

Herschel Grossman, "Was Keynes a 'Keynesian'? A Review Article," *Journal of Economic Literature*, 10 (March 1972), pp. 26-30.

John Maynard Keynes, *The General Theory of Employment, Interest, and Money* (New York: Harcourt Brace Jovanovich, 1936).

Axel Leijonhufvud, *On Keynesian Economics and the Economics of Keynes* (New York: Oxford University Press, 1968).

Franco Modigliani, "The Monetarist Controversy, or, Should We Forsake Stabilization Policies?" *American Economic Review*, 67 (March 1977), pp. 1-19.

MARKET FAILURES: IMPERFECT COMPETITION, INCOME DISTRIBUTION, EXTERNALITIES, AND PUBLIC CHOICE

James Buchanan and Robert Tollison, eds., *Theory of Public Choice: Political Applications of Economics* (Ann Arbor: University of Michigan Press, 1972).

James Buchanan and Gordon Tullock, *The Calculus of Consent* (Ann Arbor: University of Michigan Press, 1974).

Edward Chamberlin, *The Theory of Monopolistic Competition*, 6th ed. (Cambridge, Mass.: Harvard University Press, 1948).

R. H. Coase, "The Problem of Social Costs," *Journal of Law and Economics*, 3 (October 1960), pp. 1-44.

E. J. Mishan, "The Postwar Literature on Externalities: An Interpretive Essay," *Journal of Economic Literature*, 9 (March 1971), pp. 1-28.

A. C. Pigou, *The Economics of Welfare*, 4th ed. (London: Macmillan, 1946).

John Rawls, *Theory of Justice* (Oxford: Clarendon, 1976).

Joan Robinson, *The Economics of Imperfect Competition* (London: Macmillan, 1959).

Paul Samuelson, "The Pure Theory of Public Expenditure," *Review of Economics and Statistics*, 36 (November 1954), pp. 26-30.

Chapter 4
The Marxian Critique

THE ECONOMICS OF MARX

One common theme unites theorists of capitalism: Capitalism, either on its own or through revisions that do not alter its basic character, can resolve the economic problem of resource allocation. Writers of the anticapitalist tradition argue that capitalism is subject to basic internal contradictions that cannot be remedied through reform of the system. Marx wrote that the capitalist system would eventually succumb to these contradictions and be replaced by a new (superior) socialist order.

Dialectical Materialism

Karl Marx (1818-1883) and his collaborator, Friedrich Engels (1820–1895), mounted the most serious challenge to capitalism in Marx's three-volume *Capital* (*Das Kapital* in German).[1] Much of *Capital* was published posthumously under the editorship of Engels.[2] *Capital* concludes that capitalism is an unstable economic organization, whose lifespan is inevitably limited.

Marx's theory of capitalism is based on his materialist conception of history,[3] which involves a belief that economic forces (called **productive forces**) determine how production relations, markets, and most generally society itself (the **superstructure**) are organized. Weak productive forces (underdeveloped human and physical capital resources) will result in one arrangement for producing goods and services (**production relations**), and strong productive forces will lead to a different, more advanced set of production arrangements. Thus, a society with underdeveloped economic resources would be expected to have similarly underdeveloped production relations and superstructure (manifested in barter exchange, serf labor, a rigid social hierarchy, and religious biases against commerce). As the productive forces improve, new economic and social relationships will begin to emerge (hired rather than serf labor, monetary rather than natural exchange, among others). These new arrangements are not compatible with the old set of economic, cultural, and social relationships. When they come into contact, tensions and conflicts mount.

Figure 4.1 Schematic Development of Marxist Thought

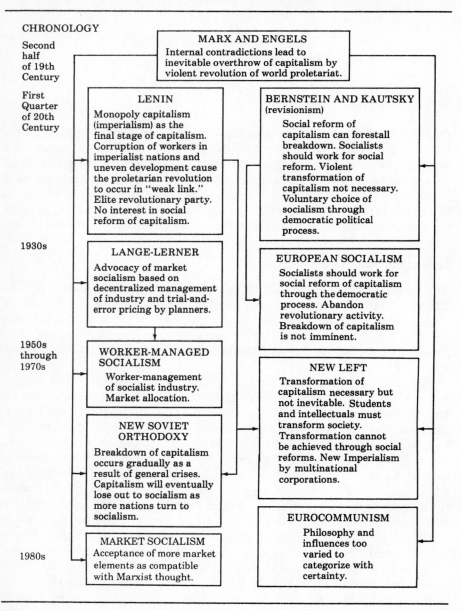

Eventually, the incompatibilities will become so great that a qualitative change (usually the result of violent revolution or war) will occur. New production relations and a new superstructure, compatible with the new productive forces, will replace the old order. These **qualitative changes** are inevitable because societies are destined to evolve from a lower to a higher order as underlying productive forces develop.

The engine of change is the conflict between the old and new, primarily in the form of class antagonisms (the emerging capitalist class versus the landed gentry in fuedal societies, the worker versus the capitalist in capitalist societies). The process of evolutionary and inevitable qualitative change through the competition between opposing forces (**thesis versus antithesis**) is the foundation of Marx's theory of **dialectical materialism**, which is based on the teachings of the German philosophers Georg Wilhelm Hegel and Ludwig Feuerbach.

The upshot of Marx's materialist conception of history was his contention that societies evolve according to an inevitable pattern of social and economic change in which lower systems are replaced by more advanced systems. In this manner, feudalism is bound to replace slavery, capitalism will inevitably displace feudalism, and socialism will eventually replace capitalism.

The Class Struggle and Surplus Value

According to the dialectic, the victory of capitalism over feudalism will represent a qualitative step forward for society. A highly efficient productive machine (capitalism) will replace an inefficient one (feudalism) based on semiservile labor and governed by traditional landed interests. Two landmarks will signal the emergence of capitalism. The first is the initial accumulation of capital (wealth) by the emerging capitalist class (the bourgeoisie) — a process Marx called **primitive capitalist accumulation**. The second indicator is the formation of a "free" labor force at the disposal of capitalist employers. This occurs when laborers are separated from control over the factors of production (land, tools, livestock) and are left with only their own labor to sell. At this point, the capitalist, who now controls the means of production, hires this free labor, and capitalist factories are established to serve as the new vehicle for commodity production. In this manner, the basic class conflict of capitalism is created — the conflict between the working class and the capitalist, who "owns" the labor services of the worker. A new superstructure will emerge in which all social, political, and religious institutions will serve to promote the interests of the new ruling class, the bourgeoisie.

Marx's **labor theory of value** and **theory of surplus value** are key to explaining the long-run dynamics of capitalism. Marx maintained that the value (true price) will be determined by the amount of labor embodied directly and indirectly in the commodity, plus profit. Marx did not deny that in the short run commodity *prices* are determined by supply and demand and could therefore diverge from their underlying labor values. Moreover, even in the long run, the prices of *individual* commodities may deviate systematically from their labor values because of differing capital intensities of production (the famous transformation problem).[4] Despite these reservations, two basic points remain: Value is generally equal to labor inputs, and only direct labor can produce profits (surplus value).

Marx's labor theory of value states that the value of a commodity (C) will equal the sum of direct labor costs (v), indirect labor costs (c), and surplus value (s) (Marx's term for profits).[5]

$$C = c + v + s \qquad (4.1)$$

Marx's definitions of fixed capital or indirect labor costs (c) and variable capital or direct labor costs (v) differ somewhat from the modern terms. Fixed capital (c) refers to outlays for the services of plant, equipment, inventories, and expenditures for materials, the common feature of which is that they embody past labor, which has already been exploited. In modern terminology, c represents the nonlabor costs of production (depreciation, material costs, insurance charges, and others). By v Marx means the direct labor costs of production, that is, wage costs.

According to Marx, the feature that distinguishes labor from the other factors of production — land, capital, and materials — is that the employer can compel workers to produce a value above the labor time required by the workers to maintain themselves. Yet the employer is not required to pay workers the full value of their production, only enough to allow them to subsist. A particular worker may have to perform eight hours of work to produce a value sufficient to meet subsistence needs; yet the employer can force the worker to create a surplus (s), which will accrue to capitalists, by working twelve hours — four hours more than are required to satisfy subsistence needs. Marx was unclear about how **subsistence needs** was to be defined; it is not clear whether he meant physical subsistence or some socially accepted consumption norm. Other factors of production (c), though essential to the production process, cannot create surplus value, for the surplus value created in their production has already been appropriated by the capitalist class. Direct labor is the sole source of surplus value (s). Workers are exploited because they produce the surplus but it accrues to the capitalist class.[6] Surplus value plays a central role in Marxian theory, for the capitalist's desire to maximize profits is the driving engine of capitalism. On the last point, Marx and conventional economists agree, although they do not agree about how profits are created.

Whether workers receive a share of the surplus value depends on whether they are paid subsistence or above-subsistence wages.[7] Marx maintained that wages would tend toward subsistence in the long run, because capitalism creates a large number of unemployed workers (called the **reserve army of the unemployed**) whose existence ensures that wages will not rise for long periods above subsistence.

Three relationships illustrate Marx's view of the dynamics of capitalism. The first is the **rate of exploitation**, s', which is

$$s' = \frac{s}{v} \qquad (4.2)$$

The rate of exploitation equals profits divided by the wage bill. If a worker is required to work 12 hours per day, of which only 8 hours are needed to meet subsistence requirements, surplus value is 4 and the rate of exploitation is 4/8 or 0.5. The worker will receive a wage equal to subsistence requirements (8 hours of production), and the employer will receive a profit of 4 hours of production.

The second relationship is called the **organic composition of capital** (q), which Marx defines as the ratio of fixed to total (fixed plus variable) capital:

$$q = \frac{c}{c + v} \qquad (4.3)$$

The third relationship is the **profit rate** (p), which Marx defines as the ratio of surplus value to total capital:

$$p = \frac{s}{c + v} \qquad (4.4)$$

or, substituting from equation 4.3,

$$p = s' (1 - q) \qquad (4.5)$$

As equation 4.5 indicates, the profit rate is the product of the rate of exploitation times $(1 - q)$. Thus, the higher s', the higher p; and the higher q (the greater the share of fixed capital), the lower p. If there were no variable capital ($v = 0$), there would be no profits (an expected result because only direct labor creates surplus value). The point is that the trend in the long-run profit rate will depend, according to Marx's definitions, directly on s' and inversely on q.

The Law of the Falling Rate of Profit, Exploitation, and Crises

Marx pictured capitalism, at least in its early stages, as a world of cut-throat competition. He also believed that the capitalist was driven to maximize profits (surplus value) and to accumulate more capital out of profits.

The forces of competition compel capitalists to increase the organic composition of capital (q), causing the profit rate to fall. Capitalists, operating in intensively competitive markets, are forced to introduce cost-saving innovations, lest their competitors do so before them and drive them out of business.[8] Capitalist A introduces a new labor-saving (thus cost-saving) technology, attracts competitors' customers through lower prices, and experiences a temporary increase in profits above "normal" levels. The profits, however, are short-lived, because competitors respond by introducing the same cost-saving techniques, and new competitors enter the market in response to windfall profits. Excess industry profits are eliminated, and no capitalist ends up better off as a consequence. But fixed capital has been subsituted for labor (q rises), and unless something happens to offset the rise in q, the profit rate will decline. There is an inherent tendency to substitute fixed for variable capital throughout the economy, even though variable capital (labor), is the sole source of surplus value. Marx predicted the profit rate would fall, with disastrous consequences for capitalism.

The proposition of the declining profit rate depends on a strong *ceteris paribus* condition that casts doubt on its inevitability.[9] For now, let us continue Marx's line of reasoning.

As the profit rate falls, internal contradictions and weaknesses in the system become apparent. In an effort to halt the decline in p, capitalists attempt to increase the exploitation of their workers (raise s'), and the alienation and exploitation of the proletariat intensifies. Moreover, the declining profit rate leads to the failure of marginal businesses, and petty (small) capitalists now swell the ranks of the unemployed, exerting even more downward pressure on the wage rate. The misery of the proletariat worsens. Those fortunate enough to be employed are exploited and alienated; those unemployed are in even worse shape.

A more ominous phenomenon is the tendency toward overproduction and disproportions.[10] Workers are kept at subsistence wages by high unemployment; capitalists, driven by the desire to accumulate more capital, are not willing to increase their spending on luxury goods. Moreover, the ranks of the capitalists are thinning, as huge monopolies drive smaller capitalists out of business. Yet all the while, the productive capacity of the economy is growing because of the growing capital-intensity of industry. Thus, aggregate demand will fall chronically short of aggregate supply; recessions and then depressions will occur, and worldwide crises become commonplace. Overproduction will be only one source of crisis. The declining profit rate will lead to declines in investment spending and to further shortfalls in aggregate demand. Disproportions in individual branches, such as steel and energy, can further intensify crises.

Marx described only generally the final stages of the capitalist break-down. Overproduction, underconsumption, disproportions, and the exploitation and alienation of workers will combine to create the conditions necessary for the violent overthrow of capitalism.[11] The proletariat unites against the weakened capitalist class and through a violent *world* revolution establishes a new socialist order. Marx and Engels had little to say about this new order (what they did relate is described in Chapter 5). Implicit in Marx's general writings on the final stage of capitalism is the point that the contradictions will be most intense in the most advanced capitalist countries; thus the proletarian revolution will be initiated there.

LENIN: MONOPOLY CAPITALISM AND IMPERIALISM

Vladimir Ilich Lenin (1870–1924), the father of the Russian Revolution, wrote primarily about the politics of revolution (prior to 1917) and the practical problems of governing the first socialist state. His most important economic works, *The Development of Capitalism in Russia* and *Imperialism, the Highest Stage of Capitalism*, were both researched and written from exile.[12]

Better known for his theory of revolutionary strategy (the concept of an elite revolutionary party),[13] Lenin studied the final stage of capitalism, which he called **monopoly capitalism** or equivalently **imperialism**. Lenin's writings on imperialism are best understood in terms of his ambition to lead a Russian Marxist revolution. Marx and Engels were counting on the German proletariat to initiate the revolution. Lenin, as a Russian revolutionary, had to demonstrate why the revolution instead began in Russia. After it was apparent that the Russian Revolution would not turn into a world revolution, Lenin had to explain why the proletarian revolution was confined to the Russian borders (**socialism in one country** versus **world revolution**).

Monopoly Capitalism

According to Lenin, Marx and Engels, writing during the intermediate stages of capitalism, did not have the opportunity to observe the mature stages of capitalism. Lenin concentrated his efforts on the final

stage of capitalism, which he called monopoly capitalism. Lenin felt
that mature capitalism will be different from the competitive system
that characterizes early and intermediate capitalism. A monopoly
capitalist system will be dominated by giant trusts, cartels, and monopolies, many operating on an international basis. In spite of their power,
monopolies will not totally eliminate competitive producers; rather a
dual economy of coexisting monopolistic giants and competitive industries will emerge. Friction between them will be considerable as the
former gradually wear down the latter.

The emergence of monopoly as the dominant economic organization
signals the final stage of capitalism. Lenin listed five characteristics of
monopoly capitalism:

1. The concentration of production in the hands of fewer and fewer
   industrial giants
2. The merger of financial and industrial capital, as the banks and
   financiers come to exercise greater control over the allocation of
   capital resources
3. The emergence of capital (rather than commodity) exports as the
   major form of international exchange
4. The division of the world into economic spheres of influence and
   control by monopoly capitalists
5. The subdivision of the world into corresponding political spheres of
   influence by the governments of mature capitalist countries[14]

Lenin's picture of maturing capitalism is not much different from
that of Marx, although it is more sharply defined. The basic Marxian
contradictions are still present: the declining rate of profits, the class
struggle between capitalist and worker, and the worsening condition of
the proletariat. But there are crucial differences between Marx's and
Lenin's visions, and these differences are closely related to Lenin's
justification of a proletarian revolution in backward Russia.

According to Lenin, the class struggle would continue even in the
mature imperialistic countries. In one sense, it would be worsened by
the merger of financial and industrial capitalism. Financial capitalists
would come to control capital resources, and the ownership and management of industrial enterprises would be separated. Instead of the
earlier system of owner-managers, professional managers would run
industries, while an idle and decadent class of rentiers would reap the
benefits of the efforts of labor. On the other hand, in the mature countries the class struggle would be softened by using trade unions to bribe
the working class with a share of surplus value. This bargain would be
necessary because the wealth of the advanced imperialist economies
would be dependent on the exploitation of the weak colonial countries.
In this manner, the proletariat is corrupted; the exploitation of the
working class is exported to weaker countries; and foreign workers are

exploited to benefit the capitalists and privileged workers in the rich countries.

The Theory of Uneven Development

The **theory of uneven development** is the cornerstone of Lenin's analysis of the locus of the proletarian revolution.[15] According to Lenin, monopoly capitalism will experience uneven development both within economic branches and among capitalist countries. Growth will be uneven within economic branches because of the friction between monopolistic and competitive branches, because the decline of competition will force the state to rescue failing monopolistic industries, and because monopolists will restrain production. On the international level, latecomers (such as the United States) will be growing rapidly, while the more mature (and decaying) capitalist countries (such as France) will be in decline. However, because the underdeveloped world has already been completely partitioned by the monopoly capitalists, the only way for a latecomer to acquire a foreign dominion is by taking it away from a declining power. Thus the law of uneven development ensures global competition and conflict among the imperialist powers as they vie with one another for the control of foreign resources and markets.[16]

These military conflicts and wars leave the imperialist powers weakened, especially the relatively backward countries. This weakness provides the working class with the opportunity to rise up against their capitalist oppressors. Because the workers in the advanced imperialist countries have already been bought off, the revolution is not likely to break out there. Rather it is likely to occur in the weakest link of the capitalist chain, for there the contradictions and class conflict between worker and capitalist will be most intense. This, according to Lenin, is why the proletarian revolution began not in Germany or England, but in Russia, the **weak link** in the capitalist chain.

Russia as the Weak Link and the Problems of Transition

According to Lenin, Russia was a peculiar mix of mature and less-advanced capitalism. In his study of Russian economic development, Lenin underscores the dual nature of the Russian economy. On the one hand, Russian heavy industry was highly concentrated and monopolistic. Thus the Russian industrial worker had already experienced the alienation and exploitation required for the formation of a revolutionary outlook. The Russian state played a prominent role in supporting heavy industry and protecting vested monopoly interests. In fact, the Russian industrial proletariat was exploited both by the monopolistic employers and the state.[17] Moreover, Russia itself acted as an imperialist power in central Asia, China, and Manchuria. Lenin, however, stressed that there were backward features of Russia as well. Russian industry depended on foreign capital and technology and was thus in a semicolonial position. Second, handicraft industry continued to dominate the production of consumer goods, in contrast to the control of heavy industry by monopolies. Finally, Russian agriculture was plagued by the vestiges of feudalism and still employed backward cultivation techniques.

From this, Lenin concluded that Russia was indeed the weak link in the capitalist chain. Its advanced features had served to create a revolutionary industrial proletariat, which, if guided by a **revolutionary elite**, the Bolshevik party, would be ripe for the overthrow of capitalism. Russia's backward features would ensure an inability to compete effectively in the imperialistic struggle, leaving Russian monopoly capitalism in a vulnerable position.

Because Russia was admittedly a less-advanced capitalist country, would it be necessary to pass through a transition period (a **bourgeois revolution**) to set the stage for the final proletarian revolution? This ideological and political issue split the leadership of the Bolshevik party. Leon Trotsky argued in favor of a **permanent revolution**, by which he meant that the Russian proletariat should carry the revolution throughout the world from the bourgeois to the socialist stage in one uninterrupted sequence.[18] Lenin argued against this position by noting that a transition period between the fall of capitalism and the introduction of socialism would be required. In fact, by allowing **state capitalism** to develop in Russia, the eventual socialist victory would be promoted.[19]

Lenin reasoned as follows. The monopolization of industry in the hands of finance capital would mean the socialization of the production process. Market forces would virtually disappear, to be replaced by a centralized structure directed by economc administrators. State capitalism could exploit the working classes only so long as the capitalists remained in control. By having a proletarian dictatorship take control of this monopoly structure (seize the "commanding heights" of the economy), the enormous productive capacity of monopoly capitalism could be turned to benefit the working classes. If the old order were to be "smashed," as the Bolshevik theoretician Nikolai Bukharin urged,[20] this would represent a step backward according to Lenin, for the socialization process would have to be started again from the beginning.

Subsequent events, most importantly the Russian civil war, rendered this controversy among Lenin, Bukharin, and Trotsky moot; the wartime emergency made a transitional alliance between the new and old orders impossible.[21] Nevertheless this Bolshevik discussion of the transition represents an important contribution to Marxist theory.

REVISIONISM

The history of Marxist thought after Marx, Engels, and Lenin is difficult to describe in an unbiased manner. In the Soviet Union, Marxism-Leninism ossified into dogma.[22] The contributions of important Marxist theorists and leaders such as Leon Trotsky and Nikolai Bukharin — older Russian revolutionaries who had fallen from favor with the Bolshevik establishment — were ignored or disparaged. Other socialist writers — Bernstein, Tugan-Baranovsky, Kautsky, Luxemburg — were written off as "revisionists" or "deviationists." Serious development of Marxist thought ended in the Soviet Union with the ascendancy of Stalin in the late 1920s. In place of substantive advances in Marxist-Leninist theory, the Soviet establishment has been content to issue periodic political economy "textbooks" on Marxism-Leninism, which serve to articulate the latest party orthodoxy. The *glasnost* of the late 1980s represents the first effort to reopen serious discussion of policy in the Soviet Union since the twenties.

Soviet Orthodoxy: The General Crisis of Capitalism

Soviet ideological textbooks have had to adapt Marxism-Leninism to capitalism's failure to break down and to the rising prosperity of capitalist workers.[23] The **theory of the general crisis of capitalism** is the official Soviet contribution to Marxist theory,[24] seeks to explain how the transition from capitalism to world socialism is to take place despite rising prosperity in the industrialized capitalist world.

The general crisis theory says there will be a general and gradual deterioration of the advanced monopoly capitalist countries as a consequence of internal and external weaknesses. The process will be accelerated by the existence of an advancing socialist world (the Soviet Union, China, Eastern Europe, and others), which will demonstrate the superiority of the Marxist alternative to weak capitalist countries. The world's population will gradually shift from capitalism to socialism: the expansion of the communist world after the Russian Revolution is the basic empirical proof of this thesis. On a political level, the general crisis theory provides the basis for the doctrine of **peaceful coexistence** between capitalism and socialism — a concept that appears to be a significant "revision" of Marxist thought. With peaceful coexistence, the capitalist world will be unable to compete with world communism and, in the long run, will lose out to its superior competitor.

What forces are expected to cause the gradual deterioration of capitalism? They are the traditional crisis factors emphasized by Marx combined with more recent historical developments: loss of colonial territories after the Second World War, wars of national liberation, continuing internal antagonisms between capitalist and worker, and uneven growth of mature capitalist countries. Over the long run, capitalism will disappear, but without the benefit of a violent proletarian world revolution.

Official Soviet sources picture the theory of the general crisis as a logical expansion of orthodox Marxism, but we consider it more than that. It appears to contradict the Marxian notion of the violent overthrow of capitalism by a revolutionary proletariat unable to bear suppression and exploitation any longer. In its place, Soviet ideologists substitute gradualism, the slow victory of socialism over capitalism.

Revisionist Thought After Marx

Socialist thought after Marx, Engels, and Lenin focuses on two themes. The first theme is the possibility of efficient resource allocation in a market socialist economy. The second theme is the possibility of changing capitalism to make proletarian revolution unnecessary. We classify as "revisionists" those who deny the necessity of the collapse of capitalism and its violent overthrow by a revolutionary proletariat.

The revisionist movement began in Germany after the death of Engels in 1895.[25] Its aim was to revise Marx in light of ongoing experience. The major question addressed was whether capitalism could be changed in a positive manner to avoid the need for proletarian revolution. In general, the revisionists were involved in the trade union movement in Europe and felt that social reform of capitalist society and promotion of democracy were more reasonable social goals than were the revolutionary politics of Lenin. The revisionists believed that the breakdown of capitalism was not imminent and perhaps would never come to pass.

Eduard Bernstein (1850-1932) was a close colleague of Engels and a member of the German social democratic movement. His revision of Marxism at the turn of the century was regarded as an important event in the history of Marxism-Leninism. Bernstein argued that the breakdown of capitalism was no longer inevitable because of recent meliorative trends in capitalist development. The severity of economic crises had lessened and the class struggle was no longer as sharply defined. In this new milder environment, the necessity of an immediate, violent, socialist revolution was no longer apparent. In its place, the evils of capitalism would gradually be eliminated as the public became more educated and enlightened. In the long run, these meliorative tendencies would become so strong that the civilized public would be allowed voluntarily to select socialism as the established economic order without the benefit of violence.

Mikhail Tugan-Baranovsky (1865–1919), an eminent Russian economist and "Legal" (moderate) Marxist, is also prominently mentioned in the revisionist movement. Tugan-Baranovsky argued that Marx's theories of the crisis and breakdown of capitalism were incorrect, primarily because there is no inherent tendency for the profit rate to fall and because underconsumption (overproduction) will not be a problem in the advanced capitalist countries. Capitalism could continue to expand indefinitely. According to Tugan-Baranovsky, humankind "will never achieve socialism as a gift of blind elementary economic forces."[26] Instead, people must work slowly and gradually in an enlightened manner for the eventual adoption of socialism without violent revolution.

Karl Kautsky (1854-1938), another prominent representative of social democracy in Germany, was at one time regarded as the most authoritative spokesman for orthodox Marxism. It was Kautsky who made the initial counterattack against Bernstein's revisionism. In 1902 he formulated the view that chronic depression would drive workers to select the socialist alternative and that social reforms would not ease class antagonisms. However, by the mid-1920s, Kautsky apparently had joined the revisionsists by challenging the inevitability of the breakdown of the capitalist system. According to Lenin, Kautsky exhibited revisionist tendencies much earlier by asserting that the working class might be able to achieve a balance of power with its class opponents through the growth of democracy.[27]

THE NEW LEFT

The New Left, which became prominent in the United States and Western Europe in the mid-1960s represents an unusual blend of orthodox Marxism-Leninism with new radical thought.[28] This movement has been influenced by numerous and disparate writers, ranging from the founders of orthodox Marxism (Marx, Engels, and Lenin) to older critics of capitalism (Paul Baran, Paul Sweezy, Maurice Dobb, Ernest Mandel, Andre Gorz, and Joan Robinson), to non-Marxist writers such as John K. Galbraith, Herbert Marcuse, and C. Wright Mills. Revolutionary leaders such as Mao, Ho Chi Minh, Fidel Castro, and Che Guevara are also prominent in New Left thinking, as are anarchist philosophers such as Bakunin and Kropotkin and utopian socialists. American New Left writers are principally young economists trained in the conventional neoclassical tradition (which they reject).[29] The New Left is more than a simple Marxist revival and, in fact, differs in important respects from orthodox Marxism.

Agreement and Disagreements

The New Left and orthodox Marxists agree that capitalist society is disharmonious and must be transformed into a new socialist society. Capitalist society is inherently corrupt and cannot be salvaged by means of social reform. The New Left agrees with the Leninist disinterest in social reforms and parts company with the revisionists who felt that social reform would obviate the need for revolution.

The basic disagreement with orthodox Marxism concerns the inevitability of socialism. The New Left concurs with the revisionist claim that the breakdown of capitalism is neither inevitable nor imminent. The working class in the industrialized capitalist countries has been integrated into capitalist society and can no longer be counted on to force the radical transformation of capitalist society. Thus a new revolutionary elite comprised of students and intellectuals must assume this function. Revolutionary senses have been dulled by rising affluence, and those directly excluded from this prosperity — the blacks and browns, women, the elderly — are too weak and disorganized to serve as an effective revolutionary core. The radical transformation of capitalist society is not only not, as Marx and Lenin had claimed, inevitable, it is, according to some writers associated with the New Left, now highly unlikely.[30]

New Left Criticism of Contemporary Capitalism

The New Left criticism of modern capitalism accepts much of the traditional Marxist critique. The unequal distribution of economic and political power under capitalism particularly provokes New Left writers. Specifically, the New Left argues that there is an intimate relationship between private economic status and political power; if income is distributed unequally, political power will be distributed unequally as well. Thus the class conflict may be viewed as a conflict over the distribution of political power. The capitalists — the monopolists, the multinational corporations, the Rockefellers — exercise undue political power. Although public officials are ostensibly subject to the dictates of the majority, capitalist democracy does not actually operate on the "one man one vote" rule; rather, those with economic power control political processes.

The control of political power by monopoly capitalists has important consequences for the world economy. The prosperity of the rich countries depends on militarism and the exploitation of poor countries. Without rising military expenditures, aggregate demand would be insufficient to maintain real incomes at their present levels; and without exploitation of the resources and workers of the underdeveloped world, the wealth of the affluent capitalist countries could not be maintained. The powerful can ensure the continued expansion of military outlays and the continued suppression of the resource-rich but economically poor countries by force. The New Left theory of imperialism agrees with Lenin that the prosperity of the rich depends on the exploitation of the poor in other countries and that the working class in the rich countries becomes corrupted. One new twist is that this "new imperialism" is engineered by multinational corporations, which transcend national boundaries, rather than by the state. In this manner, corporate imperialism replaces state imperialism.[31]

Alienation and the Quality of Life

Despite its relative affluence, the working class in the advanced capitalist countries remains alienated. The root source of this alienation is that the labor market deprives workers of control over their labor services and transfers it to those who control capital and technology. Workers are thus isolated from decision making, forced into a depersonalized work atmosphere, and subjected to the anonymity of the assembly line. Capitalist production serves as a strong instrument of social control. Moreover, freedom of choice in the capitalist labor market is strictly limited by social stratification. Women are excluded from high-paying and rewarding occupations, minorities are excluded from craft trade unions, and so on. Most importantly, entry into rewarding occupations — management, the professions, banking — depends on the wealth of one's family, because of the expense of higher education and the importance of family contacts. Wealth and inequality tend to be passed from one generation to another.

AN EVALUATION OF CAPITALISM'S CRITICS

Today, approximately one-third of the world's population lives in communist states expressing some sort of ideological allegiance to the basic notions of Marx and Engels. The radical challenge has not fallen on deaf ears.

Orthodox Marxism obviously underestimated the long-run viability of capitalism as an economic system. Capitalist economic crises have not worsened. There is no evidence of a secular decline in profit rates or of a runaway increase in unemployment rates. Workers in the advanced capitalist countries have experienced a rising real standard of living, taking them above any conceivably defined subsistence level. The proletarian revolution failed to spread beyond the boundaries of the Soviet

Union, and the introduction of socialism into Eastern Europe after the Second World War by the Soviet army did not follow the orthodox Marxist model of proletarian revolution despite Soviet efforts to cast it in this mold. The establishment of Marxist regimes in China and Yugoslavia at the end of the Second World War took place without the protection of the Red Army, but these were scarcely the mature capitalist countries of which Marx and Engels spoke.

The revisionists, who early came to doubt the inevitability of the capitalist breakdown, were more on track. It may be relevant to ask whether capitalism spared itself from the fate predicted by Marx by reforming itself (Keynesian macroregulation, the introduction of social reforms) or whether Marx was just plain wrong in his assessment of capitalism. In any event, capitalism's failure to show signs of imminent collapse has led to substantive "revisions" of Marxism-Leninism even in the Soviet Union and Eastern Europe, which purport to speak for ideological orthodoxy. The major revision has been the denial of the need for a radical transformation of capitalism into socialism by a violent world proletarian revolution — a revision forced by the continued strength of the capitalist world.

That Marx did not correctly predict the future of world capitalism does not alter his position as a giant in the history of economic thought. In fact, Marx's prognostications have proven to be no more off the mark than those of Ricardo and Malthus, who averred that capitalism would reach a stationary state because of rapid population growth and diminishing returns.[32] No one denies the importance of their contributions to the history of economic thought.

Finally, one could assess the radical challenge in terms of the economic and social organization that it proposes in place of capitalism.[33] It is easy to emphasize the weaknesses of the established order of capitalism, but one must consider whether socialism, either of the planned or market socialist variety, can do a better job. On this point, the challengers of capitalism are remarkably silent. Marx and Engels had very little to say about the new socialist order that would take the place of capitalism after its breakdown. The Soviet system of resource allocation through central planning evolved after the death of Lenin and has severe weaknesses. The New Left does not provide a clear blueprint of its ideal society; it offers, instead, some general references to decentralization and reliance on moral rather than economic incentives.

Demonstrating that capitalism has its problems does not prove that the alternative, socialism, is a superior economic system. In Chapter 5, we turn our attention to the theory of centrally planned and market socialism and the question of how well socialism will resolve the problem of resource allocation.

At the end of Chapter 3 we presented certain hypotheses concerning the expected performance of capitalism. Capitalist theory hypothesizes great productive efficiency but, on the negative side, warns against macroinstabilities. Marxian thought agrees with this assessment. Marx and even Lenin were impressed with the productive efficiency and production potential of capitalism. Lenin even suggested taking advantage of this strength during the transition period to lay the foundations for the coming socialist society. Marxism-Leninism also agrees about the inherent instability of capitalism, only in a more lethal form than that envisioned by conventional economists. In fact, it is a tenet of orthodox Marxism that the instabilities will be so severe as to cause the eventual collapse of capitalist society. Well-intentioned reforms would not prove sufficient to prevent this collapse.

SUMMARY: THE MARXIAN CRITIQUE

1. Karl Marx pictured capitalism as an unstable economic system, doomed to be replaced in a violent manner by a superior socialist order. Labor alone created surplus value; yet the capitalist system was inevitably driven to replace labor with capital, causing the profit rate to fall. As the profit rate falls, the capitalist will increase the exploitation and alienation of the worker, unemployment will rise, and crises of overproduction and disproportions will occur. In the end, the capitalist system will break down, and the proletariat will establish a new socialist order.

2. V. I. Lenin analyzed the final stage of capitalism, which he called monopoly capitalism or imperialism. Monopoly capitalism would be dominated by trusts, cartels, and monopolies operating on an international basis. Its distinguishing features would be the concentration of production, the merger of financial and industrial capital, the dominance of capital exports, and the division of the underdeveloped world into spheres of economic and political influence. The class struggle would continue, but capitalists in the advanced capitalist countries would seek to buy off the proletariat. This, combined with the uneven development of the capitalist world, would cause the revolution to break out in the weakest link in the capitalist chain.

3. In the Soviet Union, the first Marxist state, there has been little effort to expand Marxian thought. Instead, Soviet theorists have had to update Marx to account for the failure of capitalism to succumb to its inherent contradictions. The theory of the general crisis of capitalism maintains that the transition from capitalism to world socialism will take the form of a gradual victory of socialism over capitalism. We have argued that this is a significant revision of Marxism.

4. The revisionist movement began after the death of Engels and was largely associated with the social democratic movement in Germany. The common feature of revisionism is its acceptance of the fact that the overthrow of capitalism is not imminent and that one should work for reform of the capitalist system.

5. The New Left movement represents a blend of Marxism-Leninism and revisionism. The New Leftists agree with orthodox Marxism that capitalism cannot be salvaged by means of social reform. Instead, it must be transformed into a new socialist society. The working class, however, has been integrated into capitalist society and will not be prepared, unless reeducated, to be an effective revolutionary force. Intellectuals must unite those disenchanted with capitalist society to transform society, but the probability of this occurring is low.

NOTES

1. Two works that seek to describe the basics of Marx's economics in the language of conventional economic theory are Oskar Lange, "Marxian Economics and Modern Economic Theory," *Review of Economic Studies*, vol. II (June 1935); and Murray Wolfson, *A Reappraisal of Marxian Economics* (New York: Columbia University Press, 1966).

2. Karl Marx, *Capital* (Chicago: Charles Kerr and Company), vol. I, 1906; vols. II and III, 1909. For an annotated (East) German edition, see Karl Marx, *Das Kapital*, Band 1-3 (Berlin: Dietz Verlag, 1962).

3. Our discussion of the economic theories of Marx and Engels is based primarily on the following sources: Paul Sweezy, *The Theory of Capitalist Development* (New York: Monthly Review Press, 1968); Wolfson, *A Reappraisal of Marxian Economics*; Alexander Balinky, *Marx's Economics: Origin and Development* (Lexington, Mass.: Heath, 1970); John Gurley, *Challengers to Capitalism: Marx, Lenin, Mao* (San Francisco: San Francisco Book Company, 1976); William Baumol, Paul Samuelson, and Michio Morishima, "On Marx, the Transformation Problem, and Opacity — A Colloquium," *Journal of Economic Literature*, 12 (March 1974), pp. 51-77; *Grundlagen des Marxismus-Leninismus: Lehrbuch*, German translation of the 4th Russian edition (Berlin: Dietz Verlag, 1964); Karl Marx and Friedrich Engels, *The Communist Manifesto*, in Arthur Mendel, ed., *Essential Works of Marxism* (New York: Bantam Books, 1965), pp. 13-44; Paul Samuelson, "Understanding the Marxian Notion of Exploitation: A Summary of the So-called Transformation Problem Between Marxian Values and Competitive Prices," *Journal of Economic Literature*, 9 (June 1971), pp. 399-431; and Leon Smolinsky, "Karl Marx and Mathematical Economics," *Journal of Political Economy*, 81 (September–October 1973), pp. 1189-1204.

4. See Sweezy's discussion of the transformation problem in Sweezy, *The Theory of Capitalist Development*, pp. 109-130. For a mathematical discussion of the transformation problem in terms of modern economic theory, see Samuelson, "Understanding the Marxian Notion of Exploitation," pp. 399-431; and Baumol, Samuelson, and Morishima, "On Marx, the Transformation Problem, and Opacity," pp. 51-77. We provide a brief introduction to the transforma-

tion problem, using the notation in equations in Appendix 4A at the end of this chapter.

5. Marx's labor theory of value is a theory of long-run values. Marx was interested in long-term, deep, underlying price determinants and felt that labor inputs would determine values in the long run. In the short run, prices would be subject to shifts in supply and demand and could diverge from values. For a discussion of this, see Wassily Leontief, *Essays in Economics, Theories and Theorizing* (New York: Oxford University Press, 1966), pp. 72–83.

6. Other socialist economists have sought to demonstrate the existence of exploitation by using the conventional marginal productivity theory of income distribution in place of the labor theory of value. Oskar Lange, for example, argues that the receipt of the marginal products of capital and land by individual owners of capital and land resources is equivalent to the exploitation of labor. This is true because the owners of capital do not necessarily deserve to obtain the returns to capital and land that more rightly belong to labor. On this, see Oskar Lange and Fred M. Taylor, *On the Economic Theory of Socialism*, ed. Benjamin Lippincott (New York: McGraw-Hill, 1964), pp. 99-102. Another tack has been to demonstrate, using marginal productivity theory, that, under conditions of imperfect competition in either the product or labor market, workers will receive less than the value of the marginal product they produce. The gap between the value they produce and the wage they receive is regarded as exploitation. For the classic discussion of this point, see Joan Robinson, *The Economics of Imperfect Competition* (London: Macmillan, 1959).

7. There is considerable controversy over whether Marx had in mind the notion of biological subsistence or the satisfaction of necessary wants as determined by society when he wrote of "subsistence wages." According to Wolfson, *A Reappraisal of Marxian Economics*, pp. 11-94, Marx definitely had the latter interpretation in mind.

8. Another possible explanation for capital-labor substitution is given by Sweezy, *The Theory of Capitalist Development*, ch. 9. A burst of investment activity can cause a temporary reduction in the reserve army of the unemployed and a rise in wages above subsistence. The increase in the relative price of labor therefore induces capitalists to substitute capital for labor.

9. The basic problem is that an increase in the organic composition of capital is likely to lead to an increase in the rate of exploitation s'. As q goes up, labor productivity increases, and the amount of labor required to meet the subsistence needs of the worker is reduced. One cannot therefore predict what will happen to the profit rate, for these two forces tend to offset one another. Even such a devoted admirer of Marx as Sweezy concludes that "it is not possible to demonstrate a falling tendency of the rate of profit by beginning the analysis with the rising organic composition of capital" (ibid., p. 105). He concludes that other factors causing the rate of profit to fall must be considered.

10. For the analyses of Marx's theory of crises, see Sweezy, *The Theory of Capitalist Development*, chs. 8-10; and Wolfson, *A Reappraisal of Marxian Economics*, pt. IV.

11. According to Sweezy, *The Theory of Capitalist Development*, ch. 11, the Marx-Engels description of the end of capitalism and the coming of socialism was scattered and sketchy. Their failure to deal more completely with the breakdown of capitalism led to the **breakdown controversy** among socialist writers — Eduard Bernstein, M. Tugan-Baranovsky, Karl Kautsky, Rosa Luxemburg, and others. The central issue of this controversy was whether a violent overthrow of capitalism was obviated by reform of the capitalist system and the capitalist government. For Lenin's view of Kautsky and "revisionism" see V. I. Lenin,

State and Revolution, in Mendel, *Essential Works of Marxism*, pp. 103-198; and V. I. Lenin, *Izbrannye proizvedeniia*; Tom I (Moscow: Gospolitizdat, 1960), pp. 56-63 ("Marxism and Revisionism").

12. V. I. Lenin, *The Development of Capitalism in Russia* (Moscow: Foreign Languages Publishing House, 1956); V. I. Lenin, *Imperialism, the Highest Stage of Capitalism* (London: Martin Lawrence, 1933).

13. Lenin's revolutionary strategy is given in V. I. Lenin, "What Is to Be Done?" in Robert Tucker, ed., *The Lenin Anthology* (New York: North, 1975), pp. 12-114.

14. Lenin, *Imperialism*, p. 81.

15. *Grundlagen des Marxismus-Leninismus*, pp. 305-306.

16. The role of war in promoting radical revolutions was an integral part of Nikolai Bukharin's revolutionary theory. For a discussion of Bukharin's theories, see Stephen Cohen, "Bukharin, Lenin, and the Theoretical Foundations of Bolshevism," *Soviet Studies*, 21 (April 1970), pp. 436-457; and Stephen Cohen, *Bukharin and the Bolshevik Revolution: A Political Biography, 1888-1938* (New York: Knopf, 1973).

17. Lenin, *State and Revolution*, pp. 103-198.

18. Lenin's view of the state as an instrument of capitalist exploitation is related in ibid., pp. 123-198. In *State and Revolution*, Lenin justifies the necessity of a strong state apparatus after the proletariat revolution, contrary to Engels's position (in his famous anti-Dühring paper) that the state should "wither away." Lenin's main justification is that a state apparatus is necessary to oppress the previous oppressors, the capitalists. Only when the former oppressors have been eliminated will the need for a state apparatus disappear. Bukharin disagreed, arguing that a strong state could conceivably eliminate the crises and contradictions of advanced capitalism and eliminate revolutionary opposition. Thus the first order of business of the socialist revolution was to smash the existing state apparatus. For Bukharin's views, see Cohen, "Bukharin, Lenin, and the Theoretical Foundations of Bolshevism"; Cohen, *Bukharin and the Bolshevik Revolution*; and H. Ray Buchanan, "Lenin and Bukharin on the Transition from Capitalism to Socialism: The Meshchersky Controversy, 1918," *Soviet Studies*, 28 (January 1976), pp. 66-82.

19. Maureen Perrie, "The Socialist Revolutionaries on 'Permanent Revolution,'" *Soviet Studies*, 24 (January 1973), pp. 411-413.

20. This discussion is based primarily on Buchanan, "Lenin and Bukharin," pp. 66-82.

21. For our discussion of this period of Soviet economic history, see Paul Gregory and Robert C. Stuart, *Soviet Economic Structure and Performance*, 3rd ed. (New York: Harper & Row, 1986), ch. 2. For a contrary interpretation of Lenin's role during this period, see Paul C. Roberts, *Alienation and the Soviet Economy* (Albuquerque: University of New Mexico Press, 1971), ch. 2.

22. Apparently, basic intellectual research on Marxism persists in other countries of Eastern Europe, despite the example of the Soviet Union. For a study of the Polish case, see Domenico Nuti, "The Political Economy of Socialism — Orthodoxy and Change in Polish Texts," *Soviet Studies*, 25 (October 1973), pp. 244-270.

23. E. Varga's book *Changes in the Economy of Capitalism Resulting from the Second World War* was the first in a series of more realistic analyses of modern capitalism. For a discussion of Varga's work and its orthodox Stalinist critics, see Richard Nordahl, "Stalinist Ideology: The Case of the Stalinist Interpretation of Monopoly Capitalist Politics," *Soviet Studies*, 26 (April 1974), pp. 239-260.

24. See *Grundlagen des Marxismus-Leninismus.* One can also look at the series *Political Economy: A Textbook*, published by the Academy of Sciences of the Soviet Union, Department of Political Economy.

25. Our discussion of revisionism is based primarily on Sweezy, *The Theory of Capitalist Development*, chs. 11–12; and Wolfson, *A Reappraisal of Marxian Economics*, ch. 5. Of the two authors, Wolfson provides a more impartial analysis; Sweezy makes a more emotional attack on the revisionists.

26. Sweezy, *The Theory of Capitalist Development*, p. 195.

27. Lenin, *State and Revolution*, pp. 103–128.

28. The discussion of the economics of the New Left is based on these sources: Assar Lindbeck, *The Political Economy of the New Left: An Outsider's View*, 2nd ed. (New York: Harper & Row, 1977); Robert Heilbroner, "Radical Economics: A Review Essay," *American Political Science Review*, 66 (September 1972), pp. 1017–1020; Harry Magdoff, "Militarism and Imperialism," *American Economic Review, Papers and Proceedings*, 60 (May 1970), pp. 237–242; Stephen Hymer, "Discussion of Economics of Imperialism," *American Economic Review, Papers and Proceedings*, 60 (May 1970), pp. 243–246; Thomas Weisskopf, "Theories of American Imperialism: A Critical Evaluation," *Review of Radical Political Economics*, 6 (Fall 1974), pp. 41–57; Martin Bronfenbrenner, "Radical Economics in America, 1970," *Journal of Economic Literature*, 8 (September 1970), pp. 747–766; John Gurley, "The State of Political Economics," *American Economic Review, Papers and Proceedings*, 61 (May 1971), pp. 53–62; Raymond Franklin and William Tabb, "The Challenge of Radical Political Economics," *Journal of Economic Issues*, 7 (March 1974), pp. 128–140; Paul Sweezy, "Toward a Critique of Economics," *Review of Radical Political Economics*, 2 (Spring 1970), pp. 1–8; Paul Baran and Paul Sweezy, *Monopoly Capitalism* (New York: Monthly Review Press, 1968); Bruce McFarlane, "The Political Economy of the New Right," *Review of Radical Political Economics*, 4 (Summer 1972), pp. 85–89. Although most conventional economists view Lindbeck as a sympathetic observer of the New Left, the New Left is dissatisfied with his treatment of their views. McFarlane even refers to Lindbeck's critique as the "New Right" counterattack.

29. The New Left's critique of neoclassical economics is discussed in Lindbeck, *The Political Economy of the New Left*, pt. 1.

30. Paul Baran and Paul Sweezy abandoned Marx's faith in the proletariat to produce the revolutionary overthrow of capitalism. Yet the disenchanted (the old, the poor, the unemployed) are too scattered to constitute a real force in capitalist society. Thus Baran and Sweezy predict mass neurosis in place of revolution. On this, see Bronfenbrenner, "Radical Economics in America, 1970," p. 763.

31. For the New Left's theory of imperialism, consult Magdoff, "Militarism and Imperialism," pp. 227–242; Hymer, "Discussion of Economics of Imperialism," pp. 243–246; and Weisskopf, "Theories of American Imperialism," pp. 41–57.

32. For an analysis of the differences between Marx's and Ricardo's theories of declining profit rates, see Kazimierz Laski, "Zur Marxischen Theorie des tendenziellen Falles der Profitrate," *Wirschaft und Gessellschaft*, 3 (1976), pp. 27–42.

33. This is Lindbeck's strongest criticism of the New Left, and it is also echoed in Paul Samuelson's foreword to Lindbeck's book *The Political Economy of the New Left*.

RECOMMENDED READINGS

MARXISM

Alexander Balinky, *Marx's Economics: Origin and Development* (Lexington, Mass.: Heath, 1970).

John Gurley, *Challengers to Capitalism: Marx, Lenin, Mao* (San Francisco: San Francisco Book Company, 1976).

Karl Marx, *Capital*, trans. Samuel Moore and Edward Aveling (New York: Modern Library, 1906).

Karl Marx and Friedrich Engels, *The Communist Manifesto*, in Arthur Mendel, ed., *Essential Works of Marxism* (New York: Bantam Books, 1965), pp. 13-44.

Arthur Mendel, ed., *Essential Works of Marxism* (New York: Bantam Books, 1965).

Paul Sweezy, *The Theory of Capitalist Development* (New York: Monthly Review Press, 1968).

Murray Wolfson, *A Reappraisal of Marxian Economics* (New York: Columbia University Press, 1966).

LENINISM

Paul Baran and Paul Sweezy, *Monopoly Capitalism* (New York: Monthly Review Press, 1968).

Stephen Cohen, "Bukharin, Lenin, and the Theoretical Foundations of Bolshevism," *Soviet Studies*, 21 (April 1970), pp. 436-457.

V. I. Lenin, *The Development of Capitalism in Russia* (Moscow: Foreign Languages Publishing House, 1956).

——, *Imperialism, the Highest Stage of Capitalism* (London: Martin Lawrence, 1933).

——, *State and Revolution*, in Mendel, *Essential Works of Marxism, pp. 123-198.*

NEW LEFT

Martin Bronfenbrenner, "Radical Economics in America, 1970," *Journal of Economic Literature*, 8 (September 1970), pp. 747-766.

Raymond Franklin and William Tabb, "The Challenge of Radical Political Economics," *Journal of Economic Issues*, 7 (March 1974), pp. 128-140; reprinted in David Mermelstein, ed., *Economics: Mainstream Readings and Radical Critiques*, 3rd ed. (New York: Random House, 1976), pp. 30-41.

John Gurley, "The State of Political Economics," *American Economic Review, Papers and Proceedings*, 61 (May 1971), pp. 53-62.

Robert Heilbroner, "Radical Economics: A Review Essay," *American Political Science Review*, 66 (September 1972), pp. 1017-1020; reprinted in Assar Lindbeck, *The Political Economy of the New Left: An Outsider's View*, 2nd ed. (New York: Harper & Row, 1977), pp. 174-183.

Assar Lindbeck, *The Political Economy of the New Left: An Outsider's View*, 2nd ed. (New York: Harper & Row, 1977) (with polemics by George Bach, Stephen Hymer and Frank Roosevelt, Paul Sweezy, and Assar Lindbeck).

Bruce McFarlane, "The Political Economy of the New Right," *Review of Radical Political Economics*, 4 (Summer 1972), pp. 85-89; reprinted in Lindbeck, *The Political Economy of the New Left*, pp. 184-207.

Harry Magdoff, "Militarism and Imperialism," *American Economic Review, Papers and Proceedings*, 60 (May 1970), pp. 237-242; reprinted in Lindbeck, *The Political Economy of the New Left*, pp. 184-207.

Paul Sweezy, "Toward a Critique of Economics," *Review of Radical Political Economics*, 2 (Spring 1970), pp. 1-8.

Thomas Weisskopf, "Theories of American Imperialism: A Critical Evaluation," *Review of Radical Policital Economics*, 6 (Fall 1974), pp. 41-57; reprinted in Mermelstein, *Economics*, pp. 210-225.

APPENDIX 4A: THE TRANSFORMATION PROBLEM

The transformation problem involves the conversion of commodity *values* (C_i) into commodity *prices* (denoted P_i), where i now refers to commodities. The major issue is whether the prices (P_i) at which commodities exchange in the long run will be equal to their values (C_i), where the values are determined according to the labor theory of value by the direct labor costs of production (v_i), indirect labor costs (c_i) of production, and surplus value (s_i) as a fixed percentage of direct labor costs. If prices are not equivalent to labor values, then it has been argued that this is a significant deviation for a central feature of Marxist theory — the labor theory of value. In fact, the so-called Austrian school attacks the deviation of prices from values as a fundamental weakness of Marxist economics.[1]

The transformation problem follows from Marx's assumption that competition would ensure an equalization of profit rates (p_i) among commodities, for if the profit rate were higher for commodity i than for commodity j, there would be a redistribution of capital to commodity i until profit rates equalize. Let us deal with a simplified economy consisting of two commodities (branches) called commodity 1 and commodity 2. By assumption:

$$p_1 = p_2 \qquad\qquad (4A.1)$$

But

$$p_i = \frac{s_i}{v_i}(1 - q_i) \qquad \text{from (4.5)} \qquad (4A.2)$$

Therefore

$$\frac{s_1}{v_1}(1 - q_1) = \frac{s_2}{v_2}(1 - q_2) \qquad \text{from (4A.1) and (4A.2)}$$

If one assume equivalent rates of exploitation (s/v) for the two commodities, then the values of two commodities (C_i) will equal their prices (P_i) *only* if the organic composition of capital (q_i) is equal in the two branches. Because the organic composition of capital is not expected to be equal throughout the economy, values and prices will not be equivalent — that is, prices different from values must obtain in order to equalize the profit rate.

Marx's response to this criticism is given in Volume III of *Capital*. Marx argues that what is important is whether the equality of prices and values holds in the **aggregate**, not whether it holds for all commodities individually. In our two-commodity world, Marx's solution is as follows: Marx assumed that for all commodities an average profit ($\overline{p}$) on **total capital** would be earned, where $\overline{p}$ equals the economy-wide surplus value (S) divided by the economy-wide sum of total capitals ($C + V$). Thus commodity prices will equal fixed and variable capital costs plus a return on capital, where the rate of return ($\overline{p}$) is uniform across commodities:

$$c_1 + v_1 + \overline{p}\,(c_1 + v_1) = P_1$$

$$c_2 + v_2 + \overline{p}\,(c_2 + v_2) = P_2$$

Totals

$$C + V + \overline{p}\,(C + V) = P$$

But

$$\overline{p}\,(C + V) = S$$

Therefore, in the aggregate $C + V + S = P$, for example, aggregate value equals aggregate price; but for individual commodities, $c_i + v_i + s_i$ is not equal to $c_i + v_i + \overline{p}\,(c_i + v_i)$. According to this formulation, prices and values will not necessarily be equal for each commodity, although total value equals total price. Surplus value will be redistributed among the various capitalist claimants (bond holders, entrepreneurs, landlords) in different branches and will not necessarily accrue to the capitalists who have been instrumental in generating it (through the exploitation of labor in their branch of production).

Marx's solution of the transformation problem has been criticized on the ground that his procedure expresses outputs in *price* terms, while leaving fixed and variable capital in *value* terms. Thus the macroequilibrium between supply and demand is disrupted, and his solution is inconsistent. This dilemma has led to a technical literature that attempts to resolve the transformation of values into prices while preserving the sectoral equilibrium between supplies and demand for capital, consumer necessities, and luxuries.[2]

NOTES

1. E. von Böhm-Bawerk, *Capital and Interest*, vol. I-III (South Holland, Ill.: Libertarian Press, 1959).
2. Sweezy, *The Theory of Capitalist Development*, pp. 115-130; Samuelson, "Understanding the Marxian Notion of Exploitation," pp. 399-431; Baumol, Samuelson, and Morishima, "On Marx, the Transformation Problem, and Opacity," pp. 51-77.

Chapter 5
The Theory of Socialism:
Market and Plan

RESOURCE ALLOCATION UNDER SOCIALISM

Marx analyzed capitalism. He had little to say about socialism. Marx did not answer the question of how a socialist society would deal with the resource-allocation problem. Indeed, the question of rational resource allocation under socialism did not arise formally until the early 1900s. At that time the role of the state in the economic system stirred a debate known as the **socialist controversy**. There is no socialist economic paradigm[1] equivalent to the model of perfectly competitive capitalism. This fact might explain why so little attention has been devoted to socialist economics in standard works on the history of economic thought.[2]

THE MARXIST-LENINIST
VIEW OF SOCIALISM

Although Marx did not analyze the economic working arrangements of a socialist society, he did develop a framework for predicting the triumph of socialism over capitalism. For Marx, the historical evolution from primitive societies to communism was inevitable.[3] Capitalism, largely because of its exploitation of workers and internal contradictions, would be replaced by socialism. Capitalism would be an engine of economic progress, the results of which would be more evenly shared under socialism.

Socialism would be an intermediate step, a system ultimately to be replaced by communism. Communism, the highest stage of social and economic development, would be characterized by the absence of markets and money, distribution according to need, material plenty, and the withering away of the state. In the meantime, under socialism, vestiges of capitalism would continue and some familiar institutions would remain. The most important institution would be the state, which under socialism would be transformed into a **dictatorship of the proletariat**. Marx emphasized a strong role for the state, a role that was subsequently strengthened by Lenin.[4] Under socialism, though, the state would be representative of the masses and, therefore, noncoercive. The state would have ownership of the means of production as well as rights to all surplus value. Under socialism, each individual would be expected to contribute to the system according to capability, and rewards would be distributed according to that contribution. Subsequently under communism, the basis of reward would be **need** rather than contribution. However, need would presumably have a meaning rather different from the one assigned to it under capitalism, where wants are continually expanding.

Many changes and additions have been made to the Marxian model originally developed in the nineteenth century. Lenin wrote extensively on the role of the state under socialism, especially on the tactics of revolution. He also contributed to thinking on the role of the Communist party and to modern Marxian thinking on imperialism. Stalin contributed mainly to the discussion of **socialism in one country**, the question of whether socialism could be built successfully in a single country or whether world revolution was essential for the victory of socialism.

Lenin in his writings emphasized that inequalities and capitalist vestiges would still exist under socialism, hence coercive actions by the state would be necessary.[5] Lenin promoted (and applied under war communism in the Soviet Union) a peculiar view of the state in which the task of administering the economy's affairs was viewed as simple, capable of being handled by all.[6] There was no need, Lenin argued, for specialists because the tasks of management were regarded as quite routine. These views were subsequently modified, although they form the basis of later Soviet thinking on management.

Marx, Engels, and Lenin wrote about the role of the state and income distribution under socialism. They did not deal with the more fundamental issue of how scarce resources were to be allocated during the socialist phase. In the following discussion, we shall return to the two variants of socialism — market socialism, with resource allocation through the **market mechanism**; and planned socialism, with resource allocation conducted primarily through a national economic **plan**.

THE SOCIALIST CONTROVERSY: THE FEASIBILITY OF SOCIALISM

There is no single socialist economic paradigm. Socialist economics must be assembled partly from theory and partly from historical experience.

Resource allocation under socialism has been widely discussed over the past seventy-five years, a discussion loosely termed the socialist controversy. The prevailing view is that workable resource allocation under socialism is certainly possible. Present-day discussion focuses more on the comparative economic **efficiency** of socialism.

Socialist economic theory must answer how resources are to be allocated under socialism. If the socialist economy is planned, how will planners make rational decisions about the use of scarce resources? Is private ownership necessary for the proper functioning of markets?

Barone: A Theoretical Framework

The first consistent theoretical framework of resource allocation under socialism was developed by the Italian economist Enrico Barone. In 1907, Barone published "The Ministry of Production in the Collectivist State."[7] Barone argued, albeit in a limited and purely theoretical way, that prices, understood as **relative valuations**, are not bound to the market. A central planning board (hereafter designated CPB) could establish prices, or "ratios of equivalence" among commodities.

Barone's model consisted of a vast array of simultaneous equations relating inputs and outputs to the ratios of equivalence. If solved (Barone admitted that a real-world solution would be impractical), the equations could provide the appropriate relative valuations of resources required to balance demand and supply. A CPB armed with perfect computation techniques, would require perfect knowledge of all relevant variables, specifically (1) individual demand schedules, (2) enterprise production functions, and (3) existing stocks of both producer and consumer goods. Barone's principal conclusion was that the CPB's computed resource allocation would be remarkably similar to that of competitive capitalism. In fact, he saw no reason for substantial differences.

One could question the practicality of this approach, both at the time Barone was writing and even in the present state of improved computer technology. Nevertheless, it demonstrated that the relative valuations of resources essential for rational resource allocation could be discovered by imputation (solving equations) rather than through the particular institutional arrangements of the market.

The Challenge of Ludwig von Mises

The discussion of this matter went little further until the 1920s and 1930s, when three important developments took place. First, Ludwig von Mises mounted a formidable and now famous attack against the case for rational resource allocation under socialism.[8] Second, a number of Soviet authors made important contributions to the theory of planning, then in its formative stages. Third, the noted Polish economist Oskar Lange set forth his now famous model of market socialism.[9]

Mises's challenge was directed toward the problem of allocating producer goods in a socialist economic system, a task presumably in the hands of the state (with the allocation of consumer goods left to the market). Mises argued that for a state to direct available resources rationally toward the achievement of given ends (even if resource availabilities and ends are known), a knowledge of relative valuations (prices) would be essential. Mises maintained that the only way to establish these valuations would be through the market mechanism, absent in a socialist state where producer goods are owned and allocated directly by the state. If prices are the vehicle by which relative scarcities are reflected, why not artificially simulate prices via a system of equations as proposed by Barone? Mises argued that it would be difficult if not impossible to separate the allocation function from the workings of the market. Both, he suggested, are tied together through the profit motive and the existence of private property.

Much has been written about the profit motive and private property.[10] Mises argued that individuals are motivated by the urge for material self-betterment, which translates into utility and profit maximization. Second, individuals and enterprises are motivated to produce goods and services as efficiently (rationally) as possible so as to increase profits. Third, the drive for achievement cannot be socialized; that is, the urge for betterment cannot be translated from the individual to the group. Furthermore, if resources are owned by the state, profits accrue to the state, not to individuals. Thus, Mises argued, the motivation for utilizing available resources in the best (most efficient) way is lost.

The responses to Mises's original position have varied. There have been two main interpretations. The first is that Mises was saying that socialism could not "work" in the sense that resource allocation would be impossible in the absence of a market mechanism. The works of Barone and actual historical experience provide an effective repudiation to this argument.

The second and more common interpretation of Mises is that socialism cannot work *efficiently*. Consideration of the argument that resource allocation is less efficient under socialism than under capitalism is interesting, for present-day socialist systems do "work." In fact, the contemporary debate over the relative merits of socialism and capitalism focuses on the question of relative efficiency. In this sense, recent works by Bergson and others comparing productivity achievement in differing economic systems is a direct response to the original challenge by Ludwig von Mises.[11]

Kornai: Socialism and Shortage

Hayek and Mises emphasized the complexity and incentive problems of socialism. The noted Hungarian economist, Janos Kornai, focuses on the inherent tendencies of planned socialist economies to operate under conditions of shortage.

Kornai argues that the planned socialist economic system is a system of **shortage**, where shortage is a systemic, perpetual, and self-reproducing state.[12] Most Western economists have argued that persistent shortages or excess demand in the socialist systems is a function of readily identifiable, though not necessarily easily corrected, forces. For example, consumer goods are simply not a high priority in these systems, being supplanted by current high rates of economic growth, emphasis on producer goods and military production, and so on. Furthermore, errors in planning, inadequate incentives, and other system characteristics lead to shortages on a continuing basis.

From a very different perspective, Kornai argues that the economy of shortage arises from the nature of the **enterprise** in the planned socialist system.[13] The socialist enterprise operates under fundamentally different rules from the capitalist enterprise. The capitalist enterprise is motivated to maximize profits. It makes its input and output decisions on the basis of prices established in markets. As a profit maximizer, the capitalism enterprise has little incentive to overdemand resources. If it employs more resources than technology requires, its profits suffer. The capitalist enterprise experiences a hard budget constraint. Faced with input prices and output prices, the capitalist enterprise must cover its costs while offering an acceptable rate of return to invested capital. If it fails to meet its budget constraint, the capitalist firm will fail in the long run. The capitalist firm must live within its means. The hard budget constraint polices capitalist enterprise activities and effectively eliminates shortage (in the sense of excess demand for inputs).

The socialist firm operates in a supply-constrained economy. Socialist planners have as their objective the rapid expansion of outputs, and they tend to judge the performance of socialist enterprises on the basis of rates of output expansion. The manner in which socialist enterprises select inputs to meet their output objectives is of less importance than the output targets themselves. Although socialist enterprises face prices for inputs and outputs, their resource-allocation decisions are aimed at meeting output targets. Relative prices play only a minor role.

The capitalist enterprise that fails to live within its means is punished by bankruptcy. The socialist enterprise that fails to generate revenues that cover costs plus a rate of return on the state's invested capital does not suffer the same consequences. Socialist planners value enterprises for their outputs; socialist enterprises that make losses remain in business by means of state subsidies. Accordingly, socialist enterprises face a soft budget constraint. Socialist enterprises can live beyond their means, if necessary, over the long run.

The hard budget constraint on capitalist enterprises forces them to limit their demands for inputs. The soft budget constraint on socialist enterprises fails to reward them for restricting their input demands. Hence, the socialist system generates continuous excess demands for inputs. The supply of inputs falls chronically short of the demand for inputs, and persistent shortages or imbalances are the result.

Economic systems must allocate resources in an orderly fashion. Persistent imbalances and chronic shortages detract from the orderly allocation of resources. With imbalances, those who obtain resources may be those who will not put them to their best and highest use. Kornai's analysis of socialism is related to the complexity and motivation issues raised by Mises and Hayek. Kornai's conclusion is that the socialist motivation system and inattention to relative prices disrupts the orderly allocation of resources under socialism.

While Kornai's model is in sympathy with some Western observations about socialist economic systems, it explains these observations differently. Take the case of shortages in consumer goods markets. Recent Western theoretical and empirical work in this area has been based on the disequilibrium model developed in Appendix 7A. Kornai argues that it would be difficult to observe excess demand in consumer goods markets, because long-term shortages in these markets force consumers to substitute one product or service for another. Thus, while forced substitution may lower consumer well-being, one does not necessarily observe disequilibrium in the aggregate.

A PLANNED SOCIALISM

The socialist controversy raised the key issues of resource allocation under conditions of socialism. On the one hand, it raised the complexity issue for planned socialism. Barone showed that the CPB would, in theory, have to gather data and solve simultaneous equations for millions of products. Such a task would be beyond the capabilities of any real-world CPB. On the other hand, the socialist controversy raised the motivation issue for both planned and market socialism. If the means of production are owned by society at large, how are managers to be motivated to combine resources efficiently and to take innovative risks?

The discussion that follows pursues these questions for both planned socialism and market socialism. We begin with the origins of the theory of planned socialism in its first real-world experiment — the Soviet Union in the 1930s, and we then proceed to modern discussions of the theory of planning.

Origins: The Soviet Union in the 1920s

The 1920s has been described as "the golden age of Soviet mathematical economics."[14] There was relatively open discussion in the Soviet Union, including an important discussion about the appropriate path and mechanisms for economic growth under socialism.[15] The emphasis was on formulating a socialist path of development, guided by Marxist-Leninist ideological principles. Pioneers in mathematical economics, a key area for the subsequent development of the theory of economic planning, were very active. Under these conditions, it is not surprising that prior to the Stalinist crackdown of the late 1920s, Soviet planners and theoreticians pursued the theory of planning under conditions of social ownership. Possibly the most important practical work of this period was the development of **balance of the national economy**, forerunners of the input-output analysis of Wassily Leontief, and of **material balances**, the planning system used today in planned socialist economies. Clearly the development of the material balance approach remains a major (but simple) contribution to the history of economic thought and a development of immense practical importance.[16]

The notion of a material balance formulated by Soviet economists focused on the need to determine aggregate demands and supplies for basic industrial commodities and to bring them in balance without relying on market forces. More specifically, the theoretical underpinning of the material balance approach (input-output analysis) demonstrated that the productive relations of an economic system could be approximated by a system of simultaneous equations along the lines suggested by Barone.

Much of the Soviet effort of the 1920s was devoted to model building of one sort or another. In fact, some sophisticated mathematical growth models were formulated. Considerable attention was devoted to macroeconomic problems such as inflation, business cycles, and the role of money. Much of the economic analysis of the period was cast within a framework of economic growth and development, for this was the dominant concern of the time. Indeed, participants in the industrialization debate of the 1920s devoted considerable attention to problems of industrialization, sectoral balance, trade strategies, and so on.

A significant omission in the Soviet discussion of the 1920s was the matter of how enterprises might be guided at the micro level. Some Soviet economists even argued that the whole discussion of relative values (prices) under socialism was irrelevant because the **law of value** would not exist under socialism.

Although there is no necessary inconsistency between Marxian economics and mathematical economics, Stalin thought otherwise. This view ended open discussion in the Soviet Union, a situation that did not change until after Stalin's death in the early 1950s.

Principles of Economic Planning

It is not surprising that the Soviet discussions of the 1920s focused on the techniques of **national economic planning**. If market-resource allocation is to be eliminated, some alternate arrangement must be used in its place.

There has been a tendency to associate national economic planning with socialism in both a political and economic context. Actually, planning is consistent with a wide variety of organizational and ideological arrangements. Nevertheless, the idea that an economic system could be centrally planned stems in large part from the Soviet experience. Even in the countries where most national planning is done — for example, the Soviet Union — the so-called theory of planning is really only a set of pragmatic principles; there is no "theory" comparable to the paradigm of the market economy. In this sense, most real-world national planning is a pragmatic exercise.

Planning is a term with widely differing connotations. Different authors have used different definitions, but there are basic elements in common. Gerald Sirkin writes: "Planning is an attempt, by centralizing the management of the allocation of resources sufficiently, to take into account social costs and social benefits which would be irrelevant to the calculus of the decentralized decision maker."[17] The emphasis here is the appropriate *level* of decision making and the social versus the private element in the decisions taken.

Abdul Qayum defines planning as "a systematic and integrated program covering a definite period of time, approved or sponsored by the state to bring about a rationalization of resources to achieve certain national targets using direct and indirect means with or without state ownership of resources."[18] Here we have a broader and more inclusive definition, which nonetheless includes elements of the previous definition — notably, the implication of centralization in the decision-making process.

Michael Todaro, writing in the context of development planning, defines planning as follows: "Economic planning may be described as the conscious effort of a central organization to influence, direct, and, in some cases even control changes in the principal economic variables (e.g., GDP, consumption, investment, savings, etc.) of a certain country or region over the course of time in accordance with a predetermined set of objectives."[19] Todaro further emphasizes that the key concepts are influence, direction, and control, and he defines an economic plan "as a specific set of quantitative targets to be reached in a given period of time."

The concept of plan formulation has been described succinctly by G. M. Heal, who suggests that it can be viewed as "solving a constrained maximization problem."[20] In simple terms, this means that plan formulation involves doing the best one can to achieve objectives, albeit with limitations on available resources.

In contrast to the increasing specificity of these definitions, it is interesting to consider the following Soviet definition:

> Socialist planning is based upon strict scientific foundations; it demands the continuous generalization of the practical experience of the construction of Communism as well as the utilization of the accomplishments of science and technology. To operate the economy according to plan means to foresee. Scientific foresight rests on the recognition of the objective economic laws of socialism. Plans carry in socialism the character of objectives. The planned direction of the economy requires that priorities be established and the main priorities of the economic plan are the branches of heavy industry, for they determine the development of all industrial branches as well as the economy as a whole.[21]

Although some of the elements of this definition may be difficult to interpret — for example, the "objective economic laws of socialism" — the definition contains some familiar concepts such as the ability to foresee and the existence of objectives.

These definitions, though differing in specifics, differ relatively little in terms of substance. A **national economic plan** is a mechanism to guide the activity of an economy through time toward the achievement of specified goals or objectives. The notion of control is fundamental to the concept of planning. Planning is more than forecasting. Although forecasting involves projections of future economic activity, planning is substantively different: The planner attempts to *alter* the economy's direction of movement and hence to change economic outcomes. It is convenient to categorize planning as either indicative or directive. In the case of **indicative planning**, targets are set in the hope of affecting economic outcomes by providing information external to the market; typically individual firms receive no directives from planners. In the case of **directive planning**, however, targets are set by planners with the expectation of directly altering outcomes, because plan targets are legally binding on enterprises. A popular expression in the Soviet Union is that "the plan is law." Indicative planning will be discussed in more detail in a later chapter.

If the economic activity of a country is to be planned, three basic steps are required. First, a plan has to be constructed specifying the goals or objectives that are to be achieved and the means for achieving those goals. A time frame must also be specified. Second, there must be an organizational mechanism for executing the plan and, in particular, a means to guarantee that the participants in the economic system (such as households and firms) will in fact attempt to achieve plan goals. In short, there must be an incentive system to harmonize the behavior of participants with goal achievement. Finally, there must be a means to evaluate outcomes and, where they differ from targets, to ensure appropriate feedback to adjust the direction of future economic activity.

The literature on national economic planning can be conveniently divided into two parts. First, there is the literature devoted to the planning methods actually utilized in the planned socialist economic systems. This literature relates primarily to material balance planning, the Soviet origins of which have already been discussed. Second, there is the literature devoted to national economic planning models, usually employing some optimizing (mathematical) procedure. Although the basic principles of planning are common to both lines of thought, the major planned economies utilize the material balance approach.

Material Balance Planning

The material balance approach to national economic planning has been widely used in the planned socialist economic systems. The central planning board specifies a list of goods and services that are to be produced in the plan period. Once the CPB determines the inputs (land, labor, capital, and intermediate products) needed to produce one unit of output (generally on the basis of historical input-output relationships), it can draw up a list of input requirements necessary for meeting the specified output objectives. Obviously the CPB would like to produce as much output as possible, but the availability of inputs will limit how much can be produced, at least without changes in technology.

The CPB must assure a balance between outputs and inputs. For each factor input and intermediate good, the amount needed to produce output (the demand) must be equated with the amount available (the supply). If a balance between the two sides does not exist, then administrative steps must be taken to reduce demand and/or expand supply. A balance must exist for each item; in addition, there must be an aggregate balance of demand and supply.

On the supply side, there are three main sources of input: production, stocks on hand, and imports available during the planning period. On the demand side, there are two main elements: interindustry demand, where the output of one industry (for example, coal) is used as the input for another industry (for example, steel); and final demand, consisting of output that will be invested, consumed by households, or exported. Thus on both the demand and supply sides, adjustment is possible, and it is through such adjustment that demand and supply are balanced. This procedure is in basic contrast to the operation of the market in market economies, where prices adjust to eliminate imbalances.

For a modern economic system, maintaining an appropriate balance between the supplies and demands for all products would be an enormous task, a point emphasized by Hayek and Mises. In fact, the systems that use the material balance approach plan only the most important inputs and outputs, handling others on a more decentralized basis. Although this means that only a portion of total output is fully within the control of the planners, it is nevertheless sufficient to exert a major degree of influence over the economic outcomes.

Even in this more limited context, Barone's question — how to solve the equations — remains a central problem. The problem of balancing supply and demand can be conveniently formalized in the following manner:

$$\text{Sources} \qquad\qquad \text{Uses}$$

$$X_1 + V_1 + M_1 = X_{11} + X_{12} + \ldots + X_{1n} + Y_1$$
$$X_2 + V_2 + M_2 = X_{21} + X_{22} + \ldots + X_{2n} + Y_2$$
$$X_n + V_n + M_n = X_{n1} + X_{n2} + \ldots + X_{nn} + Y_n$$

where n items are included in the balance and the symbols are identified as follows:

X_i = planned output of commodity i
V_i = existing stocks of commodity i
M_i = planned imports of commodity i
X_{ij} = interindustry demand; that is, the amount of commodity i required to produce the planned amount of commodity j
Y_i = the final demand for commodity i; that is, for investment, household consumption, or export

Table 5.1 depicts a simplified material balance. Notice that for each commodity, a balance exists. For example, in the case of steel, there are three sources on the supply side: Production of 2,000 tons, no stocks on hand, and imports of 20 tons for a total supply of 2,020 tons. On the demand side, however, there are six users of steel: the coal industry using 200 tons, the steel industry using 400 tons, the machinery industry using 1,000 tons, the consumer goods industry using 300 tons, and exports of 100 tons, domestic use of 20 tons, for a total demand of 2,020 tons. Thus, in this example, supply and demand are balanced at 2,020 tons.

Table 5.1 Sample Material Balance

	Sources			Intermediate Inputs Required by				Final Uses	
	Output	Stocks	Imports	Coal Industry	Steel Industry	Machinery Industry	Consumer Goods Industry	Exports	Domestic Uses
Coal (tons)	1,000	10	0	100	500	50	50	100	210
Steel (tons)	2,000	0	20	200	400	1,000	300	100	20
Machinery (units)	100	5	5	20	40	10	20	10	10
Consumer goods (units)	400	10	20	0	0	0	100	100	230

Demonstration that a balance exists:

sources of coal: 1,010 tons   = uses of coal: 1,010 tons
sources of steel: 2,020 tons   = uses of steel: 2,020 tons
sources of machinery: 110 units   = uses of machinery: 110 units
sources of consumer goods: 430 units = uses of consumer goods: 430 units

Source: Paul R. Gregory and Robert C. Stuart, *Soviet Economic Structure and Performance* (New York: Harper & Row, 1986), p. 169. Reprinted by permission of Harper & Row. Copyright © 1974 by Paul R. Gregory and Robert C. Stuart.

The theoretical basis of the material balance approach is the input-output model developed in Appendix 5A.

Computational, administrative, and data-gathering limitations set an upper limit on the number of items that can be handled by material balance planning. Which items will be planned and which unplanned? Typically, the items that are of major significance to the achievement of state objectives will be included in the plan. Items not included in the plan will be planned at a lower level in the hierarchy. Plan authorities have discovered that the economy can be effectively controlled by manipulating a relatively small number of important inputs.

How does the CPB know how much of each input ($X_{ij}s$) will be necessary to produce a unit of output? The coefficient relating input to output is typically derived from the previous year's planning experience with some adjustment (usually upward) to allow for investment and productivity improvements. Moreover, these coefficients are normally assumed to be constant over varying ranges of output — an assumption that causes problems when an industry is expanding and experiencing increasing (or decreasing) returns to scale. Gathering the information necessary to keep the coefficients up-to-date is a real problem. Most planned socialist systems rely on communications with enterprises, a process that is time-consuming and not necessarily reliable.

Material balance planning must deal with the interrelatedness of economic sectors. Suppose, for example, that during the process of plan formulation (or execution, for that matter) there is a need to expand the output of a particular commodity or a previously unknown input shortage is discovered. If more steel is needed, so also will more coal be needed for the production of the steel. But, to produce more coal, more electricity is needed, and on, and on, and on. These second-round effects which reverberate throughout the economic system, can make it very difficult to obtain a balance. To what degree can planners take account of second-round effects? In theory, a number of reformulations of the plan would be necessary. In practice, most planners take account of the initial or most serious repercussions, leaving the remainder to be absorbed as shocks by the system.

The balancing of demands with supplies is the essence of material balance planning. But what about optimality? Optimality implies that of all possible variants achieving a balance, the *best* plan be selected. The best plan is the one that maximizes the planners' objectives. While it is mathematically possible to elaborate the criteria for selecting an optimal plan from among a number of variants, most planned socialist economies are able to prepare, at best, two or three variants, and there is no reason for the selected variants to be optimal.

When we examine Soviet planning we shall have a chance to consider further aspects of material balance planning. At this juncture, let us simply observe that material balance planning is a mechanism that works. Furthermore, it does allow the planners to select key areas on which pressure can be applied to seek rapid expansion, regional economic growth, or whatever. On the other hand, it is cumbersome, and the achievement of a balance frequently requires the existence of buffer or low-priority sectors (typically consumer goods), which can absorb planning mistakes.

Raymond Powell has examined how economies that operate through material balance planning have been able to survive and grow.[22] Powell points out that material balance planning does not prevent participants in the economy (managers, ministers, and central planners) from responding to nonprice scarcity indicators. Insofar as there will inevitably be planning errors (imbalances between output targets and allocated inputs to produce these targets), managers and planners will be confronted with various indicators of scarcity. Managers will recognize that some materials are harder to acquire than others or that some materials held by the enterprise are scarcer than others. Ministries will receive warnings from their enterprises concerning production shortfalls and material shortages and must judge the reliability of this information. On the basis of this nonprice information, resources will be reallocated within the firm according to perceived indicators of relative scarcity. Managers may allocate internal resources (personnel and trucks) to seek out and transport scarce materials. Ministries and central planners will reallocate materials to enterprises that, according to the scarcity indicators they receive, have relatively high marginal products. According to Powell, these natural responses to scarcity indicators introduce the necessary rationality into material balance planning to allow it to function and survive.

Optimization and Economic Planning

Soviet material balance planning is the actual planning method used by the Soviets to allocate resources. Material balance planning will be described in more detail in Chapter 7. As noted above, Soviet material balance planning is a pragmatic method for planning an economy by administrative means. Its objective is to provide a rough balance between supplies and demands of a relatively limited number of key industrial commodities. Because of its administrative complexity, Soviet material balance planning aims at achieving a balance; it does not aim at achieving the optimal balance.

The theory of economic planning focuses on the problem of achieving an *optimal* balance. It shows how, in theory, planners can plan for the economy to produce the optimal combinations of outputs subject to the constraint of limited land, labor, and capital resources. No

present-day economy actually allocates resources by using administrative planning techniques that select detailed optimal combinations of
outputs. Although the solution to such a planning problem is evident
in theory, the solution in practice is elusive.

The planning problem can be expressed in the following manner:

$$\text{Maximize } U = U(X_1, X_2, \ldots, X_n) \qquad i = 1, \ldots, n \qquad (5.1)$$

Where X_i are products that are produced subject to existing technology:

$$X_i = f(u_1, u_2, \ldots, u_m) \qquad (5.2)$$

where u_j are resources (land, labor, materials, and others) and are subject to

$$u_j \leqslant b_j \qquad j = 1, \ldots, m \qquad (5.3)$$

where b_j represents resource availabilities, and u_j represents the total
amount of resource j used by all producers. Moreover, resources are
employed at zero or positive levels:

$$u_j \geqslant 0 \qquad (5.4)$$

The goal of planning is to achieve the maximum value of equation
5.1, termed the **objective function**. The objective function summarizes
the planners' economic objectives and provides a precise relationship
between the utility derived by society (U) and the output of goods and
services (X_i) from which the social utility, or satisfaction, is derived. In
turn, the magnitude of goods and services available is a function of
resource availabilities (u_j) with given technology. Resources cannot be
used beyond their available supplies (b_j), either in the aggregate or for
any individual resource.

The critics of the Barone model explained why such otpimal planning is virtually impossible in practice. First, an economy produces
millions of distinct products and factor inputs. Even with powerful
computers, it is not possible to solve the millions of simultaneous
equations for the optimal combinations of inputs and outputs. To
reduce the computational problem to manageable proportions, planners
would have to work with *aggregations* of distinct commodities (such as
tons of steel, square meters of textiles). Real-world economies do not
operate with aggregated commodities. Factories require steel goods of
specific grades and qualities. To go from a planning solution based upon
aggregate inputs or outputs to real production and distribution processes is an extremely complicated problem. Second, even if planners
could gather the necessary information and make the complicated

calculations, it is still not clear how to get enterprises to actually produce the planned commodities using optimal input combinations. This is the problem of creating an incentive scheme that encourages firms to actually implement the optimal production and distribution computed by planners. A related problem is the generation and processing of data. The information burden on planners is already excessive even if there is accurate and unbiased reporting by the enterprises. However, planners might find it difficult to elicit accurate information from enterprises because their success or failure might be based upon these statistical reports.

A final problem with optimal planning is obtaining agreement on the objective function of society. How are planners to know what goods and services are more important than others? Presumably, planners would have some insights on this issue, but the more complex the economy becomes, the more difficult it might be to determine the relative social valuations of different goods and services. In a complex economy, planners must know whether industrial plastics are more important than stainless steel or ceramics, all of which might serve similar functions as substitutes. Appendix 5B explores the computation problems of planning.

Coordination: How Much Market? How Much Plan?

In our discussion of planning, two themes emerge. First, there is the matter of how much control the central planning board is to exercise over economic outcomes. Should all decisions be made from above by planners, or should there be some decentralization to lower levels? Second, there is the matter of actually solving the plan to achieve both consistency and optimality. In most planned socialist systems the practical approaches to these problems involve simplification through limitation of the formal planning procedures to important outputs and inputs, and a downgrading of the optimality criterion. Furthermore, mistakes are typically absorbed by low-priority (buffer) sectors. Also, most real-world systems utilize intermediate arrangements that combine plan and market. For sectors viewed by the planners as crucial to the achievement of state objectives (for example, steel), the CPB will play an important role; for sectors viewed as substantially less important (for example, light industrial goods), the CPB may play a minor role. Most approach planning as only a partial means for the allocation of resources. The "priority principle" (that is, focusing on important sectors such as steel and chemicals) serves to limit the range of inputs and outputs planned at the center. Plan techniques are of the material balance type, substantially distant from the more sophisticated and theoretically elegant optimization models that we have described.

Critics of the planned socialist system argue that the complexities of the real world make it impossible for the CPB to handle its tasks, let alone to expect the individual firm to follow its directives. The supporters of planned socialism, on the other hand, have argued that choices in production and consumption are in fact generally much simpler than neoclassical economic theory implies. These sorts of issues remain at the center of the debate over the relative merits of the plan versus the market.

The theory of planning stresses the *formulation* of a plan, consisting of a set of objectives and the means for achieving the objectives. Plans are of little value unless they are implemented. Implementation calls for incentives that induce economic agents to achieve the goals of planners. The record of the Soviet Union and other planned socialist economic systems shows that ensuring appropriate motivation is a serious problem. Managers frequently work with plan objectives that are poorly specified, if not contradictory. When managers are asked to execute plans with limited information under such conditions, a large element of informal (and often dysfunctional) decision making takes over where plan directives were intended to be dominant.

MARKET SOCIALISM: THEORETICAL FOUNDATIONS

The problems of optimal planning — computational difficulty and motivation — make market socialism more appealing. By allowing the market to direct a number of resource-allocation decisions, the burden on the CPB is reduced. Also, by allowing individual participants to respond to market incentives, market socialism may offer greater inducements to combine resources efficiently at the local level.

The Lange Model

The most famous theoretical model of *market* socialism is the trial-and-error model proposed by the Polish economist Oskar Lange.[23] This model focuses on the use of a general equilibrium framework (emphasized in the writings of Barone, Pareto, Walras, and others), approaching a "solution" through a number of sequential stages (emphasized by Walras).

A number of economists have made contributions to this model (most notably H. D. Dickinson and Abba Lerner), and a number of variants of the model exist.[24] Furthermore, the Lange model of market socialism differs from our definition of market socialism insofar as Lange envisioned only indirect use of the market.

What are the essential features of the Lange-type market socialist model? The model posits there levels of decision making (see Figure 5.1). At the lowest level are firms and households, at the intermediate level industrial authorities, and at the highest level a central planning board (CPB). The means of production, with the exception of labor, are state owned. Consumer goods would be allocated by the market.

The CPB would set the prices of producer goods. Producing firms would be informed of these prices and would be instructed to produce in accordance with two rules: produce the level of output at which price is equal to marginal cost, and minimize the cost of production at that output. Households would be left alone to make their own decisions about how much labor to supply.

Because the initial prices of producer goods would be arbitrarily set by the CPB, there is no reason to believe that as firms follow the rules (assuming that they do in fact follow the rules) the "right" amount of

Figure 5.1 The Organization of an Economic System in the Lange Framework

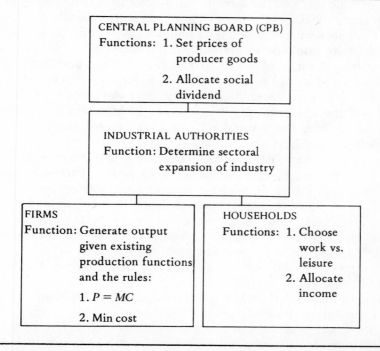

goods and services would be produced and supplies and demands would be in balance. What would the planners do if there were an imbalance?

If, at the end of the planning period, there is an excess supply of a particular good, the price of that good will be lowered by the CPB. If there is excess demand, the price will be raised by the CPB. Thus, in a sequential process through time, the CPB will adjust prices until they are at the "right" levels, that is, where supply and demand are balanced.

In addition to setting prices, the central planning board would also allocate the social dividend (rents and profits) earned from the use of productive resources owned by the state. This dividend could be distributed in the form of public services or investment, the latter decision made in conjunction with the intermediate industrial authorities. The state would have a substantial degree of power insofar as it could determine both the magnitude and the direction of investment, though Lange argued that investment funds should generally be allocated to equalize marginal rates of return in different applications.

This, in simple form, is the essence of the Lange model. Considerable central control over the economic system is maintained by the CPB. At the same time, prices are used for decision making to relieve the CPB of a substantial administrative task.

Let us examine some of the positive aspects of the Lange model. Lange envisioned that with the means of production owned by the state, both the *rate* and the *direction* of economic activity would in large part be determined by the state. Thus the returns from and the influence of private ownership would be removed. Accordingly, the distribution of income would be substanitally more even than under capitalism. Furthermore, the mix of output would be different, and insofar as the investment ratio would be a major determinant of the rate of economic growth, this rate too would be largely state determined. Both these features of the Lange model, a more even distribution of income and state control over the investment ratio, are typical characteristics of most socialist specifications.

Lange argued that externalities could be better accounted for because the state could manipulate resource prices. This is a common theme in the literature on socialist economics. Other economists — for example, Jan Tinbergen and Maurice Dobb — have argued that, in general, decisions made at higher levels rather than lower levels are likely to be "better" in terms of preventing undesirable environmental effects.[25] Lange further presumed that state control over savings and investment would reduce cyclical instability, a mainstay in the socialist critique of capitalism.

Although real-world market systems depart from the perfectly competitive model, this simulation of the market, argued Lange, would utilize the positive aspects of the market while eliminating its negative characteristics. In this context, it is ironic that Lange said little about the problems that would arise when difficulties of entry, economies of scale, or changes in technology are present. These forces are crucial in determining the degree of competition in a capitalist economic system. Might not some of these problems arise in the real-world operation of a Lange-type model?

The Lange model has captured the fancy of many observers over the years, but it has not been without critics. Lange himself recognized that the many tasks assigned to the CPB could lead to the development of a large bureaucracy, long considered to be a potentially negative feature of socialism. The most outspoken critic on this score has been the Nobel laureate F. A. Hayek. Hayek has suggested that although the task set for the CPB might be manageable in theory, it would most likely be unmanageable in practice.[26]

Abram Bergson and others have pointed to a key problem in the Lange model, namely, that of ensuring appropriate managerial motivation.[27] How will the intermediate authorities and especially the agricultural and industrial managers be motivated to follow Lange's rules of conduct even if they know marginal costs? Again, the problem of establishing a functional incentive structure has been a theme of major importance in modern socialist economic systems.

Bergson also emphasized the possibility of monopolistic behavior in the Lange framework, if not at the enterprise level, then possibly at the intermediate level. This problem and the matter of relating one level to another are substantially neglected in the original formulation of the Lange model.

Although the Lange model uses features of capitalism, it is also characterized by many elements normally associated with socialism. The scholarly literature, therefore, has tended to focus on whether the Lange model can operate in reality, and if so, how effectively. The Lange model has also sparked great interest because most existing socialist systems use a crude form of trial and error for the setting of prices, at least for consumer goods. Real-world reliance on the trial-and-error methods is important, for mathematical models of planning (and price formulation) have been of limited practical use in spite of their theoretical elegance.[28]

Market Socialism: The Cooperative Variant

A variant of the market socialist approach is the cooperative or labor-managed economy. The growing interest in worker participation stems from both the theory of cooperative economic behavior elaborated in this section and the system of worker management used in Yugoslavia and Western Europe.

The development of the cooperative model of market socialism stems from the notion that people should participate in making the decisions that affect their well-being. Jaroslav Vanek, a mjaor advocate of the "participatory economy," emphasizes this theme:

> The quest of men to participate in the determination and decision-making of the activities in which they are personally and directly involved is one of the most important sociopolitical phenomena of our times. It is very likely to be the dominant force of social evolution in the last third of the twentieth century.[29]

Vanek uses five characteristics to identify the participatory economy:

1. Firms will be managed in participatory fashion by the people working in them.
2. Income sharing will prevail and is to be equitable, that is, "equal for labor of equal intensity and quality, and governed by a democratically agree-upon income-distribution schedule assigning to each job its relative claim on total net income."[30]
3. Although the workers may enjoy the fruits of the operation, they do not own, and must therefore pay for, the use of productive resources.
4. The economy must always be a market economy. Economic planning may be used through indirect mechanisms, but "never through a direct order to a firm or group of firms."[31]
5. There is freedom of choice in employment.

In essence, therefore, resources are state owned but are managed by the workers in the enterprises whose objective is to create a maximum dividend per worker. Cooperative socialism belongs to the more general category of market socialism, since there is state ownership of the means of production but also an exchange of goods and services in the market without intervention by central planners. Producer goods would use market prices, as opposed to prices manipulated by the CPB in the Lange framework. The cooperative form of socialism is viewed as an important and path-breaking addition to socialist thinking, especially by those who would identify with democratic socialism as a political system.

Theoretical analysis of the cooperative model dates from an article by Benjamin Ward published in 1958 and the subsequent elaboration of the participatory economy by Vanek.[32] Resources (with the exception of labor) are owned by the state and will be used by each firm, for which a fee will be paid to the state. Prices for both producer goods and consumer goods will be determined by the interplay of supply and demand in the market. Enterprises will be managed by the workers (who may hire a professional manager responsible to them), who will attempt to maximize the dividend per worker (net income per worker) in the enterprise. With this objective, management must decide on input and output combinations.

In addition to levying a charge for the use of capital assets and for land, the state will administer the public sector of the economy and may levy taxes to finance cultural and industrial development. In this environment, how will the cooperative firm behave? Let us examine two cases: first, the short run where there is a variable supply of labor but capital is fixed; second, the long run where both labor and capital are variable.

The cooperative model assumes that the enterprise manager wishes to maximize net earnings per worker (Y/L), and that output (Q) is solely a function of the labor input (L) in the short run. The output can be sold on the market at price (P) as dictated by *market* forces. The firm must pay a fixed tax (T) on its capital. In the short-run variant, capital is fixed; so is the tax. Under these conditions, the firm would seek to maximize the following expression:

Maximize
$$Y/L = \frac{PQ - T}{L} \tag{5.5}$$

where

$$Y/L = \text{net income per worker}$$
$$P = \text{price of the product}$$
$$Q = \text{quantity produced}$$
$$T = \text{fixed tax levied on capital}$$
$$L = \text{labor input}$$

Maximum net income per worker in equation 5.5 will be achieved when the amount of labor hired (L) is such that the value of the marginal product of the last worker hired is the same as average net earnings per worker or, in terms of the notation of equation 5.5, when the following balance is achieved:

$$P \cdot MP_L = \frac{(PQ - T)}{L} \tag{5.6}$$

where

$$MP_L = \text{marginal product of labor}$$

The logic of this solution is quite simple. If, by hiring another worker, the enterprise can increase average net revenue — that is, if the marginal product of the last worker hired is greater than average net revenue — then the worker should be hired and average net revenue can be increased. The addition of workers should continue until the value of the marginal product of the last person hired and the average net revenue are the same. If the manager were to hire, at the margin, a worker whose value of marginal product were less than the average net revenue per worker, than the net income of remaining workers would fall.

In the *long run*, the cooperative must select its optimal capital stock (K), on which it will pay a rental charge (r) per unit of capital used. The firm now seeks to maximize its average net revenue as given by the following expression:

Maximize
$$Y/L = \frac{PQ - rK}{L} \qquad (5.7)$$

where

K = amount of capital used
r = the charge per unit of capital used

The maximum value of this expression (average net revenue per worker) will be achieved in a manner similar to that of the short-run case. As long as the value of the marginal product of capital $(P \cdot MP_K)$ is greater than the rental rate (r) paid to hire the capital, more capital should be hired and utilized until the return and the cost are equalized $(P \cdot MP_K = r)$. This rule applies to the perfectly competitive capitalist firm and the Lange-type firm, as well. The same rule as equation 5.6 would apply for the hiring of labor, except that the charge for variable capital would have to be deducted as follows:

$$P \cdot MP_L = \frac{PQ - rK}{L} \qquad (5.8)$$

These two cases, the short run and the long run, are both simple variants of the cooperative model. The short-run case is elaborated diagrammatically in Figure 5.2. It should be emphasized that the model assumes that both product and factor markets are perfectly competitive and that there is no interference by the state.

The cooperative model works through product and factor markets. Households will supply labor services as a consequence of maximizing household utility in the choice of work versus leisure. In so doing, labor supply schedules will be determined, as will demand schedules for consumer goods. Firms will attempt to maximize net revenue per worker and in so doing will be prepared to supply goods and services at various prices and at the same time purchase inputs at various prices.

There is a close relationship between the cooperative model and the competitive capitalist and Lange models. In essence, the cooperative model captures the efficiency features of both, a major appeal for many of its advocates. In the Lange model, the firm will follow two rules equating price and marginal cost and minimizing average cost of production. In the cooperative model, these two rules are replaced by a single rule (in the short run represented by equation 5.6). In the case of the capitalist market economy, the firm will follow the rule of equating marginal cost and marginal revenue, which in the case of perfect competition reduces to the Lange rule; so here also, the cooperative variant simply replaces this rule with equation 5.6.

There is now a considerable body of literature on the cooperative model and its variants. Many pertinent issues have been raised by the model's critics as well as by its admirers.

Figure 5.2 The Cooperative Model

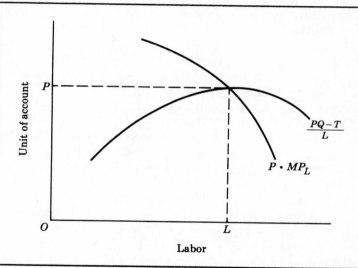

Explanation:

$$\frac{PQ - T}{L} = net \text{ receipts per worker}$$

$$P \cdot MP_L = \text{marginal value product of labor}$$

If the cooperative wishes to maximize the value of net receipts per worker, it should hire labor until the value of the marginal product of the last worker hired is the same as the net receipts per worker. In the diagram, the cooperative would hire OL labor, and each worker would receive OP.

Criticism of the Cooperative Model

The basic cooperative model has been analyzed in detail by Benjamin Ward. Ward notes that the two key features of the model are "individual material self-interest as the dominant human motivation" and "the resort to markets as the means of allocating resources."[33] Ward has devoted considerable attention to analyzing the response of the cooperative to various changes in capital charges, taxes, input prices, and product prices.[34] For the capitalist and Lange-type firm, an increase in price will induce an increase in output, that is, a positively sloped supply curve. Ward has demonstrated that the cooperative supply curve may well be negatively sloped (that is, an increase in product price generates a *decrease* in output), especially in the short run.[35] If true, this would certainly be a perverse and undesirable result, especially in an economy where resources are allocated by the market. Such a result might (though not necessarily) present problems of both existence and stability of equilibrium in product markets.

Ward has also argued that if two cooperatives producing an identical product use different technologies, there will be a misallocation of labor and capital that would not occur if the two were capitalist firms.[36] In the case of the capitalist firms, both would hire labor until the wage is equal to the value of the marginal product ($W = P \cdot MP_L$), for both face the same market-determined wage (W) and hence generate the same value of marginal product. In the case of the cooperative, however, unless the production functions are identical, the average net revenue per worker will differ between the two cooperatives. Although each cooperative equates average net revenue per worker with the marginal product of the last worker hired, overall output could be increased by moving workers to the cooperatives where the value of the marginal product is higher.

Ward has also argued that the cooperative might be undesirable if it existed in a noncompetitive environment.[37] Specifically, he argues that the monopolistic cooperative would be less efficient than either its competitive cooperative twin or its monopolistic capitalist twin. The monopolistic cooperative would hire less labor, produce less output, and charge a higher price for its output than either the competitive cooperative or the monopolistic capitalist firm.

Critics of the Lange model raised the issue of how to ensure appropriate managerial motivation. To the extent that the cooperative utilizes hired professional management, the problem of how to motivate and regulate managers will exist. As we shall see later, this matter has been of central importance in the Yugoslav case. Ward has noted that in some cases the cooperative will have the incentive to expand, although in the absence of private property holding, it is not clear who the entrepreneur will be.[38] It is possible that the state would play an important role here because it would control some of the investment funds.

Advantages of the Cooperative Model

Strong support for the cooperative model comes from Jaroslav Vanek, who argues that the participatory economy is an element of social evolution that will be especially important in future years.[39] In addition to prescribing the participatory economy for the present-day capitalist and planned socialist systems, Vanek also argues that it is the best alternative for the developing economies.

Vanek does not agree with Ward's technical criticisms. He argues that if the technology available to two cooperative firms is identical, and if there is free entry and exit, the input-output decisions of the cooperative will be identical to those of two capitalist firms operating under the same conditions.[40] Morevoer, Vanek argues, the result would be much more desirable socially, because in the capitalist case the workers would be rewarded according to the value of the marginal products, whereas under the cooperative case, workers will be rewarded according to the decision of the collective, over which they themselves have control.

Vanek also maintains that under certain likely cases, the supply curve of the cooperative firm will not be negatively sloped as Ward suggests. If the cooperative is a multiproduct firm, or if it faces an external constraint (for example, on the available supply of labor), Vanek shows that the firm's supply curve will be positively sloped.

Vanek argues that the imperfectly competitive cooperative firm will be superior to the imperfectly competitive capitalist firm because it will have no incentive to grow extremely large and hence to dominate a particular market. Further, the cooperative will have no incentive to act in a socially wasteful manner — for example, by creating artificial demand for a product through advertising. Finally, Vanek maintains that both the demand for investment and the supply of savings will tend to be greater in the cooperative than in the competitive capitalist environment.

Many of the issues surrounding the comparative performance of cooperative and capitalist firms seem highly abstract and theoretical. They are, however, of basic importance to the efficiency of each system. The response of the cooperative firm to market signals will determine the extent to which it can meet consumer goals and, in the long run, the extent to which an appropriate industrial structure is established in line with long-term development goals and aspirations.

Many of the supporters of the cooperative model, especially Vanek, argue that beyond these specific performance characteristics, the crucial features of the cooperative are its "special dimensions." Among the most important would be the elimination of the capitalist dichotomy between management and labor. It is also argued that there would be greater social justice in the distribution of rewards.[41]

Over the years, there has been a great deal of interest in various forms of what might be broadly termed market socialism. In part, the appeal of market socialism rests on the appeal of socialism per se — that is, greater equality in the ditribution of income, more attention to the public sector, and so on. In another dimension, however, the appeal rests on the perception that these features of socialism can be combined with a useful resource allocation mechanism, namely the market, and that this can be done with a substantial amount of personal freedom and participation.

THE PERFORMANCE OF SOCIALIST ECONOMIC SYSTEMS: HYPOTHESES

In Chapter 3, we put forth several hypotheses concerning the expected performance of capitalist economic systems with respect to the performance criteria of economic growth, efficiency, income distribution, stabilty, and development objectives. We shall now attempt to do the same for socialist economic systems.

As we have no paradigm of socialist economic systems, the formulation of hypotheses is especially difficult. It is made even more difficult by the fact that we are dealing with two models of socialism: market and planned socialism. Nevertheless, preliminary working hypotheses do suggest themselves.

Income Distribution

The first hypothesis is an obvious one and applies to both socialist models. It is that income will be more equally distributed under both models of socialism than under capitalism. In both planned and market socialist economies, the state (society) will typically own capital and land, and the returns on these assets will go to the state. It is conceivable, but not likely, that the state will distribute this nonlabor income more unequally than capitalist societies.

Efficiency

The efficiency of market socialism is a matter of some controversy; therefore, it would be unwise, at this stage, to adopt a strong posture. Lange and Vanek have argued that market socialism is potentially more efficient than real-world capitalist systems. Equally strong theoretical arguments have been raised on the other side (by Hayek, Mises, Bergson, and Ward) to demonstrate the inherent inefficiency of market socialism. In the absence of compelling theoretical evidence, we must leave the relative efficiency of market socialism to be decided empirically.

The efficiency of planned socialism is another matter. Planning techniques that aim at optimality still have limited real-world applicability, and planned socialist economies have had to use material balance planning procedures that are unlikely to place them on their production possibilities schedules. In fact, the aim of material balance planning is consistency, not optimality. Thus the hypothesis that the planned socialist economies will not perform well in terms of both dynamic and static efficiency appears to be a fairly safe one.[42]

Economic Growth

In both market and planned socialism, the state will be able to exercise greater control over the investment and savings rates than under capitalism. This is true because virtually all nonlabor income accrues to the state. One would therefore expect a higher savings rate under both forms of socialism, because the socialist state will likely have rapid growth as a priority objective (the building of socialism). In market socialist economies, however, the allocation of resources would proceed primarily according to the dictates of the market, and there is no particular reason to expect resources to be directed in a distinctive fashion into growth-maximizing pursuits. On the other hand, the use of the market may yield (and this is a question we have not been able to answer) a higher degree of efficiency to compensate for this.

In the planned socialist economies, rapid growth will be promoted both by the high savings rate and by the direction of resources by planners into growth-maximizing pursuits. At first glance, therefore, it would appear that one should hypothesize a higher growth rate for the planned socialist economies. The complicating factor is the hypothesized lower efficiency of the planned socialist economies. Thus, we again must refrain from stating a strong hypothesis concerning the relative growth of planned socialism, which must be left as an empirical issue.

Stability

We hypothesize that the planned socialist economies will be more stable than their market socialist and capitalist counterparts. In making this statement, we do not deny the fact that significant concealed instabilities (repressed inflation, underemployment) will be present in the planned socialist economies. We base our hypothesis of greater stability on the following considerations. First, investment spending will be subject to the control of planners and will likely be maintained at a fairly stable rate. Thus fluctuations in investment spending — a major source of instability in capitalist economies — will probably be small. Second, material balance planning will lead to an approximate balance of labor supplies and demands, for unemployed labor will lead to an underutilization of growth potential. Third, supplies and demands for consumer goods will be subject to a great deal of state control (planners set industrial wages and determine the output of consumer goods). Moreover, the state will be less subject to popular pressures to pursue inflationary monetary policies.

The market socialist economies will likely be more stable than their capitalist counterparts but less stable than their planned socialist counterparts. We do not suggest this as a strong hypothesis. Our reasoning is much like Lange's. In a market socialist economy, the state (CPB) will exercise a greater degree of control over savings and investment than in a capitalist economy. Large cyclical fluctuations in investment spending are therefore unlikely. However, insofar as the market allocates resources, market socialist economies will be subject to the same instabilities as capitalist economies (within the framework of more stable investment spending). Moreover, in democratic socialist societies, the state will be subject to popular pressures toward monetary expansion, much like their capitalist counterparts.

Development Objectives

We refrained from suggesting a hypothesis concerning capitalism's ability to achieve development objectives, because this can be done only in a comparative setting. Despite the arguments raised by Vanek, we fail to see any particular advantages of market socialism over market capitalism. The possible exception is the greater control over the savings and investment rates in the former.

The planned socialist economies appear to have one advantage — their ability to concentrate available resources on developmental objectives. The ability to direct resources to specific aims could result in more rapid structural changes and higher growth — which would lead to an acceleration in the pace of economic development above what it would have been under market capitalism. Again, countervailing forces render the verdict uncertain. Can the hypothesized higher efficiency of market capitalism outweigh these advantages? This is one of the major questions in the field of comparative economic systems, and we obviously cannot provide any unequivocal answers at this point.

SUMMARY: THE THEORY OF SOCIALISM

1. This chapter examines socialism in the form of the two pure models — market socialism and planned socialism. These variants of socialism differ insofar as the first relies primarily on the *market* as the mechanism through which resource allocation is conducted, and the second relies on the *plan* as the mechanism for resource allocation.

2. There is no socialist paradigm; instead, the economic theory of socialism must be gathered from various sources. One is the Marxist-Leninist view of socialism and communism and the role of the state. Another is the socialist controversy, a debate over the relative merits of socialism as an economic system. A third is the set of principles developed in socialist systems. The initial contribution was made by Barone, who demonstrated in theoretical terms the possibility of efficient resource allocation under conditions of state ownership of the means of production. He failed, however, to demonstrate its feasibilty. Mises and Hayek pointed out sources of inefficiency in socialist economic systems, emphasizing problems of motivation and coordination in the absence of private ownership and market resource allocation. Kornai explains why shortages are persistent under conditions of socialism.

3. Lange's trial-and-error model of market socialism was an important attempt to demonstrate the feasibility of efficient resource allocation with public ownership. The cooperative variant of market socialism represents a more recent contribution to the theory of socialism. Its efficiency features and "special dimensions" have been the subject of considerable controversy.

4. The theory of planned socialism is more difficult to deal with than the theory of market socialism. The theory of planning can, to some extent, serve as the model of planned socialism, although planning itself need not be tied to any particular institutional arrangement. One can also look at the theory of planning by examining the practical experiences of centralized planning in the planned socialist countries. The technique of material balance is the only operative planning model for entire economic systems.

5. Hypotheses concerning the performance of market and planned socialism were formulated, although in some instances theory suggests ambiguous results. It was argued that both planned and market socialism would have a more equal distribution of income than market capitalism, that planned socialism would be more stable than market socialism, which would be more stable than market capitalism, and that planned socialism might be less efficient than either market socialism or market capitalism.

Countervailing forces prevented us from deriving hypotheses concerning economic growth and the achievement of developmental objectives. In both instances, the greater ability of the socialist economies to marshal savings and investment was weighed against the presumed greater efficiency of market capitalism.

NOTES

1. See, for example, A. C. Pigou, *Socialism Versus Capitalism* (New York: St. Martin's, 1960), ch. 1. For a definition emphasizing brevity, see Benjamin N. Ward, *The Socialist Economy* (New York: Random House, 1967), ch. 1; for a broader definition, see J. Wilczynski, *The Economics of Socialism* (London: Allen and Unwin, 1970), ch. 1.

2. See, for example, the treatment in E. Ray Canterbery, *The Making of Economics* (Belmont, Calif.: Wadsworth, 1976); or Robert Lekachman, *A History of Economic Ideas* (New York: McGraw-Hill, 1976). For a treatment in the context of the history of economic thought, see Edmund Whittaker, *Schools and Streams of Economic Thought* (Chicago: Rand McNally, 1966), chs. 10–11; for a collection of important original sources, see Alec Nove and D. N. Nuti, eds., *Socialist Economics* (Harmondsworth, England: Penguin Books, 1972).

3. It is worth noting at this juncture a contradiction that will arise frequently in the present book. In the Marxian schema, capitalism is the engine that was to create the developed and industrialized economy; socialism would be concerned with the provision of an "equitable" distribution of the productive capacity developed under capitalism. Although socialism was never intended to be the mechanism through which economic development would take place, this is precisely the role into which it has been cast in almost every real-world instance.

4. For a survey, see R. N. Carew Hunt, *The Theory and Practice of Communism* (Harmondsworth, England: Penguin Books, 1963), chs. 6, 15.

5. Lenin's views on this matter are elaborated in his *State and Revolution*, published in 1917.

6. This view, though largely discredited during the period of war communism in the Soviet Union, has remained influential and forms an important element in present-day Soviet attitudes toward industrial and agricultural management. This attitude is used to support the argument for technical rather than managerial training for the performance of leadership functions in large enterprises.

7. The important articles in this debate can be found in F. A. Hayek, ed., *Collectivist Economic Planning*, 6th ed. (London: Routledge and Kegan Paul, 1963).

8. See Ludwig von Mises, "Economic Calculation in Socialism," in Morris Bornstein, ed., *Comparative Economic Systems*, rev. ed. (Homewood, Ill.: Irwin, 1969), pp. 61–68.

9. The best source for the original article by Oskar Lange and related discussion is Benjamin Lippincott, ed., *On the Economic Theory of Socialism* (Minneapolis: University of Minnesota Press, 1938), reprinted by McGraw-Hill in 1964.

10. See, for example, Pigou, *Socialism Versus Capitalism*, ch. 1.

11. Bergson's original essay can be found in Abram Bergson, *Essays in Normative Economics* (Cambridge, Mass.: Harvard University Press, 1966), ch. 9; for a

return to the same theme, see Abram Bergson, "Market Socialism Revisited," *Journal of Political Economy*, 75 (October 1967), pp. 663-675.

12. Kornai has been a prolific contributor to the literature on shortage. See Janos Kornai, *Economics of Shortage* vols. A and B (New York: North-Holland, 1980). For a recent discussion of some of the issues raised by Kornai, see Paul G. Hare, "Economics of Shortage and Non-Price Control," *Journal of Comparative Economics*, 6 (1982), pp. 406-425. An excellent summary is J. Kornai, "Resource Constrained Versus Demand Constrained Systems," *Econometrica* 47, 4 (July, 1979), pp. 801-819.

13. See Janos Kornai, *Anti-Equilibrium: On Economic Systems Theory and the Tasks of Research* (Amsterdam: North-Holland, 1971); and Janos Kornai, *Rush Versus Harmonic Growth* (Amsterdam: North-Holland, 1972); *Overcentralization in Economic Administration* (London: Oxford University Press, 1959); and *Growth, Shortage, and Efficiency: A Macrodynamic Model of the Socialist Economy* (Berkeley: University of California Press, 1983).

14. See Leon Smolinski, "The Origins of Soviet Mathematical Economics," in Franz-Lothar Altmann, ed., *Jahrbuch der Wirtschaft Osteuropas* [Yearbook of East European Economics, Band 2 (Munich: Gunter Olzog Verlag, 1971), pp. 137-154.

15. The most famous Soviet growth model is by P. A. Feldman and is discussed in Evsey Domar, *Essays in the Theory of Economic Growth* (New York: Oxford University Press, 1957), pp. 233-261. The classic work on the Soviet industrialization debate is Alexander Erlich, *The Soviet Industrialization Debate, 1924-1928* (Cambridge, Mass.: Harvard University Press, 1962).

16. R. W. Davies and S. G. Wheatcroft, eds., *Materials for a Balance of the National Economy 1928/29* (Cambridge: Cambridge University Press, 1985).

17. Gerald Sirkin, *The Visible Hand: The Fundamentals of Economic Planning* (New York: McGraw-Hill, 1968), p. 45.

18. Abdul Qayum, *Techniques of National Economic Planning* (Bloomington: Indiana University Press, 1975), p. 4.

19. Michael P. Todaro, *Development Planning: Models and Methods* (Nairobi: Oxford University Press, 1971), p. 1.

20. G. M. Heal, *The Theory of Economic Planning* (New York: American Elsevier, 1973), p. 5.

21. *Political Economy: A Textbook*, 4th ed. (Berlin: Deitz, 1964), pp. 496, 499.

22. Raymond Powell, "Plan Execution and the Workability of Soviet Planning," *Journal of Comparative Economics*, 1, no. 1 (March 1977), pp. 51-76.

23. See Lippincott, *On the Economic Theory of Socialism*.

24. See, for example, F. M. Taylor, "The Guidance of Production in a Socialist State," *American Economic Review*, 19 (March 1929); reprinted in Lippincott, *On the Economic Theory of Socialism*, pp. 39-54; H. D. Dickinson, *Economics of Socialism* (London: Oxford University Press, 1939); and Abba P. Lerner, *The Economics of Control* (New York: Macmillan, 1944).

25. See the discussion in Maurice Dobb, *The Welfare Economics and the Economics of Socialism* (Cambridge: Cambridge University Press, 1969), p. 133 and footnotes thereto.

26. F. A. Hayek, "Socialist Calculation: The Competitive Solution," *Economica*, n.s. 7 (May 1940), pp. 125-149; reprinted in Bornstein, *Comparative Economic Systems*, pp. 77-97.

27. See the sources cited in note 11.

28. The sophisticated works of Soviet mathematical economists have been brought to Western readers by Zauberman, Ellman, and others. See, for example, Alfred Zauberman, *The Mathematical Revolution in Soviet Economics* (London: Oxford University Press, 1975); Michael Ellman, *Soviet Planning Today*

(Cambridge: Cambridge University Press, 1971); Martin Cave, Alastair McAuley, and Judith Thornton, eds., *New Terms in Soviet Economics* (Armonk, N.Y.: M. E. Sharpe, 1982).

29. Jaroslav Vanek, *The Participatory Economy* (Ithaca, N.Y.: Cornell University Press, 1971), p. 1.
30. Ibid., p. 9.
31. Ibid., p. 11.
32. For Ward's original contribution, see Benjamin Ward, "The Firm in Illyria: Market Syndicalism," *American Economic Review*, 48 (September 1958), pp. 566-589. See also E. Domar, "The Soviet Collective Farm as a Producer Cooperative," *American Economic Review*, 56 (September 1966), pp. 734-757; and Walter Y. Oi and Elizabeth M. Clayton, "A Peasant's View of a Soviet Collective Farm," *American Economic Review*, 58 (March 1968), pp. 37-59. For a general treatment of Vanek's argument, see Vanek, *The Participatory Economy*; and for a detailed analysis see Jaroslav Vanek, *The General Theory of Labor-Managed Market Economies* (Ithaca, N.Y.: Cornell University Press, 1970). For a more recent collection, see Jaroslav Vanek, *The Labor-Managed Economy: Essays* (Ithaca, N.Y.: Cornell University Press, 1977).
33. Ward, *The Socialist Economy*, p. 183.
34. Ibid., chs. 8-10.
35. Ibid., pp. 191-192.
36. Ibid., pp. 184 ff.
37. Ibid., pp. 201 ff.
38. Ibid., ch. 9.
39. For the general treatment, see Vanek, *The Participatory Economy*.
40. See Vanek, *The General Theory*.
41. For background on participatory socialism, see for example Ellen Turkish Comisso, *Worker's Control Under Plan and Market* (New Haven: Yale University Press, 1979), chs. 1-2; Hans Dieter Seibel and Ukandi G. Damachi, *Self-Management in Yugoslavia and the Third World* (New York: St. Martin's, 1982); Howard M. Wachtel, *Workers' Management and Workers' Wages in Yugoslavia* (Ithaca, N.Y.: Cornell University Press, 1973), ch. 2.
42. P. J. D. Wiles, *The Political Economy of Communism* (Oxford: Oxford University Press, 1962), ch. 11.

RECOMMENDED READINGS

SOCIALISM IN HISTORICAL PERSPECTIVE

G. D. H. Cole, *Socialist Economics* (London: Gollancz, 1950).
R. N. Carew Hunt, *The Theory and Practice of Communism* (Harmondsworth, England: Penguin Books, 1963).

THE SOCIALIST CONTROVERSY

F. A. Hayek, ed., *Collectivist Economic Planning*, 6th ed. (London: Routledge and Kegan Paul, 1963).
Benjamin N. Ward, *The Socialist Economy* (New York: Random House, 1967).

MARKET SOCIALISM: TRADITIONAL VIEWS AND COUNTERTHOUGHTS

Abram Bergson, "Market Socialism Revisited," *Journal of Political Economy*, 75 (October 1967), pp. 663–675.

H. D. Dickinson, *Economics of Socialism* (London: Oxford University Press, 1939).

Abba P. Lerner, *The Economics of Control* (New York: Macmillan, 1944).

Benjamin Lippincott, ed., *On the Economic Theory of Socialism* (New York: McGraw-Hill, 1964).

MARKET SOCIALISM: THE LABOR-MANAGED VARIANT

Jaroslav Vanek, *The General Theory of Labor-Managed Market Economies* (Ithaca, N.Y.: Cornell University Press, 1970).

——, *The Labor-Managed Economy: Essays* (Ithaca, N.Y.: Cornell University Press, 1977).

——, *The Participatory Economy* (Ithaca, N.Y.: Cornell University Press, 1971).

Benjamin N. Ward, *The Socialist Economy* (New York: Random House, 1967).

ECONOMIC PLANNING

Morris Bornstein, ed., *Economic Planning, East and West* (Cambridge, Mass.: Ballinger, 1975).

Roger A. Bowles and David K. Whynes, *Macroeconomic Planning* (London: Allen and Unwin, 1979).

Phillip J. Bryson, *Scarcity and Control in Socialism* (Lexington, Mass.: Heath, 1976).

G. M. Heal, *The Theory of Economic Planning* (New York: American Elsevier, 1973).

Zoltan Kenessey, *The Process of Economic Planning* (New York: Columbia University Press, 1978).

Abdul Qayum, *Techniques of National Economic Planning* (Bloomington: Indiana University Press, 1975).

Gerald Sirkin, *The Visible Hand: The Fundamentals of Economic Planning* (New York: McGraw-Hill, 1968).

Nicolas Spulber and Ira Horowitz, *Quantitative Economic Policy and Planning* (New York: Norton, 1976).

Michael P. Todaro, *Development Planning: Models and Methods* (Nairobi: Oxford University Press, 1971).

GENERAL WORKS

Alec Nove, *The Economics of Feasible Socialism* (Winchester, Mass.: Allen and Unwin, 1983).

J. Wilczynski, *The Economics of Socialism*, 4th ed. (London: Allen and Unwin, 1982).

APPENDIX 5A: THE INPUT-OUTPUT
MODEL AND ECONOMIC PLANNING

For our examination of differing economic systems, the static input-output model is useful in at least two important respects. First, it illustrates in a precise and graphic manner the nature of the interdependence among the various sectors of an economic system. Second, this model can help us to appreciate how a change in one sector will have an impact on some or all other sectors in the system.

An input-output table is a graphic presentation of the national accounts of an economic system and illustrates the flows among the various sectors of the economic system. The economy is divided into sectors, of which there are two broad types — those that produce output (final output for consumption or intermediate output for utilization in the production of final goods) and those that use final output (either as an intermediate input to further production or as a final consumption item). Sectors may correspond to industries, the number of which will depend on the degree of disaggregation in the table. Naturally, the greater the number of sectors the more accurately the table will reflect the real economic system. At the same time, data and computational problems normally place severe limits on size. A simple input-output format is presented in Figure 5A.1.

Recall from basic national accounting procedures that the sum total of goods and services produced in any year and valued at market prices (gross national product) is equal to the sum total of factor incomes (gross national income) generated in the production of this output. This concept is illustrated in the input-output table. For example, the sum of all inputs used in, say, agriculture (sum of entries in the second column) will be numerically equal to the total output of the agricultural sector (sum of entries in the second row). Thus each column in the input-output table illustrates both the source and the amount of input that will be used from each source in the generation of the output of the agricultural sector. The inputs as noted will be of two types, those of a **primary** nature (labor, for example) and those of an **intermediate** nature (those from industry, for example). At the same time, each row shows how the output of the particular sector (agriculture in this case) is distributed among the various users of agricultural products. In this simple table, there are two types of users: industries that will use agricultural products as intermediate inputs for additional manufacturing, and final consumers who will utilize agriculture products directly without further processing.

The input-output table is a simple yet highly useful picture of resource flows in an economic system. We should emphasize, however, that the model presented here relies on several crucial and limiting assumptions:

1. *Aggregation:* Obviously the fewer the sectors, the easier it is to manipulate the table. At the same time, a sector labeled "manufacturing" would tell us little about the input-output relationships of the steel industry.
2. *Time frame:* The simple model presented here is *static* and does not, therefore, allow for change through time. Thus the amount of labor required to produce a unit of steel is assumed not to change over time.
3. *Returns to scale:* We are assuming constant returns to scale. That is, the input-output ratios are the same, regardless of the *volume* of output being produced.

Our interest in this table focuses largely on Quadrant I, for here are the **technical coefficients** relating inputs to outputs. Specifically this quadrant tells us how much of a particular input is required to produce a unit of a particular output. Clearly this technical relationship is crucial for specifying what will be produced and what inputs will be available for this production activity. How are these coefficients determined?

Figure 5A.1 Schematic Input-Output Table

| USING SECTOR / PRODUCING SECTOR | INTERMEDIATE USE | | | FINAL USE | | | TOTAL OUTPUTS |
	Steel	Agriculture	Other branches	Consumption	Exports	Other branches	
Steel							
Agriculture	INTERINDUSTRY, QUADRANT I			FINAL USE, QUADRANT II			
Other branches							
Land							
Labor	VALUE ADDED, QUADRANT III			DIRECT FACTOR PURCHASE, QUADRANT IV			
Capital							
TOTAL INPUTS							

If we assume that there are i rows and j columns in the input-output matrix, then any cell can be described as a_{ij}, which represents the amount of i that is used to produce a unit of j as a proportion of the total output of j. These technical coefficients are readily computed in the following manner:

$$a_{ij} = \frac{x_{ij}}{X_j}$$

where

x_{ij} = the amount of input i used in industry j
X_j = the total output of industry j

What is the relationship among the input-output framework presented here, material balance planning as practiced in the planned socialist economic systems, and the more general planning problem? First, as we have noted, knowledge of the matrix of technical coefficients is crucial to the development of a plan, whether that plan is constructed by a simple material balance technique or by more sophisticated methods, and whatever criteria of an acceptable plan are utilized. For example, if a plan is to be feasible, input availabilities must be sufficient to generate desired outputs. Clearly, knowledge of the technical coefficients can assist in making such a determination.

Second, if one knows the relation between inputs and outputs, then with a given feasible objective, one in effect knows the relative worth (value) of different inputs in the production process. Thus a set of relative prices can be determined from the input-output model.

Third, it should be emphasized that although the model presented here is simple, the restrictive assumptions can be relaxed to some degree. Although the realism achieved is attractive, present and future research must devote substantial attention to overcoming pervasive problems of data, computational facilities, and so on. Clearly the basic input-output model, even with a fair degree of aggregation, provides the planner with important information about the relationship between inputs and outputs in the economic system. But, how is this information put to use? As we have noted, the planning process begins with the specification of an objective function. Planners, on whatever grounds, must determine *what* is to be produced, and when they do so, they will want to achieve maximum production consistent with available inputs. Suppose that the technical coefficients (a_{ij}) are available. How can the planner determine if a particular objective is possible with available inputs?

The basic input-output model says that for a number of sectors (in our case n sectors), the total production in the system is the sum of intermediate demand and final demand. In notational form, this relationship can be expressed as follows:

$$\sum_{j=1}^{n} x_{ij} + Y_i = X_i \qquad (5A.1)$$

But we know something about the amount of i needed to produce a unit of j. Specifically, this relationship is as follows:

$$x_{ij} = a_{ij}X_j \qquad (5A.2)$$

Substituting equation 5A.2 into equation 5A.1 we derive the following relationship:

$$\sum_{j=1}^{n} a_{ij}X_j + Y_i = X_i \qquad (5A.3)$$

Rearranging terms, we get

$$Y_i = X_i - \sum_{j=1}^{n} a_{ij}X_j \qquad (5A.4)$$

Equation 5A.4 expresses the basic relationship between final demand, interindustry demand, and total production. This basic relationship can be more conveniently expressed in matrix notion as follows:

$$X = AX + Y \qquad (5A.5)$$

or by rearranging terms

$$Y = (I - A)X \qquad (5A.6)$$

where

I = identity matrix
X = a vector of planned outputs
A = the matrix of technical coefficients
Y = a vector of final outputs

If the matrix of technical coefficients (A) is known to the planner, then the feasibility of a given vector of plan targets (X) can be readily determined by matrix multiplication. Clearly, even if the focus of the planner should change, knowing any two of the three components of this relationship makes it easier to determine the third component. How useful is this model in practice? Although aggregation reduces the realism and the practical applicability of the model, it nevertheless remains useful as a method of checking the feasibility of alternative scenarios. In addition, problems of *scale* may be less of a problem when this sort of model is used with short planning horizons. In the early stages of development, however, scale economies might be expected to be important. Finally, the absence of input substitution possibilities in the basic input-output model has never been a major issue in the socialist context. Socialist planning advocates have generally argued that the more typical pattern in production is a corner solution, rather than the usual neoclassical assumption of infinitely continuous factor substitution (the downward sloping isoquant).

REFERENCES

H. B. Chenery and P. G. Clark, *Interindustry Economics* (New York: Wiley, 1959).

R. Dorfman, P. Samuelson, and R. Solow, *Linear Programming and Economic Analysis* (New York: McGraw-Hill, 1958).

W. W. Leontief, *Input-Output Economics* (New York: Oxford University Press, 1966).

Michael P. Todaro, *Development Planning: Models and Methods* (Nairobi: Oxford University Press, 1971).

Vladimir Treml, "Input-Output Analysis and Soviet Planning," in John Hardt et al., eds., *Mathematics and Computers in Soviet Planning* (New Haven: Yale University Press, 1967).

APPENDIX 5B: THE PLANNING PROBLEM

We have emphasized that the competitive market model, though a theoretical construct, nevertheless serves as a useful basis for analyzing both the structure and the function of the capitalist market economy. In recent years, there have been increasingly sophisticated attempts to construct a similar paradigm for the planned economy. Although the theory of planning is beyond the scope of this book, we shall present here a brief outline of the direction in which this analysis is proceeding.

The text of this chapter showed that an economic plan is simply an application of maximization under constraints. It also pointed out the difficulty of actually solving for an optimal plan. This appendix discusses price and nonprice solutions to an optimal plan problem.

The planning problem, then, is conceptually quite straightforward. With given objectives and constraints, how is the objective function to be maximized? The plan, as we have outlined, it thus far, tells us what we would like to do, and what means are available for the achievement of these objectives. It does not, however, tell us what to do to achieve these goals. At this juncture, a solution for the planning problem must be found. A variety of methods, known as **planning routines**, are available.

Planning Routines

The planning problem is similar to a maximization model for a single firm and can be solved by well-known procedures. However, the matter of aggregation and the large number of inputs and outputs introduce a degree of complexity that makes it necessary to look for different solution routines. Much of the literature on planning is devoted to a discussion of these routines, their various positive and negative features, and different models of application. Most planning routines are one of three basic types: price guided, nonprice guided, or some mixture of the two. Before we turn to an examination of these different routines, some general observations are necessary.

Because the task of determining the solution to a national economic plan is so large, it is usually approached in a number of steps known as **iterations**. A simple example of an iterative approach is an auction. When the auctioneer holds up an item to be sold, he or she does not known who will purchase the item or what the price will be. Both pieces of information (the solution in this case) are obtained by a series of sequential steps in which the auctioneer hears bids from various potential buyers. The auctioneer (and the seller of the item) would like to obtain the highest possible price, and to do so with the least expenditure of time. The iterative approach to solving a planning problem is similar, and analogous criteria can be used for evaluating the effectiveness of planning routines: Which planning routine achieves the "best" solution in the smallest amount of time (or, in this case, the smallest number of iterations)? These are important questions when one is dealing with a national economic plan for which vast amounts of computational inputs are required. The material balance approach solves this problem by accounting for only the most serious reverberations resulting from imbalance.

As planners move through a series of iterations to approach a final solution, how do they know that the initially nonoptimal values of the choice variables will improve as they are adjusted? The ability of a planning routine to move closer and closer toward the maximum value of the objective function is known as **convergence**. A matter of substantial theoretical complexity, convergence is also of great practical importance. Recall that in the Lange model of market socialism if there is excess demand for a particular producer good, the CPB will raise the price. Will this adjustment necessarily (under all conditions) reduce the excess demand? As the auctioneer appeals to additional bidders in sequence, will the selling price necessarily increase at each stage? Reaching the "best" value of an objective function in the most efficient manner possible is at the heart of selecting the planning routine most appropriate for a particular application. Procedures for optimization are the subject of a vast body of literature in economics and related disciplines, generally described as mathematical programming.

In addition to obtaining the maximum value of the objective function, the plan must be **feasible**. A plan that is feasible is one whose objectives can be realized with the available inputs, technology, and so on. The concept of feasibility seems simple enough. The feasibility conditions are given in equations 5.2 to 5.4. In fact, as we have seen, feasibility is the most important criterion of good plan formulation in material balance planning. There are, however, two important complications. First, plan objectives are necessarily based on data that are probabilistic, so methods that can handle errors appropriately must be chosen. Second, there is the element of uncertainty when plan objectives are established for some future time period (as they usually will be). It is not clear that the methods viewed as appropriate for handling existing data will also be appropriate for handling projections into the future.

There are a wide variety of planning routines. The most fundamental distinctions among them, however, are the nature of the *information* that will be derived from the exercise and the manner in which the information will be utilized. *Prices* are the most familiar information mechanism in the market economy. A planning routine may be designed to give the planners prices, which can be used in varying ways to allocate resources in the system. An alternative model solves only for physical quantities of inputs and outputs, information that would then be conveyed to producing units in the system for action. Obviously it would be possible to combine the price and nonprice approaches.

The distinction between price and nonprice planning can be illustrated using equations 5.1 through 5.4. Both, in theory, should yield the same result, namely, an allocation of resources that maximizes the objective function. Nonprice planning requires planners to solve directly for the X's and the u's and then order producers to produce this mix of outputs (X's) with the prescribed mix of inputs (u's). Price planning requires the planners to solve for the set of factor prices that will induce producers to supply the same mix of outputs using the same mix of inputs. Let us now examine the main variants of price-guided and nonprice-guided planning routines.

Planning with Prices

We have already examined resource allocation in the market economy, and we need not emphasize further the important role of prices. Prices are similarly important in the market socialism model. Indeed, much of the discussion of market socialism revolves around the basic issues of how prices are to be formed and, once formed, how they will be used to manipulate economic outcomes. Under centrally planned socialism, price-guided planning models seek to find a set of scarcity (equilibrium) prices to which enterprises are allowed to respond or that help planners establish resource allocation directives.

The most famous price-guided planning routine is the Lange model, which we have already examined. From a theoretical point of view, the crucial question in the Lange model is the procedure for finding equilibrium prices. Specifically, if the initial prices quoted to firms turn out to be wrong (result in excess demand or supply), will the price adjustment procedure followed by the CPB necessarily eliminate the imbalance? To use planning language: one is interested in whether there exists an equilibrium solution and, in addition, whether the adjustment procedure being used (trial and error) will lead to convergence. Although the technical literature on this matter is beyond the scope of our present discussion, the Lange trial-and-error algorithm is likely to lead to an equilibrium solution.

The Lange model is only one variant for determining equilibrium prices in a price-guided model. However, it is not necessary at least in theory to simulate the market process to form prices. This brings us to a fundamental point in our discussion of price-guided planning, namely, the possibility of generating equilibrium prices directly from the planning process without the use of a market mechanism. How can prices be formed in this way? To maximize an objective function, there are two problems, which economists describe as the **primal** and the **dual**. The primal solution is the set of X's (and the distriubtion of the u's to produce them) that yields the maximum value of the objective function. The dual solution is the set of resource prices that will induce producers (following, say, the Lange rules) to produce the optimal set of X's.

Let us cast the relationship between the primal and dual solutions in a framework familiar to every student of microeconomic theory. Consider the case of a single firm. The maximization of output implies the minimization of inputs for a given output. If such a firm were not using the minimum amount of inputs for a given output, then clearly it could rearrange its inputs and expand the volume of output. In a formal sense then, the objective of the firm can be specified as achieving a given output with minimum inputs or, alternatively, as maximizing output with a given amount of inputs. What is the importance of this duality to planning?

If output is maximized under given technology, then under these circumstances the ratios in which the inputs are being used at the margin represent their relative values as determined by their availability and their usefulness in the productive process. From this, relative scarcities can be established, which is what prices are intended to reflect. These relative scarcities can be established as the result of a mathematical exercise and quite apart from any particular set of institutional or organizational arrangements. The most important implication is that the *market is not necessary* for the formulation of rational prices.

When a constrained maximization problem of the sort we have been discussing is solved, there will be both a primal and a dual solution. The latter provides a set of shadow prices, which, under appropriate conditions, have the same meaning as prices generated under a perfectly competitive market economic system. What exactly is a shadow price? A **shadow price** represents the increase in the maximum value of the objective function generated by a one-unit increase in the particular factor. Thus if a one-unit increase in factor b_j (*ceteris paribus*) fails to increase the value of the objective function, then the shadow price of the factor is zero. On the other hand, if a one-unit increase in b_j increases the value of the objective function, then b_j will have a positive shadow price. Thus the marginal product of the factor b_j will be positive.

The logic of the procedure for calculating shadow prices is straightforward. However, when it is applied to an entire economic system, a number of problems must be confronted.

First, for the model to be computationally feasible, a considerable amount of aggregation is necessary. Having added together a number of products and factors and treated them as if they were homogeneous, it is then difficult to draw inferences about the valuation and use of specific products and factors from a model in which they no longer have individual indentities.

Second, there are always problems pertaining to data. In particular, a great deal of data is needed, not only of the right type, but also updated through time as underying conditions change. Hayek and Mises argued that the task of gathering such data would be too immense for any planning agency.

Third, the complexity of the interrelationships in a modern economic system tends to grow as the economy grows in size and maturity, creating massive computational problems. Even if data could be gathered in sufficient detail, it is questionable whether existing computational techniques could supply solutions. Although it is theoretically possible to break up (decompose) a model consisting of systems of equations, decomposition techniques are complex and have had limited real-world applicability.

Thus far we have considered two price-guided approaches to solving the planning problem. Both are extremes. The Lange model indirectly utilizes the market mechanism; the computation of shadow prices utilizes an abstract mathematical model and is not tied to the market or to other particular organizational arrangements. Instead, the solution of mathematical equations, presumably by computer, fully substitutes for the functioning of the market.

Nonprice Planning

The alternate approach to price planning is nonprice planning. Nonprice planning could be interpreted in two ways. The first interpretation is that nonprice planning involves the primal solution for the optimal set of inputs and outputs. Planners will accordingly send directives concerning these physical inputs and outputs to producing enterprises. Throughout the process, planning will be conducted without reference to prices, although, as we have seen, underlying resource valuations are implicit in this exercise.

A second interpretation of nonprice planning is quantity planning, where prices are irrelevant. The most notable example of this is quantity planning using a static input-output model, where prices are irrelevant because factor proportions are presumed rigidly fixed by existing technology. The strict relationship between inputs and outputs will not change when input prices change. The input-output model is described in Appendix 5A. We have already noted the close resemblance between input-output planning and the material balance approach.

The foundation of input-output planning is the **technology matrix** or a matrix of technological coefficients such that all inputs can be related to all outputs, necessarily with a fairly high degree of aggregation for an entire economy. Assuming that this sort of information is available, how does one solve the planning problem? The CPB must first specify the objectives it wishes to achieve. Then, with the aid of the appropriate technological coefficients, the inputs required to meet the stated objectives can be established. Firms would then be assigned (directly) input and output targets. For those familiar with the algebra of input-output economics, these points can be illustrated succinctly. Gross output (X) is utilized either as intermediate inputs AX (where A is the technology matrix) or for final uses (Y), or

$$X = AX + Y$$

Final uses, however, can be related to gross outputs as

$$Y = (I - A)X$$

where I is an identity matrix. Thus once planners have specified the desired final output mix (Y), they can calculate the gross outputs (X) necessary by branch to produce the final outputs. The availability of primary resources will constrain the choice of final outputs. For more on this, see Appendix 5A.

Nonprice planning differs substantially from the price-guided procedures. In the nonprice variant, firms have little freedom of decision making. There are, in the extreme, no prices. Firms are told in detail what to produce and what inputs to use. This is, in effect, the basis of the material balance approach. With the appropriate amounts of information, it is theoretically possible to achieve a balance of supplies and demands in this framework.

As with other plan algorithms, the crucial question here is the nature of the adjustment process through time. The CPB would be involved in the gathering and processing of vast amounts of information, a procedure with practical limitations. Computation techniques would dictate a fairly high degree of aggregation with all the attendant problems that aggregation implies. Finally, as with the Lange model, it is a strong but necessary assumption that firms will follow instructions and thus always exhibit function (goal-oriented) behavior.

REFERENCES

G. M. Heal, *The Theory of Economic Planning*, ch. 2. See also Roger A. Bowles and David K. Whynes, *Macroeconomic Planning* (London: Allen and Unwin, 1979), ch. 3.

G. B. Dantzig and P. Wolfe, "A Decomposition Principle for Linear Programs," *Operations Research*, 8 (January–February 1961), pp. 101–111; for a summary, see Nicolas Spulber and Ira Horowitz, *Quantitative Economic Policy and Planning* (New York: Norton, 1976).

PART II

ECONOMIC SYSTEMS IN PRACTICE: THE MAJOR EXAMPLES

Chapter 6
Resource Allocation in the American Economy

Having outlined the theories of capitalism, planned socialism, and market socialism, we are now ready to see how each works in practice. The theories of capitalism and socialism provide the foundations for our discussion of real-world capitalist and socialist economies.

Chapters 6 and 7 examine the American and Soviet economies. In terms of size, economic and political power, and general leadership roles, the United States and the Soviet Union are the two most important representatives of their respective systems. Moreover, scholars have devoted more attention to the American and Soviet economies than to any other pair of socialist and capitalist countries. Both the United States and the Soviet Union provide a reasonable laboratory for evaluating their respective systems. Both possess rich natural resources, massive military power, and large domestic markets — factors that have allowed each to pursue its own economic course relatively free from outside influence and controls.

The United States and Soviet Union are not equivalent in all respects other than the economic system. In fact, their differences are substantial. The United States is one of the world's most advanced industrial nations. The Soviet Union is not. The United States has been a relatively advanced country for more than a century; the Soviet Union became an industrialized country only in the 1930s. Moreover, there are striking differences in climate, culture, and nationality, and such differences must be "held constant" before one can begin to evaluate the relative merits of economic systems.

In Chapters 6 and 7 we shall describe how resources are allocated by the American and Soviet economies. In each case, we shall try to determine how closely the theoretical models of capitalism and planned socialism are approximated. Our emphasis is on *how* resources are allocated by each economy; we avoid comparisons of *how well* each economy performs.

We present American and Soviet resource allocation arrangements on as parallel a basis as possible. For each economy, we shall discuss the manner in which materials, labor, and capital are allocated. Then, in the American case, we turn to the role of the state in economic affairs. In the Soviet case, we turn to the role of the market. Surprisingly, it is much more difficult to describe resource allocation in the American economy, as this is largely accomplished through the market without the outside influence of a hierarchy of authorities. The Soviet case is easier to describe, for it works on the basis of concrete institutional and bureaucratic procedures.

RESOURCE ALLOCATION IN THE PRIVATE SECTOR

The role of government is more limited in the United States than it is in most industrialized capitalist countries. Government ownership has been limited even in the case of natural monopolies and transportation, which in most other countries are government owned and operated. The United States has no apparatus for economic planning. The market makes the overwhelming majority of resource allocation decisions in the United States.

The **private sector** refers to the business sector, where private ownership prevails and government regulation is not pervasive. According to Milton Friedman's calculations for 1939, some one-fourth of economic activity in the United States was government operated or supervised, leaving a residual of three-fourths for the private sector.[1] This breakdown is representative for the 1980s as well.[2]

Business Organization

Business enterprises in the United States (and in capitalist countries in general) are divided into three categories on the basis of legal organization: sole proprietorships, partnerships, and corporations.

The sole proprietorship is owned by one individual, who makes all the business decisions and receives the profits (or losses) that the business earns. A partnership is owned by two or more partners, who make all the business decisions and share in the profits and losses of the business. The major advantages of these forms of business organization are their relative simplicity (the proprietorship is simpler than the partnership) and the fact that, under existing tax law, their profits are taxed only once. They have two major disadvantages: (1) the owners are personally liable for the debts of the business, and (2) the ability to raise capital is limited, dependent on the owners' ability to borrow against personal assets.

The third form of business organization, the corporation, is owned by its stockholders and has authorization to act as a single person. A board of directors, elected by the stockholders, appoints a professional management team to run the corporation. The advantages of the corporation are: (1) its owners (the stockholders) are not personally liable for the debts of the corporation (limited liability), (2) its management team can be changed if necessary, and (3) it has more options for raising capital (through the sale of bonds and additional stock). A major disadvantage of the corporation is that its income is taxed twice if corporate earnings are distributed to stockholders as dividends. Double taxation gives American corporations an incentive to reinvest earnings rather than pay out dividends.

These three forms of business organization are supplemented in the United States by innovative legal arrangements (such as limited liability partnerships) designed to circumvent a variety of weaknesses; yet the threefold classification remains valid. Figure 6.1 and Table 6.1 show the distribution of U.S. enterprises according to legal form of business organization. Although sole proprietorships account for the bulk of American businesses (70 percent), they account for only 6 percent of business revenues. Corporations, though few in number (about 20 percent of the total) account for 90 percent of business revenues. The larger size of the corporation is explained by limited liability and the greater ability of the corporation to raise capital. The proprietorship is important in agriculture, retail trade, and services; the partnership is important in finance, insurance, real estate, and services; the corporation is the dominant form in other sectors.

Figure 6.1 Proprietorships, Partnerships, and Corporations, 1983

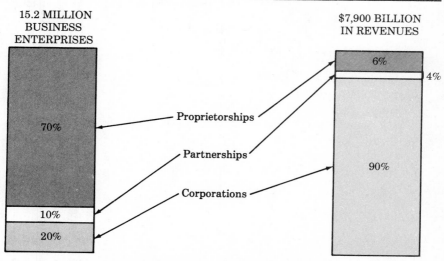

Source: *Statistical Abstract of the United States*, 107th ed., 1987.

Table 6.1 Proprietorships, Partnerships, and Corporations, by Industry, 1983

Industry	Number (in thousands)			Business Revenues (in billions of dollars)		
	Proprietorships	Active Partnerships	Active Corporations	Proprietorships	Active Partnerships	Active Corporations
Total	10,535	1,537	2,977	460.8	277.7	6,330.6
Agriculture, forestry, and fishing	304	137	92	10.0	5.9	55.1
Mining	153	60	37	12.2	17.1	122.5
Construction	1,273	64	284	51.8	21.6	280.9
Manufacturing	331	26	262	15.4	14.2	2,418.3
Transportation, public utilities	483	20	122	25.4	7.2	627.8
Wholesale and retail trade	2,415	194	852	195.7	59.9	2,071.3
Wholesale	203	24	284	26.2	17.2	1,056.2
Retail	2,094	170	566	164.0	42.6	1,011.6
Finance, Insurance, Real Estate	930	730	480	25.8	76.8	362.6
Services	4,646	306	848	124.5	75.1	392.1

Source: *Statistical Abstract of the United States*, 107th ed., 1987.

The Product Market

Resource allocation arrangements depend significantly on the degree of **market power** in different product markets. There is no accurate measure of market power, but the most frequently used measure is the **concentration ratio**. The concentration ratio gives the percentage of industry sales accounted for by the largest four, eight, or twenty firms. For example, a four-firm concentration ratio of 80 percent means that the four largest firms account for 80 percent of industry sales. An industry with a very low concentration ratio is generally a "competitive" industry; one with a very high concentration ratio is an "oligopoly" or near-monopoly. (The comparison is not exact for various reasons: the difficulties of defining industry boundaries; the availability of competitive substitutes from domestic or foreign producers; the fact that some firms operate in regional and local markets, others in national and international markets; and so on.)

The competitiveness of the private sector of the U.S. economy is a hard thing to measure. Most concentration studies relate to manufacturing, which is the most visible branch of U.S. industry, yet it accounts for only one-fourth of national income. Many industries that produce raw materials, such as agriculture, forest products, and coal, are organized competitively. But even here, one must be cautious, for government price-support programs in agriculture have affected the behavior of agricultural procedures, and the owners of coal mines often band together into associations, at least to deal with labor. Retail stores and most services operate in primarily local markets and operate largely in a competitive environment, although there are exceptions to this rule as well.

Estimates of the overall level of competitiveness in the private sector (including agriculture, manufacturing, trade, and services) are few and far between. Milton Friedman's estimates for the year 1939 indicate that the private sector of our economy then was between 15 and 25 percent "monopolistic" and between 75 and 85 percent "competitive."[3] A recent study finds that the degree of competition has increased for the U.S. economy as a whole since the 1960s.[4] See Table 6.2.

Competitive Industries

Competitive producers are **price takers**. They cannot influence prices, so they maximize profits by expanding their output to the point where marginal cost is equal to the product price. If, for some reason (say, an unexpected shift in demand) above-normal profits are being made, excess profits will disappear as new firms enter the market.

Prices are formed in competitive industries by the interplay of supply and demand. Let us take the case of basic agricultural products (wheat, pork bellies, soy beans, frozen orange juice), which are traded on international commodity markets. These markets are called **perfect markets** because at any point in time, all buyers of a homogeneous product pay a uniform price. All potential buyers and sellers are participants in the national market, and information concerning prices is available almost instantaneously to all potential buyers and sellers. Thus, all participants will know, for example, the price of a bushel of wheat at any point in time.

Buyers and sellers come together in commodity markets, and commodity prices are determined by supply and demand. Producers and users of these commodities, however, are not the only participants in the market. Commodity speculators buy and sell commodities in the hope of buying at a low price then selling high. Commodity markets establish not only prices of commodities for immediate delivery, but also prices (called **futures prices**) for deliveries at some specified date in the future. Thus, an American wheat farmer can contract to sell next

Table 6.2 Trends in Competition in the U.S. Economy, 1939-1980

Sectors of the Economy	Share of Each Sector That Was Effectively Competitive (percent)		
	1939	1958	1980
Agriculture, forestry, and fisheries	91.6	85.0	86.4
Mining	87.1	92.2	95.8
Construction	27.9	55.9	80.2
Manufacturing	51.5	55.9	69.0
Transportation and public utilities	8.7	26.1	39.1
Wholesale and retail trade	57.8	60.5	93.4
Finance, insurance, and real estate	61.5	63.8	94.1
Services	53.9	54.3	77.9
Total	52.4	56.4	76.7

Note: In this table, an effectively competitive industry is one in which the 4-firm concentration ratio was below 40 percent, entry barriers were low, market shares were unstable, and prices were flexible. The extent of oligopoly in the economy is the measure of the combined shares of dominant-firm and tight-oligopoly industries.

Source: William G. Shepherd, "Causes of Increased Competition in the U.S. Economy, 1939-1980," *Review of Economics and Statistics*, November 1982, pp. 613-626. Used by permission of Elsevier Science Publishers, Amsterdam.

year's harvest at a specified price in the commodity market even before the crop has been planted.

In the real world of the U.S. economy, most competitive industries are not perfectly competitive because they sell slightly differentiated products. Most of the rules just described, however, apply in general terms. Even though a product is differentiated, producers have little control over price because various local or regional markets form in which slightly different prices are charged. In each market, prices are established by supply and demand, and **arbitrage** (buying in the cheap market and reselling in the expensive market) prevents large price disparities between these markets. Although these markets are not perfectly competitive, they closely approximate perfect competition.

Imperfectly Competitive Industries

Competitive markets work in a fairly invisible and low-key manner. Highly concentrated, noncompetitive industries follow a wide variety of behavior patterns.

The surprising feature of U.S. manufacturing is that the degree of concentration appears to have scarcely changed since the turn of the century (see Table 6.3). According to G. Warren Nutter's famous study,

Table 6.3 Trends in Concentration in American Manufacturing: Two Measures

Year	Percentage of Output by Firms with 4-Firm Concentration Ratio of 50 percent or Above (1)	Percentage of Output of 100 Largest Firms (2)
1895–1904	33	n.a.
1947	24	23
1954	30	30
1958	30	32
1972	29	33
1977	28	34
1982	24	—

Sources: G. Warren Nutter, *The Extent of Enterprise Monopoly in the United States, 1899-1939* (Chicago: University of Chicago Press, 1951), pp. 35-48, 112-150; F. M. Scherer, *Industrial Market Structure and Economic Performance* (Boston: Houghton Mifflin, 1980), pp. 68-69; *Concentration Ratios in Manufacturing, 1977 Census of Manufacturing*, MC77-SR-9.

in 1900 roughly one-third of manufacturing net output came from industries whose four largest firms accounted for one-half or more of industry output. In 1963, the figure was still one-third and in 1972, the figure was 29 percent. Morris Adelman reports similar findings for the period 1947–1958, when the average concentration ratio of the four largest firms in each industry rose only from 35 to 37 percent. Between 1931 and 1960, the share of the 117 largest manufacturing firms in total manufacturing assets remained stable at 45 percent.[5]

Economic theory suggests that concentrated industries with a great deal of market power will enjoy larger profit rates than unconcentrated (competitive) industries. Joe S. Bain and H. Michael Mann have shown that profit rates in the 1930s and 1950s tended to rise with concentration and with barriers to entry, although this effect was more pronounced in the 1950s.[6] Studies of more recent periods find that at concentration ratios above 70 percent, concentration is strongly related to profit rates. Barriers to entry appear to have an even stronger positive effect on profit rates. At lower rates of concentration, the relationship among profits, concentration, and entry barriers appears weak or even nonexistent.[7] Higher profits are explained by the fact that concentrated industries are protected by economies of scale and barriers to entry.

Concentrated industries are mutually independent. Some concentrated industries, such as steel and automobile, use **price leadership,** in which case a particular producer, without formal agreement, acts as the price leader in a particular product line. Informal arrangements (termed conscious parallelism) such as market sharing, licensing, market division, and nonprice competition are also used. Concentrated industries have learned to live with mutual interdependence among major producers and only rarely engage in price-competitive battles.

Another gauge of competitiveness of the U.S. economy is how much national output would increase if monopoly power were eliminated. Researchers have calculated such "monopoly welfare losses," notably Arnold Harberger and David Schwartzman.[8] These researchers conclude that if monopoly power were to disappear from the American economy, national income would increase by less than 1 percent. These calculations do not consider the fact that the distribution of income between the holder of monopoly power and the consumer is seriously affected by monopoly. Rather, what is calculated is the "deadweight loss" of monopoly, that is, the loss of output due to monopoly.

Critics of monopoly like Gordon Tullock and Anne Krueger have pointed out that monopoly rent-seeking raises society's losses above deadweight losses.[9] Examples of monopoly rent-seeking include bribing public officials to gain monopoly franchises and lobbying to gain protection from foreign imports. Because substantial profit gains accrue to the monopolist, people are prepared to expend substantial resources to turn a competitive industry into a monopoly. Another critic of monopoly, Harvey Leibenstein, has emphasized the "organizational slack" or "X-inefficiency" of monopoly. Because monopolists are faced with less competition, they are under less pressure to minimize costs of production. The competitive firm that fails to minimize costs may be forced out of business, but the monopoly may overlook means of holding down costs. If one takes monopoly rent-seeking and X-inefficiency into account, society's losses from monopoly may be considerable.

John K. Galbraith argues that monopoly has not led to a significant loss of output, but for entirely different reasons. Galbraith maintains that concentrated industries are more efficient than competitive industries. In fact, competitive industries are at a severe disadvantage relative to monopolistic industries because they cannot control their markets or engage in long-term planning.

Harold Demsetz argues in a different vein that the higher profits of large enterprises result from their superior cost performance.[10] If prices are set competitively so that each firm acts like a price taker, then economic profits accrue to those firms that have lower costs of production. The higher profit rates found in highly concentrated industries are the result of the superior efficiency of large firms.

The Labor Market[11]

Labor is allocated largely through labor markets in the United States. In competitive labor markets, employers demand larger quantities of labor at low wages. The supply of labor is a positive function of the wage rate offered, and a wage rate equating the supply and demand for labor is established automatically in the marketplace.

There are no measures to indicate how competitive the U.S. labor market is. Obvious examples of highly competitive labor markets are markets for domestic servants, farm labor, most white-collar occupations, and banking employees. Labor market analysis focuses on the causes of deviations from the competitive model — union power, government intervention, and discrimination.

Unions

Only a minority of the U.S. labor force belongs to a labor union; currently, it is less than 20 percent of the total labor force. In the 1930s, union members accounted for 6 to 7 percent of the labor force. The union membership rose in the 1940s and peaked at 25 percent in the mid-1950s. Since then, the percentage of union membership has declined — despite the notable increase in union membership among public employees — largely because of the rapid growth of white-collar employment. The American trade union movement is more decentralized than its counterparts in the advanced European capitalist countries. More authority rests with local unions and the movement has failed to produce its own political party. Thus, the American union movement consists of loose federations of local unions banded into national unions. Bargaining over wages, with notable exceptions, proceeds on a company-by-company basis. In recent years, however, the trend has been toward collective bargaining at the national level and bargaining over local issues at the local level.

Most American unions are associated with the AFL-CIO (American Federation of Labor–Congress of Industrial Organizations). The AFL–CIO currently accounts for almost 80 percent of all union members. The United Automobile Workers is the largest union not affiliated with the AFL–CIO.

Unions were not an important part of the American labor scene until the 1930s. In the late 1880s, the traditional craft unions banded together into the American Federation of Labor under the leadership of Samuel Gompers. Gompers favored a nonpolitical and nonsocialist approach to unionism and promoted the exclusion of unskilled workers from the AFL. Unskilled workers joined together into the Knights of Labor. That organization experienced rapid growth in the 1880s until violence in Chicago's Haymarket Square in 1887 turned public opinion against organized labor. After 1887, the Knights of Labor, the representative of unskilled labor, disappeared from the scene. Industrial unionism made a comeback in the 1930s under the leadership of John L. Lewis, who organized unskilled and semiskilled labor into the Congress of Industrial Organizations. In 1955, the AFL and CIO merged.

American workers were slower to organize than their European counterparts because of unfavorable legislation until the early 1930s: The Sherman Antitrust Act of 1890 was initially applied against "monopolistic" labor unions; court orders prohibited union activity; and "yellow dog" contracts required employees to agree not to join a union. The Norris-LaGuardia Act of 1932 and the Wagner Act of 1935 supplied the legislative foundation for the growth of unionism.

How much have unions altered the process of labor allocation described by the competitive model? On this, there are wide differences of opinion. Some (Milton Friedman, for example) argue that unions have had only a minimal impact on employment and wages, that unions simply act as highly visible **intermediaries** between the forces of supply and demand, and that the net result is a pattern of wages and employment virtually identical to that which would have prevailed without unions. Collective bargaining cannot negate the forces of demand over the long term because too high wages would result in a substitution of other factors of production for labor.

Most studies show that unions raise wages in unionized industries. Unions control wages through their power to strike and to control the supply of (and in some cases, through work rules, the demand for) labor. The most-cited estimate of the effect of unions on wages in the **unionized** sector is that they raised wages some 25 percent during the mid-1930s, 5 percent during the late 1940s, and some 10 to 15 percent during the 1950s. The most recent studies show that unions raised wages 15 to 18 percent higher than they would have been in the absence of unions. For the entire economy, it is virtually impossible to estimate the impact of unionization, but it is probably small. Union wages are emulated in the nonunionized sector, and higher union wages reduce employment in the unionized branches and hence place downward pressure on wages in nonunionized branches.

What has been the effect of unions on productivity? Economists have traditionally believed that unions exert a negative effect on productivity. Unions were thought to limit output per worker through disruptive strikes, through featherbedding practices that kept employers from using labor efficiently, and by distorting union-nonunion wages. In recent years, some economists have questioned this view. Albert Hirschman, Richard Freeman, and James Medoff maintain that unions actually raise productivity by giving union members a collective voice in the enterprise. Without union representation, the only voice workers have against bad employers is to exit — that is, to leave the enterprise. With unions, workers can gain effective representation and can work from within to improve conditions. According to this new view, unions can have a positive effect on productivity in three ways: unions reduce worker turnover and thus limit hiring and training costs; senior workers are more likely to provide informal training and assistance; and the union provides for an improved information flow between workers and managers.

Government Intervention

A second extramarket force is government. Government can affect wages through licensing and other procedures that regulate the supply of labor in particular occupations. It also affects the supply of labor in the long run through its policies toward public education and job training. Moreover, antidiscrimination legislation, hiring quotas, and the like, also affect employment practices. Probably the most disputed role of government is minimum wage legislation. Its opponents argue that minimum wages disrupt the market process and create unemployment among the poor workers the legislation seeks to assist. Supporters argue that minimum wages are unlikely to have a significant effect on employment and are necessary to protect weak workers, who are at a disadvantage in the bargaining process.

Discrimination

The third extramarket force is discrimination by race and sex, which excludes particular races and sexes from particular occupations (such as specific craft unions) and channels them into overpopulated occupations. An example is the channeling of women into public school teaching. A great deal of research has attempted to estimate the effect of discrimination on earnings of blacks, Mexican-Americans, and women. The general consensus is that discrimination does exist, once other factors such as background and education are held constant, but that its overall effect on wages in the United States has been limited. Within specific occupations, the discrimination effect on the observed minority wage differential is small. The most significant impact of race and sex discrimination results from the exclusion of minorities from specific occupations.

In Chapter 7, we shall compare the allocation of labor in the United States and in the Soviet Union. We shall see that it is in the area of labor allocation that the two economies are most alike in their resource allocation procedures, although substantial differences still exist.

The Capital Market

The purpose of our discussion of the U.S. capital market is to provide an overview of how investment decisions are made and financed in the United States. This overview can then be contrasted with Soviet investment planning in Chapter 7.

Businesses contemplating investment in plant, equipment, and inventories will be prepared to undertake investment projects as long as the anticipated rate of return exceeds the "cost" of financing the project, the cost being the **interest rate**. Businesses undertake investment projects as long as the anticipated rate of return exceeds the cost of acquiring capital funds (the interest rate). At the margin, projects will be undertaken whose rates of return just equal the cost of borrowing. Accordingly, the lower the cost of acquiring investment funds, the higher the demand for investment will be.

The supply of investment funds depends on the savings of individuals, government surpluses or deficits, and the amount of funds that businesses retain out of profits and for depreciation. In the U.S. capital market, the supply of investment funds is seldom channeled directly from the saver to the investor. Such transactions are normally handled by **financial intermediaries**, such as commercial banks, savings banks, and insurance companies. In the corporate sector (which accounts for some three-fourths of business borrowing), there are three sources of investment finance. The corporation can raise capital by issuing debt, by issuing additional stock; or by using retained earnings. The supply of investment funds varies positively with the interest rate.

Demanders and suppliers of investment funds meet in generally well-organized capital markets. Supply and demand determine the interest rate. Although interest rates are determined freely in the capital market, the Federal Reserve System is in a position to alter this interest rate through its control of credit.

A striking feature of American capital markets (and capital markets in general in industrialized capitalist countries) is the prevalence of financial intermediation. Financial intermediaries borrow funds from one set of economic agents (people or companies with savings) and lend to other economic agents. Financial intermediaries serve a useful purpose by making it unnecessary for borrowers and lenders to seek each other out. A commercial bank, for example, borrows from its depositors (by accepting checking and savings account deposits) and then lends to a corporation building a new plant. The ultimate borrower and ultimate lender do not have to find each other. If borrowers and lenders had sought each other out, the lender would have received a higher rate of interest and the borrower would have paid a lower rate of interest. The fact that lenders and borrowers pay for financial intermediation suggests that the service performed is a valuable one. Of the private domestic funds advanced for private investment in 1981, only 12 percent was supplied directly from the ultimate lenders to the ultimate borrowers. The remaining 88 percent was supplied through financial intermediaries.

The U.S. capital market is a well-organized market in the sense that national securities markets (the New York and American Stock Exchanges, markets for federal funds, and others) bring together all potential borrowers and suppliers of investment funds, and information concerning investment alternatives is readily and almost instantaneously available to all participants in the capital market. It is misleading to speak of a U.S. capital market, for there is an interrelated international capital market. International banks are not limited to national boundaries; U.S. corporations borrow in the European capital markets; and so on. The huge amount of international data in the financial section of the daily newspaper demonstrates this fact. The net result is an approximate equalization of rates of return on all investments at the margin once they are adjusted for risk.

This equalization of rates of return at the margin is considered to be an important positive feature of the U.S. capital market because it leads to an efficient allocation of capital resources. If rates of return were not equal at the margin, then capital funds could be redistributed from projects with a low rate of return to those with higher rates, and output could be increased without an increase in capital resources.

There are exceptions to the rule of equal rates of return. In some instances (low-cost loans to small businesses, disaster relief loans, preferential home mortgage rates to veterans), government programs finance investment projects whose rates of return at the margin are below the equilibrium rates established by the capital market. Such projects are undertaken in the pursuit of social rather than economic goals. We should also mention that, because investment projects are uncertain in nature, rate of return calculations depend on guesses about what the future will bring. Thus, what is equalized at the margin is the **anticipated** rate of return. There is no guarantee that these expectations will be met.

THE ROLE OF GOVERNMENT IN THE AMERICAN ECONOMY

Just as it is fitting to consider the role that the market plays in the planned socialist economy, so is it fitting to consider the role of non-market forces, primarily the public allocation of resources, in predominantly market-oriented economies.

In so doing, we ask several questions: Just how important is resource allocation by the public sector of the U.S. economy? How does this compare with the experiences of other industrialized capitalist countries? *How* are resources allocated by the public sector in the United States? And *how well* are they allocated? Our survey of the theory of capitalism (in Chapter 3) indicated several economic functions for government but noted that different capitalist societies have different attitudes toward the appropriate scope of government activity. We shall see that the scope of government activity has been more limited in the United States than in most advanced capitalist countries. In fact, the American experience may suggest the minimal functions of government compatible with modern industrial capitalism.

There is little dispute that government must provide **public goods,** commodities that are consumed jointly and that nonpayers (free riders) cannot be excluded from enjoying. There is more debate about the other functions suggested by capitalist theory; in the United States considerable controversy still surrounds them. These functions are the correction of monopoly power, the correction of external effects, macroeconomic stabilization, and the redistribution of income. A further role for government, not discussed in Chapter 3, is the provision of **merit goods,** commodities that the public holds to be so meritorious (or demeritorious) that their use should be encouraged (or discouraged) by government.[12]

These are the governmental functions suggested by standard economic theory. How far the government should go in fulfilling them is a matter of dispute.[13] Different capitalist societies have resolved this question differently. But at a minimum, economic theory suggests that modern capitalist economies must mix private and public economic activity.

The Scope of the Public Sector

The data presented in Tables 6.4 through 6.8 and summarized in Figure 6.2 shed light on the role of government in the American economy. One key indicator is the government's claim on labor and capital resources, as this indicates how productive resources are divided between government and business uses. Government (federal, state, and local) today employs approximately 16 percent of the American labor force

Table 6.4 Percentage of National Income Produced and Employment by General Government and Government Enterprises in the United States, 1869–1985

Year	Percentage of National Income			Percentage of Persons Engaged in Production		
	Federal Govt.	State and Local Govt.	Combined	Federal Govt.	State and Local Govt.	Combined
1985	4.5	10.3	14.8	2.7	12.3	15.0
1981	3.8	8.7	12.5	2.8	13.2	16.0
1970	6.7	9.2	15.9	3.3	11.8	15.1
1960	6.2	7.6	13.8	3.3	8.8	12.1
1950	6.4	5.3	11.7	3.1	6.6	9.7
1940	7.6	10.1	18.7	1.8	5.7	7.5
1929	1.7	8.7	10.4	1.0	5.1	6.1
1918–1920 [a]	—	—	8.5	—	—	4.6
1899–1903 [a]	—	—	6.0	—	—	2.0
1889	—	—	5.2	—	—	—
1869	—	—	4.2	—	—	—

[a] Data are averages for the period.

Sources: U.S. Department of Commerce, *Historical Statistics of the United States: Colonial Times to 1970* (Washington, D.C.: Government Printing Office, 1975), Series F250-61; U.S. Bureau of the Census, *Statistical Abstract of the United States, 1987.*

Table 6.5 Government (Federal, State, and Local) Shares of National Wealth in the United States, 1900–1985 (in Current Prices)

Year	Structures (%)	Inventories (%)	Land (%)
1985	16	—	—
1980	18	—	—
1958	21	6	13
1955	20	6	15
1950	20	3	18
1939	18	3	19
1929	12	0[a]	13
1920	6	0[a]	13

[a] Zeros denote less than one half of 1 percent.

Sources: U.S., Department of Commerce, *Historical Statistics of the United States: Colonial Times to 1970* (Washington, D.C.: Government Printing Office, 1975), Series F422–445; *Statistical Abstract of the United States, 1987.*

Table 6.6 Percentage of National Income by Legal Form of Organization in the United States, 1929–1985

Year	Origin of Shares			
	(1) Business	(2) Government Enterprises	(3) General Government	(4) (2) and (3) Combined
1985	80	1.5	13.1	14.6
1979	81	1.5	12.6	14.1
1970	81	1.5	14	15.5
1960	85	1	11.5	12.5
1950	88	1	9	10
1940	88	1	10	11
1929	91	1	5	6

Note: Income originating abroad and in households and institutions is omitted.

Sources: U.S., Department of Commerce, *Historical Statistics of the United States: Colonial Times to 1970* (Washington, D.C.: Government Printing Office, 1975), Series F192–209; U.S., Bureau of Census, *Statistical Abstract of the United States, 1987.*

Table 6.7 Percentage of Government Purchases of Gross National Product in the United States, 1929–1985 (in Current Prices)

Year	(1) Total Federal	(a) Federal Defense	(b) Federal Nondefense	(2) State and Local	(3) (1) and (2) Combined
1985	8.1	5.9	2.2	9.9	18.0
1980	7.5	5.0	2.5	12.8	20.3
1970	9.5	7.5	2	13	22.5
1960	11	9	2	9	20
1950	6	5	1	7	13
1940	6	2	4	8	14
1929	1.5	—	—	7.5	9

Sources: U.S., Department of Commerce, *Historical Statistics of the United States: Colonial Times to 1970* (Washington, D.C.: Government Printing Office, 1975), Series F47–70; U.S., Bureau of Census, *Statistical Abstract of the United States, 1987.*

Table 6.8 Government Spending as a Percentage of Gross Domestic Product in the United States and Other Industrialized Countries, 1960 and 1973

Country	1960 Government Spending, Total	1973 Government Spending, Total	Defense	Nondefense
United States	25	31	6	25
Belgium	28	36	3	33
Canada	25	34	2	32
Denmark	21	35	2	33
Finland	22	28	1.5	26.5
France	29	32	4	28
West Germany	28	34	3	31
Ireland	24	33	1	32
Italy	27	38	3	35
Japan	13	14	1	13
Netherlands	25	44	3	41
Norway	28	39	3	36
Sweden	27	43	3	40
Switzerland	15	—	2	—
United Kingdom	29	36	5	31
Average	24.4	34.3	2.8	31.7

Sources: The World Bank, *World Tables, 1976* (Baltimore: Johns Hopkins Press, 1976), p. 446; Central Intelligence Agency, *Handbook of Economic Statistics, 1976* (Washington, D.C.: CIA Office of Research, 1976), p. 41. The defense figures are from the CIA publication.

and owns approximately 18 percent of the stock of structures, one-eighth of all land, and one-twentieth of all inventories. Using rough calculations, we estimate that government owned approximately 15 percent of the national wealth of the United States and accounted for some 7 percent of total labor, capital, and land inputs into the economy in the late 1950s (Table 6.5).

Government's share of productive resources has increased steadily over the last one hundred years. At the turn of the century, government accounted for some 4 percent of employment and owned 6 percent of the stock of structures and 13 percent of the stock of land. By 1939, the government's share of the national wealth had increased substantially (to 18 percent of structures and 19 percent of land), while its share of the labor force rose to about 10 percent. Since the late 1930s, government's share of employment has increased by 80 percent, but its share of national wealth has risen only slightly. Thus, the United States appears to have reached a national consensus concerning the distribu-

Figure 6.2 Indicators of Government Participation in Economic Activity and Wealth in the United States, 1900–1985

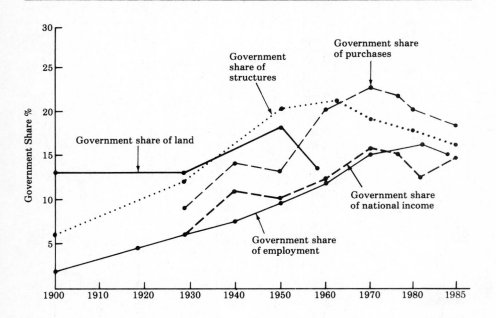

Source: Tables 6.2, 6.3, 6.4, and 6.5. The dots (·) indicate the years of observations.

tion of private and public wealth, which has remained fairly stable for about fifty years. There is now little serious talk of major nationalizations, and most of the major decisions in this area (broadcasting, communication satellites, atomic energy) have come down on the side of private ownership.

One should emphasize that these statistics do not provide a definitive picture, for the dividing line between government and private activity is often ill defined. A defense contractor producing military hardware exclusively for the government would enter these statistics as a private employer, while a municipal utility company is classified as a public employer, even though it may conduct its business just like the private utility in the next city.

Another way of looking at the scope of government is to consider the portion of national output produced by government (Tables 6.4 and 6.6, summarized in Figure 6.2). Currently, government produces about 14 percent of national income, of which the overwhelming portion is produced not by government enterprises but by "general government." On the other side, the business sector accounts for over 80 percent of national income, the remainder is accounted for by government and nonprofit institutions. The encroachment of government enterprises (primarily publicly owned utilities and the post office) on private business has been minimal. Government enterprises account for less than 2 percent of the national income not produced by general government and nonprofit institutions. Rather than government enterprises supplanting private enterprises, it has been the expansion of general government activities that has accounted for rising government output.

The government's share of national income has been rising steadily over the last one hundred years (4 percent in 1869 to 8.5 percent in 1919 to 15 percent in 1985). Since the 1930s, the increase in the federal government's share has been more substantial than that of state and local government. Since 1929, business's share of national income has fallen from 91 percent to 81 percent at the expense of the rise in general government and nonprofit institutions.

We now come to the crucial issue of the government's claim on the output of final goods and services (Table 6.7). Currently, government purchases account for slightly over one-fifth of the total. Interestingly, most of the historical increase in the share of government purchases has been due to rising state and local government spending and federal defense spending. Expenditures by the federal government for nondefense purposes remains a small portion of the GNP.

It is important to view these U.S. developments in the perspective of other industrialized capitalist countries. An examination of other industrialized capitalist countries (Table 6.8) indicates that the U.S. experience is average or even below average if one considers that most of these countries do not bear a substantial defense burden. If one looks only at nondefense spending, the U.S. government's share of total spending appears to be relatively small by international standards. The rising share of government output and expenditures is also unexceptional; it has characterized the economic growth of capitalism for over a century.

Some people view the rising share of government with alarm; others consider it too small. All one can say is that the allocation of resources between the public and private sectors is basically a matter of public choice in the United States. If the mix is badly out of line, a change will be forthcoming.

The Provision of Public Goods:
The Case of National Defense

Government in the United States bears the principal responsibility for providing public goods, although it must be noted that in the real world there are few "pure" public goods. The activity that dominates the so-called public goods market in the United States is national defense, which is also the best theoretical example of a public good; we shall therefore use it to illustrate how the U.S. government deals with public goods.

Two issues must be considered. The first is how decisions are reached concerning national defense's share of total public resources. The second issue is the market structure under which defense goods are produced.

Resource Allocation by the Defense Industry

The share and product mix of national defense are decided by the political process. The connection between the government and the large manufacturers of military hardware has come to be called the **military-industrial complex** by some. Three explanations of weapons procurement by the military-industrial complex have been offered: the strategic, the bureaucratic, and the economic.[14]

The strategic explanation is that defense planners determine weapons procurement on the basis of rational calculations about the foreign military threat. The bureaucratic explanation is that defense spending is the product of a disorganized tug of war among the various interests that make up the military-industrial complex, not of any rationally calculated plan of national security. One branch of the military exerts pressure to obtain the weapons system it favors, while a rival branch applies similar pressure in favor of its project. Or one systems manufacturer exerts pressure through strategic members of Congress or lobbyists in favor of its design for a major new weapons system. According to the bureaucratic explanation, the overall distribution of resources depends on the outcome of this struggle of vested interests.

Economics provides the final explanation. According to this view, defense spending is based on its impact on the overall economy. In the view of the New Left, an expanding defense budget is necessary to preserve full employment and economic stability. According to another view, contracts for major weapons systems will be granted, not on the basis of which company will produce the most effective system, but in order to preserve established contractors located in politically important states.[15]

A related consideration is the extent to which the private defense contractors themselves are able to determine or at least influence defense spending. According to Galbraith and the New Left, the economic and political power of the major defense contractors is sufficient to exert significant control over the allocation of defense resources.[16] Although these observers have likely overrated the power of defense contractors, there is strong evidence that their view is at least partially true.[17]

The Market Structure of the Defense Industry

Defense contracting procedures and the consequences of cost-plus pricing have been the subject of intense scrutiny. Most observers agree that these procedures violate the principle that national defense should be provided at a minimum cost of society's resources. Some authorities, in fact, argue that the current system leads to excessive cost and subsidies. The market structure of the U.S. military-industrial complex consists of the U.S. government, as a monopsonistic buyer, purchasing from a small number of giant defense contractors. The government purchases a weapons system from a single supplier, who is granted a monopoly to develop the system. Often there is no serious negotiation with potential competitors. Defense contracts are typically let on a cost-plus basis, whereby the manufacturer agrees to supply a particular weapons system at a negotiated cost plus an agreed-upon profit margin. Because there is little competition among producers and the manufacture of a new weapons system is surrounded by technological uncertainty, the government is in a poor position to judge whether the manufacturer is operating efficiently.

Most suggestions for reform of the military procurement system center on either the nationalization of the defense industry or the introduction of more competition into the existing system.[18] The major disadvantage of nationalization is that the monopoly over new weapons systems would then reside directly with the U.S. government; pressure to seek out cost-effective techniques would still be lacking. The second approach does not appear to be politically feasible because strong vested interests favor the existing system of protecting and subsidizing established defense contractors.

Manpower and National Defense

Until 1973, the manpower needs of the armed forces were met by a national draft operated by the Selective Service System. Conscription was employed to fill the gap between the number of volunteers joining the military at established wage rates (the supply) and the quotas established by the armed services (the demand). The costs of maintaining the armed forces therefore consisted of payments to armed service personnel *plus* the loss of income incurred by those draftees who had to forgo higher incomes outside the military. To some extent, however, individuals with higher earning capacities were excluded from the draft by educational and occupational exemptions.

Military manpower prior to 1973 was handled largely outside of the labor market. With the winding-down of the Vietnam War, the U.S. government turned to a voluntary army in 1973. Military manpower needs were to be met by raising military pay and benefits to the level required to bring the supply of and demand for military personnel into approximate balance. This use of the market represents a return to the practice of using hired troops. It has the advantage of relying on freedom of choice of occupation and avoiding the economic inefficiency of conscripting individuals with high earning capacities. Its disadvantages are that the armed forces are made up primarily of the disadvantaged, for whom military pay scales are attractive, and that the whole notion of national service is circumvented.

The Provision of Merit Goods:
Health, Education, and Welfare

The American public's support of merit goods has been limited primarily to public education, some low-cost health care for the poor, and social security insurance for retirement, disability, and unemployment. Such services are typically supplied on a mixed private enterprise–public service basis with the user paying a portion of the cost.

The mix of private versus public merit goods has been shifting toward public provision and reflects a changing public attitude toward government responsibility. Over the last half century, this change has been most dramatic in the areas of health expenditures, social welfare expenditures, and social insurance (Table 6.9), which had been regarded as private or charitable obligations. Prior to the 1930s, almost all retirement, health, and unemployment insurance was purchased on a voluntary private basis; in 1929 only 10 percent of personal health expenditures were funded by governmental agencies. Public elementary and secondary education has dominated the American education system for quite a while, but the government share of support for higher education has increased substantially over the last fifty years. During that time public universities have supplanted private universities as the dominant institutions in higher education.

Two general rules have governed the allocation of merit goods in the United States. The first is that, if feasible, merit goods should be provided on an "in-kind" basis (for example, subsidized school lunches and food stamps) rather than income payments. This suggests an unwillingness to rely on freedom of choice when it comes to merit goods and a feeling that the poor are not to be trusted to allocate their incomes wisely. The second general rule is that families should not have the power to shop around for merit goods, despite arguments that this

Table 6.9 Expenditures on Merit Goods in the United States, 1890–1985

Year	Public Personal Health Care Expenditures as a Percent of Total	Public Social Welfare Expenditures as a Percent of GNP[a]	Public Social Insurance Expenditures as a Percent of GNP	Public Higher Education Expenditures as a Percent of Total
1985	36	18.9	10.1	65.0
1980	39	18.5	8.0	66.3
1970	35	15.3	5.7	67.5
1955	26	8.6	2.6	64.0
1929	10	3.9	.2	41.0
1920	—	—	—	38
1900	—	—	—	—
1890	—	2.4	—	—

[a] Social welfare expenditures include social insurance and public aid, education, veterans' programs, child nutrition, and rehabilitation programs.

Source: U.S., Department of Commerce, *Historical Statistics of the United States: Colonial Times to 1970* (Washington, D.C.: Government Printing Office, 1975), Series B236-247, H1-31, H412-432, H716-727; *Statistical Abstract of the United States, 1987.*

practice would force suppliers to be more efficient and responsive to the consumer.

U.S. GOVERNMENT POLICY
TOWARD MONOPOLY

In the United States, government monopoly policy has been neither uniform nor consistent. In some instances, government policy restricts competition (tariffs, licensing, agricultural price supports); in others, it seeks to restrain monopoly power and to promote competitive behavior.

Government Ownership

Several options are open to government with regard to natural monopolies, which for a variety of reasons must serve as the sole suppliers of a product. The government can nationalize them in the "public interest." It can also tax them in order to transfer monopoly profits to the state and to guarantee an output/price combination more consistent with competitive standards. A third alternative is state regulation. A fourth is for the government to auction exclusive franchises to operate natural monopolies. This option would transfer much of the monopoly return to the state and then leave the natural monopoly alone.[19]

In the United States, all of these approaches have been employed, although discriminatory monopoly taxation and franchise auctions are rare. Public ownership of natural monopolies is common at the local and state levels but rare at the federal level. Municipal services such as local transportation, garbage collection, water, electricity, gas, public wharves, and state transit authorities are often owned and operated by state and municipal government. Over 20 percent of all electrical energy is generated by government or cooperative arrangements and 10 percent of all utility payments go to government enterprises. In only two of the ten largest cities is the municipal transit system privately owned. Approximately 3 percent of all residential housing construction has been undertaken by public authorities.[20]

Government enterprise operated by the federal government is more limited: operating the post office (now a semigovernmental operation), administering public lands (the Forest Service), lending and guaranteeing loans (the FHA and VA programs), providing insurance against various risks (social security), generating electricity (the Tennessee Valley Authority) and engaging in limited manufacturing activities (Redstone Arsenal, the U.S. Government Printing Office).[21]

Local, state, and federal government enterprises account for less than 2 percent of national income (see Table 6.6) and are therefore of minor economic importance. The public's decision to leave natural monopolies in the hands of private owners has been in marked contrast to the European pattern, where the state owns and operates most natural monopolies — and even enterprises that are not natural monopolies (automobile manufacturing, national airlines, railroads).

Despite their small scope, it is nevertheless important to consider how well U.S. public enterprises perform and, in addition whether they improve economic performance. In public enterprises, the incentive to restrict output and raise prices should not be as strong as under private ownership. On the other hand, the pressures to reduce costs and to innovate are generally weaker, because private enterprises must protect themselves from the long-run competition. Moreover, red tape and civil service restrictions may impede efficiency in the public enterprise. At the empirical level, the evidence is mixed. One authority concludes (after reviewing the European experience as well) that "the evidence is presently insufficient to support a sharp choice between the alternatives on straightforward economic performance grounds."[22]

In industries where public and private enterprises coexist, the former represent a potential yardstick for evaluating the private sector. The prime example is the Tennessee Valley Authority (TVA), the largest electrical utility in the United States. The exceptionally low costs of the TVA have been used to challenge the rates of private utilities. Yet TVA's lower costs do not prove unambiguously the greater efficiency of public ownership, for, as the private utilities point out, the TVA enjoys certain privileges not open to the private companies.

Public enterprise could conceivably improve resource allocation by forcing private producers to behave more competitively and efficiently. Strategies available to the public enterprise would be price undercutting and the threat to expand capacity. According to one authority, these strategies have rarely been used because of the opposition of private enterprises and the reluctance of managers of public enterprises to compete with private industry.

Regulation

The overwhelming political choice has been to regulate industries that possess monopoly power rather than to use public ownership.[23] Regulation has been exercised by a wide variety of local, state, and federal agencies. Other kinds of regulation — control by the courts or by the terms of franchises, charters, and city ordinances — have proven to be ineffective in the United States, and the public has turned instead to administrative regulation, either by an official of executive government or by semi-independent commissions operating under general legislative authority.[24]

Regulation at the state and local level is principally directed at natural monopolies — specifically, the electric, gas, and telephone companies. At the federal level, federal commissions have regulated both monopolistic industries (such as local telephone service) and those with a potentially significant degree of competition (such as trucking and airplanes). The stated rationale for federal regulation has been to ensure quality of service and to guarantee the public "reasonable" prices without unfair discrimination among users. A degree of monopoly power, however, is generally a necessary but insufficient condition for regulation. Buyers would have to be at a disadvantage in bargaining by virtue of the fact that the service is an essential, nonpostponable one for which there are few good substitutes. Although the American automobile industry is much more concentrated than the natural gas or rail industry, the latter two are regulated, while the other is free from direct regulation. There are historical reasons for regulation as well. The railroads were placed under the supervision of the Interstate Commerce Commission at a time when the railroads possessed considerable monopoly power. Motor and air transport lessened this power, yet the commission could not continue to regulate railroads without extending federal regulation to other forms of transport.

Generally, the regulatory commissions have controlled entry into the industry by granting franchises and licenses — for a new airline route or a new interstate natural gas pipeline, for example. Rarely are these licenses or franchises actually sold (for the purpose of diverting some of the ensuing profits to the public). Rather, it is assumed that regulation will prevent excessive profits.

It is the responsibility of the regulators to set "reasonable" rates for the services of regulated producers. In this, the regulatory commissions have been guided by the principle, guaranteed by the Fifth and Fourteenth Amendments protecting private property, that rates should be sufficient to cover operating costs plus a "proper" rate of return on invested capital. A second principle is that the rate structure should not discriminate among buyers, except when justified by cost differences.

To apply this pricing formula several important matters must be resolved: How are operating costs to be defined? What is an appropriate rate of return on invested capital? How is the rate base (the value of tangible and intangible assets of the company) to be measured? The regulated price is essentially a cost-plus price, and additions to cost will, in time, be passed on to the user. This may well reduce the incentive to seek out cost economies. Moreover, there is the problem of dealing with illegitimate or padded costs, such as buying materials from an unregulated affiliate at inflated prices in order to increase that company's profits.

Determining an appropriate rate of return to regulated firms has been another area of controversy. One principle that regulators have used is that the rate of return should be high enough to attract new capital; accordingly, the interest rate on recently floated debt has often been used as the rate of return. According to one authority, however, the rates of return that regulatory commissions and the courts have historically allowed have been "conventional or arbitrary, bearing no apparent relation to any statement of principles...usually based upon expert testimony with little pretense of economic analysis."[25] The rates allowed have varied from state to state and from time to time, falling between 5½ percent in the 1940s and 11 percent and higher during the 1970s and 1980s.

An Assessment of Regulation

Most authorities give regulation relatively poor marks, especially in industries that are not natural monopolies.[26] Regulation of natural monopolies has had a remarkably small effect on the prices charged consumers. Opponents of regulation argue that operating costs will fall when potentially competitive industries are freed from regulation (deregulated).

Why have the regulatory commissions not had a more beneficial impact on the industries they regulate? There are several possible explanations. The first is that the balance of power between the regulators and the regulated is uneven. The regulated industries have well-paid staffs, while the regulatory commissions are understaffed and underpaid, the state commissions particularly. Regulated industries appear to be able to circumvent regulations if necessary. Moreover, the commissioners themselves tend to be in close contact with the industries they regulate, not with the consumers they are supposed to represent and tend to take on a proindustry attitude. But the regulatory crisis goes beyond these considerations. The very *methodology* of regulation remains a problem. A commission has no way of knowing what operating costs would be if the most efficient production techniques were used. Even if it did know, it would lack the authority to mandate use of these techniques. Instead, it must simply accept the actual operating costs of the utilities as given, except in obvious cases of corruption or gross mismanagement.

To show that regulation has been less than optimal does not establish that a superior alternative exists, especially in the case of natural monopolies. Because they cannot be organized on a competitive basis, they will possess significant monopoly power. Despite its weaknesses, direct regulation may still be the best alternative.

An alternative is to deregulate all industries, even natural monopolies. Some conservative economists believe that regulation is so ineffective that unregulated natural monopolies would offer better prices and services to the consumer. Government could sell franchises to the highest bidder and thereby capture some of the monopoly profits for the public. Another suggestion is to place representatives of consumer interests on the boards of directors of natural monopolies to act as consumer watchdogs.

Deregulation[27]

The Airline Deregulation Act was signed in October 1978. Under this act the airlines, rather than the Civil Aeronautics Board, set their own fares and chose their own routes (subject to the important availability of landing slots). The Civil Aeronautics Board went out of existence at the end of 1984. This first major deregulation act was followed in 1980 by the Motor Carrier Act (which curbed the Interstate Commerce Commission's control over interstate trucking), the Staggers Rail Act (which gave the railroads more choice in setting rates and selecting routes), and the Depository Institutions Deregulation and Monetary Control Act (which eliminated government-set interest rate ceilings and reduced differences between commercial banks and thrift institutions).

The deregulation movement is designed to remove the government from the business of regulating potentially competitive businesses like the airlines, trucking, and banking. In all cases, opponents of deregulation warned that deregulation will lead to deteroriating service, pricing wars, and an unstable industry. Such warnings intensified in the late 1980s with regards to the airline industry. Advocates of deregulation predict improvements in service and generally lower prices.

It is too early to judge deregulation. Airline deregulation was carried out during a period of soaring energy prices and costly recessions. The public did indeed benefit from lower prices, but it is difficult to say whether the economic problems of the airlines in the early 1980s are attributable to deregulation or to the generally bad economic climate of the period. Deregulation of banking has increased competition in the banking industry and has allowed the small investor to receive, for the first time, the higher interest rates previously reserved for large investors. It remains to be seen whether banking deregulation will lead to increased concentration in banking as smaller banking institutions are unable to compete with larger institutions. The unions and the major trucking companies have fought deregulation, and most interstate trucking is still subject to a great deal of federal regulation.

U.S. experience has shown that deregulation leads to lower prices for most — but not all — consumers. Consumers in small markets characterized by high costs are no longer protected and now have to pay prices closer to costs. Deregulation has increased the diversity of services offered, and has given consumers more freedom of choice. Firms that had been protected by regulation have lowered their costs substantially, and these lower costs are being passed on to their customers. Deregulation has also had its losers. Firms that could not meet competitive pressures have gone out of business or have been acquired by more successful firms. Employees have seen their earnings fall as firms have sought ways to lower their costs.

Antitrust Legislation

The major alternative to direct regulation of monopoly is legislation to control market structure and market conduct.[28] The most important piece of federal antitrust legislation, the Sherman Antitrust Act of 1890, confronts these issues. The Sherman Act was the government's reaction to public hostility toward the trust movement of the late nineteenth century in the transportation, steel, tobacco, and oil industries. The Sherman Act contains two sections. Section 1 declares "every contract, combination...or conspiracy" in restraint of interstate commerce illegal. Section 2 makes the attempt to monopolize interstate commerce a federal offense. Section 1 prohibits a particular type of market *conduct* (conspiring to restrain trade), while Section 2 enjoins a particular market *structure* (monopoly). The language of Section 2 is vague, and this imprecision has led to varying court interpretations over the years. According to the language of Section 2, **monopolization** is prohibited, not **monopolies**. The Sherman Act clearly bans the act of creating a monopoly but is ambiguous on the legality of existing monopolies.

The Sherman Antitrust Act of 1890 forms the foundation of American antitrust legislation. The Clayton and Federal Trade Commission acts of 1913 established a commission to investigate "unfair" business practices (the Federal Trade Commission) and prohibited specific illegal business practices. The Wheeler-Lea Act of 1938 gave the Clayton Act more teeth by declaring unfair or deceptive business practices illegal. The Celler-Kefauver Act of 1950 tightened up the antimerger provisions of the Clayton Act.

American antitrust policy is made by Congress and by the courts, for it is in the courts that actual antimonopoly policy has been set. The basic issue confronting the courts was whether certain forms of market conduct were prohibited or whether the monopoly market structure was illegal *per se*. If so, it was then up to the courts to decide what constituted a monopoly. In the early court rulings (the American Tobacco and Standard Oil cases of 1911 and the U.S. Steel case of 1920), the courts interpreted the Sherman Act as enjoining anticompetitive market conduct (price cutting to eliminate competition, mergers, price fixing) but not the existence of monopoly per se. This became known as the "rule of reason."[29]

The rule of reason appeared to be reversed when the courts ruled in 1945 that Alcoa was in violation of the Sherman Act because it controlled over 90 percent of U.S. aluminum output. Although Alcoa had not used its monopoly power to restrain trade unfairly, the courts ruled that size alone was a violation of antitrust statutes. Thus, an important inconsistency appeared to be removed. The rule of reason had implied that companies engaging in practices that would ultimately lead to monopoly were in violation of the Sherman Act, but existing monopolies, if they behaved well, were not in violation.

The Alcoa ruling was gradually eroded by court decisions of the 1970s and 1980s. The basic problem with the Alcoa decision was that it appeared to punish all monopolies, even those that became monopolies by means of superior innovation and management. The Eastman Kodak case of 1972 and the FTC ruling in favor of DuPont in 1978 established that monopolies created through superior management and innovation were not in violation of the Sherman Act. The Alcoa decision was also weakened when the Justice Department dropped its thirteen-year-old suit against IBM in 1982. U.S. antitrust legislation is summarized in Table 6.10.

Price Fixing and Mergers

In the United States, the courts have generally found price-fixing agreements among producers and mergers of large companies engaged in the

Table 6.10 An Overview of U.S. Antitrust Legislation

Act	Date	Provisions
Sherman Act	1890	Section 1: restraint of interstate commerce illegal Section 2: attempt of monopolizing illegal
Clayton Act	1914	Declared specific business practices illegal
Federal Trade Commission Act	1914	Established the FTC to secure compliance with Clayton Act
Wheeler-Lea Act	1938	Banned deceptive business practices
Celler-Kefauver Act	1950	Broadened ban on mergers

same line of business to be in violation of the antitrust laws.[30] There are significant exemptions. Agricultural cooperatives are exempted from price-fixing statutes, and organized labor's right to bargain collectively for higher wages is guaranteed by the Norris-LaGuardia Act of 1932 and the Wagner Act of 1935. Moreover, the legality of resale price maintenance agreements (fair trade pricing) was established with the Miller-Tydings Act of 1937.

With these exceptions, formal arrangements for fixing prices have consistently been ruled illegal restraints of trade. The United States stands virtually alone among the industrialized capitalist countries in holding that formal arrangements for price fixing are illegal per se, even if the resulting prices are "reasonable." The courts have thus avoided the difficult issue of distinguishing "reasonable" from "unreasonable" price fixing.

The more difficult enforcement issue, however, has been collusion without outright agreement on pricing policy. Prior to 1948, the courts held that informal price coordination was illegal even if a formal price conspiracy could not be shown. After 1948, in order to demonstrate an illegal conspiracy, it had to be shown that the pattern of pricing could not conceivably have occurred if each firm had acted independently in its own self-interest. This interpretation established the legality of price leadership arrangements and other forms of oligopoly pricing, which led to parallel behavior without requiring formal agreements among producers.

The basic legislation against mergers is found in the Clayton Act of 1914 and the Celler-Kefauver Act of 1950. Especially since 1950, the courts have adopted a virtual prohibition of mergers between firms with substantial market shares. The only exceptions appear to be mergers where one firm takes over another on the verge of bankruptcy and conglomerate mergers, where one firm takes over another in a different line of business. In various rulings, the courts have decided that mergers involving combined market shares of 20 percent and even lower constitute an undue lessening of competition.

In its strict interpretation of antimerger statutes, the United States stands alone among the industrialized capitalist countries, most of which encourage mergers that serve to increase the scale of production. In Western Europe, for example, the burden of proof is on the government to establish that the social costs of a proposed merger exceed its benefits. In the United States the burden of proof lies with the merging firms, and if significant market shares are involved, the merger will be declared illegal per se.

It is difficult to establish the effect of antimerger legislation on the market structure of the American economy. It is likely, however, that the strict interpretation of the merger laws has reduced the number of mergers taking place in the United States.

An Evaluation of Antitrust Policy

How successful has U.S. government policy toward monopoly been? There are three lines of criticism of existing antitrust policy. The first is that the standard of workable competition toward which government policy strives cannot be met, even with rigorous enforcement of existing legislation. At best, the end result will be an economy dominated by oligopolies, and it is not clear that oligopolies are "better" than the monopolies they replace. A variant of this argument is that monopoly power is not so bad after all, for monopolies and oligopolies can take advantage of economies of scale, can afford substantial research and development programs, and so on. The upshot of these arguments is that we would probably be better off if we would just leave monopolies alone.

The second line of criticism is often expressed by big business — namely, that the antitrust laws are too vague and this imprecision makes voluntary compliance difficult. Moreover, they argue, the appropriate standard for judging market conduct is performance. Do price fixing or mergers lead to undesirable economic outcomes? Conduct should be judged on the basis of its effects, rather than being barred per se.

The final criticism of antitrust policy is that the government has been too soft on violators. The staffs of the Department of Justice and the Federal Trade Commission are too small to prosecute more than a small percentage of violations, and they generally select only open-and-shut cases. Penalties for violators are small; prior to 1959, no offender was sentenced to a term in jail. More substantively, there has been a general reluctance to require divestiture, although this is the most potent remedy to the exercise of monopoly power.

The most relevant criterion for evaluating government policy toward monopoly is its effect on U.S. economic structure and performance. Since the antitrust laws have been in effect, there has not been a significant increase in the concentration of American industry, whereas the second half of the nineteenth century did witness a substantial increase in concentration. (The government's inability to prevent the conglomerate mergers of the 1960s and 1970s, however, has likely led to an increased concentration of ownership.) One can speculate on the manner in which the antitrust laws contributed to the stability of concentration in the twentieth century. According to one authority, antitrust legislation made three important contributions to the maintenance of workable competition: it prevented European-type cartelization of American industry; it prevented consolidations that would have led to dominant industries; and it helped to preserve freedom of entry and equality of opportunity.[31]

Although it does appear that government policy has contributed to the maintenance of workable competition in the U.S. economy, one should not gain the impression that all policy has been consistent. In fact, one can list a great many government activities designed to reduce the competitiveness of the American economy: protective tariffs for selected industries, price supports for agricultural products, the patent system, licensing, and so on.

GOVERNMENT AND MACROECONOMIC STABILITY

Planning for macroeconomic stability in the United States is limited to the use of the indirect tools of monetary and fiscal policy. No national economic plan is drafted by government. The United States deviates significantly from other industrialized capitalist countries, most of which have some form of national economic planning. (Our case studies of capitalist variants study national economic planning in France and Britain.) Congressional proposals to introduce a rather mild form of economic planning have raised considerable controversy.[32]

Prior to the Great Depression the prevailing notion in government circles was that monetary and fiscal policy should be as neutral as possible. "Neutral" meant interfering as little as possible with private economic activity. After the Great Depression and the acceptance of Keynesian economics, this view changed; by the 1960s both major political parties came to accept the view that discretionary monetary and fiscal policy should be actively used to counter cyclical unemployment and inflation. Although some American monetarists and rational expectations theorists have spoken out in favor of a return to the traditional neutralist view, monetary and fiscal planners continue to engage in countercyclical demand management.

The Federal Reserve System is in charge of formulating monetary policy. Established in 1913, the Federal Reserve System consists of twelve Federal Reserve district banks coordinated by the board of governors in Washington, D.C. In the United States the "central bank" is more decentralized along regional lines than is common for central banks, but it nonetheless performs the functions of a central bank — regulating the money supply through open market operations, managing the discount rate, setting reserve requirements, and so on.

Authority over fiscal policy is diffused among the various executive and legislative bodies in charge of government spending and taxation, and the balance of authority has tended to shift over time. It is therefore difficult to describe briefly how important fiscal decisions are made. The president can propose budgets, but only Congress can approve them. The Treasury Department can propose changes in the tax structure, but it is the Congress that amends and approves such executive suggestions.

One point is fairly clear in comparing the existing machinery for conducting monetary and fiscal policy: the conduct of monetary policy is more divorced from the business of day-to-day politics than is the conduct of fiscal policy. Members of the board of governors of the Fed are appointed for fourteen-year terms and, although they owe their ultimate responsibility to the Congress, a tradition of independence for the Fed has emerged. Recurring proposals call for greater congressional control of the Fed, and there is evidence that the Fed does seek to pursue a monetary policy consistent with that of the current administration. The conduct of fiscal policy is very much a matter of politics in the United States, and accordingly, it has proved difficult to conduct counter cyclical fiscal policy. This is especially true during periods of inflation, when politically unpopular budget cuts and tax increases are shunned.

The postwar period has witnessed a battle between monetarists and Keynesians over the conduct of monetary policy. The Keynesians argue that the Fed should aim at controlling interest rates, while the monetarists argue that the Fed should, instead, control the rate of growth of the money supply. In a historic decision, the Fed decided in 1979 that it would reverse its policy of controlling interest rates and turn to controlling the money supply — a clear-cut victory for the monetarist position. In the 1980s, the Fed returned to a more pragmatic policy of interest rate targets and monetary-growth targets.

On the whole, the distinctive feature of economic planning in the United States is its virtual absence. Price and wage controls have been applied during periods of inflation, in the form of either voluntary guidelines or mandatory wage and price limitations. The most dramatic examples of this were the price freezes of 1971-1973, after which the economy returned to more voluntary measures.

Government Activity and Externalities

We now turn to the problem of externalities. No comprehensive program for dealing with externalities exists at the federal level, and the responsibility for environmental protection is diffused among a wide variety of federal, state, and local agencies. Some of these agencies have an exceptional record of environmental protection, for example, the U.S. Soil Conservation Service. Others, such as the U.S. Environmental Protection Agency, are young and seem to lack sufficient authority to correct serious cases of misallocation.

Three themes should be stressed in assessing the role of the state in dealing with the externality problem. The first is that the division of authority and responsibility among local, state, and national agencies (control of air pollution, for example) has made it difficult to devise effective programs. In many cases, external effects transcend local political boundaries; they thus require some form of national or regional coordination for their correction. The second theme has been the general reluctance to use market forces (such as taxes on polluters). Fines, prohibitions, and other administrative orders have been the principal means of enforcement. The third theme is the general unwillingness to consider "optimal" levels of environmental disruption —namely, the level of pollution reduction one should aim for, given the fact that it can be attained only at the expense of society's resources.[33]

The record of environmental protection varies by locality and region. In some areas, heavy emphasis has been placed on environmental protection, and enforcement of meaningful pollution regulations is strict. Examples are the efforts to prohibit additional refining capacity and offshore drilling in the Northeast and the furor over nuclear power generation in different parts of the country.

Government Policies and the Distribution of Income

To what extent does government in the United States redistribute income through taxation and the distribution of social services? The distribution of income is measured by the Lorenz curve (defined in Chapter 2), which compares family income by rank (say, the lowest to highest fifth of all families) with their percentage share of income either before or after taxes. Some studies adjust the Lorenz curve by adjusting for age differences, for differences in family size, and for the distribution of government services.[34]

As measured by the Lorenz curve before taxes and any other adjustments, there appears to have been little change in the U.S. distribution of income since 1950. In 1950, the lowest and highest fifth of families accounted for 5 and 45 percent of all income, respectively. By 1982, the figures were 5 and 42 percent. The change since 1929 has been more substantial: The share of the highest fifth of U.S. families declined from 54 percent to 43.5 percent in all income between 1929 and 1985.[35] It has been argued that if one adjusts these figures for differences in age and family size, then the trend toward greater equality is even more evident.[36]

The traditional view is that government has not played a significant role in redistributing income from the upper to lower income groups. Although the federal tax system is progressive (upper-income families pay a higher percentage of their income in taxes than do lower-income families), state and local taxes are regressive (upper-income families pay a lower percentage of income). On balance, therefore, the total tax system is roughly proportional (each income group pays the same percentage of its income in taxes), and the after-tax distribution of income will not be that much different from the before-tax distribution. Remember, though, that all such calculations are inexact because of the difficulty of determining what proportion of business and property taxes are passed on to the consumer in the form of higher prices. Joseph Pechman and Benjamin Okner have found that if one assumes such taxes are almost entirely passed on to the consumer, then the tax system is indeed largely porportional. If one assumes they are borne by the producer, Pechman and Okner find that the tax system becomes progressive, but only at the very top and very bottom of the income distribution.[37]

According to some, the state plays a greater redistributive role than is commonly thought.[38] The basis for such claims is that lower income groups receive larger shares of government in-kind benefits (food stamps, welfare, public education) than their shares of money income. If one includes the value of these benefits in income and then subtracts income and payroll taxes, the distribution of disposable income is much more equal than the unadjusted figures suggest. Table 6.11 and Figure 6.3 show calculations from a study by Edgar Browning to illustrate this position. Even with these recalculations, we must question whether this is a significant redistribution of income. Chapter 12 shows that the

Table 6.11 Income Distribution in the United States, Unadjusted and Adjusted, 1972

	Lowest Quintile	2nd Quintile	3rd Quintile	4th Quintile	Highest Quintile
1. Unadjusted income distribution	5.4	11.9	17.5	23.9	41.4
2. Share of benefits in kind including public education	30.5	17.3	16.2	16.6	19.4
3. Income distribution adjusted for benefits in kind	8.6	12.6	17.3	23.0	38.6
4. Income distribution adjusted for income and payroll taxes	9.9	13.9	18.0	23.0	35.2

Source: Calculated from Edgar Browning, "The Trend Toward Equality in the Distribution of Net Income," *Southern Economic Journal*, 43 (July 1976), 914. By permission of *Southern Economic Journal*.

redistributive role of government in the United States is probably much less significant than in other industrialized capitalist countries; so, relatively speaking, the government plays a modest role in the redistribution of income in the United States.

SUMMARY: RESOURCE ALLOCATION IN THE AMERICAN ECONOMY

1. Resource allocation is determined primarily by market forces in the United States; that process conforms well both to our definition of market capitalism and to the theoretical description of capitalist resource allocation. Exceptions to the rule of competitive resource allocation are monopoly, trade unions, government intervention. The forces of supply and demand are the principal determinants of resource allocation in the American economy.
2. Government plays a significant role in the resource allocation process. Major government activities are the regulation and control of industries possessing some degree of market power.

Figure 6.3 Lorenz Curves: U.S. Income Distribution Before and After Income and Transfer Payments, 1972

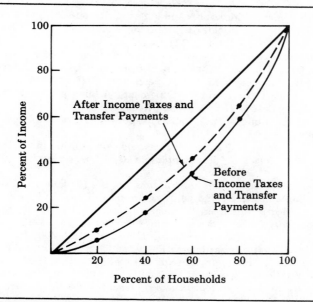

Source: Based on Edgar K. Browning, "The Trend Toward Equality in the Distribution of Net Income," *Southern Economic Journal* 43, (July 1976), 914.

Government enterprises, unlike those of many other advanced industrialized countries, constitute an insignificant share of economic activity. Some 25 percent of economic activity is directly affected by government activities (that is, government spending and government-regulated industries). The remaining economic activity is conducted by the "private sector."

3. Government affects economic activity in the United States principally by regulation and by antitrust policy. The amount of government ownership in the United States is less than in other industrialized capitalist countries. The impact of regulation on the prices of regulated monopolies has been limited, and potentially competitive industries have been deregulated. The Sherman Antitrust Act is the major antitrust act of the United States, and it has been subject to differing court interpretations over time. In the United States, the government's effect on the distribution of income has been limited. Government redistribution works primarily through the unequal distribution of in-kind services rather than through the tax system. In the next chapter, we shall turn to resource allocation arrangements in the Soviet economy. We shall see that Soviet arrangements differ radically from those of the United States.

NOTES

1. Milton Friedman, "Monopoly and Social Responsibility of Business and Labor," in Edwin Mansfield, ed., *Monopoly Power and Economic Performance*, 3rd ed. (New York: Norton, 1974), pp. 57–68.
2. According to Frederic Scherer, *Industrial Structure and Economic Performance*, 2nd ed. (Boston: Houghton Mifflin, 1980), p. 519, the government-regulated sector accounted for 11 percent of GNP in 1965. The government sector accounted for another 12 percent, yielding a total of 23 percent in 1965, a figure close to the 25 percent figure for 1939.
3. Friedman, "Monopoly and Social Responsibility of Business and Labor," pp. 57–68.
4. William G. Shepherd, "Causes of Increased Competition in the U.S. Economy, 1939–1980," *Review of Economics and Statistics*, November 1982, pp. 613–26.
5. See Scherer, *Industrial Market Structure*, pp. 68–70; James V. Koch, *Industrial Organization and Prices*, 2nd ed. (Englewood Cliffs, N.J.: Prentice-Hall, 1980), p. 181; in Morris Adelman, "Changes in Industrial Concentration," in Mansfield, *Monopoly Power and Economic Performance*, pp. 83–88.
6. Joe S. Bain, *Barriers to New Competition*, pp. 192–200; H. Michael Mann, "Seller Concentration, Barriers to Entry, and Rates of Return in Thirty Industries," *Review of Economics and Statistics*, 58, 3 August 1966, pp. 296–307.
7. Leonard W. Weiss, "Quantitative Studies of Industrial Organization," in Michael D. Intrilligator, ed., *Frontiers of Quantitative Economics* (Amsterdam: North Holland, 1971); Leonard Weiss, "Concentration-Profits Relationship and Antitrust," in Goldschmidt et al., eds., *Industrial Concentration: The New Learning* (Boston: Little, Brown, 1974), pp. 184–233.

8. The Harberger results can be found in Arnold Harberger, "Monopoly and Resource Allocation," *American Economic Review*, vol. 44 (May 1954), pp. 77-87.

9. Anne Krueger, "The Political Economy of the Rent-Seeking Society," *American Economic Review*, 64 (June 1974), pp. 291-303; Gordon Tullock, "The Welfare Cost of Tariffs, Monopolies, and Theft," *Western Economic Journal*, 5 (June 1967), pp. 224-232; Harvey Leibenstein, "Allocative Efficiency vs. X-Inefficiency," *American Economic Review*, 56 (June 1966), pp. 392-415.

10. Harold Demsetz, "Industry Structure, Market Rivalry, and Public Policy," *Journal of Law and Economics*, 16 (April 1973), pp. 1-10.

11. Our discussion of the U.S. labor market and the figures cited are from the following sources: William Bowen and Orley Ashenfelter, eds., *Labor and the National Economy*, rev. ed. (New York: Norton, 1975); H. Gregg Lewis, *Unions and Relative Wages in the United States* (Chicago: University of Chicago Press, 1963); Stanley Masters, *Black-White Income Differentials* (New York: Academic, 1975); Cynthia Lloyd, ed., *Sex, Discrimination and the Division of Labor* (New York: Columbia University Press, 1975); Michael Boskin, "Unions and Relative Real Wages," *American Economic Review*, 62 (June 1972), pp. 466-472; George Johnson, "Economic Analysis of Trade Unionism," *American Economic Review, Papers and Proceedings*, 65 (May 1975), pp. 23-28; Albert Rees, *The Economics of Trade Unions* (Chicago: University of Chicago Press, 1963); C. J. Paisley, "Labor Union Effects on Wage Gains: A Survey of Recent Literature," *Journal of Economic Literature*, 18 (March 1980), pp. 1-31; and Richard Freeman and James Medoff, "The Two Faces of Unionism," *The Public Interest*, 57 (Fall 1979), pp. 73-80; and Ronald G. Ehrenberg and Robert S. Smith, *Modern Labor Economics*, 3rd ed. (Glenview, Ill.: Scott, Foresman, 1988).

12. The original statement of the merit goods (wants) concept is found in Richard Musgrave, *The Theory of Public Finance* (New York: McGraw-Hill, 1959).

13. For a classic debate over the proper scope of government and "nongovernment," see Paul Samuelson, "The Economic Role of Private Activity," *A Dialogue on the Proper Economic Role of the State*, in Paul Samuelson, ed., *Readings in Economics*, 7th ed. (New York: McGraw-Hill, 1973), pp. 78-84; and George J. Stigler, "The Government of the Economy," *A Dialogue on the Proper Economic Role of the State*, ibid., pp. 73-77.

14. For more on the various explanations of the U.S. weapons procurement system, see James Kurth, "The Political Economy of Weapons Procurement: The Follow-On Imperative," *American Economic Review, Papers and Proceedings*, 62 (May 1972), pp. 304-311.

15. Seymour Melman, *Pentagon Capitalism* (New York: McGraw-Hill, 1970); and Kurth, "The Political Economy of Weapons Procurement," pp. 304-311.

16. For Galbraith's view, see John Kenneth Galbraith, "Power and the Useful Economist," *American Economic Review*, 63 (March 1973), pp. 1-11.

17. For a more moderate view of the power of the military-industrial complex, see Adam Yarmolinsky, "The Industrial-Military Complex: II," in Edwin Mansfield, ed., *Defense, Science, and Public Policy* (New York: Norton, 1968), pp. 42-43.

18. For suggestions on how to improve the current procurement system, see Carl Kaysen, "Improving the Efficiency of Military Research and Development" with comments by Paul Cherington, in Mansfield, *Defense, Science, and Public Policy*, pp. 114-131.

19. For arguments in favor of the fourth approach, see Friedman, "Monopoly and Social Responsibility of Business and Labor," pp. 57-68; and George Stigler and Claire Friedland, "What Can Regulators Regulate? The Case of Electric-

ity," in Paul MacAvoy, ed., *The Crisis of the Regulatory Commissions* (New York: Norton, 1970), pp. 39–52.

20. These statistics are from Department of Commerce, *Historical Statistics of the United States: Colonial Times to 1970* (Washington, D.C.: Government Printing Office, 1975), Series N15–29, S86–94, 6416–469, Y505–521; and Clair Wilcox, *Public Policies Toward Business*, 3rd ed. (Homewood, Ill.: Irwin, 1966).
21. Wilcox, *Public Policies Toward Business*, ch. 20.
22. Scherer, *Industrial Structure and Economic Performance*, p. 421.
23. The following discussion of regulation is based on these sources: Wilcox, *Public Policies Toward Business*, part III; Scherer, *Industrial Structure and Economic Performance*, ch. 18; and Paul MacAvoy, "The Rationale for Regulation of Field Prices of Natural Gas," in MacAvoy, *The Crisis of the Regulatory Commissions*, pp. 152–168; Robert E. Litan and William D. Nordhaus, *Reforming Federal Regulation* (New Haven: Yale University Press, 1983); and Lawrence J. White, *Reforming Regulation* (Englewood Cliffs, N.J.: Prentice-Hall 1981).
24. The first of these commissions was established in New England before the Civil War with authority over the railroads and in the Midwest in the 1870s. Commissions for the regulation of public utilities were set up only in the early twentieth century (1907); in some instances, public utility supervision was entrusted to the already established railroad commissions. Federal regulation was initiated first in 1887 with the Interstate Commerce Commission, the first major federal regulatory commission.

   State commissions in almost all states have jurisdiction over railroads, motor carriers, water, electricity, gas, and telephones; and about one-half have the authority to regulate urban transit, taxicabs, and gas pipelines. Commissioners are either elected or appointed by the governor of the state. The staffs of the commissions are generally small and are generally poorly funded relative to the legal staffs of the industries they regulate.

   There are five federal commissions. The Interstate Commerce Commission (established in 1887) regulates railroads, interstate oil pipelines, interstate motor and water carriers. The Federal Power Commission (established in 1920) has jurisdiction over power projects and the interstate transmission of electricity and natural gas. The Federal Communications Commission (established in 1933) regulates interstate telephone and telegraph and broadcasting. The Securities and Exchange Commission (established in 1934) regulates securities markets. The Civil Aeronautics Board (established in 1938) supervises domestic and international aviation. These federal commissions are staffed by commissioners appointed by the U.S. president for terms of five to seven years, and their staffs range from 1,000 to 2,000 employees. In general, the professional staffs on the federal commissions are better paid and more qualified than their state counterparts, but their salaries are not competitive with those paid by the regulated industries.
25. Wilcox, *Public Policies Toward Business*, p. 326.
26. See, for example, the selections by Merton Peck (on transportation), Richard Caves (on air transport), and Paul MacAvoy and E. W. Kitch (on natural gas) in MacAvoy, *The Crisis of the Regulatory Commissions*, pp. 72–93, 131–151, 152–186.
27. This discussion is based on Roy J. Ruffin and Paul R. Gregory, *Principles of Microeconomics*, 3rd ed. (Glenview, Ill.: Scott, Foresman, 1988), ch. 14; Elizabeth E. Bailey, "Price and Productivity Change Following Deregulation: The U.S. Experience," *The Economic Journal* 96 (March 1986): pp. 1–17. See also C. Winston, "Conceptual Developments in the Economics of Transportation," *Journal of Economic Literature* 23 (1985): pp. 57–94; T. Keeler, *Rail-*

roads, Freight, and Public Policy (Washington, D.C.: Brookings, 1983); A. F. Friedlander and R. H. Spady, *Freight Transport Regulation* (Cambridge, Mass.: MIT Press, 1981).

28. This discussion is based on Scherer, *Industrial Structure and Economic Performance*, ch. 19 and pp. 469–494; A. D. Neale, *The Antitrust Laws of the United States of America* (Cambridge: The University Press, 1962), pp. 2–5; Eugene Singer, *Antitrust Economics* (Englewood Cliffs, N.J.: Prentice-Hall, 1968), ch. 2; Marshall C. Howard, *Antitrust and Trade Regulation* (Englewood Cliffs, N.J.: Prentice-Hall, 1983); Oliver Williamson, *Markets and Hierarchies: Analysis and Antitrust Implications* (New York: The Free Press, 1975); and Howard, *Antitrust and Trade Regulation*.

29. The landmark cases were the Standard Oil and American Tobacco cases of 1911. In both instances, the courts ruled that these companies, both accounting for some 90 percent of industry output, should be dissolved into smaller companies. The courts' reasoning, however, was that Standard Oil and American Tobacco were in violation of the Sherman Act not because they accounted for such a large share of industry output (that is, not because they were monopolies), but because they had engaged in "unreasonable" restraints of trade. The implication of this ruling was that if these companies had behaved better toward their competitors, they would not have been held in violation of the Sherman Act. This so-called rule of reason was the prevailing interpretation of the Sherman Act until 1945. The rule of reason was upheld in 1920 with the U.S. Steel case. The company controlled over one-half of industry output, yet had not treated its competitors unfairly or sought to control steel prices. In this case, the courts upheld the rule of reason, stating that the law does not make mere size or the existence of unexerted power an offense.

30. This discussion is based on material in Wilcox, *Public Policies Toward Business*, ch. 11; and Mansfield, *Monopoly Power and Economic Performance*, pt. II.

31. These conclusions are from Simon Whitney, *Antitrust Policies*, vol. II (New York: Twentieth Century Fund, 1958), p. 429; summarized in Wilcox, *Public Policies Toward Business*, p. 281.

32. Richard Musgrave, "National Economic Planning: The U.S. Case," *American Economic Review, Papers and Proceedings*, 67 (February 1977), pp. 50–54.

33. Edwin Mills, "Economic Incentives in Air-Pollution Control," in Marshall Goldman, ed., *Controlling Pollution: The Economics of a Cleaner America* (Englewood Cliffs, N.J.: Prentice-Hall, 1967), pp. 100–108.

34. See, for example, Morton Paglin, "The Measurement and Trend of Inequality: A Basic Revision," *American Economic Review*, 65 (September 1975), pp. 598–609; and Edgar Browning, "The Trend Toward Equality in the Distribution of Income," *Southern Economic Journal*, 43 (July 1976), pp. 912–923.

35. These figures are from Department of Commerce, *Historical Statistics of the United States*, series G; and *Statistical Abstract of the U.S.*

36. Paglin, "The Measurement and Trend of Inequality," pp. 598–609.

37. Joseph Pechman and Benjamin Okner, *Who Bears the Tax Burden?* (Washington, D.C.: Brookings, 1974).

38. Browning, "The Trend Toward Equality," pp. 912–923. Also see Edgar Browning and William R. Johnson, *The Distribution of the Tax Burden* (Washington, D.C.: American Enterprise Institute, 1979).

RECOMMENDED READINGS

William Bowen and Orley Ashenfelter, eds., *Labor and the National Economy*, rev. ed. (New York: Norton, 1975).

Edgar Browning and William R. Johnson, *The Distribution of the Tax Burden* (Washington, D.C.: American Enterprise Institute, 1979).

Richard Caves, *American Industry: Structure, Conduct, and Performance*, 4th ed. (Englewood Cliffs, N.J.: Prentice-Hall, 1977).

Lance Davis et al., *American Economic Growth, An Economist's History of the United States* (New York: Harper & Row, 1972).

Ronald Ehrenberg and Robert Smith, *Modern Labor Economics*, 3rd ed. (Glenview, Ill.: Scott, Foresman, 1988).

Richard Freeman and James Medoff, "The Two Faces of Unionism," *The Public Interest*, 57 (Fall 1979).

W. G. Friedman and J. F. Gardner, eds., *Government Enterprise, A Comparative Study* (New York: Columbia University Press, 1970), ch. 11.

James V. Koch, *Industrial Organization and Prices*, 2nd ed. (Englewood Cliffs, N.J.: Prentice-Hall, 1980).

H. G. Lewis, *Unionism and Relative Wages in the United States* (Chicago: University of Chicago Press, 1963).

Paul MacAvoy, ed., *The Crisis of Regulatory Commissions* (New York: Norton, 1970).

Edwin Mansfield, ed., *Monopoly Power and Economic Performance*, 3rd ed. (New York: Norton, 1974).

Joseph Pechman and Benjamin Okner, *Who Bears the Tax Burden?* (Washington, D.C.: Brookings, 1974).

Frederic Scherer, *Industrial Structure and Economic Performance*, 2nd ed. (Boston: Houghton Mifflin, 1980).

Eugene Singer, *Antitrust Economics* (Englewood Cliffs, N.J.: Prentice-Hall, 1968).

Simon Whitney, *Antitrust Policies* (New York: Twentieth Century Fund, 1958).

Clair Wilcox, *Public Policies Towards Business*, 3rd ed. (Homewood, Ill.: Irwin, 1966).

Chapter 7
Resource Allocation in the Soviet Economy

Having compared American capitalism to the theoretical model of pure capitalism, we now compare the Soviet socialist planned economy with the theory of planned socialism outlined in Chapter 5. Our approach is similar to that in the previous chapter. We first examine output determination and materials allocation and then see how inputs (land, labor, and capital) are allocated. In contrast to capitalism, where market forces are pervasive and state intervention an (important) exception, the roles of the state and the Communist party are pervasive and market forces an exception in the Soviet economy.

The Soviet Union merits our consideration as a major case study because, although the Soviet economic system differs in important respects from planned socialism, most observers would characterize the Soviet system as *the* major example of centrally planned socialism. In addition, the Soviet economic system has been in operation for a relatively long time. The Soviet government has been in power since 1917; the system of central planning has been in place since 1928. This time span provides a unique opportunity to examine the nature of the Soviet economic system, its operation under varying conditions, and its influence on outcomes.

Our concern in this chapter is the structure of the Soviet economy and its operation over time — in particular, Soviet organizational arrangements for resource allocation.[1] We look at the traditional features of the Soviet economic system and touch on major changes suggested by Mikhail Gorbachev in mid-1988 in terms of their relation to traditional aspects of the system. However, a full discussion of economic reform in the Soviet Union and other planned socialist systems is deferred to Chapter 14.

HISTORICAL PERSPECTIVES

Our approach toward American capitalism was not historical. The Soviet economic system and the society in which it is embedded, however, represent sharp departures from the Russian (prerevolutionary) experience. To understand the Soviet system, a brief historical review is required.

At the time of the Bolshevik revolution in 1917, the era of the czars came to a close and the era of the Soviets began. Although the Soviet economic system as we know it today generally dates from 1928, analysis and assessment of the Soviet era must begin with some understanding of the base from which it grew: the *level* and *rate* of economic development at the end of the czarist era.

Economic development as of 1917 was at a relatively low level, judged by indicators such as per capita gross national product. However, there had been considerable increase in rate of growth, especially industrial growth, during the last three decades of czarist rule and the Soviets could therefore build on an attractive base (transportation, industrial capacity, minerals, and so forth).

At the end of the 1920s the Soviet leader, Joseph Stalin, made two important decisions. First, a comprehensive system of central economic planning based on compulsory state and party directives was established. An abrupt end to the prevailing system of market relations in industry ensued; and there was a sudden shift in industrial production away from consumer goods toward producer goods. Second, the agricultural sector was collectivized. A vast net of collective farms (*kolkhozy*) was created in which more than 90 percent of Soviet peasant households were living by the mid-1930s.[2] These two major decisions, though sudden at the time, did not arise out of a vacuum.

Two economic "experiments" were conducted in the period immediately following the revolution of 1917: war communism (1917–1920) and the New Economic Policy (1921-1928).[3] Both responded to the need to consolidate power and at the same time to marshal economic resources in a time of crisis.[4]

War communism, implemented by Lenin during the Russian Civil War, saw the introduction of substantial state ownership (nationalization), an attempt to eliminate market relationships in industry and trade, and the gathering of agricultural products from the peasants by forced requisitioning. In a sense, it seemed that Lenin was attempting to by-pass socialism and move directly from a capitalist to a communist system. Whatever the intent, the economic consequences were a disaster by the end of the civil war; the economy was in ruin.[5]

In an attempt to instill economic recovery, the New Economic Policy (NEP) was introduced by Lenin in 1921. NEP signaled a partial return to private ownership (the so-called commanding heights of industry remained nationalized), reintroduction of the market as a primary mechanism for resource allocation, and implementation of a more viable tax system on agriculture. By 1927, the Soviet economy had recovered from the losses of war communism and was at or in some cases above the prewar level.[6]

The period of Soviet history from 1917 to 1928 provided some important lessons — lessons that permeate Soviet thinking today. First, it became apparent that if the market were to be eliminated, some mechanism for coordination had to take its place. During war communism Lenin nationalized industries and eliminated the market, but he did not replace the market with a plan or some other substitute mechanism. Second, as a result, at least in part, of inept state policies, the peasants came to be viewed as holding considerable power over the pace of industrialization.[7] After all, the economy was largely agricultural, so both product and labor force would have to come primarily from the rural sector. Third, the response to Lenin's attempt to introduce payment in kind and to downgrade the importance of money during war communism made it obvious that, whatever the system, material incentives would be crucial to motivate labor.

In addition to the experience of war communism and NEP, the 1920s witnessed open and important discussions, the "great industrialization debate" and the beginnings of the theory of planning (discussed in Chapter 5).[8] The debate on industrialization focused on modes of industrialization and, in particular, differing roles for the agricultural and industrial sectors. All participants agreed that industrialization was essential and that the peasants would play a key role. The end result, however, was not readily foreseen by the debate's participants.

The economic system that Stalin put in place in the late 1920s and early 1930s was radically different from then existing systems. It remains largely intact to the present day and differs sharply from the systems of the pre- and immediate postrevolutionary periods.

The Setting

Before we examine the Soviet economic system, it is necessary to become familiar with some basic features of the country in which this system functions.

First, the Soviet Union is very large, a fact important to its economic development. It occupies over 8.6 million square miles, an area more than twice that of the United States. Furthermore, the 1981 population of the Soviet Union, at just over 266 million, is roughly 15 percent greater than that of the United States. The United States is predominantly urban (approximately 77 percent); the urbanization level of the Soviet Union is approximately 63 percent.

Second, the Soviet Union is a diverse nation. It consists of fifteen union republics, of which the Russian Republic is dominant, accounting for over 50 percent of the population. The remainder of the population, however, accounted for by such diverse peoples as the Latvians, the Ukrainians, and the Uzbeks, provides the Soviet nation with important ethnic, cultural, and historical diversity. In terms of sheer physical dimensions and natural diversity one must note sharp differences within the Soviet Union. Its climate ranges from the hot, dry areas of central Asia to the cold expanses of Siberia to the wet, cool plains of the West.

Third, the Soviet Union is very wealthy in terms of its natural resource base. In addition to being a major producer of fish and forest products, the Soviet Union is amply endowed with minerals and is the world's largest producer of petroleum, coal, and iron ore. Indeed, there are few minerals for which the Soviet Union has inadequate domestic supplies.

THE SOVIET ECONOMY:
A FRAMEWORK FOR ANALYSIS

Differences in outcomes can be related to differences in economic systems. System differences fall into four basic and important categories: decision-making *levels*, mechanisms of information (*market* and *plan*), property rights (*public* versus *private*), and finally, the nature of incentives (*material* versus *moral*).

As we examine the Soviet economy and, in particular, the organizational arrangements used to allocate resources, it is important to ask two questions: How does this system differ from the ideal of planned socialism? How can the actual system be categorized in terms of the four criteria?

In terms of the decision-making structure, the Soviet economy is organized in a vertical hierarchical fashion. The Soviet state, operating through government ministries, and the Communist party, operating through party groups and cells, share authority and responsibility. There are a number of decision-making layers, beginning with the state and party structure at the top, the ministries and regional authorities (and sometimes trust organizations) in the middle, and the basic production units (enterprises and farms) at the local level. The Soviet Union is clearly a **centralized economic system**.

Turning to the matter of information, the Soviet economy is a **planned economy** in the sense that, for most units in the system, whether a ministry or a factory, the national economic plan and its subcomponents supply information on the key issues of what to produce and how to produce. At the same time, market influences exist in some segments of the Soviet economy, for example in the allocation of labor and in the second, or underground, economy. While planning is the predominant mechanism, it is not universal.

The most striking difference between the Soviet economy and the capitalist market systems is in the area of property rights. The Soviet state is the dominant owner of property in the Soviet Union, and thus the utilization of property, whether a machine in a factory or a piece of land, is determined by the state. Exceptions to state ownership and control, such as property held by Soviet collective farms, are not especially important.

Finally, given the fact that income from property accrues exclusively to the state, it should not be surprising to learn that **wage income** is the dominant source of earnings for the Soviet worker. In addition to material incentives, however, the Communist party and other organizations place considerable emphasis on moral incentives, which become important in the Soviet system.

Organizational Features

The main organizational features of the Soviet economy are shown in Figure 7.1. The Soviet Union is nominally governed by an elected government, the operative organ of which is the Council of Ministers at the federal and republican levels.[9] A parallel structure, the Communist Party of the Soviet Union (CPSU), is the principal organ of control and supervision, operating largely through a complex centralized structure

Figure 7.1 The Organization of the Soviet Economy

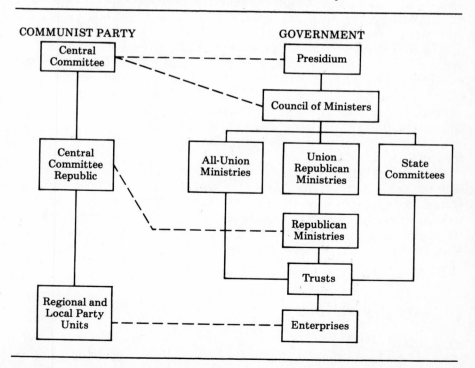

beginning at the national level and terminating with individual party cells in every Soviet enterprise, farm, and organization.[10] Regional party organizations are important in the allocation of resources at the regional level. The means of production, with very limited exceptions, are owned by the state. The agricultural sector is organized into state and collective (cooperative) farms, and both allot private plots to families. These plots are, however, state property, the use of which is granted to individual families under strict regulation.

From an economic point of view, two additional properties of the system require comment. First, the major organization around which the industrial activity of enterprises and the agricultural activities of farms are organized is the **ministry**. Ministries are hierarchically organized by type of production — steel, agriculture, and so on. The ministerial structure was changed to a *regional* basis in 1957 under the leadership of Nikita Khrushchev. The purpose, apparently, was to break down the tendency of ministries to become self-sufficient and ignore interactions with other ministries. The reform did not work and was abandoned when Khrushchev fell from power in 1964. Ministries differ in importance depending on their function. For example, the most important branches of industry are governed by all-union ministries. Important decisions concerning, for example, steel production facilities are made at the center. Union republican ministries disperse a measure of decision-making authority to the level of the republic (of which there are fifteen). The ministries, then, are the organizational superiors of the industrial and agricultural enterprises. Organizational reforms over the past decade have experimented with combining enterprises into trusts, which are intended to serve as an intermediary between the enterprise and the ministry.

Second, planning is done by Gosplan, the state planning agency. Gosplan is the agency responsible for converting general directives of the Communist party into operative plans with the help of the ministries and individual enterprises.

The way in which the Soviet economy operates in practice has remained remarkably stable over the years. A hierarchical command system with public ownership of the means of production and substantial material incentives remain the key mechanisms for achieving state and party directives. It is only in the Gorbachev era that reforms far-reaching enough to lessen the powers of Gosplan and the ministries have been suggested.

PLANNING IN PRACTICE

The allocation of resources in the Soviet Union is conducted primarily through the plan. There are short-term (one year), longer-term (five or seven years), and even twenty-year "perspective" plans. The five-year and annual plans, which direct economic activity, are of central interest here.

The essence of plan formulation is the material balance technique, the theoretical basis of which was examined in Chapter 5.[11] The plan is formulated in the following (highly simplified) manner. General directives on the economy are provided by the CPSU and are converted into control figures by Gosplan. The control figures, or tentative production targets, are transmitted through the ministries down to the level of individual enterprises, comment and informational input being sought from each level in the hierarchy. The control figures move back up through the hierarchy and at the Gosplan level are "balanced"; that is, for major items in the plan, supply and demand must balance. Once balance is achieved, the plan is disaggregated and the targets are once again disseminated down through the ministries to the individual enterprises. The final result is the **techpromfinplan** (technical-industrial-financial plan), which is legally binding and contains detailed directives for enterprise operations during the forthcoming year.

In practice, the formulation of this plan takes considerable time, is complex, and clearly cannot approach the theoretical ideals posed in Chapter 5. Our own brief description cannot do justice to the bargaining, haggling, interplay among the various units, and delays that have become integral parts of Soviet planning. Frequently the new plan is late in arriving, and consequently the enterprise must continue to operate under the guidance of the old plan. The material balance system works in large part because it has built-in flexibility. The planning process does not start from scratch each year. Thus the plan for year t is, in effect, little more than a revision and update of the plan for year $t - 1$. This practice has been described as "planning from the achieved level." While this simplifies the planning process considerably, it does build in considerable inflexibility. In addition, Soviet planners do not plan all items produced by the economy; they plan at the center only a relatively small number of items. Major commodities such as steel and machinery are called **funded** or **limited commodities** and are planned at the center. Their number has varied over time from a few hundred to a few thousand. Other commodities are planned at progressively lower and lower levels in the hierarchy, depending on their importance in the economy. This simplifies the planning process while leaving much to be done at the lower levels, for example, in the various republics.

In constructing balances for major materials planners face a dilemma. On the one hand, they would like the balance to be achieved at the highest possible level; on the other hand, they know that the more *taut* the plan — that is, the closer the targets are to maximum capacity — the more likely are errors and supply imbalances.[12] The approach is, in practice, to attempt to find a balance at a reasonably high level through adjusting input usage, manipulating final demand, adjusting stocks, and/or seeking foreign supplies. All are devices for ensuring that the plan can be demanding yet at the same time in balance. Soviet planners do not employ sophisticated planning techniques to "balance" supplies and demands. In fact, ad hoc tallies of sources and material requirements are maintained, and past experience is the principal guide to what is justified. Accordingly, Soviet planners are usually satisfied if they are able to come up with a *consistent* plan, but they do not have the luxury of seeking out the *optimal* plan from among all possible consistent plans.

In addition to these formal mechanisms to adjust supply and demand, informal patterns of managerial response also serve to manipulate plan patterns, sometimes in undesirable directions. Also, buffer sectors, typically consumer goods, have been used to absorb shortages as they arise.

Our picture of Soviet planning is a distortion of reality, for it suggests an economy rigidly planned and controlled by central authorities. In relative terms this is correct. All economies do combine some mix of market and plan, and the Soviet economy does lean most heavily in the direction of planning by directive. Most facets of the Soviet economy are planned and there is almost total public ownership of the means of production, but beneath the façade of rigid centralized planning rest numerous informal and some quasi-market mechanisms affecting resource allocation. We know relatively little about the scope and workings of these informal mechanisms, although we do have some hints about them.

We know that the formal plan is really only the initial blueprint of economic activity both at the economy-wide and the enterprise level. The manner in which the plan is revised in the course of plan fulfillment is probably as important as the initial plan itself. In fact, the changes and revisions that take place after the plan is finalized are so great that some analysts question whether it is appropriate to call the Soviet economy a planned economy. We also know that a variety of unofficial markets (to be examined later in this chapter) exist and are important, yet they have little to do with the formal planning process.[13] Most products, in fact, are planned at regional or local levels or are not planned at all. In some instances, indirect signals (for example, prices) do play roles in allocating resources, especially at the managerial level.

It is not possible to draw a balance between the formal and informal forces affecting resource allocation in the Soviet Union. What we do know is that relative to market economies the balance is strongly in favor of centralized administrative allocation, but the role of informal forces is just now coming to be recognized.[14]

Our earlier examination of the theory of planning emphasized three important stages in the planning process: plan development, implementation, and feedback. In the Soviet case, the individual enterprise or farm is responsible for **plan implementation**. We next examine the Soviet enterprise's role in plan implementation, bearing in mind the question developed in Chapter 5: What sort of rules are needed to ensure that each enterprise, in following plan directives, will be motivated to achieve the wishes of the central planners?

THE SOVIET ENTERPRISE

All enterprises have a plan, which is usually specified in annual terms but broken down into monthly (and even shorter) periods. First, the plan is a comprehensive document covering many facets of the firm's operations, and it carries the force of law. Second, the plan specifies both inputs and outputs in physical and financial terms; it specifies the sources and the distribution of funds for the firm; and so on. However, it would be erroneous to think that the Soviet manager is fully regimented, mechanically follows instructions, and has little freedom of action. In fact there is quite a bit of managerial freedom. To understand Soviet management and plan fulfillment one must understand how managers respond in this environment and what impact they have on the plan and its fulfillment.

Much of the Soviet managerial milieu can be summed up as "the managerial success indicator problem." In short this means that Soviet managers are offered substantial rewards for the achievement of a number of planned (often conflicting) objectives, but those objectives are fuzzy and often ill defined, leading at times to peculiar and dysfunctional managerial behavior.[15]

Historically, **gross value of output** (or, in later years, gross sales) has been the most important target from the manager's viewpoint. The manager's performance has been judged on the basis of the fulfillment of this target. But, even if prices accurately reflected relative scarcities, it would be difficult for planners to specify output objectives in unequivocally clear terms. For example, if managers are told to maximize the gross value of output, they will ignore items that make a small contribution (relative to their claim on scarce resources) to gross value and overproduce items that make a large contribution. The *mix* of goods within the plan (assortment) will be ignored if necessary to meet the gross output target. Within existing patterns of Soviet managerial bonuses, such behavior, though potentially disruptive to the system, is rewarding to the manager and the enterprise. The bonus system has typically paid little or nothing until achievement of 100 percent fulfillment of the output plan, then additional rewards are paid for production over this level, resulting in an average managerial bonus of possibly 25 or 35 percent of base salary.[16] Top managers receive bonuses in excess of 50 percent. Moreover, managerial perks and job tenure depend on fulfillment of the gross output target. Thus we find a combination of generally taut targets, uncertain supply especially for "limited" goals, and substantial rewards for fulfillment of planned output targets. The result has been informal and frequently dysfunctional managerial behavior, a problem not anticipated by the socialist economic theorists who assumed that managers would obey all rules handed down by superior authorities.

How do Soviet managers protect themselves and prosper in such an environment? First, managers can, during the plan formulation stage, attempt to secure "easy" targets, that is, targets that are relatively low vis-à-vis the actual capacity of the enterprise. This is a problem of any system in which participants can manipulate the objectives against which they will be measured. This, in a nutshell, is why the reward system is so important in a planned economy.

Second, managers can emphasize what is important (in terms of their rewards) and neglect or ignore other areas. Thus cost-saving targets may be sacrificed along with assortment targets for the sake of ensuring fulfillment of gross output targets. This is a major explanation for the shortage of spare parts in the Soviet industrial sector: Their manufacture disrupts production lines and does not contribute sufficiently to rewards. Third, managers can seek "safety" in various other practices. For example, managers can stockpile materials that are expected to be in short supply; they can avoid change, notably innovation; or they can establish unplanned (informal or "family") connections to ensure a supply of crucial inputs when needed.

Many features of the informal Soviet managerial milieu are disruptive and shift the results of production away from those envisaged by the planners. Others are necessary to correct for errors made by planning authorities and for breakdowns in the supply system. Plan execution, therefore, is subject to a substantial measure of flexibility and variation not envisaged in the theoretical models: People simply do not do what they are told. But, the state does not stand idle; it can and does exercise control over enterprise management.

Planners monitor enterprise performance, though this is not a simple task in an economy the size of the Soviet Union. The CPSU is an important institution for this purpose. Most organizations contain party cells, and enterprise managers are almost always party members. They will therefore be aware of the priorities specified by the party. Nevertheless, at almost all levels of the Soviet economy there is a bias in favor of reporting successful results. If local enterprises perform well, the careers of local party officials are advanced and so on up the hierarchy. Another very different but important monitoring device is the state bank

(Gosbank).[17] Most Soviet enterprises are budget financed, which means that funds both to and from enterprises flow through the state bank into and out of the state budget. The state budget is a major source of enterprise investment funds, or, for an enterprise that loses money, of subsidy funds. Profits, too, are channeled through the state bank, and profit taxes form an important part of Soviet budgetary revenue. Each enterprise is required to hold accounts with the state bank where all transactions are recorded. Not only is the quantity and type of labor that a firm can use specified in the plan, the fund used to pay for the labor must be held and monitored by the state bank.

Second, managerial behavior can be manipulated by the nature of rewards, both material and moral.[18] We have noted that Soviet managers can earn substantial monetary bonuses for meeting targets; also, there are other rewards such as housing, vacations, automobiles, and promotion. On the negative side, managers who do not perform can be dismissed, a sanction that was far more widely used in the early days of Soviet planning than it is today.[19]

We have seen that Soviet plans coexist in both physical and money terms. The financial plans are derived by applying prices to the physical plans. In recent years, increasing attention has been paid to the financial variables and accordingly to the matter of price formation. In theory and reality, the capitalist economy uses prices to allocate resources. If prices are to be useful in achieving social objectives, they must accurately reflect the relative scarcities. If financial variables grow more important in the Soviet system (for example, if costs and profits are used in the decision-making process), what can be said about Soviet prices?

PRICES AND THE ALLOCATION OF LAND, LABOR, AND CAPITAL

Soviet Prices: General Features

Soviet prices, with some exceptions, are set by administrative authorities.[20] In the case of the collective farm markets and services provided by moonlighting workers, prices are the result of supply and demand forces. Soviet industrial prices are largely set to equal average cost by industrial branch plus a small profit markup. **Branch average cost** generally excludes rental and interest charges, and its use as a standard has resulted in enterprises making both planned profits and planned losses within the same branch. Pricing authorities have sought to raise prices sufficiently through periodic price "reforms" to make enterprises profitable. This presumably means that enterprises at the margin will break even and others will make substantial profits when the price reform is introduced. But the administrative difficulty of making frequent price reforms has meant that historically prices have been allowed to lag behind real cost increases, and at times the majority of enterprises in particular branches have made planned losses. During the last quarter century, major price reforms have been rare. Wholesale prices established in 1955 remained generally in effect until 1966. The 1966–1967 price reform remained in effect until the general price reform of 1982. Price reform is a major component of Gorbachev's proposed reform.

As far as interenterprise relations are concerned, wholesale prices play primarily an accounting role, for supplies and demands are administratively planned and are not functions of prices. However, when a product leaves the wholesale level to be sold at the retail level, the matter is not so simple. Figure 7.2 illustrates retail price formation.

The supply of consumer goods at the retail level is determined largely by the planners, although producers, if they have a choice in output mix, may choose to produce a product with a higher relative price. Thus we draw the supply curve (S) with a steep upward slope. The demand curve (D) is a function of relative prices, incomes, and tastes

Figure 7.2 Soviet Turnover Tax

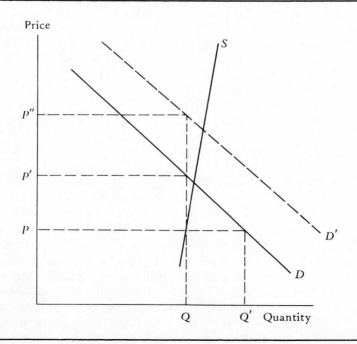

and cannot be controlled by the planners. How can the planners ensure that supply and demand will balance at the retail level? Typically, the retail price is established at or near market-clearing level by adding a tax (the **turnover** tax) or subsidy (if the wholesale price is above the clearing level). If the retail price were set at the wholesale (cost-based) price (P in Figure 7.2), there would be an excess demand of $Q'Q$, for OQ would be produced and OQ' demanded. Some form of rationing would have to be found.

In addition to administrative rationing and tolerating an excess demand (as shown by long lines to purchase goods), Soviet authorities have relied heavily on the turnover tax to balance supply and demand. If the authorities choose to ration via price, the retail price would be set at OP' and approximate equilibrium would prevail. It is important to note that raising the retail price *does not* raise the quantity supplied above OQ because the enterprise continues to receive the wholesale price OP for the product. The difference between the retail and wholesale price (ignoring trade margins) is the turnover tax.

The turnover tax, in this case PP', is an important component of Soviet budgetary revenue. Unlike Western sales taxes, its proportion differs widely from one product to another, and it is included in the price rather than being added on at the time of sale. Its share of retail prices has declined slowly over time as planners have increased supplies of consumer products and have raised the wholesale prices of farm products.

Although prices approach equilibrium at the retail level, it should be emphasized that this mechanism is very different from that prevailing in the capitalist market economy. What we see in the Soviet case as a tax would in effect be a profit accruing to the capitalist producer, which serves as a signal to existing producers to expand supply and to new producers to enter the market. There is no such signal in the Soviet case because what would be profit in the capitalist context accrues as tax revenue to the state. The producer at the wholesale level is unaware and largely uninterested in retail prices. Thus the link between consumer demand and the producer is broken. Assume an increase in demand from D to D'. As the producer continues to receive the wholesale price OP, the quantity produced remains at OQ. But at the old retail price OP', there is now an excess of demand over supply. The state reacts eventually by raising the turnover tax by $P'P''$.

It is fair to say that in the Soviet case, the value and mix of consumer goods is determined by planners' preferences, not by consumer demand, although in the long-run planners may well consider consumer signals when establishing plan targets. Thus it is argued that in the Soviet case prices play only a very limited **allocative** role and are used primarily for functions such as measurement, control, and the manipulation of the income distribution.

Soviet price policy has always emphasized the desirability of pricing some goods and services relatively "low" and others relatively "high." This policy reflects a very different (socialist) attitude toward the appropriate ("equitable") distribution of income and toward determining what is a necessity and what a luxury. Thus the prices of books, housing, medical care, and transportation are very low, and the prices of automobiles and vodka are very high. Price policy affects the distribution of real incomes in accordance with state objectives.

The issues surrounding prices and pricing policies in the Soviet economy are complex. Price reforms in recent years have generally focused on making Soviet prices more realistic, in that they now reflect costs more accurately and promote greater efficiency in input usage than they did in the past. If prices are to play a greater role in decision making under Gorbachev, major reform will clearly be necessary.

Input Prices: Land and Labor

The prices of inputs — land, labor, and capital — reflect a peculiar combination of Marxian orthodoxy, pragmatism, and allocative necessity. There is, for the most part, no rental price for agricultural land. Land is allocated to collective and state farms administratively. Land utilization is determined within the framework of the plan taking into account the technical and local conditions of the agricultural enterprise. The absence of land charges makes farm accounting a questionable exercise, the result of which has been an endless debate over the role of land rent under socialism. Despite some interest in land valuation problems, the Soviet Union has not formalized a system such as that used in East Germany, for example, where land is valued on a point system. Historically, however, Soviet planners have attempted to extract a rent from the Soviet countryside by using regionally differentiated procurement prices and differential charges for machine services provided by the State.

The allocation of labor in the Soviet Union is a very different case, for there is a price for labor in the form of a wage rate. How are wages set in the Soviet Union, and what role do wages have in allocating labor among its various occupations, uses, and regions?[21]

Historically, differential wages has been one of several mechanisms utilized to allocate labor in the Soviet Union. The demand for labor is primarily plan determined. Once output targets are established, labor requirements can be determined by applying technical coefficients, representing the amount of labor required per unit of output under existing technology. On the supply side, however, households are substantially free to make occupational choices and to decide between labor and leisure. The state has set wage differentials — for example, by occupation and by region — in an attempt to induce appropriate supplies to meet planned demands.

The basic wage-setting procedure is straightforward. For an industrial branch, a base rate is established. This rate determines the wage level for that branch relative to other branches. A schedule gives all rates above this level as a percentage of the base and establishes the pattern of wage differentials within the branch. Thus the level and differential can be adjusted by manipulating the base or the schedule. Soviet trade unions and individual workers play virtually no role in setting wages; wages are set by administrative authorities. But, unlike many other areas in the Soviet economy, planners have been quite willing to *use* these differentials to manipulate labor supply. There is a substantial degree of market influence on the structure of Soviet wages.[22]

In addition to wage differentials, other devices are used to manipulate labor supply. Higher- and technical-education institutions are expanded in direct relation to the desired composition of the labor force, and this is a matter under state control. In addition, nonmonetary rewards, adulation in the press, social benefits, and other such methods (moral incentives) have been used to affect the supply of labor. Organized recruitment by special organizations and the party has been important in the past but has declined in importance in recent years with the possibly important exception of the seasonal needs of agricultural production.[23] The Soviet system, therefore, combines both material and moral rewards, with the emphasis on the former.

Soviet labor policies, including the forced labor campaigns of the 1930s, have ensured a very high rate of labor force participation to provide rapid economic development. In recent years, the participation rate, defined as the civilian labor force as a portion of the able-bodied population, has generally exceeded 90 percent. On the other hand, structural problems have recently become more serious and will be a major test of the efficacy of central planning as a mechanism for allocating labor. For example, a very rapid even if controlled rate of urbanization has left shortages in some areas, surpluses in others. These imbalances are especially true for the regional distribution of labor, where Soviet authorities have not been able to meet the labor needs of Siberia and the Far North. In addition, the rather restrictive role of Soviet trade unions and the policy of "full employment" have resulted in underemployment — artificially high levels of staffing at the enterprise level. Under present conditions, it is quite difficult to lay off workers even if they are redundant. This problem has prompted the state to experiment with new programs to encourage the firing of unproductive workers. The Soviet economy has not solved the problem of microeconomic allocation of labor resources for a modern economy. The crucial question that arises is whether a full (or "overfull") employment policy can be maintained and at the same time ensure allocative efficiency. This is an important area for reform in Soviet planning methods. It is noteworthy that Gorbachev has placed heavy emphasis on labor discipline and morale in his efforts to improve economic performance.

Capital Allocation

We turn now to the matter of pricing capital, or the determination of an interest charge.[24] As we saw in Chaper 4, capital is not a value-creating input in the Marxian scheme. Why then should its use generate a reward in the form of a capital (interest) charge? Even if capital has no value-creating capacity, less is available than is demanded. Some means must be devised for its allocation. Furthermore, even if a "price" is used in this allocation function, it will perform *only* this function. Where all capital is owned by the state, the "income" from capital accrues directly to the state, not individuals.

In the Soviet case, investment is largely controlled by central planning authorities and the ministries. In drawing up the output plan, planners apply technical coefficients to determine the amounts of capital investment necessary to produce the planned output, and investment funds are authorized. Some funds will be available from internal enterprise funds, but even these funds remain under control of the banking system. The aggregate supply of investment funds is largely under the control of planners. It is not surprising, therefore, that the ratio of saving to gross national product is very high in the Soviet Union — much higher, for example, than in the United States. Indeed, this illustrates a basic feature of planners' preferences. In a market capitalist economy, saving is influenced by government but is largely determined by individuals and businesses as they choose between consumption in the present and greater consumption in the future. In the Soviet context, the state controls the amount of saving (primarily by the state and by enterprises). In a capitalist economy, saving arises as undistributed profits in enterprises and as income that is not consumed in households. Both *types* of saving exist in the Soviet case, but because wages and prices are set by the state, the state can itself accumulate savings at whatever rate it chooses without recourse to the indirect method of taxation. This ability to control saving and investment is a powerful mechanism to promote a more rapid rate of capital accumulation than would likely be tolerated in an economy directed by consumer sovereignty.

Since the late 1960s Soviet enterprises have paid an interest charge for the use of capital. This charge has typically been small (6 percent), designed to cover the administrative costs of making the capital funds available to the enterprise.

At the enterprise level, Soviet authorities have devised rules to choose among investment projects. Suppose there is a directive to raise the capacity to generate a certain volume of electric power. Will the capacity be hydroelectric, nuclear, coal fueled, or what? How can one compare the capital-intensive variant that has low operating costs to the variant requiring less capital initially but having high annual operating costs? Although quasi-market techniques for making this sort of decision were rejected by Stalin in the 1930s in favor of planners' wisdom, these methods surfaced again in the late 1950s and have been widely used in recent years.

Since 1958, planners have accepted the principle that the selection among competing project variants should be based on cost-minimizing procedures. To illustrate, a general formula (the coefficient of relative effectiveness) to compare project variants has been in use since 1958:

$$C_i + E_n K_i = \text{Minimum}$$

where

C_i = current expenditures of the ith investment project
K_i = the capital cost of the ith investment project
E_n = the normative coefficient

This formula has been used to weigh the tradeoff between higher capital outlays (K_i) and lower operating costs (C_i). The notion underlying this formula is that that project variant should be selected that yields the minimum full cost, where an imputed capital charge is included in the cost calculation. The capital cost (charge) is calculated by applying a "normative coefficient" (E_n) to the projected capital outlay.

For example, assume that a choice must be made between two projects, the first having an annual operating cost (C) of 10 million rubles and a capital cost (K) of 30 million rubles; the second having a C of 7 million rubles but a K of 50 million rubles. Applying a normative coefficient of, say, 10 percent yields a full cost of 13 million rubles for the first and 12 million rubles for the second. The second project therefore should be chosen because it is the minimum cost variant. However, suppose a normative coefficient of 20 percent is applied. In this case, the full cost of the first variant will be 16, that of the second variant 17. In this case, with a change in the normative coefficient, the first variant will be chosen.

An important feature of this formula should be noted. The higher the normative coefficient, the higher the imputed capital cost, and the *less* likely that capital-intensive variants would be selected. This is exactly what occurred between 1958 and 1969, when a system of differentiated normative coefficients was used. The pattern of differentiated norms followed the established principle of giving priority to heavy industry by applying low E_ns to heavy industrial branches (thereby encouraging the selection of capital-intensive variants of projects in these branches) and high E_ns to light industry. In 1969, a new *Standard Methodology*[25] replaced the earlier differentiated system with a standard normative coefficient of 12 percent. It was supposed to be applied equally to all branches of the economy.

The principle that capital should be allocated among project variants on the basis of such rate of return calculations should not obscure the fact that the basic allocation of capital still proceeds through an administrative investment plan, which itself is a derivative of the output plan. These rate of return calculations are used only to select among the variants of projects that follow planners' preferences in the first place. Thus they are used to decide what type of plant should be used to generate electricity, not whether the investment should be in electricity generation or, for example, steel production. In fact, the standardized coefficient introduced in 1969 has been watered down since then by numerous exceptions for particular branches of heavy industry and for various regions.

Financial Planning

The Soviet economy is run by largely administrative rules and instructions. Although value categories (prices, costs, profits, and so on) have always existed, they have played only a limited role in allocating resources. Even in a centralized economy where few decisions are made at local levels, households make decisions concerning labor participation and consumer spending. How can planners ensure that there will be a macroeconomic balance of consumer goods in the economy? Aggregate consumer demand and supply can be illustrated in the following framework:

$$D = WL - R \tag{7.1}$$

$$S = P_1 Q_1 \tag{7.2}$$

where

D = aggregate demand
S = aggregate supply
W = the average annual wage
L = the number of worker-years of labor used in the economy
R = the amount of income not spent on consumer goods
(equal to the sum of direct taxes and savings)

Q_1 = the real quantity of consumer goods produced
P_1 = the price level of consumer goods

The problem here is conceptually quite simple. As the Soviet socialist economy developed rapidly in the early plan years, it paid labor increasingly large salaries to motivate higher participation and greater effort; but the state wanted that labor to produce producer goods, not consumer goods (Q_1). Thus the state permitted wages (W) to rise rapidly to encourage labor inputs (L) to rise. In the absence of sharp increases in Q_1, however, it was necessary to pursue alternate steps to achieve a balance between S and D, notably to let P_1 rise along with R (the latter rise engendered through forced bond purchases). However, prices were not allowed to rise fast enough to absorb the full increase in demand; an imbalance between aggregate supply and demand was allowed to develop. This technique, typical for any less-developed economy during the early stages of development, is known as **repressed inflation** and has been used widely in the Soviet Union.[26] Repressed inflation was prominent during the 1930s and early 1950s.

In the postwar era, the real quantity of consumer goods has increased, and excess demand has been reduced. However, complaints about shortages of consumer goods in the Soviet Union persist and scholars such as Janos Kornai have considered why shortages continue to exist despite rising production of consumer goods.

Although the focus of discussion has been the issue of repressed inflation, there has been increasing emphasis on the examination of this phenomenon in a **disequilibrium framework**. It is argued that persistent excess demand in consumer goods markets may well have feedback effects throughout the system. Thus if wage earnings cannot be effectively transformed into consumer goods, there may be an impact on savings (in effect, forced savings). In addition, there is the possibility of secondary effects, for example, reduction of labor force participation. This sort of investigation is in its early stages (see Appendix 7A). Researchers have devoted a great deal of attention to the saving behavior of the Soviet public in an effort to establish the causes of increases in aggregate saving. Some scholars view increases in saving as proof of massive disequilibrium (people save because there is nothing to buy at prevailing prices). Other scholars find that Soviet saving behavior is consistent with that in capitalist countries.[27]

THE ROLE OF MARKET FORCES

The American economy is a market economy in which the state has come to play a growing and frequently controversial role. The Soviet economy, on the other hand, is a planned economy in which market forces are of moderate and secondary importance. Just as we had to view state economic activity as the exception in the U.S. case, market resource allocation in the Soviet Union is the exception to resource allocation by the plan.

In an economic system, ownership and control are closely related. The Soviet state as the primary owner of the means of production is assumed to exercise control over the direction of economic activity through the national economic plan. Our discussion of the Soviet economy has been cast in these terms.

Paul Craig Roberts has argued that the Soviet economy is a "polycentric" system in which control is diversified.[28] He maintains that the interaction of enterprises at the local level, their informal interrelationships, and the generation of local information flows, not the plan, are the main forces determining economic activity. Eugene Zaleski has concluded from his analysis of plan fulfillment that administrative adjustments made after the plan is finalized have a stronger bearing on resource allocation than do the plans themselves. Zaleski refers to the Soviet economy as an administratively managed (not planned) economy.[29]

A number of other Western analysts have come to question whether the Soviet economy is indeed a "planned" economy. John H. Wilhelm argues that the original plan typically is not workable, is continuously changed in the course of plan fulfillment, and in the end is revised to correspond to expected fulfillment. Under these circumstances, Wilhelm argues, it is inappropriate to call the Soviet economy a planned economy.[30] Available evidence does not allow us to draw a firm conclusion on this question, but we would reject the argument that the plan is not a critical determinant of economic activity. Rather, the relevant issue is whether and how much additional forces affect economic outcomes.

Western economists have long argued that in some areas of the Soviet economy — for example, labor allocation — planners have used market-type mechanisms to influence observed outcomes. Thus wage differentials are used to influence the distribution of labor by region, by season, and by profession; retail prices are used to allocate available consumer goods. The fact that wages and retail prices are set by planners does not rule out market forces. In such instances planners are actually acting as market intermediaries.

A third role for market forces is the "second economy." The second economy has been analyzed extensively by Gregory Grossman, Dimitri Simes, and Aron Katsenelinboigen.[31] It consists of a number of market-type activities of varying importance and degrees of legality, all facilitating "unplanned" exchange among consumers and producers. According to Grossman, second economy activities must fulfill at least one of the two following tests: (1) the activity is for private gain; (2) the activity knowingly contravenes existing law.

Examples of second economy activities abound. A physician may treat private patients for higher fees. A salesperson may set aside quality merchandise for customers who offer large tips. The manager of a textile firm may reserve goods for sale in unofficial supply channels. A collective farmer may divert collective farm land and supplies to his private plot. Black marketeers in port cities may deal in contraband merchandise. Owners of private cars may transport second economy merchandise. In some cases, official and second economy transactions are intertwined. A manager may divert some production into second economy transactions to raise cash to purchase unofficially supplies needed to meet the plan. The official activities of an enterprise may serve as a front for a prospering second economy undertaking.

According to available accounts, second economy activities are concentrated in collective farms and in the transportation network. Apparently, the supervision of collective farms is more lax; they therefore serve as better fronts for the second economy. Transportation enterprises are critical to the second economy, for its merchandise must somehow be moved. The increase in private ownership of automobiles has apparently enhanced the operation of the second economy.

We cannot establish how important the second economy is, say, as a percentage of retail sales, but those who have studied the second economy argue that it is quite significant. To take isolated examples, where estimates are available: In 1970, one-fourth of all alcohol consumed in the Soviet Union was produced and supplied through the second economy; in the mid-1970s, the overwhelming portion of fuel for private autos was purchased in the second economy.[32] The significance of the second economy should come as no surprise, for the official planning system has assigned low priorities to nonessential services (beauty shops, appliance repairs, and so on), and expenditures on these items typically rise with rising income. Moreover, the official supply system has failed to offer the Soviet consumer sufficient supplies of quality merchandise, and the second economy serves as a means of channeling available quality merchandise to the highest bidder.

The second economy has its advantages and disadvantages as far as the planners are concerned. It helps to preserve incentives because higher wages and bonus payments can be spent in the second economy. Moreover, the second economy serves to reduce inflationary pressures on the official economy. On the negative side, the second economy diverts participants in the economy from planned tasks and loosens planners' control over the economy. Soviet authorities have long tolerated the second economy. Reforms of the late 1980s have moved to legalize a number of second economy activities that do not involve the use of hired labor.

A fourth area of market influence is the private sector of Soviet agriculture. The farm family, under restricted conditions, can use a plot of land, hold animals, and raise crops. The resulting products are sold in markets (the kolkhoz market) tolerated by the authorities. Prices are freely established by supply and demand and provide a substantial portion of the farm family's income. It is not by accident that the private plots produce farm products that are poorly suited to planning, such as fruits, vegetables, and dairy products — all of which require great personal care and motivation.

How important are market forces in the Soviet economy? There is little doubt that market forces exist and are important in a number of dimensions. It is, as we have emphasized, very difficult to give a quantitative estimate of their importance (other than the case for the private sector of agriculture), let alone to know the direction of change over time. However, a recent study of Soviet emigrants to Israel assesses the magnitude of the private sector at roughly 10 percent of family income, though income from this source is unevenly distributed, being centralized mainly in the service sector.

SOVIET AGRICULTURE

Organizational Arrangements

In the course of Soviet industrialization, agriculture has been of paramount importance. Its organizational aspects are in many respects unique, and even today agriculture accounts for a relatively large portion of output and labor force. Centralized planning of agriculture has been an illuminating if not always successful experience.

The agricultural sector of the Soviet economy is, like industry, within the purview of the planning apparatus. Were it not for its special dimensions, it would not need to be singled out for special treatment.

As far back as the 1920s, the so-called peasant problem was viewed as central to any development effort. During war communism and the New Economic Policy, various forms of organization existed, but private peasant agriculture dominated.[33] The rural sector was seen as crucial to any Soviet development effort because industrialization would depend on agricultural deliveries. Whether or not the perception of agriculture in the 1920s as the key to industrialization was correct, it was the rationale for Stalin's decision to collectivize in 1929.[34]

Two major institutions have been dominant in Soviet agriculture since the 1930s. The collective farms (**kolkhozy**) were to operate like cooperatives; the state farms (**sovkhozy**), in which the farmers would be paid like industrial workers, would be a "factory in the fields." The sovkhoz was and is a state enterprise with state-appointed management.[35] The kolkhoz was and is (in theory) a cooperative with elected management. Sovkhoz workers are state employees and therefore receive fixed wages like other state employees. Kolkhoz peasants, on the other hand, received a dividend instead of a wage. Because this unique payment system was the cornerstone of Stalin's attempt to extract a surplus from the countryside, dwelling on it for a moment is worthwhile even though it was abandoned in 1966.[36]

Prior to 1966, payment for peasants in the kolkhoz was established in the following fashion. For a particular task assigned to a peasant by, say, a brigade leader, a certain number of labor days would be "paid" and recorded in the peasant's work book. The labor day was not necessarily a measure of time or effort, but rather an often arbitrary measure of work input. At the end of the year, the *value* of one labor day would be determined by the following formula:

Value of one labor day = farm income after required deliveries and other expenses ÷ total number of labor days for entire kolkhoz

Having determined the value of a labor day, it would then be possible to pay each individual a "dividend" by multiplying the number of labor days accumulated by the value of the labor day.

This system of payment was highly arbitrary. The work demanded for one labor day could and did vary regionally, seasonally, and from farm to farm. Furthermore, contrary to the principles of any good incentive system, the peasant had little idea in advance what she or he would earn per labor day. The labor day system was finally abandoned in 1966 and was replaced by a guaranteed wage.

Collective Farm and State Farm Differences

Most input and output determinations in the kolkhoz and the sovkhoz are planned in a fashion similar to that used in an industrial enterprise. There are, however, some noteworthy differences. First, the method of payment for labor in the kolkhoz was, until 1966, very different from that in the sovkhoz. Second, the manner in which capital investment has been provided is different: kolkhoz investments have been largely self-financed; sovkhoz investment funds come directly from the state budget.[37] Third, until the late 1950s, machinery and equipment were maintained in the Machine Tractor Stations and were provided to the collective farms for a payment.[38] This mechanism served as an important external control over the management of the kolkhozy. Fourth, the method of distribution of output has been different. The sovkhoz, as a state enterprise, distributes the bulk of its output through the normal state trade channels as an industrial enterprise might do. The kolkhoz, in contrast, has been required to make compulsory deliveries to the state, often at very low fixed prices; but the remainder of its output has been free for sale either to the state at higher prices or on the collective farm markets. This two-tier pricing arrangement has allowed the state to extract the product from the kolkhoz.

In both the kolkhoz and the sovkhoz, families are entitled to small plots of land for their private use (typically about half an acre).[39] The produce from this land, very important in the case of some products (typically truck-garden products), can be consumed on the farm, sold to the state, or sold by the peasants in the collective farm markets. It is difficult to summarize the importance of the private sector in a few numbers. However, to give some idea of its impact we note that in the 1960s the private sector accounted for roughly 60 percent of total potato output, 70 percent of total vegetable output, and 30 percent of total milk output. In the postwar period, the private sector has accounted for approximately 40 percent of family income on collective farms. Peasants are also entitled to hold some animals, although the permitted number of each type has varied over time. For example, roughly 40 percent of all cows were owned privately in the 1960s.

Changes in Soviet Agriculture

Organizational arrangements in agriculture have changed substantially since the 1930s, although the kolkhoz, sovkhoz, and the private sector remain at least in name to the present day. We note the main trends of change.[40]

First, since the 1940s, a program of merger and consolidation has sharply reduced the number and importance of kolkhozy; at the same time, the number of sovkhozy has increased, and their average size is greater. In 1940, there were 237,000 kolkhozy in the Soviet Union with an average sown area of 1,235 acres. By the mid-1980s, the number of kolkhozy had been reduced to just over 26,000, while each kolkhoz had an average sown area of just over 8,600 acres. As for sovkhozy, in 1940 there were 4,200, averaging just over 6,900 acres of sown area on each farm. By the mid-1980s, the number of sovkhozy had increased to almost 22,700 with an average sown area of almost 12,000 acres per farm.[41] In 1940, roughly 78 percent of all sown area was accounted for by kolkhozy; this was reduced to 44 percent by the mid-1980s.

Possibly the most important organizational change in contemporary Soviet agriculture has been the introduction of **agro-industrial integration** on a major scale.[42] Begun with renewed emphasis in the 1970s, agro-industrial integration has brought both kolkhozy and sovkhozy together with industrial-type activity (for example, processing) into integrated production units with centralized management. These

changes, along with organizational changes on the regional level introduced with the Brezhnev "Food Program" of 1982, set the scene for
further changes to occur with **perestroika** under Gorbachev.

Second, there have been changes in planning and supervisory organs
and in the farm managerial system. The Machine Tractor Stations were
abolished in 1958, and their equipment was sold to the farms, a move
that gave farm managers enhanced control over farm equipment. In
addition, the quality of managerial personnel has improved dramatically
in recent years.

Third, rural incomes have increased sharply since the 1950s, generally more rapidly than industrial incomes. In addition, a pension system
introduced in the 1960s substantially improved the welfare of rural
workers and peasants and reduced the rural-urban income differential.[43] However, expanded production costs at the farm level and
unwillingness to raise retail food prices significantly have resulted in a
very large subsidy to the agricultural sector.[44]

Fourth, after a period of extensive campaigns by Nikita Khrushchev
in the 1950s (the Virgin Lands Campaign, the corn program, and so on)
designed to expand inputs, the emphasis in the 1960s and 1970s shifted
to improvement of productivity, in part through significant increases
in the volume of investment provided by the state.

Fifth, there has been an ongoing program to examine seriously the
problems of agriculture in an urban industrial economy. For example,
Soviet planners have devoted considerable (though not always successful) attention to the problems of supplying large cities with vegetables.
Also, efforts have been made to stem the continuing rapid flow of
young males from the rural areas and hence to alleviate the problem
of labor shortages and imbalances.

Soviet agriculture has always been of more than passing interest to
Western observers. Catastrophic crop failures, minimal supplies of meat,
and the virtual absence of produce in Soviet cities in winter are puzzling
in a heavily industrialized nation. Many observers have laid the blame
for uneven Soviet agricultural performance on unique Soviet organizational arrangements or limited investment in agriculture.

We must ask whether the agricultural sector of the Soviet economy
has been neglected in some sense and what sorts of policies have been
developed in the 1970s and early 1980s. The Brezhnev years saw important developments in Soviet agriculture, though change was implemented less flamboyantly than it had been under his predecessor.
Capital investment increased from roughly 15 percent of aggregate
investment to almost 27 percent, a substantial increment by any standard. At the same time, agricultural productivity remains a problem,
imports remain very important, and Gorbachev criticizes agricultural
performance. Clearly, productivity must be improved. But, possibly
more important, the infrastructure of Soviet agriculture must be im-

proved, especially food processing, storage, and distribution arrangements. As we shall see, Gorbachev has begun to address the problems of Soviet agriculture, though with rather traditional approaches — incentives through the collective contract brigade, relaxation of rules for the private sector, and streamlining of the upper-level administrative structure.

INTERNATIONAL TRADE

No coverage of the Soviet economy could be complete without some discussion of how the Soviet economic system participates in the world economy.

Chapter 11 is devoted to international trade in different economic systems. We limit our discussion here to some specifics of the Soviet case, leaving for later consideration more general issues of trade, planning, and markets.[45]

Decision making — in terms of what will be traded, with whom, and on what terms — is relatively centralized in three major areas: the Ministry of Foreign Trade (MFT), the *Vneshtorgbank* or Bank for Foreign Trade (BFT), and the various foreign trade organizations (FTOs). The formal organization of Soviet foreign trade is represented by Figure 7.3. The Ministry of Foreign Trade, like other Soviet ministries, is a relatively centralized body concerned with issues of foreign

Figure 7.3 The Organization of Soviet Foreign Trade

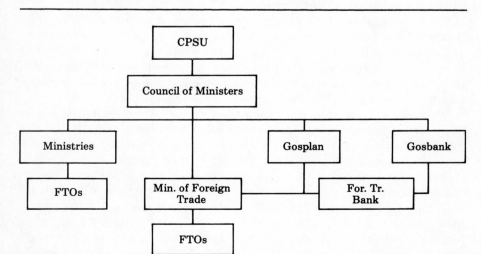

trade planning — the development of import/export plans, material supply plans, and balance of payments plans — all of which form an integral part of the Soviet material balance planning system.

Individual Soviet enterprises have generally not dealt with the external world, although reforms proposed by Gorbachev in the summer of 1987 would change this posture. Rather, for both imports and exports, enterprises have dealt with the FTOs in domestic currency at domestic prices, and the FTOs have dealt with the external world, with financial arrangements handled by the Ministry of Foreign Trade and the BFT. In the Soviet case, a monopoly in the hands of the Soviet government conducts foreign trade. The domestic users or producers of goods entering the foreign market are substantially isolated from foreign markets by this foreign trade monopoly. As viewed by Western economists, Soviet foreign trade has operated according to formal rules: Export what is available to be exported to pay for necessary imports, and limit the overall volume of trade to control the influence of market forces on the Soviet economy.

Most Soviet trade, even with other socialist countries, is bilateral, that is, directly negotiated for each trade deal with each trading partner. Bilateral trade means that Soviet exports and imports are handled largely on a barter basis. The well-known difficulties of operating according to offsetting barter deals have hampered Soviet trade turnover through the years. In part, bilateral trading arrangements arise from and contribute to the nonconvertibility of the Soviet ruble, which is not accepted as a medium of exchange in world financial markets.

Soviet organizational arrangements are not conducive to maintaining an expanding and competitive position in world markets, but Western economists have generally argued that the Soviet Union has followed a policy of deliberate "trade aversion."[46] What are the justifications for trade aversion? Dating from the late 1920s and early 1930s, Soviet trade ratios (that is, the ratio of imports and exports to gross national product) generally declined. For many years they remained "low" by world standards. In part, this pattern may have resulted from the Soviet Union's adverse position in world markets at that time, or it may have been in part a deliberate policy response. In any event, for the trade that *was* conducted, a very successful effort was made to redirect Soviet imports away from consumer goods and toward producer goods that contributed to the development effort.

Recent decades have witnessed changes in Soviet foreign trade. These changes might be indicative of a changing trade posture, in particular a more aggressive posture in world markets.

First, Soviet trade ratios have been rising in recent years, signaling an increased participation in the world economy. The extent of this rise is difficult to estimate because of the peculiarities of Soviet foreign trade accounting,[47] but there is little doubt that Soviet participation in foreign trade in the 1980s is well above the rates of the 1950s and 1960s.

Second, the 1960s and 1970s saw important organizational changes. To take one major example, there has been continuing discussion in the Soviet Union about the need to make its enterprises more responsive to world markets and to streamline the FTOs as the mechanism through which enterprise contacts with world markets are channeled. These themes have become important components of reform in the Gorbachev era.

Third, there has been a revolution in Soviet attitudes toward foreign trade, with renewed interest in Western, or neoclassical, trade theory and, most important, development and application of useful criteria on which to base trade decisions.

Fourth, the Soviet Union, though fundamentally conservative compared to most of its East European neighbors, has, nevertheless, displayed increasing interest in participating in world trade arrangements and organizations.

Past interest in Soviet foreign trade frequently centered on the role of trade in the Soviet development experience. Today, when the Soviet economy is moving from an extensive to an intensive mode of production, the role of technology is crucial. It is not surprising, therefore, that Soviet interest in the world market is growing, despite political tensions between East and West. Although trade between the United States and the Soviet Union is small and destined to remain so, trade between planned socialist and market capitalist economic systems is another matter, one that receives close attention in Chapter 11.

SUMMARY

1. The Soviet economic system was put in place in the late 1920s and early 1930s with the introduction of centralized planning and collectivization in agriculture. The system has remained remarkably stable.
2. The Soviet economy is a centralized economic system run by a bureaucracy that consists of Gosplan, ministries, and enterprises and trusts. The Communist party plays an important role in resource allocation both at the national and regional levels.
3. Soviet planning uses material balances to equate supplies and demands of key industrial commodities. Material balancing is a crude procedure that emphasizes consistency and not optimality.
4. Soviet enterprise managers respond to the prevailing incentive system. In the absence of a price system that reflects opportunity costs, the incentive system often leads managers to engage in dysfunctional behavior.

5. Prices serve primarily an accounting function in the wholesale area. Prices are used as resource-allocating mechanisms in retail markets and in labor markets. Although capital is allocated by rules that resemble rates of returns, capital is primarily allocated by administrative decree.

6. Financial planning is used to balance aggregate supplies and demands for consumer goods.

7. Market allocation is used in the second economy, collective farm markets, and in the allocation of labor.

8. Soviet agriculture is based upon the collective farm and the state farm. The private plot is an important supplier of food products despite its small share of total acreage.

9. Foreign trade is conducted by a trade monopoly that largely insulates Soviet firms from foreign markets.

NOTES

1. For a general treatment of the Soviet economy and references to the specialized literature see, Paul R. Gregory and Robert C. Stuart, *Soviet Economic Structure and Performance*, 3rd ed. (New York: Harper & Row, 1986); and Alec Nove, *The Soviet Economic System*, 2nd ed. (London: Allen and Unwin, 1981). For useful background papers, see U.S., Congress, Joint Economic Committee, *Soviet Economy in the 1980s: Problems and Prospects*, Parts 1 and 2 (Washington, D.C.: Government Printing Office, 1982). For a briefer treatment of the Soviet economy, see Franklyn D. Holzman, *The Soviet Economy: Past, Present, and Future* (New York: Foreign Policy Association, 1982); James R. Millar, *The ABC's of Soviet Socialism* (Urbana: University of Illinois Press, 1981).

2. For a discussion of these years, see M. Lewin, *Russian Peasants and Soviet Power* (London: Allen and Unwin, 1968); for a brief survey, see Gregory and Stuart, *Soviet Economic Structure and Performance*, ch. 5.

3. A considerable amount has been written about the Soviet economy during these early years. See, for example, Alec Nove, *An Economic History of the U.S.S.R.*, rev. ed. (London: Penguin Books, 1982); Eugene Zaleski, *Planning for Economic Growth in the Soviet Union, 1928–1932* (Chapel Hill: University of North Carolina Press, 1971); Maurice Dobb, *Soviet Economic Development Since 1917*, 5th ed. (London: Routledge and Kegan Paul, 1960); E. H. Carr and R. W. Davies, *Foundations of a Planned Economy, 1926–1929*, vol. I, pt. 2 (New York: Macmillan, 1969); Roger Munting, *The Economic Development of the USSR* (London: Croom Helm, 1982); R. W. Davies, *The Socialist Offensive, the Collectivization of Soviet Agriculture 1929–30* (London: Macmillan, 1980); Thomas F. Remington, "Varga and the Foundation of Soviet Planning," *Soviet Studies*, 34 (October 1982), pp. 585–600.

4. There is considerable debate about the *level* of economic development in the Soviet Union in 1917 and hence the readiness of that country, in the Marxian schema, for the introduction of socialism. For a discussion of this issue, see Gregory and Stuart, *Soviet Economic Structure and Performance*, ch. 2; for more detail, see Paul R. Gregory, "Economic Growth and Structural Change in Tsarist Russia: A Case of Modern Economic Growth?" *Soviet Studies*, 23

(January 1972), pp. 418-434; and Paul R. Gregory, *Russian National Income 1885-1913* (New York: Cambridge University Press, 1983).

5. By 1920, the index of industrial production (1913 = 100) had fallen to 20; the index of agricultural production had fallen to 64; and the index of transportation had fallen to 22. See Gregory and Stuart, *Soviet Economic Structure and Performance*, p. 58.

6. By 1928, the index of industrial production (1923 = 100) had risen to 102; the index of agricultural production had risen to 118; and the index of transportation had risen to 106. See ibid., p. 56.

7. For a discussion of the policy issues of this period, see Jerzy F. Karcz, "From Stalin to Brezhnev: Soviet Agricultural Policy in Historical Perspective," in James R. Millar, ed., *The Soviet Rural Community* (Urbana: University of Illinois Press, 1971), pp. 36-70; and Davies, *The Socialist Offensive*.

8. The classic work is Alexander Erlich, *The Soviet Industrialization Debate, 1924-1928* (Cambridge, Mass.: Harvard University Press, 1960). For a translation of original contributions to the debate, see Nicolas Spulber, *Foundations of Soviet Strategy for Economic Growth* (Bloomington: Indiana University Press, 1964); for a companion volume summarizing the issues, see Nicolas Spulber, *Soviet Strategy for Economic Growth* (Bloomington: Indiana University Press, 1964).

9. There is, however, only a single candidate for each position, although Gorbachev has proposed changes. For a comprehensive discussion of the Soviet government and party structure, see Jerry F. Hough and Merle Fainsod, *How the Soviet Union Is Governed* (Cambridge, Mass.: Harvard University Press, 1979).

10. For a study of the Communist party of the Soviet Union, see Leonard Shapiro, *The Communist Party of the Soviet Union* (New York: Random House, 1971); and Hough and Fainsod, *How the Soviet Union Is Governed*. For a statistical survey of party membership, see T. H. Rigby, *Communist Party Membership in the U.S.S.R., 1917-1967* (Princeton, N.J.: Princeton University Press, 1968). For further evidence, see T. H. Rigby, "Soviet Communist Party Membership Under Brezhnev," *Soviet Studies*, 28 (July 1976), pp. 317-337; and Jan S. Adams, *Citizen Inspectors in the Soviet Union: The People's Control Committee* (New York: Praeger, 1977).

11. The material balance technique has been analyzed in some detail. The classic article is J. M. Montias, "Planning with Material Balances in Soviet-Type Economies," *American Economic Review*, 49 (December 1959), pp. 963-985; for a summary, see Gregory and Stuart, *Soviet Economic Structure and Performance*, p. 163 ff. For a theoretical discussion, see Raymond P. Powell, "Plan Execution and the Workability of Soviet Planning," *Journal of Comparative Economics*, 1 (March 1979), pp. 51-76.

12. This is an important point and represents a sharp difference between the functioning of a planned economy and a market economy. In the market economy, the producing enterprise will normally have supply contracts for required inputs. However, the firm can, with limitations, enter the market either to secure better contractual arrangements or to find a replacement if existing arrangements are interrupted for some reason. In the planned economy, the producing enterprise relies on an interenterprise delivery specified in the annual plan. If this delivery is interrupted for any reason, the producing enterprise has no market to which it may turn. In such cases production is typically interrupted. Unless formal or informal stopgap measures can be taken, the imbalances tend to cumulate throughout the economy.

13. See, for example, A. Katsenelinboigen, "Coloured Markets in the Soviet Union," *Soviet Studies*, 29 (January 1977), pp. 62-85; Vladimir G. Treml, "Alco-

hol in the USSR: A Fiscal Dilemma," *Soviet Studies*, 27 (April 1975), pp. 161–177; and Boris Rumer, "The 'Second' Agriculture in the USSR," *Soviet Studies*, 33 (October 1981), pp. 560–572.

14. The role of the Soviet second economy has been the focus of a major research effort undertaken by Gregory Grossman and Vladimir Treml. The Grossman-Treml project involves interviews with recent Soviet émigrés concerning their personal experiences in the second economy. Gur Ofer and Aaron Vinokur have conducted studies of second economy earnings among Soviet émigrés to Israel and the ongoing Soviet Interview Project headquartered at the University of Illinois is studying second economy earnings among recent Soviet emigrants to the United States.

15. There is a substantial body of literature on the problems of Soviet enterprise management. See Joseph Berliner, *Factory and Manager in the USSR* (Cambridge, Mass.: Harvard University Press, 1957); David Granick, *The Red Executive* (New York: Doubleday, 1960); David Granick, *Managerial Comparisons of Four Developed Countries: France, Britain, United States and Russia* (Cambridge, Mass.: M.I.T. Press, 1972); William J. Conyngham, *The Modernization of Soviet Industrial Management* (New York: Cambridge University Press, 1982); Jan Adam, "The Present Soviet Incentive System," *Soviet Studies*, 32 (July 1980), p. 360.

16. Gregory and Stuart, *Soviet Economic Structure and Performance*, pp. 222–224.

17. Unfortunately, relatively little research has been done on the structure and functions of the Soviet state bank. For a survey, see Paul Gekker, "The Banking System of the USSR," *Journal of the Institute of Bankers*, 84 (June 1963), pp. 189–197; and Christine Netishen Wollan, "The Financial Policy of the Soviet State Bank, 1932-1970" (Ph.D. diss., University of Illinois, Urbana, 1972).

18. Incentives — How to make enterprises do what the center wants — have been the subject of a considerable amount of research. See David Conn, special ed., *The Theory of Incentives*, published as vol. 3, no. 3, *Journal of Comparative Economics* (September 1979); and J. Michael Martin, "Economic Reform and Maximizing Behavior of the Soviet Firm," in Judith Thornton, ed., *Economic Analysis of the Soviet-Type System* (New York: Cambridge University Press, 1976).

19. The rate of turnover of Soviet industrial managers has declined quite significantly in recent years. For evidence, see Granick, *Managerial Comparisons*.

20. For a basic survey of Soviet price policy and citation of the important literature, see Gregory and Stuart, *Soviet Economic Structure and Performance*, pp. 193-202; for an update, see Morris Bornstein, "Soviet Price Policy in the 1970s," in U.S., Congress, Joint Economic Committee, *Soviet Economy in a New Perspective* (Washington, D.C.: Government Printing Office, 1976), pp. 17-66; and Morris Bornstein, "The Administration of the Soviet Price System," *Soviet Studies*, 30 (Octover 1978), pp. 466-490; Morris Bornstein, "Soviet Price Policies," *Soviet Economy* 3, 2 (1987), pp. 96-134.

21. For a discussion of Soviet wage-setting procedures, see Leonard J. Kirsch, *Soviet Wages: Changes in Structure and Administration Since 1956* (Cambridge, Mass.: M.I.T. Press, 1972).

22. See Abram Bergson, *The Economics of Soviet Planning* (New Haven: Yale University Press, 1964), ch. 6.

23. The provision of appropriate manpower to the Soviet economy is a matter of both interest and complexity insofar as it involves analysis of Soviet demographic trends. For a summary of statistical trends, see Murray Feshbach and Stephen Rapawy, "Soviet Population and Manpower Trends and Policies," in

Joint Economic Committee, *Soviet Economy in a New Perspective*, pp. 113–154; for the specific case of agriculture, see Karl-Eugen Wadekin, "Manpower in Soviet Agriculture — Some Post-Khrushchev Developments and Problems," *Soviet Studies*, 20 (January 1969), pp. 281-305. Recent evidence is presented in Murray Feshbach, "Population and Labor Force," in Abram Bergson and Herbert S. Levine, eds., *The Soviet Economy: Towards the Year 2000* (Winchester, Mass.: Allen and Unwin, 1983), pp. 79-111; Jan Adam, ed., *Employment Policies in The Soviet Union and Eastern Europe*, 2nd ed. (New York: St. Martins, 1987).

24. For a brief summary of the socialist attitude toward an interest charge for capital, see A. C. Pigou, *Socialism Versus Capitalism* (London: Macmillan, 1937), ch. 8. For a discussion of Soviet investment planning, see Gregory and Stuart, *Soviet Economic Structure and Performance*, ch. 8. For details, see David A. Dyker, *The Process of Investment in the Soviet Union* (Cambridge: Cambridge University Press, 1983).

25. For a discussion of the rules, see Alan Abouchar, "The New Soviet Standard Methodology for Investment Allocation," *Soviet Studies*, 24 (January 1973), pp. 402-410; P. Gregory, B. Fiedlitz, and T. Curtis, "The New Soviet Investment Rules: A Guide to Rational Investment Planning?" *Southern Economic Journal*, 41 (January 1974), pp. 500-504; Frank A. Durgin, "The Soviet 1969 Standard Methodology for Investment Allocation Versus 'Universally Correct' Methods," *The ACES Bulletin*, 19 (Summer 1977), pp. 29-53; Frank A. Durgin, Jr., "The Third Soviet Standard Methodology for Determining the Effectiveness of Capital Investment (SM-80, Provisional)," *The ACES Bulletin*, 24, no. 3 (Fall 1982), pp. 45-61; and Janice Giffen, "The Allocation of Investment in the Soviet Union: Criteria for the Efficiency of Investment," *Soviet Studies*, 33 (October 1981), pp. 593-609.

26. Recently there has been debate over the extent of repressed inflation in the Soviet Union. See D. H. Howard, "The Disequilibrium Model in a Controlled Economy: An Empirical Test of The Barro-Grossman Model," *American Economic Review*, 66 (December 1976), pp. 871-879; Richard Portes, "The Control of Inflation: Lessons from East European Experience," *Economics*, 44 (May 1977), pp. 109-130; Richard Portes and David Winter, "A Planners' Supply Function for Consumption Goods in Centrally Planned Economies," *Journal of Comparative Economics*, 1 (December 1977), pp. 351-365; and Richard Portes and David Winter, "The Demand for Money and for Consumption Goods in Centrally Planned Economies," *Review of Economics and Statistics*, 60 (February 1978), pp. 8-18.

27. Joyce Pickersgill and Gur Ofer have conducted empirical studies of Soviet saving behavior and have concluded that Soviet citizens appear to save for the same reasons as Westerners do. On this, see Gur Ofer and Joyce Pickersgill, "Soviet Household Saving: A Cross-Section Study of Soviet Emigrant Families," *Quarterly Journal of Economics*, 95 (August 1980), pp. 121-144; and Joyce Pickersgill, "Soviet Household Saving Behavior," *Review of Economics and Statistics*, 58 (May 1976), pp. 139-147. Other scholars see increases in excess demand as the cause of increases in saving. On this, see D. W. Bronson and Barbara S. Severin, "Recent Trends in Consumption and Disposable Money Income in the USSR," U.S., Congress, Joint Economic Committee, *New Directions in the Soviet Economy*, Part II-B (Washington, D.C.: Government Printing Office, 1966); and Igor Birman, *Secret Income and the Soviet State Budget* (Boston: Kluwer, 1981).

28. Paul Craig Roberts, "The Polycentric Soviet Economy," *Journal of Law and Economics*, 12 (April 1969), pp. 163-181.

29. Eugene Zaleski, *Stalinist Planning for Economic Growth, 1932-1952* (Chapel Hill: University of North Carolina Press, 1980).

30. John Wilhelm, "Does the Soviet Union Have a Planned Economy?" *Soviet Studies*, 31 (April 1979), pp. 268-274.

31. Gregory Grossman, "The 'Second Economy' of the USSR," *Problems of Communism*, 26 (September-October 1977), pp. 25-40; Aron Katsenelinboigen, "Coloured Markets in the Soviet Union," *Soviet Studies*, 29 (January 1977), pp. 62-85; Dimitri Simes, "The Soviet Parallel Market," *Survey*, 21 (Summer 1975), pp. 42-52.

32. Vladimir Treml, "Alcohol in the USSR: A Fiscal Dilemma," *Soviet Studies*, 41 (October 1973), pp. 161-177; Dennis O'Hearn "The Consumer Second Economy: Size and Effects," *Soviet Studies*, 32 (April 1980), p. 221.

33. For a discussion of the various forms of agricultural organization, see D. J. Male, *Russian Peasant Organization Before Collectivization* (Cambridge: Cambridge University Press, 1971); and Robert G. Wesson, *Soviet Communes* (New Brunswick, N.J.: Rutgers University Press, 1963).

34. For a survey of thinking on this issue, see Karcz, "From Stalin to Brezhnev."

35. Because the sovkhoz is a relatively straightforward state enterprise operating under the same general principles as the industrial enterprise, relatively little attention has been given to its structure and operation. It is important to note, however, that the sovkhoz is state-owned property but the kolkhoz is an ideologically inferior form of property holding known as kolkhoz-cooperative property. The future legal basis of the kolkhoz is uncertain. Many of the recent changes in the kolkhoz can be explained by the implementation of state policy designed to "improve" the kolkhoz and raise it to the same level as the sovkhoz. It is, however, a matter of speculation whether the kolkhoz will ultimately disappear. In a real sense, its original image has already disappeared.

36. For a detailed discussion of the kolkhoz and the labor day mechanism, see Robert C. Stuart, *The Collective Farm in Soviet Agriculture* (Lexington, Mass.: Heath, 1972). Recent research has supported the view that during the introduction of the collectives there was no increase in the net surplus generated by agriculture. For a discussion of this question, see James R. Millar, "Soviet Rapid Development and the Agricultural Surplus Hypothesis," *Soviet Studies*, 22 (July 1970), pp. 77-93; and M. J. Ellman, "Did the Russian Agricultural Surplus Provide the Resources for the Increase in Investment in the USSR During the First Five Year Plan?" *Economic Journal*, 85 (December 1975), pp. 844-863. For a summary, see Gregory and Stuart, *Soviet Economic Structure and Performance*, ch. 5.

37. For a discussion of the financing of the kolkhozy, see James R. Millar, "Financing the Modernization of Kolkhozy," in Millar, *The Soviet Rural Economy*, pp. 276-303.

38. The standard work on the Machine Tractor Stations is Robert F. Miller, *One Hundred Thousand Tractors* (Cambridge, Mass.: Harvard University Press, 1970).

39. For an in-depth discussion of the private sector in Soviet agriculture, see Karl-Eugen Wadekin, *The Private Sector in Soviet Agriculture* (Berkeley: University of California Press, 1973).

40. For a survey of postwar developments in Soviet agriculture and references to the specialized literature, see Gregory and Stuart, *Soviet Economic Structure and Performance*, ch. 9.

41. Robert C. Stuart, "The Changing Role of the Collective Farm in Soviet Agriculture," *Canadian Slavonic Papers*, 26 (Summer 1974), pp. 145-159.

42. For a survey, see K. E. Wadekin, *Agrarian Policies in Communist Europe: An Introduction* (Totowa, N.J.: Allanheld and Osmun, 1982), ch. 12.

43. Rural income levels are discussed in David W. Bronson and Constance B. Krueger, "The Revolution in Soviet Farm Household Income, 1953-1967," in Millar, *The Soviet Rural Economy*, pp. 214-257; and in more general terms in

Gertrude E. Schroeder and Barbara S. Severin, "Soviet Consumption and Income Policies in Perspective," in Joint Economic Committee, *Soviet Economy
in a New Perspective*, pp. 620-660.

44. For a discussion of subsidies, see W. G. Treml, "Subsidies in Soviet Agriculture:
Record and Prospects," in U.S. Congress, Joint Economic Committee, *Soviet
Economy in the 1980s: Problems and Prospects* (Washington, D.C.: U.S.
Government Printing Office, 1982), pp. 171-186.

45. For a survey of Soviet foreign trade and references to the literature, see Gregory and Stuart, *Soviet Economic Structure and Performance*, ch. 10.

46. For a different view, see Steven Rosefielde, "Comparative Advantage and the
Evolving Pattern of Soviet International Commodity Specialization, 1950-
1973," in Steven Rosefielde, ed., *Economic Welfare and the Economics of
Soviet Socialism* (New York: Cambridge University Press, 1981), pp. 185-220.

47. On this, see Vladimir Treml and Barry Kostinsky, *Domistic Value of Soviet
Foreign Trade: Exports and Imports in the 1972 Input-Output Table*, Foreign
Economic Report No. 20, U.S. Department of Commerce, October 1982.

RECOMMENDED READINGS

GENERAL WORKS

Robert W. Campbell, *The Soviet-Type Economies: Performance and Evolution*, 3rd
ed. (Boston: Houghton Mifflin, 1981).

Paul R. Gregory and Robert C. Stuart, *Soviet Economic Structure and Performance*, 3rd ed. (New York: Harper & Row, 1986).

Franklyn D. Holzman, *The Soviet Economy: Past, Present and Future* (New York:
Foreign Policy Association, 1982).

James R. Millar, *The ABC's of Soviet Socialism* (Urbana: University of Illinois
Press, 1981).

Alex Nove, *The Soviet Economic System*, 2nd ed. (London: Allen and Unwin,
1981).

United States Congress, Joint Economic Committee, *Gorbachev's Economic Plans*,
vols. I and II, (Washington, D.C.: U.S. Government Printing Office, 1987).

SOVIET ECONOMIC HISTORY

E. H. Carr and R. W. Davies, *Foundations of a Planned Economy, 1926-1929*, vol.
I, pts. 1 and 2 (New York: Macmillan, 1969).

R. W. Davies, *The Industrialization of Soviet Russia*, vols. I and II (Cambridge:
Harvard University Press, 1982).

Maurice Dobb, *Soviet Economic Development Since 1917*, 5th ed. (London:
Routledge and Kegan Paul, 1960).

Alexander Erlich, *The Soviet Industrialization Debate, 1924-1928* (Cambridge,
Mass.: Harvard University Press, 1960).

Paul R. Gregory, *Russian National Income, 1885-1913* (New York: Cambridge
University Press, 1983).

Gregory Guroff and Fred V. Carstensen, *Entrepreneurship in Imperial Russia and
the Soviet Union* (Princeton, N.J.: Princeton University Press, 1983).

Moshe Lewin, *Political Undercurrents in Soviet Economic Debates: From Bukharin
to The Modern Reformers* (Princeton, N.J.: Princeton University Press, 1974).

Roger Munting, *The Economic Development of the USSR* (London: Croom Helm,
1982).

Alec Nove, *An Economic History of the U.S.S.R.*, rev. ed. (London: Penguin Books, 1982).

Nicolas Spulber, *Soviet Strategy for Economic Growth* (Bloomington: Indiana University Press, 1964).

THE COMMUNIST PARTY AND THE MANAGER

Donald D. Barry and Carol Barner-Barry, *Contemporary Soviet Politics: An Introduction*, 2nd ed. (Englewood Cliffs, N.J.: Prentice-Hall, 1982).

William J. Conyngham, *The Modernization of Soviet Industrial Management* (New York: Cambridge University Press, 1982).

David Granick, *Managerial Comparisons of Four Developed Countries: France, Britain, United States and Russia* (Cambridge, Mass.: M.I.T. Press, 1972).

Jerry F. Hough and Merle Fainsod, *How the Soviet Union Is Governed* (Cambridge, Mass.: Harvard University Press, 1979).

David Lane, *Politics and Society in the USSR*, 2nd ed. (London: Martin Robertson, 1978).

Leonard Shapiro, *The Government and Politics of the Soviet Union*, 6th ed. (Essex, England: Hutchinson Publishing Group, 1978).

SELECTED ASPECTS OF THE SOVIET ECONOMY

R. Amann and J. M. Cooper, eds., *Industrial Innovation in the Soviet Union* (New Haven: Yale University Press, 1982).

Joseph S. Berliner, *The Innovation Decision in Soviet Industry* (Cambridge: Cambridge University Press, 1983).

Morris Bornstein, ed., *The Soviet Economy: Continuity and Change* (Boulder, Colo.: Westview Press, 1981).

Robert W. Campbell, *Soviet Energy Technologies* (Bloomington: Indiana University Press, 1980).

David A. Dyker, *The Process of Investment in the Soviet Union* (Cambridge: Cambridge University Press, 1983).

Franklyn D. Holzman, *International Trade Under Communism* (New York: Basic Books, 1976).

Alastair McAuley, *Women's Work and Wages in the Soviet Union* (London: Allen and Unwin, 1981).

Mervyn Matthews, *Education in the Soviet Union* (London: Allen and Unwin, 1982).

——, *Poverty in the Soviet Union* (New York: Cambridge University Press, 1987).

James R. Millar, *Politics, Work, and Daily Life in the USSR* (New York: Cambridge University Press, 1987).

Henry W. Morton and Robert C. Stuart, eds., *The Contemporary Soviet City* (Armonk, N.Y.: M. E. Sharpe, 1984).

Robert C. Stuart, ed., *The Soviet Rural Economy* (Totowa, N.J.: Roman and Allenheld, 1983).

Murray Yanowitch, *Social and Economic Inequality in the Soviet Union* (London: Martin Robertson, 1977).

Eugene Zaleski, *Planning Reforms in the Soviet Union, 1962–1966* (Chapel Hill: University of North Carolina Press, 1967).

FOR THE ADVANCED READER

Alan Abouchar, ed., *The Socialist Price Mechanism* (Durham, N.C.: Duke University Press, 1977).

Edward Ames, *Soviet Economic Processes* (Homewood, Ill.: Irwin, 1965).

Abram Bergson and Herbert S. Levine, eds., *The Soviet Economy: Towards the Year 2000* (London: Allen and Unwin, 1983).

Martin Cave, Alastair McAuley, and Judith Thornton, eds., *New Trends in Soviet Economics* (Armonk, N.Y.: M. E. Sharpe, 1982).

Michael Ellman, *Soviet Planning Today: Proposals for an Optimally Functioning Economic System* (Cambridge: Cambridge University Press, 1971).

David Granick, *Job Rights in the Soviet Union: Their Consequences* (New York: Cambridge University Press, 1987).

Donald W. Green and Christopher I. Higgins, *SOVMOD I: A Macroeconometric Model of the Soviet Economy* (New York: Academic, 1977).

John Hardt et al., *Mathematics and Computers in Soviet Planning* (New Haven: Yale University Press, 1977).

Steven Rosefielde, ed., *Economic Welfare and the Economics of Soviet Socialism* (New York: Cambridge University Press, 1981).

Robert C. Stuart, ed., *The Soviet Rural Economy* (Totowa, N.J.: Roman and Allenheld, 1983).

Judith Thornton, ed., *Economic Analysis of the Soviet-Type System* (New York: Cambridge University Press, 1976).

Alfred Zauberman, *Mathematical Theory in Soviet Planning* (Oxford: Oxford University Press, 1976).

APPENDIX 7A:
MEASUREMENT OF OUTCOMES

THE NONMARKET CONTEXT

Throughout this book are many instances in which we wish to examine a particular outcome in an economic system using tools familiar to the market case. For example, suppose that we wish to give empirical content to the familiar proposition that in the Soviet Union there is persistent excess demand for consumer goods, or repressed inflation. In the past, the evidence on this question has largely been partial and anecdotal. Thus we would seek to learn about the complaints of consumers in the Soviet press, opinions about changes in the length of waiting lines, and growth rates of consumer goods output. This approach, which may be inevitable in the absence of data, is nevertheless unsatisfactory.

THE MARKET CONTEXT

If we wish to examine outcomes of the supply of and demand for, say, consumer goods in the market context, a familiar approach would be the specification and estimation of demand and supply equations representing the particular market. Equations 7A.1 and 7A.2 illustrate the demand and supply equations respectively.

$$Q_d = a + bP + cY + u \qquad (7A.1)$$

$$Q_s = d + eP + fC + u' \qquad (7A.2)$$

This model, designed only for illustrative purposes, would allow us to give empirical content to the demand and supply relationships where demand is viewed as a function of prices (P) and incomes (Y) and supply is a function of prices (P) and some measure of production capacity (C). Familiar techniques are available for the estimation of this sort of model.[1]

While this sort of model is generally not discussed in an introductory text in economics, an important proposition underlying the model *is* generally discussed, namely the identification problem. As most discussions of supply and demand emphasize, when we observe prices and quantities in the real world, let us say over time, we are in fact observing a series of equilibrium positions, or intersections of supply curves and demand curves. To take a simple case in which demand is unchanged, but supply is increasing through time, the price-quantity combinations that we would observe would be those represented, for convenience, by the letters A, B, and C in Figure 7A.1.

It is important to note that in this approach, the market clears; at each point in time equilibrium prevails. Suppose, however, that the market does not clear. Let us consider the disequilibrium case.

Figure 7A.1

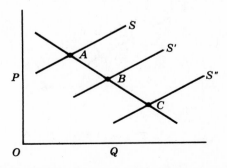

THE DISEQUILIBRIUM CONTEXT

In recent theoretical and empirical work, it has been argued that the equilibrium approach outlined above may be inappropriate due to persistent excess demand.[2] For example, if we consider a simple static case where the price is set by state authorities, the outcome could be represented by Figure 7A.2, where the magnitude of excess demand is given by the distance $Q_s Q_d$ and the prevailing price is set by the state at OP'.

It is quite obvious that in this case we would not, in the real world, observe the intersection of the supply and demand curves when we examined price-quantity combinations. Under the conditions specified in Figure 7A.2, we would observe the state-set price of OP', some rationing device (about which we may or may not have information), and a resulting quantity actually sold, probably Q_s. If we move from this simple case to a more realistic case with persistent excess demand through time, it is clearly possible that the magnitude of the excess demand may change. Could we capture the increased complexity of this disequilibrium case in a formal model? One approach that has been suggested can be represented by equations 7A.3, 7A.4 and 7A.5 below:

$$Q_d = a + bP + cY + u \qquad (7A.3)$$

$$Q_s = d + eP + fC + u' \qquad (7A.4)$$

$$Q = \min(D, S) \qquad (7A.5)$$

Figure 7A.2

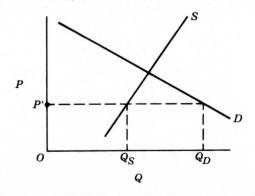

In this particular case, equation 7A.5 is introduced to provide a rule by which the suspected shortage will be handled. Once again, various methods of estimation are available, with price (P) assumed to be exogenous. In this approach, interest centers on the appropriate specification, alternative methods of estimation, and, finally, empirical verification of whether in fact a disequilibrium specification is appropriate.[3]

A more sophisticated variant would include the possibility that if there is excess demand in a particular market at a particular time, planners may (a) have some knowledge about this excess demand and (b) take some steps to lessen its magnitude through time. A number of attempts have been made to construct macroeconometric models of planned socialist economic systems. It is particularly appealing on a number of grounds to consider a model in which planners have available and utilize various policy controls for manipulation of the economic system through time. Although one can imagine a wide array of possible contols, let us, for sake of illustration, cosnider a basic approach suggested by Richard Quandt.[4] Thus, to consider the response of planners over time, we specify a more complex model as follows:

$$Q_t^d = a + bP_t + cY_t + u \qquad (7A.6)$$

$$Q_t^s = d + eP_t + fC_t + u' \qquad (7A.7)$$

$$Q_t = \min(D_t, S_t) \qquad (7A.8)$$

$$P_t - P_{t-1} = g(D_t - S_t) + u'' \qquad (7A.9)$$

In the model presented above in equations 7A.6 through 7A.9, price (P) is again exogenous and is assumed to be the mechanism through which planners make adjustments. Specifically, planners vary price through time depending on the magnitude of the excess demand. While other approaches could be considered, this particular model captures the essence of the Lange adjustment and is thus of more than passing interest.

The disequilibrium approach outlined here is of recent vintage. While there are problems of both specification and estimation, especially in the more complex models, it is nevertheless a promising approach, which has already been applied in a number of cases.

NOTES

1. These models are discussed in any basic econometrics textbook. See for example Henri Theil, *Introduction to Econometrics* (Englewood Cliffs, N.J.: Prentice-Hall, 1978), ch. 20.

2. For example, Western interpretations of the Soviet consumer goods market have generally suggested that while there is excess demand, the turnover tax has been used to bring prices close to the point of equilibrium. One could argue, however, that if prices are in fact "close" to equilibrium, planners would have sufficient knowledge and power to raise prices to equilibrium, thus eliminating the persistent complaints about shortgages. The possibility of persistent excess demand deserves our attention, especially since it is a basic underpinning of the work of Kornai described in Chapter 5.
3. See, for example, Richard E. Quandt, "Tests of the Equilibrium vs. Disequilibrium Hypothesis," *International Economic Review*, 19, no. 2 (June 1978), pp. 435–452.
4. Ibid.

REFERENCES

R. J. Barro and H. I. Grossman, "A General Disequilibrium Model of Income and Employment," *American Economic Review*, 61 (March 1971), pp. 82–93.

W. Charemza and M. Gronicki, *Plans and Disequilibria in Centrally Planned Economies* (New York: Elsevier, forthcoming).

S. M. Goldfeld and R. E. Quandt, "Estimation in a Disequilibrium Model and the Value of Information," *Journal of Econometrics*, 3 (November 1975), pp. 325–348.

———, "Single Market Disequilibrium Models: Estimation and Testing," *The Economic Studies Quarterly*, 32, no. 1 (April 1981), pp. 12–28.

———, "Some Properties of the Simple Disequilibrium Model with Covariance," *Economic Letters*, 1, pp. 343–346.

David H. Howard, *The Disequilibrium Model in a Controlled Economy* (Lexington: Lexington Books, 1979).

———, "The Disequilibrium Model in a Controlled Economy: An Empirical Test of The Barro-Grossman Model," *American Economic Review*, 66, no. 5 (December 1976), pp. 871–879.

Richard Portes and David Winter, "The Demand for Money and for Consumption Goods in Centrally Planned Economies," *Review of Economics and Statistics*, 60, no. 1 (February 1978), pp. 8–18.

———, "The Supply of Consumption Goods in Centrally Planned Economies," *Journal of Comparative Economics*, 1, no. 4 (December 1977), pp. 351–363.

Richard E. Quandt, "Tests of the Equilibrium vs. Disequilibrium Hypotheses," *International Economic Review*, 19, no. 2 (June 1978), pp. 435–452.

H. S. Rosen and R. E. Quandt, "Estimation of a Disequilibrium Aggregate Labor Market," *Review of Economics and Statistics*, 60 (1978), pp. 371–379.

Chapter 8
Yugoslavia: Market Socialism in Practice

Market socialism is one of the three major paradigms discussed in the early chapters of this book. Market socialism is characterized by the combination of some socialist principles (for example, public ownership of the means of production and a rather egalitarian distribution of income) with other typically nonsocialist elements (for example, market allocation and substantial decentralization of decision making).

The market socialist model has considerable appeal because it is often thought to combine the best features of differing systems. A socialist finds it appealing because of the equitable manner in which rewards are distributed, while the nonsocialist finds the efficient utilization of the market attractive. Market socialism is seen as a means of avoiding the bureaucratization of economic life under socialism while at the same time taking into account socialist concerns regarding income distribution, public goods, and externalities.

But, if Yugoslavia is *the* example of market socialism, it is much more than this. Yugoslavia is the major case study of **worker management**, a system in which some control, and hence authority and responsibility over enterprise decision making, rests with the workers or their direct representatives.[1] There is a great deal of interest in worker management, not only in its theoretical underpinnings, but also in its real-world operating characteristics.

At least two other aspects of the Yugoslavian system merit attention. First, Yugoslavia is a relatively underdeveloped country. Yugoslavia ranks closest to Greece and Portugal in per capita income. As a middle-income developing country, Yugoslavia serves as a case study of economic development under market socialism. Second, Yugoslavia's size and regional diversity present a challenge both in its international economic arrangements and its persistent attempts to reduce regional differences.

HISTORICAL PRECEDENTS

The historical evolution of the Yugoslav economic and political system differs from that of other socialist economic systems that we consider in this book. During World War II, the Nazi occupation of Yugoslavia brought with it substantial destruction and considerable population loss. The resistance movement was led by Josip Broz, better known in the West as Tito. Under Tito's leadership, the Yugoslavs liberated virtually all occupied territory themselves. He emerged as the postwar head of the Yugoslav Communist party — or the League of Communists of Yugoslavia (LCY) as the party would later be known. Unlike other rulers in Eastern Europe, Tito was not brought to power by Soviet force. His personal popularity and leadership during the war years were confirmed by a subsequent election. Tito remained as Yugoslavia's leader until his death in 1980.

In spite of these facts, Yugoslavia at war's end began to put together an economic system very similar to that of the Soviet Union. The organizational structure was based on the ministerial system and the Federal Planning Commission had wide powers to implement a national economic plan, the first of which was to begin in 1947. In 1948 without much public discussion, the Soviet Union and Yugoslavia severed relations, and Stalin expelled Yugoslavia from the Cominform (the Communist Information Bureau, precursor of the Warsaw Pact). From 1949 onward, Tito began to build a political and economic system that would one day be viewed as a different road to socialism.

As we examine the contemporary Yugoslav economic system, it is important to bear in mind several facets of its development in the 1950s and thereafter. First, in the absence of any clearly defined theoretical model of a worker-managed economic system, the Yugoslav economic system, like the Soviet system, was carved out largely through practical experience.[2] From its inception, organizational change and experimentation have been the rule rather than the exception. Second, while Yugoslavia is a single-party state, it is very different from the Soviet Union. The precise role of the Communist party in the Yugoslav economic system is still a matter of contention. Yugoslavia's leaders have demonstrated a willingness to change where necessary and to do so with some recognition of pluralistic interests. Regional diversity and strong ethnic differences have precluded the extreme centralization of the Communist party practiced in the Soviet Union and Eastern Europe.

Economic growth has been a major thrust of Yugoslav economic policy since the early 1950s. Thus while Western interest frequently centers on Yugoslav worker management, Yugoslavia is a test also of the degree to which market socialism can generate rapid growth of GNP and an increased standard of living for the population.

THE SETTING

Yugoslavia's population in the mid-1980s of just over 23 million persons is divided equally between rural and urban residence. With a land area of just under 100,000 square miles, Yugoslavia has a mountainous territory roughly the size of the state of Colorado. The country is divided into six republics: Bosnia-Hercegovina, Croatia, Macedonia, Montenegro, Serbia, and Slovenia. Yugoslavia has six distinct regions, six ethnic groups, and three official languages. Yugoslavia also has a long history of ethnic and regional enmity and jealousies.

Although Yugoslavia is not well endowed with natural resources, it does have fossil fuels, coal, iron ore, and bauxite. The natural setting of Yugoslavia plays an important role in understanding its economic system. Endowed with a scenic countryside and beaches, Yugoslavia has maintained a thriving tourist industry.

THE YUGOSLAV ECONOMY: ORGANIZATIONAL ARRANGEMENTS

Yugoslavia began its pursuit of worker management in the early 1950s. Since that time, change has been frequent, but the principle of self-management has endured. (See Table 8.1.) While we wish to avoid the minutiae of political and economic change over time, it is necessary to consider major shifts in economic policy to appreciate the evolution of the Yugoslav system.

As with most reform programs in socialist systems, changes in the Yugoslav economy are identified with formal decrees. Associating changes with formal decrees is artificial. Changes are usually introduced slowly in practice, and seldom follow formal decrees in their entirety.

Between 1952 and 1965, Yugoslavia pursued the development of the worker-managed enterprise. Controls were exercised by an essentially indicative planning system and by state and party mechanisms to promote plan implementation. Basic economic objectives were rapid economic growth, the reduction of regional differences, and integration into the world economy.

The early years of worker management were characterized by a reluctance to decentralize decision making in such areas as investment allocation and the distribution of enterprise profits between worker compensation and retained earnings. In addition, state authorities were inclined to interfere in the price-setting process.

Prior to 1965 the state budget was the major dispenser of capital funds, which were acquired principally through high taxes on industry and agriculture. Investment funds were allocated largely on an administrative and political basis, often to promote regional equality. In fact, the investment decision was the last one to be decentralized and largely freed from strict government control, although state influence has remained strong. Throughout the years, authorities feared that workers would allocate too large a portion of enterprise net income to themselves and too little for reinvestment in plant and equipment. There is theoretical support for this argument as well as empirical evidence that enterprise saving rates have fallen during periods of less strict government rules concerning the distribution of enterprise income.[3] Given the priority attached to the growth objective, one can understand official concern over enterprise saving decisions.

By 1965 the need for reform was apparent. Modifications of the existing system were inadequate to stem the mounting problems. In part, the problems were familiar — inflation, unemployment, and balance of payments problems. In another sense, however, the problems were less familiar. Ellen T. Comisso called the reforms of 1965 "more a decision by default than an act of positive policy."[4] Why describe them in that manner? Simply put, Yugoslav economic policies, particularly the system of controls and external constraints designed to achieve these policies, were not working effectively under changing conditions.

Table 8.1 Yugoslav Economic Reform

Period	Reform Measures
1: End of war to 1948	Rigid centralized planning; emphasis on collective agriculture; minimal use of market resource allocation.
2: 1948-1965	Movement toward worker self-management; privatization of agriculture; indicative planning with extensive state and party interference in management appointments and in price, wage, and capital allocation decisions.
3: 1965 to the mid-1970s	Increased reliance on market allocation; greater freedom for enterprises to make price, wage, and investment allocation decisions; less state and party interference; devolution of government activities to lower levels; continued use of indicative planning.
4: Mid-1970s	Creation of new enterprise arrangements and interenterprise arrangements; indicative planning from the ground up; further devolution of political authority; enlarged role of party and state in promotion of harmony of interests; social compacts and SMAs as instruments of social harmony.
5: 1988	Announced reforms of the tax system, foreign debt rescheduling, and austerity programs in response to the economic crises of the mid-1980s.

Although the state had considerable power over the allocation of investment funds, it did not know how best to distribute these funds to lessen regional differentials. In addition to the ongoing debate on investment policy, there was lack of agreement on macroeconomic policy and on the types of controls that were appropriate to achieve policy objectives.

The economic reform of 1965 introduced two important changes in the Yugoslav economy. First, there was substantial devolution of decision-making authority to the enterprise level and increased reliance on the market as the coordinating mechanism. Second, the role of the state shifted significantly, again in the direction of lessening state control of the economy.

For example, while national economic plans continued to be prepared, they played no directive role in the economy. In addition, control of state funds was shifted downward in the political structure, and efforts were made to reduce the role of the state in enterprise decision making. The enterprise gained increased independence in the distribution of enterprise funds, and a new and more meaningful relationship with banks was established. Less reliance was placed on price controls. Finally, the 1965 reform called for a reformulation of the appropriate role of the Communist party in Yugoslav economic life.

Simply stated, the 1965 reform can be viewed as an effort to establish a truly decentralized model of worker self-management. Enterprises were to be allowed to make most of their own decisions in a market context. The process of resource allocation was to be turned over to the "neutral" mechanism of the market. Some observers even date the real beginning of self-management to the 1965 reform, citing the strong external constraints imposed on enterprises prior to that date.

The reforms of the 1970s were in part political and in part economic.[5] In the political sphere, reform arose largely out of the need to define an appropriate role for the Communist party in Yugoslav society. Its mission was to be rather different from the mission frequently observed in other East European systems. The task of the party would be to harmonize widely divergent interests and to do so with a degree of pluralism — not an easy task.

With Tito's death in May of 1980, the political decentralization of Yugoslavia increased. Lacking a national leader who could overcome the strong regional enmities, the Yugoslavs turned to a collective presidency comprised of representatives from six republics and two regions. This arrangement reflected the wish of the different regions not to be dominated by a strong central government. Each republic and region has veto power over central government action.

It is not difficult to isolate the forces leading to economic reform. The 1970s and early 1980s were difficult periods for most economies, Yugoslavia's included. Many felt that the market was misapplied, and there was considerable dissatisfaction with the increased dependence on market forces introduced in 1965. Yugoslavia suffered from unemployment, inflation, energy shocks, growing internal inequality, and increasing difficulties in the international sphere. Against this background we examine the working arrangements of the Yugoslav economy, beginning with a description of the worker-management system prior to the changes of the 1970s. Then, we examine the impact of recent changes on the system. Finally, we consider more broadly the Yugoslav economy of the 1970s and 1980s, how it has changed, and where it is going in the 1990s. The latter period is especially important as the economic reversals of the 1980s raise questions about the workability of the system.

MICROECONOMIC ORGANIZATION

With the exception of agriculture and enterprises employing fewer than five persons, Yugoslav enterprises are organized as producer cooperatives with worker management as the operational system. Private ownership in retail trade is not allowed. Even government offices and communal and service organizations such as schools and the post office are worker managed.

In the Yugoslav system, the workers do not own outright the assets of the enterprise, rather they hold these assets in trust for society. The highest governing body of the Yugoslav enterprise is the workers' council, a committee of workers elected through secret ballot by the workers at large. In very large enterprises, the workers' council may elect a smaller management committee to handle routine operational matters.

Responsibilities of the workers' councils normally focus on long-range enterprise policy. They include setting wage differentials, establishing smaller decision-making units within the enterprise, and allocating net income among personal incomes, incentive funds, and reinvestment (within limits allowed by law). In a sense, the functions of a workers' council are similar to those of the board of directors of a firm in a capitalist system. However, the members of the workers' council are elected by the workers, not shareholders, and turnover is maintained by not permitting a member to serve more than two consecutive terms.

The enterprise director is chosen by the workers' council generally for a contract period of four years, though the director is usually re-appointed.[6] Openings are supposed to be publicly advertised with a competition for the available positions. However, government officials, the Communist party, and the trade unions have reportedly played an important role in the nominating process. In the early years, many managers were drawn from party ranks.

The enterprise director is charged with overseeing day-to-day operations and is typically empowered to manage production, integrate the work of different production units, make financial reports to the workers' council, and so on. Directors are apparently reappointed regardless of the enterprise's performance, and rarely is a director seeking reappointment subjected to serious competition for the job.

The influence of the enterprise director is generally greater than one might infer. From the point of view of the average worker (revealed in a survey of workers), the manager, his or her staff, and the skilled workers exercise considerably more influence over enterprise decisions than do rank-and-file workers. The director, however, has to contend with a number of outside forces such as the party, the trade unions, and government and bank officials.

What is the prime objective of the Yugoslav enterprise? As we noted in Chapter 5, the theory of worker-managed economies assumes that the objective of worker-managed firms is to maximize an enterprise's net income per worker. According to Joel Dirlam and James Plummer, "There is no doubt that Yugoslav enterprises give heavy weight to the importance of maximizing their workers' incomes. . . . Nevertheless, a remarkably high proportion of enterprises appears to have emphasized growth and, at least since the 1965 reforms, modernization."[7] According to these authors, this is so because Yugoslav workers have had to be concerned with the long-term health of their enterprises, especially in a socialist country with a relatively high unemployment rate. This concern, coupled with official interest in enterprise reinvestment, explains adherence to the growth objective.

Continued losses usually mean the eventual demise of capitalist firms. In Yugoslavia there has been a strong tendency for local authorities and the banks to bail out failing enterprises. The bail-out is typically accomplished by subsidies, tax exemptions, and low-interest loans. In 1968, for example, almost 1,800 enterprises failed to cover personal income obligations and charges and had to be subsidized by the banks and government authorities.[8]

At the other end of the spectrum, a new enterprise can be formed by individuals or partnerships if total employment is less than five. As the enterprise grows, it must be converted into a socialized worker-managed firm, and the former owners are compensated. In other cases, municipal, regional, or national government bodies start up new enterprises and then turn them over to the workers for self-management.

Yugoslav antitrust (cartel) laws are lax. Not only are enterprises allowed to enter into business associations, the structure of the Yugoslav economy does not promote competition among firms. Concentration ratios in Yugoslav manufacturing are probably above those of its Western European neighbors, and the major competitive force is foreign imports,[9] which are subject to numerous restrictions and controls.

Although the system of worker management we have described is fundamental to the Yugoslav economic system, the changes of the 1970s and 1980s have been important and far reaching. While the context of recent changes spans a number of decrees whose ultimate outcome is unknown, we must nevertheless examine these reforms in some detail.

CHANGE IN CONTEMPORARY YUGOSLAVIA

The Yugoslav economy of recent times has been guided by three main acts. First, and possibly most important, a new constitution was promulgated in February 1974. The fourth constitution since World War II, this lengthy document provides for major organizational changes in the Yugoslav economic system. Second, the Associated Labor Law of November 1976 is the fundamental document pertaining to economic activity. Finally, the Foreign Trade Act of 1978 attempts to regularize the conduct of foreign trade in a new framework. The reform proposals issued in 1988 seek to deal with the external and internal macro imbalances that emerged in the 1980s.

The new constitution is important in two main dimensions. First, the overall emphasis on decision making and resource allocation is through **decentralization** at all levels. Powers and responsibilities formerly exercised at the federal level are to be shifted to the republican level, and from the republican level to the local level. In addition, new arrangements within the enterprise and other organizations attempt to shift decision making downward toward the work collective. Indeed, as we shall see, under the new arrangements the issue of defining the enterprise takes on new importance. Second, in addition to shifting the focus of decision making to lower levels within the hierarchy, there is a new emphasis on information flows — specifically on horizontal consultation among subunits in the system. This emphasis, to be achieved through the creation of new organizational and consultative arrangements, must be viewed as an important step in light of the socialist experience with local decision making.

The most important change within the enterprise and other organizations is the creation of a new labor organization at the most basic level. The BOAL or *Basic Organization of Associated Labor* is an association of workers in a factory.[10] Large enterprises may have more than one BOAL. As an example, separate BOALs might be created for the major divisions of the enterprise. The BOALs combine together contractually to form WOALs or *Work Organizations of Associated Labor*. Within the WOAL, however, each BOAL maintains its independence. The members of the constituent BOALs elect the workers' council, which in turn appoints executives. Workers must attend monthly and annual meetings of the BOALs. Rotation of worker council positions (a worker may only serve two consecutive terms) is designed to guarantee widespread participation over time.

In addition to the BOAL and WOAL, the *Composite Organization of Associated Labor* (COAL) is a vertical or horizontal organization consisting of several WOALs.[11] This organization is designed to pursue commercial ventures in which vertical and/or horizontal integration is important. Once again, the autonomy of the participating units is maintained.

In addition to the organizational arrangements within and above the enterprise, all enterprises (and other organizations) belong to the Economic Chambers. These chambers exist at three levels above business associations: first, under federal law, there is the *Yugoslav Chamber of the Economy*; second, there are similar units at the republican and regional levels; and finally, there are chambers at the district and local level.

Broadly speaking, the economic chambers are intended to foster better economic performance. The economic chambers try to enhance productivity by holding discussions in delegate assemblies, the delegates being elected from the participating enterprises. Although the chambers do not have administrative authority or the power to coerce enterprises, it is assumed that contractual arrangements will arise. For example, enterprise plans for firms working in a similar sector of the economy may be harmonized by discussion of plan objectives in the appropriate economic chamber. Agreements of both a binding and a nonbinding nature may arise from these discussions, the intent of which is to guarantee plan fulfillment.

Decision making under these new organizational arrangements is designed to include substantial consultation, both horizontally and vertically. Discussion and consultation among government units, enterprises, social organizations, and other units are formalized in nonbinding agreements or **social compacts**. These social compacts, while nonbinding, give formal expression to policy objectives and focus constituent action on these objectives.

A second and rather different expression of agreement is the SMA or *Self-Management Agreement*. Unlike the social compacts, the SMAs are formal binding agreements, nonfulfillment of which can bring recourse in the courts. The SMAs cover agreements on basic and important questions. For example, within an enterprise, the BOAL would decide how to distribute enterprise income; that decision would be implemented through an SMA. This SMA will then become the guiding law on this particular question with the enterprise.

The basic goal of these reforms is apparent. In a country (and world) wracked by stagflation, oil shocks, and external financial disturbances, "social" controls over enterprise pricing decisions, profit distribution, and investment allocations appear to be essential. Moreover, the increased decentralization of the late 1960s appeared to exacerbate the problem of regional inequality, and autonomous worker-managed enterprises revealed their inclination to favor the allocation of enterprise profits to wage increases rather than to investment. However, from the point of view of identifying the firm, these arrangements are complex.

The Yugoslav policy problem in the mid-1970s and early 1980s was not unlike that of the industrialized capitalist world: how to deal with rampant inflation, rising unemployment, and external disruptions without sacrificing market resource allocation? Like most of the capitalist countries, Yugoslavia has settled on a form of **incomes policy**. The social compacts and SMAs, which call for consultation and negotiation between enterprises and government, attempt to require economic agents to consider the social consequences of output, pricing, and investment decisions. The key to the Yugoslav experiment with incomes policy is the emphasis on the harmonization role played by the state and party and the reliance on voluntarism.

These changes can also be viewed as an effort to deal with a persistent problem of the Yugoslav self-management system; namely, the tendency of workers to prefer wages over reinvesting profits in the enterprise. Obligatory distribution formulas were abandoned in the 1960s, but initially nothing was put in their place. The SMA solves this dilemma because, unlike the nonbinding social compacts, the SMA is a formal binding agreement on the distribution of enterprise profits.

The changes thus outlined clearly will have important long-run and as yet unknown consequences for the Yugoslav economy. The formal thrust is clearly decentralization of decision making, enhanced horizontal consultation, and harmonization of diverse interests through formal and informal agreements.

These reforms did not solve Yugoslavia's problems.[12] On balance, the main difficulties involved decision-making arrangements at the local and enterprise levels. The social compacts, for example, were slow and cumbersome and were unable to function smoothly in light of local differences and local powers. The process of negotiating social compacts and SMAs proved to be very time consuming. Agreements were often concluded after the period under consideration had elapsed. Lack of speedy action was of particular concern where specific problems required timely action.

Problems also arose in other areas. For example, a major goal of Yugoslav economic policy has been to improve the capital allocation process. While the role of the bank in enterprise financial decisions has been reduced, it was not clear that the new arrangements dramatically improved capital allocation. Specifically, to the extent that capital outlays are substantially financed from within the enterprise, the state role in shifting capital funds from one enterprise, sector, or region to another was absent, and local mechanisms such as pooled financing must arise in the case of joint enterprise ventures.

Finally, it remains to be seen whether the price system can play an effective role in enterprise functions. The question of enterprise specialization, size, and structure rests heavily on interenterprise connections, especially the nature of price signals being received by the enterprise. If enterprise decisions are to result in the most effective use of available resources, transfer prices must reflect relative scarcities. It is not clear that this is now the case.

The most interesting feature of the reforms discussed here is the experimentation with building social consensus. Indeed, many economies have striven for this goal. One need only recall the consensus-building aspects of French indicative planning and of West German codetermination. Will the Yugoslav experiment succeed? Observers have already noted a number of sources of friction that make social consensuses difficult: Regional and local authorities want to keep their investment resources at home. Workers prefer to distribute enterprise profits as wages rather than to plow them back as investment. Rates of return may actually be higher in the more developed region; yet national policy calls for investment in the backward regions. In this environment, social consensus will not come easily, especially if the principle of voluntarism is observed.

Unfortunately, it is extremely difficult to build consensus in troubled economic times. When we turn to the performance issue, we see that Yugoslav economic performance was generally good in the 1970s, but markedly less so in the 1980s. This fact, combined with the external search for balance between local institutions and the power of the Communist party, has created an air of uncertainty in the 1980s.

Although our discussion of Yugoslav economic reform has included organizational change beyond the enterprise itself, the important changes external to the enterprise deserve additional attention.

THE YUGOSLAV ENTERPRISE AND EXTERNAL FORCES

In most socialist economic systems, the national economic plan is an important mechanism for allocating resources. The plan includes important directives for all units in the economy and, in addition, provides authorities with the tools necessary to ensure movement toward plan objectives.

Yugoslav planning in the era of worker management has had limited influence on resource allocation, and that influence has declined in recent years. Traditionally, the Federal Planning Office has prepared a five-year and an annual national economic plan setting forth objectives (output, input, employment, prices, and so on) in major sectors of the economy disaggregated to the industry level. The function of this plan has been informational (indicative); it has not been the source of directives for influencing enterprise behavior.

In the 1970s, in addition to the development of competing forecasting arrangements, the planning process changed direction. In the past, plans were prepared at the top and disseminated through the system. Now, the plan is prepared as a consolidation of information flowing up from the bottom, but as before, only for informational purposes. To the extent that local objectives derive from local decision-making arrangements (for example, the SMAs) the accuracy and timeliness of plan information will presumably rely heavily on the success of these local arrangements.

Most systems that use some form of indicative planning rely on fiscal, monetary and other controls to, at a minimum, influence enterprises to achieve plan directives. These sorts of controls have never been particularly strong in Yugoslavia, and their role has declined dramatically in recent years.

The case of monetary policy in general, and investment finance in particular, is instructive.[13] Prior to the 1960s, federal authorities had substantial control over investment in the Yugoslav economy through the General Investment Fund, which was derived in large part from taxation and enterprise profits. In the 1960s, power over the creation and distribution of investment funds was largely shifted to the banks, even though some federal controls were maintained until the late 1960s. Finally, in the 1970s, the thrust was toward reduction of bank influence over enterprises and expansion of the enterprise role in investment financing. The evidence on this issue is unclear, though there seems to have been little increase in the importance of investment financing at the enterprise level.

The usual instruments of monetary control have not been particularly important in the Yugoslav case. While monetary policy is carried out by the National Bank of Yugoslavia at the federal level and by eight banks at the republican and provincial levels, its increased control over credit expansion in the 1960s was not matched by control over enterprise credit expansion. As we have noted, the trend of the 1970s was to expand the enterprise role in this area.

Finally, most observers would agree that a major tool of monetary policy, namely interest rates, has not been important in Yugoslavia. Only in the late 1970s and early 1980s were interest rates raised as a means to control undesirable credit expansion. Low interest rates contributed to capital misallocations.

Fiscal policy in Yugoslavia has primarily aimed at achievement of long-term objectives, not control or elimination of short-run cyclical fluctuations. The reforms of the 1970s reduced significantly the fiscal role of government. Budgets below the federal level account for 80 percent of aggregate government spending in Yugoslavia.[14] Furthermore, in a formal sense, lower levels of government are not permitted to run deficits, which limits their role in stabilization policy. Even funds devoted to promoting economic development in the less-developed regions were shifted from the federal to the republican level in the mid-1970s. The main source of budgetary revenue, the turnover tax, has also been shifted to the republican level.

Another major instrument of control in Yugoslav society is the Communist party, or LCY. Obviously, party members, operating at all levels in the system, are in a position to be an important guiding force, yet the evidence on the nature of this role is mixed. More than any other Eastern European nation, Yugoslavia has attempted to harmonize the relations between the regime and the population. How strong is the LCY in this scenario? Western views differ. Laura D'Andrea Tyson in recent works suggests a limited role for the LCY, arguing that in the past, where differences emerged, the LCY was not able to harmonize diverse interests.[15] John H. Moore, on the other hand, views the LCY as a much more powerful coordinating mechanism, and indeed views past Yugoslav economic growth much more as a policy of the state and the LCY than as a policy of the people.[16]

A recent study of Yugoslavia by Harold Lydall focuses in part on the inherent conflict between self-management and a single monopoly party. Indeed, this conflict remains unresolved as we end the 1980s.

If past experience is any guide, there will be continuing changes in the Yugoslav economic system. Indeed, only after consolidation of the reforms of the 1970s and 1980s will it be possible to understand the role of the LCY. However, its role certainly seems at this time to be different from, and rather less than, that played by similar parties in other East European systems.

LABOR AND CAPITAL ALLOCATION

Capital

Our examination of the Soviet economy singled out labor and capital for discussion largely because of our interest in allocation procedures under central planning and their impact on performance. Since Yugoslavia is fundamentally a market system, we would expect allocation procedures to be more akin to those with which we are familiar.[17] In part this is true, though there are some important and interesting distinctions.

Yugoslavia has generally maintained a very high investment rate more typical of centrally planned systems of Eastern Europe and the Soviet

Union than of market systems.[18] For example, gross domestic investment as a portion of gross domestic product increased from 30 percent
in 1965 to 39 percent in 1985.[19] Between 1965 and 1980, gross domestic investment grew at an average annual rate of 6.5 percent, though
this rate dropped to -.3 percent between 1980 and 1985.[20] As John H.
Moore points out, measurement problems aside, it is evident that
capital accumulation has been a major part of Yugoslav development
strategy and a major contributor to Yugoslav economic growth.[21] Since
we normally associate such high investment ratios with a fairly substantial degree of state and/or plan control over the economy (and in
particular control over investment), it is interesting to speculate on the
respective roles of the state, plan, and enterprise worker-management
system in Yugoslav investment practice.

It will be recalled that some have argued that under a system of
labor-managed enterprises, there may be a tendency to favor distributions to labor rather than capital accumulation. Is there any evidence
on this question in the Yugoslav case?

Although there have been fluctuations, enterprise accumulation has
been important over the years — generally accounting for about one-
third of the funds invested in industry and mining. However, there is
some evidence to suggest in the absence of controls or regulations of
some sort, wage increases tend to be favored over increases in accumulation.[22] In the Yugoslav case, however, evidence on this issue is
clouded by the fact that there are substantial profitability variations by
region, and by industry and enterprise, largely the result of wide performance differences.

The allocation of capital by region and by sector is invariably the
focus of attention. In addition to maintaining a high rate of accumulation, a cornerstone of Yugoslav economic policy has always been the
pursuit of economic growth and the reduction of regional income differentials through the promotion of economic growth and development in
the poorer regions. Although this type of regional policy has tended to
be controversial, a recent study by Tyson suggests that there has been
considerable capital misallocation in Yugoslavia, most notably the
tendency to concentrate further accumulation in sectors that are
already capital intensive.[23] This result, she argues, stems in part from
enterprise regulations, but it can also be attributed to organizational
arrangements that have hampered the regional mobility of capital in
spite of persistent bank power in the allocation process.

In keeping with the general reform program of the 1970s, the investment process has also been decentralized in anticipation of expanded
horizontal consultation at the local level. In addition to decentralization in the control of funds channeled through the government sector,
banks have raised interest rates and have put pressure on enterprises to
finance larger portions of their capital investment programs.

One may wonder why Yugoslav authorities remain so concerned about capital allocation when the Yugoslav investment rate is one of the highest in the world (see Chapter 12). The answer is that the concern is not with the volume of investment but rather with the enterprise's unwillingness to plow back profits and with the misallocation of investment funds. Regional authorities appear to be unwilling to invest their funds in other regions, preferring to keep investment funds within their own boundaries. Although Yugoslavia, as a developing country, is labor rich, enterprises and political authorities appear to favor capital-intensive projects. Why? The Yugoslav system taxes enterprise labor usage heavily and capital lightly. In addition, capital-intensive projects serve to raise the incomes of workers remaining with the enterprise over the long run.

Labor

Labor allocation in Yugoslavia is fundamentally a market process, though the mechanism of worker management and the peculiarities of Yugoslavia present some special problems.

In Yugoslavia, workers in self-managed enterprises are guaranteed a minimum annual wage. The remainder of the annual wage payment depends on enterprise performance. If the enterprise fails to earn enough net income to cover the guaranteed wages, the enterprise must cover them out of reserve funds or the state must subsidize the wage bill. It is the responsibility of the workers' council to establish the system of wage differentials within the enterprise (within limits set by law). This is supposed to be done, as far as possible, on the basis of the employee's contribution to the success of the enterprise (according to the socialist principle of "to each according to his contribution").

Some enterprises are more successful than others, sometimes because of factors having little to do with workers' performance; thus it has been common for workers performing the same task but belonging to different enterprises to receive different wages. This is especially true of enterprises operating with high capital-labor ratios or occupying a dominant market position. However, according to a study by Howard Wachtel, wage differentials are narrower in Yugoslavia than in most Western European countries; so worker management does serve, to some extent, to level the distribution of wages among workers.[24] Evidence from the 1970s and 1980s suggests that Yugoslavia has a distribution of labor income very much like that of Eastern Europe.[25]

Reforms introduced in 1970 established the principles that wage differentials should capture present labor contributions and the portion of *past* labor reinvested in the enterprise, but that differentials due to monopoly power should not be allowed.[26]

Although Yugoslav enterprises are worker managed, this has not eliminated strikes, often called by specific groups of workers, say, unskilled workers, to protest the wage differentials established by the workers' councils. These strikes are often undertaken for their political impact rather than to influence enterprise policy.

Rigidities in the Yugoslav labor market prevent it from being highly fluid. Some rigidities arise from the system of employee compensation. Positions in enterprises with high net income per worker are not freely available and are often rationed out to relatives and friends. Regional enmities prevent workers of one nationality from moving into a region populated by another nationality. On the positive side, one can note that, due to its open border policy, Yugoslavia is a part of the Western European labor market, and this has acted as a pressure valve for young unemployed workers.

Yugoslavia is basically a labor surplus economy, in the sense that labor is more abundant than capital. In spite of the export of Yugoslav workers to Western Europe, unemployment has been a persistent problem at home, a scenario rather different from that of other East European systems. Although the unemployment rate grew in the 1970s and 1980s and regional differentials worsened (suggesting some immobility of labor), nevertheless there was considerable expansion in the number of jobs available and hence the number of Yugoslavs employed in the domestic economy. In part this must have resulted from self-management agreements designed to enhance employment.

Although the supply of labor has typically exceeded the demand for labor in the aggregate, it is difficult to know to what extent market forces influence labor allocation in Yugoslavia. Sharp earnings and unemployment differentials by region and by sector on a continuing basis might suggest that market forces are not strong.

As we have already noted, the distribution of enterprise earnings has increasingly come under the control of the individual enterprise. Thus, the accumulation of revenues is associated with the BOAL typically as a part of a WOAL. While there is a minimum wage and, typically, advances based on anticipated enterprise earnings, adjustments to the advance will be included in an overall self-management agreement covering the particulars of income distribution.

The extent to which wage increases beyond productivity gains may have contributed to inflation in Yugoslavia is a matter of contention.[27] While the distribution of enterprise income seems broadly to conform to the theory of the worker-managed enterprise, pressure exists to expand wage payments rather than accumulation. Empirical evidence supports the view that much strike activity is motivated by the desire for higher wages rather than other social issues handled by the trade unions.[28]

It remains to be seen whether Yugoslavia can create employment and limit wage increases to productivity growth while making more effective use of labor resources. This was a major issue addressed by the reforms of the 1970s.

THE FOREIGN SECTOR

Foreign trade is important to the Yugoslav economy. Like other small and relatively open systems, the Yugoslav economy faced a difficult period in the 1970s when world markets generally collapsed and energy prices soared. The scenario is familiar: In the face of slackening world markets, the Yugoslav economy faced increasingly tight export markets; at the same time, as a major importer of energy and manufactures, imports grew — resulting in persistent annual deficits and the accumulation of a large external debt, the bulk of which is in hard currency. To understand these developments and the Yugoslav response, we must look at the composition of Yugoslav foreign trade, the changing nature of Yugoslav trading arrangements, and the nature of trade policies in the 1970s and 1980s.

Yugoslavia has generally experienced deficits in the merchandise trade balance. These deficits were lessened and sometimes eliminated by surpluses in services, particularly tourism and remittances from Yugoslav workers abroad. The net result, however, was a growing external debt that reached approximately $20 billion by the end of 1985.[29] The bulk of the Yugoslav external debt was financed in world commercial markets although the World Bank and the International Monetary Fund were also involved. What were the major forces underlying this unenviable trade posture?

First, the Yugoslav economy has not performed well in commodity trade. While there were continuing fluctuations in the 1970s, there was a net slackening in the growth of commodity exports with no comparable slackening in the growth of imports.[30] Indeed, recent studies have emphasized the long-term dependence of the Yugoslav economy on imports — especially in key growth areas, such as intermediate goods for industrial production.[31] In addition, Yugoslavia has been heavily dependent on foreign energy sources (the USSR and Iraq) and has also been a major importer of capital goods.

The unattractive posture in merchandise trade has led to and is reflected in important shifts in the regional distribution of Yugoslav trade. In the 1970s and 1980s, the centrally planned economies and especially the Soviet Union grew more important as trading partners of Yugoslavia for two basic reasons. First, Yugoslav exports of manufactures, not particularly competitive in Western markets (and especially noncompetitive in times of Western recession), found ready markets in the East, especially in the Soviet Union. Second, the traditional Western markets for Yugoslav exports weakened substantially. The net result has been an expansion of trade between Yugoslavia and the Soviet Union, which is not attractive as a means to generate hard currency.

Although many would agree that this period has been peculiar in a number of dimensions clearly beyond the control of Yugoslav authorities, the more fundamental question is why Yugoslav exports are not more competitive in world markets. Is this simply a peculiarity of the time or is it a more fundamental (and thus more troubling) feature of the Yugoslav economy?

First, protectionist policies have contributed to difficulties in export markets. For example, even though Yugoslavia has a special agreement with the European Economic Community (EEC), limitations imposed by the EEC are a particular problem for Yugoslavia because its exports are predominantly those of a less-developed nation — that is, food products, raw materials, and the like.

Second, aspects of the domestic Yugoslav economy have hindered the development of competitive exports. Inflation in Yugoslavia during the 1970s substantially raised the cost of Yugoslav products for potential importers.

Third, Yugoslav authorities have not aggressively developed competitive export industries. The mechanisms for domestic capital allocation have favored domestic industries and potential sources of comparative advantage, for example in labor-intensive industries, have not been pursued.

Although specific steps were taken in the late 1970s and 1980s to stabilize the Yugoslav economy and to improve its debt position, the more interesting aspect of the 1970s was the reforms in the foreign trade arrangements and regulations. It is difficult if not impossible to judge the extent to which these changes may be effective in the future.

In keeping with the general trend toward decentralization arising from the new constitution of 1974 and subsequent decrees and laws, decentralization of foreign trade arrangements has also been pursued. In 1977, Communities of Interest for Foreign Economic Relations (CIFERs) were established in the republics and regions (but not at the local level). The BOALs, as members of these CIFERs, would be responsible for planning foreign trade — that is, imports, exports, and the articulation of an overall foreign trade policy at the federal level. Indeed, the Trade Act of 1978 envisaged that any enterprise engaged in foreign trade should become a foreign trade organization with foreign earnings distributed through the CIFER mechanism. The CIFERs have considerable power over the conduct of foreign trade, including planning, import controls, the promotion of exports, distribution of foreign trade earnings, and supervision of self-management agreements in the trade sector. However, it is not yet known whether the CIFERs will be able to harmonize successfully the diverse interests of the enterprises and other groups, develop and articulate a consistent trade policy, and carry out such a policy to the benefit of the Yugoslav economy.

Another major factor in Yugoslav foreign trade has been its exchange rate policy. The Yugoslav dinar is not a fully convertible currency, though convertibility has been a long-term objective. Yugoslav manipulation of the dinar is really dictated by market forces. For example, the dinar was devalued vis-à-vis the U.S. dollar four times in recent years: in 1965, 1971, 1974, and again in 1980. The fact that the dinar was not pegged to the dollar resulted in an average annual depreciation of 1.7 percent. However, as Tyson and Eichler have pointed out in a recent study, when the extent of inflation in Yugoslavia's principal trading partners is taken into account, the dinar turns out to have appreciated relative to the currencies of those countries.[32]

Yugoslavia is an associate in the Organization for Economic Cooperation and Development (OECD) and has a preferential trade agreement with the EEC. In addition, Yugoslavia has been an associate member of COMECON since 1964 and participates in a number of the latter's commissions and banking arrangements. Yugoslav trade policy and posture of the late 1970s and 1980s has been aimed at handling an immediate problem — a mounting external hard currency debt with associated debt-service charges. The foreign trade mechanism of the Yugoslav economy was altered significantly in the 1970s. Only time will tell to what extent the combination of new policies and new trading arrangements can improve the Yugoslav position in the international economy.

AGRICULTURE IN YUGOSLAVIA

During the years immediately following World War II, a reform program implementing producer cooperatives developed in Yugoslavia, though never at the pace exhibited by the Soviet Union during its earlier collectivization drive.[33] At the peak of this movement in 1950, roughly 36 percent of the agricultural land in Yugoslavia was part of a cooperative or a state farm (that is, socialized). However, a law passed in 1953 spelled out the conditions under which peasants could depart from cooperatives, and a steady decline in the number of cooperatives and their membership began. Small peasant farms have been replacing the cooperatives as the dominant form of ownership. Today, approximately 16 percent of agricultural land in Yugoslavia is socialized. The state sector, utilizing worker management, includes large-scale operations and agro-industrial complexes. Although the number of producer cooperatives is limited, Yugoslavia does have a number of general agricultural cooperatives whose functions include technical advice, marketing arrangements, and deliveries of inputs such as fertilizer.

In recent years, agriculture's share in the Yugoslav economy has declined significantly, not unexpected during a period of economic development. For example, between 1965 and 1979, agriculture's share of the Yugoslav labor force declined from just under 50 percent to 34 percent, while agriculture's share of gross national product for the same period fell from just over 25 percent to 20 percent.[34] The average annual rate of growth of agricultural output in the 1970s was approximately 3.6 percent. There were substantial year-to-year fluctuations, however, and for the 1970s, per capita agricultural output grew at an average annual rate of slightly better than 2.5 percent.[35] Average annual growth for the 1980s has been only 1.3 percent.

Although overall output performance of Yugoslav agriculture has been reasonable in recent years, the agricultural sector suffers from a lack of modernization, and especially a dichotomy between the socialized and the private sectors. The basic statistics tell the story. For example, the share of gross fixed agricultural investment in aggregate investment has stood at just over 9 percent for the past fifteen years. This is the lowest share of any country in Eastern Europe and is well below the product share of Yugoslav agriculture. It is not surprising, for the same period, that the level of agricultural output per capita is the lowest in Eastern Europe. Furthermore, in the area of important inputs, for example, fertilizer and tractors, Yugoslavia generally falls well behind other East European countries. Although the rate of growth of these inputs to Yugoslav agriculture has been good, a lot remains to be done.

Through the years, considerable effort has been expended to stimulate Yugoslav agriculture, especially through improvement of prices, expansion of incentives, and so on. At the same time, Yugoslav agriculture has failed to move toward a modern footing in which it would have a smaller share in the economy and a higher level of economic development. This has been a central issue in discussions of the Federal Council for the Problems of Economic Stabilization and doubtless will be the basis of future agricultural policy. That policy, in whatever specific form it may take, will surely focus on the modernization of Yugoslav agriculture, particularly modernization based on agro-industrial integration.

YUGOSLAV ECONOMIC PERFORMANCE

This chapter has listed the economic objectives of the Yugoslav leadership. Rapid economic growth has been a consistent goal because of the underdeveloped nature (relative to Western Europe) of the Yugoslav economy. The maintenance of a "socialist" distribution of income has been another consistent goal, particularly in a socialist country in which much resource allocation is left to the market. A special Yugoslav goal, in light of the vast regional differences in the ethnically diverse nation, has been to reduce regional income differences. Added to these goals are the common macroeconomic goals of full employment, reasonable price stability, and balance of payments equilibrium.

To what extent has Yugoslavia been able to achieve these objectives? Although we compare Yugoslav economic performance with that of other countries in Chapter 12, it is useful to note basic trends here. In doing so, we must emphasize that assessment of economic performance is always difficult because of the problems of measurement. In the Yugoslav case, there is also the serious problem of relating observed performance patterns to the periods when particular Yugoslav economic institutions of worker management existed.

From the 1950s through the 1970s, Yugoslav economic performance, judged by the average annual growth of total and per capita gross national product, was very good. The pace of structural change was rapid and Yugoslavia achieved a "socialist" distribution of income similar to that of other Eastern European systems. Yugoslav economic performance in other areas was less satisfactory. Unemployment was a continuing problem, and the average annual rate of inflation accelerated into the double-digit range. Moreover, regional inequalities apparently sharpened, in spite of policies intended to lessen them.

The decade of the 1980s has been difficult for Yugoslavia. The negative trends noted above have continued, and many of the positive trends have been reversed — partly as a result of recession elsewhere in the world and continuing energy problems. For example, while gross domestic product grew at an average annual rate of 6.5 percent between 1965 and 1980, growth slipped to .8 percent for the period 1980 to 1985.[36] In the same two periods, the average rate of inflation increased from 15.2 percent to 45.1 percent. Moreover, export growth has slowed in the 1980s, and import growth became negative. Yugoslavia's long-term debt increased dramatically from 15 percent of gross national product in 1970 to 35.3 percent in 1985. In addition to new regulations pertaining to foreign exchange, foreign investment in Yugoslavia has been made more attractive. The value of the dinar has fallen steadily against the dollar in the 1980s.[37] Domestic demand has been constrained largely through investment. Gross domestic investment grew at an average annual rate of 6.5 percent between 1965 and 1980, but fell to a rate of negative .3 percent between 1980 and 1985.

The reversals of the 1980s have once again called attention to the relationship between the economic system, reform of the system, and performance. This issue is particularly critical in the Yugoslav case, given the continuing search for a fully workable participatory market socialism.

The Reform Proposals of 1988

The 1965 reforms were aimed at strengthening the role of market resource allocation in Yugoslavia. The reforms of the 1970s were aimed at resolving the macroeconomic instabilities caused by the combination of worker-managed socialism, which were intensified by the world-wide inflations of the 1970s and early 1980s and the stagflation of the same period. Tito's death in 1980 crippled Yugoslavia's ability to map out further economic reforms because regional diversity and enmity reduced the role of the central government, and the Yugoslav communist party disintegrated into regional factionalism.

The 1980s saw rampant inflation, growing foreign debt, and actual declines in real per capita income. The unemployment rate averaged above 10 percent in the 1980s, and real personal income fell a whopping 39 percent between 1980 and 1986. Clearly, the goal of the 1970s reforms to achieve workable social compacts that would resolve the inflation and unemployment problems had not been realized. The root causes of the economic crisis of the 1980s were the tendency of Yugoslav firms to overexpand capacity (higher capital intensity meant more net income per worker), the provision of credit by regional branches of the state bank at low interest rates and according to political needs, the inability of the divided regions to agree on demand-management fiscal policies, the overvaluation of the dinar, and the lack of a strong central bank to control the growth of the money supply.[38]

The crises of the late 1970s and 1980s mobilized the split in Yugoslav leadership to devise a new set of economic reforms in 1988, designed specifically to deal with the macroeconomic imbalances of inflation, unemployment, and trade deficits. A price freeze was put into effect in early 1988. Yugoslavia entered into negotiations with the International Monetary Fund to achieve a rescheduling of Yugoslavia's soaring foreign debt in return for an austerity program that would put Yugoslavia's financial house in order.

The reforms put forward by the collective Yugoslav leadership in 1988 call for import restrictions, incentives to increase domestic savings, reductions in government expenditures on social services, higher interest rates and cost of capital, slower growth of the money supply and the restriction of "grey market" financial transactions, and a more progressive tax system. The Yugoslav national bank is to have greater autonomy and authority and the federal government is to play a larger role in coordinating the budgets of republican and regional governments.

YUGOSLAVIA'S ECONOMIC FUTURE

The Yugoslav market socialist economy is an interesting social experiment. It asks whether the benefits of market allocation can be effectively combined with the social policies of socialism. The difficulties of achieving this mix are apparent from the Yugoslav experience over the past 30 years. It may be that the great regional diversity of Yugoslavia spawned market socialism in the first place because the different regions did not want a strong central authority. It now appears that the lack of central regional authority has created substantial macroeconomic imbalances that defy easy correction. Without a strong central monetary authority, the Yugoslav money supply has been allowed to expand at hyperinflationary rates. Without a national budgeting process, regional budgets have been allowed to expand at inflationary rates. Price controls and interest-rate controls have prevented prices from sending out key scarcity signals, and worker-managed enterprises have been allowed to borrow from sympathetic regional banks at interest rates that do not reflect the scarcity of capital. Attempts to hold worker-managed enterprises to social compacts concerning employment and pricing policies have not succeeded.

Yugoslavia is not the only economy that has suffered economic difficulties in the 1970s and 1980s, but Yugoslavia's problems appear to be especially severe. Whereas inflation has been brought under control in Western Europe, it remains at hyperinflation proportions in Yugoslavia in the absence of price freezes. Unemployment has remained high in Western Europe in the 1980s, but it has remained even higher in Yugoslavia.

NOTES

1. Worker participation can take many forms. The system we have in mind is one in which workers have a voice in decision making within the enterprise but do not own the assets of that enterprise. Though certain types of guarantees and minimums may prevail, the worker is, fundamentally, a residual claimant (after expenses and taxes) to enterprise income.
2. For a discussion of earlier arrangements, see Joel B. Dirlam and James L. Plummer, *An Introduction to the Yugoslav Economy* (Columbus, Ohio: Merrill, 1973); Deborah Milenkovitch, *Plan and Market in Yugoslav Economic Thought* (New Haven: Yale University Press, 1971); Howard Wachtel, *Workers' Management and Workers' Wages in Yugoslavia* (Ithaca, New York: Cornell University Press, 1973); Harold Lydall, *Yugoslav Socialism: Theory and Practice* (Oxford: Clarendon Press, 1984).
3. Laura D'Andrea Tyson, "The Yugoslav Economy in the 1970s: A Survey of Recent Developments and Future Prospects," in U.S., Congress, Joint Economic Committee, *East European Economies Post Helsinki* (Washington, D.C.: Government Printing Office, 1977), p. 945.
4. Ellen Turkish Comisso, *Workers' Control Under Plan and Market* (New Haven: Yale University Press, 1979), p. 75.
5. An excellent survey of the 1970s can be found in Laura D'Andrea Tyson, *The Yugoslav Economic System and Its Performance in the 1970s* (Berkeley: Institute of International Studies, 1980); Laura D'Andrea Tyson and Gabriel Eichler, "Continuity and Change in the Yugoslav Economy in the 1970s and the

1980s," in U.S., Congress, Joint Economic Committee, *East European Economic Assessment*, Part 1 (Washington, D.C.: Government Printing Office, 1981), pp. 139-214.

6. For additional discussion of the role of enterprise directors in Yugoslavia, see David Granick, *Enterprise Guidance in Eastern Europe* (Princeton, N.J.: Princeton University Press, 1975), chs. 11-13.

7. Dirlam and Plummer, *An Introduction to the Yugoslav Economy*, p. 57.

8. Ibid., p. 50.

9. Ibid.

10. In addition to Tyson, *op. cit.*, an excellent source is Janez Prasnikar and Jan Svejnar, "Economic Behavior of Yugoslav Enterprises," in *Advances in the Economic Analysis of Participatory and Labor-Managed Firms*, vol. 3 (Greenwich, CT: JAI Press, Inc., 1988).

11. Ibid.

12. See, for example, Comisso, *Workers' Control*, ch. 6; Tyson, *The Yugoslav Economic System*, ch. 2; Stephen Sacks, "Transfer Prices in Decentralized Self-Managed Enterprises," *Journal of Comparative Economics*, 1, no. 2 (June 1977), pp. 183-193; Prasnikar and Svejnar, *op. cit.*

13. Past investment procedures are discussed in John H. Moore, *Growth with Self-Management* (Stanford, Calif.: Hoover Institution Press, 1980), ch. 8.

14. OECD, *Yugoslavia* (Paris: OECD, 1982), p. 34.

15. See Tyson, *The Yugoslav Economic System*, pp. 27-30.

16. See, for example, Moore, *Growth with Self-Management*; also John H. Moore, "Self-Management in Yugoslavia," in Joint Economic Committee, *East European Economic Assessment*, Part 1, pp. 215-229.

17. A great deal has been written on these issues, especially on capital allocation. For a recent survey of developments and an introduction to basic issues, see Tyson and Eichler, "Continuity and Change in the Yugoslav Economy," pp. 156-164.

18. Ibid., p. 157.

19. World Bank, *World Development Report, 1987* (New York: Oxford University Press, 1987), Table 5.

20. Ibid., Table 4.

21. Ibid., p. 216.

22. See Laura D'Andrea Tyson, "A Permanent Income Hypothesis for the Yugoslav Firm," *Economica*, 44, no. 4 (November 1977), pp. 393-408.

23. See Tyson, *The Yugoslav Economic System*, pp. 39-51.

24. Wachtel, *Workers' Management and Workers' Wages in Yugoslavia*.

25. John R. Moroney, *Income Inequality Trends and International Comparisons* (Lexington, Mass.: Heath, 1979), p. 5.

26. Milenkovitch, *Plan and Market in Yugoslav Economic Thought*, pp. 57-58.

27. For an analysis and discussion of the issue of inflation and unemployment in Yugoslavia, see Laura D'Andrea Tyson, "The Yugoslav Inflation: Some Competing Hypotheses," *Journal of Comparative Economics*, 1, no. 2 (June 1977), pp. 113-146; Michael L. Wyzan and Andrew M. Utter, "The Yugoslav Inflation," *Journal of Comparative Economics*, 6 (1982), pp. 396-405.

28. Abram Bergson, "Entrepreneurship Under Labor Participation: The Yugoslav Case," in Joshua Rosen, ed., *Entrepreneurship* (Lexington, Mass.: Lexington Books, 1982), p. 199.

29. World Bank, *World Development Report, 1987*, p. 233.

30. Between 1965 and 1980, exports of merchandise grew at an average annual rate of 5.6 percent, while imports grew at 6.6 percent. Comparable figures for the period 1980 to 1985 were 2.1 and -3.3 percent respectively. See World Bank, *World Development Report, 1987*, p. 221.

31. For a discussion of recent developments in the foreign sector, see Tyson and Eichler, "Continuity and Change in the Yugoslav Economy," pp. 174-211. This section is based on the discussion by Tyson and Eichler.

32. Ibid., p. 190.

33. For a discussion of these years, see Theodor Bergmann, *Farm Policies in Socialist Countries* (Lexington, Mass.: Lexington Books, 1975), pp. 129-152; Robert F. Miller, "Group Farming Practices in Yugoslavia," in Peter Dorner, ed., *Cooperative & Commune* (Madison: The University of Wisconsin Press, 1977), pp. 163-197.

34. Gregor Lazarcik, "Comparative Growth, Structure, and Levels of Agricultural Output, Inputs, and Productivity in Eastern Europe, 1965-79," in Joint Economic Committee, *East European Economic Assessment*, Part 2, p. 592.

35. Ibid., Table 2; World Bank, *World Development Report, 1987*, p. 205.

36. Data here are from the World Bank, *World Development Report, 1987*, text tables.

37. The Economist, Intelligence Unit, *Country Profile: Yugoslavia 1987–88* (London: The Economist, 1987), p. 9.

38. Kenneth Zapp, "Economic Reforms in Yugoslavia," paper presented at Midwest Economic Association Meeting, Chicago, IL, April 1988.

RECOMMENDED READINGS

GENERAL WORKS

Abram Bergson, "Entrepreneurship Under Labor Participation: The Yugoslav Case," in Joshua Rosen, ed., *Entrepreneurship* (Lexington, Mass.: Lexington Books, 1982)

Ellen Turkish Comisso, *Workers' Control Under Plan and Market* (New Haven: Yale University Press, 1979).

——, "Yugoslavia in the 1970s: Self-Management and Bargaining," *Journal of Comparative Economics*, 4, 2 (June 1980), pp. 192-208.

Milojko Drulovic, *Self-Management on Trial* (Nottingham: Spokesman Books, 1978).

Vinod Dubey, ed., *Yugoslavia: Development with Decentralization* (Baltimore: Johns Hopkins Press, 1975).

Branko Horvat, "Yugoslav Economic Policy in the Post-War Period: Problems, Ideas, Institutional Developments," *American Economic Review*, 61 (June 1971), pp. 70-169.

——, *The Yugoslav Economic System* (White Plains, N.Y.: M. E. Sharpe, 1976).

Harold Lydall, *Yugoslav Socialism: Theory and Practice* (Oxford: Clarendon Press, 1984).

Deborah Milenkovitch, *Plan and Market in Yugoslav Economic Thought* (New Haven: Yale University Press, 1968).

John H. Moore, *Growth with Self-Management: Yugoslav Industrialization, 1952–1975* (Stanford, Calif.: Hoover Institution Press, 1980).

——, "Self-Management in Yugoslavia," in U.S., Congress, Joint Economic Committee, *East European Assessment*, Part 1 (Washington, D.C.: Government Printing Office, 1981), pp. 215-229.

Laura D'Andrea Tyson, *The Yugoslav Economic System and Its Performance in the 1970s* (Berkeley: Institute of International Studies, 1980).

——, "The Yugoslav Economy in the 1970s: A Survey of Recent Developments and Future Prospects," in U.S., Congress, Joint Economic Committee, *East*

European Economies Post Helsinki (Washington, D.C.: Government Printing Office, 1977), pp. 941-998.

Laura D'Andrea Tyson and Gabriel Eichler, "Continuity and Change in the Yugoslav Economy in the 1970s and the 1980s," in U.S., Congress, Joint Economic Committee, *East European Economic Assessment*, Part 1 (Washington, D.C.: Government Printing Office, 1981), pp. 139-214.

THE YUGOSLAV ENTERPRISE

David Granick, *Enterprise Guidance in Eastern Europe* (Princeton, N.J.: Princeton University Press, 1975).

Janez Prasnikar and Jan Svejnar, "Economic Behavior of Yugoslav Enterprises," in *Advances in The Economic Analysis of Participatory and Labor-Managed Firms*, vol. 3 (Greenwich, CT: JAI Press, Inc., 1988).

Stephen Sacks, "Divisionalization in Large Yugoslav Enterprises," *Journal of Comparative Economics*, 4, no. 2 (June 1980), pp. 290-325.

——, *Self-Management and Efficiency: Large Corporations in Yugoslavia* (Boston: George Allen and Unwin, 1983).

Laura D'Andrea Tyson, "Incentives, Income Sharing and Institutional Innovation in The Yugoslav Self-Managed Firm," *Journal of Comparative Economics*, 3, no. 3 (September 1979), pp. 285-301.

INFLATION

Laura D'Andrea Tyson, "The Yugoslav Inflation: Some Competing Hypotheses," *Journal of Comparative Economics*, 1, no. 2 (June 1977), pp. 113-146.

Michael L. Wyzan and Andrew M. Utter, "Comment: The Yugoslav Inflation," *Journal of Comparative Economics*, 6 (1982), pp. 396-405.

AGRICULTURE

FAO, *The Development of Agriculture in Socialist Yugoslavia* (Rome: FAO, 1976).

Miles J. Lambert, "Yugoslav Agricultural Goals for 1976-85," *ACES Bulletin*, 20, no. 3-4 (Fall-Winter 1978), pp. 37-64.

Gregor Lazarcik, "Comparative Growth, Structure, and Levels of Agricultural Output, Inputs, and Productivity in Eastern Europe, 1965-79," in U.S., Congress, Joint Economic Committee, *East European Economic Assessment*, Part II (Washington, D.C.: Government Printing Office, 1981), pp. 587-634.

OECD, *Agricultural Policy in Yugoslavia* (Paris: OECD, 1980).

FOREIGN TRADE

Laura D'Andrea Tyson and Egon Neuberger: "The Impact of External Economic Disturbances on Yugoslavia: Theoretical and Empirical Explorations," *Journal of Comparative Economics*, 3, no. 4 (December 1979), pp. 346-374.

RECENT WORKS

The Economist, Intelligence Unit Ltd., *Country Profile: Yugoslavia 1987–88* (London: The Economist, 1988).
OECD, *Yugoslavia* (Paris: OECD, 1988).

Chapter 9
Variants of Capitalism

We have examined the theories of capitalism and planned socialism, and discussed the major real-world cases — the capitalist economy of the United States, the planned socialist economy of the Soviet Union, and the market socialist system of Yugoslavia. In this chapter, we look at five major variants of the market capitalist model — France, Great Britain, West Germany, Japan, and India. These countries have been chosen because of certain distinguishing features that make each country especially interesting to comparative economists. We discuss these features and present background material about each country so that its special characteristics can be placed in proper historical and analytical context. The structural features of these countries (and of the United States and Soviet Union as well) are presented in Table 9.1.

All of these countries can be classified as market capitalist systems in which the market is the primary mechanism for resource allocation, private ownership is the dominant form of property holding, and material incentives are used to motivate people.

If the economies of these countries are broadly similar, what are their distinguishing characteristics? France is a market capitalist system in which a national economic plan has been used to influence resource allocation. The French plan has been of particular interest as a form of noncoercive or **indicative planning**, although it is difficult to decide whether the improved French economic performance after World War II was achieved because of or in spite of the plan. French indicative planning is an attempt to combine market and plan in a capitalist economic system.

Great Britain is an example of **mature capitalism**. The industrial revolution began in Great Britain in the eighteenth century, so the nation has had almost 200 years' experience as an industrialized capitalist country. Great Britain has experimented with state ownership of basic industries, with redistribution of income through the tax system, with the provision of public services by the state, and with using incomes policies to stabilize the economy. British politics is characterized by strong differences in economic policy between the two dominant political parties that have held power alternately over recent decades. Labor Party governments have favored public ownership and an aggres-

Table 9.1 Selected Structural Features of Economic Systems: A Statistical Overview

Feature	France	Great Britain	West Germany	Japan	India	U.S.	USSR
1. Per capita GNP in U.S. dollars, 1986	13,770	12,680	14,890	13,660	270	17,220	8,370
2. Percentage of population in urban areas, 1985[a]	73	92	86	76	25	74	66
3. Percentage of GDP derived from industry, 1985	34	36	40	41	27	31	34
4. Percent of GDP of public consumption, 1985[b]	18	21	20	10	12	18	20
5. Gross domestic investment as a percentage of gross domestic product, 1985	19	17	20	28	25	19	30
6. Man-days lost to strikes in industry as a percentage of man-days worked in industry, 1975[c]	2.8	1.8	.03	2.5	n.a.	7.0	0[d]
7. Labor force participation rate of women, 1970[e]	50.6	50.8	48.1	55.4	n.a.	48.9	71.0
8. Defense expenditure as a percentage of gross national product, 1980	2.8	4.6	2.7	1.0	2.8	4.9	11.8–15.0[f]

[a] The definitin of *urban* is that which is used in each country and will therefore differ from case to case.

[b] Public consumption is current expenditure by all levels of government for the purchase of goods and services (including capital expenditures for defense) as a percentage of gross domestic product.

[c] These estimates were computed by the authors. They should be regarded as crude estimates, indicating only general orders of magnitude. The problems of definition and measurement are discussed in International Labor Organization, *International Recommendations on Labour Statistics* (Geneva: II O, 1976). Note also that although the incidence of strikes in German manufacturing has been relatively very low, 1975 was an especially low year.

[d] Assumed to be zero.

[e] Data cited in Frederic Pryor, *A Guide Book to the Comparative Study of Economic Systems* (Englewood Cliffs, N.J.: Prentice-Hall, 1985), p. 83.

[f] Computed from U.S., Congress, Joint Economic Committee, *USSR: Measures of Economic Growth and Development, 1950–80* Washington, D.C.: Government Printing Office, 1982), tables A-1, C-4. For discussion of measurement problems, see Abraham S. Becker, "Overview" in U.S., Congress, Joint Economic Committee, *Soviet Economy in the 1980s: Problems and Prospects*, Part 1 (Washington, D.C.: Government Printing Office, 1982), pp. 287–295.

Sources: Unless otherwise noted above, data are from *World Development Report, 1987* (New York: Oxford University Press, 1987). GNP data are from Central Intelligence Agency, *Handbook of Economic Statistics, 1987* (Washington, D.C.: U.S. Government Printing Office, 1987).

sive government role in income redistribution. Conservative govern-ments have favored privatization, deregulation, and a less aggressive state role in redistributing income.

West Germany, which describes itself as a **social market economy**, is of interest because of its attempts to combine market allocation with worker participation and government intervention to achieve social goals. The strong performance of the postwar German economy makes the social market economy model especially interesting.

The Japanese economy is of interest because it has achieved the highest growth rate among the major industrialized capitalist countries. This was accomplished through high rates of capital formation and rapid technological progress. Japan's strong economic performance has made it one of the most important industrialized economies in the world. In considering the sources of Japanese economic success we look at the role of Japanese lifetime-employment policy, state industrial policy in promoting new industries, and government capital formation programs.

India is an example of capitalism in a poor country. In contrast to China, India has chosen a capitalist economic system in combination with a significant degree of state influence through controls and plan-ning to achieve growth and development. Unlike the other capitalist economies that we examine, India demonstrates the role that the capitalist economic system and associated controls play in the early stages of the development process.

In each of these countries, we examine the features that have been of interest to Western observers. Because these features differ considerably so too will our method of examination differ. We focus on the nature of planning in France, but on the broad pattern of development in Japan. We do not attempt to force the cases into a unifying mold as we examine their distinguishing features.

Furthermore, our examination is for the most part divorced from the economic problems occupying current headlines. For example, French indicative planning is less important in the 1980s than it was in the early postwar era, yet it is the experiment with indicative planning and its success or failure that interests comparative economists. Moreover, Great Britain has had a Conservative government from the mid-1970s through the 1980s that has introduced economic policies that could change the basic nature of British capitalism. If these policies are carried through, some of the features of British capitalism highlighted in this chapter may have faded by the 1990s.

FRANCE: INDICATIVE PLANNING IN A MARKET ECONOMY

The post–World War II French economic system is viewed as a signifi-cant test of whether national economic planning and a democratic capitalist society can be effectively and harmoniously combined.[1] For those who believe that some or all of the ills of capitalism require some form of state intervention, the French example has been cited on both practical and theoretical grounds.[2] French planning uses noncoercive intervention while preserving the market economy. Moreover, the French planning mechanism has remained modest in size, an important issue raised by Hayek and others in the socialist controversy.

It is ironic that our primary interest in the French economy centers on its indicative planning, for there has been a significant decline in French interest in planning since the late 1960s. Nevertheless, in the period when the French planning system was being structured and restructured (1949–1969), the economy grew at an average annual rate of 4.7 percent, a very good performance by international standards.[3] Did the French economy achieve this substantial economic progress after the war because of or in spite of national economic planning? To pursue this question, let us examine the background of the French case, the planning mechanism, and its impact on economic outcomes.

France: The Setting

Countries, as representatives of economic systems, possess unique features such as location, size, cultural and historical characteristics, all of which influence the economic system. Although such features of economic development frequently cannot be measured, they may be of great importance in molding the course of events. France, a country whose history and traditions bore heavily on its acceptance of national economic planning, is certainly a case in point.

France is a major world power with a long, rich, and varied history. France has a population of roughly 55 million people residing predominantly in urban areas and a total land area just over twice the size of the state of Colorado. Although France enjoys excellent agricultural conditions, agriculture represents a relatively small portion of gross domestic product (as it is in most developed countries). By international standards, France is a developed country with a high standard of living and a contemporary record of good economic growth.

To understand the French economic system, one must understand the French political system. France is a republic whose president is elected to serve for a term of seven years. The president in turn appoints the prime minister. The National Assembly or Parliament is elected.

Although one might look to earlier times to discover the roots of French thought on the appropriate economic role of the state, it is worth emphasizing that during the Fifth Republic, under the leadership of Charles De Gaulle (1958–1969), the power of the French presidency was substantially enhanced.[4] This power has been retained during the post-De Gaulle era, though its impact on the economy has varied over time.

During the 1970s, with growing concern for inflation, unemployment, and balance of payments problems, austerity was imposed under the leadership of Georges Pompidou and Valery Giscard d'Estaing. This was a period of declining interest in planning as a mechanism to guide recovery. In short, France became less and less interesting as a case of indicative planning.[5]

In the spring of 1981 Francois Mitterrand, a socialist, was elected to the French presidency and a socialist majority was sent to the French National Assembly. Mitterand was reelected in 1988. Although one might have expected a socialist government to be more sympathetic to planning, it is not clear that this has been the case as we shall show.

France and Indicative Planning: The Background

France has a long history of a strong state and, more important, acceptance of a strong role for the state in the management of the nation's economic affairs.[6] This historical experience contrasts sharply with that of the United States, Canada, and Great Britain, where it is an article of faith, at least in most business circles, that the least government is the best government.[7] French history was an important element in the widespread postwar acceptance of planning by many segments of the French population. Indeed, the early development of the plan by M. Jean Monnet (the founder of the European Common Market) was predicated on the acceptance of the plan mechanism by influential business leaders.

The French have tended to view their economy in a rather long-term perspective, emphasizing the primary importance of balanced economic growth and development.[8] Faith in the ability of the unfettered market mechanism to produce economic harmony is not strong. Even within the framework of national economic planning, the French have been willing to utilize mechanisms that are often viewed with skepticism in other countries. For example, the mixed enterprise in which the state and the private sector combine their entrepreneurship and managerial skills has a long history in France. The pattern of interchanging executives between the public and the private sector has facilitated a better understanding of the problems in each sector.[9] For example, the recruitment of top executives for the public sector from the upper echelons of management creates a managerial style very different from that found in Britain.[10]

Although these characteristics of the French economy may have facilitated the introduction and operation of a planning mechanism, such a step represents both practical and theoretical problems for the market economy. Witness, for example, the widespread discussion generated by proposals to introduce mild forms of planning in the United States.[11] Although the U.S. case may be exceptional, the path to national economic planning in capitalist economic systems has generally been slow and unsure.

The basic case for indicative planning — the theoretical underpinning of the French system — rests on the manner in which information guides the economic system in the face of uncertainty.[12] Specifically, it is argued that decision making can be improved if some agency (a "planning" agency) collects, processes, and disseminates information to any and all decision-makers in the economy. The mechanisms for plan implementation are also important. Indicative planning is nonauthoritarian, in the sense that no directive targets are issued and economic agents are encouraged to pursue plan objectives by indirect incentives.

French planning began immediately after World War II, when countries such as England and West Germany were dismantling the controls and planning of the war years. As in other countries that began to experiment with planning at that time, the planning experiment in France subsequently underwent significant change, especially as the economy moved away from the immediate postwar problems toward a period of more "normal" operation. The first plan, begun in 1946 and subsequently extended to 1952, was essentially a transitional plan, closely associated with the name of Jean Monnet.[13] Monnet headed the General Planning Commissariat, working closely with the Marshall Plan, and utilized direct controls to manipulate economic activity.

French planning has changed significantly over the years, largely in response to the changing needs of the French economy. The changes, however, have been mostly in terms of *goals* and the *means* to achieve these goals rather than in the administrative machinery of the plan. In effect, each plan on a five-year horizon has had a theme. The first plan focused on the development of key sectors: transportation, agricultural machinery, steel, electricity, coal, and cement. The second five-year plan emphasized the improvement of productivity. The third was devoted to economic growth and the foreign sector. The plans thereafter departed from the traditional sectoral emphasis and focused instead on improved economic performance in general. They also placed strong emphasis on social goals, lessening income differentials, redressing regional economic imbalances, and so on.

Vera Lutz argues that one should really distinguish between the Monnet and the post-Monnet plans. The former, she argues, were expedient at the time and were based on direct controls. The latter, on the other hand, relied on the indirect mechanisms for implementation that ultimately became the hallmark of French planning.[14]

The Plan Mechanism

The organizational arrangements of French planning remained relatively unchanged from after World War II until the early 1980s, at which time substantial modifications were made. Because the pre-1980s arrangements are important to any assessment of the planning system, we discuss them before noting recent changes.

Historically, French planning relied on an unpretentious institutional structure to forge a social consensus among various interest groups, such as business, trade unions, regions, and so on. The main planning organ was the General Planning Commissariat, a small and relatively modest operation. Under the General Planning Commissariat some thirty "vertical" and "horizontal" modernization commissions were responsible for sectoral projections. The "vertical" commissions dealt with various sectors of the economy, while the "horizontal" commissions dealt with economy-wide matters such as finance. Consultation, a major feature of the French system, was achieved through the work of the Economic and Social Council.

The plan itself was based on a series of alternative projected growth paths for the French economy, including major state priorities, which were formulated by the Planning Commissariat. Subsequent elaboration was developed by the modernization commissions with help from various state agencies. In essence, then, the French plan consisted of rather broad sectoral growth targets relating to input, output, investment, productivity, and so on. These targets were derived from macroeconomic projections for the aggregate economy and included state objectives, but they also recognized important constraints, such as the foreign sector.

Basically, despite the changes made in the 1980s, French planning continues to rely on many traditional features.

Characteristics of Indicative Planning

The traditional French plan, unlike its Soviet counterpart, does not order firms to do things. The plan is indicative; it offers suggested targets at a fairly high level of aggregation. The plan projections are a source of information that, along with traditional market signals, can be used by firms to make decisions. Why would a firm bother to look further at the French plan if it is not compulsory? The mechanisms for plan implementation, both direct and indirect, are another distinctive feature of French planning, a feature that outside observers have discussed with praise and scorn.[15]

The state has two major vehicles for influencing economic outcomes, namely, the budget and public ownership. Not all forms of investment that flow through the state are governed by the national economic plan. Furthermore, the degree of control exercised by the plan agencies over state investment differs substantially, depending on the particular case.[16] Plan control over investment in large public enterprises is considerable, but such control is limited in the case of local government investments.

It is difficult to untangle the budgetary process to measure the impact of the state on investment, especially in light of various changes as plan emphases have changed over the years.[17] Investment by the state (not including public enterprises) has averaged roughly 12 percent of aggregate investment compared to 20–23 percent in Great Britain. French public investment, moreover, has been concentrated in key sectors such as housing.

Like state investments, public ownership in France is concentrated in key sectors such as banking, coal, gas and electricity, transportation, auto and aircraft production. As a producer, consumer, and financier, the state sector of the French economy is in a position to influence economic activity in both the public sector and in the private sector. These mechanisms have varied over time, but the state has influenced the availability and terms for credit, the availability of crucial inputs such as electricity, the regional distribution of resources, tax incentives, and so on.

Plan fulfillment depends on whether firms tend to follow the plan. The logic of the plan suggests that the plan is designed to achieve the best possible French economic performance, consistent with intersectoral harmony. Thus a firm, especially a large firm, operating in harmony with plan directives should be able to do *its* best and to avoid unpredictable constraints. This, if true, is an attractive feature of French planning: the creation of a predictable and harmonious business environment.[18] Evidence suggests that French firms have in fact paid attention to the plans, especially firms sufficiently important to know that the plan may influence their operation.

Monnet argued that a plan is likely to be carried out if those who will be implementing it have a voice in its creation.[19] This aspect of the French system is exemplified by the administrative structure of the plan mechanism, especially the modernization commissions, where traditionally diverse interests (particularly labor, the state, and business) come together to discuss differences and to forge a consensus. The relation between business and the state in France is said to foster an interchange of ideas and understanding where there would otherwise be antagonism — in Great Britain and the United States, for instance.

Events of the 1970s — especially external shocks to the economy — resulted in a loss of interest in the planning mechanism. Then, election of a socialist president in 1981 presented the opportunity for renewed planning activity. Although domestic economic problems and external events continued to keep planning on a back burner throughout the 1980s, some signs of interest in planning appeared.[20]

In the early 1980s, a special commission was set up to assess the French planning system. While this assessment was in progress, external economic conditions resulted in termination of the eighth five-year plan (1981-1985) and its replacement with an interim plan (1982-1983). (Ultimately there was a new, ninth, five-year plan for the years 1984 to 1988.) Although the interim plan reflected the socialist government's policy of expanding the role of the public sector, conditions created by the worldwide recession took priority. French economic policies, therefore, were designed primarily to meet the realities of weak foreign markets, inflation, and unemployment.

The socialist government created a Ministry for Economic Planning and Regional Policy in 1981. Next, a National Planning Commission was established to bring together, in addition to the Minister of Planning, interest groups such as trade unions, regions, and employers for the purpose of spelling out plan priorities and methods of plan fulfillment. Along with these organizational changes, procedural changes were introduced. The new planning process distinguishes between, firstly, the identification of plan objectives and, secondly, designation of the methods by which plan objectives will be achieved. The first phase places new emphasis on realistic macroeconomic projections, while the second is concerned with such mechanisms as regional development, technological advancement, and so forth.

Another change of the 1980s is that regional plans are developed and incorporated into the national plan. In addition, contracts have become an important mechanism for achieving plan fulfillment. One might argue that the recent changes are more an attempt to revitalize planning than to change its basic nature. However, the organizational *framework* of French planning clearly *has* undergone change. The notion of achieving objectives that are spelled out in a national consensus is given new force through the use of contractual arrangements. Moreover, in addition to emphasizing better planning in a number of dimensions, the arrangements of the 1980s harmonize regional and national objectives.

Has French Planning Worked?

The features that have made the French planning system attractive to many, especially its apparent consistency with the values of a Western pluralistic society, would be of little value if the plan did not work. Most observers of the post-World War II French economy would argue that in spite of some problems, the French economic record has generally been very good. Has indicative planning, albeit in a limited form, contributed to that performance?

There are many reasons why it is difficult to assess the impact of the French planning system on economic performance. However, three major issues stand out.

First, the planning system has changed in many ways. For example, in the 1950s planners were concerned with rather specific sectoral goals in what was almost a developmental context. During the 1960s the plan grew more sophisticated and plan objectives broadened. By the 1970s, especially under conservative leadership, interest in planning waned. During that period traditional economic difficulties such as inflation, unemployment, and trade deficits were countered largely by using traditional monetary and fiscal policy.[21] Market allocation was strengthened through the reduction of controls, less emphasis on the public sector, and more attention to the development of efficient capital markets. In a very real sense, it was an era of reduced state intervention in the economy and movement toward an "industrial policy."

Although considerable attention has been paid to changing the planning arrangements in the 1980s the need to resolve macroeconomic problems has overshadowed improvement of the planning system.

A second and closely related issue is the effectiveness of the plan mechanism over time. Some observers argue that French planning has been of limited importance, especially in recent years, because planning is poorly done.[22] Only limited amounts of information are used to generate the plan, and plan objectives are much too simplistic, consisting of single projections. Furthermore, it has been argued that this sort of information has been of little value to industrial firms, even state-owned firms, operating independently of state control. Finally, the 1970s witnessed declining coordination in the business sector, further lessening the potential usefulness of the plan to decision makers.

In the 1980s, there is renewed emphasis on plan execution. Procedures have been established to monitor plan performance. In addition, both public and private sectors are to be more involved in monitoring plan performance, and to receive more information. It is too early to assess the effect of these changes, though preliminary signs indicate that they have done little to enhance the importance of planning.

Third, in a mixed economy like that of France, what indicators can we use to judge the effectiveness of the plan? When specific results are examined, for example sectoral growth targets in the 1950s, there tends to be considerable difference between plan and actual achievement. On this basis, plan performance is rather poor. Other observers, however, focus on more general outcomes, such as the rate of growth of output. There is a tendency to argue that the plan must have had something to do with improved growth.

One way to look at the impact of the plan is to ask business firms, both public and private, the extent to which they have been influenced in their decision making by plan directives. Hans Schollhammer found that, on balance, French firms did consider the plan to be important, especially for the provision of useful information and for the creation of a dynamic business environment.[23] The firms that did pay attention to the plan were for the most part large, capital-intensive, and domestically owned. One could argue that this evidence, in combination with good economic performance in the postwar years, presents a circumstantial case in favor of the French planning system.

Another test would be the record of plan fulfillment. Have the mechanisms of plan implementation been sufficiently strong and the targets sufficiently realistic that plan fulfillment has generally been achieved?

In a study of plan fulfillment, Vera Lutz, a critic of French planning, argues that, on balance, the achievement record of French planning has been dismal.[24] In fact, Lutz argues, the French system of planning is not central planning at all. It is little more than "collective forecasting." Lutz's examination of the plan target and achievement data suggests that the degree to which targets were achieved has varied widely from one target to another and, on balance, has probably not improved over time.

In another major study of French planning, John J. McArthur and Bruce R. Scott argue that "the national planning process did have some influence on the *general* measures and macro-economic programs used by the state to shape the economic environment in which companies and industries worked."[25] McArthur and Scott contend that the plan mechanism has influenced economic outcomes through its *indirect* use of state influence. They suggest that the plan has had very little direct influence on corporate decision making, nor has it had indirect influence through the state's manipulation of selective means of control. They argue that this lack of influence can at least in part be explained by the inability of the planning mechanism to adapt to the changing needs and circumstances of the French economy.

A survey by J. R. Hough suggests that the planning system may have been a factor creating a favorable climate for the good economic growth that France has achieved, at least prior to the energy crisis of the 1970s.[26]

In a survey of the literature on indicative planning and its relation to the French experience, Saul Estrin and Peter Holmes argue that in spite of its theoretical basis, planning in France "lost practically all practical relevance after 1965."[27] Thus Estrin and Holmes emphasize the growing lack of interest in planning, poor planning, and inadequate mechanisms to implement plans.

A useful consensus on the French experience is provided in a study by Stephen S. Cohen.[28] Cohen points out that when economic progress is rapid, it is easy to be generous in interpreting the economic impact of planning. Although we have stressed improved French economic performance, that record changed for the worse in the 1970s. It may be that the plan mechanism did not adapt from its original objective of postwar recovery to the needs of what Cohen describes as "general resource allocation planning." With adverse macroeconomic conditions, the French government has turned to traditional techniques to manipulate economic activity. Failure of those economic policies combined with growing lack of interest in planning, resulted in a virtual cessation of plan adaptation.[29]

Will the reforms of the 1980s change the importance of planning in the French economy? Although it is too early for an answer, Martin Cave suggests that pessimism may be appropriate.[30] Cave notes that many of the reforms of the 1980s (for example, the National Planning Commission) have simply not worked. Moreover, the Mitterand government has not placed confidence in the plan, preferring traditional macroeconomic tools. There is very little evidence to suggest that French planning has regained a position of importance in the French economy.

The French Economy: Approaching the 1990s

The 1980s has been a period of change in the French economy, and yet it would seem that planning has yet to play a major role, even under a socialist government. One might suggest that in the face of continuing economic difficulties, Mitterrand has pursued austerity (or *riguer*) along with change in a socialist context. The latter has involved expansion of the state role through further nationalization and a new social policy.

Although there were some signs of improvement in the French economy by 1983, trends of the 1970s and the early 1980s under the impact of world recession and the domestic energy crisis were viewed as unacceptable. The growth of gross domestic product slowed from an average annual rate of 5.6 percent in the period 1967–1973 to an average annual rate of 2.8 percent in the period 1973–1980.[31] For the period 1980–1985, gross domestic production grew at an average annual rate of 1.1 percent. Unemployment rose from 2.8 percent in 1974 to 8.6 percent in 1982.[32] Inflation increased from an average annual rate of 8.0 percent (1965–1980) to 9.5 percent (1980–1985). For the same two periods, the rate of growth of both exports and imports declined sharply.

In the interim plan (1982–1983), the Socialist regime moved to raise taxes, restrict consumption, and reduce balance of payments deficits, the latter by concentrating on import reduction, export expansion (especially to underdeveloped nations), and devaluations.

The initial years of the Mitterrand government witnessed a substantial increase in the role of government in the French economy. Beginning in late 1981 and early 1982, a policy of nationalization was announced, especially in relation to the large industrial trusts where state involvement was already substantial. Substantial nationalization took place in the banking sector as well.[33]

In a study of the early years of the Mitterrand government, Bela Balassa notes that the public sector share "has risen from zero to 71 percent in iron ore, from 1 to 79 percent in iron and steel, from 16 to 66 percent in other metals, from 16 to 52 percent in basic chemicals, and from zero to 75 percent in synthetic fibers."[34] This certainly constitutes a trend toward greater government involvement in the French economy, evident even in the 1970s. For example, total government expenditure as a portion of gross domestic product grew from 36.7 percent in 1960–1962 to 45.6 percent in 1977–1979. This growth in government share is comparable to that experienced by Great Britain over the same period, but well below that of the United States where the government share grew from 28.5 percent to 33.9 percent. During the period from 1960–1962 to 1977–1979, real public expenditure in France grew at an average annual rate of 6.22 percent.[35]

While it is quite clear that the socialist government of François Mitterrand has moved on a course different from that of his immediate predecessors, there is little agreement on whether these changes are fundamental and far reaching or are of rather minor importance. Throughout the 1980s, France has been faced with the need to address basic and traditional economic problems. Revisions in French economic policies and organizational changes in the planning system, have not fundamentally altered the operation of the French economy.

GREAT BRITAIN: MATURITY, INSTABILITY, AND INCOMES POLICY

Whether rightly or wrongly, the postwar French economy carries an image of success through indicative planning. In contrast, Britain has projected an image of poor economic performance, which is blamed on so-called socialism and, to a lesser degree, the rise of economic planning and control. In fact, Great Britain has had experience with national economic planning only since the early 1960s. Britain's popular classification as a socialist economy derives from general acceptance of the public provision of services such as medical care, use of highly-progressive taxes, and the nationalization of important sectors of the British economy.[36] Postwar British economic performance was generally poor until the 1980s, and the economy has suffered from cyclical instability, imbalance in the foreign sector, and substantial inflation and unemployment.[37]

The 1970s was a difficult decade for Great Britain. There was evidence of stagnation and a continuing search for its causes. Some observers were concerned about the growing role of the state in the economy.

The election of a Conservative government under the leadership of Margaret Thatcher in 1979 was a pivotal point in contemporary British economic history. British economic performance improved in the 1980s under a package of Conservative economic reforms focusing on deregulation, privatization, incentives, and a redefined role for trade unions. It is difficult at this early stage to separate out the effect of these policies from other events, such as the discovery of North Sea oil and gas.

Britain is neither a planned economy, nor a socialist system, according to our definition. The role of the state is significant but not exceptional by European standards (see Table 9.1). It is, however, a mature economy in the sense that it was the first to experience industrialization in the eighteenth century. In addition, it remains at a high level of development in terms of the structure of production, urbanization ratios, and demographic characteristics.[38] Other economies in Western Europe and North America, however, have surpassed Great Britain in terms of some conventional development indicators. Thus by maturity we mean in the British case the longer experience with economic development.

Comparative analysts who look at the British economy often do so for the wrong reasons — for example, to study nationalization, public services, and sharply progressive taxes. These features are important components of the British economy, but they are not unique. Other more successful economies resemble Britain in terms of nationalization, public services, and progressive taxes. We consider a broader question: In the long run, are maturity and stagnation an inevitable combination? What we are looking for is whether a particular combination of economic and political forces can account for Britain's apparent inability to deal with maturity, although a full assessment of the 1980s may eventually change this focus on stagnation.

Great Britain: The Setting

Great Britain is an island economy; its land area is slightly greater than that of the state of Minnesota. Britain's history of achievement and rise to world power has not been matched by good economic performance in contemporary times. Much of the modern literature on the British economy focuses on the reasons for this modest performance, indeed relative decline, in an era of advance for many West European countries.

Great Britain has a population of just over 56 million persons, of which roughly 75 percent live in urban areas. Although Great Britain was the home of the Industrial Revolution and the source of much innovative industrial activity, the resource base of the economy is quite limited. Thus it is not surprising that in modern times the fate of the British economy is very closely tied to performance in the foreign sector. Like other developed countries, the British economy is dominated by the service and industrial sectors. The agricultural sector contributes only a very small fraction of gross domestic product.

Great Britain has limited amounts of good agricultural land. With a relatively large population, intensive land use is essential. While Great Britain has substantial deposits of coal and iron ore, these deposits have been heavily exploited and are not of high quality. From the 1960s through the 1980s attention focused on the discovery of substantial reserves of oil and natural gas in the North Sea and the extent to which these reserves could be effectively utilized to improve and to sustain British economic performance.

Background of the British Economy

Great Britain is an open economy, particularly vulnerable to external shifts over which it has no control. Problems in the foreign sector have been an important theme of the postwar period. As a rough indicator of the importance of the foreign sector to the British economy, note that in 1985, the sum of merchandise imports and exports represented 46 percent of British gross domestic product, while the comparable figure for the United States was 15 percent.

The British concept of an appropriate role for the state in economic affairs is very different from that prevailing, for example, in France.[39] France had experienced economic difficulties in the prewar years and was acutely aware of the need for economic recovery. Whatever the motivating force, the state would play an important role in the direction of the French economy, with planning viewed as the appropriate mechanism. In Britain, however, in spite of substantial war damage, the immediate postwar emphasis was on preserving the independence of small business and interfering with the economy only through fiscal and monetary policy. The Keynesian revolution convinced the British of the superiority of "demand management" over central economic planning. Though impossible to quantify, this attitude about the role of the state has been an important factor in the divergent economic paths taken by France and Britain.

Britain has suffered from rather significant regional inequalities.[40] Certainly, regional inequalities have always existed. Modernization has required the increased mobility of labor and urbanization and has brought the problems of regional differences to the attention of policy makers and the public. The regional question has been at the forefront of British economic policy.

The British political structure is based on strong conservative and labor parties, both of which have a role in the parliamentary structure, thus providing a testing ground for the capitalist and socialist ideologies. Labor policy is said to be basically socialist, particularly on questions of nationalization and income distribution. But there is an erroneous tendency in the West to associate socialism with planning, and this is completely contrary to the British socialist tradition. As Andrew Schonfield points out, "By 1948, the basic elements of modern planning were present in Britain as in no other major Western country."[41] But there it ended until the limited introduction of planning in the 1960s. The basic elements of planning to which Schonfield refers are the Development Councils set up in the late 1940s to exert state control over the private sector, the nationalized sectors, state ownership of the Bank of England, and the wartime experience with planning.[42] All could have been important elements in a comprehensive planning system, but with the advent of a Conservative government in 1951, national economic planning was not seriously discussed for more than a decade.

Probably the most important reason for this delay was the British Labour Party's view of socialism, based on old-style ideological convictions that had no connection to modern economic planning. Furthermore, wartime planning was short-term crisis planning that had little to do with long-term planning of the entire economy. After the war, the wartime controls were phased out, though the nationalized industries (in varying degrees) remained. However, nationalization does not mean planning unless there is a mechanism to coordinate economic activity. In postwar Britain the mechanism was to be predominantly the market.

War damage in Britain (as in France, West Germany, and Japan) was extensive. The war years called for special means to direct British economic activity toward the single purpose of military victory. During the transition to peace, wartime controls were largely replaced by the market mechanism, but there was growing concern for the health of the economy. This concern became, in the middle and late 1950s, an obsession with poor economic performance.[43]

The British experience is, like that of France, a special case. It is a case for which the theoretical underpinning — the economics of maturity — is limited.[44] It is, however, interesting because it is a case that may ultimately be relevant for other mature economic systems.

The British Economy: The Early Postwar Era

When a market economy has been operating for some period under controls, release of those controls can create adjustment difficulties. Such was the case in the immediate postwar British economy. Although British economic performance was relatively good in the late 1940s and early 1950s, the roots of subsequent inadequate economic performance were evident even in these early years. Policy measures taken to offset the subsequent malaise were at best useless and at worst harmful.[45] What were the roots and the dimensions of the impending economic problems?

British economic problems of the 1950s and 1960s are now familiar. The most visible was a growing balance of payments deficit produced in large part by Britain's declining ability to compete in export markets and its overextended aid program. This problem was combined with growing home demand for imports, a slackening though respectable rate of economic growth, and growing regional inequalities surfacing through inadequate mobility of labor and growing unemployment. Rather than treat underlying causes, the British government chose to stimulate and stabilize economic growth through the traditional macroeconomic policy of demand management. Subsequent evidence suggests that the experience was destabilizing, and sufficiently so to describe it as a period of "stop-go" policies.[46] In a sense, however, it was a continuation of the immediate postwar concern for the short run and a neglect of long-run policy remedies.

There have been many explanations of the poor performance of the British economy in the first decade and a half after the war. The main explanations put forward were: inadequate (inflexible) supplies of labor, inadequate investment, poor distribution of investment in non-growth-producing areas, inability of the British economy to move ahead technologically, the burden of progressive taxation, and a heavy defense burden. In addition, demand management was inept and a cause of poor performance. Attention has focused on the foreign sector, notably the growing pressure of imports, worsened by the role of sterling as a key world currency and the apparent inability of Britain to maintain a strong competitive position in world export markets.

Many would consider these features symptoms rather than causes. True, the inability of exports to keep up with the growth of imports was obviously a factor in the balance of payments problems, but why this backsliding in the growth of exports? Above all, why was the British economy in the early postwar years unable to adapt to change? The British managerial structure in industry and the civil service power structure are both molded by tradition, which has for years served in place of expertise. Trade unions, on balance, have probably tended to be skeptical of technological change, seeing it as a factor leading to unemployment. In short, the British economy proved incapable of adapting to its new role in the world economic community and to the new role of the British consumer, whose expectations were high in the 1950s.

The British Economy: Planning in the 1960s

Although the main elements of national economic planning were present in the immediate postwar British economy, the subject received no attention after the election of a Conservative government in 1951 and languished until 1961, when the Conservative government itself introduced a measure of planning to the British economy. Alarm over economic difficulties caused this policy shift, though the instigation of planning meant very little under Conservative guidance and continued to mean little under subsequent Labour leadership.

In a period of generally poor economic performance, a balance of payments crisis in 1961, and concern for the shape of future relations with the emerging European Economic Community, the Conservative government in 1962 established the National Economic Development Council.[47] Both labor and industry generally supported the idea of planning, though each had a different concept of what shape planning might assume. Both, however, shared a rather peculiar view that there must be an "arm's length" relationship between the state and the plan. In addition to the creation of the main plan organization, the NEDC, a professional staff was organized in the newly created National Economic Development Office. Economic development committees (initially about 30) were created as well to serve as a forum for planning discussions by leaders of labor, business, and government.

There were really two economic plans prepared for the 1960s. One, begun in 1962, was to govern the growth of the economy through 1966. The second plan, introduced in 1965 and abandoned in 1966, was to govern the growth of the economy through 1970. Both plans were essentially a sectoral elaboration of a projected aggregate growth rate. According to observers, both were based on inadequate information and had no means of implementation. Both were considered failures.

As Werner Z. Hirsch observes, the years that followed were not really years of economic planning. They were, at least until the mid-1970s, merely a continuation of the British government's effort to develop macroeconomic forecasting and use it to manipulate economic outcomes.[48] The culmination of this exercise was the passage under the Labour government of the Industry Act of 1975, which created the National Enterprise Board and Planning Agreements. The National Enterprise Board was provided with funds to assist private industry and also to extend the scope of the public sector. The Planning Agreements were designed to increase collaboration between the private sector and government and to coordinate government assistance.

In most respects, the British experience with national economic planning was a failure. It did not alter economic outcomes in desired ways. However, as Hirsch points out, it might be more appropriate to consider the experience as one designed to improve communication, information flows, and hence decision making, but not as an exercise in planning per se. What were some of the more general problems of this experience?

First, any planning system must have accurate and up-to-date information. Furthermore, the planners must be privy to state decision making, especially the state budget, which is a crucial element in both plan formulation and execution in a pluralistic society. During the early years of planning, there was no close relationship between NEDC and those making the important decisions in government, especially the treasury. Planners were not even informed of government financial and budgetary decisions.

Second, there was a continuous struggle over how various interest groups — notably unions, corporations, and the state — would be represented. Even if one is skeptical about French claims of harmony, the contrast between the British and the French experience is striking. In Britain, instead of a state plan formulated with the inputs of interest groups and with built-in incentives for fulfillment, the planning structure proved to be a bargaining arrangement with an arm's-length relationship between the state and the planners. Schonfield notes that "the crucial issue in modern capitalist planning, which is the relationship between public power and private enterprise, remains open and undecided in the British case."[49]

Third, powerful tools — bank control over investment, tax incentives, and others — used for plan implementation in France were not brought to bear in Britain. In the British case the state did have a substantial degree of control over state spending and the rate and pattern of investment, but both were directed within a traditional framework of monetary and fiscal policy and neither had much to do with the plan.

Fourth, organizational change, surely a destabilizing element, was frequent, especially with the shifts between Labor and Conservative governments. Throughout the 1960s traditional policy measures continued to be used. Discussion focused more on the necessity for formulating an incomes policy. Personal income rose much more rapidly than gross domestic product.[50] To bring the two into line and to stabilize economic activity, fiscal and monetary policy were used along with efforts to reach agreements with labor and management concerning wage and price increases. Such policies were described as "stop-go" policies in the 1950s, "incomes policies" in the 1960s, and "demand management" thereafter.

The British Disease

Observers of the British economy have identified a number of specific problem areas — investment levels and patterns, a noncompetitive position in export markets, a high burden of taxation, problems in the allocation of labor, and the defense burden — as manifestations or causes of Britain's economic difficulties of the postwar era.

Investment as a proportion of gross domestic product was between 16 and 20 percent, rising somewhat during the 1950s and 1960s. This ratio was well below that of France and West Germany. Furthermore, although government and public enterprises accounted for over 40 percent of domestic capital formation, there is little evidence that the government played any useful role in directing investment activity toward growth-producing sectors or regions. Moreover, the British capital stock (per worker) has been unusually small compared with that of the other countries.[51]

The British tax system has also been singled out as a cause of economic problems. Is the tax burden of the British economy unusually high? The answer to this question is probably in the affirmative. The progressive tax on personal income has been higher in Great Britain than in the United States, but it has been significantly lower in Britain than in the United States for corporations. Furthermore, the disparity between the British personal and corporate tax widened between the 1950s and the 1960s, a change that depressed personal incentives. The loss of skilled professionals (physicians, engineers, and so forth) to other countries during this period is certainly consistent with this interpretation. The outcome of steeply progressive taxation — namely, a lessening of income differentials — can be seen in the British case. Data for the mid-1960s suggests that the income distribution in Britain was narrower than that in West Germany, France, or even Yugoslavia.[52]

Compared to countries such as France, Germany, and Italy, the British economy did not do well in obtaining economic growth from increases in the quality and quantity of the labor force. At the same time, the process of collective bargaining in Britain has been pinpointed as a factor contributing to low industrial productivity. Contrary to the popular concept that Britain is plagued by strikes, for the period 1955–1964 many fewer days were lost (as a portion of employment in key sectors) in Britain to strikes than in France, West Germany, Italy, or the United States.[53] However, this statistic may simply indicate a greater willingness on the part of private and public management to accede to wage and work-rule demands.

Finally, turning to the question of defense burden, the share of gross domestic product devoted to defense in Great Britain has been smaller than that of the United States but considerably larger than that in West Germany, France, or Italy. Although this share of defense spending shifts resources away from other potential uses, it is not clear that it has depressed economic growth.

Nationalization and the Market

To assess British economic performance, it is useful to return to our basic classification of economic systems in terms of the decision-making structure, the mechanisms for information and coordination, property rights, and the incentive system. How might we describe the postwar British economy in terms of these characteristics?

Britain is frequently described as a socialist, if not a planned socialist, economic system.[54] This identification is based on the perception of a substantial role for the state through the budgetary process, nationalized firms in key sectors, and, to a lesser degree, the existence of national economic planning. Although there is no single indicator of the state's role in an economic system, most available evidence supports the view that the role of the state in the British economy has been smaller than generally perceived and does not justify classification of the system as socialist.

A study by Frank Gould of public expenditure patterns in a number of Western industrialized countries sheds light on the growth of government spending.[55] General government spending as a portion of gross domestic product in 1960/62 was 37 percent for France, 33 percent for the United Kingdom, and 28.5 percent for the United States. By the years 1977/79, these shares had risen to 46 percent, 45 percent, and 34 percent, respectively. During this period, real general government expenditures grew at an average annual rate of 6 percent in France, 4 percent in the United Kingdom, and almost 5 percent in the United States. Gould concludes that while state and local government spending has assumed greater importance, the major explanation for the rise in general government spending can be found in the growth of government transfers. As a portion of general government spending, government transfers in 1977/79 represented 60 percent in France, 47 percent in the United Kingdom, and 41 percent in the United States. Public expenditure patterns in the United Kingdom do not appear to be different from other industrialized countries at the aggregate level.

The public sector in Britain has played a substantial role in both savings and investment. Public saving as a portion of aggregate saving in the economy fluctuated from a low of 21 percent (1960) to a high of 46 percent (1950) over the period 1950 to 1966. For the same years, public investment as a portion of total investment fluctuated from a low of 31 percent (1950) to a high of 56 percent (1952) and in recent years has been just over 40 percent. Over these years, public savings has averaged 31 percent of total savings, while public investment has averaged 42 percent of total investment. Judged by the experience of other industrialized countries, these ratios are average or, at best, slightly above average.[56]

Although public enterprise is highly visible in some sectors of the British economy, its overall contribution is really not large.[57] Although the share of public corporations in the capital formation of the public sector has grown (largely at the expense of capital formation by the central government), the contribution of public enterprises to output remains small. In 1950, for example, the net output of the public enterprise sector in Britain accounted for just over 8 percent of British gross domestic product; the equivalent figure for 1967 was just over 7 percent.[58]

It is difficult to judge the overall success of the nationalization experience because in most cases nationalization came about as a result of problems in the particular sectors involved. However, in spite of a continuing conflict among objectives — that is, between financial health and some interpretation of public service or benefit — the former has generally prevailed and it is not clear that the nationalized industries have been especially important in carrying out government economic policies.

The British Economy in the 1970s and 1980s: An End to Stagnation?

Our discussion so far has rated contemporary British performance as rather poor. Indeed this has been the prevalent view. Some have argued that the problems plaguing the British economy are unique to that system, representing the "British disease."[59] Others have argued that the British economy is in a phase of deindustrialization, thought of as a decline in importance of manufacturing.[60]

The negative picture might be summed up in the following way: In spite of a persistent effort to manipulate aggregate demand, economic performance has been inadequate relative to other industralized European economies. This performance gap, it has been argued, stems from a poor labor-management system, poor work attitudes, and a management system incapable of growth and change. These forces, which are deeply ingrained in the British system, resulted in low growth of productivity in manufacturing, an inability to compete in export markets, a growing domestic demand for imports, and the like.

To some degree, the assessment of British economic performance depends on the standards chosen for judgment. For example, the rate of growth of output in Britain in the 1960s was modest when compared to other Western industrialized economies. However, the same can be said for the United States. What seems to be distinctive is the British pattern of change in the 1970s. While most economies experienced problems in the 1970s, British performance was inferior relative to that of other industrialized countries, in particular those of the OECD group.[61]

Real gross domestic product per person grew by 2.4 percent per annum in Britain in the 1960s and by 1.9 percent in the 1970s. Comparable figures for the United States were 2.9 percent and 1.8 percent; for Japan they were 15.9 and 4.8 percent, respectively.[62] In the 1970s Britain lost ground. For example, in 1967, per capita gross domestic product of Great Britain was 86 percent of the OECD average; by 1978, the comparable figure was 72 percent.[63]

Most countries experienced rapid inflation in the 1970s. However, the British rate of inflation generally exceeded that of other Western industrialized economies. Indeed, for most years from the late 1960s through the late 1970s, the rate of inflation in Britain exceeded the average in all OECD countries.

Turning to the question of labor market performance, unemployment increased substantially in the 1970s, though not always to levels experienced in other countries. At the same time, wages increased without concomitant rises in labor productivity. The increasing unit labor costs made British exports less competitive abroad. This latter trend was partially offset by the declining value of the pound sterling. For example, between 1966 and 1977, the average annual increase in unit labor costs in Britain was 11.5 percent, while the comparable figures for Japan, France, and the United States were 8.1 percent, 7.7 percent, and 4.4 percent, respectively.[64] Britain's share in the world export of manufactures declined between 1951/55 and 1973/77 by 11.4 percent. While the United States experienced a comparable decline of 7 percent, West Germany's share grew by 8 percent, Japan's by 9.8 percent, and France's by 0.3 percent.[65]

The analysis of such numbers can proceed indefinitely. What are we to conclude from this exercise? In a study of British economic performance in the 1970s, W. B. Reddaway concluded that the "sick man" view is one-sided, saying that while other economies had done better, "Even in the less satisfactory 1970s the economy made faster progress, in real terms, than in any pre-war decade, and the two previous decades might be regarded as a golden age."[66] At the same time, a Brookings study argued that in the decade between 1967 and 1978, Britain lost ground among OECD countries, markedly so after 1973. The authors conclude: "Britain's economic malaise stems largely from its productivity problem, whose origins lie deep in the social system."[67]

Despite a wide variety of views on the health of the British economy, most agree that British economic performance was poor in the 1970s. The discovery of North Sea oil in the late 1970s and early 1980s was an important factor limiting the bad economic news for Britain. This positive input has a finite life span, however, and continuing improvement must rest on more fundamental changes in the British economy.[68]

As we look at the British economy of the 1980s, much of what has been said above might be viewed as an exercise in economic history. If so, is it a useful exercise? Many would answer in the affirmative, for while the Thatcher programs of the 1980s brought important changes to the performance of the British economy, there is still a nagging feeling that it is, after all, a troubled economy temporarily strengthened by North Sea oil.

British economic policies of the 1980s clearly represent a significant departure from those of earlier years. Such a departure is difficult to evaluate in the short run, although the volume of literature on the subject is already large.[69]

It is not surprising that the conservative focus of the Thatcher government places much of the blame for past performance failures squarely on past economic policies, especially the ambitious role of the government in the British economy. Accordingly, economic policies in the 1980s have been designed to reduce the role of government, and to do so in four important areas.[70]

First, to improve market stability, a monetary policy designed to reduce the rate of inflation was instituted. A reduction in the rate of growth of the money supply was combined with less public-sector borrowing and less use of fiscal policy. This aspect of the Thatcher economic policy became known as a monetarist macroeconomic policy, understandably to be compared to policies of the Reagan administration in the United States. It came to be known officially as the "Medium Term Financial Strategy."

Second, to reinstitute a competitive market economy, government controls and regulations were reduced. This policy, designed to stimulate private market initiative, applied to both the domestic and the international economy.

A third area of focus, related to the issue of a competitive market economy, involved "privatization" or the return of the public sector (especially nationalized industries) to private ownership and operation.

Finally, steps were taken to reduce the powers of trade unions and make them more responsive to their members.

The implementation of these policy measures in the 1980s generated a discussion of great importance. Obviously, the Thatcher government has found implementation difficult. At the same time, British economic performance has improved, though critics suggest that the improvement will be short-lived.[71]

Some success has been achieved in control of inflation: The average annual rate of inflation in Great Britain was 11.2 percent for the period 1965–1980, while for the period 1980–1985, the rate was reduced to 6.4 percent.[72] However, critics charge that this reduction was achieved only at a significant price. First, manufacturing output fell sharply in the early 1980s, although it has recovered in the mid- and late 1980s.

The average annual rate of growth of industrial output fell from 1.2 percent for the period 1965–1980 to 0.6 percent for the period 1980–1985.[73] Second, unemployment increased steadily through the mid-1980s, from single-digit numbers in the 1970s to double-digit numbers in the 1980s.

Have deregulation and the privatization of the British economy succeeded? To the extent the British effort to deregulate can be described as an industrial policy, it has been selective and difficult to evaluate. As one author has noted, British policy is based in large part on the notion that private ownership is in itself sufficient to generate efficient markets; at the same time, however, government support, albeit selective, has increased.[74] For example, the British government has attempted to invigorate regional policy, stimulate industries where advanced technology is important, and stimulate the quality of investment. There has also been substantial privatization of firms, ranging from British Petroleum in the early 1980s, to British Airports, British Airways, and automobile producers in the mid- and late 1980s. The impact of privatization remains unclear. The British government has in effect divested itself of a variety of assets, but it is uncertain whether this transition in ownership will effect major changes in the management of these assets in the future.

Finally, with respect to trade unions, the government has instituted a number of changes in union rules in order to limit unions' power in the economy. In addition, certain social policy reforms aimed at stimulating individual effort have been implemented. These include a reduced tax burden and a strengthened social-security net for specific groups, such as the unemployed. It is difficult to assess the effectiveness of these changes, since they are still in transition. Although there has probably been a reduction of trade union power, critics suggest that this outcome is the result of the economic downturns rather than any specific changes made by the government.[75] Nevertheless, the government can point with pride to a reasonably good rate of economic growth in the 1980s, along with significant gains in productivity.

As we assess the prospects for the future, a number of considerations seem relevant. First, for the economist interested in different economic systems, Britain in the 1980s is clearly making a significant departure from the past. While stagnation and the "British disease" were dominant themes of the 1970s, a shift to the right has introduced new organizational arrangements, new policies, and an underlying faith in the free market economy as a mechanism to stimulate British economic performance. Clearly this experiment bears watching. Many have argued that the gains that have been made are inherently short run, and will not be able to stand the test of time. Critics suggest that gains — the reduction of inflation and the enhancement of productivity — have been made at the expense of other objectives, considered less important by the government, for example, full employment.

Finally, our analysis of the 1980s has not emphasized the international sector. Although foreign competition has had a strong impact on British domestic industry, prevailing trade arrangements, for example, through GATT and the European Economic Community, have dictated stable international economic policies. As many have noted, North Sea oil has been a major bonus to the British economy. For example, the share of fuels and minerals in British exports increased from 7 percent in 1965 to 24 percent in 1985.[76] But, at the same time, while the share of industry in general and manufacturing in particular in British domestic product has slipped considerably in the past twenty years, there has been a sharp reduction in the share of machinery products in British exports.

Thus, time will help us to unravel the significance of the Thatcher experiment of the 1980s, but it will still be difficult to assess the gains and the losses, and even more difficult to place these in perspective vis-à-vis the international sector of the British economy.

WEST GERMANY: THE SOCIAL MARKET ECONOMY[77]

The economy of West Germany, the Federal Republic of Germany, belongs in a discussion of the variants of capitalism for two reasons. The first is that the economic performance of the West German economy is generally perceived to be the strongest of the major European countries throughout the postwar era. West Germany has emerged as the economic leader of Europe. The second reason is West Germany's combination of free market forces with significant state intervention to achieve desired social goals. The Germans label this combination the **social market economy** (soziale Marktwirtschaft) of the Federal Republic.[78] The combination of good economic performance with some of the ideals of a welfare state make Germany an interesting case study.

Background

The Federal Republic of Germany (Bundesrepublik Deutschland) came into existence in the late 1940s as the three allied occupation forces (the United States, England, and France) converted their occupation zones into a unified economic area (Vereinigtes Wirtschaftsgebiet) in 1947. A 1948 currency reform established the three occupation zones as a single currency area; Soviet authorities kept the Soviet occupation zone out of this currency union. This event signaled the splitting of Germany into two Germanys. The Basic Law for the Federal Republic of Germany was passed on June 23, 1949. It established West Germany as federal republic consisting of a federal government (with two legislative houses and a federal bureaucracy of ministries), the states (Länder), and the local governments (Gemeinden). The Federal Republic is a democracy with two major parties, the Christian Democratic Union (CDU) and the Socialist Party (SPD), that have dominated the political scene throughout the postwar era. Along with governmental bodies and agencies, a number of quasi-state organizations such as labor unions, employer organizations, and chambers of commerce are active in economic affairs.

The Federal Republic with its population of 61 million is the largest Western European country, and its GNP is the largest in Western Europe. A member of the European Economic Community and the OECD, it has played an important role in expanding international trade organizations over the past thirty years. West Germany accounts for about 16 percent of the exports and 11 percent of the output of the industrialized capitalist world.

Origins of the Social Market Economy

The social market economy originated in the immediate postwar years. Its intellectual heritage can be traced to the so-called Freiburg school of neoliberalism, the most important representatives being Walter Eucken and Alfred Muller-Armack.[79] The Freiburg school believed that the state should play an active role in ensuring the workability of the competitive market system and the market system should serve as the major instrument for allocating resources. The state should be prepared to intervene, however, to achieve important social goals. Intervention should be compatible with the underlying market order; thus policies that disrupt the working of the market (direct orders, price freezes, and so on) should be avoided.

The political background of the social market economy can be traced to the immediate postwar years of Allied occupation. The initial Allied policy was to continue the wartime controls. Until 1947 the objective of allied policy was to enforce reparations payments and to destroy the German military industry potential. When the emphasis turned to long-term rehabilitation and recovery, direct controls were dismantled and the running of the country's economy was gradually returned to German hands. Ludwig Erhard, the minister of economics during the Adenauer years, was a strong proponent of the teachings of the Freiburg school. He strongly favored decontrol and deregulation and the turning of economic decisions over to the impersonal hands of the market.[80] The choice of market versus plan was heatedly debated, with the social democrats coming out in favor of strong state planning. Memories of the chaos of the inflationary 1920s and the depression of the 1930s had convinced many German politicians of the dangers of a market economy. Two major political events signaled the return to market resource allocation: the Currency Reform and Price Reform of June 1948 and the passage of the Basic Law (Grundgesetz) of the Federal Republic in May 1949, the latter serving as the German constitution. Those events established the principle of the sanctity of private property, which was to serve as the foundation of economic policy in the postwar era.

Unlike the United States, where national economic goals (with the exception of full employment) are unwritten, the economic goals of the Federal Republic have been written into law. These goals are price stability (a stable currency) and full employment, balance of payments equilibrium, and stable economic growth. Three social goals, closely associated with the notion of the social market economy, are also identified in German law — namely, the goals of social equity, social security, and social progress. The social goals provide much of the basis for state intervention in economic affairs in the Federal Republic.[81]

Characteristics of the Social Market Economy

The principal features of the social market economy have evolved over the years. The first principle remains the sanctity of private property. The second is that resource allocation should follow the dictates of the market unless there is a serious confict with national social objectives. In West Germany, there is no significant planning apparatus and the macroplanning that does exist works through traditional monetary and fiscal policy, with principal emphasis on monetary policy as carried out by the Bundesbank (the central bank).[82] German fiscal policy coordinates the budgets of the different levels of government (federal, state, and local). Unlike the United States, where fiscal policy is the responsibility of the federal government, the German "stability law" sets up a Business Cycle Commission (Konjunkturrat) and Finance Planning Commission (Finanzplanungsrat) to coordinate the federal, state, and local budgets for fiscal policy goals. In the area of monetary policy, German policy makers were never strongly caught up in the Keynesian revolution. The Bundesbank is more politically independent than the American Federal Reserve, and a country that has experienced hyperinflation is more likely to see inflation as a monetary phenomenon. Monetarism has been a long-run feature of German macropolicy. The economic forecasting of macroeconomic variables is a relatively recent phenomenon and is done by semi-independent research institutes, which serve as consultants for the federal government. In fact, a striking characteristic of the West German economic apparatus is the virtual absence of planning machinery at the federal level.

In view of the emphasis placed by the Freiburg school on the state's responsibility to ensure the workability of competition, it is informative to see what procompetition arrangements have emerged. Government policies in favor of competition are based on the anticartel law of 1957.

The Law Against Limitations on Competition (Gesetz gegen Wettbewerbsbeschränkungen) makes an interesting contrast with American antitrust legislation. First, the German law is quite specific, and the courts have played a relatively minor role in interpreting the law. Second, the German law singles out labor unions as a clear exception to the anticartel rule. Labor is recognized as being unlike other commodities, and labor's right to form unions is clearly authorized. Third, the German law uses both the Verbotsprinzip (outright prohibition) and the option to correct market abuses. Horizontal cartel contracts and agreements are illegal outright, while firms that occupy market-dominating positions are subject to the control and scrutiny of the cartel authorities. The law provides detailed definitions of "market-dominating" firms based on market shares (33 percent single-firm concentration ratio), financial power, and barriers to entry. Cartel authorities are supposed to disallow mergers if the merger produces a market-dominating firm.

The Law Against Limitations on Competition allows exceptions and exemptions that appear to contradict the basic principles of the social market economy. Agricultural, credit, insurance, transportation, rebate, "structural crisis," and "rationalization" cartels are exempted from the cartel laws. A "structural crisis" cartel, for example, is permitted if there has been a long-term decline in demand that requires the creation of a cartel to salvage an industry. A rationalization cartel can be formed if a cartel is deemed necessary to introduce new technologies into the industry. Critics point out that cartel authorities are placed in the position of having to judge when a structural crisis exists or whether a new technology will be introduced only if a cartel is formed. This practice tends to lessen competition during economic downturns.[83]

The state actively limits competition in a number of areas based on its social responsibilities to the public. Examples of such interventions are strict state regulation of business hours, state support of minimum price legislation for brand-name articles, rent controls, laws that give renters virtual property rights, and government rules on the firing of employees, none of which is very unusual by European standards.

One type of state activity should be singled out — the extensive role played by state (Länder) governments in managing the occupational training of young workers. The chambers of commerce allocate young people into apprenticeships in industry and establish rules whereby local industries are responsible for the training of young workers, at the expense of these industries.

Social Correctives of the Market Economy

In the Federal Republic social correctives of market resource allocations are actively pursued in cases of conflict between private economic
decision making and national social objectives. Such social correctives
occur in five major areas: (1) the security of employment, (2) the protection of employees, (3) insurance against the risks of workers, (4) improvement of the distribution of income, and (5) other measures having
a significant impact on social policy.

The first three instances are typical of most industrialized capitalist
countries and involve programs of employment services; protection
against dangerous employment conditions and protection of teen-age
workers; unemployment, hospitalization and accident insurance; and so
on. The unusual aspects of the German case are that such programs
were instituted so early (under Bismarck in 1881) and that they are so
comprehensive in contemporary terms.

The West German welfare state is highly developed and rapidly expanding. State expenditures as a share of GNP rose from 32.5 percent
in 1960 to about 50 percent in the late 1980s. The share of social expenditures of GNP rose in the same time period from 21 percent to 30
percent. Between 1960 and the mid-1980s expenditures for the state
health insurance system rose by a factor of 10. Critics of the rising
share of government expenditures point to the inefficiencies that such
government programs will eventually produce.

Correctives aimed at improving the distribution of income are more
unusual. In West Germany, progressive income taxes do not serve as the
principal vehicle for making the market-determined distribution of
income more equal. Rather, the objective has been to use other instruments — the promotion of asset formation among lower-income groups,
direct transfer payments (examples are child allowances and subsidization of rental payments), and direct state intervention (government
funding of public housing and obligatory health insurance). Finally,
the state has supported programs to allow workers to share in the
profits of their enterprises as well as to have a say in the conduct of
enterprise affairs (codetermination) — all of which may affect the real
distribution of income.

Let us first consider state policies to promote capital formation in
general and savings of lower income groups in particular. In some instances, the state supplements the savings of low-income families
through a schedule of premiums, especially for savings, that cannot be
withdrawn for seven or more years. Savings for home purchases receive
similar treatment, and employer contributions to employee life insurance or other savings programs receive favorable tax treatment. These
two features, in addition to government programs to ensure workers'
access to the distribution of enterprise profits, seek to render even the

lower-paid workers less dependent on their wage income. Earnings from assets should serve as income supplements. One might note that a side benefit of such pro–capital-accumulation (and anticonsumption) policies is to encourage a high domestic savings rate and a higher domestic growth rate.

In addition to these policies to promote capital formation even among working families, the income distribution is made more equal by direct government interventions. A prime example is the fact that most apartment construction in contemporary West Germany is funded (or sponsored) by state organizations for the purpose of making low-cost housing available to lower income groups.

Codetermination and Labor Unions

An important aspect of government social policy is codetermination (Mitbestimmung). Codetermination means having worker representatives on the boards of directors of corporations. The objective of this policy is "industrial democracy," or forcing management to take workers' interests into consideration when making policy. Initially applied only to selected industries, German law was revised in 1976 to apply codetermination to almost all industry.[84] Firms with two thousand or more employees fall under the codetermination legislation. A separate codetermination law applies to the coal, iron, and steel industries.

According to the law, stockholders and workers should have an equal number of representatives on the board of directors. For example, if the board consists of twelve members, six would be representatives of the stockholders and six would represent the employees. Of the latter, two must be representatives of the labor union and at least one must be a "leading employee" (such as a foreman). The codetermination law requires the election of a chairman (Vorsitzender) of the board of directors. In the absence of a majority, the chaiman is elected by the representatives of the stockholders. In this way, the codetermination law seeks to avoid a stalemate by giving the chairman the deciding vote in the case of an evenly split board. Although labor and stockholders appear to have parity on the board of directors, the stockholders actually have the advantage because of the way in which the chairman is selected and because "leading employees" often side with the stockholders.

The 1976 regulations are still being tested in the German courts. Because codetermination rules call for a nearly equal labor voice, they call into question the protection of private property guaranteed in the German constitution. Another challenge raised against the codetermination legislation is that it puts labor representatives on both sides of the collective bargaining table and thus gives labor an unfair advantage. In steel industry negotiations, however, labor representatives on the management boards have sided with management against the steel workers' demand for a 35-hour workweek. It is not obvious, therefore, how labor representatives will behave when they in fact join management.

The codetermination law provides labor with a voice in major policy decisions, but the board of directors rarely deals with shop-level issues. The Enterprise Constitution Law (Betriebsverfassungsgesetz or BVG) of 1972 gives labor a voice in shop-floor decisions. The BVG requires the election of an enterprise council in enterprises employing five or more workers; "leading employees" are not eligible for election to that council. The enterprise council has codetermination responsibilities in the following areas: wages, length of the working day, firings, and layoffs. The influence of the enterprise council is strongest in personnel areas where every termination requires the approval of the enterprise council.

The BVG law of 1972, on paper at least, substantially constrains management in the area of personnel decisions. How the law works in practice remains to be fully researched. It is not yet known whether most enterprises actually follow the letter of the BVG law. Also, its effect on productivity remains to be measured. On the positive side, worker participation may raise worker loyalty and enthusiasm and reduce turnover; on the negative side, worker participation may prevent management from making necessary personnel changes.

Labor and Collective Bargaining

The right of workers to join together to form trade unions is recognized in the German constitution and the cartel laws. Workers have the freedom to contract with management or management organizations through collective bargaining. The "closed shop" (whereby all workers must belong to the union) is not allowed in Germany. The percentage of the labor force belonging to unions in Germany is approximately 41 percent, much higher than the current American ratio of less than one in five. German unions are organized on an industry basis to prevent competition among individual unions for members. German unions are grouped into federations, the most important being the German Federation of Unions (Deutscher Gewerkschaftsbund), which accounts for 84 percent of all union membership.

Collective bargaining between unions and management generally proceeds at a realtively high level. Unions have the right to strike, and management has the right to lock out (Aussperrungen), or close down, firms in which workers are striking. The volume of strikes is relatively low in Germany (58 days per 1,000 workers per year for the period 1970 to 1979), but it is noteworthy that management has been willing to respond to strikes by lock-outs. For example, 1971 and 1978 were years of relatively high strike activity in Germany. In both years, the number of workdays lost through lock-outs was about two-thirds of the number of workdays lost through strikes. German labor laws do not require compulsory arbitration, but this device is commonly used to settle stalemates. Once unions and management agree to arbitration, they mut hold their peace. Arbitration proposals are not binding, but they do impose strong psychological pressure on the parties to agree.

The low frequency of strikes in Germany and the relatively low nominal wage increases agreed to by unions in the postwar period point to comparatively successful labor-management relations in postwar Germany. Many factors could contribute to this success: the codetermination laws, the role of the enterprise council, and the traditional German fear of inflation.

An interesting feature of German social policy is the notion that problems of income distribution should not be solved by collective bargaining for higher nominal wages by unions and management. Although German workers are organized into powerful unions and the German social democratic party is strongly influenced by organized labor, collective bargaining in West Germany has been more quiescent than it has been in other European countries. Whether the government's social policies can be credited for this fact or whether fear of inflation is at the root, we cannot determine; but the failure of German unions to be more demanding has likely been an important factor in accounting for the lower rates of inflation in West Germany.

Public Enterprise

The role of public enterprise is greater in West Germany than in the United States. State enterprises dominate not only transportation and communication and the construction of apartment dwellings, but there is significant state participation in mining and metallurgy.[85] In some cases, government participation is indirect (as in the recent case of the Krupp industries); in others it is carried out through holding companies. Nevertheless, one cannot cite government enterprise as a unique feature of the German social and market economy, for German experience is quite typical of Europe in general.

In fact, the West German experience with nationalization has been the reverse of the British experience at least prior to the 1980s. In Germany, the emphasis has been upon denationalization (Privatisierung). The Federal Treasury Ministry (Bundesschatzministerium) was established in 1957 to deal with public enterprises. It was set up not as an instrument of central management but rather to lay the foundations for denationalization. The management of public enterprises has typically been decentralized to the enterprise itself. Two methods of denationalization have been used: (1) the sale of formerly public enterprises to private persons or private groups, and (2) social denationalization, which is achieved by establishing a new type of equity, the so-called popular share, to be sold to low-income citizens on a preferential basis. The main denationalizations were those carried out at Volkswagen and Veba.

Union-owned and organized enterprises represent a mix of public and private enterprise. For example, the union-owned Gruppe Neue Heimat was once the largest European apartment construction firm, the Bank fur Gemeinwirtschaft is the fourth largest German interregional bank, and the Coop-Unternehmen forms the second largest retail trade organization in Germany. Officially, these firms were founded to serve the common good, not to maximize profits.

Performance

The annual growth rate of the West German economy averaged 4.5 percent between 1950 and 1987. Its most rapid growth came in the immediate postwar era, with a 1950–1960 growth rate of 8.5 percent The West German investment rate has remained consistently around 25 percent of GNP — one of the highest of an industrialized country. A relatively low unemployment rate accompanied this rapid growth. In the 1950s and 1960s unemployment rates at or below 1 percent were common. The German unemployment rate (like that in other Western countries) has increased since the mid-1970s, reaching 7 percent range in 1987. Consumer prices increased at remarkably low rates for such rapid growth and low unemployment. In the 1950s consumer prices increased at a 2.6 percent rate. In the inflationary 1970s, the German inflation rate was a relatively low 5 percent per annum. In the 1980s, German inflation was under one percent per annum. Relative price stability led to a stable and generally rising exchange rate and a positive trade balance. The outstanding performance of the West German economy, especially during the late 1940s and 1950s has caused analysts to speak of the German "economic miracle" (Wirtschaftswunder).

There is no doubt that the economic performance of West Germany in the postwar era has been excellent, with high rates of economic growth, relatively low rates of inflation, a stable balance of payments, and relatively harmonious labor-management relations. To what extent is this performance the consequence of the choice of the economic system just described?

As is usual in such instances, one cannot provide any unambiguous answers, but one can speculate. One unusual feature of the German system has been the rather intense effort on the part of state policy to promote capital formation, even among lower income groups, while avoiding a steeply progressive income tax. The Federal Republic today has one of the highest national savings rates of the industrialized countries (along with Japan), and this is at least a partial consequence of state policy. The concerted effort to promote investment while restraining consumption seems to have paid off in terms of economic growth and price stability — two of the hallmarks of the German Wirtschaftswunder.

Moreover, German state policy has sought to prevent discord between worker and employer, principally by ensuring the social security of the German worker. Contemporary developments in the area of codetermination can be viewed as a continuation of social reforms begun in the Bismarck era. These policies, combined with the traditional German fear of hyperinflation, have perhaps served to limit the wage demands of German unions, despite their enormous economic and political power.

Prospects

The key problem that faces West Germany in the late 1980s and early 1990s is the potential conflict between the goals of efficiency and social justice. According to its original conception, the social market economy was to be based on market resource allocation combined with social correctives that do not fundamentally alter the principle of market allocation. As in other countries, social correctives are becoming more expensive and more frequent. Social expenditures account for 30 percent of GNP, and the conservative coalition government that has been in power in the 1980s shows few signs of significantly reversing this trend. Medical services and, to a lesser extent, apartment construction are no longer handled by market resource allocation. The key issue, therefore, is whether market allocation will play a less prominent role in the social market economy.

JAPAN: GROWTH THROUGH THE MARKET

Japan is a capitalist economy with a record of exceptional economic performance. Japan's postwar rate of economic growth is the highest of the major industrialized countries. For the admirer of high rates of economic growth, thought to be a hallmark of the early years of planned socialist systems, Japan is cited as a capitalist alternative to the Soviet model for the developing nations. However, in Japan, as in other countries, growth rates have slowed. In the 1980s attention has focused on how, and how well, the Japanese economy can adjust to external shocks from the world economy.

Our discussion of Japan stresses three areas: the historical traditions and special circumstances of Japan; its economic performance; and finally, the explanations by various observers of Japan's impressive growth record.

Background of the Japanese Economy

Japan is a small country with adequate labor but generally limited supplies of natural resources and land. Prior to the Meiji restoration, which began in 1868, Japan was "a fossilized and closed society."[86] Interest in Japanese economic performance centers, therefore, on the period since 1868, though the roots of modern development may be found in the Tokugawa period prior to the Meiji restoration.[87]

Japan, like Great Britain, is an island economy. With a population of approximately 121 million, 75 percent of whom live in urban areas, and a land area slightly smaller than that of the state of California, Japan is densely populated. Japan is a developed economy dominated by the service sector, the industrial sector, and a small agricultural sector.

Japan has a long, varied, and controversial history. Since its defeat in the Second World War, Japan has been governed under a democratic policital system established by the Allied occupation forces. The Japanese parliament (Diet) is elected by the people; it chooses the prime minister, who is the leader of the country.

The Japanese have achieved rapid growth in a country whose natural resource base is minimal. Japan is not well endowed with minerals or fertile agricultural land. Thus Japanese performance must be explained by its economic system, its organizational arrangements, and the people who operate within this system.[88] Between the late 1860s and the early 1900s, Japan developed policy measures for economic growth based on special features of the Japanese system.

There was (and still is) a unity of purpose among the Japanese population, fostered by the state but facilitated by Japanese cultural traditions and history. There is a discipline and devotion to work on the part of the laborers and a degree of paternalism on the part of employers unlike that of other countries. Although it is difficult to pinpoint the sources of this unity, one observer has suggested that a long period of development of the labor market, based on the discipline of the home production process, and the generation of information for an efficient market combined to create an efficient and disciplined worker.[89]

Second, the state has performed important functions. The figures in Table 9.1, with the possible exception of state ownership, suggest a rather modest role for the state in the Japanese economy. Such statistics may understate the role of the state in the postwar Japanese economy. For example, in the crucial area of capital formation, the government has played a key role, not only in promoting savings and investment, but also in encouraging foreign capital, important in the early years of Japanese development.

Although the rate of capital formation in postwar Japan has been much higher than in other capitalist economies, the *direct* state role has been smaller than in other nations. Government purchases have also been smaller proportionally than in any of these countries. The state role, then, has been the stimulation of *private* investment through strong incentives such as low tax rates, proinvestment state financial policy, and a limited state role in the provision of social services.

The role of the Japanese state as a purchaser was important in earlier times, especially in its capacity as an entrepreneur — a role that carries over to present-day Japan. This state function has been important not only in getting industry started, but also in focusing investment in growth sectors, at the best scale of operation, and utilizing the best available technology.

Third, historical experience is crucial to understanding modern economic growth in Japan. During the Meiji restoration, the Japanese economy was opened up to Western technology. Enrollment in formal educational programs increased rapidly, as did participation in the labor force, and a "dual economy" developed. The dual economy consisted of a large, increasingly modern, industrial sector requiring skilled labor alongside relatively primitive industrial operations using labor with minimal skill levels.

Agricultural development accelerated during this period, and technological progress and the expansion of conventional inputs (labor and fertilizer) were important to creating an agricultural surplus. Agriculture's role in Japanese development — in particular, the use of high taxation to extract the surplus — remains a matter of controversy.[90]

Fourth, military activity has been an important factor. The rapid pace of development after the 1860s through World War I was fostered in part by military spending. Thereafter, at least until 1946, war was a dominant theme. The Second World War warped the structure of production and led to an economy governed by controls and, later manipulated by the American occupation forces. American occupation policies were primary land reform (large holdings were broken up), deconcentration of industrial ownership, the introduction of trade unionism, and an end to the military commitment.[91] All had important implications for Japan's development in the postwar period. No simple set of features can explain Japanese growth.

Japanese Economic Growth

Japanese economic growth is compared to that of other countries in Chapter 12. However, since rapid growth is a salient feature of the Japanese case, let us consider its underlying features.

Although the Japanese economy has been growing rapidly for a long time, the interesting facet of this record, as Kazushi Ohkawa and Henry Rosovsky emphasize, is the accelerating trend of economic growth at a particularly high level. The rate of growth of output of the Japanese economy in the postwar years has been exceptionally high by international standards, averaging close to 10 percent per annum. This rate meets or exceeds even those of such rapidly growing countries as West Germany and the Soviet Union. However, as noted earlier, growth rates through the 1980s have been much slower, though certainly respectable by international standards.

The Japanese economy is a capitalist market economy, in which national economic planning has played only a marginal role. One cannot look to extramarket mechanisms, like planning, to explain Japanese growth. What, then, has led to this impressive economic performance? It is very difficult, in any economic system, to isolate the key features that have influenced economic performance. However, the path-breaking work of Ohkawa and Rosovsky identifies two general influences: those that are narrowly economic and those of a broader nature.[92] Let us examine each in turn.

The economic explanations for postwar (and earlier) Japanese economic development, according to Ohkawa and Rosovsky, were a technology gap, a high rate of capital formation, and the availability of appropriate labor supplies. Being a closed economy, Japan had a technology gap and thus could benefit in a major way from the absorption of Western technology. Technology assimilation was facilitated by sharp increases in the size of the capital stock (through imports of capital, a high propensity to save, and the state's promotion of capital formation) and by elastic supplies of labor. Furthermore, the dual labor market permitted the shift of labor from the primitive to the modern sector at a rate dictated by the needs of the advanced sector, with wage increases kept behind productivity advances.[93]

At the same time, the Japanese economy was able to promote a growing role in foreign markets. During the early stages of development while modern industry was growing, exports were derived primarily from traditional industries such as textiles. As modern technology was assimilated, Japanese exports shifted away from the traditional products toward the high-technology products that Japan could produce with comparative advantage, owing to its productive but relatively inexpensive labor. In part, industrial development at home was enhanced by the state's policy of starting import-competing industries.

These factors, combined with reparations from China and an aggressive external posture, made the foreign sector an important contributor to Japan's growth.

The factors emphasized by Ohkawa and Rosovsky are familiar — technology, capital creation, development of the labor force. The difference may be Japan's ability to assemble these features in a harmonious way. Ohkawa and Rosovsky place great emphasis on the noneconomic or special features of the Japanese nation. What are the important noneconomic features of the Japanese development experience?

First, we must again emphasize the important and multidimensional role of the state. The state gave impetus and direction to the drive for economic growth. The state intervened selectively and has been an important catalyst for ensuring not only a high rate of investment but also its proper distribution. For example, beyond the approval of general economic policies by the Diet, government is also involved in business on a more direct basis. Government offices (genkyoku) supervise indivdual industries, and ministries supervise sectors of the economy. Also, there are ministries (such as the Ministry of Finance) whose interests cross specific industrial borders. Finally, the government is directly involved in a wide range of economic matters — the encouragement of designated industrial projects through low-interest loans from the Japan Development Bank, regulation of antitrust matters by the Fair Trade Commission, and so on.[94]

The role of the state in the Japanese economy is difficult to classify. It remains one of the intriguing aspects of the Japanese economic system. In terms of readily quantifiable indicators of state economic activity such as revenue and expenditure, the role of the state is small relative to most other industrialized capitalist systems. At the same time, the state has been very important as a facilitator of the market process, as the creator of a harmonious business environment, and as an entrepreneur and overseer of the development process.

Second, what Ohkawa and Rosovsky describe as the "human element" has been a very important factor in the Japanese story. In Japan, labor has a peculiar and growth-conducive attitude toward industry — the "permanent employment" system and the submissive attitude of labor toward the industrial establishment.[95] In addition, rising family incomes have produced unusually high levels of savings, most appropriate for rapid growth but hard to explain on other than traditional and cultural grounds.

Prior to World War II, the government suppressed the growth of the trade union movement, although it did grow to some degree along with the development of government regulations concerning the labor market. Having gained recognition in the postwar period, trade unions have a voice in wages, supplemental benefits, and working conditions. They are constrained, insofar as they are enterprise unions, enrolling long-term employees. Their primary strength is in the largest industrial enterprises.[96]

Third, one could cite a number of other factors — some narrowly economic, others less so — which have been important: favorable population growth and hence labor supplies, the end to military expenditure, and the limiting of low-growth sectors (such as housing).

Industrial Organization

An economy's industrial organization can affect its performance, and most capitalist theories associate competition with "good" economic performance. The Japanese economy presents a test case, for it appears to have combined an industrial structure dominated by giant vertical and horizontal trusts with rapid economic growth.

Prior to the Second World War, Japanese industry was dominated by giant holding companies, called *zaibatsu*, which represented a complex maze of interlocking directorships, banking relationships, and family ties.[97] At the end of the war, this concentration of ownership had proceeded to the point that less than four thousand zaibatsu-connected families owned almost 50 percent of total outstanding shares. The American occupation forces sought to eliminate zaibatsu dominance by outlawing holding companies, breaking up monopolies, and making mutual shareholdings among zaibatsu firms illegal.

In the postwar era, shareholding in industry and banking has become more evenly distributed among the population. New industrial groupings called *kieretsu* have replaced the old zaibatsu organizations. Kieretsu can be either vertical or horizontal, either a large firm in charge of smaller ("children") firms or a horizontal grouping of interest groups. These new groups are less powerful than the old zaibatsu, and it is possible for a firm within a grouping to place its own interests above that of the group, an impossible action before the war.

One enduring feature of the large Japanese company is its emphasis on industrial paternalism. Established employees of large companies are, in effect, guaranteed lifetime employment. They are taught to think of the company as their family, and they believe that if they work hard for the company, the company will take care of them. John M. Montias singled out this characteristic of the Japanese enterprise for study, and found that this "permanent employment" constraint on Japanese management is likely to alter resource allocation patterns, at least in theory.[98]

Clearly, arrangements for the allocation of labor in the Japanese economy differ from those familiar to Western students. Indeed, the Japanese economy has been characterized as a **share economy**, based on a framework suggested by Martin Weitzman.[99] The evidence for this characterization — the bonus system in Japan — is not strong, though differences in the allocation system make Japanese labor markets of great interest to the comparative analyst.[100]

The concepts of industrial paternalism and lifetime employment have received a great deal of attention, in large part because the system seems so different from other capitalist countries. How can labor be allocated in a rapidly changing environment if it is not mobile?

The answer to this question lies in large part in the difference between appearance and substance. In fact, there are a number of forces at work in the Japanese economy that limit the impact of guaranteed employment.[101] First, not all members of the Japanese labor force are covered by guaranteed employment. One study suggests that roughly 30 percent of the industrial labor force is covered by some form of guaranteed employment.[102] Second, Japanese firms have ways to create flexibility in employment. For example, a temporary labor force can be utilized, and the payment system, where bonuses can be important, does serve as an inducement for employees to work hard. Third, Japanese firms can rely on subcontracting for industrial parts, thus lessening the need to hire the labor force necessary to produce these parts on a sustained basis. Finally, guaranteed employment does not mean that inefficient firms are in some way maintained. On the contrary, both the pressures of the market and the role played by government agencies encourage the productive sectors and discourage the unproductive sectors. All of these factors substantially mitigate what would otherwise appear to be a starkly different system of labor-management relations.

Japanese Planning

Economic planning has not been an important element in the Japanese economy. Japan has had a planning agency since the late 1940s and has assembled numerous plans. Japanese plans have been highly pragmatic, with frequently shifting goals. They have been highly aggregative and based on a simple extension of the national accounts. The plan targets (in addition to being highly aggregative) have been projected only to terminal years of the five-year planning period, making them of minimal value to private firms even when those firms want to be integrated into the plan projections.

One measure of the value of a plan is how closely it is fulfilled. Japanese economic performance has typically been better than that called for by the plan. Plan targets have typically been exceeded, sometimes by very large amounts. This sort of inaccuracy makes the plan targets of little use for purposes of coordination and leads to skepticism about the plan and the necessity for continued corrections by individual firms.

Although the discipline of Japanese firms and their management would make them look at and consider the plan, the real force of intervention in the life of the economy has been the state, not the planning agency.[103] Although we have emphasized this fact, it is worth noting again that discussion of intervention in the Japanese economy focuses not on the Economic Planning Agency, but on the Ministry of International Trade and Industry, where the real power lies. In this sense, the state, its agencies, and its budget are the focus of attention.

All this is not to say that planning may not be an important force in the future. In recent years, there has been a growing interest in the mathematical modeling of the economy. Should performance deteriorate, one could surmise that planning would play a more important role.

Japan: Industrial Policy?

Thus far we have traced the development of the Japanese economy by focusing on features that are thought to have contributed to rapid economic growth. It has been difficult, if not impossible, to render any substantive judgment on the role of government in the Japanese economy. Let us examine this question further.

First, Japanese social structure differs markedly from the United States. Above all, Japan is a country dominated by both vertical and horizontal organization, where group allegiance, formal and informal, is very important. Japanese society might be likened to a family, where the role of the individual contrasts markedly with the sort of individualism familiar to us in the United States.

Second, government does play an important role in the Japanese economy, yet its role is difficult to measure.[104] The Japanese ministerial structure has a substantial impact on the economy, not only through direct participation in key aspects of economic life, but also through its indirect influence. The Ministry of Finance, for example, is responsible for the traditional functions of monetary control along with the Bank of Japan. To the outside world, however, it is the Ministry of International Trade and Industry (MITI) that receives most attention.[105]

MITI has an impressive formal role, being responsible for international trade, domestic production, and domestic industrial structure. Whether formal or informal, though, MITI is frequently viewed as the purveyor of an "industrial policy" geared to promoting rapid economic growth.[106] MITI is responsible for guiding and influencing economic decisions by promoting key sectors of the economy and carefully phasing out other low-productivity sectors. MITI uses public funds for research and development and provides assistance for organizational change, such as mergers. While MITI is an important vehicle for transmitting information in the Japanese economy, few describe this function as planning.

Beyond the ministerial system, there is considerable government involvement in the economy. This activity ranges from the traditional provision of "public goods" to activities in less traditional areas, for example, special financial institutions that provide supplementary services to the private industrial sector.

Traditional measures of government involvement in an economic system probably don't capture the essence of the Japanese system. In the absence of a major formal role for government and planning, the government is nevertheless able to influence both short- and long-run decision making. Rather than formal and powerful involvement in a few traditional and noticeable areas, the government exerts its influence through a myriad of arrangements that guide economic growth. Enthusiasts of an industrial policy cite the Japanese experience.

During the 1970s, American admiration for the Japanese economic system grew. In a time of general economic turmoil, the Japanese were perceived to have found the keys to sustained economic growth. Many writers attempted to discover the precise identity of the growth forces, whether industrial policy, a special role for the government, the managerial system, the labor-management arrangements, or the nature of Japanese society and the Japanese work force. This admiration has been limited only by an apparent inability to transplant these growth forces and continuing friction in Japanese-American trade relations.

The 1970s, however, were not a tranquil decade for the Japanese economy. The early 1970s brought Japan two major shocks. The first was the move by the Nixon administration to end the long-fixed exchange rate between the American dollar and the Japanese yen and move toward a flexible exchange rate.[107] The second event was the initial impact of the energy crisis in 1973. The average annual rate of growth of real GNP declined from above 10 percent in the late 1960s to generally lower rates in the mid 1970s. The average annual rate of inflation reached almost 25 percent in 1974. Other performance indicators showed similar trends. Productivity (output per hour) in manufacturing declined, and manufacturing unit costs increased dramatically.

The late 1970s brought on a second if less severe energy crisis and, possibly more important, a sharply increasing positive balance on the current account. Once again, the problem of balancing Japanese-American trade became a major issue.

Nevertheless, the condition of the Japanese economy was generally positive: Although the rate of economic growth declined in the 1980s, performance was still impressive. Between 1965 and 1980, gross domestic product grew at an average annual rate of 6.3 percent, and from 1980 to 1987, 3.7 percent. For the same periods, the average annual rate of inflation declined from 7.5 to 1.5 percent.[108] Policies of restraint, intended to bring inflation under control and to restore economic growth and balance of payments equilibrium, were largely successful.

For the student of comparative economic systems, interest in the Japanese economic system and its economic policies has shifted. Through the 1960s and into the 1970s, interest centered on the impressive growth of the Japanese economy and its relationship to Japanese institutions and policies. Through the 1970s and 1980s, however, students have instead tried to understand how the Japanese economy has been able to handle the shock of oil price increases while maintaining economic growth with low rates of inflation and unemployment.[109] Therefore, current discussion of the Japanese economy focuses on adjustment, and in particular, adjustment to new international economic conditions.

INDIA: THE QUEST FOR ECONOMIC DEVELOPMENT

Early in this book, we posed the question: Does any one economic system appear better suited to solving the development problems of low-income countries? It is therefore incumbent on us to include a low-income country among our capitalist variants. There are more poor countries than affluent ones. In fact, affluence is limited to a very small portion of the world's population. The difficulty is that there is more diversity among the less-developed countries (the LDCs) than there is among the industrialized economies. Some LDCs are only a step removed from the economic arrangements that have prevailed over centuries of time; others appear to be on their way to transforming themselves into developed countries. Moreover, the LDCs have diverse political and social institutions. In some, tribal or traditional authority still prevails; other LDCs have adopted Western democratic political institutions; still others are controlled by dictatorships of one kind or another.

What common features can be extracted from this diversity? LDCs possess the characteristics generally associated with low levels of income: the dominant role of agriculture, high fertility and mortality rates, limited use of advanced technology and lower saving rates. In addition to these features, LDCs share other common characteristics: concentration of the ownership of wealth, reliance on indirect taxes, extensive government control of international transactions, poorly developed capital markets, and monopoly power in the limited industry sector.[110]

Rather than attempt to deal with the LDCs as a group, we have selected one, India. We believe that the Indian economy is reasonably representative of the operation of the capitalist economic system at low levels of economic development; moreover, this populous and strategically important country provides the closest capitalist counterpart to China, the planned socialist LDC discussed in Chapter 10.[111]

Basic Characteristics[112]

India is the world's second most populous country (over 765 million in 1985), with approximately 15 percent of the world's population. On the other hand, India accounts for under 2 percent of world GNP. These two facts highlight India's very low per capita income (under $270 in 1985 dollars). Approximately 31 percent of India's GNP originates in agriculture, and only one in four persons lives in urban areas. Some 70 percent of the labor force works in agriculture. Population has tended to grow at a rate of over 2 percent per annum (as compared to about 0.5 percent in the industrialized countries), and life expectancy is under fifty years. Only one in every three adults is literate.

India has been called the world's largest democracy. Its government is patterned on the English parliamentary system, and over the years Indian politics has been dominated by the Congress party. India is comprised of a multiplicity of ethnic groups, who speak different languages, and has suffered over the years from ethnic and regional strife.

The Indian Economy: Historical Background[113]

The Indian economy prior to independence from Britain in 1947 makes an ideal case study of a traditional society with a long history of colonial domination. Prior to British rule (first under the British East Indies Company and then under the Crown), the Indian moghul economy (so called because a Moslem minority was the ruling elite) operated according to long-standing traditional rules. Society was divided into castes, with the religious leaders, warlords, and their retainers at the top and the small peasant and untouchable castes at the bottom. In this hierarchical system, one's place in society, as well as one's occupation, was determined at birth. Occupations were not distributed according to the skills, qualifications, and wishes of individuals or according to the needs of society. Moreover, work was considered beneath the dignity of the upper castes; physical labor could be engaged in only by the lower castes.

The ruling class itself generally did not own and was not involved in the management of agricultural production, as in other feudal societies. Instead, the actual land cultivators paid taxes (tribute) to the ruling classes (often 50 percent of the harvest) according to custom and in return for protection, which was necessary in an area torn by regional factionalism, warlordism, and civil strife. Agricultural taxes were levied not only to meet the needs of general government but also to support the high living standards of the upper castes. In the village community, the ruling class controlled the land, but because property rights were poorly defined, the farm family (and the landlords) had little incentive to undertake land improvements. In the farm family, an extended family system prevailed whereby income was shared among brothers, counsins, uncles, and so on.

The wealthy classes were not motivated to make productive investments; instead, their savings were devoted to acquiring precious metals, and little social overhead investment (such as in irrigation) was undertaken. Foreign trade was conducted primarily by foreigners, who traded Indian spices and handicrafts for gold and silver. The limited education that did exist was purely religious in character, and the education of women was proscribed.

Economic progress under the moghul economy was limited. Population did not increase for two thousand years. In the sixteenth century it is likely that per capita income in India was on a par with that of Western Europe and contemporary European visitors even felt that average living standards were higher in India than at home. By the time of British rule, however, per capita income in India was very low relative to Western Europe. Thus during the era when Europe was preparing for its initial industrialization and population expansion, the Indian moghul economy was becoming relatively backward. The reasons for this declining economic position are not hard to see: the rigid caste system, religious restrictions, uncertain property rights, barriers against productive investment, and civil strife. It was the last, particularly the enmity between the majority Hindu population and their Moslem rulers (as well as regional factionalism) that allowed the British to turn India easily into a colonial dominion.

The Indian economy under British rule was not dramatically different, but the British did remove the old moghul warlord aristocracy, replacing it with a new indigenous ruling elite (supportive of the British) and a professional British bureaucracy, both designed to preserve law and order. Britain's objective was not to promote the economic development of India but to use India as a guaranteed market for British products. Tariff barriers were erected against Indian textiles abroad, and the removal of the moghul princes reduced the demand in India for the traditional luxury products of Indian handicraft. The British accepted and even intensified the caste system by establishing themselves as a separate ruling class. After 1930, native Indians gradually infiltrated the bureaucracy. This native bureaucracy became a wellspring of nationalism and was instrumental in achieving independence for India in 1947.

During British rule, the population of India began to grow for the first time over an extended period, and the economy grew along with population. Nevertheless, per capita income failed to increase perceptibly. Although British colonial rule did establish conditions for the growth of output and population, it did not allow output growth to exceed population growth. The positive economic features of the colonial period were the creation of a professional bureaucracy, the introduction of a secular education system to replace the system of religious education, a reduction of the tax burden on agriculture, and the creation of some property rights in agriculture (for the new ruling class). Under British rule, the proportion of national income going to the nonvillage economy declined somewhat with the elimination of the moghul elite, and a lower proportion of national income went to the new ruling elite (British officials, native princes, and their retainers). However, the share of income received by those at the bottom of the ladder did not increase.

The Modern "Socialist" Indian Economy

The modern Indian economy is the creation of the Congress party and its leaders, Mahatma Gandhi and Jawaharlal Nehru, who referred to India as a "socialist" economy, though they differed on the appropriate course of Indian socialism. Gandhi extolled the traditional village community as the ideal economic organization and downgraded industrialization and the profit motive. Nehru favored industrialization and emphasized heavy industry as the appropriate path for Indian socialism. According to our definition, socialism is largely a misnomer in the case of India except for government ownership in industry and commerce. Indian leadership has not pursued a socialist distribution of income. India is still primarily an agricultural country, and the distribution of income depends primarily on the distribution of agricultural property. Since independence, only limited progress has been made in land reform. Although there have been some efforts to distribute land to the poor peasants, land is unequally distributed and there is no evidence that the range of income inequality has been reduced.[114] It is true that the pensioning off of the native princes and limitations on landholdings have reduced the number of enormous estates; but the land-limiting legislation has been circumvented, and many Indian states have not been able (or willing) to push land reform because of the strength of vested landed interests. The tax system continues to be regressive; direct taxes are rarely levied on land; and the nominally high urban income taxes are ameliorated by evasion and by numerous exemptions.

The pretax income distribution figures sum up the failure to establish a more equal distribution of income. In 1960, the bottom 10 per-

cent of families accounted for less than 1 percent of all income, while
the top 10 percent accounted for over one-third. This income distribution is more unequal than in the industrialized capitalist countries (a
more unequal distribution is characteristic of less developed countries).[115] The after-tax distribution is not significantly different from
this pretax distribution because of the predominance of regressive indirect taxes. A native Indian elite of civil servants, the military, and
capitalists has replaced the British and native prices at the top of the
income distribution. Landless agricultural laborers, small landholders,
and the urban poor remain at the bottom.

Rather than seeking to achieve "socialist" objectives through income
redistribution, the architects of the modern Indian economy emphasized state ownership in industry. The feeling was that socialism could
be achieved through state control of industry, which would serve as a
surrogate for social change. The strategy was that state promotion of
heavy industry (through ownership and government controls) would
lead to economic development and limit the concentration of wealth in
private hands, and economic development would inevitably bring about
necessary social change. In the early postwar period, the Indians
adopted one basic feature of the Soviet development model (discussed
in Chapter 7), namely, the priority of heavy industry over light industry
and agriculture. It was argued that the creation of a domestic heavy
industry base would lead to more rapid development, would promote
domestic savings, and would make India less dependent on the outside
world (allowing India to pursue an independent political course).[116]

India's heavy-industry strategy was reflected in the public ownership
of heavy industries and banking. Steel, heavy machinery, chemicals,
power, fuel, communication, transportation, and life insurance were
nationalized in the early 1950s. In the 1970s the state moved to enlarge
the public sector by nationalizing the large banks, the copper industry,
the wholesale grain and jute trade, and a number of coal mines and textile mills. In some instances, the Indians followed the British pattern of
nationalization to rescue failing private companies. In others (such as
the wholesale grain trade), nationalization was undertaken to expand
state control over the private economy. Nationalization in most instances was accomplished by compensation (rather than expropriation)
of previous owners, and there has been an increasing Indianization of
industrial ownership as foreign owners have been displaced.

Despite substantial nationalization, the scope of the public sector
remains limited. Private enterprise still accounts for some 90 percent of
industrial output.[117] The public sector (general government and public
enterprises) accounts for approximately 15 percent of national output.[118] The government's share of savings is 13 percent.[119] These
figures indicate that the role of the public sector in India is below
average or small relative to the industrialized countries.[120] Thus the

strategy of pursuing socialism through public ownership has had only a limited effect on the aggregate economy. However, one must bear in mind that the Indian economy is still highly underdeveloped, and most of the labor force remains concentrated in agriculture and personal services. This means that the share of the heavy industry sector (the focal point of nationalization) must necessarily be limited. Moreover, the impact of public policy on economic affairs may be greater than the public sector share figures indicate because of a pervasive system of indirect controls and planning.

The organization of the private industrial sector is quite concentrated in India, and the objective of limiting industrial wealth holdings has not been achieved. At the end of the 1950s, the twenty largest industrial groups owned one-third of the share capital of the private corporate sector.[121] Although measures have been introduced since then to reduce this concentration of private wealth and power (the most significant being the nationalization of large banking interests), large private interests are probably promoted by the existing system of economic control. In addition, major industrialists are key figures in the Congress party.

Economic Planning in India[122]

Economic planning in India has attracted considerable attention because it is one of the few LDCs to have well-organized and sophisticated planning machinery. The planning apparatus in a typical LDC is as underdeveloped as the economy; so the Indian example serves as a useful test case of the potential contribution of planning in an LDC.

According to the definitions developed in Chapter 5, Indian planning would be classified as indicative. It is a noncompulsory form of planning, in keeping with the Indian philosophy that the use of force is contrary to Indian democracy. This does not suggest that Indian plan directives have not been implemented. In the industrial sector a wide range of enforcement mechanisms has been available. Much heavy industry is directly owned by the state and can be expected to follow plan guidelines; industrial credit is largely state controlled; import licenses are also granted by the state. The fact that the Indian economy has developed a relatively large heavy industry sector for an LDC demonstrates better than anything else that planning has mattered. Nevertheless, India continues to be an agricultural country, and agriculture, which cannot be planned in any effective way, remains largely out of the control of planners.

India has concentrated on long-term plans, typically of five years' duration. Attempts to devise annual operational plans have not been successful. Planning goals and planning methods have changed over the years, although the general objectives (raising the rate of economic growth and the investment ratio, reducing inequalities, stimulating employment) are familiar to observers of national economic planning. The first plan was based on simple Keynesian growth models. The second plan (1956–1961) emphasized the priority of heavy industry. Later plans have concentrated on multisectoral balances and have to some extent moved away from the emphasis on heavy industry.

Balances for the major industrial sectors have been constructed (using either rudimentary methods or input-output tables) to determine the consistency of the plan. A crucial component of the plan is the investment subplan, which indicates the growth rates of investment in the public and private sectors. The investment plan, which determines the basic direction of the economy, is most amenable to enforcement because of the state's control of public enterprises, raw-material allocations, investment credit, and imports.

Economic planning in India is carried out on an aggregated level; specific output directives are not normally issued to the private industrial sector. In the public sector, an industry often consists of a small number of publicly owned enterprises; therefore, the aggregate directives can be converted into actual production and investment targets. On the surface, it would appear that Indian planners are in a better position to influence the behavior of industry with the arsenal of controls at their disposal, but it is difficult to establish the degree of control they actually do exercise over the private sector.

Economic Controls[123]

Governmental controls over resource allocation are more extensive in India than in the industrialized capitalist countires. In addition to the planning apparatus, a whole range of extramarket controls are utilized. The rationale for these controls is the widespread belief that the free market cannot be trusted to allocate resources in a low-income country.

The basic instrument for control of private industry was the Industries Act of 1951 (covering almost all manufacturing, mining, and power). It gave the government authority to grant licenses for capacity expansion and to control the allocation and prices of raw materials and, in some instances, the prices of finished products. The prices of basic agricultural products are controlled by the state, and a complex zonal pricing system exists to regulate the flow of agricultural products from surplus to deficit regions. Moreover, the state disburses food products received under foreign aid programs and in this way exercises further influence over agricultural prices.

A most important instrument of state control is state regulation of foreign exchange and imports. From the mid-1950s, India has been on a strict import and exchange control system. Imported capital equipment, crucial to industrial expansion, has been regulated by industrial licensing, and input and raw-material licenses have regulated the disbursement of imported materials to industrial users. The import control system has operated on the principles of essentiality and indigenous nonavailability. In order to justify an import, the domestic user has to demonstrate that the commodity is essential and that it cannot be purchased at home. Import restrictions, when strictly applied, have given automatic protection to domestic industry and, according to many economists,[124] have decreased the efficiency of the Indian economy.

In the late 1960s, the Indian system of economic controls was reexamined, and an attempt was made to limit controls (except for agricultural pricing) to large firms. The retention of controls, despite the growing recognition of their inefficiency, can be attributed to three factors.[125] The first is that many large firms actually like controls because they reduce risk and guarantee profits. Second, controls enhance the power and positions of bureaucrats. Third, distrust of the market is ingrained in the Indian bureaucracy.

It is difficult to quantify the effect of government controls on Indian resource allocation because one cannot know to what extent they are circumvented. What one can say is that the system of state controls is more comprehensive than that in the advanced capitalist countries.

Growth Performance

The growth of the Indian economy after 1947 represents a marked improvement over historical performance. As we already noted, the moghul economy was stagnant for centuries, and per capita income failed to grow during British colonial rule; therefore any growth of per capita income is an improvement over historical standards. The difficulty in evaluating Indian growth performance is that the world economy experienced accelerated growth after the Second World War, and India's participation in this acceleration would be expected.

India's per capita GNP has average a 1.7 percent growth for the period 1965–1985. According to Angus Maddison, the reasons for this per capita growth rate are the expansion of government services (education and credit assistance), a high investment rate, the increase in both public and private investment, foreign aid, and the importation of advanced technology.

On the positive side of the ledger, one can point to the steady but unspectacular rise in per capita income despite substantial population pressures. In the crucial agricultural area, output has expanded slightly more rapidly than population (at a per capita rate of about one-half of 1 percent per year). India's dependence on imported grains has declined over the years and now India is largely self-sufficient in basic food grains. On the negative side, India's per capita income growth has been slow relative to the performance of other developing countries (whose per capita growth tended to be around 2 to 3 percent per year). India's growth performance has been well below that of China, although China and India began their postcolonial development from an equivalent point. Because of lower growth, India's per capita income today is only three-quarters that of China.[126] Additional negative features are persistent high unemployment (and underemployment), rapid inflation, and susceptibility to external shocks (such as the oil price explosion of the 1970s).

Maddison and Malenbaum argue that Indian growth has been substandard for the LDCs in the postwar era, and Maddison calculates that the Indian growth rate has been 25 percent below its potential.[127] The reasons for this underutilization of growth potential are India's extremely low per capita income, relatively small per capita receipts of foreign capital, poor natural resources, the drain of a large military, the retention of institutional constraints (caste restrictions, maldistribution of agricultural land, taboo on slaughter of livestock), and the inefficiency of public enterprise, which has been operated at a loss throughout most of the postwar era.

Capitalism in India

Notwithstanding the large share of government ownership of heavy industry and finance, India is a capitalist economy. The public enterprise sector comprises a small share of the total economy, and private ownership prevails throughout the rest of the economy. The dominant sector, agriculture, is characterized by private ownership of land. There has been no significant change in the distribution of income, and the inequality of income distribution is greater in India than in the advanced capitalist countries either on a pretax or posttax basis. Economic planning is primarily indicative, although planning of the public enterprise sector may carry with it some compulsory elements. Nevertheless, noncoercion remains the foundation of Indian planning.

The amount of government intervention in private economic decision making is probably more extensive in India than in the advanced capitalist countries, although the actual degree of compliance is difficult to establish. Government controls have been placed on prices, imports, foreign exchange, raw materials, and capacity expansion. One reason for these controls is a rather deep-seated distrust of market resource allocation. On the other hand, controls seem to be a characteristic feature of capitalism under conditions of underdevelopment, and, in this sense, India conforms to the general pattern of underdevelopment.

Problems and Prospects

The basic challenge facing India over the coming decades is to improve the utilization of its abundant resource, labor. Endemically high rates of unemployment and underemployment attest to labor's underutilization, but the best means of correcting the situation remains a heatedly debated issue: Should there be more or less planning? Should government intervention and controls be increased or reduced? Can ways be found to remove the remaining vestiges of feudalism and the caste system? Can centuries-old regional and ethnic factionalism be removed? Can there be any narrowing in income inequality? In a sense, the grand decision facing India appears to be whether to choose more market or more plan. Should resource allocation be more fully entrusted to the market with government acting on the sidelines to protect property rights and promote competition? Or is it dangerous to trust market guidance in a developing country?

SUMMARY: THE VARIANTS OF CAPITALISM

This chapter examines five capitalist systems, selected because of their differing systemic arrangements of interest to the comparative economist. While there are significant variations in the contemporary economic performance of these systems, it is important to emphasize one underlying fact. For most systems, the 1950s and 1960s were relatively tranquil decades, and thus they were years in which basic system characteristics could be studied. On the other hand, the 1970s and 1980s have been anything but tranquil, with energy shocks and recession as major world events. In these decades, most systems have had to develop a response to world market forces. These responses have differed from case to case, as have the outcomes. To summarize each case briefly:

1. France used indicative planning in the 1950s and 1960s to promote economic growth. French indicative planning issues non-binding plans based on a social consensus. Indirect means are used to promote plan fulfillment. In recent years, there has been a move away from indicative planning toward traditional monetary and fiscal policy.

2. Traditionally the economic role of government has been important in Great Britain, not so much because of its planning activities, but rather through the budgetary process and public ownership. Britain was viewed as a case of economic stagnation until recently, but the Conservative government of Margaret Thatcher has significantly improved the nation's economic performance in the past decade. The Thatcher policy is based on the use of monetary policy, stimulation of incentives and com-

petitive markets, and privatization. Debate over this record centers first on its costs, for example, in terms of unemployment. Second, critics question the economy's potential for the long run, given the crucial role of North Sea oil in the British economic equation.

3. West Germany is described as a "social market economy" in which there is a strong combination of government intervention and worker participation. The contemporary economic performance of the West German economy has been very good, although it also has had to respond to external shocks, and these are especially significant in an open economy.

4. Japan's is a unique system, combining interesting organizational arrangements, especially an important role for the state, with a social structure and social values that facilitate the state's role in decision making. Traditionally, the Japanese economy has been of interest for its exceptional growth peformance. Although the Japanese economy continues to perform well in the 1980s, it has gone through a period of major adjustments designed to sustain its leading role in the world economy.

5. As a large and quite poor country, India has pursued economic growth and development largely through the market mechanism, but with a socialist overlay in a number of dimensions. India has managed to sustain reasonable rates of economic growth, but it has a long way to go along the development path. Since the 1970s, the traditional comparison of India with China is of even greater interest in light of major changes within the Chinese economy.

NOTES

France

1. There is a large body of literature on the French economy. For an overview, see J. R. Hough, *The French Economy* (New York: Holmes & Meier, 1982); Stephen S. Cohen, *Modern Capitalist Planning: The French Model* (Berkeley: University of California Press, 1977); Stephen S. Cohen and Peter A. Gourevitch, eds., *France in a Troubled World Economy* (Boston: Butterworth, 1982); for a discussion of the French economy and survey of the literature on indicative planning, see Saul Estrin and Peter Holmes, *French Planning in Theory and Practice* (Boston: Allen and Unwin, 1983); for a survey of recent events, see Bela Balassa, *The First Year of Socialist Government in France* (Washington, D.C.: American Enterprise Institute, 1982). For a discussion of planning institutions, see John and Anne Marie Hackett, *Economic Planning in France* (Cambridge, Mass.: Harvard University Press, 1963). For an examination of the effectiveness of French planning, see John H. McArthur and Bruce R. Scott, *Industrial Planning in France* (Boston: Graduate School of

Business Administration, Harvard University, 1969). For a critical view, see Vera Lutz, *Central Planning for the Market Economy: An Analysis of the French Theory and Experience* (London: Longmans Green, 1969). For an in-depth treatment of French economic performance, see J.-J. Carre, P. Dubois, and E. Malinvaud, *French Economic Growth* (Stanford, Calif.: Stanford University Press, 1975); for a historical survey, see Richard F. Kuisel, *Capitalism and the State of Modern France* (New York: Cambridge University Press, 1981).

2. In market economic systems where planning has been introduced, or in planned economies where economic reform has meant the introduction of market forces, there have tended to be difficulties bringing the two different sorts of instruments together. This case has been argued in David Granick, "An Organizational Model of Soviet Industrial Planning," *Journal of Political Economy*, 67 (1959), 123-124; for an analysis see Benjamin N. Ward, *The Socialist Economy: A Study of Organizational Alternatives* (New York: Random House, 1967), pp. 178-181.

3. Carre, Dubois, and Malinvaud, *French Economic Growth*, p. 21.

4. For background, see Richard F. Kuisel, *Capitalism and the State in Modern France*; Andrew Schonfield, *Modern Capitalism: The Changing Balance of Public and Private Power* (New York: Oxford University Press, 1965).

5. See for example the discussion in Saul Estrin and Peter Holmes, *French Planning in Theory and Practice*, ch. 8.

6. This case is argued in Andrew Schonfield, *Modern Capitalism: The Changing Balance of Public and Private Power*, ch. 5.

7. For a detailed examination of the growth of the public sector in different countries, see Frederic L. Pryor, *Public Expenditures in Communist and Capitalist Nations* (London: Allen and Unwin, 1968). Recent evidence is discussed in D. Cameron, "The Expansion of the Public Economy: A Comparative Analysis," *American Political Science Review*, 92 (1978), pp. 1243-61; Frank Gould, "The Development of Public Expenditures in Western Industrialized Countries: A Comparative Analysis," *Public Finance*, 38, 1 (1983), pp. 38-69.

8. Schonfield, *Modern Capitalism*, pp. 156-157.

9. The importance of technical planning experts in different planning efforts has been emphasized: a major role in the French case, a minimal role in the British case. For a comparison, see ibid., pp. 155-156.

10. The differing national styles of executive development have been examined in David Granick, *The European Executive* (New York: Doubleday, 1962). For a recent comparative analysis, see David Granick, *Managerial Comparisons of Four Developed Countries: France, Britain, United States and Russia* (Cambridge, Mass.: M.I.T. Press, 1972).

11. For a survey of views on planning in the United States, see Zoltan Kenessey, *The Process of Economic Planning* (New York: Columbia University Press, 1977). For a comparative viewpoint, see Morris Bornstein, ed., *Economic Planning, East and West* (Cambridge, Mass.: Ballinger, 1975). On the relevance of the French planning experience to the United States, see Stephen S. Cohen, *Recent Developments in French Planning: Some Lessons for the United States* (Washington, D.C.: U.S. Government Printing Office, 1977).

12. For an excellent survey of views, see Estrin and Holmes, *French Planning in Theory and Practice*, chs. 1-2.

13. See Schonfield, *Modern Capitalism*, ch. 7.

14. Lutz, *Central Planning for the Market Economy*, ch. 6.

15. Any discussion of the French planning system invariably devotes a great deal of attention to the mystique of the planning system; the ability of the state

and the planners to get things done in the absence of coercive power; flexibility and strength; democracy and direction. For a generally balanced treatment of these features of French planning, see Schonfield, *Modern Capitalism*, ch. 7; for a critical view, see Lutz, *Central Planning for the Market Economy*; for a brief but useful discussion of pro and con views and references to the literature, see Hough, *The French Economy*, ch. 5.

16. See Hans Schollhammer, "National Economic Planning and Business Decision Making: The French Experience," in Moeris Bornstein, ed., *Comparative Economic Systems: Models and Cases*, 3rd ed. (Homewood, Ill.: Irwin, 1974), pp. 52-76.

17. For a useful discussion of the relationship among the state, the sources of investment funds, and the plan, see Carre, Dubois, and Malinvaud, *French Economic Growth*, ch. 10.

18. Changing the nature of the business environment and the extent to which planning (as opposed to simple forecasting) is useful has been controversial. For a discussion of information flows and the French planning system, see ibid., ch. 14; for a discussion of the theoretical question of reducing uncertainty through planning, see J. E. Meade, *The Theory of Indicative Planning* (Manchester, England: Manchester University Press, 1970); see also Estrin and Holmes, *French Planning in Theory and Practice*, chs. 1-2.

19. Lutz, *Central Planning for the Market Economy*.

20. For a discussion of changes in the French planning system, see Martin Cave, "Decentralized Planning in Britain: Comment," *Economics of Planning* 19, 3 (1985) pp. 141-144; Martin Cave, "French Planning Reforms, 1981-1984," *The ACES Bulletin* 26, 2-3 (1984), pp. 29-38; Saul Estrin, "Decentralized Economic Planning: Some Issues," *Economics of Planning*, 19, 3 (1985), pp. 150-156.

21. Robert Eisner argues that obsession with trade deficits has been a major focus of policy in the early 1980s. See his article "Which Way for France?" *Challenge*, 20, no. 3 (July/August, 1983), pp. 34-41.

22. Such a case is made in Estrin and Holmes, *French Planning in Theory and Practice*.

23. See Schollhammer, "National Economic Planning and Business Decision Making," pp. 52-76.

24. Lutz, *Central Planning for the Market Economy*.

25. McArthur and Scott, *Industrial Planning in France*, pp. 26-27.

26. Hough, *The French Economy*.

27. Estrin and Holmes, "Preface," *French Planning in Theory and Practice*, p. vii.

28. Cohen, *Modern Capitalist Planning*.

29. Ibid., pp. 238-279.

30. Martin Cave, "French Planning Reforms."

31. Eisner, "Which Way for France?" pp. 35-37.

32. Ibid.

33. A. Dupont-Fauville, "Nationalisation of the Banks in France: A Preliminary Evaluation," *The Three Banks Review*, 139 (September 1983), pp. 32-41.

34. Balassa, *The First Year of Socialist Government in France*, pp. 2-5.

35. Measures of government involvement are from Gould, "The Development of Public Expenditures in Western Industrialized Countries: A Comparative Analysis," pp. 42-43.

Great Britain

36. For a discussion of the British economy in the socialist mold, see Allan G. Gruchy, *Comparative Economic Systems*, 2nd ed. (Boston: Houghton Mifflin, 1977), ch. 11. For a recent statement, see Michael Meacher, *Socialism with a Human Face* (London: Allen and Unwin, 1982).

37. The following are useful sources: John and Anne Marie Hackett, *The British Economy: Problems and Prospects* (London: Allen and Unwin, 1967); Richard E. Caves and Associates, *Britain's Economic Prospects* (Washington, D.C.: Brookings, 1968); and Sir Alec Cairncross, ed., *Britain's Economic Prospects Reconsidered* (Albany: State University of New York Press, 1970); Richard E. Caves and Lawrence B. Krause, eds., *Britain's Economic Performance* (Washington, D.C.: Brookings, 1980); W. P. J. Maunder, ed., *The British Economy in the 1970s* (London: Heinemann Educational Books, 1980); Sidney Pollard, *The Wasting of the British Economy* (New York: St. Martin's, 1982). A useful introductory survey is National Institute of Economic and Social Research, *The United Kingdom Economy* (London: Heinemann Educational Books, 1976); for a helpful update, see W. B. Reddaway, "Problems and Prospects for the U.K. Economy," *The Economic Record*, 59, no. 166 (September 1983), pp. 220-231.

38. For a statistical comparison of development patterns including Great Britain, see Hollis Chenery and Moises Syrquin, *Patterns of Development, 1950-1970* (New York: Oxford University Press, 1975).

39. Andrew Schonfield, *Modern Capitalism: The Changing Balance of Public and Private Power* (New York: Oxford University Press, 1965), ch. 6.

40. On the regional question, see B. E. Coates and E. M. Rawstron, *Regional Variations in Britain* (London: Batsford, 1971).

41. Schonfield, *Modern Capitalism*, p. 88.

42. For an interesting discussion of a particular case of British wartime planning, see Ely Devons, *Planning in Practice* (Cambridge: Cambridge University Press, 1950).

43. In the period when British concern for poor economic performance, especially unemployment, was growing rapidly, actual peformance was quite good though possibly not on a par with the fast-growing nations of the period. For example, between 1959 and 1966, the average annual rate of unemployment was 2.6 percent in Britain, 5.4 percent in the United States, and 5.5 percent in Canada. For the period 1955-1964, per capita national income grew in Britain at an average annual rate of 2.1 percent, compared to 1.4 percent in the United States, 4.7 percent in Italy, and 4.3 percent in West Germany.

44. For a discussion, see Carlo M. Cipolla, ed., *The Economic Decline of Empires* (London: Methuen, 1970); see also Frank Blackaby, ed., *De-industrialisation* (London: Heinemann Educational Books, 1979).

45. We shall not discuss the details of British stabilization policy in this short survey. The interested reader should refer to the discussion in Hackett, *The British Economy*, ch. 1; for a recent brief survey, see G. D. N. Worswick, "Fiscal Policy and Stabilization in Britain," in Cairncross, *Britian's Economic Prospects Reconsidered*, pp. 36-60; for useful background, see Charles Feinstein, ed., *The Managed Economy* (Oxford: Oxford University Press, 1983). See also G. D. N. Worswick, "The End of Demand Management?" *Lloyd's Bank Review*, 123 (January 1977), pp. 1-18.

46. Worswick, "Fiscal Policy and Stabilization in Britain."

47. For a brief but excellent survey of the British experience with national economic planning, see Werner Z. Hirsch, *Recent Experience with National*

Economic Planning in the United Kingdom (Washington, D.C.: Government Printing Office, 1977).

48. Ibid., pp. 13-15.
49. Schonfield, *Modern Capitalism*, p. 173.
50. Hackett, *The British Economy*, p. 162.
51. Caves and Associates, *Britain's Economic Prospects*, pp. 271-274.
52. Chenery and Syrquin, *Patterns of Development*, table 5-4.
53. Caves and Associates, *Britain's Economic Prospects*, ch. 8.
54. Meacher, *Socialism with a Human Face*.
55. The data presented here are from Frank Gould, "The Development of Public Expenditures in Western Industrialized Countries: A Comparative Analysis," *Public Finances*, 38, no. (1983), pp. 38-69.
56. See World Bank, *World Tables*, 2nd ed. (Baltimore: Johns Hopkins Press, 1980).
57. A great deal has been written about the nationalized industries in Great Britain. For a brief survey, see Richard Pryke, "Public Enterprise in Great Britain," in Morris Bornstein, ed., *Comparative Economic Systems: Models and Cases*, 3rd ed. (Homewood, Ill.: Irwin, 1974), pp. 77-92. For in-depth treatment, see R. Kelf-Cohen, *Twenty Years of Nationalisation* (London: Macmillan, 1969); R. Kelf-Cohen, *British Nationalisation, 1945-1973* (New York: St. Martin's, 1973); and Leonard Tivey, ed., *The Nationalized Industries Since 1960: A Book of Readings* (Toronto: University of Toronto Press, 1973). For a discussion of issues in the 1970s, see T. G. Weyman-Jones, "The Nationalised Industries: Changing Attitudes and Changing Roles," in W. P. J. Maunder, ed., *The British Economy in the 1970s*, ch. 8.
58. Steel (denationalized in 1954 and nationalized again in 1965) is not included. See Pryke, "Public Enterprise in Great Britain," p. 82.
59. See, for example, the discussion in Reddaway, "Problems and Prospects for the U.K. Economy."
60. For a useful discussion, see Blackaby, *De-industrialisation*.
61. Poor performance after 1973 is emphasized in Caves and Krause, *Britain's Economic Performance*.
62. Reddaway, "Problems and Prospects for the U.K. Economy," table 1.
63. Computed from Caves and Krause, *Britain's Economic Performance*, table 2, p. 3.
64. Pollard, *The Wasting of the British Economy*, table 3.3, p. 53.
65. Ibid., table 1.2, p. 12.
66. Reddaway, "Problems and Prospects for the U.K. Economy," p. 225.
67. Caves and Krause, *Britain's Economic Performance*, p. 19.
68. For interesting background, see Bernard N. Nossiter, *Britain — A Future That Works* (Boston: Houghton Mifflin, 1978).
69. Useful sources include David S. Bell, ed., *The Conservative Government, 1979-84: An Interim Report* (London: Croom Helm, 1985); Paul Hare, *Planning the British Economy* (London: Macmillan, 1985); Grahame Thompson, *The Conservatives' Economic Policy* (London: Croom Helm, 1986); Alan Walters, *Britain's Economic Renaissance* (New York: Oxford University Press, 1986); "Planning in Britain," *Journal of Comparative Economics* 19, 3 (1985).
70. Alan Walters, *Britain's Economic Renaissance*, pp. 4-5.
71. For a critical view, see David S. Bell, *The Conservative Government*.
72. World Bank, *World Development Report 1987* (New York: Oxford University Press, 1987), p. 203.
73. Ibid., p. 205.
74. Grahame Thompson, *The Conservatives' Economic Policy*, ch. 7.

75. David S. Bell, *The Conservative Government*, ch. 3.
76. World Bank, *World Development Report 1987*, p. 223.

West Germany

77. Our discussion is based on the following sources: Heinz Lampert, *Volkswirt-schaftliche Institutionen* (Munich: Verlag Franz Vahlen, 1980); G. Gutman, W. Klein, S. Paraskewopolous, and H. Winter, *Die Wirtschafts-Verfassung der Bundesrepublik Deutschland*, 2nd ed. (Stuttgart: Fischer, 1979); Hannelore Hamel, ed., *Bundesrepublik Deutschland-DDR, Die Wirtschaftssysteme*, 4th ed. (Munich: C. H. Beck, 1983); Gerhard Brinkman, *Okonomik der Arbeit*, vol. I (Stuttgart: Ernst Klett Verlag, 1981).
78. This label is credited to A. Muller-Armack, "Soziale Marktwirtschaft," in *Handwörterbuch der Sozialwissenschaften*, Band IX (Stuttgart: Fischer, 1956), p. 390.
79. H. Jorg Thieme, *Soziale Marktwirtschaft: Konzeption und wirtschafts-politische Gestaltung in der BRD* (Hanover: Berenberg, 1973), pp. 21–28; and Wolfram Engels, *Soziale Marktwirtschaft: Verschmähte Zukunft* (Stuttgart: Seewald, 1973), pp. 40–45.
80. L. Erhard and A. Muller-Armack, *Soziale Marktwirtschaft* (Frankfurt am Main: Ullstein, 1972).
81. See Gutman, et al., *Wirtschaftsverfassung*, ch. 8.
82. Thieme, *Soziale Marktwirtschaft*, pp. 83–87.
83. Lampert, *Institutionen*, pp. 31–49.
84. Martin Schnitzer and James Nordyke, *Comparative Economic Systems*, 2nd ed. (Cincinnati, Ohio: Southwestern 1977), p. 328.
85. J. H. Kaiser, "Public Enterprise in Germany," in W. G. Friedman and J. F. Garner, *Government Enterprise: A Comparative Study* (New York: Columbia University Press, 1970).

Japan

86. Angus Maddison, *Economic Growth in Japan and the USSR* (London: Allen and Unwin, 1969), ch. 1.
87. For an excellent survey of the early years of Japanese economic development, see Kazushi Ohkawa and Henry Rosovsky, *Japanese Economic Growth* (Stanford, Calif.: Stanford University Press, 1973).
88. For an examination of the Japanese growth experience, see Lawrence Klein and Kazushi Ohkawa, eds., *Economic Growth: The Japanese Experience Since the Meiji Era* (Homewood, Ill.: Irwin, 1968); Japan Economic Research Center, *Economic Growth: The Japanese Experience Since the Meiji Era*, vols. I and II (Tokyo: Japan Economic Research Center, 1973); and Hugh Patrick and Henry Rosovsky, eds., *Asia's New Giant: How the Japanese Economy Works* (Washington, D.C.: Brookings, 1976). For a discussion of Japanese economic planning, see Shuntaro Shishido, "Japanese Experience with Long-Term Economic Planning," and Tsunshiko Watanabe, "National Planning and Economic Growth in Japan," both in Bert G. Hickman, ed., *Quantitative Planning of Economic Policy* (Washington, D.C.: Brookings, 1965); and William Lockwood, ed., *The State and Economic Enterprise in Japan* (Princeton, N.J.: Princeton University Press, 1965). For an analysis of

Japanese labor markets, see Koji Taira, *Economic Development and the Labor Market in Japan* (New York: Columbia University Press, 1970). For a discussion of Japanese multinationals, see Ozawa Terutomo, *Multinationalism Japanese Style* (Princeton, N.J.: Princeton University Press, 1979); Yoshi Tsurumi, *The Japanese Are Coming: A Multinational Interaction of Firms and Politics* (Cambridge, Mass.: Ballinger, 1976); M. Y. Yoshino, *Japan's Multinational Enterprises* (Cambridge, Mass.: Harvard University Press, 1976). For a general discussion of the Japanese economic system, especially its organizational features, see G. C. Allen, *The Japanese Economy* (London: Weidenfeld and Nicolson, 1981).

89. Taira, *Economic Development*.

90. For a brief discussion, see Allen, *The Japanese Economy*, ch. 5; for background, see I. J. Nakamura, *Agricultural Production and the Economic Development of Japan, 1873-1922* (Princeton, N.J.: Princeton University Press, 1966).

91. Maddison, *Economic Growth in Japan and the USSR*, ch. 4.

92. For a survey of Japanese economic growth, see Ohkawa and Rosovsky, *Japanese Economic Growth*, ch. 2.

93. Various aspects of the Japanese labor market are discussed in Allen, *The Japanese Economy*, ch. 9; Taira, *Economic Development*.

94. For a useful survey of organizational features of the Japanese economic system, see Kanji Haitani, *The Japanese Economic System* (Lexington, Mass.: Heath, 1976).

95. Ohkawa and Rosovsky, *Japanese Economic Growth*, ch. 5.

96. In addition to Taira, *Economic Development*, see Robert E. Cole, *Japanese Blue-Collar: The Changing Tradition* (Berkeley: University of California Press, 1971); for a summary, see Robert E. Cole, "Industrial Relations in Japan" in Morris Bornstein, ed., *Comparative Economic Systems, Models and Cases*, 3rd ed. (Homewood, Ill.: Irwin, 1974), pp. 93-116.

97. Kozo Yamamura, "Entrepreneurship, Ownership and Management in Japan," in M. M. Postan et al., *Cambridge Economic History of Europe*, vol. VII, pt. 2 (Cambridge: Cambridge University Press, 1978), pp. 215-264. See also Eleanor M. Hadley, *Antitrust in Japan* (Princeton, N.J.: Princeton University Press, 1970); Richard E. Caves and Masu Uekusa, *Industrial Organization in Japan* (Washington, D.C.: Brookings, 1976); and Haitani, *The Japanese Economic System*.

98. John M. Montias, *The Structure of Economic Systems* (New Haven: Yale University Press, 1976), pt. 5.

99. Martin Weitzman, *The Share Economy* (Cambridge: Harvard University Press, 1984).

100. Merton J. Peck, "Is Japan Really a Share Economy?" *Journal of Comparative Economics* 10 (1986), pp. 427-432.

101. For a recent discussion, see Gregory B. Christainsen and Jan S. Hagendorn, "Japanese Productivity: Adapting to Changing Comparative Advantage in the Face of Lifetime Employment Commitments," *Quarterly Review of Business and Economics*, 23, no. 2 (Summer 1983), pp. 23-39. For a discussion of the labor-management issue in a growth context, see Harry Oshima, "Reinterpreting Japan's Postwar Growth," *Economic Development and Cultural Change*, 31, no. 1 (October 1982), pp. 1-43.

102. Christainsen and Hagendorn, "Japanese Productivity," p. 30.

103. The classic work on the Japanese factory is J. G. Abegglen, *The Japanese Factory* (Glencoe, Ill.: Free Press, 1958).

104. Assessing the role of government on the importance of the "public" sector in the Japanese economy is difficult for definitional reasons. For a discussion,

see Chalmers Johnson, *Japan's Public Policy Companies* (Washington, D.C.: American Enterprise Institute, 1978).

105. Much has been written about MITI. For basics, see Haitani, *The Japanese Economic System*; for more detail, see Chalmers Johnson, *MITI and The Japanese Miracle* (Stanford, Calif.: Stanford University Press, 1982); Christainsen and Hagendorn, "Japanese Productivity."

106. For a more restrained view of the role of MITI in the 1970s, see Kozo Yamamura, "Success That Soured: Administrative Guidance and Cartels in Japan," in Kozo Yamamura, ed., *Policy and Trade Issues of the Japanese Economy* (Seattle: University of Washington Press, 1982), pp. 77–112. On the role of the state in supporting key sectors, see also Gary R. Saxonhouse, "What Is All This About 'Industrial Targeting' in Japan?" *The World Economy*, 6 no. 3 (September 1983), pp. 253–273.

107. The movement from fixed to flexible exchange rates was, of course, much more an issue than U.S.–Japanese trade. See Patrick and Rosovsky, *Asia's New Giant*, ch. 6. See also Takafusa Nakamura, *The Postwar Japanese Economy* (Tokyo: University of Tokyo Press, 1981), pt. 3; for specific references to the impact of oil shortages, see Yoichi Shinkai, "Oil Crises and Stagflation in Japan," in Yamamura, *Policy and Trade Issues of the Japanese Economy*, pp. 173–193.

108. Data are from World Bank, *World Development Report 1987* (New York: Oxford University Press, 1987), pp. 202–205.

109. Useful sources for analyzing contemporary adjustment policies include Ronald Dore, *Flexible Rigidities* (London: The Athlone Press, 1986); Chikara Higashi and G. Peter Lauter, *The Internationalization of the Japanese Economy* (Boston: Kluwer Academic Publishers, 1987); Edward J. Lincoln, *Japan: Facing Economic Maturity* (Washington, D.C.: The Brookings Institution, 1988); Yoshio Suzuki, *Money, Finance, and Macroeconomic Performance in Japan* (New Haven: Yale University Press, 1986).

India

110. The literature on the economic characteristics of LDCs is summarized in Marvin Miracle, "Comparative Market Structures in Developing Countries" (Association for Comparative Economics, Proceedings in Conjunction with the Midwest Economic Association, Detroit, April 1970). Also see John Due, *Indirect Taxes in Developing Countries* (Baltimore: Johns Hopkins Press, 1970).

111. Comparison of Indian and Chinese economic growth is provided by Subramanian Swamy, "Economic Growth in China and India, 1952–1970: A Comparative Appraisal," *Economic Development and Cultural Change*, 21 (July 1973), pp. 1–84; and Wilfred Malenbaum, "Modern Economic Growth in India and China: The Comparisons Revisited," *Economic Development and Cultural Change*, 3, no. 1 (October 1982), pp. 45–84.

112. Data here are compiled from World Bank, *World Development Report 1987* (New York: Oxford University Press, 1987), pp. 202–267.

113. This discussion is based principally on Angus Maddison, *Class Structure and Economic Growth: India and Pakistan Since the Moghuls* (New York: Norton, 1971), chs. 2–4.

114. Raj Krishna and G. S. Raychaudhuri, "Trends in Rural Savings and Capital Formation in India, 1950–51 to 1973–74," *Economic Development and Cultural Change*, 30, no. 2 (January 1982), pp. 289–294.

115. Maddison, *Class Structure and Economic Growth*, ch. 6.

116. For a discussion of the Indian controversy over planning priorities, see Jagdish Bhagwati and Sukhamoy Chakravaty, "Contributions to Indian Economic Analysis: A Survey," *American Economic Growth*, 59 (September 1969), pp. 4-29; and V. V. Bhatt, "Development Problem, Strategy, and Technology of Choice: Sarvadaya and Socialist Approaches in India," *Economic Development and Cultural Change*, 21, no. 1 (October 1982), pp. 85-100.

117. Maddison, *Class Structure and Economic Growth*, p. 119.

118. Allan G. Gruchy, *Comparative Economic Systems*, 2nd ed. (Boston: Houghton Mifflin, 1977), p. 638.

119. World Bank, *World Tables, 1976*, p. 428.

120. Ibid., summary tables.

121. Maddison, *Class Structure and Economic Growth*, p. 127.

122. Our discussion of Indian planning is based on Gruchy, *Comparative Economic Systems*, pp. 639-653; and Bhagwati and Chakravaty, "Contributions to Indian Economic Analysis," pp. 2-73.

123. This discussion is based on Maddison, *Class Structure and Economic Growth*, pp. 120-125.

124. Bhagwati and Chakravaty, "Contributions to Indian Economic Analysis," pp. 60-66.

125. Maddison, *Class Structure and Economic Growth*, pp. 122-124.

126. Malenbaum, "Modern Economic Growth in India and China," pp. 45-84; World Bank, *World Tables, 1980*, pp. 372-375.

127. Maddison, *Class Structure and Economic Growth*, p. 81.

RECOMMENDED READINGS

FRANCE

Bela Balassa, *The First Year of Socialist Government in France* (Washington, D.C.: American Enterprise Institute, 1982).

J.-J. Carre, P. Dubois, and E. Malinvaud, *French Economic Growth* (Stanford, Calif.: Stanford University Press, 1975).

Stephen S. Cohen, *Modern Capitalist Planning: The French Model* (Berkeley: University of California Press, 1977).

——, *Recent Developments in French Planning: Some Lessons for the United States* (Washington, D.C.: Government Printing Office, 1977).

Stephen S. Cohen and Peter A. Gourevitch, eds., *France in a Troubled World Economy* (Boston: Butterworth, 1982).

Saul Estrin and Peter Holmes, *French Planning in Theory and Practice* (Boston: Allen and Unwin, 1983).

John and Anne Marie Hackett, *Economic Planning in France* (Cambridge, Mass.: Harvard University Press, 1963).

Stanley Hottman and William Andrews, eds., *The Fifth Republic at Twenty* (New York: State University of New York Press, 1980).

J. R. Hough, *The French Economy* (New York: Holmes & Meier, 1982).

Richard F. Kuisel, *Capitalism and the State in Modern France* (New York: Cambridge University Press, 1981).

Vera Lutz, *Central Planning for the Market Economy: An Analysis of the French Theory and Experience* (London: Longmans Green, 1969).

John H. McArthur and Bruce R. Scott, *Industrial Planning in France* (Boston: Graduate School of Business Administration, Harvard University, 1969).

John Sheahan, *An Introduction to the French Economy* (Columbus, Ohio: Merrill, 1969).

W. Allen Spivey, *Economic Policies in France 1976–1981* (Ann Arbor: University of Michigan Graduate School of Business Administration, 1983).

GREAT BRITAIN

David S. Bell, ed., *The Conservative Government, 1979–84: An Interim Report* (London: Croom Helm, 1985).

Frank Blackaby, ed., *De-industrialisation* (London: Heinemann Educational Books, 1979).

Richard E. Caves and Associates, *Britain's Economic Prospects* (Washington, D.C.: Brookings, 1968).

Richard E. Caves and Lawrence B. Krause, eds., *Britain's Economic Performance* (Washington, D.C.: Brookings, 1980).

Carlo M. Cipolla, ed., *The Economic Decline of Empires* (London: Methuen, 1970).

B. E. Coates and E. M. Rawstron, *Regional Variations in Britain* (London: Batsford, 1971).

Charles Feinstein, eds., *The Managed Economy* (Oxford: Oxford University Press, 1983).

John and Anne Marie Hackett, *The British Economy: Problems and Prospects* (London: Allen and Unwin, 1967).

Paul Hare, *Planning the British Economy* (London: Macmillan, 1985).

Werner Z. Hirsch, *Recent Experience with National Economic Planning in Great Britain* (Washington, D.C.: Government Printing Office, 1977).

R. Kelf-Cohen, *British Nationalization, 1945–1973* (New York: St. Martin's, 1973).

W. P. J. Maunder, ed., *The British Economy in the 1970's* (London: Heinemann Educational Books, 1980).

F. V. Meyer, D. C. Corner, and J. E. S. Parker, *Problems of a Mature Economy* (London; Macmillan, 1970).

National Institute of Economic and Social Research, *The United Kingdom Economy* (London: Heinemann Educational Books, 1976).

Sidney Pollard, *The Wasting of The British Economy* (New York: St. Martin's, 1982).

Grahame Thompson, *The Conservatives' Economic Policy* (London: Croom Helm, 1986).

Alan Walters, *Britain's Economic Renaissance* (New York: Oxford University Press, 1986).

WEST GERMANY

Ludwig Erhard, *The Economics of Success* (London: Thames and Hudson, 1963).

G. Gutmann et al., *Die Wirtschaftsverfassung der Bundesrepublik Deutschland*, 2nd ed. (Stuttgart: Gustav Fischer Verlag, 1979).

Hannelore Hamel, ed., *Bundesrepublik-DDR, Die Wirtschaftssysteme*, 4th ed. (Munich: C. H. Beck, 1983).

Jack K. Knott, *Managing the German Economy* (Lexington, Mass.: Heath, 1981).

Heinz Lampert, *Volkswirtschaftliche Institutionen* (Munich: Verlag Franz Vahlen, 1980).

Martin Schnitzer, *East and West Germany: A Comparative Economic Analysis* (New York: Praeger, 1972).

Kurt Sontheimer, *The Government and Politics of West Germany* (New York: Praeger, 1973).

Gustav Stolper et al., *The German Economy, 1870 to the Present* (New York: Harcourt Brace Jovanovich, 1967).

Henry Wallich, *Mainsprings of the German Revival* (New Haven: Yale University Press, 1955).

JAPAN

J. G. Abegglen, *The Japanese Factory* (Glencoe, Ill.: Free Press, 1958).

G. C. Allen, *The Japanese Economy* (London: Weidenfeld and Nicolson, 1981).

Edward F. Denison and William K. Chung, *How Japan's Economy Grew So Fast: The Sources of Postwar Expansion* (Washington, D.C.: Brookings, 1976).

Ronald Dore, *Flexible Rigidities* (London: The Athlone Press, 1986).

Kanji Haitani, *The Japanese Economic System* (Lexington, Mass.: Heath, 1976).

Japanese Economic Research Center, *Economic Growth: The Japanese Experience Since the Meiji Era*, vols. I and II (Tokyo: Japanese Economic Research Center, 1973).

Chalmers Johnson, *Japan's Public Policy Companies* (Washington, D.C.: American Enterprise Institute, 1978).

——, *MITI and The Japanese Miracle* (Stanford, Calif.: Stanford University Press, 1982).

Lawrence Klein and Kazushi Ohkawa, eds., *Economic Growth: The Japanese Experience Since the Meiji Era* (Homewood, Ill.: Irwin, 1968).

Edward J. Lincoln, *Japan: Facing Economic Maturity* (Washington, D.C.: The Brookings Institution, 1988).

William Lockwood, ed., *The State and Economic Enterprise in Japan* (Princeton, N.J.: Princeton University Press, 1965).

Angus Maddison, *Economic Growth in Japan and the USSR* (London: Allen and Unwin, 1969).

Ryōshin Minami, *The Economic Development of Japan* (London: Macmillan, 1986).

Takafusa Nakamura, *The Postwar Japanese Economy* (Tokyo: University of Tokyo Press, 1981).

Mieko Nishimizu and Charles R. Hulten, "The Sources of Japanese Economic Growth, 1955-71," *Review of Economics and Statistics*, 60 (August 1978), pp. 351-361.

Kazushi Ohkawa and Henry Rosovsky, *Japanese Economic Growth* (Stanford, Calif.: Stanford University Press, 1973).

Hugh Patrick and Henry Rosovsky, eds., *Asia's New Giant: How the Japanese Economy Works* (Washington, D.C.: Brookings, 1976).

M. M. Postan et al., eds., *Cambridge Economic History of Europe*, vol. VII, pt. 2 (Cambridge: Cambridge University Press, 1978), chs. 3-5 on Japan.

Ozawa Terutomo, *Multinationalism Japanese Style* (Princeton, N.J.: Princeton University Press, 1979).

Yoshio Suzuki, *Money, Finance, and Macroeconomic Performance in Japan* (New Haven, Conn.: Yale University Press, 1986).

Yoshi Tsurumi, *The Japanese Are Coming: A Multinational Interaction of Firms and Politics* (Cambridge, Mass.: Ballinger, 1976).

Kozo Yamamura, ed., *Policy and Trade Issues of the Japanese Economy* (Seattle: University of Washington Press, 1982).

M. Y. Yoshino, *Japan's Multinational Enterprises* (Cambridge, Mass.: Harvard University Press, 1976).

INDIA

A. N. Agrawal, *Indian Economy*, 2nd ed. (New Delhi: Vikas Publishing House, 1976).

Jagdish Bhagwati and Sukhamoy Chakravaty, "Contributions to Indian Economic Analysis: A Survey," *American Economic Review*, 59 (September 1969), pp. 4–29.

Pramit Chaudhuri, ed., *Aspects of Indian Economic Development* (London: Allen and Unwin, 1971).

Francine R. Frankel, *India's Green Revolution* (Princeton, N.J.: Princeton University Press, 1971).

———, *India's Political Economy, 1947-1977* (Princeton, N.J.: Princeton University Press, 1978).

Raj Krishna and G. S. Raychaudhuri, "Trends in Rural Savings and Capital Formation in India, 1950-1951 to 1973-1974," *Economic Development and Cultural Change*, 30, no. 2 (January 1982), pp. 271-298.

William A. Long and K. K. Seo, *Management in Japan and India* (New York: Praeger, 1977).

Angus Maddison, *Class Structure and Economic Growth: India and Pakistan Since the Moghuls* (New York: Norton, 1971).

Wilfred Malenbaum, "Modern Economic Growth in India and China: The Comparison Revisited, 1950-1980," *Economic Development and Cultural Change*, 31, no. 1 (October 1982), pp. 45-84.

C. H. Shah and C. N. Vakil, eds., *Agricultural Development of India: Policy and Problems* (New Delhi: Orient Longman, 1979).

Subramanian Swamy, "Economic Growth in China and India, 1952-1970: A Comparative Appraisal," *Economic Development and Cultural Change*, 21 (July 1973), pp. 1-84.

Chapter 10
Variants of Socialism

In this chapter, we discuss important variants of planned socialism in three countries: Hungary, China, and East Germany. Each has distinctive features that differentiate it from the basic Soviet model.

We include Hungary because of its ongoing effort to decentralize planned socialism and introduce market-type modifications under its New Economic Mechanism. These modifications are designed to combine market and plan in a system where foreign trade is important.

China is included as an example of a Marxist alternative to the Soviet Union and as a representative of planned socialism in a large and very populous poor country. China is, therefore, interesting in a contemporary development context, especially as it undergoes major change in the post-Mao era.

East Germany is a relatively successful industrialized planned socialist economy, forced by resource endowment to follow an intensive path of economic development. East Germany's attempts to improve the planning system without altering its basic character are of special interest.

Each of these economies possesses the classic features of planned socialism: social ownership of the means of production, great emphasis on moral incentives, and an active government role in the control of the economy. The focus of this chapter is not so much on common features as on diversity among socialist economic systems: the extent to which market mechanisms are allowed to play coordinating and informational roles, the manner in which the planning system deals with the problems of advanced and underdeveloped socialist economies, and finally, the decentralization of decision making in these systems. The three countries discussed in this chapter have diverse economic characteristics, as shown in Table 10.1.

HUNGARY: SOCIALIST PLANNING AND ECONOMIC REFORM

Early works in comparative economic systems devoted little attention to the Hungarian economy. Over the last twenty years, however, Western economists have begun to pay more attention to Hungary.

As one prominent observer of Hungary and other East European systems has noted: "The Hungarian reform experience says as much about central planning as it does about Hungary, and therefore an understanding of that experience is important for those interested in the prospects for reform in all of Eastern Europe, and indeed, in the Soviet Union."[1] In other words, Hungary is a prototype of economic reform for the planned socialist economic systems of Eastern Europe, and presumably elsewhere. Why is this so?

Table 10.1 Selected Features of Some Socialist Economic Systems

Feature	Yugoslavia	Hungary	East Germany	China	Soviet Union
1. Percentage of GNP derived from industry, 1982	46[a]	41[a]	45.4[b]	47[a]	34[c]
2. Gross investment as a percentage of GNP, 1985	39	25	21.7[b]	38	30[c]
3. Working-age[d] population as a percentage of total population, 1985	68	66	67	65	66
4. Per capita GNP (1986) measured in U.S. dollars	6,220	7,920	11,300	260	8,370
5. Urban population as a percentage of total population (1985)	45	55	76	22	66

[a] 1985, percentage of gross domestic product.
[b] From Thad P. Alton, "East European GNPs: Origins of Product, Final Uses, Rates of Growth, and International Comparisons," in U.S. Congress, Joint Economic Committee, *East European Economies: Slow Growth in the 1980s* (Washington, D.C.: U.S. Government Printing Office, 1985), p. 89; East German investment is total accumulation as a share of net material product for 1981, p. 97.
[c] 1985 from CIA, *Handbook of Economic Statistics, 1987* (Washington, D.C.: U.S. Government Printing Office, 1987), Tables 39, 41.
[d] Defined as age 15–64.

Sources: Data with the exceptions noted are from World Bank, *World Development Report 1987* (New York: Oxford University Press, 1987), pp. 195–283.

Prior to 1968, Hungary applied the Soviet model of centrally planned socialism in a typical fashion. However, in 1968, Hungary began to introduce by far the most radical economic reform attempted in Eastern Europe (with the exception of Yugoslavia). In the words of one early observer of this reform: "It clearly represents the most radical postwar change, in the economic system of any Comecon country, which has been maintained over a period of years and give promise of continuity."[2]

Although the reform program in Hungary has met with only partial success, the problems that have arisen (persuading participants to actually change their ways and conflicts of objectives, for example) are fundamental to the reform experience of planned socialist systems.

Hungary shares many features with other Eastern and Southeastern European countries, such as Yugoslavia. It provides a refreshing contrast to the Soviet Union, which in some important respects is atypical. Hungary is a small country heavily dependent on foreign trade. The Hungarian experience with reforming foreign trade, and in particular its efforts to become integrated into the world economy both East and West, is prototypical. The difficulties of reforming the foreign trade mechanism are crucial to the Hungarian economy as well as to the economies of many other planned socialist systems of Eastern Europe.

We discuss economic reform in depth in Chapter 14. However, Hungarian reform is presented in this chapter because an understanding of the Hungarian experience at this point will prepare the reader for our later analysis of other reform models.

Hungary: The Setting

Hungary is located in central Europe. Its land area of approximately 36,000 square miles makes it roughly the same size as the state of Indiana. Its population of about 11 million is comparable in size to the population of Illinois. Although Hungary is not self-sufficient in energy, it does have supplies of coal, oil, and a number of minerals, including important bauxite deposits.

Although it has some rolling hills and low mountains, Hungary is basically a flat country with good agricultural land and a favorable climate. As in other East European countries, the period since the Second World War has seen a continuing flow of population from rural to urban areas and a changing balance of industrial and agricultural activity. Today, approximately half the population lives in urban areas.

Hungary is not particularly prosperous. While the reader is referred to Table 12.1 for additional detail, suffice it to say that most estimates of gross national product or per capita gross national product place Hungary in the middle of the East European countries.[3] It is generally wealthier than Bulgaria and Yugoslavia, and certainly wealthier than Albania. At the same time, it ranks behind East Germany and Czechoslovakia. Hungary's per capita income appears to be close to that of Greece. In this sense, economic development remains a key issue in Hungary. By the standards of Western Europe, Hungary remains relatively poor; by the standards of the Third World, Hungary ranks among the more affluent countries.

The Hungarian Economy: Prereform

The postwar reconstruction of the Hungarian economy began quite modestly in 1945.[4] Prior to the implementation of a three-year plan in 1947 (1947–1949), the main policies included stabilization of the currency, changes in the nature of rural landholdings, and the beginnings of nationalization. The first three-year plan was designed primarily to bring the economy up to prewar levels of economic activity. During this plan, a planning mechanism was created and the share of national income going to investment increased sharply. On balance, however, the changes were not radical, and balanced development was envisioned.

The era of balanced development came to an end with the introduction of a five-year plan in 1950. The share of national income devoted to investment was increased substantially and the bulk of new investment was directed toward heavy industry. This policy was partially reversed toward the end of the plan period, but it was reaffirmed in 1955–1956.

A number of economic trouble spots called for attention. There was an observed need to improve industrial labor productivity, especially through the development of a better incentive system to offset the declining supply of labor from rural areas. Suppy-demand imbalances were growing increasingly severe. Waste and imbalance in the material-technical supply system created the need for a substantially modified coordinating mechanism among enterprises.[5]

In addition, excess demand for investment led to substantial amounts of unfinished new construction and lack of attention to old facilities. Some mechanisms for the more rational allocation of capital investment had to be found. Adoption and diffusion of technological advances were seen as inadequate. Technological improvement was considered crucial for continued development of the economy.

This background seems familiar: a small country, the Soviet (Stalinist) model of industrialization, overcentralization, emphasis on extensive growth, rigidities of the plan mechanism, incentive problems, and the resulting difficulties. Against this background, the New Economic Mechanism initially promulgated in a party resolution in 1966 was introduced in practice in 1968. Over twenty years later, it remains one of the most important reform programs of planned socialist systems.

Intent of the New Economic Mechanism

There is disagreement as to the importance and effect of the Hungarian reform program. The New Economic Mechanism (NEM) has generally been interpreted as leaving the power to direct and manipulate the main lines of economic activity (volume and direction of investment, consumption shares) with the central authorities while relying on the market to execute the routine activities of the system.[6] The NEM called for substantial decentralization of decision-making authority and responsibility from upper-level administrative agencies to the enterprise level. In a general way, NEM bears a close resemblance to the Lange model. Let us consider the original blueprint of the NEM.

The objective of NEM was to combine the central direction of key variables with local responsibility for the remaining decisions. The first change was a significant reduction in the number and complexity of the directives emanating from the central planners. Although annual and five-year targets remained in force and determined the overall directions of change, individual enterprises were allowed to respond to the largely uncontrolled forces of supply and demand. The market was to assume a new role in determining both the input and output mix and in coordinating interenterprise activities. In most instances, enterprises were to be freed from compulsory output targets. The plans became considerably less detailed; greater emphasis was to be placed on five-year plans, less on one-year plans.

Second, an elaborate array of financial mechanisms was developed. The prevailing theme was less control from above, the use of profits as an indicator of success, and above all, the utilization of profits by the enterprise. Profits were to be used in an incentive system for both managers and workers and also for financing decentralized investment. The latter was to become an important share of total investment in the economy under NEM.

In general, the decreasing emphasis on administrative controls would be replaced by what Istvan Friss termed the "economic regulators."[7] These economic regulators would include a price policy, enterprise wage policy, investment policy, credit policy, trade policy, and fiscal and budget policy. The use of such regulators would facilitate enterprise autonomy while keeping enterprise activities within bounds acceptable to state planners.[8] For example, price flexibility would prevail, but within the limits of tolerable inflation. Wage policy would also be flexible, but within the policy goal of full employment. Decentralized investment at the enterprise level would be encouraged, but investment through the state budget would exercise state influence over the general direction of economic activity.

Foreign trade reform was a major component of NEM. In general, NEM called for less detailed planning in the foreign trade sector; in particular, a new role was envisioned for producing enterprises vis-à-vis the Foreign Trade Corporations. Individual enterprises would be encouraged to engage directly in foreign trade. To facilitate this shift, price flexibility was introduced so that some domestic prices could respond to changes in foreign currency prices. As one observer of the reform noted, even with the maintenance of various types of controls in the foreign trade sector, this program was of major importance, for it implied a genuine economic (as opposed to accounting) function for the exchange rate in a socialist planned economy.[9]

The potential appeal of the Hungarian economic reform is evident. As one analyst has noted, its development represents a clear-cut alternative to the East German reform.[10] Hungary has attempted by far the most radical reform in the planned socialist systems. Although NEM has not been without problems, it has remained in effect for two decades, a sufficient period to judge its effectiveness.

From a theoretical point of view, the Hungarian reform represents a significant departure from the Soviet model and a real attempt to combine decision making at the center and the periphery as suggested by the Lange model. The center retained responsibility for certain important decisions, but lesser decisions were left to individual producing and consuming units. In particular, market influences were to determine prices, though in many cases — especially for products deemed important by planners — central price controls were maintained and limits on the magnitude of most price changes were instituted.

Problems of Implementation: The Early Years

The Hungarian reformers have encountered three main types of difficulties.[11]

First, political constraints, notably Soviet concern and vested domestic interests, have limited the extent to which central control over key variables could be replaced by decentralized decision making. The political constraint also affected foreign trade. The political setting necessarily circumscribed what could be realistically attempted and achieved. (Hungary watched with interest the abortive attempt at economic reform in Czechoslovakia suppressed by the Soviets in the late 1960s.)

Second, it was quite evident that the structure of the Hungarian economy, like other planned socialist systems, would be molded by the priorities of the Soviet model. No reform program, regardless of political flexibility, could expect to avoid serious transitional problems. Indeed, the fundamental problem of effectively combining market and plan mechanisms in a manner consistent with central priorities would have to be resolved through considerable experimentation.

Third, planned socialist systems typically operate under different policy objectives than those of market capitalist systems. We have examined the problem of comparing economic systems when both objectives and constraints differ. In the Hungarian case, there were important constraints on the achievements of the reform program. David Granick, in his analysis of the Hungarian reform, identifies a number of them — limited tolerance of unemployment and inflation and a lack of desire for sharply expanded mobility of the labor force.[12] These constraints, though important, were not sufficiently severe to lead to abandonment of the reform scheme, although they have led to various modifications of original intentions.

For example, the market mechanism was intended to generate prices to which the industrial enterprises would respond, but intolerance of inflation led to the subsequent imposition of rather severe price controls. Fear of inflation also led to controls on wages, a measure that doubtless helped to control inflation but also damaged the incentive structure.

The reform was implemented with the existing industrial structure. Hungarian industrial enterprises, after the amalgamation of the early 1960s, were large; unlike other socialist countries, Hungary had not developed intermediate-level industrial authorities. Thus by 1970, there were only 812 industrial enterprises in Hungary with an average of seven plants each and with relative geographic concentration. As Granick notes, this meant an oligopolistic industrial structure in which planners could talk to enterprises rather easily without going through intermediate agencies.[13] In this framework, it is unclear to what extent NEM actually improved information flows; nor is it clear what impact the oligopolistic structure had on the rationality of decentralized price setting.

The sharp changes in world oil prices in the early 1970s made it necessary to connect external and internal prices on a permanent basis. Staged adjustments of internal prices (both producer and consumer prices) and revaluation of the Hungarian currency to keep internal price increases below external price increases offered a reasonable means for accomplishing the goals, in the view of Bela Csikos-Nagy.[14]

To summarize, in the early years of NEM, that is into the early 1970s, Hungarian economic performance, especially growth performance, was good. However, by the mid-1970s, it was harder to achieve domestic policy objectives (in particular the growth of consumption and the growth of exports) in the face of an increasingly unattractive world economic situation. Hungary responded, to some degreee, by reversing NEM. During this period, the use of market-type mechanisms (prices for example) declined, while state intervention in the economy increased.[15] For example, domestic prices became less meaningful as taxes and subsidies were introduced to shelter the domestic Hungarian economy from troubling world market forces. Controls over enterprise financial behavior were strengthened. The result was a slowdown of economic performance, accumulation of foreign debt, and a less positive outcome for NEM.

The NEM in the Seventies and Eighties

World economic conditions of the 1970s inhibited the progress of economic reform. At the same time, however, the reform programs were significantly limited by domestic considerations, in fact by problems typical of the centrally planned socialist systems. As Edward Hewett observes: While it is true that economic decision making is far more decentralized in Hungary today than it was two decades ago (and more decentralized than it is in any of the other CMEA countries), Hungary's economy is still more centralized than would have been anticipated in 1968.[16]

Although Hungary was able to translate past economic performance into enhanced levels of living for the population, performance slipped in the 1970s. According to official statistics, the average annual rate of growth of net material product in industry was 7.6 percent for the period 1970–1975, 5.7 percent for the period 1975–1978, and 2.8 percent in 1979. From 1980 to 1982, economic growth averaged about 1 percent per year.[17] In addition, according to United Nations calculations, the domestic consumer price index was increasing during the 1970s at just under 6 percent on an average annual basis. This was an astronomical inflation rate by the standards of the pre-1968 period.[18]

Most important, the terms of trade with both the West and COMECON countries turned sharply against Hungary in the mid-to-late 1970s.[19] The inevitable result was a growing annual external deficit and an accumulating external hard currency debt for a country that relied on imports and was less than competitive in world export markets.

As Hewett has noted, Hungary faced two major problems as a result of the problems of the 1970s.[20] First, to restrain inflationary pressures, there was a need for demand management, which had to take place primarily within the enterprise sector; it could not act on aggregate consumption as is typical in Western economies. Second, there was a need to improve the organization of supply at the microeconomic level, a system closely but uncontrollably tied to the foreign sector.

Faced with these difficulties, Hungarian leaders altered their economic policies to reflect the basic economic problems in the system.

The changes of the late 1970s and early 1980s seemed once again to move the economy closer to the original goals of NEM. However, as with earlier reform efforts, bureaucratic inertia and the inherent difficulty of implementing new procedures stood as obstacles to success.

Hungarian economic policy of the late 1970s and early 1980s was directed toward the achievement of two broad objectives.[21] First, an effort was made to maintain the achieved standard of living of the Hungarian people, despite an inevitable slowdown, which Hewett describes as "austerity." Second, to bring the trade imbalance under control, a set of procedures that would control the advancement of the domestic economy within the realistic limits of its trade potential was instituted.

Specifically, a stabilization program was introduced, and familiar measures enacted to bring debt under control. Steps were taken to improve Hungarian access to credit (Hungary joined the IMF and the World Bank in the early 1980s), and limits were placed on domestic demand so that import growth could be constrained and export growth expanded. Curbs on the growth of domestic demand limited the growth of both consumption and investment. Investment could be controlled through changes in the state budget, and consumption through the state's ability to limit wages.

Total gross domestic investment declined from an index of 100 in 1978 to 68.5 in 1984.[22] Real earnings of wage earners and employees declined from an index of 100 in 1978 to 97.2 in 1982, although real consumption grew in the same period due to slippage in the private sector. During these years, the convertible currency trade balance improved as a result of a variety of measures. The objective in the 1980s has been a gradual but continuing reduction in the convertible currency debt. The average annual rate of growth of gross domestic product slipped from 5.5 percent for the period 1965–1980 to 1.8 percent for the period 1980–1985, a combination of improvement in agriculture, with sharp declines in industrial and service growth rates.[23]

The NEM proposed to use economic regulators (prices, investment rules, credit arrangements, and so forth), to improve the efficiency of industrial enterprises. As both Hungarian and Western observers have emphasized, however, Hungarian industrial enterprises have been protected by a myriad of regulations (implemented by the planners, the banking system, state agencies, and others) and protective policies such as subsidies.[24] This system, kept largely intact in the 1970s and 1980s, had a number of negative consequences.

First, the investment component of aggregate demand was largely out of control and grew rapidly.[25] The drive by individual enterprises to expand investment to achieve plan targets and the willingness of the state to support this behavior led to overexpansion of investment. Second, there was excess demand for investment goods. Furthermore, with imports playing a major role in Hungarian industrial inputs, and with little effective control over enterprise purchases of inputs from the foreign sector, inefficiencies were bound to arise. Third, Hungarian industrial enterprises, protected in the domestic market and from world markets, had little incentive to develop effective exports or, for that matter, substitutes for imports.

In light of these developments, government policy began to emphasize equilibrium in the domestic economy and control of the foreign trade imbalance. In the late 1970s and early 1980s, some controls were expanded, for example direct controls over certain types of enterprise investment. At the same time, emphasis was placed on enterprise self-financing of investment, a policy designed to wean the industrial enterprise from its protective cover. Finally, substantial price adjustments were made in the early 1980s.

Since the use of the price mechanism as an economic lever is of fundamental importance, the matter of prices bears further consideration. One of the basic goals of NEM was an expanded role for prices as regulators in the system. Put another way, prices were to be gradually adjusted so that they would come, more or less, to reflect relative scarcities in the system. This adjustment was to come about by using world market prices as a guide. These pricing goals have not been accomplished.

After many years of isolation from market forces, domestic Hungarian prices at the time of the reform bore little relation to world market prices and even less relation to relative scarcities. Fundamental adjustments in relative prices were required if Hungarian prices were to reflect relative scarcities. The various programs of price controls and price freezes precluded these changes, and dramatic shifts in the world economy (rising energy prices in the 1970s) exacerbated the Hungarian adjustment problem.[26] Nevertheless, pricing policies of the late 1970s and 1980s once again moved in the general direction of adjusting Hungarian prices toward world market prices.[27]

Further adjustment of prices is to take place in two general steps. First, prices of Hungarian producer goods are to be gradually adusted to reflect world market prices. Second, Hungarian consumer goods prices are to be adjusted to cover domestic producer goods prices. Some subsidies and taxes (a major source of past distortions) will cushion the initial impact. Ideally, these changes will force enterprises to face economic reality rather than rely on subsidies. In addition, where highly profitable enterprises have been a major source of government revenue, new revenue sources will have to be found. In the 1980s, price increases have been implemented. The price of many consumer goods has risen.

The adjustment of prices in the foreign trade sector is equally complex. A major, though largely unachieved, aim of NEM was to move enterprises out of their protective cover and place them in an aggressive posture vis-à-vis the world economy. Achievement of this goal was retarded by a number of factors. First, protective subsidies remained in effect for many enterprises engaging in foreign trade. Second, fundamental adjustments in domestic and foreign trade prices were slow in coming. Third, means had to be found to coordinate the NEM system of trade with that of its planned socialist trading partners.

Hungarian enterprises cannot make rational decisions as long as meaningful comparisons of domestic and foreign prices are impossible. Initial steps have been taken to bring the forint (the domestic Hungarian currency) into line with world currencies, in order to set a meaningful, though controlled, exchange rate that would reflect the purchasing power of the forint.[28] Multiple exchange rates, long typical of the Hungarian foreign exchange system, were abandoned in 1982. These steps seek to strengthen the rationality of enterprise decision making by making it possible to compare domestic costs and prices with foreign costs and prices.

Many economic systems have had to respond to external market shocks in the 1970s and 1980s, but in the Hungarian case, the common East European problem of hard currency debt has been a major driving force. At the same time, although some traditional macroeconomic tools have been used in the adjustment process, interest in reform continues in Hungary. Indeed the replacement of Janos Kadar by a much younger leader, Karoly Grosz, in May of 1988 may well signal a more rigorous pursuit of reform. Recent developments in the Hungarian reform process are further discussed in Chapter 14.

CHINA: SOCIALISM, PLANNING, REVOLUTION, AND ECONOMIC DEVELOPMENT

China has fascinated the West for centuries. Western economists are interested in modern China for three principal reasons. First, the characteristics of Chinese industrialization distinguish it from other cases that we have examined. After the Chinese Communist party came to power in 1949, a period of socialist industrialization began. The Chinese applied the Soviet model, with alterations, in a highly underdeveloped setting.[29] Second, the easing of Chinese-American hostilities in the early 1970s sharply expanded communication between the two countries.[30] This era provided Americans a long-denied opportunity to examine the Chinese system on a firsthand basis. This opportunity was enriched in the late 1970s and early 1980s when the Chinese began to release a substantially increased volume of information about their economy.[31] The result has been a sharply expanded and productive dialogue, considerably enhancing our knowledge of the Chinese economy. Third, the post-Mao era has seen major changes in the Chinese economic system. These changes are of great interest to the comparative economist, not only for their impact on Chinese development, but also for the enrichment they provide to our understanding of the traditional Soviet model of development.

There is much more to the Chinese economy than reform, although changes of the late 1970s and 1980s clearly dominate current interest. In this chapter, we discuss the basic working arrangements of the Chinese economy; focus on and interpretation of reform are covered in Chapter 14.

The Setting

First, China is a very large country by any definition. It is sobering to compare China with Canada, another large country. Canada, with a population of approximately 25 million, has a land area of 3.8 million square miles. China, with a population of slightly more than one billion, has a land area of just over 3.6 million square miles. Indeed, if the Chinese population should continue to increase at the average annual rate of 2.1 percent of the past two decades, a new Canada, in terms of population, would arise in China roughly every fifteen months![32] Both land and population are resources that can contribute to economic development, but people must eat, and considerable portions of China's land are inappropriate for increasing the food supply, at least in the absence of capital investment.

Second, China is a resource-rich country, but, once again, its resources must be exploited to support the objective of economic development. While coal is a major source of energy, only recently has China initiated a major effort to utilize its oil riches. In addition, sharp variations in climate and fertility, along with large areas of rough terrain, make the application of large amounts of capital essential to raise agricultural output, despite China's vast land area.

Third, China is a poor country. While substantial economic progress has been made since the industrialization drive began in the early 1950s, China in 1987 had a per capita income of about $500.[33] China's per capita income, while above its immediate neighbors India and Pakistan, ranks well below that of Taiwan, South Korea, and Malaysia. From the standpoint of the economy, then, the major goals are still industrialization and economic development.

Finally, a nonsystemic feature is the unique Chinese historical experience. China is the oldest existing civilization in the world, a source of great pride to the Chinese people. While there are numerous ethnic minorities in China (primarily in the western part of the country), the dominant nationality group is the *han* nationality. The Chinese language with many varying dialects is dominated by the Mandarin dialect. The rich heritage of the Chinese people must be an important if unmeasurable influence on their attitudes toward and participation in the modernization process.

China and the Soviet Model

The economic, social, and cultural differences between China and the other socialist countries are striking. To the extent that we wish to make comparisons between China with its low income and, say, the United States, with its high income, great caution must be taken. Comparisons of China with India, or even contemporary China with the Soviet Union of the 1930s make more sense. Even in this latter comparison it is important to note that China in 1949 was probably much more backward than Russia in 1917.

In looking back on the problems that must have faced Chinese leaders and planners in adapting the Soviet model, the key questions are: How could the Chinese economy, in the absence of the advantages enjoyed by Russian leaders in 1917 (a basic industrial capacity, a transportation network, and so on), institute a planned socialist economic system in a large and very poor peasant economy? In developing such a planned socialist economy, what modifications of the Soviet model would have to be made to account for the very large Chinese population, its relative poverty, and its primarily rural character? To what extent would the Chinese natural resource base support industrial development, especially in view of sharp regional disparities and the likelihood that foreign trade would play a relatively small role? Could the Soviet model of rapid industrialization, used twenty years earlier under rather different circumstances, be transplanted in whole or in part to the Chinese case?

China at the time of the 1949 revolution was a classic LDC: low per capita income, significant population pressure on arable land and other resources, and an absence of institutions appropriate for economic development. China, with a land mass slightly larger than that of the United States and about half that of the Soviet Union, and with a population roughly four times that of the United States and about three and one-half times that of the Soviet Union, began to implement the Soviet model in 1949 with important and interesting modifications. The result has been substantial economic growth and development that has, however, been interrupted when ideological and political factors have gained supremacy over economic factors.

In looking at different economic systems in action, we have varied the format from case to case in order to highlight the system's salient features. Chinese economic development can best be understood in terms of its historical evolution since 1949 and, in particular, as a modification of the Soviet model of economic development.[34] What we wish to learn from the Chinese experience is, above all, the extent to which a system of planned socialism is a suitable vehicle for economic development in a large country of extreme poverty.

The Beginnings of Industrialization: The 1950s

The Chinese People's Republic was proclaimed by Mao Zedong in 1949. Between 1949 and 1952 a period of consolidation ensued. Two main goals were pursued. First, the redistribution of land to individual households was implemented in preparation for ultimate collectivization. The latter, however, was to be pursued without undue haste. Second, nationalization and consolidation of the holdings in the industrial sector took place in preparation for the development of national economic planning. Other steps were taken — financial reform, educational reform, and other changes deemed necessary to stabilize the economy in preparation for the beginning of the first five-year plan in 1953. However, the basic steps were toward changing the ownership base and the means of guiding the economy. In this respect, China's first steps were much like those of the Soviet Union in the aftermath of the revolution.

Inevitably, the Chinese experience with change in the rural sector is compared to the Soviet experience of the late 1920s and early 1930s, especially insofar as Soviet collectivization brought with it a number of important negative consequences.[35] Did the Chinese leadership modify the Soviet approach? On the surface both countries utilized initial land reform and similar experimental forms of organization — the elimination of class differences at a rapid pace, the distribution of machinery and equipment through centralized facilities, and pressure to hold down rural food consumption levels. At the same time, there were differences. Possibly the most important achievement was the avoidance of substantial destruction (of cattle, facilities, and so on) in China.[36] This factor alone has led most observers to believe that the extremes of the Soviet model were avoided. Possibly the Chinese countryside was better prepared in terms of ideological and organizational factors, though certainly not in terms of machinery and equipment. Also, the state farm, a key feature of the Soviet experience, was not introduced until later in China.

In sum, the Chinese adopted the basic Soviet model of land reform and subsequent collectivization; the differences, however, were sufficient to preclude the extreme negative consequences experienced in the Soviet Union. However, the success of Chinese collectivization in transferring resources to the needs of industrialization remains an open question, just as it remains an open issue in the Soviet Union.

The Planning Apparatus

The second important policy of the early years was the nationalization of industry and the development of a system of national economic planning. During the early 1950s there was a gradual transition from private industry toward socialist industry — certainly more gradual than in the Soviet Union after 1928, but probably less gradual if one includes the Soviet periods of war communism and the New Economic Policy. The shift from private to socialist industry in China was targeted to be slow, though toward the latter part of the first five-year plan it proved to be rapid. The pattern of change was from private ownership to elementary state capitalism, then to advanced state capitalism, and finally to socialist industry.[37] However, by 1955, 68 percent of the gross value of output could be accounted for by state industry and only 16 percent by joint state-private enterprises.[38] Indeed, even handicraft production was brought under state control in moves reminiscent of the excessive nationalization of Soviet war communism. Thus, although the plans for the socialist transformation in both agriculture and industry called for a relatively gradual pace, the experience in 1955–1956 demonstrated that ideology and political considerations could accelerate the rate of change.

Soviet leaders learned from their experiences between 1917 and 1928 that if the market is to be abolished, a substitute mechanism must be developed for economic activity to continue in a coordinated fashion. The Chinese planning structure, put in place in the early 1950s and subsequently modified, was initially similar to the Soviet model.[39] The basic unit of production activity was the enterprise. As in the Soviet Union, a dual party-state administrative structure drew up and implemented (often interrupted) five-year plans for both agriculture and industry. Chinese plans are formulated largely by the State Planning Commission, which like Gosplan in the Soviet Union, operates through an industrial ministry system communicating with regional and enterprise officials and ultimately assembling a plan. Once it is approved by the State Council, that plan becomes law for all enterprises.

Output targets are expressed in value and physical terms. A material balance is worked out in a time sequence utilizing both central directive and local information. Control figures are established. After they are assembled and "balanced" at the national level, those figures become plan targets. Inevitably, this system produced problems similar to those found in the Soviet case — imbalance and shortages, poor quality, late plans, and deviation of results from targets. Chinese thinking on reforming this system began to surface in the mid-1950s, but was overshadowed by the political and ideological upheavals of the late 1950s.

The early 1950s was a period of unrest. Then, after the liberal Hundred Flowers Campaign (1956-1957), during which there was open discussion and criticism of the system, the Great Leap Forward was launched (1958-1960).[40] The Great Leap was a massive resurgence of ideology, which replaced rationality. Campaigns were instigated with revolutionary fervor to emphasize a new role for the peasantry, especially through small-scale industry in the countryside and the introduction of communes. Development of water resources was also stressed.

For a variety of economic, political, and ideological reasons, the Great Leap was abandoned by 1960, but the commune system, introduced in 1958, remained, with modifications.[41] The Rural Peoples Communes were initially set up as very large units combining a number of collectives (advanced cooperatives) to produce agricultural and handicraft products and to serve as local units of government. The original communes (roughly 26,000 in number and averaging about 4,600 households each) faced difficulties. Basically, agricultural units encompassing some 50,000 households were too difficult to coordinate, and individual incentives were overshadowed by the size of the collective. Subsequent modifications improved the commune system.

The First Ten Years

How can we appraise the first ten years of the Chinese industrialization experience? As one observer has noted: "In general, it can be said that during 1953-57, the Chinese followed the broad outlines of the Stalinist strategy of selective growth under conditions of austerity with three important qualifications."[42] First, less pressure was placed on the agricultural sector, possibly a recognition of the important underlying element of the Chinese case: a large, rural, poor population. Presumably the Chinese leaders had learned from the Soviet experience with rapid collectivization, for despite many similarities between the two cases, the extreme costs of the Soviet case were avoided in China.

Second, unlike the Soviet case, where state resources were directed toward the agricultural sector through state farms, Machine Tractor Stations, and so on, agriculture in the early years of the new Chinese regime was largely self-financed. This may have reflected the much lower level of economic development in China in 1949 than in the Soviet Union in, say, 1928.[43]

Third, the Chinese relied heavily on the state enterprise as a revenue source from which state investment funds would be derived. In 1953, for example, revenue from state enterprises accounted for roughly 35 percent of total budgetary revenue, rising to 46 percent by 1957. In comparison, by far the most important source of budgetary revenue in the early years of Soviet industrialization was the turnover tax, with revenues from enterprises playing a minor role. The decision not to rely on taxes forced from the peasants represented a realization that such a policy could not be applied to a subsistence agriculture.

During the 1950s, the Chinese generally followed the Soviet "industry first" strategy. Between 1953 and 1957, heavy industry in China absorbed an average of 85 percent of industrial investment. At the same time, only 8 percent of state investment was devoted to agriculture, while aggregate investment accounted for roughly 20 to 25 percent of the national product.[44] These figures suggest, on balance, a relatively high rate of accumulation for a poor country (though not nearly as high as the comparable rate for the Soviet Union in the early 1930s), with emphasis on industry in general and heavy industry in particular.

China's economic performance during the 1950s was generally strong, though uneven. There was an impressive doubling of GNP per capita, a ninefold increase in industrial production, a modest increase in agricultural production. Overall, the early years were ones of consolidation. The first five-year plan witnessed substantial growth of production; the latter part of the 1950s saw a mixture of progress and retrogression in both industry and agriculture.

The striking feature of Chinese economic performance in the 1950s was the impact of ideological disruptions. According to Subramanian Swamy's calculations, Chinese GNP grew at an annual rate of 6 percent from 1952–1956.[45] The 1958 level of GNP, however, was not regained until 1963. Thus, the Great Leap caused an enormous setback in Chinese growth.

The Great Leap Forward was abandoned in the late 1950s at a time when relations between China and the Soviet Union were deteriorating rapidly. The ideological (and economic) break between the two countries was almost complete by 1960. Although the role of outside aid in the Chinese development experience was minimal, the Soviet contribution was important in the early years, especially in the area of technical assistance. The break would prove to be a sobering experience for Chinese leaders and planners.

The 1960s: Development and Disruption

Like the earlier decade, the 1960s can be conveniently divided into two very different periods: moderation in the early 1960s, upheaval in the late 1960s.

The early 1960s was a period of relative calm in which there was a tendency to look toward balance in economic development, modernization in the agricultural sector, and recovery from the aftermath of the Great Leap. In industry, the 1960s was a period of rather substantial reform — a movement away from the overwhelming importance of gross output, the major success indicator of the 1950s, toward quality in production and the elimination of major deficiencies in the planning system.

In a sense, both central control and local initiative were variables to be changed. The center tried to put pressure on enterprises to improve quality, to be concerned with efficiency, to enhance the role of technical expertise in the decision-making process. At the same time, there was a tendency to shift many decisions, especially minutiae, to the local level. For example, local industrial establishments were set up to serve local (especially rural) needs. Although the emphasis on enterprise efficiency and profitability came under sharp attack during the Cultural Revolution of the late 1960s, evidence suggests that in the 1960s the Chinese industrial structure was modified to suit peculiar Chinese conditions, and the modifications for the most part withstood later upheavals.

During the early 1960s, new emphasis was placed on agriculture's role in the economy and the need for mechanization and reorganization in that sector. The communes underwent substantial change. Because communes were found to be too large, the intermediate (brigade) and lower-level (team) units assumed new importance. Emphasis on non-material rewards, a hallmark of the earlier commune system, was changed in favor of material incentives and the reintroduction of private plots. Although the number of communes was reduced during the 1960s, their role in the social, cultural, and political affairs of the countryside remained intact through the 1970s.

In addition to organizational changes and policy shifts, the 1960s witnessed a widespread educational campaign among the Chinese people. There was an effort to re-educate the population in the ways of Mao. This campaign laid the foundations for the Cultural Revolution.

If the early 1960s was a period of rationality — reform and change along a well-defined continuum — the opposite could be said of the Cultural Revolution of 1966–1969. The Cultural Revolution, difficult for the Western observer to fully comprehend, was an upheaval of ideas, an abandonment of much that had preceded it. Emanating from a Communist party struggle, the Cultural Revolution was not a debate over economic ideas. In fact, its economic implication, the disastrous disruption of economic activity, became apparent only later. However, although economic activity was substantially disturbed, the basic organizational arrangements in industry and in agriculture do not seem to have been altered in significant ways.

Like the Great Leap, the Cultural Revolution had a disastrous effect on output. Disruption was so great that meaningful GNP estimates during the Cultural Revolution are not available. Swamy's estimates show that GNP failed to increase between 1965 and 1970, a loss of output equal to or more severe than that of the Great Leap.[46]

China After the Cultural Revolution

Ironically, examination of events relating to the Chinese economy in the 1970s and 1980s reveals a pattern of twists and turns and an intermix of ideology and economics reminiscent of earlier years. Notwithstanding the rapprochement between China and the United States and a sharply increased flow of information about the Chinese economy, it remains difficult to assess with any certainty the impact of programs and policies developed during these eyars.

The early 1970s was a period of recovery from the Cultural Revolution.[47] Western scholars have generally argued that the Cultural Revolution was a major setback to Chinese economic development and modernization. Furthermore, the attempted return to normalcy of the early 1970s was interrupted. Zhou Enlai, a long-term advocate of a moderate path of industrialization, died in January 1976. The following September, Mao Zedong, the father of the revolution and the advocate of a continuation of the revolutionary mentality, died. Shortly thereafter, in October 1976, the "Gang of Four," representing the revolutionary left and continuation of the Stalinist mode of industrialization, were arrested amid great ideological fervor.[48] These events paved the way for what would turn out to be fundamental changes in Chinese economic policy. The resurgence of conservative elements, however, meant an immediate resumption of the drive toward industrialization and modernization.

In 1978, a ten-year plan for China's modernization was announced by Hua Guofeng. This plan, covering the period 1975–1985, was to pursue the "Four Modernizations" — namely, industry, agriculture, sicence and technology, and defense. The initial plan was grandiose. The average annual rate of growth of industrial output was to be 10 percent, of agricultural output, 4–5 percent. The stress would be traditional: industry at the forefront, in particular heavy industry. By the end of 1978, however, imbalances in the economy led to important shifts. Hua Guofeng announced a major program of economic reform and effectively scrapped the ten-year plan. In effect, one-year plans replaced the defunct ten-year plan. In 1982, a five-year plan was announced for 1981–1985, though this plan actually covered the period from 1983 to 1985. What were the imbalances, and what steps were taken to reform the system?

Fundamentally, the problems that plagued the Chinese economy in the 1970s and 1980s derived from the unyielding pursuit of the Stalinist model of industrialization. Material incentives were weakened by the continuing emphasis on accumulation. Moreover, the lion's share of that accumulation was devoted to heavy industry. As a result, there were growing problems in the areas of energy, transportation, and consumer goods.

Although the Chinese have tended to modify their working arrangements without a formal and specific reform program, the program announced at the end of 1978 and subsequently subsumed under the "eight-point program" really amounted to a major modification and consolidation of the system. Reforms were directed at a number of problems.

First, priorities were changed. Light industry, agriculture, and infrastructure were to receive new attention. For example, the share of investment devoted to heavy industry fell from 54.7 percent in 1978 to 40.3 percent in 1981.[49]

Second, there was to be a substantial attempt to decentralize decision making in industrial enterprises. Industrial enterprises were to become responsible for their own operations. They were given greater authority and more responsibility for, among other things, the distribution of enterprise revenues. Increasingly, enterprise profits could be retained for enterprise investment, worker bonuses, and so forth.

Third, substantial changes were to be implemented in agriculture. These reforms focused on changes in the mechanism of payment and the importance of material incentives.

China: The Rural Economy

In our examination of different economic systems, we have not always paid special attention to the rural economy. By most definitions, however, agriculture (broadly defined to include rural economic activity in general) is the dominant sector of the Chinese economy. Moreover, the **commune** is an interesting and important organizational unit, that is worthy of considerable attention.

Prior to 1978, the commune was the best-known unit of organization in rural China.[50] The conduct of basic economic activity was in the hands of the **production team**, a combination of a number of households; within a village, production teams would combine to form a brigade; brigades would combine to form a commune. Above the commune, the county has been the state unit responsible for directing agricultural activity. It has played a major role in implementing the national economic plan administered by the Ministry of Agriculture and Forestry.[51]

The commune had a reward system not unlike that used prior to 1966 in Soviet collective farms. Individuals would accumulate points for work done on a daily basis. Their renumeration would then be based on the residual income of the commune, which consisted of revenues less expenses (the latter including investment in the commune).

In 1978, two major reforms were introduced that significantly changed production arrangements in the Chinese countryside. First, the production team became the basic accounting unit. Second, the **responsibility system**, which tied rewards directly to production, replaced the former point system. Although this description is a simplification, and there are significant variations, it is fair to say that both changes have been implemented throughout much of rural China.[52]

There were also important policy changes in the countryside. First, the responsibility system introduced significant decentralization to decision-making authority. Sowing targets were replaced with contracts, and since 1985, with only a few exceptions, fixed purchase quotas have been abolished.[53] Second, there was a marked shift in favor of expanded material incentives. Not only was the point system replaced, but also prices were increased, leading to a much more favorable incentive structure for the rural sector. Finally, with a relaxation of restrictions on private economic activity, nonagricultural activity increased significantly in rural areas.

The reforms have not been without problems, which are discussed in Chapter 14. Nevertheless, agricultural output during the 1980s has grown at better than 12 percent on an average annual basis, though impending difficulties may lower this rate in the latter years of the decade.[54]

China at the Crossroads

As the decade of the 1980s comes to an end, the story of China for the immediate future is one of economic reform. According to estimates of the World Bank, growth of the Chinese population declined from an average annual rate of 2.2 percent in the period 1965 to 1980 to 1.2 percent in the period 1980 to 1985.[55] The rate of urbanization in these two periods was 2.6 and 3.3 percent respectively, generating a balance of only 22 percent urban population in 1985.

However, when one examines the record of economic growth, the results are impressive, even on a per capita basis. For the period 1965 to 1980, gross domestic product grew at an average annual rate of 6.4 percent, and for the period 1980 to 1985, 9.8 percent. Performance was good in all sectors of the economy, although the greatest gains were made in agriculture.

Although the dollar value of gross national product remains very modest, at U.S. $310 in 1985, nevertheless structural changes are significant. Between 1965 and 1980, the share of industry in gross domestic product increased from 38 to 47 percent, while for the same period, the share of agriculture declined from 39 to 33 percent.

For the period 1965 to 1980, the average annual rate of growth of private consumption was 5.3 percent, and for the period 1980 to 1985, it was 7.7 percent. The share of investment in gross domestic product was 25 percent in 1965, increasing to a very high level of 38 percent in 1985.

There has been a significant rate of growth of merchandise trade, although in the 1980s the rate of growth of imports has been notably higher than the rate of growth of exports.

Judged by simple performance numbers, the contemporary Chinese record is impressive. However, as we discuss in more detail in Chapter 14, this performance record has been achieved in the face of significant difficulties in the Chinese economy. Can this record of economic progress be sustained? Will imbalances and political forces threaten continuation of the reform? These are a few of the issues that must be considered in a full assessment of the status of Chinese reform.

EAST GERMANY: INTENSIVE
GROWTH WITH PLANNING

There are two reasons for considering the economy of East Germany, the German Democratic Republic (GDR), here. First, the GDR typifies a planned socialist economy that has been forced to develop along an intensive rather than extensive growth path. Throughout the postwar era, the GDR has experienced a decline in population because of the flight of its population to West Germany, extremely low birthrates, and wartime population losses. Ample labor reserves were simply not available in East Germany to support a rapid expansion of employment. Moreover, East German authorities were constrained by the proximity of the West German *Wirtschaftswunder* and could not allow unduly large differentials in living standards to develop between the two countries. The higher standard of living in West Germany is well known in the East because of access to West German television and the flow of visitors from the Federal Republic. Thus, despite a relatively high per capita income, the East Germans have had below-average investment rates (by Soviet-bloc standards) throughout the postwar period. Accordingly, the East Germans have not had the benefit of exceptional rates of growth of capital stock. Even if capital had grown rapidly, however, the question of whether it could have effectively substituted for deficient labor would be unanswered. As other planned socialist economic systems move away from an extensive and toward an intensive pattern of growth, the East German experience may be a crucial bellwether.

The second reason for analyzing East Germany is that the GDR is the one Soviet-bloc country to have attempted a full-fledged experiment with so-called **Libermanism** — the notion that central planning can be made more efficient by **devolution** of planning authority. This experiment, called the New Economic System, began in 1963 and ended in the early 1970s. Although short-lived, the New Economic System provided an interesting case for the study of attempted devolution of decision-making authority in a planned socialist system. These two points, and the fact that GDR economic performance has been strong by the standards of the planned socialist countries, require its inclusion in our discussion of variants of socialist economic systems.[56]

Historical Setting

The historical evolution of the East German economic system is an integral part of the story of the postwar division of Germany. The Potsdam Conference, held in the late summer of 1945, created four occupation zones (Soviet, French, British, and American) and produced the agreement that postwar Germany would continue to be treated as one country. It became apparent, even before the conclusion of the conference, that the social, political, and economic policies of the Soviets and the Western allies would be markedly different in their respective occupation zones. The Soviet Military Administration in Germany (SMAD) has already nationalized much of industry and banking and expropriated estates of more than 100 hectares. By July 1945, SMAD established the German Central Management for Industry, Transportation, Agriculture and Forestry, Fuels, and Energy (*Deutsche Zentralverwaltung*) which became the German Economic Commission (*Deutsche Wirtschaftskommission*) in 1947. In April 1946 the Socialist Unity party (SED) was formed by SMAD under the leadership of Walter Ulbricht (who returned to Germany after spending the war years in the Soviet Union).

The initial policy of both the Soviet and the allied occupation forces was to hold back the economic development of Germany. The allies shared a common fear of a strong German economy. In the Soviet zone, an active policy of reparations collection was pursued. Many factories were dismantled and their equipment sent to the Soviet Union. The Soviets also collected war reparations by claiming shares of current production of German industry. In the allied zones, there was a significant change in policy in 1947 with the realization that the economic recovery of Europe was strongly dependent on the recovery of the German economy. The Marshall Aid program was announced by the United States, and, in May of 1947, the allied zones were merged into the United Economic Region. In June 1948, separate currency reforms were carried out in the Soviet and allied occupation zones, an act that formalized the division of postwar Germany. In the spring and summer of 1949, separate constitutions for the Federal Republic of Germany (FRG) and for the German Democratic Republic were adopted.

The changes in the economic system of East Germany that occurred during the political division of Germany were predictable. By the late 1940s, virtually all of industry, transportation, and banking was nationalized and placed under the control of central planning. In agriculture, the process of collectivization began in earnest in 1952 and was completed by 1960. Only in handicraft production and retail trade was private ownership permitted, so that even today roughly 75 percent of workers in handicraft work for privately owned firms.

The Contemporary Setting

East Germany has slightly less than one-half the area of West Germany. Its population of 17 million is about one-fourth that of West Germany. The northern part of East Germany is sparsely populated and specializes in agricultural production; the industrial regions are located in the south. In terms of natural resources, East Germany has brown coal reserves and potash; but on the whole, East Germany must be regarded as a resource-poor country whose industry is dependent on raw material imports.

More than one-half of the East German population is employed, one of the highest ratios in the world. The participation rate of women is over 80 percent, and two-thirds of all employed persons have completed occupational training or higher education. The major economic sector of the East German economy is industry. The most important industrial branches are chemicals, machine building and transportation equipment, and electrotechnics. East Germany's per capita income places it at the top of the planned socialist economies, but it is approximately one-half that of West Germany.

The East German Economic System Prior to the
New Economic System

The model of planning and enterprise management introduced into East Germany at the end of World War II deviated only slightly from the Soviet mold. The names of the various administrative organs and management practices were translated directly from the Russian into German. Prior to 1963, the deviations from the Soviet pattern consisted of a greater retention of private ownership in certain sectors — for example, in handicraft and retail trade and to a smaller extent in agriculture.[57] Moreover, up to 1971, mixed (*halbstaatlich*) enterprises, of which the state is part owner, were important in industry and retail trade, accounting for some 10 percent of output in these sectors.[58] After 1971, they were converted into state enterprises.

With these small exceptions, the East German system of planning and enterprise management is virtually identical to that described for the Soviet economy in Chapter 7. A monopoly communist party (the Socialist Unity party) dictates priorities to a state planning commission, which, in conjunction with the ministries, establishes binding plans and balances that govern enterprise operations during the plan period. The enterprise plan contains a mass of detail concerning enterprise operations, ranging from output and input targets to financial and labor force directives; nevertheless, the principal criterion for success is the fulfillment of the output plan.

Not only do the administrative details of the GDR economy match those of its Soviet model, but economic reforms carried out prior to 1963 followed closely the lead of the Soviet Union. Thus when Khrushchev turned away from the ministerial system in the mid-1950s, substituting in its place a regional management system, the East Germans followed. Not until 1963 did the East Germans strike out on their own in an attempt to improve their system of planning and economic control. Even in this instance, they again followed the Soviet decision to allow open discussion of economic reform: the so-called Liberman debate.

The New Economic System

The East German New Economic System,[59] announced by the GDR leadership in 1963, was the first major economic reform of a centrally planned socialist economy (not including the Yugoslav move to worker self-management). It centered on the reform proposals enunciated by the Soviet economist Evsei Liberman and thus provided a testing ground for his ideas on devolution. In addition, some of the reform principles attempted in East Germany found their way into the 1965 reforms in the Soviet Union. One can ask whether the Soviets took their lead from the East German experiments.

The major Liberman proposal was that planning could be made more efficient if the administrative burden on central planners were diminished by allowing intermediate planning bodies and the enterprises themselves to make more decisions. Liberman was seeking to strengthen administrative planning, *not* to eliminate it, and he believed that devolution of planning decisions to lower administrative levels, particularly to enterprise managers, would accomplish that end. Under the Liberman system, it was never questioned that binding output planning would be maintained.

In order to accomplish devolution, Liberman proposed that the multitude of targets established at the center be limited to outputs and assortment of output, leaving the enterprise essentially free to make its own input decisions through the wholesale trade network. The incentive system was to be revised to elevate profitability to the most important success criterion, contingent upon successful implementation of the output targets. Enterprises were to be rewarded for attempting difficult profitability targets and were to be given long-term targets that would not suddenly shift upward after a particularly successful year. Enterprises were to pay an interest charge for the use of capital to encourage the more economical use of that input, and a general price reform was to be instituted to ensure that enterprise decisions would be based on a "rational" set of prices.[60]

In the midst of the discussion that followed Liberman's proposals the East German authorities launched their New Economic System.[61] Concern over the declining growth of output and productivity after 1960 was the stimulus for this reform, as growth, measured by official statistics, all but ground to a halt in 1962 and 1963. In 1963, the number of centrally planned output targets and balances was reduced, and responsibility for their planning and pricing was handed over to lower planning authorities and to the enterprises themselves. In this regard, the Unions of State Enterprises (the VVBs) secured much of the authority over planning and establishing the balances for the products produced under their own jurisdiction. It should be stressed that the total amount of output and delivery planning was not reduced; decision making was simply shifted to lower levels.[62]

Having determined to devolve planning tasks, the East Germans had to contend with one of the basic weaknesses of the Liberman system. If the number of centralized balances was to be reduced, how would the state ensure a macrobalance between supplies of and demands for industrial commodities? That is, if industrial authorities and enterprises assumed responsibility for planning and balancing their own inputs and outputs, how could one be sure that the outputs and inputs (especially those transcending the narrow boundaries of the authorities) would balance at the national level? Liberman's own hope was that a rational pricing system and the formation of a wholesale trade network would solve this problem.

The East Germans responded to the problem of macrobalance by emphasizing a system of contracts between suppliers and users. Balancers, using information about outstanding contracts, would attempt to equate supplies and demands. If the balancers (the VVBs, the enterprises, the ministries) found that the existing contracts for a particular commodity were not consistent with a macrobalance, they could order changes in the contracts. Contractees would have to be compensated out of a special fund at the disposal of the balancers; otherwise, contracts were to be strictly enforced. The unique feature about the proposed GDR system of contracting under the New Economic System was that the contract was not to be an outcome of the balance, but the reverse. One could say that the East German contribution to the Liberman system was the substitution of a contract system for the wholesale trade network.

As Liberman himself had pointed out, the devolution of planning authority requires change in the incentive system and reform of the price system. Both were carried out in the GDR between 1963 and 1968. During this period the role of profits increased. Initially, profits were to be the sole success indicator; later, bonuses for profit targets were contingent on the fulfillment of basic output targets. Otherwise, profit bonus funds would be drastically cut. Moreover, again true to Liberman's suggestions, long-term profit norms were introduced to protect managers from the ratchet effect; residual profits were placed in an enterprise investment fund; and an interest charge on capital was introduced. A price reform was completed in 1967. In order to ensure that prices remained reflective of costs over time, price-setting authority was, in many instances, handed down to industrial authorities and to the enterprises themselves. Provisions were established for more frequent changes in prices.

Demise of the New Economic System

Students of the East German economy agree that the New Economic System was abandoned after 1970.[63] As Michael Keren shows in his studies of the GDR reform, most of the important features of the 1963 reform had been reversed by 1971. The number of centrally determined targets and balances had been increased. The contract system had been weakened. There was a return to gross output targets and a downplaying of profitability targets, and price-setting authority was recentralized. East German authorities have never officially repudiated the New Economic System; thus it is difficult to pinpoint the date of its demise.

One might rightly ask why the East Germans felt compelled to abandon their experiment. Growth rate difficulties cannot be cited as the reason, for the period 1964–1970 witnessed a revival of high rates of economic growth, although official growth rates were slightly higher after 1970.[64] According to Keren, the main factor behind the abandonment of the New Economic System was the increasing tautness of planning after 1968 and the attempt to split the economy into a centralized-priority sector and a lower-priority sector.

In 1968 a significant exception was made to the New Economic System. The proclamation of "planning according to structure-determining tasks" returned high-priority branches and activities (largely associated with modernization and exports) to the old system of centralized control. These "structure-determining" activities were to be exempted from the New Economic System; less important activities were to be handled by lower administrative authorities and by the enterprises themsleves. Thus a dual system of management was established that created internal contradictions and made it difficult to continue the experiment with Libermanism.

There followed a period of overambitious planning. Central authorities tried to plan "structure-determining" activities but left other activities to be regulated according to New Economic System principles. Generally overambitious targets led to shortages, especially in raw materials and energy. Substantial deficits with the Soviet Union piled up, and plan discipline showed signs of breaking down. In response to these shortages and bottlenecks, which spread throughout the economy, the state recentralized control over the planning activities that had devolved to lower authorities and enterprises. This recentralization spelled the demise of the New Economic System. Centralization and devolution proved incompatible. In any case, the GDR experiment with Libermanism, while not unsuccessful from the point of view of economic growth, failed to last more than seven years, suffering a fate similar to that of the 1965 Soviet reforms, which were also abandoned around this time.

It is difficult to evaluate the New Economic System because of its limited life span and because one cannot determine how faithfully it was implemented. Most accounts of the reform are based on official pronouncements and decrees, and it is well known that vested interests against reform and change tend to be strong in such planned economies. Was this a true test of Libermanism and the notion that planning could be significantly improved by devolution? The decision in 1968 to recentralize priority branches certainly was a significant step away from Libermanism. One cannot, therefore, regard the East German experiment as a reasonable test. The fact that the reform was abandoned, however, suggests that a Liberman-like reform will fail in the absence of truly significant changes in industrial prices and in interenterprise relations and enterprise incentives. There was never any serious attempt to turn wholesale prices into "scarcity" prices, and the combination of a centralized priority sector with devolved authority over lower-priority sectors made the problem of finding an equilibrium even more difficult. Decentralization without some form of balancing mechanism (such as a system of scarcity prices) will likely result, as it did in the East German case, in widespread shortages and confusion, unless the planned tasks are very easy. But a system that requires "easy" targets would not prove acceptable over the long run.

The 1970s and 1980s: Efficient
Planning Through Combines[65]

The abandonment of the New Economic System signaled the end of the experiment to increase economic efficiency through greater freedom of decision making for managers. The East German economy, however, remained just as dependent on growth through efficiency improvements after the New Economic System as before. If substantive decentralization to the enterprise level was ruled out, what could take its place?

The East German quest in the 1970s and 1980s has been for efficiency improvements through better planning. History has repeated itself. East German authorities have once again begun to emulate Soviet experiments. The East Germans have concluded that strong intermediate planning and management authorities (called *obedinenie* in the Soviet case) can markedly simplify and improve planning.

In the early 1970s, the process of developing intermediate planning authorities began. The intermediate management authority in the East German case is the combine (*Kombinat*), which differs considerably from the intermediate organizations (VVBs) established under the New Economic System. The combines have considerable authority over member enterprises and can merge enterprises from different branches (ministries) if their union forms a rational economic unit. Combines are formed to gain the benefits of economies of scale, to establish more effective supply relationships, and to provide more efficient investment allocation. In East Germany today, one can find four or five types of combines ranging from giant single firms, to vertically integrated combinations of manufacturers and their suppliers, to horizontal combinations of manufacturing enterprises.

The rate of combine formation has been rapid. In 1973, there were 37 combines. By the start of the 1980s, virtually all industry and construction enterprises had been brought together into combines (there were some 157 combines in 1981). Combines account for well over 90 percent of employment in centrally managed industry. Four industrial ministries — electronics, heavy engineering, chemicals, and light industry — are in charge of 50 percent of all existing combines. The organization chart of the East German economy in the 1980s, provided in Figure 10.1 emphasizes the fact that the eleven ministries deal directly with the combines under their control. Notable is the absence of lines of authority from the ministries to the enterprises.

What roles do the combines play in the East German economy? The combines are supposed to take over many of the responsibilities previously exercised by the ministries. In particular, combines have been given extensive responsibilities in plan development, material balancing, and the management and coordination of plan fulfillment. The

Figure 10.1 Organization of the East German Economy, 1981

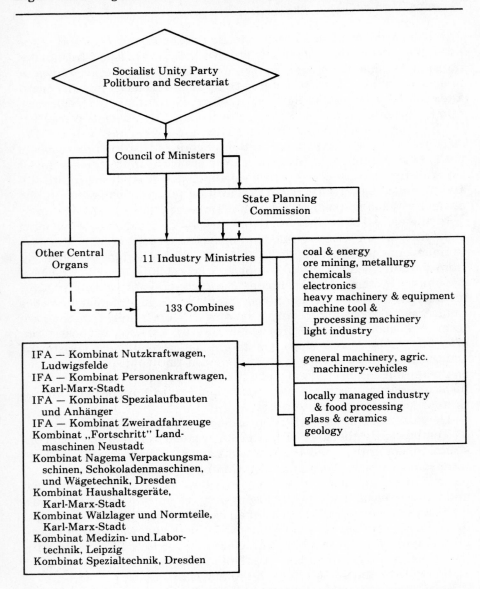

Source: Adapted from Angela Scherzinger, "Planungssystem," in DDR und Osteuropa, Ein Handbuch (Opladin: Leske Verlag, 1981), p. 41.

ministries and state planning commission now hand down fewer and more aggregated targets to the combines. It is the combine's responsibility to work out the operational details.

Simply put, the basic intent of the combine movement is to replace the existing three-level management system (enterprise-intermediate authority-central authority) with a more manageable two-level system (combine-central authority). In this way, rather than having enterprises planned and managed by central authorities (the ministries and the state planning commission) with the assistance of an intermediate authority, the combine coordinates and manages its member enterprises. In effect, the combine is envisioned as a huge firm with which the central authorities can deal directly. Central authorities no longer have to plan and coordinate thousands of individual enterprises; instead, they need only to deal with the less than 200 combines. In such a scheme, the planning and coordination tasks of the ministries are reduced considerably; they should be free to concentrate on macro goals, leaving the combines to transform these general goals into operational practice.

The role of the enterprise within the combine is a particularly sensitive one. Official pronouncements stress the continued legal autonomy of the enterprise. Reality seems to differ, however. As long as enterprises remain autonomous within the combine, the three-level management system will persist. If enterprises can make independent resource allocation decisions, they must still be monitored and controlled by both intermediate and central authorities. According to students of the East German combine system, most enterprises have had to give up much of their autonomy upon joining the combine. The general director of the combine appears to have the legal right to control the resource allocation decisions of its member enterprises. The combine appears to operate on the one-man-rule principle, characteristic of the enterprise, although certain provisions for collegial decision making by committees of leading technical experts and enterprise managers have been put in place.

We do not yet know whether the relocation of authority to combines interposed between the enterprise and the central authorities will provide the solution for East Germany. Will a planned economy based on a small number of large, integrated concerns with central authorities pay off in growth and efficiency gains? The success or failure of the combine idea, it appears, will depend on how unresolved power relationships are eventually worked out. The division of authority between the ministry and the combine has yet to be clearly defined. The overall idea is for the ministry to confine itself to broad aggregate decisions and for the combine to work out the details. Whether ministries will be content to let the combines work in this way remains to be seen. Events of the late 1970s and early 1980s suggest that the ministries are attempting to recover lost authority. For example, ministries have set up a number of control mechanisms to monitor the combines. Various ministerial control commissions have been established to check on combine planning and plan fulfillment. The second unresolved issue is what happens when combines cross ministerial boundaries. Ministries have resisted the amalgamation of enterprises previously under their control into combines subordinated to another ministry, even if the amalgamation makes sense on economic grounds. The combine threatens to disrupt long-established domains of the ministries. The third unresolved issue is the realtionship between the combine and the enterprise. If the enterprise surrenders its autonomy upon entry into the combine, it would appear that more decisions will be made above the enterprise level than before. It is not known whether this will improve decision making. Moreover, the combines leave unresolved the whole issue of dysfunctional behavior. How will combine performance be evaluated? What will prevent the combines from adopting the same safety factors that the enterprises have relied on over the years? It is these safety factors that must be eliminated before major efficiency gains can be achieved.

The Performance of the East German Economy[66]

We turn now from the New Economic System to a discussion of the performance of the GDR economy. The two are related because it was poor economic growth in the early 1960s that prompted the introduction of the East German reform, and it is also true that economic growth was generally satisfactory during the New Economic System.

Throughout the postwar period, East German economic growth has had to come in large part from the growth of output per unit of labor and capital input (intensive growth) rather than from an increasing volume of inputs (extensive growth). How well has the GDR succeeded in this endeavor? An examination of East Germany's growth after recovery from the dislocations following the Second World War reveals growth that has been quite impressive by international standards. Between 1955 and 1985, real GNP grew at an annual rate of 3.1 percent; because of declining population during this same period, per capita growth was even higher at 3.4 percent. Comparing this growth rate with that of West Germany during the same period, one finds that the West German rate of GNP growth (3.7 percent) was higher, but that the per capita GNP growth rates were about the same (see Table 13.1). Because of the zero or negative growth rates of the East German population, the per capita comparison is probably more relevant.

What are the sources of East German growth? One finds a pattern quite similar to the experiences of the industrialized capitalist countries but unlike those of the other planned socialist countries: The expansion of factor productivity explains the most significant portion of GDR economic growth. In fact, in the East German case, increases in productivity account for about three-fourths of GDR economic growth.[67] In the Soviet Union, the comparable percentage would be one-fourth.[68]

It is beyond the scope of this book to establish why the East Germans have successfully promoted an intensive pattern of economic growth, but their experience does indicate that it is possible for a planned socialist economy to grow intensively. Several explanations have been offered. The first is that the limited supply of labor has forced East Germans to pay much more attention to motivating labor and management with material incentives. This is evident from the ample (by East-bloc standards) supplies of automobiles, television sets, and other consumer durables owned by the East German population and the fact that the living standard in East Germany has not been allowed to lag unduly behind that of West Germany. In fact, the devolution of planning authority during the New Economic System probably had as one of its objectives bringing producers and consumers closer together to enhance material incentives. A second explanation is the traditional industriousness of the German worker, which has nothing to do with the East German system of planning and enterprise management. A final explanation relates to the proximity of the two Germanys, which has ensured that East German industry would have knowledge of West German technology and business practices and could use these as standards.

How impressive is East Germany's economic performance? The answer depends on one's yardstick. If one were to use West Germany as the standard, East German performance would not be appealing. At the end of the war, the two German economies started out at near parity, but since then significant (in the range of one-fourth to one-half) gaps in productivity, living standards, and per capita income have emerged. Although one cannot attribute the gaps directly to the economic systems set up in the two Germanys, the systems have in all probability played an important role.[69]

SUMMARY: VARIANTS OF SOCIALISM

1. This chapter deals with three important variants of centrally planned socialism: Hungary, China and East Germany. While the historical and other non systemic features of these cases differ significantly, their economic systems nevertheless represent important applications of the Soviet model including significant

attempts to implement economic reform in the face of lagging economic performance and the presence of external shocks in the 1970s and 1980s.

2. The Hungarian economy was, prior to the beginning of the New Economic Mechanism (NEM) in 1968, a fairly typical example of centrally planned socialism in a small, resource-poor, trade-oriented country. Hungary in the reform era is a classic example of the problems of implementing economic reform, especially the difficulties of combining various elements of plan and market while attempting to achieve long standing economic objectives such as job security and improvements in the standard of living. At the end of the 1980s, Hungary remains an important case of socialist economic reform.

3. China is an interesting case of utilizing a modified Soviet model of centrally planned socialism in a large, poor country with rich resources. While our past interest has centered on the issue of economic development in China and especially the role of ideology, attention since the late 1970s has focused on Chinese economic reform. The reform process in China is important since it represents major reform in a large planned socialist system at an early stage of the development process with an initial focus on change in the rural sector and subsequent attention to the industrial and foreign sectors.

4. East Germany is an important case study of centrally planned socialism in a small, yet relatively mature economy which pursued economic reform soon after implementation of the Soviet model. In addition to the important comparisons which have been made between East Germany and West Germany partially controlling for non-systemic features, East German reform is of interest for its change of approach over time. Initially, the approach could be broadly described as decentralization, while more recently, East German experiments have generally attempted to find a more effective mode of central planning.

NOTES

Hungary

1. Edward A. Hewett, "The Hungarian Economy: Lessons of the 1970s and Prospects for the 1980s," in U.S., Congress, Joint Economic Committee, *East European Economic Assessment*, Part 1 (Washington, D.C.: Government Printing Office, 1981), p. 522.
2. David Granick, "The Hungarian Economic Reform," in Morris Bornstein, ed., *Comparative Economic Systems: Models and Cases*, 3rd ed. (Homewood, Ill.: Irwin, 1974), p. 219.

3. See, for example, Paul Marer, "Economic Performance and Prospects in Eastern Europe: Analytical Summary and Interpretation of Findings," in U.S., Congress, Joint Economic Committee, *East European Economic Assessment*, Part 2 (Washington, D.C.: Government Printing Office, 1981), pp. 19-95.

4. For background information on these years, see Bela A. Balassa, *The Hungarian Experience in Economic Planning* (New Haven: Yale University Press, 1959).

5. A classic work on the problems of overcentralization in the Soviet-type economy is J. Kornai, *Overcentralization in Economic Administration* (London: Oxford University Press, 1959).

6. Much has been written about the Hungarian economic reform. Works devoted to the initial reform movement include Granick, "The Hungarian Economic Reform"; Richard Portes, "Hungary: Economic Performance, Policy, and Prospects," in U.S., Congress, Joint Economic Committee, *East European Economies Post Helsinki* (Washington, D.C.: Government Printing Office, 1977), pp. 766-815; I. Friss, ed., *Reform of the Economic Mechanism in Hungary* (Budapest: Akademai Kiado, 1969); P. G. Hare, "Industrial Prices in Hungary, Part I," *Soviet Studies*, 28 (April 1976), pp. 189-196; P. G. Hare, "Industrial Prices in Hungary, Part II," *Soviet Studies*, 28 (July 1976), pp. 362-390; Bela A. Balassa, "The Firm in the New Economic Mechanism in Hungary," in Morris Bornstein, ed., *Plan and Market: Economic Reform in Eastern Europe* (New Haven: Yale University Press, 1973), pp. 347-372; and William F. Robinson, *The Pattern of Reform in Hungary: A Political, Economic and Cultural Analysis* (New York: Praeger, 1973). For more recent developments, see Hewett, "The Hungarian Economy"; P. G. Hare, H. K. Radice, and N. Swain, eds., *Hungary: A Decade of Economic Reform* (London: Allen and Unwin, 1981); and Paul Marer, "Exchange Rates and Convertibility," in Joint Economic Committee, *East European Assessment*, Part 1, pp. 525-548.

7. Friss, *Reform of the Economic Mechanism in Hungary*, pp. 18-21.

8. For a discussion of constraints, see David Granick, *Enterprise Guidance in Eastern Europe* (Princeton, N.J.: Princeton University Press, 1975), pp. 245-254.

9. Thomas A. Wolf, "Exchange Rate Adjustments in Small Market and Centrally Planned Economies," *Journal of Comparative Economics*, 2 (September 1978), pp. 226-245.

10. Granick, "The Hungarian Economic Reform," p. 232.

11. Portes, "Hungary."

12. Granick, "The Hungarian Economic Reform," p. 221.

13. Ibid., p. 224.

14. Bela Csikos-Nagy, "The Hungarian Economic Reform After Ten Years," *Soviet Studies*, 30 (October 1978), pp. 540-546.

15. Bela Balassa, "The Hungarian Economic Reform, 1968-82," *Banca Nazionale Del Lavori Quarterly Review*, 145 (June 1983), pp. 163-184.

16. Hewett, "The Hungarian Economy," p. 485.

17. Marer, "Economic Performance," p. 38.

18. The Economist Intelligence Unit Ltd., *Quarterly Economic Review of Hungary: Annual Supplement, 1982* (London: The Economist, 1982), p. 15; Thad Alton et al., *Occasional Paper*, no. 75.

19. Hewett has computed that the net barter terms of trade for Hungary (that is the export price index divided by the import price index) declined between 1970 and 1978 (with most of the decline coming after 1974) by roughly 20 percent for trade with CMEA countries. See Hewett, "The Hungarian Economy," p. 496.

20. Ibid., pp. 500 ff.

21. F. Havasi, "The Sixth Five-Year Plan of the Hungarian National Economy (1981-1985)," *Acta Oeconomica*, 26, no. 1-2 (1982), pp. 1-16.

22. Paul Marer, "Hungary's Balance of Payments Crisis and Response, 1978-84," in U.S., Congress, Joint Economic Committee, *East European Economies: Slow Growth in the 1980's*, vol. 3 (Washington, D.C.: Government Printing Office, 1986), p. 313.

23. World Bank, *World Development Report 1987* (New York: Oxford University Press, 1987), pp. 195-283.

24. See, for example, Hewett, "The Hungarian Economy"; M. Tardos, "Options in Hungary's Foreign Trade," *Acta Oeconomica*, 26, 1-2 (1981), pp. 29-49.

25. According to recent computations made by Edward Hewett, the ratio of investment to gross domestic product grew from just over 20 percent in the early 1960s to just over 30 percent in the late 1970s, while the ratio of consumption to gross domestic product declined over the same period from just over 65 percent to just over 55 percent. Hewett, "The Hungarian Economy," p. 495.

26. For example, if domestic prices for food products in Hungary were to reflect world market prices, generally subsidies would have to be removed and prices would in many cases increase significantly. Such a result, while appealing on efficiency grounds might well run counter to the rather general East European distaste for inflation.

27. Price increases (competitive wholesale) for industry were introduced in January 1980. Consumer goods prices have been increased on a regular basis. In 1982, the prices of basics such as housing (rent) and rail transit were increased.

28. The question of convertibility of the forint is complex. For an excellent summary of the basic issues, the present state of the debate, and prospects for the future, see Paul Marer, "Exchange Mechanism," in Joint Economic Committee, *East European Economic Assessment*, Part 1, pp. 525-548; Paul Marer, "Hungary's Balance of Payments Crisis."

China

29. Although cross-country comparison of GNP must be interpreted with caution, a per capita gross national product of $131 (measured in 1980 dollars) must rank China as a very poor country on the eve of the socialist industrialization drive. For a useful long-term comparison of basic economic and developmental indicators, see Arthur G. Ashbrook, Jr., "China: Economic Modernization and Long-Term Performance," in U.S., Congress, Joint Economic Committee, *China Under the Four Modernizations*, Part 2, Section V (Washington, D.C.: Government Printing Office, 1982), pp. 151-368.

30. For a detailed discussion of the path of Sino-American normalization, see Joint Economic Committee, *China Under the Four Modernizations*, Part 1, pp. 171-223.

31. For a discussion, see K. Chao, "The China-Watchers Tested," *The China Quarterly*, 81 (1980), pp. 97-104; Erik Dirksen, "Chinese Industrial Productivity in an International Context," *World Development*, 11, no. 4 (April 1983), pp. 381-387. Since 1982, China has published an annual statistical handbook.

32. For recent population estimates from the Chinese census, see "Chinese Population Census — 1982," *Communist Affairs — Documents and Analysis*, 2, no. 3 (July 1983), pp. 319-321; for greater detail, see John S. Aird, "Recent Demographic Data from China: Problems and Prospects," in Joint Economic Committee, *China Under the Four Modernizations*, Part 1, pp. 171-223. For an update, see Kuan-I Chen, "China's Food Policy and Population," *Current History* 86, 521 (September 1981), pp. 257-260, 274-276.

33. *Handbook of Economic Statistics 1987*, Fig. 1.

34. There is now a very large body of literature on the Chinese economy. A most useful assessment can be found in the volumes published under the auspices

of the Joint Economic Committee, the most recent of which is *China Under the Four Modernizations*, Parts 1 and 2.

35. Although collectivization may have been a factor in the consolidation of Soviet power in the countryside, recent evidence suggests that collectivization had little influence on the magnitude of the surplus shifted into the industrialization effort. For evidence, see James R. Millar, "Mass Collectivization and the Contribution of Soviet Agriculture to the First Five-Year Plan: A Review Article," *Slavic Review*, 33, no. 4 (December 1974), pp. 750-766.

36. There was some unrest and disruption in China, but markedly less than that which occurred in the Soviet Union. For a comparison, see Jan S. Prybyla, *The Political Economy of Communist China* (Scranton, Pa.: International Textbook, 1970), ch. 5.

37. For a discussion of the transitional phases, see Prybyla, *The Political Economy of Communist China*.

38. Ibid., p. 175.

39. For a useful outline of the basic features of the Chinese administrative structure and changes through time, see Thomas G. Rawski, "China's Industrial System," in U.S., Congress, Joint Economic Committee, *China: A Reassessment of the Economy* (Washington, D.C.: Government Printing Office, 1975), pp. 175-198. For a recent comparison of the Chinese experience and the Soviet experience, see Robert F. Dernberger, "The Chinese Search for the Path of Self-Sustained Growth in the 1980s: An Assessment," in Joint Economic Committee, *China Under the Four Modernizations*, Part 1, pp. 19-76.

40. For a discussion of this period, see Roderick MacFarquhar, *The Hundred Flowers Campaign and the Chinese Intellectuals* (New York: Praeger, 1960).

41. For a discussion of the early commune, see Kenneth R. Walker, "Organization of Agricultural Production," in Alexander Eckstein, Walter Galenson, and Ta-Chung Liu, eds., *Economic Trends in Communist China* (Chicago: Aldine, 1968), pp. 440-452. For a study of the private sector, see Kenneth R. Walker, *Planning in Chinese Agriculture: Socialization and the Private Sector, 1956–1962* (Chicago: Aldine, 1965). For an update of organizational changes into the 1970s, see Frederick W. Crook, "The Commune System in the People's Republic of China, 1963-74," in Joint Economic Committee, *China: A Reassessment of the Economy*, pp. 366-410; a useful recent source is Frederic M. Surls and Francis C. Tuan, "China's Agriculture in the Eighties," in Joint Economic Committee, *China Under the Four Modernizations*, Part 1, pp. 419-448.

42. Prybyla, *The Political Economy of Communist China*, pp. 144-145.

43. For example, in terms of agricultural performance, we might make the following crude comparison. In China in 1949 grain production was 0.20 metric ton per capita; in the Soviet Union in 1928-1929, grain production was 0.47 metric ton per capita. Chinese data are from Ashbook, "China: Economic Modernization and Long-Term Performance," p. 104; Paul R. Gregory and Robert C. Stuart, *Soviet Economic Structure and Performance*, 3rd ed. (New York: Harper & Row, 1986) p. 244; and TsSU (Central Statistical Administration), *Naselenie SSSR 1973* (Moscow: Statistika, 1975), p. 7.

44. These data are from Prybyla, *The Political Economy of Communist China*, pp. 135 ff.

45. Subramanian Swamy, "Economic Growth in China and India 1952-1970: A Comparative Appraisal," *Economic Development and Cultural Change*, 21, no. 4, pt. II (July 1973), p. 62.

46. Ibid.

47. An excellent survey of these years can be found in Dernberger, "The Chinese Search for the Path of Self-Sustained Growth," pp. 19-76.

48. For a discussion of the revolutionary left in the economic context, see Robert F. Dernberger and David Fasenfest, "China's Post-Mao Economic Future," in U.S., Congress, Joint Economic Committee, *Chinese Economy Post-Mao* (Washington, D.C.: Government Printing Office, 1978), pp. 3–47.

49. Chu-yuan Cheng, "China's Industrialization and Economic Development," *Current History*, 82, no. 485 (September 1983), p. 266.

50. A useful source on the communes is Frederick W. Crook, "The Commune System in the People's Republic of China, 1963–1974," in U.S., Congress, Joint Economic Committee, *China, A Reassessment of the Economy* (Washington, D.C.: Government Printing Office, 1975), pp. 411–437.

51. For a discussion of prereform arrangements, see, for example, Henry J. Groen and James A. Kilpatrick, "China's Agricultural Production," in U.S., Congress, Joint Economic Committee, *Chinese Economy Post-Mao*, vol. I (Washington, D.C.: Government Printing Office, 1978), pp. 607–652.

52. For a discussion of changes in the rural economy, see for example Kuan-I Chen, "China's Changing Agricultural System," *Current History* 82, 485 (September 1983), pp. 259-263, 277-278; Kuan-I Chen, "China's Food Policy and Population," pp. 257-260, 274-276; Yak-Yeow Kueh, "China's New Agricultural-Policy Program: Major Economic Consequences, 1979–1983," *Journal of Comparative Economics* 8, 4 (December 1984), pp. 353-375; Nicholas R. Lardy, *Agriculture in China's Modern Economic Development* (Cambridge: Cambridge University Press, 1983); Dwight Perkins and Shahid Yusuf, *Rural Development in China* (Baltimore: Johns Hopkins Press, 1984); Kenneth R. Walker, "Chinese Agriculture During the Period of Readjustment, 1978–83," *China Quarterly*, 100 (December 1984), pp. 783-812; Kenneth R. Walker, *Food Grain Procurement and Consumption in China* (Cambridge: Cambridge University Press, 1984).

53. Kuan-I Chen, "China's Food Policy and Population."

54. Based on agricultural output data in World Bank, *World Development Report 1987* (New York: Oxford University Press, 1987), pp. 204–205.

55. Ibid., pp. 202–283.

East Germany

56. Our discussion up to the late 1970s is based on the following sources: Deutsches Institut für Wirtschaftsforschung, *DDR-Wirtschaft: Eine Bestandsaufnahme* (Frankfurt am Main: Fischer, 1974); Michael Keren, "The New Economic System in the GDR: An Obituary," *Soviet Studies*, 24 (April 1973), pp. 554-587; Michael Keren, "The Return of the Ancien Regime: The GDR in the 1970s," in U.S., Congress, Joint Economic Committee, *East European Economies Post Helsinki* (Washington, D.C.: Government Printing Office, 1977), pp. 720-765; Karl Thalheim, *Die Wirtschaft der Sowjetzone in Krise und Umbau* (Berlin: Duncker and Humblot, 1964); Gert Leptin and Manfred Melzer, *Economic Reform in East German Industry* (Oxford: Oxford University Press, 1977).

57. Ernst Birke and Rudolph Neuman, eds., *Die Sowjetisierieng Ostmitteleuropas* (Frankfurt am Main: Metzner Verlag, 1959), pp. 333-372. Gert Leptin, *Die deutsche Wirtschaft nach 1945: Ein Ost-West Vergleich* (Opladen: Leske Verlag, 1970), pp. 24-27.

58. *Statistiches Jahrbuch der DDR* (Berlin: Staatsverlag, 1975), p. 107.

59. Walter Ulbricht, *Das Neue Okonomische System der Planung und Leitung der Wirtschaft in der Praxis* (Berlin: Dietz Verlag, 1963).

60. Keren, "The New Economic System in the GDR," pp. 555-557. For a more detailed discussion of Libermanism, see Paul R. Gregory and Robert C. Stuart,

Soviet Economic Structure and Performance, 3rd ed. (New York: Harper & Row, 1986), pp. 302-305.

61. The following discussion is based in large part on Keren, "The New Economic System in the GDR," pp. 555-569; Keren, "The Return of the Ancien Regime," pp. 720-765; and Gert Leptin, "The German Democratic Republic," in H. Hohman, M. Kaser, and K. Thalheim, eds., *The New Economic Systems of Eastern Europe* (London: C. Hurst, 1975).

62. On this, see Keren, "The New Economic System in the GDR," table 1, p. 56.

63. For a minority viewpoint, see Jacob Naor, "How Dead Is the GDR New Economic System?" *Soviet Studies*, 25 (October 1973), pp. 276-282.

64. Keren, "The New Economic System in the GDR," p. 569.

65. This discussion is based on the following sources: Manfred Melzer, "Combine Formation in the GDR," *Soviet Studies*, 33, no. 1 (January 1981), pp. 88-106; Hanelore Hamel, ed., *Bundesrepublik Deutschland — DDR: Die Wirtschaftssysteme*, 4th ed. (Munich: C. H. Beck, 1983); Gernot Gutman, ed., *Das Wirtschaftssystem der DDR* (Stuttgart: Fischer, 1983); and *DDR und Osteuropa: Ein Handbuch* (Opladen: Leske Verlag, 1981).

66. This section is based on Paul Gregory and Gert Leptin, "Similar Societies Under Differing Economic Systems: The Case of the Two Germanys," *Soviet Studies*, 29 (October 1977), pp. 519-542. Also see Irwin Collier, "East and West Germany" (Panel on Different Strategies, Similar Countries, Annual Meeting of the American Economic Association, New York, December 1982).

67. Ibid., table 1.

68. Gregory and Leptin, "Similar Societies Under Differing Economic Systems."

69. For a lengthy discussion of East and West German comparisons, see Gregory and Leptin, "Similar Societies Under Differing Economic Systems"; Collier, "East and West Germany"; and Hamel, *Bundesrepublik-DDR*, ch. 13.

RECOMMENDED READINGS

HUNGARY

Bela A. Belassa, "The Firm in the New Economic Mechanism in Hungary," in Morris Bornstein, ed., *Plan and Market: Economic Reform in Eastern Europe* (New Haven: Yale University Press, 1973), pp. 347-372.

———, "The Hungarian Economic Reform, 1968-82," *Banca Nazionale Del Lavoro Quarterly Review*, 145 (June 1983), pp. 163-184.

———, *The Hungarian Experience in Economic Planning* (New Haven: Yale University Press, 1959).

Alan A. Brown and Paul Marer, "Foreign Trade in the East European Economic Reforms," in Morris Bornstein, ed., *Plan and Market* (New Haven: Yale University Press, 1973), pp. 153-206.

L. Csapo, "The Hungarian Reform, Towards a Planned, Guided Market Economy," in E. S. Kirschen, ed., *Economic Policies Compared: West and East*, vol. II (New York: North Holland, 1975), ch. 6.

Bela Csikos-Nagy, "The Hungarian Reform After Ten Years," *Soviet Studies*, 30 (October 1978), pp. 540-546.

David Granick, "The Hungarian Economic Reform," in Morris Bornstein, ed., *Comparative Economic Systems: Models and Cases*, 3rd ed. (Homewood, Ill.: Irwin, 1974), pp. 218-232.

———, *Enterprise Guidance in Eastern Europe* (Princeton, N.J.: Princeton University Press, 1975).

P. G. Hare, "Economic Reform in Hungary: Problems and Prospects," *Cambridge Journal of Economics*, 1 (December 1977), pp. 317-333.

———, "Industrial Prices in Hungary, Part I," *Soviet Studies*, 28 (April 1976), pp. 189-196.

———, "Industrial Prices in Hungary, Part II," *Soviet Studies*, 28 (July 1976), pp. 362-390.

P. G. Hare, H. K. Radice, and N. Swain, eds., *Hungary: A Decade of Economic Reform* (London: Allen and Unwin, 1981).

Edward A. Hewett, "The Hungarian Economy: Lessons of the 1970s and Prospects for the 1980s," in U.S., Congress, Joint Economic Committee, *East European Economic Assessment*, Part 1 (Washington, D.C.: Government Printing Office, 1981), pp. 483-524.

Joseph C. Kramer and John T. Danylayk, "Economic Reform in Eastern Europe; Hungary at the Forefront," in U.S., Congress, Joint Economic Committee, *East European Economic Assessment*, Part 1 (Washington, D.C.: Government Printing Office, 1981), pp. 549-570.

Paul Marer, "Economic Reform in Hungary: From Central Planning to Regulated Market," in U.S., Congress, Joint Economic Committee, *East European Economies: Slow Growth in the 1980's*, vol. 3 (Washington, D.C.: Government Printing Office, 1986), pp. 223-297.

———, "Hungary's Balance of Payments Crisis and Response, 1978-84," in U.S., Congress, Joint Economic Committee, *East European Economies: Slow Growth in the 1980's*, vol. 3 (Washington, D.C.: Government Printing Office, 1986), pp. 298-321.

———, "Exchange Rates and Convertibility in Hungary's New Economic Mechanism," in U.S., Congress, Joint Economic Committee, *East European Economic Assessment*, Part 1 (Washington, D.C.: Government Printing Office, 1981), pp. 525-548.

Paul Marer and John M. Montias, *East European Integration and East-West Trade* (Bloomington: Indiana University Press, 1980).

Michael Marrese, "Hungarian Agriculture: Moving in the Right Direction," in U.S., Congress, Joint Economic Committee, *East European Economies: Slow Growth in the 1980's*, vol. 3 (Washington, D.C.: Government Printing Office, 1986), pp. 322-340.

Thomas A. Vankai, "Hungarian Agricultural Performance and Prospects During the Eighties," in U.S., Congress, Joint Economic Committee, *East European Economies: Slow Growth in the 1980's*, vol. 3 (Washington, D.C.: Government Printing Office, 1986), pp. 341-364.

CHINA

Richard Baum, ed., *China's Four Modernizations: The New Technological Revolution* (Boulder, Colo.: Westview Press, 1980).

William Byrd, *China's Financial System: The Changing Role of Banks* (Boulder, Colo.: Westview Press, 1983).

Kang Chao, *Man and Land in Chinese History: An Economic Analysis* (Stanford: Stanford University Press, 1987).

Kuan-I Chen, "China's Food Policy and Population," *Current History*, 86, 521 (September 1987), pp. 257-260; 274-276.

Chu-yuan Cheng, *China's Economic Development: Growth and Structural Change* (Boulder, Colo.: Westview Press, 1982).

———, "China's Economy at the Crossroads," *Current History*, 86, 521 (September 1987).

China: Review of Agricuture in 1982 and Outlook for 1983 (Washington, D.C.: Department of Agriculture, 1983).

Gregory Chow, *The Chinese Economy* (New York: Harper & Row, 1984).

Robert F. Dernberger, ed., *China's Development Experience in Comparative Perspective* (Cambridge: Harvard University Press, 1980).

Audrey Donnithorne, *China's Economic System* (New York: Praeger, 1967).

Alexander Eckstein, *China's Economic Development: The Interplay of Scarcity and Ideology* (Ann Arbor: University of Michigan Press, 1975).

——, *China's Economic Revolution* (New York: Cambridge University Press, 1977).

——, *Communist China's Economic Growth and Foreign Trade* (New York: McGraw-Hill, 1969).

Alexander Eckstein, Walter Galenson, and Ta-Chung Liu, eds., *Economic Trends in Communist China* (Chicago: Aldine, 1968).

The Economist, Intelligence Unit, *Country Report: China, North Korea* no. 1 (1988) London: The Economist Intelligence Unit, 1988.

John K. Fairbank, *The United States and China*, 4th ed. (Cambridge, Mass.: Harvard University Press, 1979).

Christopher Howe, *China's Economy: A Basic Guide* (New York: Basic Books, 1978).

——, *Wage Patterns and Wage Policy in Modern China, 1919-1972* (Cambridge: Cambridge University Press, 1973).

Yak-Yeow Kueh, "China's New Agricultural-Policy Program: Major Economic Consequences, 1979-1983," *Journal of Comparative Economics*, 8, 4 (December 1984), pp. 353-375.

Nicholas Lardy, *Economic Growth and Distribution in China* (New York: Cambridge University Press, 1979).

Nicholas R. Lardy, *Agriculture in China's Modern Economic Development* (Cambridge: Cambridge University Press, 1983).

Thomas P. Lyons, *Economic Integration and Planning in Maoist China* (New York: Columbia University Press, 1987).

Colin MacDougall, "The Chinese Economy in 1976," *China Quarterly*, no. 70 (June 1977), pp. 355-370.

Feng-hwa Mah, *The Foreign Trade of Mainland China* (Chicago: Aldine, 1971).

Dwight H. Perkins, *Agricultural Development in China, 1368-1968* (Chicago: University of Chicago Press, 1969).

——, ed., *China's Modern Economy in Historical Perspective* (Stanford, Calif.: Stanford University Press, 1975).

——, ed., *Rural Small-Scale Industry in the People's Republic of China* (Berkeley: University of California Press, 1977).

Elizabeth J. Perry and Christine Wong, *The Political Economy of Reform in Post-Mao China* (Cambridge: Harvard University Press, 1987).

Jan S. Prybyla, *The Chinese Economy: Problems and Policies*, 2nd ed. (Columbia: University of South Carolina Press, 1981).

——, *The Political Economy of Communist China* (Scranton, Pa.: International Textbook, 1970).

U.S., Congress, Joint Economic Committee, *China: A Reassessment of the Economy* (Washington, D.C.: Government Printing Office, 1975).

——, *China Under the Four Modernizations* (Washington, D.C.: Government Printing Office, 1982).

——, *Chinese Economy Post-Mao* (Washington, D.C.: Government Printing Office, 1978).

——, *An Economic Profile of Mainland China*, vols. I and II (Washington, D.C.: Government Printing Office, 1967).

Andrew G. Walder, *Communist Neo-Traditionalism: Work and Authority in Chinese Industry* (Berkeley: University of California Press, 1986).

——, "Wage Reform and the Web of Factory Interests," *The China Quarterly*, 109 (March 1987), pp. 22–41.

Kenneth R. Walker, *Planning in Chinese Agriculture: Socialization and the Private Sector, 1956–1962* (Chicago: Aldine, 1965).

Derek J. Waller, *The Government and Politics of the Peoples Republic of China* (New York: New York University Press, 1982).

Lim Wei and Arnold Chao, eds., *China's Economic Reforms* (Philadelphia: University of Pennsylvania Press, 1983).

Gordon White, "The Politics of Economic Reform in Chinese Industry: The Introduction of the Labour Contract System," *The China Quarterly*, 11 (September 1987), pp. 365–389.

Christine P. W. Wong, "The Economics of Shortage and Problems of Reform in Chinese Industry," *Journal of Comparative Economics*, 10, 4 (December 1986), pp. 363–387.

Yaun-Li Wu, *The Economy of Communist China: An Introduction* (New York: Praeger, 1965).

EAST GERMANY

Irwin L. Collier, ed., "Symposium on the German Democratic Republic," in *Comparative Economic Studies*, 29, 2 (Summer 1987), pp. 1–70.

Deutsches Institut für Wirtschaftsforschung, *Handbuch DDR-Wirtschaft*, rev. ed. (Hamburg: Rowolt, 1977).

Paul Gregory and Gert Leptin, "Similar Societies Under Differing Economic Systems: The Case of the Two Germanys," *Soviet Studies*, 29 (October 1977), pp. 519–542.

Gernot Gutman, ed., *Das Wirtschaftssystem der DDR* (Stuttgart: Fischer, 1983).

Hanelore Hamel, ed., *Bundesrepublik Deutschland — DDR: Die Wirtschaftssysteme*, 4th ed. (Munich: C. H . Beck, 1983).

Michael Keren, "Concentration and Devolution in East Germany's Reforms," in Morris Bornstein, ed., *Plan and Market: Economic Reform in Eastern Europe* (New Haven: Yale University Press, 1973), pp. 123–151.

——, "The New Economic System in the GDR: An Obituary," *Soviet Studies*, 24 (April 1973), pp. 554–587.

——, "The Return of the Ancien Regime: The GDR in the 1970's," in U.S., Congress, Joint Economic Committee, *East European Economies Post Helsinki* (Washington, D.C.: Government Printing Office, 1977), pp. 720–765.

Gert Leptin and Manfred Melzer, *Economic Reform in East German Industry* (Oxford: Oxford University Press, 1978).

Manfred Melzer, "Combine Formation in the GDR," *Soviet Studies*, 33, no. 1 (January 1981), pp. 88–106.

Hartmut Zimmermann et al., eds., *DDR Handbuch* (3rd revised and expanded edition) 2 volumes (Cologne, FRG: Verlag Wissenschaft und Politik), 1985.

PART III
INTERRELATIONSHIPS, PERFORMANCE, AND PROSPECTS OF ECONOMIC SYSTEMS

Chapter 11
The Interrelationship Among
Economic Systems:
International Trade

Up until now we have dealt with each economic system in isolation. Yet the systems of capitalism and socialism share one globe and interact in the arenas of international politics, cultural exchange, tourism, and international trade. Interrelationships among national economies are widely recognized. National monetary and fiscal policies must be coordinated. The leaders of the major capitalist powers meet regularly to coordinate their economic policies. Inflation in one country is transmitted to others. One nation's balance of payments depends on the budgetary policy of another.

This chapter focuses on international trade between the industrial capitalist systems of the West and the planned socialist systems of the East. When we speak of the "socialist world" or the "East," we refer to the European members of the Council for Mutual Economic Assistance (CMEA) unless otherwise noted. How do economic systems conduct trade and with what results? The two fundamental differences between East and West are the inadequacy of prices as measures of scarcity values and the prohibition against private ownership of the means of production in the East. At the end of the chapter, we deal briefly with East-West competition for economic and political influence in the Third World.

THE FORCES INFLUENCING TRADE:
COMPARATIVE ADVANTAGE VERSUS
TRADE AVERSION

In discussing international trade, distinctions among the various kinds of capitalist economic systems are not important. By and large, all Western nations belong to a set of organizations that lay down the rules of the game for their members. Although trade policies vary from one capitalist country to another, it would be difficult to identify differences in policy with different capitalist economic systems as such. The investment behavior of all capitalist nations is fairly well ordained by capital markets, and common Western capital markets allow individuals and businesses in different capitalist nations to invest as they see fit.

Regulations against international borrowing exist in some instances, but it would be difficult to identify these along systemic lines within the group of Western nations.

Similarly, among the planned socialist economies of the East, differences in institutional arrangements for the conduct of trade are relatively unimportant. They basically adhere to the same set of institutions and rules, and one can speak of a uniform Eastern model of international trade without undue distortion of reality. As we noted in Chapter 10, Hungary appears to be deviating increasingly from the Eastern model of trade. Yet it would be premature to speak of a distinct Hungarian model. Thus we deal here with an Eastern and a Western model of international trade without worrying about systemic differences within blocs.

Capitalism and planned socialism have radically different approaches to international trade. The basic force explaining the development of trade among capitalist nations is the principle of **comparative advantage**, described long ago by the classical economists. Participants in trade seek to maximize profits and compare relative prices or costs of foreign and home-produced goods. At existing exchange rates, the commodities that can be obtained abroad at lower prices will be imported; others will be produced at home. The notion underlying comparative advantage is that free international trade will benefit both trading partners by allowing each partner to specialize in commodities it can produce at lower relative costs. The respective trading partners exchange commodities at lower relative costs than would be possible in the absence of trade, thereby raising welfare in both countries.

The policy prescription to be drawn from the principle of comparative advantage is that trade among countries should be free from government control, for free trade will maximize the welfare of the trading partners. Furthermore, the more trade the better, for increases lead to even more specialization and greater efficiency of world production.

The socialist approach to international trade is called **trade aversion**.[1] The basic socialist notion is that international trade should be employed to supply the domestic economy with certain necessary imports called for by the economic plan. The emphasis is on the use of international trade to acquire *imports*; exports serve only as the means for acquiring them. This does not mean that the objective of socialist trade is to maximize imports. Rather the emphasis has been on averting trade and relying on the domestic economy to supply essential materials, using foreign imports as a "safety valve" to obtain certain (limited) material requirements. The socialist economy avoids heavy reliance on foreign suppliers, even though a product may be acquired more economically abroad. If possible, reliance on imports whose presence or absence will jeopardize overall plan fulfillment is limited.[2] In part, trade aversion stems from a view that the world market is subject to disturbances and fluctuations that planners cannot predict. Deliveries from other planned socialist economies could be irregular or late due to planning shortfalls and imbalances.

This difference in approach is reflected in the way the respective economic systems conduct foreign trade. The comparative advantage doctrine suggests that foreign trade should be free of both external and internal restrictions and that decisions on what to buy and sell abroad should be made by businesses motivated by the desire to maximize profits. The decision rule for conducting trade under this system is simple: If one can purchase a product abroad more cheaply (at prevailing exchange rates) than the commodity can be made at home, it should be imported (taking the cost of transporting the good and various risks into account, of course). When trade proceeds according to this simple rule, the eventual result will be an equalization of prices of traded goods among trading partners. Thus, instead of national prices, **world prices** will emerge for the operation of the capitalist world economy.

The true picture of capitalist trade differs from this idealized description because of tariffs and quotas and restrictions on factor mobility, but it is nevertheless a reasonably accurate description of capitalist reality. Despite restrictions on international trade, one basic point remains valid: Under capitalism, the flow of goods among countries is determined by individual producers and consumers.

In the planned socialist economies the conduct of foreign trade is much different. Planners determine what imports will be purchased from other nations, and a foreign trade monopoly is charged with implementing import and export plans. No simple decision rule, such as trading according to comparative costs, is used. Instead, a whole series of criteria, both political and economic, determine the socialist country's imports and exports. The producers and users of the traded commodities have little to do with export and import decisions; rather the foreign trade monopoly (the collection of noncompeting foreign trade enterprises) makes such decisions.

East-West trade fits into this book's emphasis on the effect of the economic system on economic outcomes. The effectiveness with which a particular economic system conducts its trade will affect economic outcomes. On the one hand, a system that trades according to comparative advantage will be able to specialize its production in areas with relatively high average productivity. A system that underutilizes its trade potential will deny itself the advantages of specialization and will be forced to produce at home a wider range of products, some at low efficiency relative to world standards. Systemic underutilization of trade potential could result in a loss of output achievable from a given volume of factor inputs — that is, a loss of static efficiency.

Trade should have a direct bearing on the economic efficiency of a system.

A system's conduct of trade can affect economic performance in other areas in ways that are sometimes hard to predict. The decision to avoid heavy reliance on foreign suppliers and world markets may make the domestic economy less subject to external fluctuations (that is, more stable),and economic stability is one criterion by which economic performance is judged. Trade underutilization can also be justified on military grounds, the argument being that military self-sufficiency requires a diversified domestic economy even if this contradicts the law of comparative advantage. Moreover, there is the issue of compromising economic and political independence. Does the economic dependence of one system on another ultimately lead to a loss of political independence?

East-West trade also hinges on the Marxist-Leninist position that the affluence of industrialized capitalism can be maintained only by exploiting less-developed countries (the LDCs). This formulation is most clearly expressed in Lenin's theory of imperialism and the contemporary theories of the New Left. Can these imperialist tendencies be observed in the dealings of the industrialized countries with the Third World? To what extent has economic competition between the industrialized West and the communist East for Third World influence affected this outcome? These are difficult and emotional issues, and we can only raise these questions and make some preliminary comments.

Finally, again with reference to the issue of underdevelopment, there is the basic issue of competition for the choice of economic system. Capitalism and market and planned socialism compete for Third World influence not only through trade and aid but also in terms of the development example they set. Should the Third World countries develop on the basis of capitalist market institutions, market socialism, or the centralized planning of resource allocation by a monolithic party (planners)?

TRADE IN EAST AND WEST: SOME DATA

The characteristic feature of Eastern trade in general and East-West trade in particular has been its limited nature despite rapid growth in recent years. As shown in Figure 11.1, the developed capitalist nations (the West) accounted for 65 percent of world trade and 65 percent of world national income in the mid 1980s. The socialist nations (including China) accounted for only 10 percent of world trade but some 24 percent of world national income.[3] These figures illustrate that the East conducts less than one-half as much international trade per dollar of national income as does the West. This marked underutilization of trade potential (trade aversion) by the socialist nations is confirmed by econometric studies for the 1950s and 1960s, which find that if the socialist countries had participated in trade to the same degree as a capitalist country at the same stage of development, their trade ratios (trade as a percentage of GNP) would have been as much as 50 percent higher.[4]

One distinguishing feature of trade in the East is its limited magnitude relative to its potential as measured by capitalist economy

Figure 11.1 Some Indicators of East-West Trade

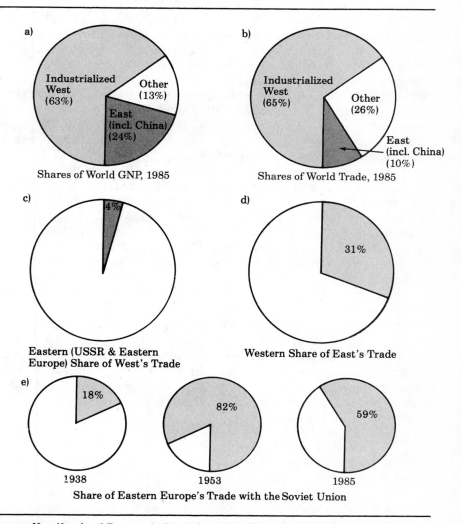

a) Shares of World GNP, 1985
- Industrialized West (63%)
- Other (13%)
- East (incl. China) (24%)

b) Shares of World Trade, 1985
- Industrialized West (65%)
- Other (26%)
- East (incl. China) (10%)

c) Eastern (USSR & Eastern Europe) Share of West's Trade — 4%

d) Western Share of East's Trade — 31%

e) Share of Eastern Europe's Trade with the Soviet Union
- 1938 — 18%
- 1953 — 82%
- 1985 — 59%

Source: *Handbook of Economic Statistics 1987*, Figure 2, Table 3, Table 66.

standards. This is true today despite the rapid expansion of the trade of the East between 1960 and the present. Between 1960 and 1980, Eastern trade (excluding the Asian communist countries) grew by a factor of 10, almost apace with Western trade, which grew by a factor of 14.[5] Thus, the Eastern share of world trade continued to decline (although at a slower pace), starting from a low percentage of trade relative to national income in the immediate postwar period.

Turning to East-West trade, we begin by stressing its low magnitude, despite an eight-fold increase since 1960. According to Franklyn Holzman, writing in 1976: "East-West trade is not very important quantitatively and could be overlooked if it were not for its political implications."[6] In fact, East-West trade in the mid 1980s accounted for only 3 percent of world trade, down considerably from its pre–World War II rate of over 6 percent. As a proportion of world trade, the flow of goods and services between socialist and capitalist economic systems is relatively minor, albeit expanding. One should add that because of low overall trade volumes in the East, East-West trade is proportionally more important to the East than to the West.[7] East-West trade accounts for only 5 percent of the trade of the West, but for almost 31 percent of the Eastern trade. Thus, in the East at least, East-West trade has assumed a position of some importance.

When discussing quantitative trends in East-West trade, one should also mention the major restructurings of Eastern European trade since the Second World War. In 1938 only 18 percent of Eastern Europe's imports came from Eastern Europe and the Soviet Union; by Stalin's death in 1953, this figure had risen to 82 percent. In 1982, imports from Eastern Europe and the Soviet Union accounted for 59 percent of the total for Eastern Europe and reflected a substantial shift toward the West since 1953.[8]

The most important point to be drawn from these figures is that, despite the rapid growth of trade over the past two decades, the Eastern countries still account for a relatively small share of world trade and grossly underutilize their trade potential. A similar conclusion can be drawn concerning East-West trade. Despite its marked increase since 1960, it remains a minuscule share of world trade; however, from the point of view of the East (with its lower trade volumes), East-West trade now accounts for a fairly significant proportion of the total trade of the socialist countries.

FOREIGN TRADE PLANNING
UNDER PLANNED SOCIALISM

What lies behind trade aversion in the planned socialist economies? One key is the method of foreign trade planning.[9] In the planned socialist states, foreign trade planning is integrated into the overall planning process. A state planning commission establishes output targets for enterprises and compiles balances of important funded commodities. The foreign trade plan emerges from these targets and balances. Targeted imports are used to fill deficits in material balances; technology imports are employed to supply new planned technology; domestic enterprises are given supply and delivery plans for the foreign sector. A committee for material and technical supply typically deals with the actual allocation of important producers' goods and may have some barter dealings with other socialist countries. A committee on science and technology handles the acquisition of foreign technologies. The finance ministry monitors the effect of foreign trade on the state budget.

Typically, two types of organizations assist the planning organizations in constructing and implementing the foreign trade plan. They are the ministry of foreign trade (MFT) and the foriegn trade organizations (FTO). Both are charged with working out the details of the generalized import and export plans, and both are responsible for making the actual contacts with domestic and foreign producers and determining the means of payment. The MFT, the state bank, and the foreign trade bank construct a balance of payments account to plan for the payment of international transactions. In the Soviet Union another organization, the State Committee for Foreign Relations, administers the Soviet foreign aid program. Figure 11.2 shows an organization chart for the Soviet foreign trade planning apparatus.

Together, the state planning commission, the state bank, the foreign trade bank, the MFT, and the FTOs make up a **foreign trade monopoly**, which conducts all the foreign trade of the socialist countries. There is little or not contact between the domestic producer and foreign user or between the foreign producer and domestic user; all contacts proceed through the foreign trade monopoly. The domestic producer knows little about the requirements of the foreign user. The enterprise is simply told by the planning commission to deliver a certain portion of its planned output to a particular foreign trade organization, which is charged with making the sale abroad. The domestic enterprise receives the same proceeds from the sale abroad as from any other sale (the domestic wholesale price) and, unless special bonus arrangements are in effect, is no more interested in this sale than in a domestic sale. In fact, domestic enterprises may seek to avoid production for foreign customers because the FTO is in a position to exercise more arbitrary authority over it in this case.[10]

In trade with Western countries, world market prices will be used. Due to its small share of world trade, the foreign trade monopoly will have no monopoly power over world market prices and must buy and sell at established world prices. In the case of trade among socialist

Figure 11.2 The Foreign Trade Bureaucracy

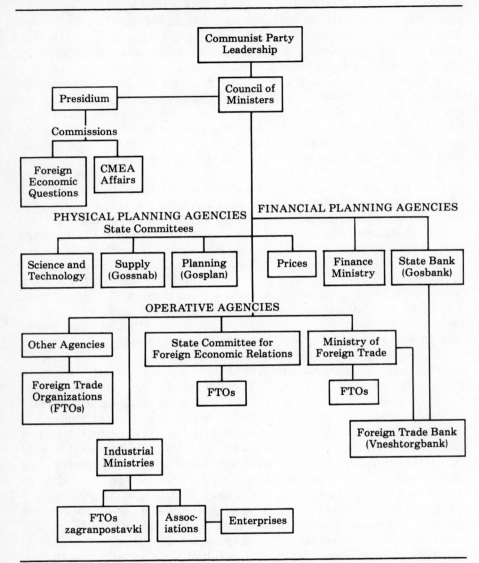

Soucre: H. Stephen Gardner, *Soviet Foreign Trade: The Decision Process* (Boston: Kluwer-Nijhoff, 1982), p. 2.

countries, averages of past world market prices are generally used as price benchmarks. In a few instances current world market prices are used. For the period 1971–1974, for example, 1965 to 1969 averages of world market prices were used. Because of increases in raw materials and other prices in the 1970s, it was agreed that prices would be based on an average of world market prices for the previous five years, with prices to be negotiated annually.[11] The use of lagged world prices is dictated by deficiencies in the domestic prices of the East-bloc countries and the lack of meaningful exchange rates among the countries, which prevent one (say, Soviet prices) from being accepted as a standard for East-bloc transactions. Although intra-CMEA trade is reported in so-called transferable rubles, they are used only as a unit of account; world market prices are the basis for the transaction. In the case of homogeneous products like oil or coal, it is not difficult to determine their world market prices. For heterogeneous products like machinery, prices are often established through bilateral negotiations.

The system of foreign trade planning contributes to the underutilization of trade potential by the centrally planned economies. Rigid quantity-oriented systems are tempted to limit risks by minimizing dependence on outside suppliers. This tendency toward autarky or trade aversion can be observed in centrally planned firms, which seek to make themselves as self-sufficient in supplies as possible. It can also be observed in the international trade dealings of these economies. To include a foreign supplier in the balancing system, especially a supplier of a commodity essential to the overall material balance of the economy, makes plan success dependent on outside forces and increases the risk of plan underfulfillment. To some extent, such pressures are less severe in the case of Western suppliers, for the capitalist market is viewed as being sufficiently flexible to guarantee on-time deliveries. But the scarcity of foreign exchange limits the use of Western suppliers.

Bilateralism and Inconvertibility[12]

No East-bloc currency is freely convertible into a western currency or into gold. Nor are East-bloc currencies convertible into another East-bloc currency in any operational sense. Moreover, private citizens in many Eastern countries are prohibited from holding Western currencies, and the state trading monopoly possesses a monopoly over foreign exchange. The same is generally true of the relationships among currencies within the East bloc, except for tourists. One Eastern currency is not freely convertible into another at an established rate of exchange, and these currencies are not accepted as a means of payment for exchanged commodities in dealings among FTOs. If a Bulgarian FTO arranges a sale to a Czech FTO, the Bulgarians cannot use the proceeds to buy freely the imports they desire from Czechoslovakia. If Czechoslovakia sells more to Bulgaria than it buys, the Czechs could not select Bulgarian commodities to use up the surplus. It follows that it is not possible for the Bulgarians to use Czech currency to pay for imports from a third country, say, the Soviet Union.

Even if a third country were willing to make goods available, they would likely be so-called soft goods — that is, goods bartered at terms less favorable than the recipient country could obtain in the world market. Hard goods, such as raw materials, which can be readily sold in world markets, would not be made available on a multilateral basis.

Commodity inconvertibility characterizes the trade among the planned socialist economies. Even if one country has a trading surplus with another, it will not be able to buy goods freely from that country. If the country with the surplus could freely purchase goods on an unplanned basis, the domestic supply plan would be disrupted. The prices at which traded goods exchange hands are often out of line with opportunity costs. If surplus countries could freely select goods from a deficit country, they could opportunistically choose goods that exchange for irrationally low prices.

Commodity inconvertibility has a substantial impact on the manner in which trade is conducted within the East bloc. Between any pair of countries, sales are negotiated on a barter basis, so that the value of commodities exchanged in both directions will balance. Thus if Bulgaria wants to sell fruit to Czechoslovakia, a barter deal must be made whereby Bulgaria receives from Czechoslovakia commodities of an equivalent value as measured by past world prices. Only rarely are non-balancing exchanges made (for credit) within Eastern Europe. Arrangements between two countries according to negotiated exchanges of equivalent values are termed **bilateral** (as opposed to multilateral agreements). Most intrabloc trade is bilateral. Estimates vary, but probably 5 to 10 percent of intra-CMEA trade is handled on a multilateral basis.[13]

In the case of East-West transactions, barter arrangements involving equivalent values are desired by the Eastern trading partner, but they do not occur as frequently. Instead, East-West trade is generally cleared on a **multilateral** basis. Purchases and sales are cleared in a convertible Western currency (say, West German marks) or are financed by a credit arrangement (say, a German bank agreeing to finance a Bulgarian purchase). In the case of a sale to a Western country, the Eastern seller can generally use the hard currency proceeds to purchase commodities from a second Western country.

Although the East-bloc countries have attempted in the past to establish some type of clearing arrangement within their bloc (for example, the International Bank for Economic Cooperation), such efforts have not succeeded, and most intrabloc trade continues to be conducted on a bilateral basis. The bilateralism of intrabloc trade is a major factor behind trade underutilization. Bilateralism means that it is impossible to achieve the most profitable level of trade between two countries because of the necessity to balance the value of imports and exports. Accordingly, the Eastern countries do not always sell on the market where they could obtain the highest price; nor do they buy on the cheapest market. Bulgaria and Czechoslovakia must balance their sales to each other, even though a better arrangement might have called for an imbalance between them.

Balance of Payments Problems

On a formal level, the East-bloc countries do not suffer from a balance of payments problem. Exports and imports are planned by the state trade monopoly, and the foreign trade plan includes a plan to balance international payments. If the projected receipts of foreign (convertible) currencies fall short of requirements, projected imports (or exports) are reduced (or increased) and a trade balance is thereby achieved. In the case of intrabloc trade, there is usually no balance of payments problem because exchanges of commodities are balanced by bilateral agreements. The balance of payments problem concerns supplies and demands for convertible currencies.

On a more substantive level, the balance of payments problem relates to the fact that historically (in the absence of credits) purchases from the West have had to be limited to the value of sales to the West. Unlike the Western countries, the Eastern countries cannot pay for the excess of purchases over sales with their own currencies. But historically the East-bloc countries have been unable to compete in Western markets because of quality and service problems, which are functions of both systemic and policy elements. The burgeoning demand for Western technology since 1960 has meant that the Eastern countries have often had to purchase less from the West than they may have desired in the absence of balance of payments problems.

One must note that the normalization of East-West trade relations in the 1970s and 1980s has served to ease (but not solve) these payments balance problems. The West European countries, in particular, competed among themselves in granting government-guaranteed credits to gain Eastern markets. Moreover, increases in the price of raw materials raised the Soviet Union's earnings of convertible currencies.[14] Eastern Europe's hard currency debt grew by a factor of almost three between 1975 and 1980, spurred by détente and Western recessions. It is now recognized that a number of Eastern countries have severe debt service problems; moreover, the recessions of the late 1970s and early 1980s restricted international lending. These factors have slowed Western lending to the East. Between 1980 and 1985, East European hard currency debt rose only by 4 percent.[15] The inability of the East-bloc countries to compete in hard currency markets is one reason for the low foreign trade proportions of the planned economies and the low volume of East-West trade.

Several explanations have been advanced for the marketing difficulties experienced by the socialist economies, especially in the area of manufactured exports. One is the inflexibility of foreign trade planning and the lack of contact between the planned producer and the Western consumer.[16] The reluctance of Eastern enterprises to produce for export and to produce spare parts can be cited as another factor. One point raised by the East-bloc countries themselves is that some Western governments discriminate against socialist exports, and such favoritism is cited as a cause of hard currency difficulties.[17]

Foreign Trade Criteria in Socialist Countries.[18]

In deciding what commodities are to be imported and exported and from whom, the foreign trade organizations of planned socialist economies rely on a series of rules and agreements, many of which have little to do with comparative costs. Some decisions are based on political considerations, such as the allocation of scarce Soviet raw materials among Eastern European countries. Others are based on long-term cooperative and trade agreements. Other decisions, however, can be made independently of political and military considerations, and it is in this area that almost all the Eastern countries have adopted economic criteria for making import and export decisions. Although these criteria differ in detail, they can be reduced to the principle that imports and exports should be selected on the basis of comparisons of domestic and foreign relative costs. In its simplest form, the standard index of foreign trade effectiveness of imports (E) is

$$E = \left(\frac{Pd}{Pf}\right)k \tag{11.1}$$

where

Pd = the domestic cost of producing the product at home
Pf = the cost in foreign exchange of importing the commodity
k = the amount of foreign exchange earned from exports per unit of domestic costs of producing the exports

This formula is best illustrated by an example. Let us say that East Germany can import steel from Poland at a price of 400 "valuta marks" per ton (Pf in our formula), and the domestic cost of producing a ton of steel at home is 800 marks (*Pd*). Thus the ratio of the domestic price to the foreign exchange (valuta mark) price is 2 — a seemingly advantageous purchase. This price ratio must be adjusted however, by *k*, which measures the cost in domestic resources of earning foreign exchange from exports to Poland to pay for this import. Clearly, the higher the domestic cost of earning foreign exchange from Poland (the lower the *k*), the less desirable the purchase.

To calculate *k*, one determines the *average* ratio of the foreign exchange value of East German exports to Poland to the *average* cost in domestic prices of producing these exports. The careful reader will note the resemblance between *k* and the Western concept of an exchange rate, although the resemblance is remote. Let us assume that the *k* ratio is 1.2, which should be interpreted as meaning that 1.2 valuta marks of foreign exchange can be earned from 1 mark's worth of production (measured in domestic prices) from East German exports to Poland. The overall efficiency index therefore is 2 × 1.2 or 2.4.

Let us now see how this formula can be used to select imports and trading partners. Two examples should suffice. Assume that East Germany must choose between importing coal or steel from Poland. The choice would be made according to which product yielded the highest *E* index (that is, the highest ratio of the domestic to the imported price). Let us say that the domestic price of coal is twice the foreign exchange price (*E* =2), but that the domestic price of steel is only one and one-half times the foreign exchange price (*E* = 1.5). If no other considerations are involved, coal rather than steel should be imported from Poland.

Our second example illustrates the choice of trading partners and is more complicated. Assume that East Germany must buy steel either from Poland or Czechoslovakia. The valuta mark prices (*Pf*) are 400 marks for Poland and 450 marks for Czechoslovakia, and the domestic price (*Pd*) is again 800 marks. On the other hand, whereas 1.2 valuta marks can be earned per mark of domestic production from exports to Poland (*k*), a higher value (say, 1.4) can be earned from exports to Czechoslovakia. The calculated *E* indexes are 2.4 for the Polish steel and 2.49 for Czech steel, leading to the conclusion (*ceteris paribus*) that the steel import should come from Czechslovakia. A similar index is used for selecting products to export and export trading partners and is analogous to the import efficiency index. Only here, the lower the efficiency index *E* the more desirable the export.

Both import and export indexes recognize the principle that trade should proceed according to comparative costs, but one should emphasize their limited use and inherent problems. As Lawrence Brainard writes with respect to Soviet trade: "Much of the Soviet trade...reflects basic political commitments, e.g., to supply raw materials to CMEA [see next section], and the bilateralism inherent in such trading relations limits the scope of application of any economic efficiency criteria."[19] There is, however, some evidence that the FTOs do indeed attempt to use these rules when planning exports and imports within narrow product groups.[20]

The use of foreign trade efficiency criteria is limited not only by the political nature of Eastern trade but also by problems inherent in the criteria themselves. The primary difficulty has to do with the pricing of imports, exports, and domestic goods. Socialist prices generally fail to reflect scarcity values and, in most instances, fail to capture the "true" domestic costs of production because of the omission of capital and rental charges. Thus comparisions of import and export prices with domestic prices may yield a distorted picture of optimal trading patterns.

The difficulty of comparing domestic and foreign costs is another factor accounting for the low trading proportions of the planned socialist countries. As long as internal prices do not reflect relative scarcities, it is not obvious to planners what should be imported or exported or what the costs are to the economy of not developing an optimal pattern of foreign trade. Even if socialist planners decided to conduct all their trade according to the principle of comparative advantage, the weaknesses of their domestic price systems would not permit them to determine where their comparative advantage would be. Moreover, the criteria are based on average valuations. They may tell planners what products to buy and sell but not how much. Only marginal criteria that give the costs and benefits of buying and selling at the margin would allow planners to determine the optimal mix. There is the further problem of information and computational requirements. Planners at the center simply do not have the information, time, and expertise to plan all imports and exports effectively. Thus the so-called microirrationality of foreign trade has come to be cited as a further source of irrationality in the planned socialist system. Surprisingly, when one examines the macrorationality of Soviet trade patterns the Soviet Union does broadly appear to trade on the average, according to relative resource endowments.[21] Such evidence of average trade patterns does not prove, however, that the crucial marginal trade decisions are rational.

TRADE POLICY IN EAST AND WEST

We now turn to trade policy, in particular, to the formation of trading blocs and the gradual dismantling of barriers to trade, in the West and between the East and West after the Second World War. The specific issue treated in this section is the degree to which trade barriers have inhibited the growth of trade between East and West. In the final part of this section, we discuss innovative arrangements that have evolved to facilitate East-West trade.

Postwar History: The West

The postwar period witnessed the rapid growth of world trade. In the West, this rapid growth was a consequence of both the high growth rates of the industrialized capitalist world and the dismantling of trade barriers that had been erected during the Great Depression. Moreover, the founding of a customs union in Western Europe — the European Economic Community (EEC) — in 1958 and the European Free Trade Association (EFTA) led to a marked integration of the West European economy and contributed to increased intra-European trade.

The industrialized capitalist countries entered the postwar era behind the high tariff walls of the 1930s but joined in 1947 into an organization committed to reducing those barriers — The General Agreement on Tariffs and Trade (GATT). Under the auspices of GATT, multilateral tariff reductions have been negotiated among participating countries, the most important being between the United States and the European Economic Community. In such tariff negotiations, the **most favored nation** (MFN) principle has been applied, whereby the participating parties agree to extend any negotiated reduction to all parties holding MFN status. This simplifies the negotiation of tariff reductions by eliminating the complicated task of renegotiating tariff agreements with all affected parties.

The United States has participated in GATT tariff negotiations under periodic legislation. The Trade Expansion Act of 1962 gave the president of the United States authority to reduce U.S. tariffs by as much as 50 percent on articles accounting for some 80 percent of world trade. Negotiations were begun with the EEC on the basis of the Trade Expansion Act, called the "Kennedy Round." These and other negotiations served to reduce substantially tariffs on commodities traded between the United States, Western Europe, and Japan. The latest such negotiations, called the "Tokyo Round," were held in 1980. The 1984 Trade and Tariff Act authorized the president to enter into a new round of negotiations to reduce trade barriers (called the "Uruguay Round"). The success of the Western program of tariff reductions through multilateral negotiation remains a signal achievement. In 1932, the average tariff rate was 59 percent. After the Tokyo Round it had fallen to less than 7 percent (Figure 11.3).

As one might expect, protectionist substitutes for tariffs are widely used and pose the most significant threat to free trade. Nontariff barriers such as quotas, import specifications, and the like are the major instruments in use today for the protection of domestic industries.

The basic framework for the postwar capitalist monetary system was created at the Bretton Woods Conference of 1944. The major capitalist countries agreed to establish a system of fixed rates of exchange among their currencies, with the U.S. dollar serving as the central currency.

The International Monetary Fund (IMF) was established to oversee the system. Member countries agreed to peg their currencies around declared par values to the dollar by purchasing and selling their own currencies in the international foreign exchange market. For its part, the United States pledged to convert dollars held by foreign governments into gold at a fixed rate of exchange. Credit arrangements were also established to assist member countries in keeping their currencies at par. Only in the case of a fundamental disequilibrium would members be allowed to change the values of their currencies vis-à-vis the dollar.

The notion behind this system of fixed exchange rates was that it would promote trade among countries by eliminating the risks of exchange rate fluctuations, and it is true that the postwar period did witness a remarkable expansion of trade among capitalist trading partners. According to United Nations and IMF statistics, the trade turnover of the developed capitalist countries increased by a factor of 11 between 1948 and 1973 in a period of relatively mild inflation.

Figure 11.3 Average Import Duties, 1925–1987

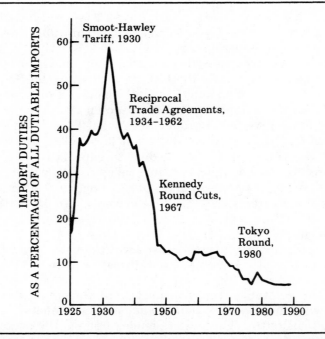

Source: *Historical Statistics of the United States; Statistical Abstract of the United States*, 1987.

Whether the Bretton Woods system can take credit for this expansion is not clear, but the system of orderly international monetary arrangements was probably conducive to expanded trade after the shocks of depression and world war.

The Bretton Woods system fell apart in August 1971 when the United States ceased converting dollars held by foreign governments into gold at a fixed rate of exchange. After attempts to return to a new fixed exchange rate parity system, by March of 1973 the major capitalist countries began to allow their currencies to fluctuate in value. A major factor behind the decision to abandon the fixed exchange rate system was the tendency for certain currencies to become over- or undervalued under the Bretton Woods system, thus placing pressure on the fixed exchange rate system. Even prior to the official abandonment of the fixed exchange rate system in 1973, there were several devaluations of "weak" currencies (the English pound) and "revaluations" of strong currencies (the German mark).

In 1976, at a conference in Kingston, Jamaica, the original IMF charter was amended to legalize the widespread system of floating currencies. Under the Jamaica Agreements, countries could adopt whatever exchange rate system they preferred (fixed or floating) but should avoid significant manipulation of their exchange rate. In 1979, the countries of the European Economic Community joined together in the European Currency Union (ECU). Member countries agreed to maintain their respective currencies at basically fixed rates relative to each other (joint floating rates).

It is still not clear whether the capitalist world will remain on a floating system or will return to a fixed system. Some authorities extol the flexibility of the floating system; others hope for a return to the stable exchange rates of earlier years. The sharp drop in the dollar exchange rate in the second half of the 1980s renewed concern over the flexible exchange rate system. Between September of 1985 and April of 1988, a series of meetings between the finance ministers of the major industrialized countries was held in New York and Europe. These meetings sought to coordinate economic policy and stabilize exchange rates.

Policies Toward the East[22]

One factor behind the limited East-West trade of the early postwar period was the effort, spearheaded by the United States, to limit the flow of strategic materials to the Soviet Union, Eastern Europe, and China. During this period, the United States used a series of measures to limit exports from the West to the East. Embargoes were placed on trade with mainland China and North Korea, and the U.S. Export Control Act of 1949 prohibited the export of a lengthy list of materials to the East. In 1947, the United States and Western Europe formed a co-ordinating committee, since called COCOM, to conduct a common embargo policy toward the communist countries. The Battle Act of 1951 called for the termination of aid to any country selling strategic materials to a communist country, and this was a potent threat during the years of the Marshall Plan. The Trade Agreement Extension Act of 1951 denied MFN status to all Eastern countries except Yugoslavia. Therefore, trade with those countries was subject to the high tariff rates of the 1930s. Moreover, the major capitalist powers agreed not to extend long-term credits to communist nations — an effective limit on Eastern imports, given the weakness of Eastern sales to the West. (Poland was granted MFN in 1960, Romania in 1975, Hungary in 1978, and China in 1980.)

After 1960, restrictions against East-West trade were eased, with the United States being one of the last countries to make trade concessions. The major changes came from Western European countries that were more dependent on trade than the United States, countries that stood to lose the most from continued restrictions on East-West commerce. The threat of U.S. countermeasures was diminished after the termination of the Marshall Plan and the end of the European "dollar shortage." One by one, the Western European nations and Japan began to expand sales to Eastern Europe and the Soviet Union and to grant long-term credits to finance such sales. Moreover, most of the Western European countries granted MFN status to their Eastern trading partners, leaving the United States as the major capitalist power failing to extend MFN to its communist trading partners. However, quantitative restrictions on Eastern imports remained an important deterrent in Western Europe.[23]

An apparent breakthrough in American trade relations with communist countries came, after extended negotiation, in October 1972, with the American-Soviet Trade Agreement. Having received concessions from the Soviet Union concerning repayment of a portion of Lend-Lease Aid, the American trade negotiators agreed to make Export-Import Bank credits available on a favorable basis and to grant MFN status to Soviet imports, subject to congressional approval. Soviet repayment of Lend-Lease debt was tied to congressional approval of MFN by 1975.

In December 1974, the Soviet Union annulled the American-Soviet Trade Agreement. Several reasons might be cited for this action. First, Congress openly tied the granting of MFN to freer emigration of Jewish citizens. To that point, such emigration had been promoted through quiet diplomacy. When this was turned into a formal condition for MFN, the Soviets interpreted the action as an excessive intrusion into their domestic political affairs. Second, Congress placed limitations on the amount of credits that could be granted under the agreement. These limitations would have prevented the Soviet Union from receiving the massive credits for major investment projects they desired from the United States and thus made the agreement less attractive. Third, the increase in the world prices of raw materials, including gold and oil, dramatically improved the hard currency earnings of the Soviet Union, rendering the granting of American credits less essential. The situation deteriorated further as the United States imposed economic sanctions on the Soviet Union for their trials of dissidents in 1978, the Soviet invasion of Afghanistan in late 1979, and the imposition of martial law in Poland in late 1981.[24] The easing of tension between the United States and the Soviet Union under Gorbachev may well lead to improved trade relations between the United States and the Soviet Union, and the eventual granting of MFN status to the USSR.

Many of the institutional restrictions on East-West trade erected in the immediate postwar period have been dismantled, and the way has been prepared for the expansion of East-West trade. The main institutional obstacles are quantitative restrictions in Western Europe and Japan, the failure of the United States to grant MFN to several of its communist trading partners,[25] and the continuing embargo on the export of "strategic" materials. The important remaining obstacles have to do with the inherent difficulties of conducting trade between capitalist and planned socialist economies — the problems of bilateralism, inconvertibility, the central planning of trade, and so on. Another such difficulty is the problem of finding suitable arrangements for cooperative projects between Eastern and Western economies that circumvent restrictions on private ownership.

It is difficult to assess the impact of Western restrictions on East-West trade. Some argue that the East chose trade aversion voluntarily, that quantitative restrictions and the failure of the United States to grant MFN have had a limited impact on Eastern sales. On the other hand, the Eastern nations emphasize these restrictions as the cause of limited East-West trade. Much attention has been devoted to the failure of the United States to grant MFN to all of the CMEA countries. Estimates of the effect of U.S. MFN vary substantially but suggest that its impact would vary widely by CMEA country. The effect would not be large in the case of the Soviet Union and Poland but would be substantial for the remainder of Eastern Europe because tariff discrimination is greater on manufactured goods, which are more important in the exports of Czechoslovakia and East Germany. There have also been efforts to assess the impact of the various sanctions (grain embargoes and the like) imposed by the United States on the Soviet Union. The consensus appears to be that their impact has been small.[26]

Postwar History: The East

The characteristic feature of postwar Western Europe has been the growing integration of its national economies. Postwar Eastern Europe, in contrast, has experienced little economic integration. Instead, the historical emphasis has been on the development of semi-independent national economies and the avoidance of regional specialization. This is true even though the European countries do have their own international organization, the Council for Mutual Economic Assistance (CMEA), founded in 1949 for the purpose of promoting economic cooperation as the Soviet counterpart to the American Marshall Plan (see Figure 11.4).

The CMEA, unlike the European Economic Community, possesses no supranational authority over its members.[27] Instead, according to its charter of 1960, all nations have an equal vote, and any one nation can veto proposals involving supranational measures. At different times, the Soviet Union has sought to give the CMEA supranational powers to promote the economic integration and specialization of Eastern Europe, but such efforts have been opposed by nations (principally, Romania and Hungary) that fear a loss of national independence and the effect that specialization would have on economic development. Despite various attempts to establish a CMEA currency (the "transferable" ruble) and the existence of a bank for multilateral clearing (the International Bank for Economic Cooperation), most negotiations on trade and technology transfers are still carried out on a bilateral basis.

The CMEA has adopted a number of programs designed to promote the economic integration of the CMEA countries.[28] The Comprehensive Program for Socialist Integration of 1971 consisted of a set of long-term proposals for bilateral economic and scientific cooperation and some voluntary joint planning. The Agreed Plan for Multilateral Integration Measures, adopted in 1975 for the period 1976–1980, is a collection of ten large joint investment projects, eight of which are located in the Soviet Union. The latest agreement, the Long-Term Special Purpose Program for Cooperation, was signed in 1979 to cover the period from 1980 to 1995. The cooperation agreements signed in the 1970s shifted the focus of economic integration in the direction of coordination of investment projects and were aimed at developing Soviet energy and raw material resources using Eastern European labor and capital equipment. These agreements do not appear to have resulted in a corresponding expansion of trade.[29]

There is controversy over whether the CMEA's presence has increased economic specialization in Eastern Europe over the years. One Western author thinks that the impact was considerable after 1964, but most authorities disagree. They find that the CMEA's impact on economic integration has been limited, especially prior to 1970.[30] Even

Figure 11.4 CMEA Organization Chart

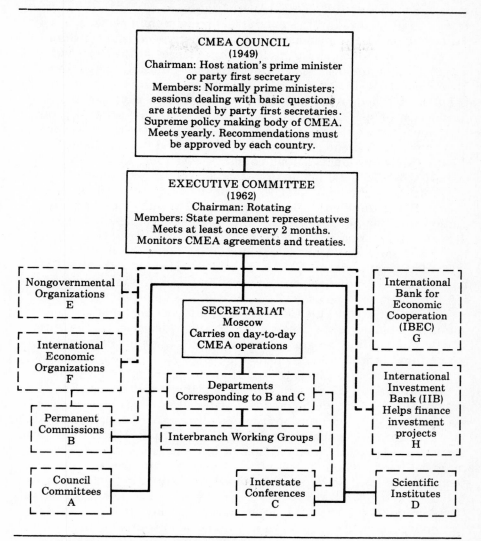

Source: Adapted from Paul Marer and John Michael Montias, "CMEA Integration: Theory and Practice," in U.S., Congress, Joint Economic Committee, *East European Economic Assessment*, Part 2 (Washington, D.C.: Government Printing Office, 1981), pp. 150–152.

though thousands of products — primarily machinery, chemicals, and metals — are covered by CMEA specialization agreements, the share of total output involved in those industries remains minimal (perhaps 6 or 7 percent of CMEA machinery output). There is no single measure of the degree of economic integration or of changes in the degree of economic integration over time. One interesting measure used by Paul Marer and J. M. Montias is analogous to the measurement of the distribution of income using Lorenz curves.[31] Basically, the shares of production of specific products accounted for by the smallest producing country, by the two smallest producing countries, and so on are calculated at different points in time. If the trend is toward a less equal distribution of products among countries over time, this would signify a move toward greater integration (that is, countries would be specializing more in specific products). According to the Marer-Montias measure (Table 11.1), there has been a general trend toward economic disintegration over the period from 1950 to 1976 — a trend halted to a small degree in the period from 1970 to 1976. On the basis of this and other evidence, Marer and Montias conclude that there has been economic "disintegration" within CMEA largely because the smaller CMEA nations began producing products that had been the monopoly of the larger planned economies.

Will the future turn the CMEA into an effective supranational organization of communist trading partners? Much depends on the success of the cooperation programs implemented between 1980 and 1990, which thus far have not had much of an effect.

Various joint investment programs are supposed to promote the economic integration of Eastern Europe and the Soviet Union. The basic pattern is for Soviet energy and raw material resources to be developed via Eastern European infusions of manpower, expertise, and equipment in return for an eventual share of the future output. Eastern European funds are supplied at nominal rates of interest, and ownership remains in Soviet hands. The long-run effects of these joint investment projects remain to be seen. Some analysts believe they are sound business investments for the CMEA nations; others speak of a revival of Soviet "exploitation" of Eastern Europe. Such joint investment projects do not now account for large shares of domestic investment (they ranged from 2 to 4 percent over the period 1976–1980). Moreover, the increasing indebtedness of the Eastern European countries to the West has made them more dependent on the Soviet Union as a lender of last resort to meet their debt service obligations. Whether these trends will continue and strengthen CMEA as a supranational organization dominated by the Soviet Union cannot be predicted.

The trade between the Soviet Union and Eastern Europe may involve hidden subsidies. If the Soviet Union, for example, sells certain goods that are traded in world markets to Eastern Europe at prices below world market, then the Soviet Union has in fact granted a hidden subsidy. The pricing formulas that govern CMEA trade certainly create an opportunity for subsidies because raw material and other prices have tended to lag behind changes in world market prices. Subsidies can also occur when one country, such as the Soviet Union, allows its trading partners to run up substantial deficits in their trade accounts.[32]

Most experts agree that, particularly in the 1970s, the Soviet Union subsidized Eastern Europe. Michael Marresse and Jan Vanous, for example, calculate that the Soviet Union sacrificed potential gains adding up to more than $5 billion per year in the period 1974 to 1978. Other estimates confirm the existence of these subsidies but find that they were not as large as the Marresse-Vanous figures.[33]

Table 11.1 Indicator of Product Specialization in CMEA:[a] Has the Distribution of Production Levels Among CMEA Members Become More Unequal?

Product	1950–60	1960–70	1970–76
Investment goods:			
Tractors	Yes	No	No
Railway cars	No	Yes	Yes
Buses	No	No	Yes
Lathes	Not available	No	No
Intermediate goods:			
Pig iron	No	No	No
Steel	No	No	No
Synthetic fertilizer	No	No	No
Consumer products:			
Shoes	No	No	No
TV sets	No	Yes	No
Radio sets	Yes	Yes	Yes
Textile fabrics	No	No	No
Cigarettes	Yes	Yes	Yes
Agricultural products:			
Butter	No	No	Yes
Meat	No	No	No

[a] The CMEA as here defined includes the U.S.S.R. and the six East European countries of Bulgaria, Czechoslovakia, the German Democratic Republic, Hungary, Poland, and Romania.

Source: Based on production data in physical units reported in various CMEA statistical yearbooks. The method of calculation is described in the text. Paul Marer and John Michael Montias, "CMEA Integration: Theory and Practice," in U.S., Congress, Joint Economic Committee, *East European Economic Assessment*, Part 2 (Washington, D.C.: Government Printing Office, 1981), p. 180.

If the Soviet Union did indeed choose to subsidize Eastern Europe, what were its motives? Marresse and Vanous argue that Soviet subsidies were granted for political reasons and represent part of the price of Soviet control in Eastern Europe.

Forms of East-West Industrial Cooperation[34]

While institutional barriers to East-West trade were falling and CMEA interest in Western imports rising, the difficult issue of accommodating the transfer of technology through capital exports between different economic systems remained unresolved. Technology transfers among capitalist nations can be financed through intergovernment loans, private loans, portfolio investment in equities, and direct investment. The last two are precluded in the East by virtue of prohibitions against private ownership. New arrangements have had to be developed. After considerable experimentation in the 1960s and early 1970s, various forms of East-West industrial cooperation have emerged, which indicates that a stage of some maturity in East-West dealings has been attained. Such industrial cooperation agreements have played an important role in the expansion of East-West trade because the East's interest in such trade is concentrated in the areas of long-term flows of capital and technology. Such arrangements have had to go beyond traditional export and import operations; they call for a relationship between the supplier and the user of the technology that will last for a number of years.

As of the early 1980s, some 2,575 industrial cooperation agreements had been signed between Western firms and CMEA nations. Hungary, Romania, and Poland have served as the pioneers in the area of East-West industrial cooperation. The Soviet Union was a latecomer to such arrangements, but now the dollar value of Soviet industrial cooperation agreements exceeds that of all Eastern Europe.

The most difficult issues in the industrial cooperation arrangements have been to find substitutes for equity ownership in the project for the participating Western firms and arrange suitable financing arrangements for the hard-currency-poor CMEA nations. There is no single model of East-West industrial cooperation. Instead, a series of models has been worked out, each one of which is suited to the requirements of the particular trading country. In 1979, China passed a joint trading law that permits the Western partner over 50 percent of equity in some cases. Hungary, Poland, Bulgaria, and Romania allow Western equity ownership up to 49 percent of equity capital, but partial equity arrangements account for only 7 percent of the cooperative agreements. The other CMEA nations have sought substitutes for Western ownership in legal guarantees of the rights of Western firms to production and profits. In no case is management control by a Western firm allowed. The various forms of industrial cooperation are licensing arrangements, turnkey agreements, coproduction, subcontracting, and other forms of joint ventures.

The dearth of hard currency in many CMEA countries has called for special attention to the matter of financing industrial cooperation. The emerging trend is for participating Western firms to receive payment in terms of a guaranteed share of future production. Thus, a Western automobile manufacturer may set up a turnkey automobile assembly plant in the Soviet Union in return for a specified share of automobile output when the plant starts operation. Or a Western oil company may agree to supply oil extraction equipment for developing Siberian oil fields in return for a share of the resulting oil production. In this manner, the need for immediate hard currency reserves or hard currency credits is circumvented, and the cooperation scheme can proceed. Another hard currency benefit to the CMEA country is the countertrade arrangement often found in such cooperative ventures. The Western firm is responsible for marketing the output in the West, and thus the CMEA producer gains access to Western markets.[35] To this point, the major problems that have come to light are Eastern complaints about the failure of their Western partners to live up to purchase agreements, the problems of accommodating cooperation agreements with the Eastern planning systems, limitations on joint management, the issue of coordinating such projects with CMEA specialization agreements, and complaints of excessive dependence on Eastern energy supplies. Despite arrangements to limit the need for Western credits, the net indebtedness of the CMEA countries to the West is considerable. In 1985, the figure was $87 billion.[36] To obtain some feel for the magnitude of CMEA indebtedness (Figure 11.5), we should note that the average per capita CMEA hard currency debt (including Yugoslavia but excluding the Soviet Union) was $485 in 1981. The average 1981 ratio of hard currency debt to annual hard currency export earnings in 1981 was 2.0, and the annual cost of financing the hard currency debt averaged 30 percent of annual hard currency earnings. These averages conceal considerable variation among CMEA countries, with the annual cost of Poland's net debt service equal to 95 percent of Poland's annual hard currency earnings.[37] A 95 percent ratio means that Poland's earnings from exports to the West are just barely sufficient to cover the service cost on debt accumulated through past borrowing. Figure 11.5 illustrates as well the rapid rise of the hard currency debt burden from more modest ratios in the early 1970s.

EAST-WEST ECONOMIC RELATIONS WITH THE THIRD WORLD[38]

To this point, little has been said about international economics and the less-developed countries (the LDCs). The LDCs tend to work as a bloc

Figure 11.5 Three Alternative Debt Burden Measures for the East European Countries, 1971, 1975, and 1979

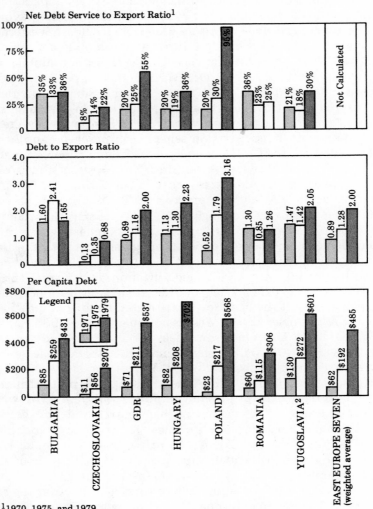

[1]1970, 1975, and 1979.

[2]Yuglosavia not strictly comparable to the other countries (see text).

Note: Debt refers to net debt; export data: sales to non-CPEs, except Yuglosavia (total exports); net debt service to export ratio: payments on medium- and long-term debt to merchandise exports to non-CPEs, except Yuglosavia (see text).

Source: Paul Marer, "Economic Performance and Prospects in Eastern Europe," copyright © 1980. Published in U.S., Congress, Joint Economic Committee, *East European Economic Assessment*, Part I (Washington, D.C.: Government Printing Office, 1981), p. 67.

through the United Nations Conference on Trade and Development (UNCTAD). Although all members of the United Nations can participate in UNCTAD, it has acted primarily as a spokesman for the LDCs in matters of trade and development. The established international organizations such as GATT and the IMF are perceived by the LDCs as representing the interests of the industrialized countries, and UNCTAD provides the organizational framework through which the wishes and demands of the LDCs vis-à-vis the developed world are made known.

Although the trade of the industrialized capitalist countries and of the CMEA countries with the LDCs is not a major element in world trade, Eastern and Western trade with and aid to the LDCs are still of considerable import. Many LDCs have sought to remain uncommitted to either the Eastern or the Western blocs; thus their political importance in world affairs far exceeds their economic importance. Moreover, they tend to be the most unstable components of the world political order; the remaining nations of the world appear to be firmly entrenched in the communist or noncommunist blocs.

The LDCs, in some instances, produce raw materials, such as petroleum, of considerable economic and strategic importance to the industrialized East and West. In fact, some observers believe that Western and Eastern policy toward the LDCs is aimed at control of their strategic raw materials. Moreover, the existence of a large and growing income gap between the rich and the poor nations is likely to contribute to political instability throughout the world. Recognition of this fact has focused attention on the development problems of the LDCs.

Capitalism and planned socialism offer competing theories to the LDCs. The established capitalist theory of development according to market resource allocation and comparative advantage states that the LDCs must be content to exchange the products (raw materials, agricultural products) they produce at a comparative advantage. By doing so, they can over time obtain at a minimum cost of their own resources the imported materials required for their economic development. As their per capita income grows, the LDCs can gradually substitute domestic production for the machinery and manufactured goods they had previously imported. The point of capitalist development theory is that the LDCs should maintain a basically capitalist economic system, albeit with stronger government controls, and should continue to produce traditional products until import substitution can be justified by sound profit-maximizing criteria.

The Marxist-Leninist theory of development paints quite a different picture: Adherence to market economics and the comparative advantage will doom the LDCs to an indefinite period of subservience to the industrialized capitalist countries. This is the upshot of Lenin's famous theory of imperialism (discussed in Chapter 4). The affluence of the industrialized capitalist countries is maintained by exploiting the labor and mineral resources of the LDCs, whose economic development is purposely retarded by the industrialized West. In order to develop, the LDCs must throw off their imperialist chains through wars of national liberation and join the ranks of the socialist countries. Then, with the assistance of the socialist world, they can begin the process of industrialization and the building of socialism. This process would require the replacement of the market with a system of central planning.

Of course, there is considerable debate over the merits of the two analyses of LDC development strategy. The LDCs themselves have contributed to this debate through the forum of UNCTAD. They have argued that they have been placed at a disadvantage in trade with the industrialized world for a variety of reasons and that it is the responsibility of the industrialized world to establish a "new international economic order," more suited to promoting LDC economic development. LDC dissatisfaction with the existing economic order centers on the fact that the LDCs have been relegated principally to the role of producing raw materials for the industrialized countries. Yet raw-material prices fluctuate more erratically than the prices of manufactured goods (often because of the competitive nature of raw-material markets). Moreover, the tariffs and quotas established by the industrialized countries discriminate against the raw-material exports of the LDCs and keep their manufactured exports (such as textiles) out of the affluent countries. The LDCs argue, therefore, that the affluent countries should increase their aid, should admit LDC manufactured goods on a preferential basis, and should assist in stabilizing the prices of LDC raw materials at levels high enough to promote their economic development. Moreover, the LDCs note that they were particularly hard hit by the increase in energy prices and the world recessions of the 1970s and early 1980s. These developments have made it difficult for the LDCs to finance their growing external debt and to pay for imports necessary for economic development.

Throughout this controversy, the Eastern countries have attempted to remain on the sidelines. They justify their inaction by saying that the problems of the LDCs are a direct consequence of the past and present imperialistic exploitation of the LDCs by the advanced capitalist nations, for which the communist world bears no responsibility. This argument is maintained despite the collapse of the colonial empires of the advanced capitalist countries after World War II. Here the Soviet (and New Left) argument is that the old form of imperialism has been replaced by a new imperialism — by an alliance between the conservative local ruling class and multinational Western corporations. Moreover, Soviet ideology has been amended to support the notion of an independent LDC nation. The "national democratic state" is an LDC that defends itself against capitalist imperialism and its military blocs but does not directly join the communist bloc. Such a state would deserve support even if it was not moving along a Soviet path of economic development. The latter type of LDC, according to the new Soviet orthodoxy, is called a "revolutionary democracy."

In sum, the nonaligned LDCs account for most of the uncommitted portion of the world's population. In this arena an ideological, economic, and military struggle for influence is being conducted between East and West. We refer the reader to the concept of the **general crisis of capitalism** (discussed in Chapter 4), whereby the Soviets argue that the world will be won for socialism not by world revolution but by the superior attractiveness of the socialist model for the nonaligned nations. Against this backdrop, it is relevant to examine the trade and aid that flow from East and West to the LDCs.

East and West Trade with and Aid for the LDCs

One would anticipate strong economic ties between the Eastern and Western countries and the LDCs as the former two vie for influence. In fact, most world trade takes place among the industrialized capitalist countries and, to a much lesser degree, among the CMEA countries. East-West trade itself accounts for an insignificant share of world trade. The trade of the East and West with the LDCs is relatively limited. In 1985, LDC exports plus imports accounted for 7 percent of total East European trade turnover and 9 percent of Soviet trade turnover. In the mid-1980s, the LDC exports and imports of industrialized capitalist countries accounted for 14 percent of their total trade turnover, excluding the OPEC countries, and for 26 percent including the OPEC countries. In terms of volume, trade between the industrialized capitalist countries and the LDCs dwarfs that of the East. In 1982, the industrialized capitalist countries bought $323 billion worth of exports from the LDCs (including OPEC); the CMEA countries bought $14 billion worth. Eastern trade with the LDCs is small relative to that of the West both in relative terms (as a percentage of total Eastern trade) and in absolute dollar terms. In fact, CMEA trade with the LDCs accounts for less than 1 pecent of world trade and for around 4 percent of total LDC trade.

What explains the limited trade of the East with the LDCs? One obvious explanation for the limited absolute volume of trade is that the East and the LDCs command only one-third of world GNP and, largely due to the East's limited participation in trade, less than one-fourth of world trade. Nevertheless, even these figures would predict larger trade volumes between the East and the LDCs than those actually observed. Another factor accounting for the low trade proportions between the East and the LDCs is that the East is a relatively new entrant into LDC markets and lacks long-established trade relationships, which are often the consequence of the past colonial rule.

One somewhat puzzling aspect of the limited amount of East-LDC trade is that there are strong economic, as well as political, grounds for such trade. In the 1950s and 1960s, the Eastern European countries embarked on national programs of industrialization, de-emphasizing the production of raw materials and agricultural products. These efforts led to a shortage of raw materials in Eastern Europe. Thus its demand for the products typically exported by the LDCs was substantial. The LDCs, on the other hand, required machinery imports for their own industrialization, but, due to the constant shortage of hard currency, they were not in a position to exercise this demand in the West. Accordingly, bilateral trade (raw materials for manufactures) appeared to represent a rational policy for both parties. If one examines the pattern of trade between the East and LDCs, the exchange of LDC raw materials and food products for Eastern manufactures and machinery does indeed predominate throughout the postwar era.

From the foregoing figures, it is apparent that the East is not in a position to exert much economic power over the LDCs. The East acts as a relatively minor buyer and seller in trade with the LDCs and does not wield the potential for economic control of the advanced capitalist nations. The same conclusion can be drawn concerning the disbursement of economic aid by East and West.

Between 1954 and 1985, the industrialized capitalist countries granted over $300 billion in economic assistance to the LDCs. Over the same period, the CMEA nations granted only $49 billion and mainland China $7 billion in economic aid. The CMEA looms larger in the area of military assistance. Between 1954 and 1985, the CMEA nations provided military assistance of $28 billion. The striking feature of CMEA exports to the LDCs is the dominant role of military hardware sales. Moreover, CMEA arms exports and military aid tend to be concentrated among fewer client countries than is Western assistance. This follows the general CMEA policy of concentrating both military and economic aid in countries where the expected political and economic benefits are highest. In this manner, the CMEA nations have sought to compensate for their lower volume of assistance.

The Soviet Development Model and
Its Influence in the LDCs[39]

Although the influence of the East in the LDCs is limited by its low volumes of trade and aid, it can exercise influence in other ways. The first is to position itself as the champion of nationalistic anti-Western tendencies and encourage the anti-imperialistic sentiments of the LDCs. Thus for many years, the Soviet Union condemned the imperialistic actions of the advanced capitalist countries and encouraged wars of "national liberation," while avoiding blame for the lack of economic development of the LDCs, which was attributed to Western imperialism. The posture of blamelessness has become less tenable in recent years with the drive of the LDCs to obtain at least 1 percent of the GNPs of the more advanced Eastern and Western countries in the form of development assistance. The lower ratios of CMEA economic assistance to their GNPs have not escaped the attention of the LDCs.

Another source of influence is potentially more influential in the long run: the offering of an alternate model of economic development for the LDCs. The major attraction of the Soviet development model is that it appears to offer to the LDCs a means of accelerating economic development through the centralized allocation of resources to specific and unbalanced growth objectives, without major reliance on external assistance. Rather than accepting the slow progress promised by the market mechanism and exchanging traditional exports for manufactured imports, LDC planners can concentrate available resources on the development of a domestic industrial base, with emphasis on domestic heavy industry if possible. They can avoid "unproductive" investments by limiting investment in services and social overhead capital. Moreover, agriculture can be placed under centralized control through collectivization. In this manner, mechanization and new techniques can be imposed on a tradition-minded peasantry. This Soviet model, while yielding certain benefits, is not without costs. The most important cost is that the population must sacrifice current consumption in order to finance the industrialization drive.

As an example, the LDCs can look to the Soviet Union of the 1930s, which made a radical transformation from backwardness to industrial power in less than one decade with virtually no external assistance. One noteworthy feature of the Soviet model, which may limit its relevance for contemporary LDCs, is the fact that rapid industrialization through high rates of capital accumulation and rapid growth of the industrial labor force was attained through forcible reductions in agricultural living standards. Such a policy requires a margin over subsistence in agriculture to cushion the blow. If this margin is not available, severe consequences (starvation, shortages of industrial raw materials, and so on) could follow.

In this regard, differences between the Soviet and Chinese development pattern are informative. The Chinese began their industrialization in the early 1950s from a much lower economic base than that inherited by the Soviets in 1917. The Chinese were not able to attain either the high rates of capital accumulation or the massive concentration of resources in heavy industry recorded by the Soviets. Instead, more attention was paid to industrial inputs into agriculture; in general, agricultural development was not starved as it was in the Soviet case. It appears that the Chinese did not have the agricultural surpluses necessary to implement the Soviet development model in its strict form. They did imitate the Soviet model in the sense that the control over resource allocation was taken out of the hands of the market and turned over to a planning apparatus, which dictated economic policy in accordance with the wishes of the Chinese Communist party.

There are no easy answers to the question of what type of development model the LDCs should adopt, and there appears to be no consensus among LDCs about how to answer that question. Some have attempted to emulate the Soviet model, others the capitalist model; most have opted for a mixed form of market with strong governmental controls. Two important points should be made about the relevance of the Soviet model for the LDCs. The first is that a principal objective of the Soviet model is the development of a relatively self-sufficient economy, namely, one that has its own industrial base. This is especially true of the Eastern European experience with the Soviet model. Each Eastern European nation has sought to develop its own domestic industrial base. In the Soviet and Chinese cases one is dealing with economies of enormous scale, rich in labor and mineral resources. Such a policy would tend to work better there than in a small, resource-poor country. It is notable that Cuba, for example, has had to forgo a broad-based industrialization effort and continues to rely on sugar production despite the adoption of Soviet-type central planning.

The second point is that the adoption and implementation of the Soviet development model, especially in its stricter form, does require a great deal of political power and control over the participants in the development effort. Typically, this control has been exercised through a monolithic party, which holds a monopoly in the area of economic and political decision making. Are the LDCs able, or perhaps more important, willing to allow such a concentration of power?

SUMMARY: INTERNATIONAL TRADE

1.   This chapter deals with the economics of East-West trade and the trade of the East and West with the developing countries. The most important systemic factors affecting trade between East and West are the manner in which Eastern trade is planned by centralized authorities, the fact that Eastern prices fail to reveal the scarcity values of domestically produced commodities, and prohibitions against private ownership. These factors have led to a system of bilateral trade and underutilization of trade potential on the part of the East, despite the rapid growth of East-West trade in recent years.

2.   Institutional barriers to East-West trade took the form of quantitative restrictions in Western Europe and failure to grant MFN

status to many Eastern countries by the United States. Institutional barriers have been lowered substantially since the 1950s, and the remaining barriers combine systemic and institutional factors.

3. Although East-West trade in products and technology has been expanding rapidly over the past two decades, it remains small relative to trading potential. Arrangements have been developed that satisfy both the desire of Western firms for equity participation and the distaste of socialist countries for private ownership. The share of East-West trade in total Eastern trade has risen substantially since 1960, yet as a percentage of world trade, East-West trade is inconsequential and is likely to remain so for many years.

4. Commercial relations are affected by the ebb and flow of East-West political relations. The remaining barriers are for the most part inherent in the economic systems of capitalism and socialism. Capitalism, with its emphasis on profit maximization and decentralized decision making, promotes foreign trade and economic specialization, once barriers are removed. The planned socialist system has not proved to be well suited to the full utilization of trade potential due to the inflexibility of the planning process, the absence of multilateralism and convertibility, the difficulty of making comparative cost evaluations, and the drive for national economic independence.

5. Most world trade is conducted among the industrialized countries; Eastern aid to and trade with the LDCs is small in both relative and absolute terms. The East is not in a position to exert much economic power over the LDCs, but may, however, press its influence in the ideological arena, through support of anti-imperialistic sentiments in the LDCs and the alternative for development it offers to the capitalist model.

NOTES

1. The standard discussions of the trade of the planned socialist economies are Frederic Pryor, *The Communist Foreign Trade System* (Cambridge, Mass.: M.I.T. Press, 1963); Franklyn Holzman, *International Trade Under Communism* (New York: Basic Books, 1976); Franklyn Holzman, *Foreign Trade Under Central Planning* (Cambridge, Mass.: Harvard University Press, 1979); P. J. D. Wiles, *Communist International Economics* (New York: Praeger, 1969); and the collection of studies in Alan Brown and Egon Neuberger, eds., *International Trade and Central Planning* (Berkeley: University of California Press, 1968).

2. For a more detailed discussion of this point, see Evsey Domar's discussion in Brown and Neuberger, *International Trade and Central Planning*, pp. 277-279.

3. These figures are from World Bank, *World Development Report, 1982* (New York: Oxford University Press, 1982), pp. 110–111; U.S., Department of State, *The Planetary Product* (Special Report No. 58, October 1979), pp. 35–36; *Handbook of Economic Statistics, 1987.*

4. Accounts of these studies are found in Frederic Pryor's discussion in Brown and Neuberger, *International Trade and Central Planning*, pp. 159–165; and in Paul Gregory, *Socialist and Nonsocialist Industrialization Patterns* (New York: Praeger, 1970), p. 120. Also see Edward Hewett's study in Josef Brada, ed., *Quantitative Analytic Studies in East-West Economic Relations* (Studies in East European and Soviet Planning and Development, Bloomington, Indiana, 1976).

5. National Foreign Assessment Center, *Handbook of Economic Statistics* (Washington, D.C.: Central Intelligence Agency, 1980), pp. 66, 67, 87–97.

6. Holzman, *International Trade Under Communism*, p. 127.

7. Ibid., p. 128.

8. United Nations, *Monthly Bulletin of Statistics*, 37, 1983, pp. xxx–xxxiii.

9. For a discussion of foreign trade planning, see Herbert Levine, "The Effects of Foreign Trade on Soviet Planning Practices," in Brown and Neuberger, *International Trade and Central Planning*, pp. 255–276; Lawrence Brainard, "Soviet Foreign Trade Planning," in U.S., Congress, Joint Economic Committee, *Soviet Economy in a New Perspective* (Washington, D.C.: Government Printing Office, 1976), pp. 695–708; H. Stephen Gardner, *Soviet Foreign Trade: The Decision Process* (Boston: Kluwer-Nijhoff, 1983).

10. Gardner, *Soviet Foreign Trade*, ch. 7.

11. Martin Kohn and Nicholas Lang, "The Intra-CMEA Foreign Trade System: Major Price Changes, Little Reform," in U.S., Congress, Joint Economic Committee, *East European Economies Post Helsinki* (Washington, D.C.: Government Printing Office, 1977), pp. 135–151; Marie Lavigne, "The Soviet Union Inside Comecon," *Soviet Studies*, 35, no. 2 (April 1983), pp. 135–153.

12. This discussion is based on Holzman, *International Trade Under Communism*, pp. 40–44.

13. Kohn and Lang, "The Intra-CMEA Foreign Trade System," p. 137; Lavigne, "Soviet Union Inside Comecon," p. 142.

14. Jan Vanous, "Soviet and Eastern European Foreign Trade in the 1970s: A Quantitative Assessment," U.S., Congress, Joint Economic Committee, *East European Economic Assessment*, Part 2 (Washington, D.C.: Government Printing Office, 1981), pp. 698–704; Allen Lang and Hedija Kravalis, "An Analysis of Recent and Potential Soviet and Eastern European Exports to Fifteen Industrialized Western Countries," in Joint Economic Committee, *Eastern European Economies Post Helsinki*, pp. 1074–1075.

15. National Foreign Assessment Center, *Handbook of Economic Statistics* (Washington, D.C.: Central Intelligence Agency, 1986), p. 48.

16. For a case study of Soviet-manufactured exports, see Paul Ericson, "Soviet Efforts to Increase Exports of Manufactured Products to the West," in Joint Economic Committee, *Soviet Economy in a New Perspective*, pp. 709–726.

17. Robert Campbell and John Hardt, eds., "The US-Soviet Agreement on Trade, Three Interpretations," *The ACES Bulletin*, 15 (Spring 1973), pp. 108–113. Also see "Commercial Relations" (contributions by Jurew, Bresnick, and Pregelj), in Joint Economic Committee, *East European Economic Assessment*, Part 2, pp. 635–684.

18. The standard discussions of foreign trade criteria in socialist countries are Andrea Boltho, *Foreign Trade Criteria in Socialist Countries* (Cambridge: Cambridge University Press, 1971); and Edward Hewett, *Foreign Trade Prices in the Council for Mutual Economic Assistance* (London: Cambridge University Press, 1974). One should also consult the discussions in Brainard, "Soviet

Foreign Trade Plannings," pp. 701–704; and Holzman, *International Trade Under Communism*, pp. 33–36.

19. Brainard, "Soviet Foreign Trade Planning," p. 704.

20. Gardner, *Soviet Foreign Trade*, ch. 7.

21. Steven Rosefielde, "Factor Proportions and Economic Rationality in Soviet International Trade," *American Economic Review*, 64 (September 1974), pp. 670–681.

22. This discussion is based on Holzman, *International Trade Under Communism*, ch. 4; Anton Malish, Jr., "An Analysis of Tariff Discrimination on Soviet and Eastern European Trade," *The ACES Bulletin*, 15 (Spring 1973), pp. 43–56; and three essays in Joint Economic Committee, *East European Economies Post Helsinki*: Edward Hewett, "Recent Developments in East-West Economic Relations," pp. 174–198; Thomas Wolf, "East-West European Trade Relations," pp. 1042–1054; Karen Taylor, "Import Protection and East-West Trade," pp. 1132–1174; and Joint Economic Committee, *East-European Economic Assessment*, Part 2, pp. 635–684.

23. T. A. Wolf, in "The Impact of Elimination of West German Quantitative Restrictions on Manufactures from Centrally Planned Economies," Band 112, *Weltwirtschaftliches Archiv* (Tübingen: J. C. B. Mohr, 1976), pp. 338–358, finds that the elimination of quantitative restrictions by West Germany between 1966 and 1976 had a significant effect on CMEA imports, especially machinery and equipment.

24. Jack Brougher, "1974–82: The United States Uses Trade to Penalize Soviet Aggression and Seeks to Reorder Western Policy," in U.S., Congress, Joint Economic Committee, *Soviet Economy in the 1980s: Problems and Prospects*, Part 2 (Washington, D.C.: Government Printing Office, 1983), pp. 419–453.

25. Taylor, "Import Protection and East-West Trade," pp. 1172–1173.

26. For an analysis of the effect of MFN on Polish-U.S. trade, see Thomas Wolf, "Effects of US Granting of Most Favored Nation Treatment to Imports from Eastern Europe: The Polish Experience," *The ACES Bulletin*, 15 (Spring 1973), pp. 3–22. For a more general study, see Helen Raffel, Marc Rubin, and Robert Teal, "The MFN Impact on U.S. Imports from Eastern Europe," in Joint Economic Committee, *Eastern European Economies Post Helsinki*, p. 1427. For a view from the other side of the cost equation, see H. Stephen Gardner, "Assessing the Cost to the U.S. Economy of Trade Sanctions Against the USSR," Conference on East-West Trade, Technology Transfer, and U.S. Export Control Policy, University of South Carolina, March 1983.

27. Our discussion of CMEA is based largely on Holzman, *International Trade Under Communism*, ch. 3; Hertha Heiss, "The Council for Mutual Economic Assistance — Developments Since the Mid-1960's," in U.S., Congress, Joint Economic Committee, *Economic Developments in Countries of Eastern Europe* (Washington, D.C.: Government Printing Office, 1970), pp. 528–542; Arthur Smith, "The Council for Mutual Economic Assistance in 1977: New Economic Power, New Political Perspectives, and Some Old and New Problems," in Joint Economic Committeee, *East European Economies Post Helsinki*, pp. 152–173.

28. Lavigne, "The Soviet Union Inside Comecon," pp. 135–140.

29. James L. Ellis, "Eastern Europe: Changing Trade Patterns and Perspectives," U.S., Congress, Joint Economic Committee, *East European Economics: Slow Growth in the 1980's*, vol. 2 (Washington, D.C.: Government Printing Office, 1986), p. 11.

30. For a discussion of this point, see Joseph Pelzman, "Trade Integration in the Council for Mutual Economic Assistance: Creation and Diversion, 1954–1970," *The ACES Bulletin*, 18 (Fall 1976), pp. 39–60; and Josef van Brabant,

"Trade Creation and Trade Diversion in Eastern Europe: A Comment," *The ACES Bulletin*, 19 (Spring 1977), pp. 79-98.

31. Paul Marer and John Michael Montias, "CMEA Integration: Theory and Practice," in Joint Economic Committee, *East European Economic Assessment*, Part 2, pp. 177-179.

32. Lavigne, "The Soviet Union Inside Comecon," pp. 145-149.

33. Michael Marresse and Jan Vanous, *Soviet Subsidization of Trade with Eastern Europe — A Soviet Perspective*, Institute of International Studies (Berkeley: University of California Press, 1983). For a different, and lower, estimate, see Raimund Dietz, "Advantages and Disadvantages in Soviet Trade with Eastern Europe," U.S., Congress, Joint Economic Committee, *East European Economies: Slow Growth in the 1980s* (Washington, D.C.: U.S. Government Printing Office, 1986), pp. 263-301.

34. Our discussion of East-West industrial cooperation is based primarily on Carl H. McMillan, "Trends in East-West Industrial Cooperation," *Journal of International Business Studies*, Fall 1981, pp. 53-67; Maureen Smith, "Industrial Cooperative Agreements: Soviet Experience and Practices," in Joint Economic Committee, *Soviet Economy in a New Perspective*, pp. 767-785; and Carl McMillan, "East-West Industrial Cooperation," in Joint Economic Committee, *East European Economies Post Helsinki*, pp. 1175-1224.

35. Janelle Matheson, Paul McCarthy, and Steven Flanders, "Countertrade Practices in Eastern Europe," in Joint Economic Committee, *East European Economies Post Helsinki*, pp. 1277-1311.

36. *Handbook of Economic Statistics 1986*, p. 48; Joan P. Zoeter, "East Europe: The Hard Currency Debt," *East European Economic Assessment*, Part 2, p. 490.

37. Zbigniew Fallenbuchl, Egon Neuberger, and Laura Tyson, "East European Reactions to International Commodity Inflation," in Joint Economic Committee, *East European Economies Post Helsinki*, pp. 54-121. For a theoretical treatment of macrodisturbances in centrally planned and modified centrally planned economies, see T. A. Wolf, "External Inflation, the Balance of Trade, and Resource Allocation in Small Centrally Planned Economies," in Egon Neuberger and Laura Tyson, eds., *The Impact of International Economic Disturbances on the Soviet Union and Eastern Europe* (New York: Pergamon, 1982).

38. The next two sections are based primarily on Holzman, *International Trade Under Communism*, ch. 5. The statistics are from Holzman; *Handbook of Economic Statistics*, various years; U.S., Department of State, *Soviet and East European Aid to the Third World, 1981* (February 1983).

39. This discussion is based on Paul R. Gregory and Robert C. Stuart, *Soviet Economic Structure and Performance*, 3rd ed. (New York: Harper & Row, 1986), ch. 11; and R. W. Davies, "Socialism in a Less Developed Country," in OECD, *Science and Technology in the People's Republic of China* (Paris: OECD, 1977), ch. 11.

RECOMMENDED READINGS

Andrea Boltho, *Foreign Trade Criteria in Socialist Countries* (Cambridge: Cambridge University Press, 1971).

Lawrence Brainard, "Soviet Foreign Trade Planning," in U.S., Congress, Joint Economic Committee, *Soviet Economy in a New Perspective* (Washington, D.C.: Government Printing Office, 1976), pp. 695-708.

Alan Brown and Egon Neuberger, eds., *International Trade and Central Planning* (Berkeley: University of California Press, 1968).

Benjamin Cohen, *Organizing the World's Money: The Political Economy of International Monetary Relations* (New York: Basic Books, 1977).

H. Stephen Gardner, *Soviet Foreign Trade: The Decision Process* (Boston: Kluwer-Nijhoff, 1983).

Phillip Hanson, *Trade and Technology in Soviet-Western Economic Relations* (New York: Columbia University Press, 1981).

Edward Hewett, *Foreign Trade Prices in the Council for Mutual Economic Assistance* (London: Cambridge University Press, 1974).

Franklyn Holzman, *Foreign Trade Under Central Planning* (Cambridge, Mass.: Harvard University Press, 1979).

——, *International Trade Under Communism* (New York: Basic Books, 1976).

Paul Marer and John M. Montias, eds., *East European Integration and East-West Trade* (Bloomington: Indiana University Press, 1980).

Egon Neuberger and Laura Tyson, eds., *The Impact of International Economic Disturbance on the Soviet Union and Eastern Europe* (New York: Pergamon, 1980).

Frederic Pryor, *The Communist Foreign Trade System* (Cambridge, Mass.: M.I.T. Press, 1963).

U.S., Congress, Joint Economic Committee, *East European Economies Post Helsinki* (Washington, D.C.: Government Printing Office, 1977).

——, *East European Economic Assessment*, Part 2 (Washington, D.C.: Government Printing Office, 1981).

——, *East European Economies: Slow Growth in the 1980's* (Washington, D.C.: Government Printing Office, 1986).

Jozef M. Van Brabant, *Socialist Economic Integration* (New York: Cambridge University Press, 1980).

P. J. D. Wiles, *Communist International Economics* (New York: Praeger, 1969).

Chapter 12
Performance of Economic Systems

THE METHODOLOGY OF
PERFORMANCE COMPARISONS

In Chapter 2, we discussed the methodology of comparing the performance of economic systems. Although certain objectives — a high standard of living, economic stability, growth, efficiency, good environmental quality — are desirable, the achievement of each goal extracts a price in terms of economic resources. Insofar as resources are limited, hard choices must be made among these economic goals. Unless different economic systems place the same weight on the various goals, it is difficult to evaluate the overall performance of the systems. The major long-term goal of the planned socialist countries has been the "building of socialism." This goal requires high rates of growth of industrial and military output; so the overriding objective of the planned socialist economies has been the achievement of rapid economic growth. This is not to say that other goals — allocative efficiency, full employment, a "socialist" distribution of income — are not also desired by the leadership; rather, that lower values have been attached to their achievement.

The ranking of economic objectives among capitalist nations is less uniform. Some emphasize economic stability; others, especially developing capitalist nations, stress economic growth; and others emphasize different goals. There is no one unifying goal that the capitalist nations have singled out as their principal objective.

If nations tend to perform relatively "better" in the areas they consider important, we would expect different economies to perform relatively well according to high-priority goals. To decide which economy or system has performed "better" would require some judgment as to which goals are more "important." Such a judgment would have to be subjective.

Another difficulty in comparing the performance of economic systems arises if we decide to eliminate the problem of ranking objectives by evaluating economic systems exclusively on the basis of economic growth. For when one examines the data on growth rates, one finds that some socialist countries during certain time periods have outgrown certain capitalist countries and vice versa. The evaluation depends on *which* countries are included in the comparison and, perhaps, on the time period investigated.

How does one select countries and time periods for comparison? One way would be to have a random selection to estimate the "true" capitalist and socialist growth rates. However, the number of countries and the historical perspective, especially on the socialist side, are too limited for random selection. Therefore, some selection criteria must be used. The criteria should result in the selection of countries most "representative" of their own system; yet it is difficult to determine the matter of representativeness. Should one compare only countries at a similar stage of economic development? Is it fair to compare the post-war rates of growth in Eastern Europe with the long-term historical growth of the capitalist nations?

For performance comparisons to be valid, the *ceteris paribus* assumption must hold; that is, that the economies compared be alike *in all other respects* with the exception of their economic systems. In the notation of Chapter 2, the *ceteris paribus* problem was described as follows: Outcomes (O) are a function of a variety of environmental factors ENV (for example, natural and human resource endowments, level of development), economic policy (POL), and the economic system (ES). Thus

$$O = f(\text{ENV, POL, ES}) \tag{12.1}$$

Because the ENV and POL values will differ by country, one cannot make a statement about the impact of ES on outcomes without a clear understanding of the role of the ENV and POL factors.

Two examples illustrate these points. Labor productivity in the Soviet Union is low relative to that in the United States and industrialized Western Europe.[1] The intriguing question, however, is whether this is a consequence of the *system* of planned socialism or a product of other (ENV, POL) factors. The level of economic development of the Soviet Union is still behind that of the United States and Western Europe, and productivity is positively associated with economic development. Can the Soviet productivity gap be accounted for entirely by these other factors, or is the economic system itself to blame? *Long-term* economic growth in the Soviet Union has outpaced that in the United States and Western Europe.[2] Is this a consequence of the economic system or of other factors unrelated to the system?

Two related approaches can be used to deal with this problem. The first is to compare economies alike in all respects other than economic system. In terms of equation 12.1, this means making performance comparisons only in instances where ENV and POL are equal so that performance differences can be attributed to the system. The nearest (yet imperfect) example of this approach would be the comparison of previously unified countries, now belonging to different economic blocs (East and West Germany, North and South Korea, for example), but such examples are rare.[3] Comparison of agricultural productivity in the Soviet Union and the United States in areas of similar land quality and climate would serve as an example of a less-aggregated approach. The basic drawback of attempting to compare similar economies is that we are denied a laboratory setting where ENV and POL are truly the same. One cannot find real-world cases where all factors other than the economic system are constant. The closest case one can find, East and West Germany, is analyzed in Chapter 13.

The econometric approach to dealing with the *ceteris paribus* problem requires the estimation of the impact of the ENV and POL factors on O. Once known, these factors can hypothetically be held constant, revealing the impact of the economic system on performance. This approach requires the investigation of *groups* of capitalist and socialist economies that differ according to ENV and POL characteristics, so that their impact can be isolated and held constant.[4]

Economic systems, either in their "pure" or real-world "mixed" forms, are multidimensional, and we have sought throughout this book to deal with economic systems in terms of their multidimensional attributes. Yet because economic systems are multidimensional and their attributes are difficult to measure, we cannot hope to formulate an *objective* and *quantitative* measure of ES which differentiates among economies according to the degree of capitalism or planned or market socialism. We cannot hope to pose or answer questions such as whether the Soviet economy is more "planned socialist" than the East German economy and whether the U.S. economy is more "capitalist" than the British economy. Therefore, we are forced to bunch real-world economies into rough political-economic groupings without being able to hold constant the effect of variations in ES *within* a particular grouping.

In this chapter, we group real-world economies into the three categories used throughout this book: capitalism, planned socialism, and market socialism. This requires combining economies that differ in important respects, a process which further obscures the impact of the economic system on economic outcomes; yet we have no choice but to make these rough divisions. For example, in the comparisons that follow, intermediate and low-income countries such as Greece, Spain, Turkey, and India are included in the "capitalist" group, despite their substantial differences from industrialized capitalist countries. Our own feeling is that there is much greater homogeneity within the planned socialist group than within the capitalist group. Yet even they have differences (ownership and control arrangements in agriculture that have been shown to affect agricultural performance, for example), so the planned socialist economics are by no means uniform.[5]

What does the performance of countries representing each economic system tell us about the performance of the system in its pure form? Since real-world economies combine elements from different economic systems, is it appropriate to try to speculate about how each economic system would have performed in its "pure" state (that is, perfectly competitive capitalism and centralized planning with perfect information and computation)? Or is it more appropriate to look at real-world mixed variants? It could be argued that representatives of a particular economic system have not performed "well" exactly because they deviate from the pure model; therefore, weaknesses should be attributed not to the economic system but to the deviations from it. If this line of argument is accepted, then performance must be evaluated in theoretical rather than empirical terms.

We reject the latter line of argument because what counts is not how an economic system would conceivably perform under ideal circumstances, but how well it can perform in a real-world setting when confronted with powerful forces (imperfect competition, external effects, imperfect planning information, computational limitations) that prevent the ideal from being realized. In our view, how well the representatives of economic systems have actually performed is the appropriate standard for evaluating the performance of economic systems, for this reflects the performance potential of the system in real-world situations.

THE PERFORMANCE OF SYSTEMS

Having expressed words of caution based on the difficulties of evaluating the performance of economic systems, we proceed to the evaluation of the performance of capitalism and socialism. We take the most important performance indicators — economic growth, economic efficiency (both static and dynamic), the "fairness" of the distribution of income, and economic stability — and attempt to determine how well selected representatives of capitalism and socialism have performed according to each individual criterion.

The Choice of Countries

The selection of representatives of capitalism and socialism is dictated by the availability of data. Data limitations dictate the principal emphasis on comparisons of the Soviet Union and Eastern European (CMEA) nations with the industrialized and near-industrialized capitalist nations.[6] The data for the Asian communist countries (North Korea, Vietnam, Cambodia, and Mongolia) are too poor to support meaningful comparisons. Yugoslavia is included to capture the performance of market socialism, but it is difficult to generalize about the performance of market socialism from the Yugoslav experience alone. Comparisons of industrialized capitalism with the planned socialism of the Soviet Union and Eastern Europe rest on firmer footing, for they are based on groups of capitalist and planned socialist countries.[7] Generalizations that emerge from these comparisons are more likely to be representative of the system because some form of average behavior is being observed.

How about the performance of China vis-à-vis its less-developed capitalist counterparts? Here the difficulty lies in estimating the degree to which China is representative of the performance of planned socialism in a large and backward economy. Chinese economic performance has been significantly affected by a series of political upheavals. We cannot establish whether these disruptions have been endemic to the system at low levels of development. There is the further difficulty of finding appropriate counterparts against which to gauge China's economic performance. Should China's performance be measured against that of Japan (an immediate Asian neighbor), India[8] (another Asian neighbor, almost equally populous), or against the large and small noncommunist Asian nations combined? If the yardstick is Japan, then Chinese performance will not be impressive; if Bangladesh, then it will appear more impressive. Our compromise is to limit our discussion of China's economic performance to Sino-Indian comparisons. However, our emphasis is on the economic performance of CMEA members vis-à-vis the performance of industrialized capitalist nations.

The number of CMEA member states (excluding Mongolia, Vietnam, and Cuba for lack of data) is seven: Bulgaria, East Germany, Poland, Hungary, Romania, Czechoslovakia, and the Soviet Union. Our selection of industrialized and near-industrialized capitalist countries is based on three considerations: the availability of comparable data, an attempt to include some countries at levels of economic development roughly comparable to that of the CMEA nations, and the desire to have the major capitalist countries (such as the United States, West Germany, and Japan) included.

The data used in this chapter are Western recalculations of CMEA national aggregate statistics. Economic aggregates, such as GNP, industrial production, and per capita consumption, are not compiled uniformly by the national statistical agencies in Eastern and Western countries, although statistical practices are fairly uniform within the two blocs. For example, the CMEA nations exclude from their definition of aggregate final output (net material product) "nonproductive" services, which do not directly support material production.[9] Thus personal transportation and communication services, government, and most professional services are excluded from net material product. Such "nonproductive" services are included in the United Nations system of national accounts statistics used by the Western nations; so direct comparisons of Western GNP or net national product with CMEA net material product would be invalid. Also net material product as defined in the socialist countries includes some double-counting of outputs.

Another problem of statistical comparability is the manner in which prices are established in planned and market economies. Economic aggregates are the sum of the products of prices times quantities; thus, substantial relative pricing differences can lead to further incomparabilities, especially if one system generates relatively high prices (large weights) for rapidly growing sectors like industry and relatively low prices for slow-growing sectors like agriculture. Differences in relative prices also complicate the determination of relative levels of output (see the chapter appendix). In the planned economy, government intervention in price setting is more substantial than in the West, and substantial turnover taxes are applied to industrial products. This practice raises the relative weight of industry in the GNP aggregate and accordingly the overall growth rate. Moreover, the CMEA nations do not include returns to capital or land in their prices, but such returns are automatically included in Western prices. This leads to further incomparabilities.

The aggregate figures cited in this chapter are recalculations that make the CMEA aggregates conform as closely as possible to standard Western national accounting practices.[10] The recalculated figures show considerably lower growth than that reported by the CMEA countries themselves. It should be emphasized that the Western recalculations have an unknown degree of reliability. Western authorities have access only to the published information released on a selective basis by the CMEA countries and must often make heroic assumptions. Yet we have no choice but to use in our comparisons figures that are at least conceptually comparable.

An Economic Profile: Structural Characteristics of East and West

Table 12.1 provides a partial economic profile of the planned socialist countries, Yugoslavia, and selected capitalist countries. This profile helps us see what factors should be held constant in performance comparisons, and it provides insights into the socialist model of industrialization. [11]

In terms of per capita income, the most widely used indicator of economic development, the Soviet Union and Eastern Europe are well behind the advanced capitalist countries. The per capita incomes in the more advanced planned socialist economies (Czechoslovakia, East

Table 12.1 An Economic Profile of Socialist and Capitalist Countries in the 1980s

	(1) Per Capita GNP, 1985 (U.S. $)	(2) Population 1985 (Millions)	(3a) Share of Industry and Construction in GNP (1982)	(3b) Agriculture	(3c) Services	(4) Proportion of Labor in Agriculture (1985)	(5) Gross Investment as a Percentage of GNP (1982)
A. Planned Socialism							
East Germany	10,440	16.7	51	13	36	10	24
Czechoslovakia	8,750	15.5	49	15	36	13	25
Hungary	7,560	10.6	38	26	36	18	29
Soviet Union	7,400	278.9	42	19	39	19	30
Poland	6,470	37.2	37	27	36	29	27
Bulgaria	6,420	9.0	46	23	31	20	28
Romania	5,450	22.7	46	26	28	29	38
China	340	1,042.4	45	35	20	68	28
B. Market Socialism							
Yugoslavia	5,600	23.1	43	12	45	20	27

C. Capitalism

Norway	16,719	4.2	41	5	54	9	26
United States	16,710	238.6	34	3	63	3	19
Canada	16,538	25.4	32	4	64	5	25
Denmark	14,603	5.1	22	5	73	7	16
West Germany	14,432	61.0	53	3	44	6	23
France	13,755	55.0	41	4	55	9	21
Japan	13,312	120.7	40	5	55	10	31
Belgium	13,219	9.9	42	4	54	3	18
Netherlands	12,741	14.5	33	4	63	5	18
Austria	12,343	7.6	39	4	57	9	26
United Kingdom	12,042	56.4	33	2	65	3	17
Italy	10,928	57.1	41	6	53	13	21
Spain	9,008	39.1	34	6	60	18	20
Greece	6,854	10.0	31	17	52	31	25
Turkey	2,135	45.1	31	22	47	60	25
India	250	767.7	26	36	38	70	25

Sources: U.S. Department of Commerce, *Statistical Abstract of the United States, 1981* (Washington, D.C.: U.S. Government Printing Office, 1981), pp. 876–879; National Foreign Assessment Center, *Handbook of Economic Statistics, 1986* (Washington, D.C.: Central Intelligence Agency, 1986); World Bank, *World Tables*, 3rd ed. (Baltimore, MD: The Johns Hopkins University Press, 1984); OECD, *Historical Statistics, 1960–1985* (Paris, OECD, 1987); Thad Alton, "East European GNPs," Joint Economic Committee, *East European Economics: Slow Growth in the 1980s, Vol. 1* (Washington, D.C., U.S. Government Printing Office, 1985), pp. 81–132. The East European investment rates are calculated by subtracting the rates of defense spending the GNP from Alton's residual expenditure category (p. 95).

Germany, Soviet Union) are well below those in Japan and the United Kingdom and between those in Italy and Spain. The intermediate (Poland, Romania, and Hungary) and less-advanced (Bulgaria) planned socialist nations are well below Italy and Spain but close to Greece. Thus the CMEA countries as a group are less advanced than the industrialized Western countries with which they are most often compared, and this difference must be considered when evaluating their performance.

Despite relatively low per capita income, the share of industry and construction in GNP in the CMEA countries is roughly equal to that of the capitalist countries. In fact, the CMEA industry share averages 43 percent; the average of capitalist countries (United States to Italy) is 36 percent. One would have to conclude that, if per capita income is held constant, the planned socialist industry share is high relative to capitalism. The CMEA shares of agriculture and services are even more different from their Western counterparts. Agriculture's share of both GNP and labor force is quite high in the planned socialist countries once per capita income is held constant, but the share of the service sector is well below that of capitalist countries at similar levels of development. The data on investment rates from 1982 (column 5 of Table 12.1), surprisingly, do not yield a clear trend. The CMEA countries do tend to have investment rates in the high ranges of 24 to 38 percent, but one can find similarly high investment rates among the capitalist countries. The East German investment rate, on the other hand, is relatively low.

Other differences, not recorded in Table 12.1, can be noted as well. If one breaks the industry sector down into heavy and light industry, the planned socialist shares of heavy industry are well *above* those of a capitalist country at a similar level of development. The shares of the urban population of the socialist countries are well *below* those of a capitalist country at a similar stage of economic development.

All of these features constitute the characteristics of the socialist industrialization model and distinguish it from its capitalist counterpart. What is the logic behind the socialist model? It aims at "building socialism" as quickly as possible. In order to do so, industrialization must be accorded priority. Activities that do not contribute to material production, such as services, should be limited; and, within industry, priority must be granted to heavy industry, for heavy industry lays the foundation for socialism. The rate of urbanization should be retarded to limit the flow of scarce investment resources into social overhead capital, a form of capital that does not lead immediately to expanded industrial capacity. Extra resources are devoted to agriculture to promote self-sufficiency, and self-sufficiency requires as well a domestic heavy industrial base, even if this works against the comparative advantage of the country. Resources are allocated away from consumption into investment in order to achieve a high investment rate, and this investment is concentrated in heavy industry.

To socialist industrialization model is important in this context for two reasons. First, it represents the major alternative for the Third World countries, which must select the socialist pattern, the capitalist pattern, or some compromise model of economic development. The model underscores the point that the planned socialist economies have not been indifferent to *what* is being produced. Their objective has not been to maximize the growth rate of output per se, but to maximize the growth of particular branches of the economy. In the planned socialist countries, heavy industry has grown at an exceptionally rapid rate; services have not. Yet the measures we use in the following sections relate to the output and efficiency of production of all types of commodities, not merely those accorded high priority by the socialist industrialization model. If our performance evaluation were carried out in terms of the socialist countries' own structural objectives, a different picture might emerge.

We have avoided generalizations concerning the one representative on Table 12.1 of market socialism, Yugoslavia. Generalizations are difficult because Yugoslavia stands alone, and central tendencies cannot be contrasted. Table 12.1 clearly demonstrates, however, that Yugoslavia is a low-income country. Its per capita income places it between Turkey and Greece, and a very high proportion of its labor force is occupied in agriculture. It appears to have a high investment rate (33 percent) for a low-income country.

Economic Growth

Table 12.2 and Figure 12.1 supply data on GNP growth rates for the postwar period in socialist and capitalist countries. One should be cautious about attaching too much importance to small differences in annual growth rates both among countries and over time, for one would expect some normal measurement error in such calculations. Moreover, there is a tendency for the measured growth rate of economies experiencing substantial structural changes to be ambiguous — the so-called problem of index number relativity.[12] This phenomenon would tend to affect the growth rates of the less-industrialized countries. On this problem, see the appendix to this chapter. Thus growth rates must be regarded as approximate and often ambiguous measures of the expansion of real goods and services, and one must be careful about their interpretation. This is especially true of East-West comparisons, where substantial adjustments must be made to render the GNP data comparable.

Table 12.2 Average Annual Growth of GNP and GNP per Capita in Socialist and Capitalist Countries, 1950–1985 (Per Capita Figures in Parentheses)

A. Socialist Countries: Planned Socialism

	1950–1960	1960–1965	1965–1970	1970–1975	1975–1980	1980–1985
Czechoslovakia	4.8 (3.9)	2.3 (1.6)	3.4 (3.2)	3.4 (2.7)	2.2 (1.5)	1.5 (1.2)
East Germany	5.7 (6.7)	2.7 (3.0)	3.0 (3.1)	3.4 (3.8)	2.3 (2.5)	1.8 (1.9)
Soviet Union	5.7 (3.9)	5.0 (3.5)	5.2 (4.2)	3.7 (2.7)	2.7 (1.8)	2.0 (1.1)
Poland	4.6 (2.75)	4.4 (3.2)	4.1 (3.4)	6.4 (5.4)	.7 (0)	.7 (-.1)
Hungary	4.6 (4.0)	4.2 (3.9)	3.0 (2.7)	3.4 (2.9)	2.0 (1.9)	
Romania	5.8 (4.55)	6.0 (5.3)	4.9 (3.7)	6.7 (5.8)	3.9 (3.0)	1.0 (.8)
Bulgaria	6.7 (5.9)	6.7 (5.7)	5.1 (4.2)	4.6 (4.2)	.9 (.9)	1.2 (1.0)
China	7.9 (5.6)	4.0 (2.5)	7.1 (4.0)	7.0 (4.5)	6.2 (4.6)	9.3 (8.0)
Unweighted average	5.7 (4.7)	4.4 (3.6)	4.3 (3.6)	4.8 (4.0)	2.6 (2.0)	2.5 (2.0)
Without China	5.4 (4.5)	4.5 (3.7)	4.1 (3.5)	4.5 (3.9)	2.1 (1.7)	1.2 (.8)

B. Socialist Country: Market Socialism

	1950–1960	1960–1965	1965–1970	1970–1975	1975–1980	1980–1985
Yugoslavia	5.6 (4.4)	6.6 (5.4)	6.2 (5.2)	5.7 (4.5)	5.9 (4.4)	1.2 (.4)

C. Capitalist Countries

	1950–1960	1960–1965	1965–1970	1970–1975	1975–1980	1980–1985
United States	3.3 (1.5)	4.6 (3.2)	3.1 (2.1)	2.3 (1.6)	3.7 (2.6)	2.4 (1.4)

Canada	4.6 (1.3)	5.7 (3.8)	4.8 (3.0)	5.0 (3.6)	2.9 (1.9)	2.2 (.9)
West Germany	7.9 (6.3)	5.0 (3.5)	4.4 (3.9)	2.1 (1.7)	3.6 (3.7)	1.1 (1.4)
Denmark	3.6 (2.9)	5.1 (4.3)	4.5 (3.7)	2.8 (2.4)	2.7 (2.4)	2.3 (2.3)
Norway	3.6 (2.5)	4.8 (4.3)	4.8 (3.9)	4.6 (4.0)	4.6 (4.2)	3.0 (2.8)
Belgium	3.0 (2.5)	5.2 (4.5)	4.8 (4.4)	3.9 (3.5)	2.5 (2.3)	.4 (.4)
France	4.4 (3.8)	5.8 (4.5)	5.4 (4.5)	4.0 (3.2)	3.2 (2.9)	1.2 (.7)
Netherlands	5.0 (3.3)	4.8 (3.5)	5.5 (4.4)	3.2 (2.0)	2.6 (1.9)	.5 (.1)
Japan	7.9 (6.6)	10.0 (9.0)	12.2 (11.2)	5.0 (3.8)	5.1 (4.2)	3.9 (3.2)
Austria	5.6 (5.4)	4.3 (3.7)	5.1 (4.6)	3.9 (3.5)	4.0 (4.0)	
United Kingdom	3.3 (2.3)	3.1 (2.4)	2.5 (2.2)	2.0 (1.4)	1.6 (1.6)	1.7 (1.3)
Italy	5.6 (4.8)	5.2 (4.3)	6.2 (5.4)	2.4 (1.5)	3.9 (3.4)	.8 (.5)
Spain	6.2 (5.3)	8.5 (7.5)	6.2 (5.1)	5.5 (4.6)	2.3 (1.3)	1.4 (.8)
Greece	6.0 (5.0)	7.7 (7.2)	7.2 (6.6)	5.0 (4.5)	4.4 (3.2)	1.0 (.4)
Turkey	6.4 (3.4)	4.8 (2.8)	6.6 (3.7)	7.5 (5.0)	3.1 (.6)	4.9 (2.7)
India	3.8 (1.9)	4.0 (1.7)	5.0 (2.6)	3.0 (1.0)	3.4 (1.6)	4.1 (1.9)
Unweighted average	5.0 (3.7)	5.5 (4.4)	5.5 (4.5)	3.9 (2.95)	3.4 (2.6)	1.9 (1.3)

Sources: Thad Alton, "Economic Structure and Growth in Eastern Europe," in U.S., Congress, Joint Economic Committee, *Economic Developments in Countries of Eastern Europe* (Washington, D.C.: Government Printing Office, 1970), p. 49; Thad Alton, "Comparative Structure and Growth of Economic Activity in Eastern Europe," in U.S., Congress, Joint Economic Committee, *East European Economies Post Helsinki* (Washington, D.C.: Government Printing Office, 1977), p. 237; Thad Alton, "Production and Resource Allocation in Eastern Europe: Performance, Problems, and Prospects," in U.S., Congress, Joint Economic Committee, *East European Economic Assessment*, Part 2 (Washington, D.C.: Government Printing Office, 1981), p. 381; U.S., Congress, Joint Economic Committee, *USSR Measures of Economic Growth and Development, 1950–1980* (Washington, D.C.: Government Printing Office, 1982), pp. 15–21; *Statistical Abstract of the United States, 1981*, pp. 878–879; Wilfred Malenbaum, "Modern Economic Growth in India and China: The Comparison Revisited, 1950–1980," *Economic Development and Cultural Change*, 31, no. 1 (October 1982), 53; *Handbook of Economic Statistics 1986*; Thad Alton et al., Occasional Papers Nos. 75–79 of the Research Project on National Income in East Central Europe (New York, 1983), pp. 7–12, 25; Rush Greenslade, "The Real Gross National Product of the USSR, 1950–75," in U.S., Congress, Joint Economic Committee, *Soviet Economy in a New Perspective* (Washington, D.C., Government Printing Office, 1975), p. 271; World Bank, *World Tables*, 3rd ed. (Baltimore: Johns Hopkins Press, 1983); OECD, *National Accounts, 1960–1985* (Paris: OECD, 1987).

Figure 12.1 Average GNP Growth Rates, Planned Socialist and Capitalist Countries, 1950–1985 (Unweighted Annual Average Growth Rates)

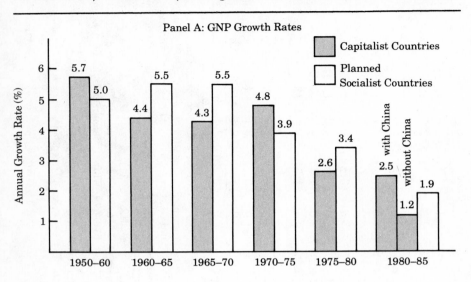

Panel A: GNP Growth Rates

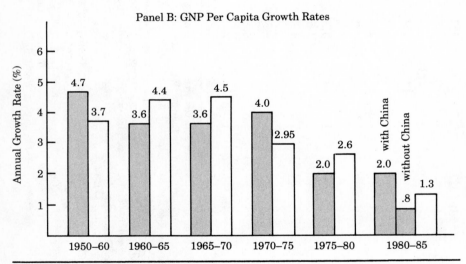

Panel B: GNP Per Capita Growth Rates

Source: Table 12.1.

In Table 12.2, we have assembled figures on growth rates of real GNP and of real GNP per capita for the entire postwar period. In panel A we supply growth rates for the Soviet Union, Eastern Europe, and China. We also supply growth rates for Yugoslavia (panel B) and for a number of capitalist countries at various stages of economic development (panel C). We include comparative growth data for China and India, two poor and populous Asian giants, one a planned socialist economy, the other a basically capitalist economy. What conclusions, if any, can we draw from these data?

The overriding question concerns the existence of systemic differences in growth rates. Has economic growth been more rapid in the planned socialist economies? Table 12.2 examines postwar economic growth from the heady growth of the 1950s and 1960s to the generally slower growth of the mid-1970s and 1980s. It illustrates the dangers of using a pair of countries (such as the United States and the Soviet Union) to judge the growth performance of capitalism and socialism. One can find capitalist countries (such as Japan) that have grown much more rapidly than most socialist countries and socialist countries (such as Bulgaria, Romania, and China) that have grown more rapidly than most capitalist countries. Moreover, some countries grow rapidly in one period (Bulgaria in the 1950s and 1960s) and then grow slowly in another period (Bulgaria in the period 1975–1980).

It is difficult to reach firm conclusions concerning the growth performance of capitalism and socialism on the basis of these data. If one simply takes unweighted averages of the eight planned socialist and sixteen capitalist countries, one finds that the socialist group grew slightly more rapidly in the 1950s at 5.7 percent per year versus 5.0 percent for the capitalist group. The capitalist group grew more rapidly in the 1960s (at 5.5 percent versus 4.4 percent in the first half and at 5.5 percent versus 4.3 percent in the second half). The capitalist group experienced severe growth recessions in the mid-1970s (1974 and 1975), whereas the socialist group appears to have enjoyed a noticeable growth advantage for the first half of the 1970s (at 4.8 percent versus 3.9 percent). The growth of the capitalist group continued to lag during the second half of the 1970s (at 3.4 percent), but the slowdown of growth was even more severe in the socialist group (falling to below 3 percent). For the period 1980 to 1985, the average socialist growth rate exceeded the average capitalist rate. Trends in per capita GNP, given in parentheses in Table 12.2, mirror these GNP growth trends.

Since only eight planned socialist countries are included in Table 12.2, the exceptionally fast or slow growth of any one would have a strong effect on the averages of the group. As Table 12.2 shows, China's growth up to the mid-1970s was not so different from that of the other socialist countries as to change average growth rates substantially. From 1975 onward, however, China's rapid growth stood in marked contrast to the slowing growth rates of the other socialist countries. If China is excluded from the socialist group, their average growth rate sinks well below that of the capitalist group from 1975 on. For example, for the period 1980 to 1985, the average socialist growth rate without China was a meager 1.2 percent per annum, versus the capitalist rate of 1.9 percent per annum. In fact, if one omits the soaring Chinese growth rates of the mid-1970s and 1980s, the decline in socialist growth rates is pronounced: from above 4 percent per annum, to 2 percent in the late 1970s, to 1 percent in the 1980s. This decline goes a long way toward explaining the efforts of planned socialist economies to effect economic reform.

In conclusion, there do not appear to be significant long-run differences in growth rates between the planned socialist countries and the capitalist countries for the postwar period. Capitalist countries have experienced periods of rapid and sustained growth (such as the period 1950–1965) as well as episodes of slow growth (such as the recessionary 1970s). Postwar history has shown that the socialist countries, while largely avoiding episodes of negative growth, can experience significant growth slowdowns, as they did in the late 1970s and the 1980s. The empirical record, at this time, shows no clear winner in the race for economic growth. The Soviet Union and Eastern Europe as a group are not reducing the per capita income gap that exists between them and their more prosperous capitalist counterparts in Western Europe and the United States.

One striking contrast between the capitalist and planned socialist growth rates, which holds over the entire postwar period, is the lesser variability of socialist country growth rates. From 1950 to 1960, for example, the gap between the lowest and highest socialist growth rate was the difference between 4.6 and 7.9 percent; for the capitalist group, the difference was between 3.0 and 7.9 percent. Thus, the capitalist averages conceal more variation among countries than do the socialist averages. This pattern has been altered somewhat by the marked contrast in growth rates between China and the other socialist countries after 1975, but it persists within the Soviet and Eastern European group. The planned socialist economies have avoided the extreme differences among countries that characterize capitalist economic performance.

Direct comparisons of planned socialist and capitalist growth rates did not reveal significant growth differences. However, if one makes a rule-of-thumb adjustment for differences in per capita income by including only the capitalist countries that fall within the approximate per capita income range of the socialist sample, say $6,000 to $3,000, some striking findings emerge. The rationale for this adjustment is that growth rates in the postwar period have tended to vary inversely with the level of development. Countries with low per capita income have grown more rapidly as a group. Unfortunately, there are few capitalist countries that fall within this income rate (four to be exact: Spain, Greece, Italy, and Venezuela), but the comparison of their average growth rates with those of the Soviet Union and Eastern Europe is nevertheless informative. For the entire postwar period, the unweighted average annual growth rate of these four capitalist economies has been almost 6 percent (4.25 percent on a per capita basis). Even including China, the planned socialist average is around 4.5 percent per annum (and 3.8 percent on a per capita basis). Thus, among countries at a similar stage of development, the planned socialist economies may have experienced slightly slower growth than their capitalist counterparts.[13]

Frederic Pryor has examined the comparative growth rates of capitalist and socialist economies for the period 1950 to 1979 using econometric methods to hold factors other than the economic system constant. Pryor finds that although the socialist-system effect is negative, the system coefficient is not statistically significant either for the growth of GNP or for the growth of GNP per capita.[14]

What about trends in capitalist and planned socialist growth rates over time? With two exceptions (Poland and Romania), the planned socialist countries were not able to maintain the respectable growth rates of the 1950s, although as the growth rates for 1965–1970 and 1970–1975 suggest, there was no further deterioration until the mid-1970s. Instead, there was a movement to a lower rate of growth after 1960, and no distinctive group trend was apparent until after 1975. As previously noted, the average planned socialist rate declined from 5.7 percent (1950–1960) to 4.3 to 4.8 percent (1960–1975). After 1975 there were further declines. For the capitalist countries, no clear pattern emerges. The majority of countries experienced rising growth rates between 1950 and 1970, although a substantial minority experienced declining growth rates during this period. In general, it appears that the capitalist countries did a better job of maintaining the high rates of growth of the early postwar period than did the planned socialist countries through 1970. After 1970, average growth rates fell in response to the recessions and growth slowdowns of the mid- and late 1970s and early 1980s. It is too early to tell whether the capitalist countries will return to the higher growth rates of earlier years in the 1980s.

Yugoslavia, the one representative of market socialism, had higher average rates of growth than the capitalist and planned socialist countries until the 1980s, but Yugoslav growth was outdistanced by some other low per capita income capitalist countries like Spain and Turkey. It is virtually impossible to generalize from the Yugoslav experience because of the diverse factors involved, but Yugoslavia does at least suggest the compatibility of market socialism with relatively high rates of growth over extended periods of time. One cannot know whether there is something unique about the Yugoslav case or whether it could be duplicated by other market socialist countries if they were to introduce the Yugoslav model.

The Chinese and Indian comparisons are included to shed light on the growth performance of capitalism and planned socialism in large and very poor countries. Although the Chinese data are fairly rough, most authorities now agree that China has outperformed India in the areas of GNP growth and per capita GNP growth. It is likely that India and China entered the postwar era with similar levels of per capita income. China's current advantage in per capita income is the consequence of its more rapid growth.

The importance of China as a development model for poor, populous countries requires a further look at Chinese economic growth in an Asian context. Table 12.3 gives the annual growth rates of seven important Asian countries for the period 1960–1985. It shows that Chinese economic growth has indeed been rapid even compared to that of other rapidly growing Asian economies, such as Japan, South Korea, and Taiwan. Chinese economic performance looks even better when compared to that of poor, populous Asian countries. For example, Chinese growth has been more than double that of India and Pakistan.[15]

There is no strong evidence that the planned socialist countries as a group have "outgrown" their capitalist counterparts. One would have to conclude, generally, that the growth rates of capitalism and planned socialism have been quite similar over the entire postwar period. Thus the planned socialist growth experience as a group has been different from the long-term experience of the first planned socialist country, the Soviet Union, whose secular growth rate (from 1928 to 1985) is higher than the secular growth rates of the industrialized capitalist countries. If one were to contrast the postwar growth rates of the planned

Table 12.3 Annual GNP Growth Rates of Selected Asian Economies, 1960–1985

China	6.8
Taiwan	8.3
South Korea	8.0
Japan	6.2
Philippines	4.5
India	3.6
Pakistan	3.5

Source: National Foreign Assessment Center, *Handbook of Economic Statistics 1986*, (Washington, D.C.: Central Intelligence Agency, 1986), Table 8 and Table 12.2.

socialist countries with the century growth rates of the industrialized capitalist countries, the former would appear to be relatively high. But the postwar period has been one of higher growth among capitalist countries, as far as our figures show; so the relevant yardstick against which to measure socialist growth performance is the experience of the postwar era, and this experience fails to demonstrate higher planned socialist growth.

The conclusion that economic growth has not been more rapid in the planned socialist economies is a strong one in view of the priority of growth in these countries and the low weight attached to economic growth by many of the capitalist countries. In fact, if one makes a crude *ceteris paribus* adjustment for differences in per capita income, capitalist growth may even have been more rapid. It is appropriate to note that the planned socialist countries have pushed for rapid growth of industry and have often neglected other components of GNP. Comparisons of industrial growth would have resulted in a somewhat more favorable picture. We cannot draw any firm conclusions concerning the growth experiences of market socialism, for we have only one representative, Yugoslavia, in our sample.

The Costs of Economic Growth:
Efficiency and Consumption

We turn now to the question of how efficiently and at what cost economic growth has been achieved. Extensive economic growth results from the expansion of the factors of production — land, labor, and capital inputs. Intensive growth is the consequence of increasing output per unit of factor input — that is, the product of increased efficiency. Economic growth is typically both extensive and intensive, for growth is normally the product of increases in both factor inputs and output per unit of factor input. At issue is which effect dominates.

Growth by means of the expansion of labor and capital inputs involves distinct economic costs. The expansion of labor inputs requires a sacrifice of leisure and time spent in household production activity; the expansion of the capital stock requires a sacrifice of current consumption in order to accumulate capital. Extensive growth is a high-cost approach to economic expansion; intensive growth, though requiring some additional (nonquantifiable) inputs, such as better managerial methods and increased knowledge, is an essentially less costly means of achieving economic growth.

In the case of East-West comparisons, it is relevant to ask which economic system has done a better job in generating economic growth, where *better* is defined in terms of the relative weights of intensive growth versus extensive growth. Two such comparisons are relevant.

The first, called *static efficiency*, involves taking a snapshot of planned socialist and capitalist countries at a particular point in time to determine how much output they are generating from a given amount of factor inputs. The second, called *dynamic efficiency*, probes the question of efficiency performance over time — that is, the extent to which output has been expanding more rapidly than inputs, the difference being the growth rate of factor productivity.[16]

It is not easy to contrast the static and dynamic efficiency of capitalism and planned socialism, for data are too limited for a fully satisfactory comparison. Bits and pieces of evidence must be analyzed over limited periods of time, but from this scattered evidence we hope to draw some conclusions concerning the relative efficiency of capitalism and planned socialism. We do not have sufficient information to include market socialism, Yugoslavia, in this investigation.

Dynamic Efficiency

In Table 12.4, we supply the available information on the dynamic efficiency of the planned socialist and the industrialized capitalist countries. Specifically, we provide the annual growth rates of aggregate employment $(\hat{L})$ and reproducible capital $(\hat{K})$, which we then compare with the growth rate of aggregate output $(\hat{Q})$. By subtracting the growth rates of employment and capital, respectively, from the growth rate of output, we obtain the growth rates of labor productivity $(\hat{Q} - \hat{L})$ and capital productivity $(\hat{Q} - \hat{K})$, respectively.

Insofar as the productivity of labor or capital is affected by substitutions between the two factors, it is desirable to have a more comprehensive measure of the growth rate of combined labor and capital productivity. One must first calculate the growth rates of labor and capital combined $(\hat{L} + \hat{K})$, or total factor input. This is typically done by taking a weighted average of the growth rates of labor and capital, where the weights represent each factor's share of national income. Thus total factor productivity is defined as $\hat{Q} - (\hat{K} + \hat{L})$, where

$$\hat{K} + \hat{L} = \hat{K} W_K + \hat{L} W_L$$

where

$$W_K = \text{capital's share of income}$$
$$W_L = \text{labor's share of income}$$

We use rates of growth of labor and capital combined $(\hat{L} + \hat{K})$, calculated in this manner. Insofar as a return to capital is typically not included in prices in the planned socialist countries, "synthetic" factor shares must be used to calculate their $\hat{L} + \hat{K}$ growth rates. We have chosen to use constant synthetic shares of .7 for labor and .3 for capital for the planned socialist countries; these shares are close to the average capitalist share.[17] Once the growth rate of combined factor inputs is calculated, it is then subtracted from the growth rate of output to obtain the growth rate of factor productivity $[\hat{Q} - (\hat{K} + \hat{L})]$. All of these figures are given in Table 12.4.

The rough nature of these productivity calculations is worth emphasizing. Factors of production, especially labor, can expand in both quantitative and qualitative terms; yet our measure captures only its quantitative advance.[18] If comparable data were available, one could have calculated a more comprehensive measure of labor's growth by adjusting for the growth in education, training, and composition of the labor force. However, data limitations do not allow such an adjustment of the planned socialist data; so we must restrict our analysis to quantitative factors. Insofar as we use employment rather than actual hours, we are not even capturing the quantitative growth of labor accurately. Moreover, the capitalist data for the period 1960–1980 do not adjust for unemployment (which rose over this period). The productivity growth of labor actually employed would therefore be slightly higher than the rates given in column 5 of Table 12.4.

We are using the official capital stock estimates of the CMEA nations, except for the Soviet Union. We have no way of knowing whether they are comparable to Western data or how reliable these estimates are, although we do know that the figures for Romania and Bulgaria are inflated (and have not been included).[19] The official capital growth rates, however, appear to be in line with the Western figures; we doubt that they involve major distortions though we have no proof.

What conclusions are to be drawn from Table 12.4 concerning the growth rates of factor inputs and factor productivity under planned socialism and advanced capitalism? The first is that during the postwar era the growth rates of capital and labor inputs have been similar for capitalism and planned socialism. The planned socialist and capitalist averages suggest roughly equivalent rates of growth of employment and, although the socialist growth rate of capital was probably slightly lower during the 1950s and higher thereafter, for the entire period capital grew on the average at roughly 5 percent in each economic system. Thus, the stereotype, fostered by the rapid growth of both labor and capital in the Soviet Union, that the planned socialist system serves to generate a more rapid rate of growth of inputs is not supported by this evidence. This conclusion is also confirmed by the rates of growth of labor and capital combined, which round to 2 percent per annum for both capitalism and planned socialism.

Table 12.4 Annual Growth of Inputs and Output per Unit of Inputs in Socialist and Capitalist Countries

		(1) Employ- ment $(\hat{L})$	(2) Fixed Capital $(\hat{K})$	(3) Labor & Capital $(\hat{L} + \hat{K})$	(4) Output $(\hat{Q})$	(5) Labor Productivity $(\hat{Q} - \hat{L})$	(6) Capital Productivity $(\hat{Q} - \hat{K})$	(7) Total Factor Productivity $\hat{Q} - (\hat{L} + \hat{K})$
			A. Planned Socialist Countries					
Czechoslovakia	1950–60	.7	3.5	1.4	4.8	4.1	1.3	3.4
	1960–83	1.0	4.7	2.1	2.6	1.6	−2.1	.5
East Germany	1950–60	.0	2.0	.5	6.1	6.1	4.1	5.6
	1960–83	.3	4.0	1.4	2.8	2.5	−1.2	1.4
Soviet Union	1950–60	1.2	9.4	3.4	5.8	4.6	−3.6	2.4
	1960–85	1.3	7.3	2.8	3.6	2.3	−3.7	.8
Poland	1950–60	1.0	2.6	1.4	4.6	3.6	2.0	3.2
	1960–83	1.5	4.7	2.5	3.3	1.8	−1.4	.8
Hungary	1950–60	1.0	3.6	1.7	4.6	3.6	1.0	2.9
	1960–83	.3	5.0	1.7	2.9	2.6	−2.1	1.2
Romania	1950–60	1.1	—a	—	5.9	4.8	—	—
	1960–85	.4	—a	—	4.6	4.1	—	—
Bulgaria	1950–60	.2	—a	—	6.7	6.5	—	—
	1960–85	.5	—a	—	3.7	3.2	—	—
Unweighted average	1950–60	.8	4.2	1.7	5.5b (5.2)c	4.8	1.0	3.5
	1960–83(85)	.8	5.1	2.1	3.3b (3.0)c	2.5	−2.1	.9

Table 12.4 (continued)

<table>
<thead>
<tr><th></th><th>(1)
Employ-
ment
($\hat{L}$)</th><th>(2)
Fixed
Capital
($\hat{K}$)</th><th>(3)
Labor &
Capital
($\hat{L}+\hat{K}$)</th><th>(4)
Output
($\hat{Q}$)</th><th>(5)
Labor
Productivity
($\hat{Q}-\hat{L}$)</th><th>(6)
Capital
Productivity
($\hat{Q}-\hat{K}$)</th><th>(7)
Total Factor
Productivity
$\hat{Q}-(\hat{L}+\hat{K})$</th></tr>
</thead>
<tbody>
<tr><td colspan="8">B. Capitalist Countries</td></tr>
<tr><td>United States 1950-60</td><td>1.4</td><td>3.6</td><td>1.8</td><td>3.1</td><td>1.7</td><td>-.5</td><td>1.3</td></tr>
<tr><td>1960-85</td><td>2.0</td><td>3.3</td><td>2.4</td><td>3.1</td><td>1.1</td><td>-.2</td><td>.7</td></tr>
<tr><td>Canada 1960-85</td><td>2.7</td><td>4.7</td><td>3.3</td><td>4.2</td><td>1.5</td><td>-.5</td><td>.9</td></tr>
<tr><td>Belgium 1950-62</td><td>.6</td><td>2.3</td><td>1.0</td><td>3.2</td><td>2.6</td><td>.6</td><td>2.2</td></tr>
<tr><td>Denmark 1950-62</td><td>.9</td><td>5.1</td><td>1.8</td><td>3.5</td><td>2.6</td><td>-1.6</td><td>1.7</td></tr>
<tr><td>1950-60[d]</td><td>.1</td><td>4.2</td><td>1.0</td><td>4.9</td><td>4.8</td><td>.7</td><td>3.9</td></tr>
<tr><td>1960-85</td><td>.7</td><td>4.8</td><td>1.8</td><td>3.9</td><td>3.1</td><td>-.9</td><td>2.1</td></tr>
<tr><td>West Germany 1950-60[d]</td><td>2.0</td><td>6.4</td><td>3.1</td><td>7.3</td><td>5.3</td><td>.9</td><td>4.2</td></tr>
<tr><td>1960-85</td><td>.0</td><td>4.8</td><td>1.2</td><td>3.1</td><td>3.1</td><td>-1.7</td><td>1.9</td></tr>
<tr><td>Italy 1950-62</td><td>.6</td><td>3.5</td><td>1.3</td><td>6.0</td><td>5.4</td><td>2.5</td><td>4.7</td></tr>
<tr><td>Finland 1960-85</td><td>.7</td><td>4.6</td><td>1.9</td><td>3.9</td><td>3.2</td><td>-.5</td><td>2.0</td></tr>
<tr><td>Sweden 1962-83</td><td>.6</td><td>3.5</td><td>1.5</td><td>2.8</td><td>2.2</td><td>-.7</td><td>1.3</td></tr>
<tr><td>Netherlands 1950-62</td><td>1.1</td><td>4.7</td><td>1.9</td><td>4.7</td><td>3.6</td><td>.0</td><td>2.8</td></tr>
<tr><td>1950-60[d]</td><td>.2</td><td>4.2</td><td>1.2</td><td>3.5</td><td>3.3</td><td>-.7</td><td>2.3</td></tr>
<tr><td>Norway 1960-85</td><td>.5</td><td>3.6</td><td>1.4</td><td>4.2</td><td>3.7</td><td>.6</td><td>2.8</td></tr>
<tr><td>United Kingdom 1950-60[d]</td><td>.7</td><td>3.4</td><td>1.2</td><td>2.3</td><td>1.6</td><td>-1.1</td><td>1.1</td></tr>
<tr><td>1960-85</td><td>.5</td><td>3.2</td><td>1.1</td><td>2.3</td><td>1.8</td><td>-.9</td><td>1.2</td></tr>
<tr><td>Japan 1953-70</td><td>1.7</td><td>9.8</td><td>3.8</td><td>10.0</td><td>8.3</td><td>.2</td><td>6.2</td></tr>
<tr><td>1970-85</td><td>.9</td><td>8.2</td><td>2.3</td><td>4.4</td><td>3.5</td><td>-3.8</td><td>2.1</td></tr>
<tr><td>Greece 1960-85</td><td><u>.4</u></td><td><u>5.8</u></td><td><u>2.0</u></td><td><u>5.1</u></td><td><u>4.7</u></td><td><u>-.7</u></td><td><u>3.1</u></td></tr>
<tr><td>Unweighted average[e] 1950-60</td><td>.9</td><td>4.7</td><td>1.8</td><td>4.8</td><td>3.9</td><td>.1</td><td>3.0</td></tr>
<tr><td>Unweighted average 1960-85</td><td>.9</td><td>4.7</td><td>1.9</td><td>3.7</td><td>2.8</td><td>-1.0</td><td>1.8</td></tr>
</tbody>
</table>

Note: All figures are annual growth rates.

$\hat{L}$ = growth rate of employment.

$\hat{K}$ = growth rate of reproducible capital.

$\hat{Q}$ = growth rate of output.

$(\hat{L} + \hat{K})$ = growth rate of labor and capital combined.

[a] The official Romanian and Bulgarian capital stock series are not cited because they are in current and not constant prices.

[b] Average of all 7 countries.

[c] Average of first 5 countries.

[d] 1950–1962.

[e] Includes Japan, 1953–1970.

Sources: Panel A: Employment: Andrew Elias, "Magnitude and Distribution of the Labor Force in Eastern Europe," in U.S., Congress, Joint Economic Committee, *Economic Developments in Countries of Eastern Europe* (Washington, D.C.: Government Printing Office, 1970), pp. 208–214; Thad Alton, "Comparative Structure and Growth of Economic Activity in Eastern Europe," in U.S., Congress, Joint Economic Committee, *East European Economies Post Helsinki* (Washington, D.C.: Government Printing Office, 1977), p. 218; *Handbook of Economic Statistics, 1980,* p. 47. *Capital Stock:* Official CMEA estimates of productive funds (*osnovnye fondy*) from *Statisticheski ezhegodnik stran-chlenov Soveta Ekonomicheskoi Vzaimopomoschi 1974* (Moscow: Statistika), p. 27; Alton, "Production and Resource Allocation in Eastern Europe," p. 372; *Handbook of Economic Statistics 1980,* p. 58; and Alton, "Comparative Structure and Growth," p. 223. *Output:* table 10.1. *Panel B: Growth Rates of Employment, Reproducible Capital, and Output:* Edward Denison, *Why Growth Rates Differ* (Washington, D.C.: Brookings, 1967), pp. 42, 190, and ch. 21; Edward Denison, *Accounting for United States Economic Growth, 1929–1969.* (Washington, D.C.: Brookings, 1974), pp. 32, 58; Edward Denison and William Chung, *How Japan's Economy Grew So Fast* (Washington, D.C.: Brookings, 1976), pp. 19, 31; OECD, Department of Economics and Statistics, *Flows and Stocks of Fixed Capital, 1960–1985* (OECD: Paris, 1987); *Handbook of Economic Statistics 1986; World Tables,* 3rd ed.

Unlike the growth-rate experience, the variability of factor-input growth by country appears to be as great under planned socialism as under capitalism. Some planned socialist countries experienced low growth of both labor and capital (East Germany, for example), while others (the Soviet Union and Poland) experienced rapid rates of growth of factor inputs. One finds similar variability among the capitalist countries, with some (notably Japan) experiencing quite rapid growth of both labor and capital inputs relative to the other capitalist countries.

Both the socialist and capitalist countries experienced a slowdown in productivity growth after the 1960s: The planned socialist growth rate of output declined after 1960 by about 40 percent; yet inputs, both labor and capital, grew more rapidly after 1960 (about one-quarter faster). Thus both labor and capital productivity and total factor productivity declined dramatically after 1960; labor productivity from an average of 4.8 to 2.5 percent and total factor productivity from 3.5 to .9 percent. Socialist efforts to stabilize the growth of output by raising the growth of inputs have not succeeded; rather than becoming more intensive, the growth of the planned socialist economies became more extensive after 1960.

The greater extensivity of socialist growth after 1960 is best seen by comparing the growth rates of total factor productivity with the growth rates of output. Taking those five socialist countries for which capital data are available, the average GNP growth rate was 5.2 percent per annum between 1950 and 1960, while the growth of efficiency (factor productivity) was 3.5 percent. Thus 3.5/5.2 or 67 percent of economic growth was accounted for by increasing output per unit of input. The corresponding figures for the 1960 to 1983 period are .9 percent and 3.0 percent. Thus from 1960 to 1983 only 30 percent of growth was accounted for by increased efficiency, and the remaining 70 percent was accounted for by increasing inputs. The declining growth of productivity was felt both by labor and capital, but the decline in capital productivity from a positive rate to a rate of −2.1 percent per annum was especially prominent.

The capitalist group also experienced a slowdown in productivity growth after 1960. Average labor productivity growth fell from 3.9 to 2.8 percent; capital productivity growth fell from zero to −1.0 percent; and total factor productivity growth fell from 3.0 to 1.8 percent. In the 1950s, some 65 percent (3.0/4.8) of growth in the capitalist group was explained by the growth of efficiency; for the period 1960–1985, 49 percent (1.8/3.7) of growth was explained by efficiency gains. Falling rates of growth of productivity have characterized the cyclical downturns of capitalist countries over the years; it is unclear whether the more modest slowdown of capitalist productivity is the result of cyclical factors or has more deep-rooted causes.

Figure 12.2 Productivity Growth in Socialist and Capitalist Countries, 1960–85

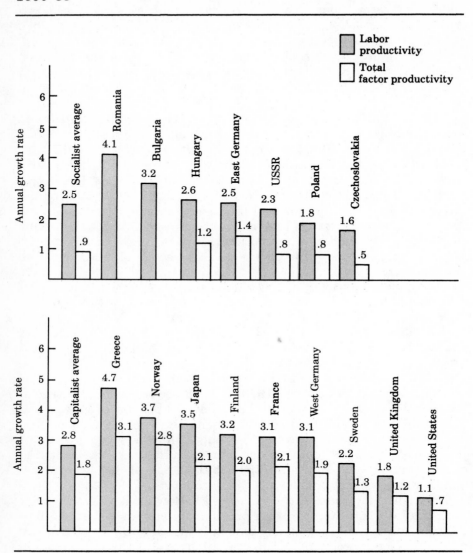

Source: Table 12.4.

What are our overall conclusions concerning the growth of efficiency (factor productivity) under capitalism and planned socialism? As in the case of economic growth, there appears to be no evidence to suggest a more rapid rate of growth of productivity under planned socialism (see Figure 12.2). Since 1960, at least, it appears that the productivity performance of planned socialism has deteriorated seriously and that socialist growth became much more extensive in character. We must emphasize that these conclusions are based on approximate data with little evidence on the qualitative growth of inputs. We believe, however, that they would hold up even under more exhaustive data.

Consumption Costs of Growth

One cost of achieving economic growth is the sacrifice in current consumption required to add to the nation's stock of capital. Although growth rates in East and West have been similar, it is not true that this growth was achieved with a similar allocation of resources between consumption and investment. Information on resource-allocation policies is summarized in Table 12.5.[20] Although the capitalist and socialist data cover slightly different time periods, they do tell an interesting story. Again, the GNP growth rates are quite similar, but personal consumption has fared relatively better than investment under capitalism. In fact, while personal consumption grew on the average at a more rapid rate in the capitalist sample (4.7 percent versus 3.6 percent), gross investment grew faster under planned socialism (6.4 percent versus 5.6 percent).

More interestingly, if one takes the ratio of the growth rate of consumption to the growth rate of investment as a measure of resource allocation, a distinct pattern emerges. Although there seems to be a positive relationship between this ratio and per capita income, the socialist consumption-investment ratios appear to be well below those of capitalist countries at a similar stage of development. Thus the achievement of similar rates of growth in East and West has required a greater sacrifice of current consumption under planned socialism. In fact, the resource-allocation pattern of the socialist countries is remarkably uniform (except in Czechoslovakia) and is closest to the pattern of the less-industrialized capitalist countries (like Turkey and Spain) and, surprisingly, of Japan and the United Kingdom.

If one starts from a position of relatively higher investment rates under planned socialism in the 1950s and 1960s, it follows that socialist per capita consumption will be lower for a given level of per capita national income *ceteris paribus*. This is the other side of the coin — namely, the cost of maintaining economic growth through expansion of capital inputs.[21] The absolute level of per capita consumption will

Table 12.5 Annual Rates of Growth of Personal Consumption, Investment, and GNP in Planned Socialist and Capitalist Countries

Country	(1) Personal Consumption	(2) Gross Investment	(3) GNP	(4) Consumption Growth as a Percentage of Investment Growth (1 ÷ 2)
A. Planned Socialist Countries				
Czechoslovakia (1950–67)	2.2	5.2	3.2	.42
East Germany (1960–75)	3.7	6.1	4.9	.61
Hungary (1950–67)	3.4	5.2	4.0	.65
Poland (1950–67)	4.2	7.9	5.1	.53
Soviet Union (1950–80)	4.3	7.7	4.7	.56
Unweighted average	3.6	6.4	4.4	.56
B. Capitalist Countries, 1950–1977				
United States	3.4	3.1	3.6	1.10
Canada	4.7	4.6	4.8	1.02
West Germany	4.7	5.0	4.8	.94
Denmark	3.5	4.9	3.8	.71
Norway	3.9	4.6	4.2	.85
Belgium	3.7	4.6	4.0	.81
France	5.0	6.1	5.0	.82
Netherlands	4.6	4.2	4.5	1.09
Japan	7.8	11.0	8.4	.71
Austria	5.4	5.1	4.9	1.06
United Kingdom	2.2	4.4	2.5	.50
Italy	4.6	5.0	4.8	.92
Greece	6.0	7.1	6.4	.85
Spain	5.2	6.7	5.6	.77
Turkey	6.1	8.2	6.3	.74
Unweighted average	4.7	5.6	4.9	.84

Sources: Thad Alton, "Economic Structure and Growth in Eastern Europe," in U.S., Congress, Joint Economic Committee, *Economic Developments in Countries of Eastern Europe* (Washington, D.C.: Government Printing Office, 1970), pp. 52–

depend on the economic potential of the country, and to argue that one country has outperformed the other simply because its standard of living is higher begs the question. The major issue is what standard of living is being supplied, given the economic resources at the nation's disposal. Such a comparison of capitalist and planned socialist living standards would show that the socialist living standards are low relative to per capita income. This reflects the decision of growth-oriented socialist planners to devote a relatively larger share of GNP to investment than under capitalism. However, the telling point is that this decision has not led to a notably higher rate of growth for the planned socialist nations. Thus the planners' consumption policies have not paid off in terms of more rapid growth.

Static Efficiency

Static efficiency is an extremely difficult concept to measure. To do so correctly requires first a notion of an economy's productive potential as defined by its total resources and then a determination of how closely the economy comes to meeting that potential. This problem is explained in Figure 12.3. To show that the Soviet Union, for example, obtains half as much output from a given amount of conventional labor and capital inputs as the United States does not unambiguously prove the greater static efficiency of the American economy, for the measurement of conventional inputs may fail to capture the full range of resources (in both qualitative and quantitative terms) at the disposal of each economy.

One way to illustrate the static efficiency measurement problem is to note the strong positive relationship between the level of economic development and output per unit of input. Thus any evaluation of the static efficiency of capitalism and planned socialism must distinguish between "normal" differences caused by unequal economic development and differences due to the choice of economic system. This is not an easy undertaking; what is missing is information on what the economy should be able to produce at maximum efficiency from its resources.

53; *Deutsches Institut fur Wirtschaftsforschung Wochenbericht*, 44 (June 1977), p. 199; Rush Greenslade, "The Real Gross National Product of the USSR, 1950–75," in U.S., Congress, Joint Economic Committee, *Soviet Economy in a New Perspective* (Washington, D.C.: Government Printing Office, 1975), p. 275; World Bank, *World Tables, 1980* (Baltimore: Johns Hopkins Press, 1980), country tables; U.S., Congress, Joint Economic Committee, *USSR: Measures of Economic Growth and Development, 1950–80* (Washington, D.C.: Government Printing Office, 1982), pp. 65–67.

Abram Bergson has made a careful study of comparative productivity under capitalism and socialism that sheds important light on the issue of relative productivity performance.[22] Bergson's data for 1975 are reproduced in Table 12.6. They give per capita outputs, labor (adjusted for quality differences), capital, and land inputs of various capitalist and socialist countries (where the socialist group includes Yugoslavia) as a percentage of the U.S. per capita figures. Bergson includes only "material sectors" in output and excludes services and housing that have a relatively low priority in the socialist countries. Table 12.6 shows, for example, that Italy has a per capita output 61 percent that of the United States, a per capita employment 75 percent that of the

Figure 12.3 Why It Is Difficult to Evaluate Static Efficiency: Different Country Production Possibilities

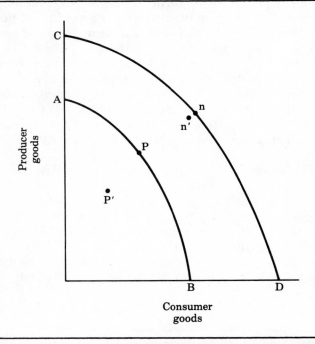

Explanation: CD represents the production possibilities frontier (PPF) of, say, the United States. AB is the PPF of, say, the Soviet Union. The U.S. PPF is to the northeast of the Soviet PPF because of greater resources and better technology. The relevant measure of static efficiency is how closely each economy comes to operating on its PPF. If, for example, the United States operates very close to n at n' and the Soviet Union operates at p', which is very far from p, the United States is statistically more efficient. In real-world measurement, all we observe is p' and n'. We have no way of knowing what p and n are.

United States, and a per capita capital stock 62 percent that of the United States. The Soviet Union has a per capita output that is 60 percent that of the United States, a per capita employment 104 percent that of the United States, and a per capita capital stock 73 percent that of the United States.

The issue is whether the socialist countries systematically obtain less output from their available inputs relative to the capitalist countries. In the data comparing Italy and the Soviet Union with the United States, Italy appears to obtain more output from its available inputs because Italy and the Soviet Union have the same per capita output, yet the Soviet Union uses more labor and capital per capita to produce this output.

Bergson demonstrates that there is a systematic tendency for the output per worker (labor productivity) in socialist economies to fall short of output per worker in capitalist countries, when inputs are held constant. According to Bergson's calculations, output per worker in the socialist group falls from 25 to 34 percent short of output per workers in the capitalist group *ceteris paribus*.

Table 12.6 Per Capita Output, Employment, Capital and Land, 1975 (U.S. = 100)

Country	Output per Capita	Employment per Capita Adjusted for Labor Quality	Reproducible Capital per Capita	Farm Land per Capita
United States	100.0	100.0	100.0	100.0
West Germany	90.9	84.0	107.3	14.8
France	92.2	88.3	83.0	40.1
Italy	61.3	75.2	61.6	24.9
United Kingdom	67.2	89.6	77.2	14.5
Japan	82.8	129.0	95.2	5.4
Spain	64.6	95.4	47.7	67.0
Soviet Union	60.0	104.1	73.2	103.5
Hungary	61.1	115.6	70.9	59.8
Poland	54.8	122.7	51.6	50.4
Yugoslavia	41.5	98.8	35.9	45.6

Source: Abram Bergson, "Comparative Productivity: The USSR, Eastern Europe, and the West," *American Economic Review*, vol. 77, no. 3 (June 1987), p. 347.

Bergson's findings are important, though of limited reliability because of the small size of his sample. At present, there is an extremely limited supply of comparable data, and it will be a long time before a similar experiment on a larger number of countries can be performed. Until then, we believe it is appropriate to conclude that socialist economies have relatively lower productivity, *ceteris paribus*, than industrialized capitalist countries.[23]

As we have shown, it is very difficult to assess the static efficiency of capitalist and socialist countries because we are not able to determine how closely real-world economies operate to their production possibilities frontier. An important study seeks to provide some evidence on this subject for Soviet industry. Padma Desai and Ricardo Martin (following a line of inquiry opened by Judith Thornton) estimate the production functions for various branches of Soviet industry. (A production function describes the technical relationships between inputs and outputs.)[24] Once the properties of these production functions are known, then it is possible to determine how closely Soviet industry approaches its production frontier. If capital and labor resources are not allocated so that marginal products are equalized across industries, less than maximum output is produced (or, stated differently, the same amount of output could have been produced with fewer resources). Desai and Martin conclude that if resources were reallocated among branches to equalize marginal products, the output of Soviet industry would be raised from 3 percent to 10 percent. Moreover, they find that misallocation inefficiencies are growing over time.

What should we make of such estimates? First, we do not know the extent of resource misallocations in nonindustrial sectors. Are they greater or smaller than in Soviet industry? Second, these estimates do not capture fully other types of inefficiencies, such as X-Inefficiency. Nevertheless, it is noteworthy that Desai and Martin are able to isolate significant inefficiencies. Western economists have been unable to locate significant inefficiencies in capitalist economies, particularly the inefficiencies associated with monopoly (the monopoly deadweight losses studied in Chapter 3). Yet in the Soviet case, we are able to find measurable efficiency losses.

What are our general conclusions concerning static efficiency under capitalism and planned socialism? We have no comprehensive measure of the productive potential of the various capitalist and planned socialist nations under investigation. All we have are rough quantitative measures of capital and labor inputs in strict quantitative terms; important qualitative variations are ignored, and other resources may be omitted. Yet our impression is one of lower output per worker under planned socialism after unsophisticated adjustments are made for differences in resource potential.

Income Distribution Under
Socialism and Capitalism

Another measure of the merit of economic systems is the distribution of income among the members of society. What constitutes a good distribution of income must be a subjective matter, but there would probably be general agreement that a distribution in which the top 5 percent of the population receives 95 percent of all income is "unfair" and that a completely equal distribution would be "unfair" because those who contribute more to society (or desire more) are under-rewarded. Marx himself rejected the notion of an equal distribution of income during the transition from socialism to communism, arguing instead for a distribution that would reflect the individual's contribution to the well-being of society.[25]

Another reason why most people reject a perfectly equal distribution of income is that rewards must be offered for differential effort and for scarce resources, or else the incentive to supply them will diminish and the economy will not produce its potential output. The issue therefore is how to construct a distribution of income that is both "fair" and provides necessary incentives. This is an issue both socialism and capitalism must face.

What differences would one expect in the distribution of incomes under capitalism and socialism? Would the socialist distribution tend to be much more equal than the capitalist distribution? In capitalist societies, the two major sources of income inequality are the unequal distributions of property ownership (land and capital resources) and of human capital. Both forms of capital yield income — the first in the form of property income from rent, interest, dividends, capital gains; the second from wages and salaries.

Under both planned and market socialism, property other than consumer durables and housing is owned by the state, and the return (income) from this state-owned property is at the state's disposal. Under capitalism, the bulk of property is owned privately and property income therefore will accrue to private individuals.

The distribution of human capital under capitalism and socialism depends, to some extent, on genetic factors, which should not vary systematically with the economic system. But it also depends on the manner in which schooling and on-the-job training are provided. Free or subsidized public schooling is available in both types of societies, although there appears to be a greater tendency for the state to pay directly for higher education in socialist societies. Nevertheless, the differences between the two systems would not be expected to be great.

The major distinction between the two systems is the virtual absence of private ownership of income-earning property under socialism.

Unless offset by higher earnings differentials, the distribution of property plus labor income should be more equal under socialism. The distribution of income after taxes will depend upon the extent to which redistributive taxes and transfers are used to equalize income distribution.

As to earnings differentials, even planned socialist societies have recognized that labor cannot be allocated administratively and must be allowed relative freedom of choice of occupation. Therefore, the distribution of wage and salary income under socialism should follow roughly the same principles as under capitalism — that is, the distribution should depend on relative scarcities.

Arguments can be made, however, that the distribution of labor incomes will vary according to the economic system.[26] Some observers argue that labor income will be more equally distributed under socialism because of the more equal distribution of education and training and because the government can control the power of strong labor groups. Another point for a more equal socialist distribution is socialist governments' greater doctrinal commitment to equality. On the other side, it has been argued that the socialist governments desire to promote priority branches of industry (by offering higher wages) will lead to greater inequality in the socialist distribution of labor income.

Frederic Pryor made an extensive econometric examination of the size distribution of labor income among workers for the late 1950s and early 1960s.[27] Pryor's finding is that the distribution of labor income is *more equal* under socialism than under capitalism, once per capita income and the size of the country are held constant. He also finds that labor incomes are distributed more unequally in the Soviet Union than in the other socialist countries; therefore, studies that generalize from the Soviet experience are likely to give a false impression.

More recent data on the distribution of earnings for full-time wage and salary earners confirm most of Pryor's findings for the 1950s and early 1960s. Persons in the top 10 percent of all U.S. earners (in the upper tenth percentile) averaged almost two times the earnings of the median earner in the late 1960s and early 1970s. In Yugoslavia, Poland, and the Soviet Union, the ratio was 1.75, while in Czechoslovakia and Hungary, earners in the upper tenth percentile earned only about 60 percent more than the median.[28] From these figures, we conclude that earnings are more equally distributed in Eastern Europe, Yugoslavia, and the Soviet Union than in the United States. For the USSR, this appears to be a relatively new phenomenon, for as late as 1957, Soviet earnings were more unequal than those in the United States.[29]

We now turn from the distribution of labor income to the distribution of total income. Table 12.7 gives data on the distribution of per capita income after income taxes in a limited number of planned socialist and capitalist countries for which data are available.[30] There are

Table 12.7 Distribution of per Capita Income Among Families After Income Taxes in Planned Socialist and Capitalist Countries

	U.K. 1969	U.S. 1968	Italy 1969	Canada 1971	Sweden 1971	Hungary 1964	Czecho-slovakia 1965	Bulgaria 1963–65	USSR 1966
Per capita income of individual in 95th percentile ÷ that of individual in 5th percentile	5.0	12.7	11.2	12.0	5.5	4.0	4.3	3.8	5.7
Per capita income of individual in 90th percentile ÷ that of individual in 10th percentile	3.4	6.7	5.9	6.0	3.5	3.0	3.1	2.7	3.5
Per capita income of individual in 75th percentile ÷ that of individual in 25th percentile	1.9	2.6	2.5	2.4	1.9	1.8	1.8	1.7	2.0

Source: P. J. D. Wiles, *Economic Institutions Compared* (New York: Halsted Press, 1977), p. 443. By permission of Basil Blackwell, Oxford.

certain weaknesses in these data. First, the socialist data generally exclude specific top income-earning families (party leaders, government officials, artists, authors), including instead only families of workers and employees. These exclusions exaggerate the equality of the socialist distributions. Second, many activities considered legal in capitalist societies (the provision of private repair and medical services, for example) must be provided on a sub rosa basis in planned socialist countries. These "second economy" activities often lead to substantial private incomes, which are not likely to be reported to the statistical authorities. Third, a relatively larger volume of resources, even excluding free educational and medical benefits, is provided on an extra-market basis — shopping privileges, official cars, vacations — and will not be included in reported income. Benefits of this kind are also provided to executives, professionals, government officials, and others in capitalist societies. Company cars, subsidized executive lunchrooms, stock options, and so on typically are not included in reported income. The distribution of money incomes may not properly reflect the true distribution of real goods and services. Although one might theoretically expect these services to be provided on a fairly egalitarian basis, there is evidence that they tend to be distributed proportionately to earned income (or to rise more rapidly than income). Finally, there is the matter of the distribution of economic power. In capitalist countries, economic power is distributed among government officials (both elected and appointed) and the owners of property resources. Thus shareholders of major corporations possess considerable economic power over the distribution of society's resources, for this wealth is highly concentrated in a few hands in capitalist societies. What about planned socialist societies? There the distribution of power is concentrated in the hands of party and government officials, and it is likely (although not evident a priori) that economic power is more intensely concentrated in planned socialist than in capitalist societies.

These considerations do enter into the calculated distributions of income, but we would guess that they would not change the overall hypothesis that income will be distributed more equally in socialist than in capitalist societies. The factor that could conceivably alter the general picture would be to apply a large weight to the distribution of economic power, for our suspicion is that economic power is concentrated in fewer hands under planned socialism.

Some data in Table 12.7 bear out these conclusions. Income is distributed more unequally in the capitalist countries in which the state plays a relatively minor redistributive role either through progressive taxation or through the distribution of social services (United States, Italy, Canada). Yet even where the state plays a major redistributive role (United Kingdom and Sweden), the distribution of income appears to be slightly more unequal than in the planned socialist countries

(Hungary, Czechoslovakia, Bulgaria). The Soviet Union in 1966 appears to have a less egalitarian distribution of income than its East European counterparts. Its distribution is scarcely to be distinguished from the British and Swedish distributions (it may even be more unequal). The Soviet distribution appears to have become more equal in recent years. Table 12.8 reveals that Soviet income distribution is more equal than that in countries like Australia, Canada, and the United States, but not much different from countries like Norway and the United Kingdom.

The Gini coefficient is a convenient summary measure of income inequality. It is the ratio of the area between the line of perfect equality and the Lorenz curve and the area of the triangle (see Chapter 1). The higher the Gini coefficient the more unequal the distribution of income. A Gini coefficient of zero denotes perfect equality; a Gini coefficient of 1 denotes perfect inequality.

Gini coefficients based on comparable income concepts support the above conclusions. Gini coefficients for Great Britain and Sweden for the early 1970s are both around .25. The Czech, Hungarian, and Polish

Table 12.8 An International Comparison of Income Shares of Selected Percentile Groups, Distributions of Households by per Capita Household Income, and GDP per Capita

Distribution, Country and Year	Percentage Income Share of			
	Lowest 10%	Lowest 20%	Highest 20%	Highest 10%
Nonfarm households (pretax)				
USSR, 1967	4.4	10.4	33.8	19.9
Urban households (post-tax)				
USSR, 1972–1974	3.4	8.7	38.5	24.1
All households (pretax)				
Australia, 1966–1967	3.5	8.3	41.0	25.6
Norway, 1970	3.5	8.2	39.0	23.5
U.K., 1973	3.5	8.3	39.9	23.9
France, 1970	2.0	5.8	47.2	31.8
Canada, 1969	2.2	6.2	43.6	27.8
U.S., 1972	1.8	5.5	44.4	28.6
All households (post-tax)				
Sweden, 1972	3.5	9.3	35.2	20.5

Source: Abram Bergson "Income Inequality Under Soviet Socialism," *Journal of Economic Literature* 22 (September 1984).

Gini coefficients for the same period are .21, .24, and .24 respectively; that is, very close to the British and Swedish coefficients. The Canadian and U.S. Gini coefficients, on the other hand, are .34 and .35 respectively, well above the socialist coefficients.[31]

Figure 12.4 provides Lorenz curves for Hungary, Sweden, West Germany, Spain, Mexico, and Yugoslavia. The reader will recall from Chapter 1 that the further the Lorenz curve departs from the line of perfect equality, the more unequal the distribution. These curves, which refer to the early 1970s (except for Yugoslavia), confirm the basic trend shown in Table 12.7: Hungary is about the same as Sweden, but is much more equal than West Germany and Spain (two capitalist countries without massive state income redistribution); Yugoslavia does not differ significantly from West Germany and Spain. However, there apparently was a narrowing of differentials in Yugoslavia between the early 1960s and early 1970s; we do not know the true relative position of Yugoslavia in the 1970s.

The Mexican Lorenz curve is included to make a general point about the Yugoslav (and Hungarian, Polish, Soviet, and Czech) distributions. As the Mexican curve shows, inequality tends to be negatively related to the level of development.[32] If one could adjust for lower per capita income, the socialist distributors would appear even more equal than they do in direct comparisons.

In general, one would have to say that the differences in the distribution of income between the planned socialist economies and the capitalist welfare states are relatively minor. This is a rather surprising conclusion. One would have expected the absence of income from the private ownership of property to make more of a difference. Nevertheless, differences are apparent when one contrasts the socialist distributions with those of the capitalist nations in which the state does not play a major redistributive role. In this instance, the expected contrast emerges rather clearly, although we must re-emphasize the difficulty of interpreting the socialist distributions because of the omitted income categories.

Economic Stability Under Socialism and Capitalism

Our final indicator of the economic performance of capitalism and socialism is the economic stability of each economic system. By economic stability, we mean the absence of movements in prices, unemployment, and output deemed undesirable or even unacceptable by relevant decision makers, be they the general population or planners. It also refers to the absence of persistent (as opposed to cyclical) high unemployment rates or inflation rates. Our discussion will be brief and is limited to several points.

Figure 12.4 Lorenz Curves on the Distribution of per Capita Income in Hungary, Sweden, West Germany, Spain, Yugoslavia, and Mexico[a,b]

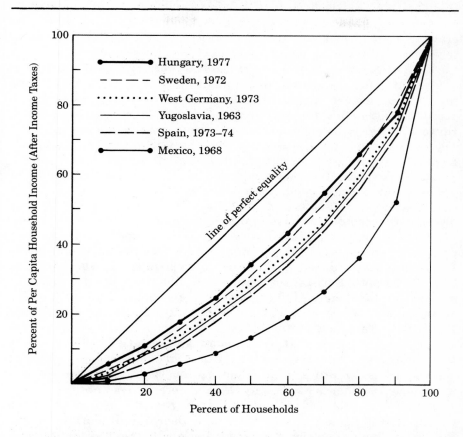

[a] For an explanation of the Lorenz curve see Chapter 1.
[b] Mexican data are prior to income taxes, but we doubt their inclusion would move the Mexican Lorenz curve dramatically.

Sources: Malcolm Sawyer, *Income Distribution in OECD Countries* (Paris: OECD, 1976), p. 17; Jan Adam and Miloslav Nosal, "Earnings Differentials and Household-Income Differentials in Hungary — Policies and Practice," *Journal of Comparative Economics*, vol. 6, no. 2 (June 1982), p. 197; Wouter van Ginneken, "Generating Internationally Comparable Income Distribution Data," *Review of Income and Wealth*, 28, no. 4 (December 1982), p. 374.

The postwar era has witnessed several recessions, the most severe occurring in the mid-1970s and the start of the 1980s, in which real GNP has actually declined in the major capitalist countries. Socialist countries experienced "growth recessions," that is, periods when the growth rate declined but remained positive, but they largely avoided recessions before 1980. In the early 1980s, however, the majority of the CMEA countries experienced at least one year of negative growth.

The literature recognizes that cyclical fluctuations are present in planned socialist economies, but it has been generally believed that socialist fluctuations are less pronounced than capitalist fluctuations. However, Frederic Pryor found (for a study covering the period 1950–1979) that socialist fluctuations in GNP, industrial output, and investment are not statistically distinguishable from capitalist fluctuations. Moreover, socialist fluctuations in agricultural output are more pronounced than those in capitalist agriculture.[33]

The socialist economies claim that socialist planning has "liquidated" involuntary unemployment. Of course, no society can eliminate unemployment entirely, for at any given point in time some people are in the process of changing jobs, but it does appear that the planned socialist economies have reduced the rate of unemployment to small proportions relative to that of the capitalist economies.[34] This is a consequence of deliberate full-employment planning. Enterprises, for example, are either unwilling or unable to release underemployed workers, creating such a problem that experiments have been attempted to encourage the laying off of redundant workers. Generally, however, enterprises are given hiring quotas for new graduates, and the planning system serves to provide employment for virtually all able-bodied individuals, whether in a necessary or an underemployed position.[35]

Moreover the planned system avoids many unemployment problems by not allowing enterprises to fail even if their output remains unsold. Enterprises have typically been rewarded on the basis of output performance rather than sales, and the existence of the enterprise appears to be guaranteed irrespective of its performance. The lack of variations in annual growth rates and low unemployment rates are the reverse sides of the same coin. As long as wage income remains stable, net output (where wages are the major component of value added) will remain stable, and growth fluctuations will be avoided.

If one examines the course of price inflation under capitalism and planned socialism, a striking contrast emerges from the official statistics (see Table 12.9). Since 1960, the major capitalist countries have experienced considerable inflation, which accelerated after 1970. According to the official planned socialist indexes, on the other hand, consumer prices have risen at a very modest pace over the last twenty years. The planned socialist economies' claims of virtual price stability in a world of rapidly rising prices rightly evokes some skepticism about the official consumer price series.[36] First, the official price series ignores substantial price increases for "new" or "higher quality" products. Often a planned enterprise can obtain a higher price by claiming superficial or nonexistent quality improvements in its products. Second, the official series fails to capture the higher rates of price increases for goods sold in legal and illegal free markets, where such sales are prompted by the

Table 12.9 Indexes of Consumer Prices in 1980, 1960 = 100 (Recalculated Socialist Indexes in Parentheses)

A. Planned Socialist Countries

Soviet Union	100	(140)
Bulgaria	130	(207)
Czechoslovakia	126	(173)
East Germany	98	(127)
Hungary	169	(210)
Poland	185	(254)
Romania	120	(—)

B. Market Socialist Country

Yugoslavia	1449

C. Capitalist Countries

United States	280
Canada	287
Belgium	261
France	382
Italy	546
Japan	420
Netherlands	295
United Kingdom	547
West Germany	213

Sources: *Statistical Abstract of the United States, 1981*, p. 881; *Economic Report of the President, 1981*, p. 355; Martin Kohn, "Consumer Price Developments in Eastern Europe," in U.S., Congress, Joint Economic Committee, *Eastern European Economic Assessment*, Part 2 (Washington, D.C.: Government Printing Office, 1981), p. 3330; Thad Alton et al., *Official Alternative Consumer Price Indexes in Eastern Europe, 1960-1980*, OP-68, Research Project on National Income in East Central Europe (New York, 1981); Directorate of Intelligence, CIA, *Soviet Gross National Product in Current Prices, 1960-80*, SOV 83-10037 (March 1983), pp. 6, 22.

unavailability of such products in official outlets. Third, the official indexes do not include the costs of standing in line for scarce commodities or the bribes often required to obtain such scarce goods. When these circumstances prevail, the demand for the particular commodity exceeds the supply at the established official price, and this is called *repressed inflation.* Supplies offered at established state prices are rationed out by standing in line, special shopping privileges, and ration coupons.

There is evidence that the official price series understates the amount of actual inflation in the CMEA countries. Recalculated price indexes (shown in parentheses in Table 12.9) suggest that prices have risen more rapidly than official sources claim. In fact, the actual rate of inflation in Eastern Europe does not appear to be much different from that of West Germany, the major industrialized Western nation with the most modest inflation rate. Inflation in the planned socialist economies seems to be below that of the capitalist countries, but we cannot prove this contention. Official consumer prices are state controlled in the planned socialist economies as is the general level of wages, and an important factor behind the apparent greater price stability of the planned socialist economies has been the fact that wage increases have been fairly closely tied to productivity increases. The relatively stable state retail prices probably conceal an unknown degree of repressed inflation, which has had a serious destabilizing effect in some planned socialist economies, such as Poland. For political and other reasons, authorities have been unwilling to raise official consumer prices to market-clearing levels. Apparent price stability has been achieved only at the cost of serious shortages, redirection of purchasing power into collective farm markets and black markets, and growing discontent.

Again, we refrain from drawing general conclusions about market socialism from the Yugoslav experience. As Table 12.9 attests, Yugoslavia has experienced a more rapid rate of inflation than any capitalist country in our sample. Moreover, the Yugoslav unemployment rate has been higher than that in the planned socialist countries.[37] Thus Yugoslavia does not appear to match the planned socialist record of stability but is more like a capitalist LDC in this regard. In fact, Yugoslav rates approximate those of Portugal and Turkey.

We should reemphasize that the planned socialist countries have become increasingly subject to external disturbances such as energy shocks, shifting terms of trade, and excessive hard-currency debt problems. Moreover, the planned countries lack some of the means (such as currency devaluation and foreign equity participation) to correct external imbalances. The CMEA countries seem threatened with increasing external instability in the future.

What general conclusions can be drawn concerning economic stability under socialism and capitalism? According to conventional

measures such as inflation rates and unemployment, the planned socialist economies appear to be more stable than their capitalist counterparts. There appears to be more job security, enterprise security, and
more stable consumer prices under planned socialism. But there is a
negative side to this picture as well. Excessive job security has led to
underemployment of the labor force, which keeps underemployed
individuals from more productive pursuits. The guaranteed existence of
socialist enterprises has reduced incentives to produce what the final
consumer desires, and official price stability has led to shortages and to
black market activities. In sum, it appears that the planned socialist
economies have purchased greater stability at the cost of economic
inefficiency.

Comparisons Between U.S. and Soviet Economic Performance

We have concentrated on broad comparisons of the economic performance of the planned socialist economies and the industrialized capitalist
countries, despite the differences among the economies within each
group. In this general comparison, planned socialism failed to score
better marks than capitalism in the areas of economic growth (despite
its high priority) and efficiency growth. The distribution of income
under planned socialism was shown to be no more equal than that of
the United Kingdom and Sweden.

In Chapters 6 and 7 we argued that the American and Soviet economies come as close as possible to representing market capitalism and
planned socialism. We refrained from emphasizing American-Soviet
performance comparisons because of the important differences in the
level of economic development and because we wished to learn something about the general behavior of economic systems. If the comparison had been based on American-Soviet economic performance, the
outcome would have been different. Soviet economic growth, both in
the historical long run and in the postwar period, has been significantly
more rapid than American growth, while Soviet productivity growth has
been roughly equal to that of the American economy. The exceptionally rapid growth rates of labor and capital inputs in the Soviet Union
have not generally taken place in the other planned socialist economies.
Moreover, labor income up to the late 1950s was more unequally
distributed in the Soviet Union than in the United States. The "atypicality" of the Soviet experience underscores the importance of examining economic systems as broadly as possible rather than concentrating
on single representatives. Yugoslavia appears to combine rapid economic growth and a fairly equal distribution of income (two goals
which it desires) with considerable instability. Over the postwar era,

Yugoslavia has had to live with extraordinary inflation and with high unemployment rates. It is our guess that its static efficiency (as judged by output per worker) may be high relative to the planned socialist economics on a *ceteris paribus* basis.

In drawing conclusions concerning the economic performance of capitalism and planned and market socialism, we have attempted to refrain from considering noneconomic criteria, such as economic and political freedom and the nonmaterial quality of life, in our assessment of economic systems, factors some observers would rate as more important than narrow economic concerns.[38] As economists, we felt we had to stick to economics. Although we were able to draw some conclusions about the economic performance of capitalism and socialism, we must remind the reader of the methodological difficulties noted at the beginning of this chapter, the most important one being the problem of isolating the impact of the economic system on performance. Throughout this discussion we made adjustments (often quite crude) for factors independent of the economic system, because there is no way to be sure that the observed performance differences are not the result of factors unrelated to the economic system. In fact, this remains a principal challenge to the field of comparative economic systems: to find better methods for determining the effect of the economic system *ceteris paribus* on economic outcomes.[39]

SUMMARY: THE PERFORMANCE OF ECONOMIC SYSTEMS

1. It is not possible to draw overall conclusions concerning the economic performance of socialism and capitalism without using subjective criteria. The performance of planned socialism and capitalism can be examined on the basis of how well each system performed according to a series of separate indicators of economic performance.

2. With per capita income held constant, industry shares are high under socialism relative to those under capitalism. Agriculture (in terms of its share of GNP and the labor force) and heavy industry are of greater importance under socialism than under capitalism; urbanization is underemphasized. Economic growth has *not* been more rapid under planned socialism despite the high importance attached to the growth objective by socialist planners. Capitalist countries have likely outgrown their planned socialist counterparts over the last twenty years and, if the level of economic development is held constant, perhaps over the entire postwar era. In any case, growth rate differences have not been substantial.

3. The growth of factor inputs has been similar under capitalism and planned socialism over the postwar era, although after 1960 factor inputs probably grew more rapidly under planned socialism, despite the declining growth rate of output. During the early postwar era, productivity growth was probably similar in the two systems. During the 1950s, efficiency growth accounted for over 60 percent of planned socialist growth — a figure close to the capitalist performance — but after 1960, planned socialist growth became more extensive. Almost 80 percent of growth was accounted for by the expansion of inputs. In the 1960s and 1970s socialist growth became quite expensive in terms of its reliance on increased factor inputs. This phenomenon is also apparent from the differential growth rates of consumption and investment, which suggest greater consumer sacrifices in the planned socialist economies. Holding other inputs constant, the planned socialist countries generally achieved less output per unit of labor input than did their capitalist counterparts.

4. Income is distributed more equally under planned socialism than in capitalist countries where the state does not play a major redistributive role. However, the differences between the distribution of income in so-called capitalist welfare states and the planned socialist economies are surprisingly small.

5. Planned socialism has been more stable in terms of conventional measures such as unemployment and inflation. These measures, however, conceal some instabilities, such as shortages and black market activities, and have likely entailed a loss of economic efficiency.

NOTES

1. Abram Bergson, *Planning and Productivity Under Soviet Socialism* (New York: Columbia University Press, 1968).
2. Paul R. Gregory and Robert C. Stuart, *Soviet Economic Structure and Performance*, 3rd ed. (New York: Harper & Row, 1986), ch. 10.
3. For studies of this sort, see Joseph Chung, "The Economies of North and South Korea" (Annual Meeting of the American Economic Association, Atlantic City, N.J., September 1976); and Paul Gregory and Gert Leptin, "Similar Societies Under Differing Economic Systems: The Case of the Two Germanys," *Soviet Studies*, 24 (October 1977), pp. 519–542. Also, see the papers on the panel: "Different Strategies, Similar Countries: The Consequences of Growth and Equity" (Annual Meeting of the American Economic Association, New York, December 1982).
4. Gur Ofer, "Industrial Structure, Urbanization, and the Growth Strategy of Socialist Countries," *Quarterly Journal of Economics*, 90 (May 1976), pp. 219–243; Gur Ofer, *The Service Sector in Soviet Economic Development* (Cambridge, Mass.: Harvard University Press, 1973); Paul Gregory, *Socialist and Nonsocialist Industrialization Patterns* (New York: Praeger, 1970);

Frederic L. Pryor, *Public Expenditures in Communist and Capitalist Nations* (Bloomington: Indiana University Press, 1973); and Fredric L. Pryor, *Property and Industrial Organization in Communist and Capitalist Nations* (Bloomington: Indiana University Press, 1973). For a discussion of the pure methodology of econometric performance evaluation, see Edward Hewett, "Alternative Econometric Approaches for Studying the Link Between Economic Systems and Economic Outcomes," *Journal of Comparative Economics*, 4, no. 3 (September 1980), pp. 274-294. For a discussion of the methodology of growth comparisons, see Gur Ofer, "Soviet Economic Growth, 1928-1985," *Journal of Economic Literature*, vol. 25, no. 4 (December 1987), pp. 1767-1833.

5. For example, Gregor Lazarcik has found that the centrally planned economies with more decentralized agriculture (such as Hungary and Poland) have performed better in terms of output and efficiency than those with centralized agriculture. On this, see Gregor Lazarcik, "Comparative Growth, Structure, and Levels of Agricultural Output, Inputs, and Productivity in Eastern Europe, 1965-79," in U.S., Congress, Joint Economic Committee, *East European Economic Assessment*, Part 2 (Washington, D.C.: Government Printing Office, 1981), pp. 587-634.

6. The major sources of data on the Soviet Union, Eastern Europe, and China are contained in various reports to the U.S. Congress prepared by the Joint Economic Committee. See, for example, *East European Economies: Slow Growth in the 1980s*, vols. 1-3 (Washington, D.C.: Government Printing Office, 1986), and *Gorbachev's Economic Plans*, vols. 1-2 (Washington, D.C.: Government Printing Office, 1987). Another useful statistical compendium is the Central Intelligence Agency, Directorate of Intelligence, *Handbook of Economic Statistics*. The most useful official East European source is the CMEA handbook: *Statisticheski ezhegodnik stran chlenov Sovet Ekonomicheskikh Vzaimopomoshichi*, various annual editions. For data on the Chinese economy, see U.S., Congress, Joint Economic Committee, *China: A Reassessment of the Economy* (Washington, D.C.: Government Printing Office, 1975); and Alexander Eckstein, ed., *Quantitative Measures of China's Economic Output* (Ann Arbor: University of Michigan Press, 1980).

7. Statistical comparisons of industrialized capitalism and planned socialism are Maurice Ernst, "Postwar Economic Growth in Eastern Europe," in U.S., Congress, Joint Economic Committee, *Economic Developments in Countries of Eastern Europe*, (Washington, D.C.: Government Printing Office, 1970), pp. 41-67; Thad Alton, "East European GNPs," Joint Economic Committee, *East European Economics: Slow Growth in the 1980s*, vol. 1, pp. 81-132. Also see Andrew Stollar and G. R. Thompson, "Sectoral Employment Shares: A Comparative Systems Context," *Journal of Comparative Economics*, vol. 11, no. 1 (March 1987), pp. 62-80; and Thad Alton, "Production and Resource Allocation in Eastern Europe: Performance, Problems, and Prospects," in Joint Economic Committee, *East European Economic Assessment*, Part 2, pp. 348-408.

8. See, for example, Subramanian Swamy, "Economic Growth in China and India, 1952-1970: A Comparative Appraisal," *Economic Development and Cultural Change*, 21 (July 1973), pp. 1-84; and Wilfred Malenbaum, "Modern Economic Growth in India and China: The Comparison Revisited," *Economic Development and Cultural Change*, 31, no. 1 (October 1982), pp. 45-84.

9. For a discussion of CMEA statistical practices, see Thad Alton, "Economic Structure and Growth in Eastern Europe, " in Joint Economic Committee, *Economic Developments in Countries of Eastern Europe*, pp. 43-45; and Alton, "Production and Resource Allocation in Eastern Europe," pp. 384-408.

10. The pioneering work on reconstructing planned socialist national income accounts was for the Soviet Union and was carried out by Abram Bergson and his associates. For an account of these efforts, see Abram Bergson, "Introduction," *Real National Income of Soviet Russia Since 1928* (Cambridge, Mass.: Harvard University Press, 1961).

11. For discussions of the socialist industrialization model, see Gregory, *Socialist and Nonsocialist Industrialization Patterns*; Ofer, "Industrial Structure, Urbanization, and the Growth of Socialist Countries" and *The Service Sector in Soviet Economic Development*; and Gregory and Stuart, *Soviet Economic Structure and Performance*, ch. 12.

12. For a discussion of index number relativity, see Bergson, *Real National Income of Soviet Russia Since 1928*, ch. 3.

13. This result was noted first by Abram Bergson in "Development Under Two Systems: Comparative Productivity Growth Since 1950," *World Politics*, 20 (July 1971), pp. 579-617.

14. Frederic Pryor, *A Guidebook to the Comparative Study of Economic Systems* (Englewood Cliffs, N.J.: Prentice-Hall, 1985), p. 78.

15. See, for example, Swamy, "Economic Growth in China and India," pp. 81-83; and Malenbaum, "Modern Economic Growth in India and China," pp. 45-84.

16. For a discussion of the measurement of static and dynamic efficiency, see Bergson, *Planning and Productivity Under Soviet Socialism*.

17. Edward Denison and William Chung, *How Japan's Economy Grew So Fast* (Washington, D.C.: Brookings, 1976), p. 30.

18. The classic treatment of the measurement of factor productivity is Edward Denison, *Why Growth Rates Differ* (Washington, D.C.: Brookings, 1967).

19. Apparently the Romanian and Bulgarian capital stock figures are in current prices. On this, see Alton, "Comparative Structure and Growth of Economic Activity in Eastern Europe," p. 223.

20. A considerable amount of research has gone into the subject of the relative growth of investment and consumption in Eastern Europe. Unfortunately, studies that cover the 1970s have not succeeded in calculating directly the real growth of investment. For a discussion of this point, see Alton, "Production and Resource Allocation in Eastern Europe," pp. 314-367. Also see Alton, "East European GNPs," pp. 94-98.

21. See the following studies of per capita consumption in the USSR and Eastern and Western Europe: Terence Byrne, "Levels of Consumption in Eastern Europe," in Joint Economic Committee, *Economic Developments in Countries of Eastern Europe*, pp. 297-315; and U.S., Congress, Joint Economic Committee, *Consumption in the USSR: An International Comparison* (Washington, D.C.: Government Printing Office, 1981).

22. Abram Bergson, "Comparative Productivity: The USSR, Eastern Europe, and the West," *American Economic Review*, vol. 77, no. 3 (June 1987), pp. 342-357. For Bergson's earlier work on this subject, see his discussion of relative Soviet output per unit of input in Abram Bergson, *The Economics of Soviet Planning* (New Haven: Yale University Press, 1964), ch. 14. Also see Bergson, *Production and the Social System: The USSR and the West* (Cambridge: Harvard University Press, 1978).

23. This view is shared by Pryor, *Property and Industrial Organization in Communist and Capitalist Nations*, p. 80.

24. Padma Desai and Ricardo Martin, "Efficiency Loss from Resource Misallocation in Soviet Industry," *Quarterly Journal of Economics*, 98, no. 3 (August 1983), pp. 441-456. Also see Judith Thornton, "Differential Capital Charges and Resource Allocation in Soviet Industry," *Journal of Political Economy*, 79 (May/June 1971), pp. 545-561.

25. For comprehensive discussions of income distribution under capitalism and socialism, see P. J. D. Wiles, *Economic Institutions Compared* (New York: Halsted Press, 1977), ch. 16; Martin Schnitzer, *Income Distribution: A Comparative Study of the United States, Sweden, West Germany, East Germany, the United Kingdom, and Japan* (New York: Praeger, 1974); and Abram Bergson, "Income Inequality Under Soviet Socialism," *Journal of Economic Literature* vol. 22 (September 1984).

26. See Pryor, *Property and Industrial Organization in Communist and Capitalist Nations*, pp. 74-75.

27. Ibid., pp. 74-89.

28. John R. Moroney, ed., *Income Inequality: Trends and International Compromise* (Lexington, Mass.: Heath, 1978), p. 5.

29. Janet Chapman, "Earnings Distribution in the USSR, 1968-1976," *Soviet Studies*, 35, no. 3 (July 1983), pp. 410-413.

30. See also a specialized study for the Soviet Union by Alastair McAuley, "The Distribution of Earnings and Income in the Soviet Union," *Soviet Studies*, 29 (April 1977), pp. 214-237.

31. Harold Lydall, "Some Problems in Making International Comparisons of Income Inequality," in Moroney, *Income Inequality*, pp. 31-33.

32. Simon Kuznets, *Modern Economic Growth* (New Haven: Yale University Press, 1966).

33. For studies of socialist business and trade cycles, see C. W. Lawson, "An Empirical Analysis of the Structure and Stability of Communist Foreign Trade, 1960-68," *Soviet Studies*, 26 (April 1974), pp. 224-238; G. J. Staller, "Patterns and Stability in Foreign Trade, OECD and Comecon," *American Economic Review* (September 1967); Josef Goldman, "Fluctuations and Trends in the Rate of Economic Growth in Some Socialist Countries," *Economics of Planning*, 4, no. 2 (1964), pp. 89-98; Oldrich Kyn, Wolfram Schrette, and Jiri Slama, "Growth Cycles in Centrally Planned Economies: An Empirical Test," Osteuropa Institute, Munich, *Working Papers*, No. 7 (August 1975); Gerard Roland, "Investment Growth Fluctuations in the Soviet Union: An Econometric Analysis," *Journal of Comparative Economics*, vol. 11, no. 2 (June 1987), pp. 192-206. Pryor's results are in Pryor, *A Guidebook*, pp. 114-118.

34. P. J. D. Wiles, "A Note on Soviet Unemployment in US Definitions," *Soviet Studies*, 23 (April 1972), pp. 619-628. David Granick, *Job Rights in the Soviet Union: Their Consequences* (Cambridge: Cambridge University Press, 1987).

35. Morris Bornstein, "Unemployment in Capitalist Regulated Market Economies and Socialist Centrally Planned Economies," *American Economic Review, Papers and Proceedings*, 68 (May 1978), pp. 38-43.

36. Authoritative discussion of official socialist price indexes and repressed inflation are found in Richard Portes, "The Control of Inflation: Lessons from East European Experience," *Economica*, 44 (May 1977), pp. 109-129. For some empirical estimates, see Richard Portes and David Winter, "The Demand for Money and Consumption Goods in Centrally Planned Economies," *Review of Economics and Statistics*, 60 (February 1978), pp. 8-18; and Martin J. Kohn, "Consumer Price Developments in Eastern Europe," in Joint Economic Committe, *East European Economic Assessment*, Part 2, pp. 328-347.

37. World Bank, *World Tables, 1976* (Baltimore: Johns Hopkins Press, 1976), Yugoslavia country tables. Also see the chapter on Yugoslavia.

38. Wiles, *Economic Institutions Compared.*

39. For a pioneering attempt to isolate the impact of the economic system on the economic performance of East and West Germany, see Peter Sturm, "The System Component in Differences in per Capita Output Between East and West Germany," *Journal of Comparative Economics*, 1 (March 1977), pp. 5-24. For

an extensive discussion of this issue, see Trevor Buck, *Comparative Industrial Systems* (New York: St. Martin's, 1982).

RECOMMENDED READING

Thad P. Alton and associates, *Economic Growth in Eastern Europe 1970 and 1975–1985*, Research Project on National Income in East Central Europe (New York: L. W. International Financial Research, Inc.), occasional paper no. 90.

Abram Bergson, "Comparative Productivity: The USSR, Eastern Europe, and the West," *American Economic Review*, vol. 77, no. 3 (June 1987), pp. 342–357.

———, *Planning and Productivity Under Soviet Socialism* (New York: Columbia University Press, 1968).

———, *Productivity and the Social System: The USSR and the West* (Cambridge, Mass.: Harvard University Press, 1978).

———, "Productivity Under Two Systems: The USSR Versus the West," in Jan Tinbergen et al., eds., *Optimum Social Welfare and Productivity: A Comparative View* (New York: New York University Press, 1972).

———, "Income Inequality Under Soviet Socialism," *Journal of Economic Literature*, vol. 22 (September 1984).

Trevor Buck, *Comparative Industrial Systems* (New York: St. Martin's, 1982).

Stanley Cohn, "The Soviet Path to Economic Growth: A Comparative Analysis," *Review of Income and Wealth* (March 1976), pp. 49–59.

Edward Denison, *Why Growth Rates Differ: Postwar Experiences in Nine Western Countries* (Washington, D.C.: Brookings, 1967).

Padma Desai and Ricardo Martin, "Efficiency Loss from Resource Misallocation in Soviet Industry," *Quarterly Journal of Economics*, 98, no. 3 (August 1983), pp. 441–456.

Irving B. Kravis, "Comparative Studies of National Incomes and Prices," *Journal of Economic Literature*, vol. 22 (March 1984).

Irving B. Kravis, Allen Heston, and Robert Summers, "Real GDP per Capita for More Than One Hundred Countries," *Economic Journal*, vol. 88 (June 1978).

———, *World Product and Income: International Comparisons of Real Gross Product* (Baltimore: Johns Hopkins University Press for the World Bank, 1982).

Sima Lieberman, *The Growth of European Mixed Economies* (New York: Halsted Press, 1977).

Alastair McAuley, *Economic Welfare in the Soviet Union* (Madison: University of Wisconsin Press, 1979).

Angus Maddison, *Economic Growth in Japan and the USSR* (New York: Norton, 1969).

Wilfred Malenbaum, "Modern Economic Growth in India and China: The Comparison Revisited," *Economic Development and Cultural Change*, 31, no. 1 (October 1982), pp. 45–84.

Paul Marer, *Dollar GNPs of the USSR and Eastern Europe* (Baltimore: Johns Hopkins University Press for the World Bank, 1985).

John Moroney, *Income Inequality: Trends and International Comparisons* (Lexington, Mass.: Heath, 1978).

Frederic Pryor, *Property and Industrial Organization in Communist and Capitalist Nations* (Bloomington: Indiana University Press, 1973).

———, *A Guidebook to the Comparative Study of Economic Systems* (Englewood Cliffs, N.J.: Prentice-Hall, 1985).

Martin Schnitzer, *Income Distribution: A Comparative Study of the United States, Sweden, West Gemany, East Germany, the United Kingdom, and Japan* (New York: Praeger, 1974).

Subramanian Swamy, "The Economic Growth in China and India, 1952–1970: A Comparative Appraisal," *Economic Development and Cultural Change*, 21 (July 1973), pp. 1–84.

U.S., Congress, Joint Economic Committee, *China: A Reassessment of the Economy* (Washington, D.C.: Government Printing Office, 1975).

———, *East European Economies: Slow Growth in the 1980s*, vols. 1–3 (Washington, D.C.: Government Printing Office, 1985).

———, *Gorbachev's Economic Plans*, vols. 1–2 (Washington, D.C.: Government Printing Office, 1987).

———, *USSR: Measures of Economic Growth and Development, 1952–1980* (Washington, D.C.: Government Printing Office, 1982).

P. J. D. Wiles, *Economic Institutions Compared* (New York: Halsted Press, 1977), ch. 16.

———, *The Distribution of Income, East and West* (Amsterdam: North Holland, 1974).

Murray Yanowitch, *Social and Economic Inequality in the Soviet Union* (White Plains, N.Y.: M. E. Sharpe, 1977).

APPENDIX 12A:
THE INDEX NUMBER PROBLEM
IN INTERNATIONAL COMPARISONS

In this chapter we cited a large number of statistics comparing the levels of GNP, output per workers, and so on among capitalist and socialist countries. For purposes of simplicity, we glossed over the fact that the price system that underlies the above valuations can have a substantial impact on the outcome. To compare levels of GNP, for example, the GNPs of all countries being compared must be valued in some common currency (dollars, rubles, marks, pounds, whatever).

Let us take the case of comparing the level of GNP of, for example, the Soviet Union and the United States in 1980. To simplify the illustration, let us say that both countries produce only two goods, wheat and lathes. In the USSR, wheat is expensive relative to lathes; in the Unites States, wheat is cheap relative to lathes (as judged by Soviet prices). Production and domestic prices of these two commodities in each country are given in Table 12A.1.

From this information, we can make two types of calculations: We can calculate the GNPs of both countries using U.S. prices or we can calculate the GNPs of both countries using Soviet prices.

In U.S. prices, we get:

$$\text{Soviet GNP} = (\$2 \times 10) + (\$2 \times 20) \quad \text{or} \quad \$60$$
$$\text{U.S. GNP} = (\$2 \times 30) + (\$2 \times 40) \quad \text{or} \quad \$140$$

Result: In U.S. prices, Soviet GNP is 43 percent (60/140) of U.S. GNP.

In Soviet prices, we get:

$$\text{Soviet GNP} = (5R \times 10) + (1R \times 20) \quad \text{or} \quad 70R$$
$$\text{U.S. GNP} = (5R \times 30) + (1R \times 40) \quad \text{or} \quad 190R.$$

Result: In Soviet prices, Soviet GNP is only 37 percent (70/190) of U.S. GNP.

The comparison is more favorable when the prices of the other country are used than when the country's own prices are used. Why is this typically the case? It is an empirical fact that the relative prices of any country tend to be inversely related to the relative quantities produced by that country. Products that can be produced relatively cheaply (due to abundant domestic resources) tend to be produced in abundance, and products that can be produced relatively expensively tend to be limited in production. Insofar as relative prices differ among countries (due to differences in human capital and natural resources), we find that each country emphasizes the production of relatively cheap commodities. Therefore, when the GNP of one country is valued using the different relative prices of another country, its total output will appear relatively large.

To take a real-world example of this index number phenomenon, we can cite studies of Soviet per capita consumption as a percentage of U.S. consumption. In 1976, Soviet and U.S. consumption per capita were 1,116R and 4,039R, respectively, when valued in rubles. In other words, the Soviet Union stood at 28 percent of the U.S. level. Valued in dollars, Soviet and U.S. per capita consumption were $2,395 and $5,598, respectively, or Soviet consumption per capita was 43 percent of the U.S. level. Which figure (28 or 43 percent) is the correct one? There is no "true" value in such comparisons. One comparison is as real as the other, for each system of relative prices will yield a different answer.

Table 12A.1

	Output		Price	
	Wheat	Lathes	Wheat	Lathes
Soviet Union, 1980	10	20	5R	1R
United States, 1980	30	40	$2	$2

It should be noted that in the comparisons used in this chapter, we consistently use dollar valuations. Dollar valuations make Soviet and East European values look more favorable than they would have if, say, ruble prices had been used.

NOTE

1. U.S., Congress, Joint Economic Committee, *Consumption in the USSR: An International Comparison* (Washington, D.C.: Government Printing Office, 1981), p. 6.

REFERENCES

Trevor Buck, *Comparative Industrial Systems* (New York: St. Martin's, 1981), ch. 5.

Irving B. Kravis et al., *A System of International Comparisons of Gross National Product and Purchasing Power* (Baltimore: Johns Hopkins Press, 1975).

Richard Moorsteen, "On Measuring Productive Potential and Relative Efficiency," *Quarterly Journal of Economics*, 75, no. 3 (August 1981), pp. 451–467.

Chapter 13
Performance of Similar Societies Under Different Economic Systems: East and West Germany

INTRODUCTION

In the previous chapter, we examined the economic performance of a large number of countries operating under different economic systems. We made some adjustments for factors other than the economic system, but relationships are too complex to hold all the relevant factors constant. Another approach is to examine economies that are alike with respect to all factors except the economic system. The economies of East and West Germany appear to offer such an opportunity.

To what extent do economic comparisons of East Germany (GDR) and West Germany (FRG) allow us to isolate the impact of the economic system on economic performance? Neither country is a perfect prototype of the system it represents; nevertheless, the two countries are close enough for our purposes.

The applicability of *ceteris paribus* to the two Germanys is critical. The strongest point in its support is the common endowment of human capital in the FRG and GDR at the end of the war, a proposition which generally holds today despite the notable divergences in population dynamics of the postwar period. The common human capital endowment could be documented with data on education, training, and the like, but it should suffice to note that the two Germanys today are inhabited by an essentially homogeneous population. Second, closely related to (perhaps inseparable from) the matter of a common population are shared culture, traditions, and tastes, which argue for equal "noneconomic" factor endowments. Third, despite some notable structural differences,[1] the two Germanys were among the most modern industrial economies at the outbreak of the war, with particular branches considered to be the world leaders. The equivalence in the level of economic development in the areas that were later to become the GDR and FRG is seen in the rough equivalence of per capita incomes and per capita industrial outputs in 1939.[2] The advanced nature of the two German economies persists to the present as is evidenced by the structure of output and capital stock (the distributions of which are

449

remarkably similar)[3] and in the advanced structure of exports and imports.

The arguments against the invocation of "all other things equal" must be weighed against the above common features. In considering nonequivalencies, one must confront a thorny issue: namely, to what extent are they truly *exogenous* to the economic system, or are they indeed *consequences* of the system?

The notably smaller scale of the GDR economy is an obvious exogenous difference. The population of the GDR territory at the end of the war was 18 million, roughly one-quarter that of the combined FRG-GDR territory. Today, it is closer to one-fifth. This difference in scale, with its potential impact on economic performance, must be weighed in any evaluation of performance. Differences in energy and resource bases are also exogenous. Although it is commonly argued that the GDR resource base is inferior to that of the FRG (owing to the loss of Silesian coal), this conclusion is not totally obvious. Population density is lower in the GDR and suggests a more favorable land-population ratio for that country. Moreover, although soft coal supplies are lacking, lignite is relatively abundant and is available for synthetic fuel production and electricity generation. The redefinition of political boundaries and the incorporation of the GDR into the communist bloc did represent a greater disruption of existing trade and production patterns for the GDR and is likely to have necessitated a longer adjustment to the new environment.

Other exogenous factors are the unequal treatment of the two Germanys at the hands of their respective occupation forces and the unequal wartime destruction of industrial capacity. It has been estimated that 50 percent of GDR and 25 percent of FRG 1943 industrial capacity had been wiped out by the end of the war;[4] thus, the GDR entered the postwar period with more substantial capacity losses. While the GDR economy was saddled with reparation payments in the early postwar period, the FRG benefited from Marshall assistance, receiving some 16 billion marks credit. On the other side, the FRG paid out some 33 billion marks as *Wiedergutmachung* payments, a sum double that of its Marshall Aid receipts. The GDR did not participate in the *Wiedergutmachung* program.[5] On the other hand, the GDR economy has enjoyed preferential energy prices (due to the implicit Soviet subsidies discussed in Chapter 11) and has received preferential tariff treatment on its exports to the West through its relationship to the FRG. Finally, the GDR has in recent years received substantial subsidies from the FRG in return for political concessions.

These exogenous forces must be considered in evaluating FRG-GDR economic performance; one must decide the extent to which they may explain the GDR's contemporary productivity, per capita income, and consumption gaps relative to the FRG. In our view, they all, with the exception of scale, represent largely transitional problems of the immediate postwar period. Scale differences are unlikely to be crucial. There are successful small economies, and there seems to be no general correlation between per capita income and size. However, the more successful small economies are intensively integrated into the world economy and owe their success to this fact. Under conditions of autarky, which is systemic to the planned socialist economies, size can play a considerable role, as can deficient resource endowments. Again, we should note that there are successful resource-poor economies (Japan, for example), but integration in the world economy is a necessary condition for their success.

Other FRG-GDR differences are less obviously exogenous to the economic system and are likely to be more important. The GDR's loss of population to the West ("republic flight") between 1945 and August 1961, ranging from 144,000 to 330,000 per year,[6] left its imprint on postwar GDR development. To some extent, this republic flight merely continued the traditional German westward migration pattern, strengthened by the strong performance of the postwar FRG economy. It was also a consequence of the choice of economic system, especially in terms of the composition of this migration. The republic flight was comprised largely of free professions, skilled technicians, and former entrepreneurs. Moreover, over one-half of the refugees during this period were under 25 years of age.[7] In these cases, the GDR economic system itself played a prominent role in prompting this flight through its income distribution policies, housing policies, and its discrimination against independent economic activity; the ensuing brain and skill drain was costly. It is not possible to separate the republic flight into its exogenous and endogenous elements, but our suspicion is that the latter dominated.

We treat divergences in participation in postwar international trade and capital flows by the FRG and the GDR as largely endogenous factors. The GDR's failure to reach its potential in international trade is evidenced by its documented low ratios of trade volume to GNP, corrected for scale and level of income.[8] Throughout the postwar era, per capita trade volume in the GDR ranged from 50 to 60 percent of that of the FRG,[9] a remarkably low figure in view of the GDR's smaller scale and less varied resource base. This policy has been costly in terms of growth and productivity performance. First, it suggests a tendency toward autarky in an economy ill-suited for self-sufficiency. Second, whereas the FRG at least initially was a recipient of advanced technology, the GDR has served throughout the postwar period as a technology exporter (a lower level of technology, to be sure) within the communist bloc and the Third World. Also lacking was the pressure of international competition to which the FRG export industries have been subjected — a weakness general to the CMEA countries.

As there are arguments both for and against *ceteris paribus*, some net evaluation must be made. The invocation of *ceteris paribus* does not unduly distort reality once *long-term* performance is considered and the interrelationships between the system and performance-related factors, especially in the areas of foreign trade and migration, are recognized. We believe that the differential treatment of the two Germanys and the disruptions of the immediate postwar period should have been overcome within a decade. The most convincing *ceteris paribus* argument is the common population of the two Germanys which should have provided the same potential for recovery, holding the impact of the system constant. The disadvantages of integration into the communist bloc should be attributed to general system-related problems and should not be regarded as exogenous to the system.

COMPARATIVE PERFORMANCE

Statistics of growth, efficiency, income, standard of living, and stability in this section, shed light on the relative performance of the FRG and GDR. Because of the greater availability of comparable statistics after 1955, we shall concentrate on this period and avoid short-term performance considerations and fluctuations.

Economic Growth

The GDR, like its CMEA counterparts, has emphasized rapid economic growth, particularly of industry, as its overriding long-term goal. The growth objective is less well defined in the FRG, where other objectives (price stability, export growth) have been accorded priority. Given the GDR leadership's intense interest in growth, it is instructive to contrast the long-term growth of the two Germanys. At the outset, we should emphasize that the FRG growth has been exceptional and that to use it as a yardstick for the GDR represents a quite ambitious criterion. The FRG and GDR are among the most successful of the systems they represent, and this fact makes our comparison an interesting one.

Table 13.1 (pp. 454–455) presents growth statistics for the 1955–1985 period. Use of this time span ensures data availability and allows some time for the countries to adjust to the disruptions of the early postwar period. This period includes the recessions of the mid- and late 1970s and early 1980s (which had a negative impact on the FRG) and the GDR's growth slowdown starting in the 1970s. The GDR aggregates have been reconstructed according to Western accounting definitions. Although independently estimated, they still rely heavily on official

GDR statistics. For this reason, we keep our conclusions as general as possible and regard small growth differentials as statistically insignificant.

According to our figures the East and West German Economies grew at similar rates between 1955 and 1985. West Germany showed a slightly higher GNP growth rate (3.7 versus 3.1 percent), but the per capita GNP rates were virtually identical (at 3.4 or 3.2 percent).

Turning to the industry and contruction growth rates, we fail to find major FRG-GDR differences. In the GDR the calculated growth (3.3 percent) is slightly higher than in the FRG (3.0 percent), but the GDR growth rate may be overstated.[10] On balance, the growth performances of the two Germanys over the past three decades have been similar, even taking into consideration the possible inflation of the GDR rate. GNP growth has been more rapid in the FRG but per capita rates are about the same. The most notable distinction is not the trend rate but deviations around this trend. The FRG growth rate shows much greater variability than the GDR rate when one looks at the annual data.[11] We return to this point later.

Data for earlier periods are less reliable, and overall conclusions depend on whose data one accepts. Reconstructions of FRG statistics to conform to GDR statistical definitions, when compared with *official* GDR statistics, yield a higher annual growth rate for the GDR between 1950 and 1960 (10 percent versus 8 percent),[12] but such data suffer from the standard weaknesses of CMEA statistical procedures. The pioneering studies by Stolper and Gleitze[13] yield a different picture. Between 1950 and 1958 the annual growth of the GDR economy was 6.5 percent, some 0.7 percent below the FRG rate. Stolper's comparisons with prewar (1936) production indicate a rather substantial decline in production in the GDR (1950 equals 73 percent of 1936) contrasted with an increase in aggregate production for the FRG (1950 equals 117 percent of 1936).

One common conclusion, however, emerges from the above statistics — both countries have grown at quite respectable rates between 1950 and 1981, and growth differences between the two economies are quite small on a per capita basis. A common pattern of resource allocation is not suggested by this conclusion. If one proceeds to a lower level of aggregation, the more typical features of the socialist industrialization model become apparent: the relative neglect of residential construction, transport, communication, and social overhead investment, and the relatively larger share of heavy industrial branches in total manufacturing output.[14]

DYNAMIC EFFICIENCY AND PATTERNS OF GROWTH

To find the sources of relatively rapid growth in the FRG and GDR, we must consider resource allocation policies and the role of technological

Table 13.1 Average Annual Rates of Growth of Output, Inputs, and Factor Productivity GDR and FRG, 1955–1985

	[1] Output	[2] Labor	[3] Capital	[4] Labor Productivity	[5] Capital Productivity	[6] Total Factor Productivity
A. GDR						
GNP	3.1	0.3	3.6	2.8	-0.5	2.0
Industry and construction*	3.3	0.7	5.9	2.6	-2.7	1.3
GNP per capita	3.4					
B. FRG						
GNP	3.7	0.2	4.8	3.5	-1.1	2.4
Industry and construction*	3.0	-0.6	4.4	3.6	-1.4	2.4
GNP per capita	3.2					

Table 13.1 (continued)

* Average annual growth rates for 1960–1985.

Note: .75 weight for labor and .25 weight for capital growth rates in computing growth of total factor productivity.

Sources: Thad P. Alton et al., "Economic Growth in Eastern Europe 1970, and 1975–1985," OP-90 (New York: Research Project on National Income in East Central Europe of L. W. International Financial Research, Inc., 1986), p. 11; Thad P. Alton, "Production and Resource Allocation in Eastern Europe: Performance, Problems, and Prospects," in U.S., Congress, Joint Economic Committee, *East European Economic Assessment*, Part 2 (Washington, D.C.: Government Printing Office, 1981), p. 383; Thad P. Alton, "Economic Growth and Resource Allocation in Eastern Europe," in U.S., Congress, Joint Economic Committee, *Reorientation and Commerical Relations of the Economies of Eastern Europe* (Washington, D.C.: Government Printing Office, 1974), p. 270 (industry and construction for 1955 estimated as average of 1950 and 1960 shares in GNP), p. 256; Statistisches Bundesamt, Lange Reihen 1950 bis 1984, Fachserie 18, Reihe S. 7 Stuttgart, FRG: W. Kohlhammer GmbH, 1985, p. (GNP on p. 41) 72 [verarbeitendes Gewerbe & Baugewerbe]; Statistisches Bundesamt, Revidierte Ergebnisse 1960 bis 1984, Fachserie 18, Reihe S. 8 Stuttgart, FRG: W. Kohlhammer GmbH, 1985, pp. 29–31; Statistisches Bundesamt, Revidierte Ergebnisse 1960 bis 1984, Fachserie 18, Reihe S. 8 Stuttgart, FRG: W. Kohlhammer GmbH, 1985, pp. 284–286 [verarbeitendes Gewerbe & Baugewerbe]; Statistisches Bundesamt, Lange Reihen 1950 bis 1984, Fachserie 18, Reihe S.7 Stuttgart, FRG: W. Kohlhammer GmbH, 1985, p. 120 [Bruttoanlagevermögen, einschl. öffentlicher Tiefbau]; Statistisches Bundesamt, Lange Reihen 1950 bis 1984, Fachserie 18, Reihe S. 7 Stuttgart, FRG: W. Kohlhammer GmbH, 1985, p. 118 [Erwerbstätige im Inland]; also Revidierte Ergebnisse 1960 bis 1984, pp. 278–282 [verarbeitendes Gewerbe & Baugewerbe]. The authors thank Irwin Collier for his assistance in preparing this table.

progress. Looking first at investment rates (Table 13.2), we find generally higher GDR rates. Recalculations according to Western concepts
and in some instances applying West German prices indicate higher
GDR investment rates with the exception of the immediate postwar
reconstruction years.

Investment rate comparisons indicate high (by international standards) investment proportions in both Germanys and show that, in
general, investment proportions have not been all that different with
the exception of the early postwar period. While the GDR investment
rate is roughly equivalent to that of the FRG, GDR output and output
per capita are well below those of the FRG (Table 13.3). The burden of
maintaining this investment rate appears to be heavier in the GDR. We
have shown in the previous chapter that the GDR investment rate is low
by CMEA standards, and more detailed studies reveal that the composition of this investment in recent years leans more toward housing construction than it does in the other CMEA countries.[15]

A brief comment is in order here concerning relative defense burdens
in the two Germanys. Although the usual statistical problems limit
accurate comparisons, the defense burden as measured by the ratio of
defense outlays to GNP has been quite similar in the two Germanys
since 1960 and has not been excessive in either area,[16] a factor which
has very likely contributed to the impressive growth of both countries.

The pattern of factor (capital and labor) growth was surprisingly similar between 1955 and 1985 (see Table 13.1). We say surprising because
of divergent trends in population growth; population declined 4 percent
in the GDR and increased by 12 percent in the FRG during this period.
Despite these divergent trends, aggregate labor force growth rates were
close, at 0.2 and 0.3 percent per year. The sectoral pattern of labor

Table 13.2 Investment Rates (Including Inventory Investment) in
Western GNP Definitions, FRG and GDR

	1950	1955	1967	1974		1980
GDR	15[a]	22[a]	25[a]	26–28[a]	(27[b])	29[a]
FRG	24	25	23	23		22

[a] FRG prices.
[b] GDR prices.

Sources: Wolfgang Stolper, *The Structure of the East German Economy* (Cam-
bridge, Mass.: Harvard University Press, 1960), pp. 426–427; "Das Sozialprodukt
der DDR–ein Ost-West Vergleich," *Wochenbericht*, no. 12 (1976), 112; I. L. Collier,
"The Estimation of Gross Domestic Product and Its Growth Rate for the German
Democratic Republic," *World Bank Staff Working Papers*, no. 773, 1985; *OECD
Historical Statistics, 1968-1981*, p. 12.

force growth was generally similar but included a more rapid decline in agriculture, a less rapid increase in service employment, and a more rapid increase in construction in the GDR. Labor force growth was achieved in the GDR despite declining population through increases in the labor force participation rates of women and older people, so that now the overall GDR participation rate (about 50 percent) and the female participation rate (84 percent of working-age women) are among the highest in the world.[17]

The patterns of capital stock growth are also similar. The overall growth of capital stock was more rapid in the FRG (4.8 percent versus 3.6 percent), but the distribution of this growth was similar. The

Table 13.3 Absolute Productivity Comparisons, GDR as a percentage of FRG, 1967 and 1980[a]

	GNP	GNP per capita	GNP per worker
Panel A			
1967			
GNP	22	78	67
Agriculture	41	141	92
Industry, Construction, Mining	24	84	72
Trade and Transport	19	65	59
Services	19	67	66
1980 GNP	15	54	44

Panel B

Relative Industrial Labor Productivity[b] in the GDR and FRG, 1970 and 1976

(FRG = 100%)

1970	48%
1976	52%

[a] GNP of the GDR in West German prices as a percentage of the FRG, in Panel A.
[b] Sales per employee for the FRG and Gross output per wage and salary employee (including apprentices) for the GDR.

Sources: "Das Sozialprodukt der DDR — ein Ost-West Vergleich," *Wochenbericht*, no. 12, 1976; Irwin L. Collier, "The Estimation of Gross Domestic Product and Its Growth Rate for the German Democratic Republic," *World Bank Staff Working Papers*, no. 773, 1985; Bundesministerium für innerdeutsche Beziehungen, *Materialien zum Bericht zur Lage der Nation im geteilten Deutschland 1987* (Bonn, 1987), p. 390.

growth rate of capital was higher in agriculture and lower in transport, communication, trade, and services in the GDR.

Because GNP growth in the FRG was slightly higher while input growth was slightly lower, FRG factor productivity growth (2.4 percent per year) was noticeably higher than GDR productivity growth (2.0 percent per year). Similarly, FRG labor productivity growth was seven-tenths of one percent higher. In the industry and construction sector, labor and capital productivity growth rates appear more favorable for the FRG. Considering the more rapid growth of labor productivity in the FRG, we would expect that the gap between FRG and GDR labor productivity has been increasing over the years (see the next section).

The remarkable feature of GDR growth performance is its intensive nature. Some 65 percent (1.2/3.1) of GDR output growth is the consequence of productivity growth; the figure is also 65 percent (2.4/3.7) for the FRG. Unlike the other planned socialist economies, the GDR has been able to generate intensive growth.

ABSOLUTE EFFICIENCY COMPARISONS

To compare absolute productivity in the two Germanys, GNP figures in a common set of prices are required. Such estimates have been made by the Deutsches Institut für Wirtschaftsforschung on the basis of 1967 West German prices. Additional calculations for 1980 have been made by I. L. Collier. The two sets of figures are not directly comparable because of the different methods used, but they portray rough orders of magnitude of change (see Table 13.3).[18] Panel B of Table 13.1 also estimates relative labor productivity in industry.

Concentrating on the GNP comparisons, we see that 1967 East German GNP in West German prices was 22 percent of that of the FRG. On a per capita basis, it was 78 percent. On a per worker basis, the relative figure is 67 percent owing to the higher labor force participation rate of the GDR. Thus GDR labor productivity was roughly two-thirds that of the FRG in 1967. In terms of sectoral productivity, the best relative performance was (surprisingly) that of GDR agriculture at 92 percent of the FRG figure, with industry (broadly defined) at 72 percent.[19] This latter figure is in accord with other estimates, which placed East German industrial labor productivity around three-quarters that of the FRG at that time.[20] Adding capital stock would not materially alter this picture. Under the most favorable assumption that capital productivity in the GDR is equal to that of the FRG, the overall productivity figure would be raised from two-thirds to three-quarters. A more likely picture, however, is lower GDR capital productivity, which would lower GDR relative productivity to less than two-thirds of the FRG. The estimates for 1980 show a widening in the GDR labor productivity gap, with GDR labor productivity falling to one-half that of the FRG. The GDR decline is from 67 percent to 44 percent of the FRG — a decline that, due to the different calculation methods, probable overstates the true GDR decline. Panel B shows that GDR relative industrial labor productivity in 1970 and 1976 remained around 50 percent.

Can the GDR productivity differential (be it 67 or 44 percent) be explained by factors exogenous to the economic system? Our subjective opinion is that the endogenous element is strong and that contemporary productivity differentials cannot be explained by the legacy of the immediate postwar period. Perhaps the most important endogenous element has been the inability of a relatively small and possibly resource-poor economy such as the GDR to integrate itself fully in the world economy. Taken together with internal allocation practices, this failure is likely to explain much of the productivity differential.

LIVING STANDARDS

Selected data on relative GDR-FRG living standards are supplied in Table 13.4. Most aggregate figures showing per capita consumption and net monthly wages of households and of income recipients indicate that the GDR living standard in the late 1960s, the early 1970s, and 1980 was roughly one-half to two-thirds of that in the FRG. The above figures fail to adjust adequately for quality differentials, the inclusion of which we believe would lower the respective GDR ratios, by how much we cannot guess. The two benchmarks from the mid-1950s and mid-1960s indicate a narrowing of the consumption differential, and this is consistent with official GDR statistics. However, the indicators of relative GDR consumption and real wages suggest declines after the mid-1960s.[21]

Despite its poor showing relative to the FRG, the GDR living standard is none the less impressive when considered both in its composition and relative to other CMEA countries. In composition, the GDR performs better, relative to the FRG, in the area of necessities excluding housing, and less well in the area of non-necessities including consumer durables. However, we should stress that the stock of consumer durables in the GDR is quite impressive both by CMEA and Western European standards.

Our conclusion therefore is that the contemporary GDR consumption gap is larger than one-third. The gap may have narrowed between the mid-1950s and mid-1960s, but it appears to widen thereafter. These conclusions are not altered by the inclusion of social services provided by the state, as such services are quite similar per capita in the two Germanys.[22] Thus, starting from a position of parity in 1936, the GDR suffered a substantial decline in consumption vis-à-vis the FRG.

Table 13.4 Various Indicators of GDR Living Standards as a Percentage of FRG (in West German DM)

Indicator	Year	GDR as % of FRG
Per capita private consumption expenditures	1955	60
	1967	69
	1980	49
Average net monthly income of households adjusted for purchasing power differentials	1967	59
Average monthly income of industrial workers adjusted for purchasing power differentials	1973	51
Average net monthly income of households	1983	50

Per capita consumption of various foodstuffs, 1970 and 1984

	1970	1984
pork	100%	116%
other meat	72%	90%
eggs	85%	110%
potatoes	149%	203%[a]
cheese	46%	55%
coffee	51%	57%
alcoholic beverages (actual alcoholic content)	73%	124%

Stocks of consumer durables per 100 households, 1973 and 1983

	1973		1983	
	GDR	FRG	GDR	FRG
cars	21	55	42	65
color television sets	1	15	38[b]	73
electrical refrigerators/freezers	4	28	29[b]	65
electrical washing machines	2	59	10	75
telephones	9	51	13	88

[a]1983.
[b]1985.

Sources: DIW, *Wochenbericht*, Stolper, p. 436; Collier, p. 60 "Bundesministerium fur innerdeutsche Beziehungen," *Materialien zum Bericht zur Lage der Nation*, 1971, pp. 103, 141; calculations by Gert Leptin; *DDR-Wirtschaft*, p. 261; Bundesministerium für innerdeutsche Beziehungen, *Materialien zum Bericht zur Lage der Nation im geteilten Deutschland 1987* (Bonn, 1987), pp. 526, 528; DIW, *Handbuch DDR Wirtschaft, 1985*, p. 280.

INCOME DISTRIBUTION

The comparison of income distributions in the GDR and FRG raises two conceptual problems. The first is that income from wealth accrues, in the GDR — with only minor exceptions — to the one major property owner, the state; whereas it accrues to the private and public owners of wealth in the FRG. It is therefore crucial to a meaningful analysis to be able to determine the claims and control that particular individuals or groups in the GDR exercise over this state wealth. Analysis of this issue must rest to a large extent on sociopolitical considerations. The second problem is that the distribution of income in the GDR will not necessarily coincide with the distribution of real goods and services. This is true because a whole series of scarce goods and services are allocated outside the market mechanism (apartments, vacations, travel to the West, and so forth) on the basis of social position, productivity, or political criteria. The third problem is one of data. For market economies such as the FRG, one has data on the distribution of income from wages and from wealth for the spectrum of societal groups, while for the CMEA countries one generally has only wage income distribution data for particular groups. In the GDR data cover workers and employees. Thus one has practically no information about the income of farm families, managers, politicians, academicians, artists, and others, who exercise an important impact on the Western distributions.

Table 13.5 cites statistics for the income distribution of worker and employee (*Arbeiter und Angestellte*) families. As such families earn income almost entirely from wages and salaries, this comparison sheds light primarily on the distribution of labor income among families and fails to deal with the broader issue of the distribution of income from wealth for society as a whole. The elites are conspicuously absent from the statistics. As is evident from Table 13.5, the distribution of wage and salary income among families was more equal in the GDR than the FRG in 1960, 1970, and 1983. However, the distribution of wage income is not dramatically different in the two Germanys, as is apparent in Figure 13.1. Wage differentiation serves as a major incentive in both countries. This point can also be seen from the close similarity of branch wage differentials in the GDR and FRG.[23] In fact, we believe that the trend toward greater equality between 1960 and 1983 is not the product of a conscious egalitarian policy in either Germany but rather the consequence of autonomous economic processes.

ECONOMIC STABILITY

The GDR has had greater economic stability throughout the postwar period than the FRG. This stability has been purchased at considerable

Table 13.5 Comparison of the Distribution of Disposable Net Income of Wage and Salary Employee Households, 1960, 1970, and 1983

Percentage of the Number of Households	Percentage of Net Income					
	1960		1970		1983	
	FRG	GDR	FRG	GDR	FRG	GDR
First Quintile	8.4	10.4	8.3	9.7	9.8	10.9
Second Quintile	12.6	15.3	12.7	16.1	14.7	16.3
Third Quintile	16.4	19.2	16.8	19.7	18.3	19.7
Fourth Quintile	22.8	23.4	22.3	23.4	22.9	22.9
Fifth Quintile	39.8	31.7	39.9	31.1	34.3	30.2
Total	100.0	100.0	100.0	100.0	100.0	100.0

Sources: Deutsches Institut für Wirtschaftsforschung, *Handbuch DDR-Wirtschaft*, 4th ed. (Hamburg, 1984), p. 272; and Bundesministerium für innerdeutsche Beziehungen, *Materialien zum Bericht zur Lage der Nation im geteilten Deutschland 1987* (Bonn, 1987), p. 503.

Figure 13.1 Lorenz Curves of FRG and GDR Income Distributions, Wage and Salary Employee Households, 1983

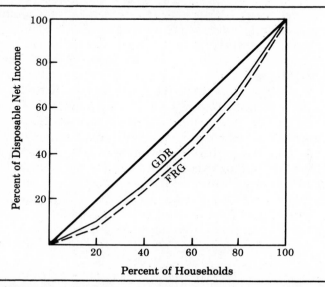

Source: Data from Table 13.5.

cost, however (Figure 13.2). By stability, we refer to the stability of economic growth and to the absence of excessive inflation and unemployment. There has been greater variation of growth in the FRG, which has experienced several recessions in the postwar era. Rather than experiencing sharp ups and downs, the GDR growth rate (along with that of the FRG) tended to decline in the 1970s. Only one year, 1982, saw slightly negative growth in the GDR.

Prices for both producer and consumer goods grew less rapidly in the GDR than in the FRG from the 1950s to the 1980s, although it is difficult to determine the real rate of producer goods inflation owing to the problem of pricing of "new" commodities and to other statistical problems. The cost of restraining the rate of inflation of producer goods in the GDR has not been too substantial in terms of allocative inefficiencies, for prices have not played much of an allocative role anyway. As far as consumer goods are concerned, the official GDR index showed a 10 percent *decrease* between 1955 and the mid-1970s. Reconstructed price indexes (Table 13.6) show that GDR prices have increased since the mid-1970s at about half the rate of FRG prices. This remarkable result is the consequence, first, of use of the formula that wage increases should be less than the rate of labor productivity growth. Second, GDR pricing authorities have been willing to accept disequilibria in particular consumer markets and the concomitant disincentive costs. Third, the state has been willing to subsidize certain products and to forfeit turnover tax revenues in cases where wholesale prices of consumer goods have risen (such as food products). Nevertheless, the political and other benefits of consumer price stability have apparently exceeded these costs. The point we would emphasize is that this apparent price stability has been achieved at the cost of disguised instabilities (subsidies, nonmarket allocation, and so on), that are hard to measure. However, in the GDR case, our impression is that such instabilities have not got out of hand (as in Poland) and do not represent a serious threat to social stability.

When prices are in disequilibrium, consumers cannot buy the mix of goods and services they would prefer. Instead, their purchases are **quantity constrained** by the limited quantities of goods with their prices held below equilibrium on the market. Irwin Collier has attempted to estimate the welfare loss suffered by the GDR population as a result of quantity constraints. He finds this loss to be about 13 percent of the value of total expenditure, measured by the amount of income the average GDR family would be willing to give up to be able to buy all goods at market prices without quantity constraints.[24]

Although one cannot estimate the aggregate unemployment rate of the GDR, we believe one can safely conclude that it is minimal by Western standards. The major cost of this minimal unemployment has been disguised unemployment, which again is impossible to measure.

Figure 13.2 Annual Growth Rate of GNP, GDR and FRG, 1961–1985

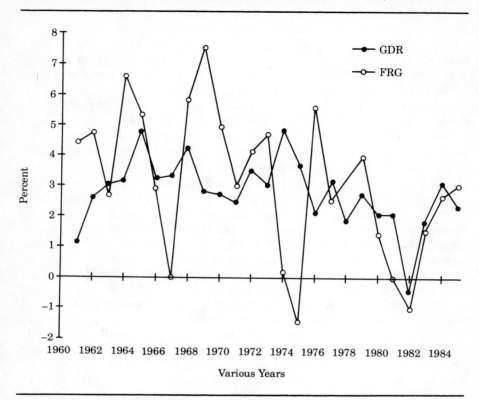

Sources: OECD, *Historical Statistics*, various years; Thad Alton, "Production and Resource Allocation in Eastern Europe: Performances, Problems, and Prospects," in U.S., Congress, Joint Economic Committee, *East European Economic Assessment*, Part 2 (Washington, D.C.: Government Printing Office, 1981), p. 381; Alton et al., "Economic Growth in Eastern Europe, 1965, 1970, and 1975–81," Research Project on National Income in East Central Europe, OP-70 (New York, 1982), p. 23; *Handbook of Economic Statistics, 1987*.

During periods of slack economic activity employment remains stable at the macro level; at the micro level, less productive individuals do not lose their jobs and excess labor is hoarded like excess materials. A major price of job security and of the ensured existence of enterprises is that quality is likely to suffer as the failure to produce quality products does not result in a loss of jobs or in the demise of the enterprise. This stability of the employment rate also helps to explain the stability of the GDR growth rate. The major component of aggregate value added is wages, and they will remain stable as long as there is stability of employment.

What are our conclusions, then, concerning economic stability? In general, we conclude that the GDR economy has been stable in terms of growth, price stability, and low unemployment. The hidden sources of instability, disequilibria in consumer markets and disguised unemployment, cannot be measured and have apparently been kept in reasonable check. There is no strong evidence to the contrary. On the other hand, we should note that the FRG economy has been among the most stable of the market economies, and that the cost of GDR stability has very likely been a relative loss of productivity and of quality.

THE RELEVANCE OF THE GDR-FRG EXPERIENCES FOR PLANNED AND MARKET ECONOMIES

We must still decide whether the East and West German experiences are typical of centrally planned socialist and market capitalist economies.

Table 13.6 Average Annual Rate of Consumer Price Inflation GDR and FRG, 1955–1983

	GDR	FRG
1950–55	−5.5	1.9
1955–60	0	1.8
1960–65	0	2.8
1965–70	0	2.3
1970–73	0	5.8
1973–77	2.8	5.2
1977–83	2.7	4.5

Source: GDR estimate from Michael Keren, "Consumer Prices in the GDR Since 1950: The Construction of Price Indices from Purchasing Power Parities," *Soviet Studies*, 39, no. 2 (April 1987), p. 263. FRG rate calculated from official FRG consumer price index.

Analysis of the West German experience is well beyond the scope of this inquiry, so we limit our remarks to the GDR.

We should begin by noting that in terms of institutional arrangements for allocating resources the GDR economy is the image of the Soviet economy, despite features of the GDR development process that make it quite different from its Soviet and CMEA counterparts. Some of these features are the consequences of the more advanced stage of economic development of the GDR; others are unique to the GDR. The issue of the atypicality of the GDR economy is relevant for two reasons. The first is that the GDR has been forced to develop without the luxury of rapidly expanding labor inputs. Thus the experiences of the GDR economy may have something to say about the future development prospects of the other CMEA countries when they, as well, exhaust their extensive development opportunities. A second reason for interest is the achievements of the GDR economy, and one would like to find an explanation for its success relative to the other CMEA countries.

Turning to the atypical features of the GDR model, we first note the need to generate economic growth with a declining population. This necessity forced the GDR authorities, in our opinion, to be more conscious of the role of incentives to ensure not only high participation rates but also the productive use of labor resources. The fact that the GDR investment rate has not been exceptionally high relative to CMEA standards despite higher per capita income, and the fairly ample (by CMEA standards) stock of consumer durables, support this conclusion. Also the distribution of investment resources in the late 1960s and early 1970s in the direction of social overhead capital and apartment construction all indicate an effort on the part of GDR authorities to improve industrial incentives and mobility. The greater toleration of private enterprise in handicraft, retail trade, and agriculture is also indicative of this trend.

An alternative explanation offers itself as well. The proximity and close emotional and family ties with West Germany made it politically and socially impossible to allow too large a gap in living standards to develop. One cannot say whether the apparent greater attention to the consumer in the GDR resulted more from the presence of the FRG or from the need to preserve labor incentives, but both forces are likely to have played important roles.

The special relationship with the FRG may have played other roles as well. The special trade relationship gave the GDR access to the Common Market on a preferential basis. A more important benefit, in view of its relatively low trade proportions with the West, may have been the role of information transfers to the GDR from the FRG. As a result of these ties, GDR managers and authorities had more knowledge of prevailing industrial practices and relative prices, which may have provided better information on which to base their own resource allocation decisions.

SUMMARY

The validity of the *ceteris paribus* assumption is the crucial issue in GDR-FRG comparisons. Our conclusion that the *ceteris paribus* assumption can be applied is based primarily on the common level of prewar economic development and the existence of a relatively homogeneous population in the two Germanys. However, the limits of the *ceteris paribus* assumption must be broadened if our assumptions concerning the endogeneity of certain negative factors are not accepted. The factors exogenous to the system, which would have to be held constant, almost all worked to the disadvantage of the GDR, but were regarded by us as largely transitional factors. The comparison of East and West German economic performance can be summarized as follows:

1. On a per capita basis, growth performance has not been all that different in the two Germanys since 1960. Since West German growth was quite strong over this period, this represents a strong achievement for East Germany. Denied the opportunity to pursue extensive growth, the East Germans somehow managed to grow intensively. Some 60 percent of their growth is accounted for by productivity growth. West Germany grew intensively as well (68 percent of its growth was due to productivity growth), but this is not unusual for the industrialized capitalist countries.

2. The major disappointment of the East German economy has been its inability since the mid-1960s to keep up with productivity growth and consumption growth in East Germany. West German labor productivity grew about one percentage point more rapidly than East German, and the gap appeared to widen substantially after the mid-1960s. One should remember that the period in question (1960–1981) includes times of considerable trouble for the industrialized West, which suffered through an energy crisis, major world recessions, and stagflation. If East Germany fell further behind in such a period, one must wonder how such a comparison will look twenty years from now, assuming that the Western business cycle returns to normal.

3. We appear to have two quite successful representatives of the two economic systems. They suggest what can be accomplished under specific conditions by each economic system. To what extent are they, then, "typical" of their systems? This question we cannot answer, for we lack a generally accepted criterion of typicality.

Our subjective conclusion is that the FRG economy, even after holding the differential experience of the immediate postwar period constant, has "outperformed" the GDR economy. For this conclusion, we rely heavily on our assignment of high significance to the productivity and consumption gaps between the two countries and the fact that these gaps do not appear to be narrowing over time. We also recognize that the use of FRG economic performance as a measuring rod for GDR performance is indeed a rigorous criterion; the GDR may have "outperformed" other major market economies in those areas to which we have subjectively attached great importance.

NOTES

1. The most authoritative study of the prewar structures of the two German economies is Bruno Gleitze, *Ostdeutsche Wirtschaft Die Wirtschaftsstruktur der Sowjetzone und ihre gegenwärtigen sozial-und wirtschaftlichen Tendenzen* (Bonn, 1951). See also Gert Leptin, *Veränderungen in der Branchen- und Regionalstruktur der deutschen Industrie zwischen 1936 und 1962* (Berlin: Ost Europa Institut, 1965).

2. According to figures supplied by Wolfgang Stopler, *The Structure of the East German Economy* (Cambridge, Mass.: Harvard University Press, 1960), p. 418, the ratio of GDR to FRG per capita income in 1936 was 0.98. On the other hand, per capita industrial output in the GDR was 16 percent higher than in the FRG in 1939, according to Gleitze, *"Die Wirtschaftsstruktur,"* p. 169.

3. On this, see Manfred Melzer, "Das Anlagevermögen der mitteldeutschen Industrie, 1955 bis 1966," *Vierteljahreshefte zur Wirtschaftsforschung*, Heft 1, 1968, *Wochenbericht*, no. 27 (1965), p. 128, and Gert Leptin, *Veränderungen.*

4. These estimates are cited by Gert Leptin, *Die Deutsche Wirtschaft nach 1945, ein Ost-West Vergleich* (Opladen: Leske, 1971), p. 51.

5. These figures are from Leptin, *Die Deutsche Wirtschaft*, pp. 56-57.

6. Leptin, *Die Deutsche Wirtschaft*, p. 61.

7. *Die Flucht aus der Sowjetzone und die Sperrmassnahmen des kommunistischen Regimes vom 13. August 1961 in Berlin*, Hrsg. vom Bundesminsterium für gesamtdeutsche Fragen (Bonn/Berlin, 1961), pp. 15-18.

8. Paul Gregory, *Socialist and Nonsocialist Industrialization Patterns* (New York: Praeger, 1970), p. 120.

9. Leptin, *Die Deutsche Wirtschaft*, p. 59. These figures are rough approximations, as the GDR figures are cited in valuta marks, whose parity is unknown.

10. Our skepticism concerning the reliability of official GDR industry statistics follows from certain unexplained contradictions. According to official sources, the index of industrial production in 1970 (1950 = 100) was 537 for the GDR and 436 for the FRG, while the industrial labor force grew more slowly in the GDR during this period (GDR = 136, FRG = 174). These indexes therefore suggest a higher rate of growth of industrial labor productivity in the GDR (GDR = 449, FRG = 291) for the period 1950-1970, that is, a substantial *narrowing* of any existing productivity gaps. This evidence conflicts not only with other sources of evidence suggesting a more rapid growth of labor productivity in the FRG, namely, the higher growth of capital per industrial

worker and of industrial energy per worker, but also with other evidence. According to the Wilkens calculations cited in Table 13.3, the productivity of the GDR industrial labor force was some 35 percent below that of the FRG in 1967. Combining this with the above-cited industry production and labor growth indexes yields the conclusion that the gap was 59 percent in 1950. Yet, official GDR statistics give the following figures (1936 = 100) for 1950: industrial production = 111 and industrial employment = 114. The corresponding FRG indexes are 110 and 116. Combining the two yields the result that labor productivity growth was almost identical in the two Germanys between 1936 and 1950 and, hence, that the 1936 productivity gap of the GDR territory in 1936 was 60 percent — a clearly implausible result in view of the roughly 15-20 percent gap shown by the German prewar statistics.

11. *Wochenbericht*, 1975, no. 16.
12. Frank Haller, *Die Wirtschaftliche Entwicklung der BRD und der DDR* (Bremen, 1974), p. 46.
13. The following figures are from Stopler, *The Structure of the East German Economy*, pp. 418-419.
14. *Materialien zum Bericht zur Lage der Nation* (Bundesministerium für innerdeutsche Beziehungen, 1971), tables 65-84.
15. Deutsches Institut für Wirtschaftsforschung, *DDR-Wirtschaft: Eine Bestandsaufnahme* (Frankfurt am Main: Fischer, 1974), p. 210f.
16. Ibid., p. 218.
17. Ibid., pp. 36-40.
18. *Wochenbericht*, no. 12 (1976); Herbert Wilkens, *Das Sozialprodukt der Deutschen Demokratischen Republik im Vergleich mit dem der Bundesrepublik Deutschland*, Sonderheft des DIW no. 115 (Berlin, 1976).
19. The finding of relatively good agricultural productivity is not consistent with other evidence for specific crops. Yields per acre in the GDR are much lower (with roughly the same factor proportions per man) and other inputs are also generally lower. We are grateful to Wolfgang Stolper for this evidence.
20. *Materialien zum Bericht zur Lage der Nation.*
21. Haller, *Die Wirtschaftliche Entwicklung*, p. 65.
22. *Materialien zum Bericht zur Lage der Nation*, p. 111.
23. Paul Gregory, "A Model of Socialist Industrial Wage Differentials: The Case of East Germany," *Quarterly Journal of Economics*, 87 (February 1973), pp. 132-137.
24. Irwin Collier, "Effective Purchasing Power in a Quantity-Constrained Economy: An Estimate For the German Democratic Republic," *Review of Economics and Statistics*, vol. 68, no. 1 (February 1986), pp. 24-32.

RECOMMENDED READINGS

Trevor Buck, *Comparative Industrial Systems* (New York: St. Martin's, 1982), ch. 5.

Bundesministerium für innerdeutsche Beziehungen, *Materialien zum Bericht zur Lage der Nation im geteilten Deutschland 1987* (Bonn, FRG: Bonner Universitäts-Buchdruckerei, 1987).

Irwin Collier, "The Estimation of Gross Domestic Product and Its Growth Rate For the German Democratic Republic," *World Bank Staff Working Papers*, no. 773, 1985.

Deutsches Institut für Wirtschaftsforschung, *Handbuch DDR-Wirtschaft*, updated and expanded 4th ed. (Hamburg, FRG: Rowohlt Taschenbuch Verlag GmbH, 1985).

Paul Gregory and Gert Leptin, "Similar Societies Under Differing Economic Systems: The Case of the Two Germanys," *Soviet Studies*, 29, no. 4 (October 1977), pp. 519–541.

Hannelore Hamel, ed., *Bundesrepublik Deutschland — DDR: Die Wirtschaftssysteme*, 4th ed. (Munich: Beck, 1983).

Gert Leptin, *Die Deutsche Wirtschaft nach 1945: ein Ost-West Vergleich* (Opladen: Leske, 1971).

Martin Schnitzer, *Income Distribution: A Comparative Study of the United States, Sweden, West Germany, East Germany, the United Kingdom and Japan* (New York: Praeger, 1974), chs. 4 and 5.

Wolfgang Stolper, *The Structure of the East German Economy* (Cambridge, Mass.: Harvard University Press, 1960).

Chapter 14
Economic Reform: Capitalism and Socialism

REFORM OF ECONOMIC SYSTEMS

Economic systems are not cast in concrete. Their characteristics —
property ownership, the incentive system, market or plan resource
allocation — can be changed. Economic reform offers the opportunity
to alter one or more characteristics in a minor way, such as by slightly
increasing the share of public ownership, or in a major way, such as
substantially shifting from market to plan allocation.

Few economic systems have experienced economic reforms that have
altered their fundamental character. However, the introduction of command planning and collectivized agriculture to the Soviet Union in the
late 1920s and the introduction of the Soviet system into Eastern
Europe and China after the Second World War are cases of fundamental
and rapid changes of economic systems. The replacement of command
planning by worker-managed socialism in Yugoslavia in the late 1940s is
another case of fundamental change of an economic system.

Rapid and fundamental change is less likely in capitalist systems. The
economic system of contemporary industrialized capitalist countries is
quite different from the system that prevailed in these same countries
500 years ago. Clearly, there were fundamental changes in that time
interval (from feudalism to capitalism). Yet these changes occurred
slowly and gradually; it would be difficult to date key transitions. When
resources are allocated by markets, changes in resource-allocation procedures are not very visible. However, in planned socialist systems,
where resources are allocated by administrative rules, changes in
resource-allocation procedures are readily identified.

CHANGE IN CAPITALIST ECONOMIES

There is no general theoretical framework for studying change in
capitalist economic systems. Karl Marx (see Chapter 3) sought to provide a general framework for the evolution of capitalism to socialism —
citing increasing concentration of wealth, worsening business cycles,
declining profits, and rising unemployment — but Marx's major predic-

tions remain difficult to verify or to deny. Moreover, Marx was interested in the transition from capitalism to socialism, not in the evolution from one form of capitalism to another. While a number of other scholars have tried to generalize the capitalist development experience (for example, Gerschenkron, Kuznets, and Rostow to name a few), the objective of a general theoretical framework remains elusive.

Lacking a theoretical framework, we can only observe actual and proposed changes in modern capitalist economic systems. We do not attempt to chronicle the many changes that have already occurred, such as the development of social welfare systems and income redistribution through taxation.

Privatization Versus Nationalization

Changes in the shares of private and public ownership, if carried to the ultimate, can alter the fundamental character of capitalism: If the state owned all capital, the economic system would no longer be capitalist. Real-world capitalist systems are mixed, some having higher shares of public ownership than others. Privatization occurs when property that had previously been publicly owned is sold to private owners. Public ownership increases when property that had previously been privately owned becomes publicly owned, or **nationalized**. The shares of public and private ownership can be changed either by government spending programs that create new government-owned capital (such as the U.S. federal government's Tennessee Valley Authority project initiated during the Great Depression) or by direct government buying or selling of existing facilities. By selling its shares of British Air, for example, the British government increases the share of private ownership in the United Kingdom. By buying a failing steel company, the British government increases the share of public ownership.

Public sentiment in favor of public ownership was highest in the United States during the Great Depression. In the United Kingdom, the election of labor governments in the 1940s and 1950s showed political support for nationalization, while the lengthy tenure of a conservative government in the late 1970s and 1980s shows support for privatization. Alternating socialist and conservative governments in France also reflect rising and falling sentiment for privatization and nationalization. In West Germany, both socialist and conservative governments have consistently favored privatization since the end of the Second World War. The German government has sold its shares of major corporations to private owners throughout the postwar era.

The figures cited in Chapter 6 for the United States showed that government shares of structures and land have not changed noticeably since the early 1930s, nor has the share of output produced by government enterprises. After a rise in public ownership in the early 1930s, the share of government ownership has remained fairly stable, despite a substantial increase in output shares consumed by government.

Table 14.1 shows the government shares of fixed capital in 1955 and 1980 in seven industrialized capitalist countries (including Greece). It should be emphasized that the wide differences in ownership shares are partially the result of different accounting procedures, but nevertheless substantial changes in government ownership shares within each country can be observed. In some countries, government ownership shares have fallen (Canada and Greece). In others, they have risen (United Kingdom and Sweden). In the majority of countries, government shares of capital have been stable over the twenty-five-year period. In France, West Germany, and Finland, government ownership shares were either unchanged or changed only slightly.

Table 14.1 reveals that overall there has been little change in private and public ownership shares in capitalist countries, suggesting that these countries have reached a basic consensus on the distribution of public and private ownership. Changes in governments over the years have not notably altered this consensus.

The conservative governments elected in the United States and Western Europe in the 1980s have brought a rising tide of privatization. It is difficult to tell whether this trend will continue long enough to fundamentally change the shares of private and public ownership in the industrialized capitalist countries, but it seems unlikely in view of the long-term stability of ownership shares.

Table 14.1 Share of Government Ownership of Fixed Capital, Capitalist Countries (percentages of total)

	1955	1980
Canada	22	19
Finland	3	3
France	16	17
Greece	3	1
Sweden	4	7
United Kingdom	11	14
West Germany	7	8
Unweighted average	9.4	9.9

Source: OECD, *Flows and Stocks of Fixed Capital, 1955-1980* (Paris: OECD, 1983).

Trends in Competition

Changes in the extent of competition alter the nature and operation of a capitalist economy, but they do not result in the system's ceasing to be capitalist. A capitalist economy in which monopoly is the prevalent form may operate inefficiently and may cause consumers to pay high prices, but it is still a capitalist economy.

The degree of competitiveness in a capitalist economy is affected by antitrust laws, regulations, trade policies, and court interpretations of antitrust policy. It is extremely difficult to generalize about trends in state policy toward competition. The best-documented trend is the postwar relaxation of international trade barriers. The industrialized capitalist countries have created international arrangement for dismantling the restrictive trade barriers that were put in place during the Great Depression, and there is little doubt that the degree of international competition has expanded at a rapid rate throughout the postwar period. Trade barriers have been lowered in both product markets and factor markets (see Figure 14.1). In the 1980s, one can speak of a

Figure 14.1 Average U.S. Import Duties, 1900–1986

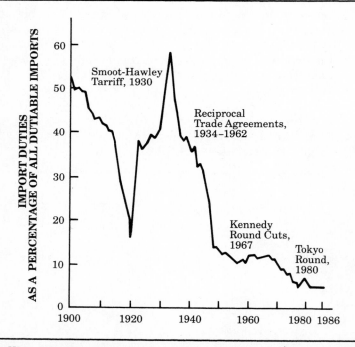

Sources: *Historical Statistics of the United States; Statistical Abstract of the United States.*

world capital market in which financial capital flows freely and quickly between Europe, North America, and the industrialized Asian countries.

The amount of deregulation is another visible indicator of state policy toward competition. If a potentially competitive industry is regulated by the state (which often results in anticompetitive behavior), the degree of competition is reduced. The trend toward deregulation started in the United States in the late 1970s, and it spread from North America to Western Europe and Japan in the 1980s. Deregulation has been most prominent in transportation, communications, and banking, but it remains to be seen whether other capitalist countries will deregulate to the extent of the United States and whether the deregulation experiment will continue in the United States.

The least visible — and most difficult to characterize — aspect of state competition policy is antitrust policy. Most industrialized capitalist countries allow more exemptions from antitrust laws than does the United States, which exempts primarily farming operations and labor unions; however, antitrust laws that prevent massive abuse of monopoly power exist in nearly every advanced capitalist country. Unlike the U.S. laws, which declare all formal price-fixing agreements illegal, other industrialized capitalist countries judge price-fixing arrangements on the basis of whether they result in reasonable prices. If they do, they are not illegal per se.

In the United States, there have been few major changes in antitrust legislation since the 1930s. The changes that have occurred have taken place in the courts. Initially, the courts interpreted the antitrust laws as outlawing anticompetitive behavior, but in the early 1950s, antitrust laws were interpreted as outlawing monopoly power per se, whether this power was abused or not. The 1970s and 1980s have seen a move toward a more liberal interpretation of antitrust laws, stemming from the recognition that businesses must compete in international markets against close substitutes and that antitrust laws should not be used to penalize competitive successes.

Growing international competition and deregulation should increase the degree of competition in capitalist countries. Moreover, rapid technological progress produces a wider variety of competitive products and promotes competition. William Shepherd has attempted to measure the changing degree of competition in the U.S. economy. He concludes that the American economy became more competitive after 1960, as a consequence of growing international competition and deregulation.[1] According to Shepherd, the share of the U.S. economy that was effectively competitive remained fairly stable at 52–54 percent between 1939 and 1958, but rose to 77 percent by 1980. Similar studies have not been conducted for the other industrialized capitalist countries, so we do not know whether the American experience is representative.

However, since virtually all industrialized capitalist countries have been subject to growing international competition, and since, according to Shepherd, growing international competition has stimulated increased competition in the U.S. economy, the impact of this development may be equally strong in other capitalist countries.

Income Redistribution

Capitalism uses material incentives to motivate economic behavior, and a move away from material incentives would signal a fundamental change in the capitalist economic system. For, if a capitalist state altered the distribution of income earned in factor markets, participants' earnings in factor markets would become less decisive in determining their command over resources. For example, if the tax system equalized the distribution of income after taxes, material rewards would cease to guide economic decision making. Changes in tax policy can indeed change the nature of the capitalist economic system.

For a tax system to have a large impact on the reward system, taxes must make up a large share of factor income, and the tax system must redistribute income. Income is redistributed with a **progressive tax** (which redistributes proportionally away from high-income earners) or a **regressive tax** (which redistributes proportionally away from low-income earners). In other words, in a progressive tax system, the tax's share of income rises with income; in a regressive system, the share falls. In order to redistribute income in a substantial way away from high-income earners, the tax system must take up a large share of factor income and be highly progressive.

Table 14.2 gives information on changes in the tax system's shares of income in 1960 and 1985 and in the shares of income taken by several different taxes. The table shows that in all the capitalist countries surveyed, taxes rose as a percentage of GNP. The most modest rise was in the United States — from 27 to 29 percent; the largest rise was in Sweden — from 28 to 51 percent.

The shares of income taxes and taxes on goods provides indirect information on the redistributive role of the tax system. Taxes on income tend to be progressive, while taxes on goods are regressive. Assuming no significant changes in income-tax rates by income bracket, the tax system would become more progressive as a whole when the share of income taxes rises. The tax system would become more regressive as a whole when the share of taxes on goods rises. Table 14.2 reveals a mixed picture. In five of the countries, the income-tax share of total taxes remained stable or fell. In the other three countries, the income-tax share rose. In only two countries (Italy's rising share and Sweden's falling share) were the changes substantial. The table also shows a generally declining reliance on taxes on goods. The share of taxes on goods fell substantially in France, Italy, and Japan. Only Canada and the United Kingdom recorded small increases in the share of taxes on goods.

Not having readily available information on income-tax rates, we can only draw cautious conclusions about this data in Table 14.2. There has been a substantial increase in the share of taxes of factor income in the industrialized capitalist countries, but there has not been a substantial shift in the form of taxation. Although there has been a slight drift away from taxes on goods to taxes on income (which should increase the progressivity of the tax system), these changes have been relatively minor, except in Italy. The overall conclusion is that the redistributive role of the tax system has not changed much in capitalist economies even though the share of taxes has been rising.

What have capitalist governments done with the increasing tax share of GNP? The last columns show the dramatic rises in the shares of social security transfers as a percentage of GNP. The effect of social security transfers on economic rewards depends on how these transfers are distributed. If they are distributed according to contributions, they

Table 14.2 Changes in the Capitalist Tax System

	Taxes as a Percentage of GNP		Share of Total Taxes				Social Security Transfers as Percentage of GNP	
			Income Taxes		Taxes on Goods			
	1960	1985	1970	1985	1970	1985	1960	1981
United States	27	29	48	42	19	18	5.3	11.5
Canada	24	34	45	43	32	33	8.0	10.2
France	32	46	18	18	38	29	13.6	24.4
Italy	27	41	17	36	38	26	9.8	17.4
Japan	20	27	41	46	22	15	3.8	10.8
Sweden	28	51	54	42	29	25	8.0	18.7
United Kingdom	28	39	40	38	29	31	6.9	13.3
West Germany	30	38	32	33	32	27	12.5	17.4

Sources: *Statistical Abstract of the United States* (international comparisons); OECD, *Historical Statistics* (Paris: OECD, 1983).

will not alter the factor distribution of income. If they are distributed in a manner unrelated to contributions (such as in poverty programs), they would alter the distribution of income.

The evidence that has been collected for the United States shows that, although the tax system does not materially alter the distribution of income, the distribution of transfers does.[2] The major instrument of state income redistribution in the United States is the distribution of transfer payments to low-income recipients. The growing GNP share of social security transfers suggests that there may have been a significant alteration in material rewards in capitalist economic systems through the distribution of social security transfers to the less advantaged.

Profit Sharing and Worker Participation

A basic characteristic of capitalism is that the owners of capital (individual proprietors, partners, or corporate shareholders) are rewarded out of profits. Workers are paid wages that do not vary directly with profits. Capitalism can change its character by sharing profits with workers.

Because profits fluctuate more than wage income, the owners of capital are, in effect, making a deal with workers that as long as the business remains solvent, workers will receive their contracted wages. Owners of capital, who bear risk in the form of fluctuating returns on capital, earn a return to reward them for risk taking. The worker accepts a nonfluctuating wage and, in return, is prepared to follow the directions of the management.

The fundamental nature of the relationship between worker and owner of capital can be altered by profit sharing. If rewards to workers depend upon the profits of the business, the worker becomes a partial capitalist and bears a part of the risk of fluctuating profits. If workers' incomes depend entirely upon the profits of the enterprise, then they basically become capitalists.

The advantages of a profit-sharing economy are that workers are more materially interested in the profitability of the enterprise. They will work more in the interests of the enterprise than before, and they will be less inclined to shirk work. A profit-sharing economy has another advantage: If workers' pay rises and falls with profits, the economy becomes more flexible. Recessions cause wages to drop, and falling wages stimulate aggregate supply.

The notion of profit sharing is not new, but it has gained increasing attention in capitalist economies because of the wide-scale use of profit sharing in postwar Japan.[3] In Japan, worker bonuses average about one-quarter of annual earnings, and they are paid out of profits. Although the relationship between profits and worker bonuses is not clear-cut,

Japanese workers certainly benefit from higher profits in the form of higher year-end bonuses.[4]

It remains to be seen whether other capitalist countries will follow the Japanese in the use of wide-scale profit sharing. Various companies in different capitalist countries do use profit sharing, but it has yet to be practiced on the same scale as in Japan.

Sharing profits with employees is one method of increasing worker interest in the outcome of the enterprise. Another approach — used in West Germany and Scandinavia — is worker participation in management decisions. In the German system of worker participation, described in Chapter 13, the actual workings of the process in the German economy remain to be determined. Will other capitalist countries move toward increased worker participation? In the United States, the path has been somewhat different. Unions have invested worker pension funds in companies — primarily companies that are ailing and need additional capital. Unions also have traded equity shares in troubled companies for labor concessions. In this manner, workers have gained representation on management boards.

Macroeconomic Management

One of the most clear-cut changes in the capitalist economic system has been this general acceptance of the notion that government is responsible for macroeconomic stability. This acceptance — also known as the Keynesian revolution — occurred in the United States in the early 1960s and in Western Europe by the mid-1960s. Although capitalist governments use different tools to stabilize the economy, there is agreement that the government is responsible for providing a reasonable level of macroeconomic performance. Countries rely on both government budgets and central banks to provide macroeconomic stability. The United States uses both monetary and fiscal policy to stabilize the economy. All capitalist countries have put in place a series of automatic stabilizers (unemployment compensation, a progressive income tax, and the like) to moderate cyclical fluctuations.

Although the reasons are unclear, capitalist countries have experienced greater macroeconomic stability in the second half of the twentieth century (despite two energy shocks in the 1970s) than in the first half of the twentieth century or in the nineteenth century. Business cycles have become less severe.

In sum, it is evident that there is continuing change in market capitalist economic systems, although the characterization of this change, as we will see, is different from that in planned socialist economic systems.

REFORMING THE PLANNED
SOCIALIST ECONOMY

Planned socialist systems have been interested in economic reform for at least thirty years. This interest has centered in the Soviet Union and Eastern Europe as well as in China. Most recently, Mikhail Gorbachev has introduced new economic programs in the Soviet Union.

We focus on four major issues of socialist reform: First, why socialist economic reform is of great importance in today's world; second, the nature of reform alternatives available to leaders of socialist economic systems; third, what problems arise and in what ways they can be overcome; finally, types of real-world economic reform in socialist countries and the future prospects for reform of these systems.

Why Economic Reform?

Reform in socialist systems differs from its counterpart in capitalist systems. We generally assume that change in capitalist systems is continuous, gradual, and decentralized, while change in planned socialist systems is discontinuous, sudden, and centralized. In socialist systems, there are formally announced reform programs, typically authorized at the highest levels, whose implementation can be watched and judged. While this contrast may be simplistic, it is nevertheless true that socialist systems have announced and have attempted to implement major programs of change at high levels.

Why Socialist Reform?

Although economic reform is of great theoretical interest insofar as it says something about the nature and feasibility of socialism as a mechanism of resource allocation, contemporary socialist reform programs are generally driven by much more pragmatic issues. The predominant force promoting economic reform in the Soviet Union and Eastern Europe has been concern about economic performance. Simply put, most indicators of economic performance reveal that the Soviet and East European systems have slipped significantly in recent years. Specifically, rates of growth of output have declined steadily between the late 1950s and the early and mid-1980s. For countries whose hallmark has been rapid economic growth, such a trend has important implications. Without improvements in productivity, the growth of consumer well-being must lag.

While many reasons have been advanced to explain the general slackening of economic performance, it would seem that the planned socialist economies have found the transformation from extensive to intensive growth very difficult. The basic Stalinist model, while draconian and possibly too costly, nevertheless served to bring idle and underused resources into the production process. However, the luxury of idle resources is, for many socialist systems, over. Thus economic growth and the expansion of consumer well-being must come from improved productivity or what socialist systems describe as **intensification**.

We do not know exactly why intensification in socialist systems has proven difficult. Clearly there are consumer pressures in these systems, and clearly they have grown more complex over time. In this sense, advances in planning methods have probably not kept pace with the demands on the planning system. But, most important, the diffusion of technology in these systems has been inadequate. These systems are not demand driven, and enterprise rules generally do not stimulate productivity growth and cost reduction. Efficiency has simply not been a hallmark of the classic Stalinist command economy.

Interest in socialist reform began in the 1960s and grew in the 1980s. By the mid-1980s, performance in most socialist systems had slipped to the point where demand simply could not be met. With inadequate incentives, there appeared to be little hope for improved productivity. Moreover, most socialist countries have not been able to compete sufficiently well in export markets to afford significant imports of consumer products. Seen in this perspective, the imperative of reform is evident.

MODELS OF ECONOMIC
REFORM OF SOCIALISM

Although there is now a large literature on economic reform in planned socialist systems, there is no general agreement on reform models. Put another way, there are no simple blueprints, a fact which greatly complicates the life of reformers. We can, however, sketch out the broad alternatives available: first, making planning work better; second, organizational reform; and third, decentralization. Let us consider each alternative.[5]

Improving the Planning Mechanism

Many Western observers consider the option of improving planning to be a weak alternative, one that signals unwillingness to make serious changes in the economic system. The arguments in support of this alternative are that problems of economic performance arise largely because planning has not been perfected, and that basic planning can be improved through the application of more sophisticated computer technology. For example, to the extent that enterprise managers make bad decisions due to lack of information, ready access to accurate information through an advanced computer network would alleviate the problem. Better planning methods, better information channels, and attention to incentive compatibility, it is believed, can perfect the planning system and improve economic performance.

Organizational Reform

Changing the organizational arrangements of the existing plan structure represents a second reform alternative. A typical organizational reform is the introduction of intermediate organizations into the organizational hierarchy. Ministries, it is argued, are too distant from the enterprises they supervise. Moreover, each ministry supervises enterprises that produce too wide and diverse an array of products. Ministries cannot keep in touch with enterprise behavior and do not truly understand the problems peculiar to the particular enterprises they oversee. Thus an intermediate agency or association should be placed between the ministries and groups of enterprises producing a similar product. The intermediate association, it is argued, could understand and manage a particular group of firms more successfully.

Another example of organizational reform would be to shift the emphasis from sectoral to regional planning. An economy planned on a sectoral basis may place the interests of the branch over national interests. A shift to regional planning might loosen the grip of an entrenched bureaucracy and encourage a better flow of information among units in the economy.

On balance, organizational reform does not change the essence of planning, but rather promotes changes in the structure of the planning framework.

Decentralization

Decentralization, our third broad category of socialist economic reform, is difficult to characterize precisely. In general terms, decentralization is a shifting of decision-making authority and responsibility from upper to lower levels. Decentralization is often viewed as "real" reform that can fundamentally change the nature of economic systems and, especially, reduce the role of central planning.

Decentralization implies that decisions about resource allocation will be shifted downward in the economic hierarchy. Most important, in a decentralized economy decisions are not made by planners, but at lower levels, using what are frequently characterized as **economic levers** — prices, profits, rates of return, and the like.

The characterization of decentralization as "real" economic reform makes sense. With true decentralization, planners do have less power, and people at local levels use economic criteria in decision making. The similarity of this type of reform to the market process is evident. Decentralization is frequently characterized as a movement away from planning toward the *market* as the fundamental allocative device. Finally, we should bear in mind that in the real world we might well expect to find significant variations and combinations of the three reform alternatives we have presented.

The Problems of Reform Implementation

Once a socialist economy selects its reform approach or package, it might encounter difficulties of implementation. A first basic difficulty is that change in any system is generally resisted, at least by some participants. It is wrong to believe that even where political power is relatively centralized, change can be brought about smoothly. In most planned socialist systems, there are many managers, administrators, and bureaucrats who have achieved success in the system. These participants seldom accept change easily. Moreover they are in a position to inhibit change when it does not conform to their interests.

Second, while the three reform alternatives may seem rather simple and attractive, there is no textbook model of socialist economic reform. Even with political will and participant support, the alternatives are not well-defined. There are no clear paths to follow. Moreover, opponents of the reform can legitimately point to the risks of failure.

Third, the timing of economic reform presents many complexities. For example, if the role of economic levers is to be enhanced, does price reform come first? What about the rules of enterprise behavior? Sequential implementation of reform has proven difficult in practice, and yet it would seem almost impossible to make all necessary changes simultaneously.

Fourth, we in the West have a tendency to view the hesitancy of reform as synonymous with the hesitancy of the political process. There are, however, fundamental economic difficulties associated with economic reform. For example, consider the case of pricing and price policies. Economists would generally agree that if prices (one of the most important economic levers) are to be used in meaningful ways, the prices must themselves be meaningful. Specifically, prices must represent rates of transformation in production and rates of tradeoff in consumption, or put another way, relative scarcities. Currently, prices in planned socialist systems have little meaning in this sense. Moreover, even if the political pressure to establish prices consistent with Marxian economic theory (whatever this means in practice) can be overcome, it is virtually impossible to introduce "rational" prices in a system where price-setting models are unavailable and markets don't exist. Although we choose price setting as an example of a serious and significant economic problem of reform programs, we shall see that much real-world reform discussion centers on this particular issue.

Fifth, even where economic reform can be introduced in a meaningful way to alleviate economic problems, it is not always clear that other problems won't arise. For example, even if planned socialist systems are amendable to a reduction of the planning power in the system, they do remain socialist systems. Socialist goals differ from those generally found in market capitalist systems. Take, for example, the case of income distribution. Clearly, income distribution is intended to be much more egalitarian under socialism than capitalism. If the economic levers were to include significant wage, and hence income, differences, in order to induce appropriate participation, could the socialist ideal be maintained? Can housing be allocated administratively if the quality of the housing stock is to be improved, and if the housing sector is to be run efficiently to "pay its way"? There are no simple answers to these sorts of questions. Many observers argue that decentralization toward the market mechanism will not always be consistent with socialist economic objectives. Put another way, it is not clear that equity, as it would be defined under socialism, is consistent with efficiency, as it would be derived from market forces.

To better understand the reform experience, let us look at reform in the socialist countries studied in this book. This will provide not only a fuller understanding of these countries, but also real-world examples of many of the issues raised above.

Economic Reform in the Soviet Union[6]

Economic reform in the Soviet Union is important because of the Soviet Union's dominant economic and political role in Eastern Europe. A successful reform that improves Soviet economic performance would have a striking effect on world affairs. Moreover, other planned socialist countries tend to take their lead from the Soviet Union; Soviet reform is often emulated elsewhere in Eastern Europe.

Soviet authorities have shown interest in economic reform since the mid-1950s. In fact, scarcely a year has passed without the announcement of some reform or experiment intended to improve economic performance. The last major economy-wide reform was introduced in 1965, after a three-year discussion of reform alternatives. The 1965 reform aimed at increasing enterprise autonomy, reducing the micromanagement of enterprises by higher authorities, creating profit-based incentive funds, raising interest in marketability of goods, and allowing some decentralized investment. This reform withered during its transition stage and largely disappeared from view in the early 1970s.

The various reforms and experiments have yet to unlock the key to improving Soviet economic performance. The declining pattern of Soviet economic performance in the 1970s and 1980s has placed increasing pressure on Soviet leadership to find new solutions. Particularly troublesome has been the inability of the Soviet economy to shift from extensive to intensive growth. The 1980s have seen years in which output per unit of factor input has actually declined. In an economy no longer able to count on rapid expansion of labor and capital inputs, growth must become intensive if it is to remain positive. Although there have been numerous changes in Soviet organizational arrangements in the 1970s and 1980s, it is only recently that the issue of major reform has once again arisen.

In the early 1980s, the Soviet leadership struggle was resolved by the rise to power of a young and vigorous general secretary of the Communist party, Mikhail Gorbachev. For the first time in more than fifteen years, the Soviet Union had a leader who was in a position to implement a long-term reform strategy. The first phase of Gorbachev's reform program, which lasted from 1985 to 1987, was a discussion of various reform alternatives. The initial reform package was settled on by the Soviet leadership in 1987 and 1988. The period 1988–1990 is envisioned as the time of transition to the new system. The 1990s is to be the decade in which the Soviet economy reaps the benefits of the economic reform.

Perestroika Provisions

The Soviets call their reform **perestroika,** or restructuring. It is designed to alter the way the Soviet economy allocates resources. The principal features of perestroika are described below.

1. Perestroika calls for an increase in enterprise autonomy. A significant portion of enterprise operations will be freed from centralized controls and allowed to make more of their own input and output decisions, set their own prices in agreements among enterprises, and use more of their profits for the benefit of the enterprise and enterprise staff. The participation of enterprise workers in enterprise decision making will increase, and workers are to have a hand in selecting the enterprise management team. In return for this increased autonomy, enterprises will be held responsible for final results. If enterprises are unable to earn a

profit (or worse, not able to cover their costs), they will not receive automatic subsidies to keep them in business. Rather, enterprises will enjoy the benefits and suffer the costs of full economic accounting, even if they have to lay off workers.

2. The responsibilities of planning authorities and industrial ministries will be fundamentally altered. Instead of planning and managing the routine operations of lower-level units, the planning apparatus will concern itself with long-term planning, technology policy, and investment policy. Ministries are to cease micromanagement of enterprises and concern themselves with coordinating activities among ministries and with technology policy. The long-term five-year plan is to become the operational plan of the economy.

3. Soviet planning authorities will continue to control directly certain priority economic activities. State planners will issue **state orders** directly to enterprises for key industrial products. Perestroika calls for the share of state orders to decline over time to give enterprises more and more autonomy, but at least initially some obligatory targets will continue. Except for state orders, planning authorities will exercise control over enterprises through indirect means. Planners will set long-term input-usage norms, norms for price setting, and norms for decentralized investments. These norms will establish the rules under which decentralized enterprises are supposed to function. Perestroika calls for these norms to be set for a five-year period. Norms will not be altered in light of successful enterprise performance to place more pressure on the successful enterprise.

4. The quality of ouptut of Soviet enterprises is to be improved by the creation of an independent inspection agency that will certify the quality of goods. In addition, fulfillment of enterprise supply plans (which are the result of negotiations among enterprises) will become a more important indicator of enterprise performance.

5. The perestroika reform opens the way for more semiprivate and private economic activity. Most small-scale service activities (not involving the use of hired labor) are to be legalized, and an income tax on private incomes has been put in place to recover a portion of private earnings for the state. Moreover, persons are allowed to enter into cooperative enterprises and to run these cooperatives for the benefit of their members. Persons holding jobs in the state sector have the right to enter into cooperatives as long as this remains a sideline activity. Pensioners and others not obligated to work in the state sector are permitted to work full time for the cooperative.

6. The perestroika reform proposes to tackle the perceived rise in worker indifference. Granting workers participatory rights within their enterprises is supposed to raise worker productivity. Moreover, by making the enterprise staff responsible for the final results of the enterprise, there will be increasing differentiation both within the enterprise and among enterprises. Allowing more open public discussion of social and economic problems (called **glasnost**, or openness) is supposed to increase worker support and enthusiasm for reform. Public enthusiasm for reform is viewed as an important counterweight to the anticipated resistance to reform by the entrenched bureaucracy.

Prospects for Perestroika

The fate of perestroika will probably not be known until the early 1990s. Much depends on the composition of the Soviet leadership and on economic performance during the transition period. A number of problems and obstacles can, however, be anticipated. How the reform leadership deals with these problems will have a large impact on perestroika's fate.

1. Perestroika calls for a mixture of centralized planning and enterprise autonomy in a framework of stable rules and norms set by the planning apparatus. It is unclear whether enterprises will make correct decisions in this mixed setting. Although perestroika calls for price reform and for the increased use of negotiated prices, Soviet reformers intend for the initial phase of perestroika to be carried out without a major price reform. Moreover, the price reform they envision is one in which planners calculate millions of prices based on costs of production. Such a price reform, we are told, will require several years of calculation. Thus enterprises will be told to make decentralized decisions in an economy in which prices still do not reflect relative scarcities. It is also unclear how negotiated prices will work. In a seller's market, suppliers will possess considerable monopoly power and will likely try to extract monopoly profits. Presumably, the pricing rules set by planning authorities will deal with this problem, but it is unclear how enterprises will be able to negotiate prices when negotiated prices and rules clash.

2. How Soviet reformers deal with bureaucratic resistance will also determine the fate of perestroika. The key bureaucratic institution is the ministry which has to date exercised detailed control over ministerial enterprises. Soviet ministries exercise petty tutelage over their enterprises because they traditionally have been held responsible for the output results of their enterprises.

An essential element of Soviet planning has been that ministries do the actual detailed planning and resource distribution for the economy. Soviet reformers have not yet worked out the new role of the ministry. As long as ministries are held responsible for final results, they have every incentive to resist reform and to continue to intervene in enterprise operations. The resistance of regional party authorities is also expected for much the same reason. As long as regional party authorities continue to be held responsible for the economic results of their region, they will resist reform. It is felt that regional party authorities will resist the laying off of workers in enterprises that fail the full-accounting test.

3. The Soviet planning system has been based upon the principle of balances. Planning authorities have administratively determined balances of key materials, labor, money, and investment resources. The perestroika system requires that fewer resources be balanced by administrative means and more by decentralized decisions. Without a price system that reflects relative scarcities, it is unclear whether balances can indeed be achieved. As imbalances emerge, it may be difficult for planning authorities to resist reintroducing administrative balances.

Perspectives

The Soviet perestroika reform involves all three basic socialist reform alternatives — improved planning, organizational changes, and decentralization. Planning is to be improved by shifting its focus to long-term matters such as technology policy, and similar concerns; instead of handing down directives, planners are to create rules and norms. Organizational reforms include combining ministries into superministries to insure that they deal with long-term issues that transcend narrow sectoral boundaries. However, the main focus of perestroika is on the third alternative — decentralization. Enterprises are to have more decision-making authority and to be responsible for the results of their decisions. Many of the decentralization ideas of perestroika were attempted more than twenty years ago in the 1965 reform. They failed then, and they might fail again. The major differences between 1965 and 1988 are the more serious economic difficulties of the Soviet economy and the apparently greater resolve of the Soviet leadership to enact meaningful reform.

Economic Reform in Hungary[7]

As we noted in our discussion of the Hungarian economy, the NEM, or New Economic Mechanism, is the major story of contemporary Hungary. The introduction of NEM in Hungary involved liberalization in a small, resource-poor country that is heavily dependent on foreign trade and influenced by world market forces. Although the NEM retains the essential features of a socialist system (in particular, public ownership of the means of production), there has been an ongoing, albeit uneven attempt to relax the control of the planners and to replace that control with economic levers. These levers imply the presence of market forces such that prices and profits can guide enterprise decision making in a setting where effort and increases in productivity can be rewarded.

There is no need to repeat our earlier discussion of the Hungarian economy. However, as we emphasized, the 1970s was not a good decade for the NEM. Indeed, it was a decade of retrenchment, though not abandonment, of the reform program. This retrenchement was substantially political, though it was driven in part by economic difficulties. Possibly most important, the micro-organization of Hungarian industry does not provide a market environment. Moreover, external factors detrimental to the Hungarian economy were difficult to overcome in the face of growing pressure for better economic performance. Administrative interference in the economy increased during this period.

During the late 1970s, a number of steps toward further implementation of reform were outlined, to be carried out in the early 1980s. Although these changes were generally implemented, it is ironic that the continuation of reform had to take place under adverse conditions, especially domestic austerity measures designed to handle a continuing hard-currency debt problem caused in part by world market conditions and the lack of competitiveness of Hungarian products in hard-currency markets.

A major focus of the 1980s has been the industrial structure in Hungary. During the early 1980s, a number of large trusts were broken up, while regulations pertaining to new enterprises and private sector activity were relaxed. This effort focused on the need for a more competitive structure. A similar decentralization of foreign trade decisions (domestic firms having direct access to foreign trade) took place in the early 1980s.

In addition to reforming its industrial structure, Hungary has attempted to reduce the importance of the ministerial apparatus. These changes, along with imporant changes of a financial nature, have significantly altered the nature of the economic system. In addition to the introduction of a limited financial market (a form of financial intermediary to provide access to capital), a bond market was authorized in 1983, though it is subject to state control.

Both price and wage reforms have been introduced along with changes in the rules pertaining to enterprise income, specifically the determination and utilization of profits. The purpose of these changes has been to improve the economic regulators while at the same time meeting the needs of austerity in the 1980s.

It is evident that, like other socialist systems undergoing economic reform, Hungary faced major problems as a result of the external shocks of the 1970s that slowed the progress of reform. In the Hungarian case, the overall focus of reform has been the desire to achieve microeconomic efficiency, macroeconomic balance, and a continuing state presence in suggesting the directions of resource allocation. Although the pressure for improved economic performance has been great, there are in Hungary, as elsewhere, forces opposing reform, including elements of the bureaucracy, fear of market evils such as inflation and unemployment, and finally, the potential impact of external forces. In light of the achievements thus far, where might we find the Hungarian reform process at the end of the 1980s?

Since the mid-1980s, developments might suggest that austerity has won over economic reform, though only time will tell if such is the case. Economic growth has been modest, though the austerity program has improved Hungary's hard-currency balance. However, in September 1987 a consolidation program designed to create short-run stability with long-term market orientation was introduced. Through the early 1990s, there is to be a consolidation of the reform with emphasis on exports and less emphasis on domestic consumption. In addition to the introduction of temporary price controls, both an income tax and a value added tax have been introduced, and price subsidies have been decreased. However, the reform is to proceed with greater emphasis on monetary methods of management, new forms of ownership, and greater freedom of enterprise decision making combined with enforcement of bankruptcy.

Finally, there is an important new political element in the Hungarian case. The replacement of Janos Kadar with Karoly Grosz, a younger leader who is generally thought to be reform-oriented, may well signal greater continuity of enthusiasm for the reform process.

In some respects, the Hungarian case is a classic example of socialist reform. Although Hungary is a small, trade-reliant country, it nevertheless exemplifies the difficulty of combining the microeconomic efficiency of the market (where a market does not really exist) with macroeconomic stability and growth in combination with longstanding socialist economic objectives. It remains to be seen whether these multiple objectives are in fact compatible.

Reform In China[8]

Reform in the Chinese economy is of interest because China is a very large country relatively rich in natural resources, although it is poor in terms of traditional indicators such as per capita gross national product. Moreover, unlike the Soviet Union during the past several decades,

China has experienced considerable political upheaval, most recently the Cultural Revolution. Thus in China we find significant shifts of the development path and limited economic growth and development. Possibly most important, productivity growth has been at best very limited. Finally, the reform process has been market oriented, involving foreign trade in a major way and, moving toward a relaxation of central control and central planning toward decentralization of decision making and the expansion of local incentives for local decisions. Thus we find in the Chinese case market reform in a large and poor socialist country, under conditions dramatically different from those in Eastern Europe.

Economic reform as we think of it in this chapter began in China after 1978. The initial focus was agriculture and thereafter the industrial and urban economy. In both cases, many would agree that the reform has produced significant performance gains, though the gains in agriculture have generally exceeded those in industry, and recent problems in both sectors have raised questions about the viability of the reform process as we enter the 1990s.

The thrust of agricultural reform has been the replacement of the commune with the contract responsibility system. Since the late 1970s, families contract with local authorities for the sale of agricultural products. Indeed, since the mid-1980s, except in selected cases, no state quotas are established. In addition to this relaxation of local decision making procedures, purchase prices were increased significantly. The net result has been, as we noted earlier, sharp increases in agricultural output at an average annual rate exceeding 12 percent through the mid-1980s.

Although industrial reform began slowly in the late 1970s, it was not until 1984 that there was a major shift of emphasis toward industrial and urban reform. In industry, the reform also moved toward decentralization — placing more decision-making authority and responsibility in the hands of individual enterprises. Possibly most important, great emphasis has been placed on the issue of appropriate incentives, in particular the notion that once basic obligations have been met, rewards will be available for distribution within the enterprise. In part the enterprise will have greater control over investment, and bonus rewards from profits tied to productivity improvement would be of major importance. In addition, enterprises were granted greater freedom in the choice of inputs including labor, although capital allocation remains a problem.

As has been the case in agriculture, prices for industrial goods have been increased. For industrial products, a three-tier price system has prevailed, with state-set prices, negotiated prices, and free-market prices. Over time, the importance of state control over output decisions and distribution has decreased. At the same time, there has been significant growth of private economic activity, although such activity is primarily in the service sector.

In addition to reforming its domestic economy, China has also taken major steps to open its economy to world trade. In addition to changing organizational arrangements in the planning of foreign trade, a substantial effort has been made through both joint ventures and foreign investment to attract foreign technology. Besides the creation of special economic zones, flexibility has also been evident in the area of ownership, though in fact the Chinese generally hold a controlling interest in joint ventures.

Although economic reform has generated significant achievements for the performance of the Chinese economy, it has also generated problems. Indeed the prevailing tendency in the mid- and late 1980s has been to question the reform, or, more precisely, the tempo of the reform. As we approach the 1990s, there is concern that problems associated with the reform will limit continuation of the reform process. What are the major problems and how can they be handled?

First, given the vast size and complexity of the Chinese economy, it would be naive to believe that the sort of market-oriented decentralization that we have outlined could be implemented with any ease. For example, there has always been a considerable amount of planning authority at regional and local levels. In this context, decentralization has proven difficult: local interests tend to prevail over larger interests, material supplies are unavailable or inadequate, larger projects requiring significant investment are neglected, and so forth. In a sense, there has been an attempt to decentralize decision-making authority through an infrastructure which, in large part, does not exist. The result has been imbalances in many dimensions of the Chinese economy.

Second, while performance has been good in agriculture, healthy increases in the output of the industrial sector have been achieved largely through increased inputs rather than through increased efficiency. To the extent that the growth of inputs has resulted from increased rewards, a number of unattractive consequences have arisen. Inflation has become a serious problem, with growth of incomes exceeding growth in supply of consumer goods. Input shortages have resulted in price increases. In 1984, a tax was introduced for those enterprises paying bonuses above a certain specified level.

The growth of capital investment has generally proceeded at a pace greater than the ability of the economy to absorb this investment. Beyond the misallocation of investment in a variety of dimensions, the financing of investment through central interference with local decisions and deficit spending have worsened the process in the absence of real capital markets.

Third, income inequality has increased significantly in rural areas, though overall, the degree of inequality has decreased due to reductions in the rural-urban income gap. The issue of growing inequality, especially in a socialist system and in combination with growing social problems, such as crime, may well serve as a brake on the pace of reform in the future.

Fourth, although steps were taken in the mid-1980s to control China's trade imbalance, it is clear that the growth of imports exceeded the growth of exports to a degree that could not be sustained. At the same time, even in the face of relaxed rules for foreign involvement in the Chinese economy, the extent of serious foreign commitment remains limited.

What lessons can we learn from these problems? Will they limit the continuation of economic reform in China?

It is quite clear that in the mid- and late 1980s some retrenchment (especially after 1986) has taken place, although the reform process continues. The Chinese experience points up many of the basic problems of socialist reform such as the lack of a blueprint, the problem of the pace of reform, and the continual interference of external (world market) forces.

Economic Reform in Yugoslavia[9]

In the literature on socialist economic reform, the Yugoslav system of worker management has received widespread attention. Yugoslavia, like the other socialist countries we have analyzed, has its unique setting and problems. But these factors aside, Yugoslavia is the most important case of market socialism because of its local decision-making arrangements and its program of devolution of authority from central to regional and local levels.

The contemporary state of Yugoslav economic reform could be assessed in a context similar to what we used for examination of the Hungarian case, in spite of important differences. In Yugoslavia, reform has proceeded along a path of uneven implementation; it has frequently been retarded by familiar forces. Although the Kraigher Commission (Commission for the Problems of Economic Stabilization) reexamined reform in the early 1980s and suggested a variety of new paths for future development, few seem to have been implemented.

Since the mid-1980s, Yugoslav economic performance has not been good. Although there has been improvement in the export/import scenario, output growth has been limited, inflation has been rapid, and unemployment persists. Thus, in spite of price controls introduced in late 1987, retail prices have risen rapidly. In 1986 foreign exchange regulations were relaxed and new rules introduced to make foreign investment in Yugoslavia more attractive. The depreciation of the dinar has been continual since 1980, when one dollar equaled 24.6 dinars, to 1986 when one dollar equaled 379.22 dinars.

The immediate problems of economic performance, in particular reactions to external conditions, will most likely be the main focus of Yugoslav economic policy for the remainder of the 1980s. If this is the case, fundamental issues of economic reform will take a back seat. These fundamental issues include Yugoslavia's willingness to tolerate the outcome of market forces in a socialist context, and if it is willing, what steps it will take to create genuine market forces. The issue of decentralization of decision making has been and will remain closely tied to reform of the Communist party structure, especially at the local level. Moreover, great emphasis will have to be placed on the creation of genuine market forces at the local level to improve microeconomic efficiency and hence the allocation of resources, for example, in the sphere of capital allocation. As we have seen in the case of Hungary, it is difficult to pursue reform in the place of austerity measures designed to come to grips with past policy problems and remaining external shocks. Such a scenario will most likely dominate the Yugoslav scene for the balance of this decade.

SUMMARY: ECONOMIC REFORM UNDER CAPITALISM AND SOCIALISM

1. The share of public ownership of the factors of production appears not to have changed significantly in the industrialized capitalist countries in the past twenty-five years.

2. Although capitalist tax systems have not significantly altered the distribution of material rewards in the various economies, the rise in the share of social security taxes suggests that the distribution of benefits to low-income people may have changed the overall distribution of income.

3. Profit sharing alters the role of the worker in capitalist economic systems. Interest in profit sharing relates to the apparent successful use of this technique by the Japanese. Other capitalist economies have experimented with worker participation in management decisions.

4. Capitalist economies have generally accepted the notion that government is responsible for providing macroeconomic stability.

5. The socialist reform cases fall reasonably within the framework developed in this chapter. The Soviet Union has been a case of very limited reform in the past. Where reform has been attempted, it has focused largely upon improvements in the planning system without any really fundamental changes in the economy. Hungary is in a sense a classic example of an attempt to decentralize through market forces while retaining a degree of central control and adherence to basic socialist economic principles. Reforms in China have also followed a path of decen-

tralization under market influence, though conditions peculiar to the Chinese case (for example, the size of the country and the level of development of China) have created unique problems of implementation. Finally Yugoslavia is a classic and in some respects a unique case due to its system of decentralization under worker management.

6. It is evident from the cases we have considered that the peculiarities of each are important, though to what degree and in precisely what dimensions is less clear. For example, the size and diversity of the Chinese economy adds a particular dimension to reform there. At the same time, even in a very small country like Yugoslavia, regional difference is very important.

7. No formal process of socialist economic reform has yet been developed. Although in many cases reform in agriculture preceded industrial reform, this may not reflect any logically developed reform sequence. Indeed, a major issue of debate among Western observers of socialist economic reform is the matter of partial versus full implementation. Can decentralization of decision making really take place to any degree before price reform? And how does the latter question relate to the complex issue of market forces?

8. There is little agreement on the effectiveness of economic reform, in part because it has tended to be, in the real world, a stop-and-go process. Thus the nature and pace of implementation of economic reform in the planned socialist systems has been driven by a wide variety of forces which vary significantly from case to case. While political forces are fundamental, external shocks have clearly been of greater importance to Hungary than, say, to the Soviet Union.

9. Can the reform experience be generalized? If so, no consensus really exists. Those countries which have tried reform over a long period of time may generate experience useful for the newcomers. But, in light of the significant differences from case to case, the transfer of reform knowledge has probably not been great.

10. In the end, Western observers tend to be very skeptical about the long-run potential for reform of planned socialist economic systems. For the reasons noted the prevailing view is that it will be extremely difficult for mixed systems, understood as reformed planned socialist systems, to achieve the efficiency of the market while retaining central control over the achievement of social objectives — especially basic socialist objectives such as egalitarian distribution of income and widespread development of public goods — without such market evils as inflation and unemployment.

NOTES

1. William G. Shepherd, "Causes of Increased Competition in the U.S. Economy, 1939-1980," *Review of Economics and Statistics* (November 1982), pp. 613-626.
2. Edgar K. Browning, "The Trend Toward Equality in the Distribution of Net Income," *Southern Economic Journal*, vol. 43, no. 1 (July 1976), p. 914.
3. The theoretical foundation for the profit-sharing capitalist economy is provided by Martin L. Weitzman, *The Share Economy* (Cambridge, Mass.: Harvard University Press, 1984); and Martin L. Weitzman, "The Simple Macroeconomics of Profit Sharing," *American Economic Review*, vol. 75, no. 5 (December 1985), pp. 937-953.
4. For analysis of Japanese profit sharing, see Merton J. Peck, "Is Japan Really a Share Economy?" *Journal of Comparative Economics*, vol. 10, no. 4 (December 1986), pp. 427-432.
5. For a useful discussion of varying approaches to socialist reform, see Paul Hare, "Economic Reform in Eastern Europe," *Journal of Economic Surveys*, 1, 1 (1987), pp. 25-58.
6. This discussion is based on sources in Recommended Readings, Soviet Union.
7. This discussion is based on sources in Recommended Readings, Hungary.
8. This discussion is based on sources in Recommended Readings, China.
9. This discussion is based on sources in Recommended Readings, Yugoslavia.

RECOMMENDED READINGS

SOVIET UNION

Timothy J. Colton, "Approaches to the Politics of Economic Reform in the Soviet Union," *Soviet Economy*, vol. 3, no. 2 (1987), pp. 145-170.

——, *The Dilemma of Reform in The Soviet Union*, revised and expanded ed., (New York: Council on Foreign Relations, 1986).

Edward A. Hewett, *Reforming the Soviet Economy: Equality versus Efficiency* (Washington, D.C.: The Brookings Institution, 1987).

Edward A. Hewett and Victor H. Winston, eds., "The First Joint Soviet Economy Roundtable," *Soviet Economy*, vol. 3, no. 4 (October-December 1987).

Maurice Friedberg and Heyward Isham, eds., *Soviet Society Under Gorbachev* (Armonk, N.Y.: M. E. Sharpe, 1987).

Marshall I. Goldman, *Gorbachev's Challenge* (New York: W. W. Norton, 1987).

Mikhail Gorbachev, *Perestroika: New Thinking for Our Country and the World* (New York: Harper and Row, 1987).

Susan J. Linz, ed., "A Symposium on Reorganization and Reform in the Soviet Economy," *Comparative Economic Studies*, vol. 29, no. 4 (Winter 1987).

Susan J. Linz and William Moskoff, eds., *Reorganization and Reform in the Soviet Economy* (Armonk, N.Y.: M. E. Sharpe, 1988).

Blair Ruble, "The Social Dimensions of Perestroyka," *Soviet Economy*, vol. 3, no. 2 (1987), pp. 171-183.

HUNGARY

Bela Balassa, "Reforming the New Economic Mechanism in Hungary," *Journal of Comparative Economics*, vol. 7, no. 3 (September 1983), pp. 253-276.

Thomas Bauer, "The Hungarian Alternative to Soviet-Type Planning," *Journal of Comparative Economics* (September 1983), pp. 304–316.

John B. Hall, "Hungary's 'Third' Model," *Economics of Planning*, vol. 20, no. 2 (1986), pp. 131–136.

"Hungary: The Third Wave of Reforms," *Journal of Comparative Economics*, special ed., vol. 7, no. 3 (September 1983).

Janos Kornai, "The Hungarian Reform Process," *Journal of Economic Literature*, vol. 24, no. 4 (December 1986), pp. 1687–1737.

Paul Marer, "Economic Reform in Hungary: From Central Planning to Regulated Market," in U.S., Congress, Joint Economic Committee, *East European Economies: Slow Growth in the 1980's*, vol. 3 (Washington, D.C.: Government Printing Office, 1986), pp. 223–297.

Ivan Schweitzer, "Some Interrelations Between Enterprise Organization and The Economic Mechanism," *Acta Oeconomica*, vol. 27, no. 3-4 (1981), pp. 289–300.

CHINA

Chu-yuan Cheng, "China's Economy at the Crossroads," *Current History*, vol. 86, no. 521 (September 1987).

Kuan-I Chen, "China's Food Policy and Population," *Current History*, vol. 86, no. 521 (September 1987).

Harry Harding, *China's Second Revolution: Reform After Mao* (Washington, D.C.: The Brookings Institution, 1987).

Yak-Yeow Kueh, "China's New Agricultural-Policy Program: Major Economic Consequences, 1979–1983," *Journal of Comparative Economics*, vol. 8, no. 4 (December 1984), pp. 353–375.

Thomas P. Lyons, *Economic Planning and Integration in Maoist China* (New York: Columbia University Press, 1987).

J. E. D. McDonnell, "China's Move to Rejoin the GATT System: An Epic Transition," *The World Economy*, vol. 10, no. 3 (September 1987), pp. 331–350.

Elizabeth J. Perry and Christine Wong, *The Political Economy of Reform in Post-Mao China* (Cambridge: Harvard University Press, 1987).

Bruce L. Reynolds, ed., "Chinese Economic Reform: How Far, How Fast?" *Journal of Comparative Economics*, special ed., vol. 11, no. 3 (September 1987).

Gordon White, "The Politics of Economic Reform in Chinese Industry: The Introduction of the Labour Contract System," *The China Quarterly*, 11 (September 1987), pp. 365–389.

Christine P. W. Wong, "The Economics of Shortage and Problems of Reform in Chinese Industry," *Journal of Comparative Economics*, vol. 10, no. 4 (December 1986), pp. 363–387.

The World Bank, *China: Long Term Development, Issues and Options* (Washington, D.C.: The World Bank, 1985).

YUGOSLAVIA

Deborah A. Bateman, Mieko Nishimizu, and John M. Page, Jr., "Regional Productivity Differentials and Development Policy in Yugoslavia, 1965–1978," *Journal of Comparative Economics*, vol. 12, no. 1 (March 1988), pp. 24–42.

John P. Burkett, "Stabilization Measures in Yugoslavia: An Assessment of the Proposals of Yugoslavia's Commission for Problems of Economic Stabilization," U.S., Congress, Joint Economic Commiteee, *East Euroepan Economies: Slow Growth in the 1980's*, vol. 3 (Washington, D.C.: Government Printing Office, 1986), pp. 561-574.

Diane Flaherty, "Plan, Market and Unequal Regional Development in Yugoslavia," *Soviet Studies*, vol. 40, no. 1 (January 1988), pp. 100-124.

Jim Seroka, "The Interdependence of Institutional Revitalisation and Intra-Party Reform in Yugoslavia," *Soviet Studies*, vol. 40, no. 1 (January 1988), pp. 84-99.

Chapter 15
Comparing Economic Systems:
Trends and Prospects

A SUMMATION OF THEMES

No two economic systems are identical, despite similarities of structure and performance. The difficulty of making comparisons does not make it any less important to try to do so, nor does it decrease the need to understand capitalism and socialism.

We have attempted to systematize comparative economic systems to provide an understanding of how the economic system influences economic outcomes. The subject is much too broad and diverse for a simple summary. Moreover, the field is undergoing such change that any summary might well be dated within a short period. We shall focus on several themes, which place our deliberations in perspective.

Three closely related questions have been asked in this book. First, what is an economic system: how can it be characterized and how can its real-world variants be isolated and identified? Second, what is the relationship between an economic system and economic outcomes? More specifically, can we identify certain system characteristics or mechanisms with specific outcomes such that the economic system itself may be considered variable and hence capable of being manipulated to alter future outcomes? Third, how do outcomes differ among economic systems?

To examine these issues, we chose a framework of system models and compared these models with real-world systems, looking for similarities and differences. We then compared the performance of different systems using a variety of performance indicators. Name tags of economic systems are important insofar as most people think in terms of the well-known systems of capitalism and socialism. The system **mechanisms** used to manipulate resource allocation are more important.

System mechanisms are organizational arrangements (plan or market), the level of decision making, property-holding arrangements, and the motivation system. Certain system characteristics affect economic outcomes in generally observable ways. Consider one example. Most observers of economic systems would agree that the level of decision making has an important effect on resource allocation and, furthermore, that the more centralized the decision-making arrangements, the greater the degree of *control* that can be exercised over economic outcomes. We found evidence to support this viewpoint in the Soviet case, where a centralized planning apparatus permitted the planners to favor rapid economic growth in the early stages of economic development at a pace that market forces probably would not tolerate. The ability to manipulate resource allocation can also be found (albeit to a lesser degree) where the plan is used in quite different settings, such as France. Within this popular classification of capitalism and socialism, we must deal with system characteristics from which we can derive expectations about economic outcomes.

Notice that even when we can relate an observed outcome to a system element, our assessment may still be largely subjective. For example, let us assume that past Soviet high growth rates have at least in part been achieved by high investment ratios, and that these high investment ratios have been achieved in large part through **central control** of investment decisions. Soviet planners would argue that such a mechanism is justified because a higher saving rate imposed on one generation will substantially benefit later generations. While such an observation may be technically correct, who is to decide which generation is to benefit and which generation is to pay? We would argue that such a decision should be made by the population at large, not by a central planner.

BEYOND THE ECONOMIC SYSTEM: POLICY, IDEOLOGY, AND NATURAL ENVIRONMENT

The economist must move beyond the narrow confines of assuming that economic outcomes are only a function of the conventional economic inputs of land, labor, and capital brought together in the immediate production process. Specifically, we have argued that the economic system must be entered into this relationship so that we can observe *its* impact on economic outcomes. In fact, we devoted Chapter 12 to assessing the system's impact on performance. The economic system has an enormous impact on economic outcomes. Economic life in the Soviet Union and the United States is obviously different because of the differing economic systems. Noneconomic forces sometimes closely related to the economic system also affect economic outcomes. The list of noneconomic forces that can influence economic outcomes is quite long — differences in policy, ideology, environment, past development experience, and so on. Let us examine some specific examples to see how such forces may influence economic outcomes.

Soviet leaders have declared that unemployment (an economic outcome) is found only in capitalist societies; they point to its eradication in the early years of Soviet rule as a characteristic feature of socialism.

Western economists point out that this Soviet claim is in part statistical myth and in part the result of an overstaffing policy by enterprises. They argue that there is frictional unemployment in the Soviet Union, though few reliable records are available,[1] while lagging productivity results from institutional arrangements that encourage Soviet enterprises to retain unnecessary employees.

Is the achievement of full employment in the Soviet Union an element of the economic system? Is it a matter of economic policy that the system could change if it desired? Is it a matter of basic ideology? Soviet leaders would probably argue that full employment is an ideological factor and that unemployment under socialism will necessarily (by definition?) be eradicated. Yet Yugoslavia, which is identified as a socialist economic system, has a continuing and substantial unemployment problem. In Hungary, under the New Economic Mechanism, the issue is how much unemployment will be tolerated as a matter of economic policy.

The Soviet system has a centralized economic system in which a particular policy objective, namely, full employment, can be achieved at the expense of efficiency. The United States has a similar policy objective (note the Full Employment Act of 1946). With the limited mechanisms in its control, the U.S. government has not been able to achieve this objective, largely because it cannot force decentralized economic units (enterprises) to accept the resulting inefficiency. In the U.S. system, the full employment objective would have to be achieved by some incentive system, such as offering enterprises subsidies to hire people they don't need. At base, we have chosen efficiency over full employment, whereas the Soviet Union has chosen full employment over efficiency. Policymakers may be forced to substitute one policy objective for another, in this case greater efficiency at the cost of some unemployment.

There is a tendency to identify system elements according to things that can be measured. Because ideology is difficult to measure or even to describe, it is unlikely to be identified as an element of the economic system. On the other hand, a system of beliefs can be a powerful driving mechanism for goal achievement. Witness the past economic disruptions in China, motivated by ideological considerations.[2]

Economic systems are embedded in a natural environment, and that environment affects economic outcomes. In this context, the Cuban economy (which we have not discussed) is particularly interesting. One historical characteristic of planned socialist systems has been a substantial degree of autarky in foreign trade. Planned Socialist systems have historically engaged in trade at rates below what one would find for capitalist market economic systems at similar levels of economic development.

Although the Cuban economic system reveals many components of the Soviet model, one would not expect Cuba to pursue a strict trade aversion strategy, given its very small size and geography.[3] Certainly if it were possible to compare Cuba with market economies that are *similar* except for their economic system, we might find that Cuba still fits the trade aversion model. However, relative to other planned socialist countries, one would not expect trade aversion to be a major component of Cuban trade policy.

In sum, it is likely that a number of forces — policy, ideology, and natural environment — will necessarily modify a particular form of economic system under differing applications. We may still wish to classify all such cases as a single economic system, but we must recognize the importance of these "nonsystem" (or "system-related") elements. In addition to the traditional inputs to the production process, a myriad of forces influence economic outcomes. In the countries we have examined, especially those with similar economic systems, some differences in outcomes can be traced to nonsystem forces. For example, economic performance in Japan, West Germany, and East Germany has probably been affected by a strong, nonquantifiable work ethic and discipline. Performance in China has been subject to ideological disruptions (the Great Leap Forward, the Cultural Revolution). The Yugoslav economy has been strongly affected by regional and ethnic factionalism. Unfortunately, because these other forces are not readily measurable, they tend to be ignored by economists and left to the attention of other social scientists.

ECONOMIC SYSTEMS: DEVELOPMENT AND CONVERGENCE

Let us turn briefly to a different theme: how economic systems change through time. Our analysis of economic systems and their impact on outcomes has been cast in static terms except for the chapter on reform of institutions. Both economic systems and outcomes change over time. A basic feature of Marxist thought is that systems and outcomes change inexorably (and predictably) over time (see Chapter 4). The realization that systems are not immutable has led many observers to suggest that we should examine not economic systems themselves but the process of economic development. Economic development, even in cases where the economic system differs, may introduce unifying characteristics. Even where the development process is initially carried out through widely varying institutional arrangements, the process of convergence guarantees similar outcomes in the long run. In this section, we examine briefly the nature of economic development, its relationship to economic systems, and the concept of convergence.

A truly dynamic analysis of economic systems would have to include an explanation of the mechanisms of change. The literature of economic development has devoted much more attention to this question than has the field of comparative economic systems. Indeed, the appeal of the Marxian idea stems, in large part, from its inclusion of inevitable stages of social and economic development. Unlike other stage theories, such as that proposed by W. W. Rostow,[4] it offers an explanation of how and why society proceeds from one stage to another. Indeed, beyond the stage theories, the development literature contains numerous other attempts to explain economic progress.

Most explanations are made without reference to the economic system. The mainstream explanation of development proceeds in terms of the dynamics of supply and demand and technological change, which cause a structural transformation from a primarily agricultural to a primarily industrial (urban) society. This literature also focuses on the mechanics of bringing inputs into the production process, ensuring accumulation, and ultimately increasing per capita incomes. Why such change comes about in the first instance (and why it has been limited to a minority of the world's population) is largely unexplained, except in very general terms — for example, the "relative backwardness" explanation proposed by Alexander Gerschenkron[5] and the even more general explanation of Simon Kuznets that development is caused by the systematic application of scientific knowledge to economic activities.[6] Development economics, for the most part, tends to downplay the potential role of institutional (organizational) characteristics in the development process, though most development economists would argue that economic development cannot take place without the simultaneous creation of an appropriate institutional infrastructure. Few general economists have given explicit consideration to the socialist development alternative in this developmental framework.[7]

If we believe that system differences have an important impact on economic outcomes, why do we not examine the process of economic development under differing economic systems? This we can do, though not with the regularity or the sorts of controls that one would like. The principal difficulty is that the exprience with economic development under planned socialism is limited to sixty-five years of Soviet growth, the postwar history of Eastern Europe, and the emerging record of China. On the other side, we have more than a century of recorded statistical history on capitalist development.

From the work of Hollis Chenery, Simon Kuznets, and others, it is quite evident that over a wide range of economic sytems, both capitalist and socialist, one can observe regularities in the pattern of economic development.[8] At the early levels of economic development, labor is concentrated in, and output generated primarily by, the agricultural sector. As development proceeds, the industrial sector gradually begins to dominate the agricultural sector. The share of the labor force in the service sector rises, and the "heavy industry" share of industrial output rises. Furthermore, regularities in other variables — the sources of capital formation (foreign versus domestic), the dynamics of population change, the role of foreign trade in development — can be observed.

Can we, in observing such regularities, control for the economic system as a variable in the development process? John M. Montias, Frederic Pryor, Paul Gregory, Gur Ofer, and others have observed regularities in the socialist development process that can be contrasted with observed regularities in the capitalist development process.[9]

Some general observations can be made about comparative industrialization patterns. The planned socialist economic systems (relative to capitalist systems at *similar* levels of development) stress capital-intensive heavy industry, downplay service-oriented activities, devote more substantial labor resources to agriculture, and maintain relatively low foreign trade proportions. The rate of consumption is depressed; proportionally more consumption needs are met by communal consumption supplied directly by the state; and investment ratios are high and are concentrated in heavy industrial activities. High employment levels are maintained, and income distribution is more even than in comparable capitalist countries. A demographic transition from high birthrates and high death rates to low birthrates and death rates occurs.

In almost all instances, the socialist model of economic development is *directionally* consistent with the capitalist pattern. The typical sector share changes occur under conditions of socialist economic development. The decline (or rise) in the consumption (or investment) share also occurs during capitalist development, as does the decline in trade proportions and the growing equality of the income distribution. What distinguishes the socialist from the capitalist development experience is the speed and magnitude of shifts in resource allocation patterns. Viewed over time, changes that require fifty to a hundred years in capitalist societies are compressed into a decade or two in socialist societies. Viewed in a cross-sectional context, planned socialist societies tend to attain resource allocation patterns typical of capitalist countries at a much higher level of economic development.

Given the speed and direction of change that we observe in contemporary socialist systems, it might be useful to compare these systems not to capitalist systems in general but to contemporary high-growth capitalist systems. Such a comparison would in part control for the fact that the socialist systems that we examine are of necessity "late developers" and thus have access to technology, for example, not readily available to earlier developers.

These sorts of patterns are observed when planned socialist and market capitalist systems are compared. However, there are problems with this sort of analysis that necessitate caution in the interpretation of these results. While we have argued that the name tags attached to differing systems are important as a mechanism for classification and hence understanding, we have nevertheless emphasized that system *mechanisms* are capable of being transplanted from one setting to another. Rather than compare economies typically labeled market capitalist and planned socialist, it might be as appropriate to compare economies that use or do not use national economic planning or that vary according to the equality of income distribution or the degree of public ownership. It is evident that there is a wide variety of dimensions for comparing industrialization patterns, many of which have not been empirically investigated.[10]

A second aspect of capitalist-socialist developmental comparisons involves the time element. Most such comparisons have been made in a limited historical time horizon, restricted by problems of classification and the availability and comparability of data. Once sufficient historical perspective is gained, comparisons of capitalist and socialist industrialization patterns through time will allow us to consider some fundamental and interesting questions. We have noted that the planned socialist economies have accelerated the process of structural change that accompanies (characterizes) economic development. Their economic structure is generally more "advanced" than their level of economic development. This pattern of resource allocation was selected because it was thought that it would lead to a higher rate of growth of output than could have been achieved by "normal" capitalist resource allocation patterns. In the future, two alternatives are possible. One is that these structural differences will persist, and then it will be apparent that they are permanent features of the economic system. The other alternative is that socialist and capitalist structural features and hence resource allocation patterns will become more similar.

The second alternative has tended to lend support to one interpretation of what is popularly termed the **convergence hypothesis**.[11] Economists and others examining the process of economic development and modernization have observed regularities, even where different systems have prevailed. The basic notion of the convergence hypothesis is that as development proceeds, social systems, their component economic systems, and even the system elements or mechanisms become increasingly similar through time. The fundamental source of such change is the alleged similarity of basic forces facing even widely differing systems — for example, modernization, the development of interest groups, factory work, urban living, the complexity of production, pluralization. The basic convergence case is as follows: Though economic systems may differ as to how they allocate resources at a point in time, the differences will tend to lessen over time as a response to unifying basic forces of economic development.

What are the merits of this hypothesis? How does one observe whether convergence is taking place? As we have stressed throughout this book, we can take the ideal case of comparing differing system *models*, one with another, or we can compare real-world economic systems. Unfortunately, this dictum is often ignored, and there is a great tendency to compare the reality of one system with the model of the other. For example, criticism is often leveled against the model of perfectly competitive capitalism, not against the reality of modern capitalism, and vice versa. The inefficiencies of Soviet planning are often contrasted with the model of perfectly competitive capitalism, and in Soviet texts descriptions of "perfect" Soviet planning are presented as if they represent the reality of Soviet planning.

A more fruitful approach would be to compare the extent to which reality differs from model, whether such divergences are greater in the capitalist or the socialist mode, and how such differences vary through time. The paradigm of the planned socialist economic system is less well developed than that of the capitalist economic system; therefore, changes in capitalist economic systems are largely couched in terms of changing *outcomes*, and changes in the planned socialist system are typically described as *economic reform*.

If we were to compare either models or real-world systems, it would be necessary to compare them at one point in time and then compare them again after change (or reform as we describe it) has occurred. Only then could we make a case for or against the convergence of systems (or system models) through time.

There are two fundamental problems in the measurement of convergence. First, whether we look at convergence in terms of system mechanisms or in terms of outcomes, how does one select the list of variables in which convergence or change will be measured and evaluated? Such a list would inevitably reflect personal value judgments. Second, even if we could agree on a list of variables, how would we aggregate them to observe change through time? Would each variable be entered with an equal weight, or would some be considered more important than others? In either case, how would the weights be selected? It is difficult to specify a model of the convergence process that is capable of unequivocally acceptable empirical verification.

Most studies of convergence select variables arbitrarily and focus on the change of these variables over time. For example, it has been argued that economic reform in the socialist planned economies of the Soviet Union and Eastern Europe has consisted primarily of the introduction of market forces and the application of profit as a managerial success criterion. At the same time, the introduction of national economic planning or, at a minimum, an expanded role for the government in the allocation of resources has been suggested as the trend in some Western market capitalist systems. Thus it is argued that the mechanisms utilized for resource allocation are growing more alike when compared over time in these two cases. Measurement problems aside, one can find some evidence to support the existence of both phenomena —

an expanded role for the government in the major capitalist economies, an expanded role for the market in the Soviet Union and Eastern Europe. However, it is difficult to jump from these isolated events (or to evaluate their magnitude and import) to a general theory of economic convergence.

The convergence literature has attempted, as well, to extend the notion of convergence into noneconomic spheres such as political and social convergence. This approach suffers from the same methodological problems: How is one to establish (measure) the convergence of multidimensional political and social phenomena and, given the multidimensionality of economic systems, make general judgments about the direction of movement of whole economic systems?

There is yet another interpretation of the convergence hypothesis, which relates to the observation of structural change.[12] If, in the Soviet case, capital-intensive heavy industry is emphasized (and the service sector depressed) at an early stage of economic development, will the shares of these sectors "converge" to some "normal" share (as determined by shares in developed capitalist countries) at a later and more mature stage of economic development? Cross-sectional examination of socialist and capitalist systems has found that when levels of development are held constant, socialist systems seem to be underurbanized relative to capitalist systems. Will this difference persist, or will socialist urbanization patterns ultimately move toward capitalist patterns of urbanization? According to this convergence concept, change in the underlying system can be observed through changes in the observed pattern of resource allocation. Although the notion of structural convergence is appealing, for it appears to be more quantifiable than other convergence concepts, the matter remains largely open for future investigation.

Although it may be difficult to prove or deny the trend toward economic convergence, the convergence hypothesis is a popular topic among analysts of differing economic systems. An important reason for the persistent interest in convergence is the continuing emphasis on economic reform in the planned socialist systems. Although we lack a general theory of economic reform in these systems, the subject bears further investigation.[13]

ECONOMIC SYSTEMS: THE FUTURE

If we knew how system differences affect economic outcomes (after controlling for nonsystem forces), we would be in a position to consider the system itself as a variable in the effort to allocate resources effectively toward the achievement of desired ends. Systems, or at least system elements, might be altered as objectives are altered; indeed, this is a common reason for attempts at economic reform in the planned socialist economic systems — the search for an optimal economic regime. Although the field of comparative economic systems is far from providing answers in this sphere, the subject will continue to be of vital importance in at least two respects.

First, comparisons between the Soviet-type socialist planned economy and the American-type capitalist market economy will continue, whether or not economists like the particular name tags. Those who attempt to develop an analytical framework for such comparisons can improve the quality of discussion by sharing their experiences and observations, however incomplete, with a wide audience.

Second, and possibly more important, even though we may not be in a position to generalize about systems and outcomes, we may be able to say quite a bit about specific system mechanisms and outcomes related to them.[14] For example, the planning mechanism has been viewed (whether rationally or not) as a mechanism that can redirect economic activity more rapidly than the market. Thus it is used to enhance the rate of accumulation in the Soviet Union, the pattern of industrial development in France, and the elimination of regional disparities in Yugoslavia, all very different social and economic systems. Certainly no particular mechanism will be generally applicable in every context. Even a particular mechanism will vary as other factors such as ideology, resource endowment, and level of development vary. In a sense, one might speak about an *optimal* economic system, one in which mechanisms are combined in varying ways to achieve varying objectives, with appropriate changes over time.

We have examined changes in economic systems largely in abstract terms — that is, with respect to modifying systems to meet changing objectives. However, among the various real-world economic systems we have discussed, what can be said about their pressing problems and about their potential for future change and adaptation?

Two broad issues will dominate discussion of market capitalist systems in the decade immediately ahead. First, can these systems overcome the seemingly intractable problems of inflation, unemployment, and balance of payments? This is really a question of the extent to which the market system, the hallmark of flexible adaptation in the past, can accommodate new circumstances in the future, especially those brought suddenly from outside. After the 1960s, a decade of seeming immunity from the business cycle, the capitalist world was shaken by a series of deep recessions, stagflation, energy crises, and disruptions of the world monetary system. The slowdowns in growth of the 1970s and 1980s appear to have been induced by both the business cycle and energy shocks. The foremost question of the 1980s has been whether the capitalist world can manage the business cycle more effectively.

Second, can the wealthy nations come to grips with the problems of generally high consumption levels when severe pockets of poverty remain within their own systems, not to mention the have-not nations? This question, just to focus on one aspect, involves not only subjective judgments about distributive justice, but also some thorny questions about which we have only a very limited knowledge. To what extent can we change the income distribution (within and among systems) without interfering with the prevailing structure of economic incentives? What role are we in capitalist market systems prepared to have government play in this process? These are the sorts of issues that will face the capitalist market systems in the years ahead.

For the socialist planned economic systems of the Soviet Union, Eastern Europe, and China, the substantive issues are really quite different. First, can economic systems that have built their wealth primarily on a pattern of extensive economic development make the transition to intensive economic development? Whether it be couched in terms of technology transfer, trade with the developed capitalist countries, or appropriate managerial rewards to encourage innovation, the key question in these countries is how to achieve productivity increases. The alarming slowdown in productivity advances in the 1970s and 1980s must be reversed if the socialist systems are to narrow their development gap vis-à-vis the industrialized West.

Second, can these systems, so long closed to the outside world and accustomed to a constrained advance in consumer spending, really open up to the norms of an advanced consumer-oriented economic and social system? Such a transformation is by no means simple and could involve fundamental changes in systems of resource allocation.

Third, can the have-not socialist nations pursue rapid economic development by means of a Soviet-type approach, or will the pressure for immediate increases in consumption lead to modifications — for example, in the role of foreign trade and aid? The importance of international interaction is evident for small countries like Hungary, and the search for a "new international economic order" will be of importance to virtually all countries, especially insofar as economic systems and system mechanisms are modified by and for expanded international economic activity. While we can observe similarities in the reform programs, it is likely that important differences will always remain. Some of these differences will be dictated by existing system differences; others will be dictated by largely noneconomic factors. It is not surprising that, in the reform sphere, the Soviet Union is very conservative; it is a large, substantially self-sufficient country, in which the impact of world developments on the domestic population has been tightly controlled. In Hungary, on the other hand, there seems to have been a genuine attempt, within limits, to integrate the system into the world economy. Finally, China, though large and potentially self-sufficient, may nevertheless be forced to pursue reform as a latecomer to development under severe population pressure. Reform has been critical.

Finally, as we have emphasized throughout this book, the 1970s and the 1980s have been decades of response to generally turbulent world market conditions. Many systems have experienced external shocks of one sort or another. For the capitalist systems, policies that could sustain reasonable rates of economic growth in the face of unemployment and inflation have been the main agenda. In the socialist systems, systemic change has led the way, with response to external shocks as a major constraint. Economic reform, a theme that languished in the 1970s, has come to the fore in the 1980s, especially in the Soviet Union and China, but also in Hungary and Yugoslavia. This revived interest in systemic change may ultimately provide us with a much better picture of the modernization process in socialist systems.

Although one can observe important day-to-day differences in the problems faced by different economic systems, there is a fundamental, underlying similarity in the drive for the economic betterment of humankind. To the extent that similarity of objectives is recognized, many will watch closely to see which economic system can best achieve the desired ends.

NOTES

1. For attempts to calculate unemployment in the Soviet Union, see P. J. D. Wiles, "A Note on Soviet Unemployment in US Definitions," *Soviet Studies*, 23 (April 1972), pp. 619-628; David Granick, *Job Rights in the Soviet Economy* (New York: Cambridge University Press, 1987); Paul Gregory and Irwin Collier, "Soviet Unemployment: Evidence From the Soviet Interview Project," *American Economic Review*, forthcoming.
2. For a discussion of ideology in the context of economic systems, see Alexander Gershenkron, "Ideology as a System Determinant," in Alexander Eckstein, ed., *Comparison of Economic Systems* (Berkeley: University of California Press, 1971), pp. 269-299.
3. For an analysis of planning in Cuba, see C. Mesa-Lago and Luc Sepherin, "Central Planning in Cuba," in Morris Bornstein, ed., *Comparative Economic Systems: Models and Cases*, 3rd ed. (Homewood, Ill.: Irwin, 1974), pp. 367-392.
4. Walt W. Rostow, *The Stages of Economic Growth*, 2nd ed. (New York: Cambridge University Press, 1971). See also Walt R. Rostow, *The World Economy: History and Prospect* (Austin: University of Texas Press, 1978). For a summary of different approaches to economic development, see Charles P. Kindleberger and Bruce Herrick, *Economic Development*, 3rd ed. (New York: McGraw-Hill, 1977), ch. 2.
5. Alexander Gerschenkron, *Economic Backwardness in Historical Perspective* (Cambridge, Mass.: Harvard University Press, 1962).

6. Simon Kuznets, *Modern Economic Growth* (New Haven: Yale University Press, 1966), ch. 1.

7. Lloyd G. Reynolds, *Image and Reality in Economic Development* (New Haven: Yale University Press, 1977).

8. See, for example, Simon Kuznets, *Economic Growth and Structure* (New York: Norton, 1965); Simon Kuznets, *Economic Growth of Nations: Total Output and Production Structure* (Cambridge, Mass.: Harvard University Press, 1971); and Hollis Chenery and Moises Syrquin, *Patterns of Development, 1950-1970* (New York: Oxford University Press, 1975).

9. See John Michael Montias, *The Structure of Economic Systems* (New Haven: Yale University Press, 1976); Frederic L. Pryor, *Public Expenditures in Communist and Capitalist Nations* (London: Allen and Unwin, 1968); Frederic L. Pryor, *Property and Industrial Organization in Communist and Capitalist Nations* (Bloomington: Indiana University Press, 1973); Paul Gregory, *Socialist and Nonsocialist Industrialization Patterns* (New York: Praeger, 1970); Gur Ofer, *The Service Sector in Soviet Economic Growth* (Cambridge, Mass.: Harvard University Press, 1973); and Paul Gregory, "Fertility and Labor Force Participation in the Soviet Union and Eastern Europe," *Review of Economics and Statistics*, 64, no. 1 (February 1982), pp. 18-31.

10. Pryor has done some pioneering work on the impact of system elements on economic outcomes. See Frederic L. Pryor, "Property Institutions and Economic Development: Some Empirical Tests," *Economic Development and Cultural Change*, 20 (April 1974), pp. 406-437; and Frederic L. Pryor, "The Impact of Social and Economic Institutions on the Size Distributions of Income and Wealth," *American Economic Review*, 57 (March 1973), pp. 50-73. Advances in both methods and data availability now permit more sophisticated analysis of socialist-capitalist comparisons. See for example John P. Burkett, "Systemic Influences on the Physical Quality of Life: A Bayesian Analysis of Cross-Sectional Data," *Journal of Comparative Economics* (June 1985), pp. 145-163; John P. Burkett, "PQLI as a Measure of Comparative Performance: Comment," *Comparative Economic Studies*, vol. 28, no. 2 (Summer 1986), pp. 59-68; Edward F. Stuart, "The PQLI as a Measure of Comparative Economic Performance," *ACES Bulletin*, vol. 26, no. 4 (Winter 1984), pp. 25-43.

11. There is a substantial body of literature on the convergence hypothesis. For a useful survey, see James R. Millar, "On the Theory and Measurement of Economic Convergence," in Bornstein, *Comparative Economic Systems*, pp. 481-492.

12. See Robert C. Stuart and Paul R. Gregory, "The Convergence of Economic Systems: An Analysis of Structural and Institutional Characteristics," in *Jahrbuch der Wirtschaft Osteuropas* [Yearbook of East European Economics], Band 2 (Munich: Gunther Olzog Verlag, 1971), pp. 425-442.

13. For an attempt to develop a theoretical framework for the analysis of economic reforms, see John Michael Montias, "A Framework for Theoretical Analysis of Economic Reforms in Soviet-Type Economies," in Morris Bornstein, ed., *Plan and Market: Economic Reform in Eastern Europe* (New Haven: Yale University Press, 1973), pp. 65-122.

14. This abstraction from ideology would not appeal to the Eastern observer of differing economic systems. For an analysis and interpretation of the field of differing systems in an Eastern perspective, see Alexander Erlich, "Eastern Approaches to a Comparative Evaluation of Economic Systems," in Eckstein, *Comparison of Economic Systems*, pp. 301-335.

RECOMMENDED READINGS

BEYOND THE ECONOMIC SYSTEM

Alexander Eckstein, ed., *Comparison of Economic Systems* (Berkeley: University of California Press, 1971).

Charles P. Kindleberger and Bruce Herrick, *Economic Development*, 3rd ed. (New York: McGraw-Hill, 1977).

P. J. D. Wiles, *Economic Institutions Compared* (New York: Halsted, 1977).

THE CONVERGENCE HYPOTHESIS

James R. Millar, "On the Theory and Measurement of Economic Convergence," in Morris Bornstein, ed., *Comparative Economic Systems: Models and Cases*, 3rd ed. (Homewood, Ill.: Irwin, 1974), pp. 481–492.

Frederic L. Pryor, *Property and Industrial Organization in Communist and Capitalist Nations* (Bloomington: Indiana University Press, 1973), pp. 356–374.

Robert C. Stuart and Paul R. Gregory, "The Convergence of Economic Systems: An Analysis of Structural and Institutional Characteristics," in *Jahrbuch der Wirtschaft Osteuropas* [Yearbook of East European Economics] Band 2 (Munich: Gunther Olzog Verlag, 1971), pp. 425–442.

Index